THE THIRD GLOBALIZATION

The Third Globalization

CAN WEALTHY NATIONS STAY RICH
IN THE TWENTY-FIRST CENTURY?

Edited by
Dan Breznitz and John Zysman

OXFORD
UNIVERSITY PRESS

Oxford University Press is a department of the University of Oxford.
It furthers the University's objective of excellence in research, scholarship,
and education by publishing worldwide.

Oxford   New York
Auckland   Cape Town   Dar es Salaam   Hong Kong   Karachi
Kuala Lumpur   Madrid   Melbourne   Mexico City   Nairobi
New Delhi   Shanghai   Taipei   Toronto

With offices in
Argentina   Austria   Brazil   Chile   Czech Republic   France   Greece
Guatemala   Hungary   Italy   Japan   Poland   Portugal   Singapore
South Korea   Switzerland   Thailand   Turkey   Ukraine   Vietnam

Oxford is a registered trademark of Oxford University Press
in the UK and certain other countries.

Published in the United States of America by
Oxford University Press
198 Madison Avenue, New York, NY 10016

© Oxford University Press 2013

All rights reserved. No part of this publication may be reproduced, stored in a
retrieval system, or transmitted, in any form or by any means, without the prior
permission in writing of Oxford University Press, or as expressly permitted by law,
by license, or under terms agreed with the appropriate reproduction rights organization.
Inquiries concerning reproduction outside the scope of the above should be sent to the
Rights Department, Oxford University Press, at the address above.

You must not circulate this work in any other form
and you must impose this same condition on any acquirer.

Library of Congress Cataloging-in-Publication Data
The third globalization : can wealthy nations stay rich in the twenty-first century? /
edited by Dan Breznitz and John Zysman.
p. cm.
Includes bibliographical references and index.
ISBN 978-0-19-991782-2 (hardback)—ISBN 978-0-19-991784-6 (pbk.)
1. Developed countries—Economic conditions.   2. Developed countries—Economic policy.
3. Economic forecasting—Developed
countries.   I. Breznitz, Dan. II. Zysman, John.
HC21.T534 2013
330.9172'2—dc23   2012025455

ISBN 978-0-19-991782-2
ISBN 978-0-19-991784-6

Printed in the United States of America
on acid-free paper

Contents

Acknowledgments vii
About the Contributors ix

Introduction: Facing the Double Bind: Maintaining a
Healthy and Wealthy Economy in the Twenty-first Century 1
    Dan Breznitz and John Zysman

PART I | THE NEW TERMS OF COMPETITION:
CHALLENGES AND CHALLENGERS
    Dan Breznitz and John Zysman

1. China's Run—Economic Growth, Policy, Interdependences, and Implications for Diverse Innovation Policies in a World of Fragmented Production 35
    Dan Breznitz and Michael Murphree

2. The Chinese Auto Industry as Challenge, Opportunity, and Partner 57
    Gregory W. Noble

3. Center-Local Politics and the Limits of China's Production Model: Why China's Innovation Challenge Is Overstated 82
    Crystal Chang

4. Services with Everything: The ICT-Enabled Digital Transformation of Services 99
    John Zysman, Stuart Feldman, Kenji E. Kushida, Jonathan Murray, and Niels Christian Nielsen

5. Platforms, Productivity, and Politics: Comparative Retail Services in a Digital Age 130
   Bartholomew C. Watson

6. A Decade After the Y2K Problem: Has Indian IT Emerged? 156
   Rafiq Dossani

7. The Dissolution of Sectors: Do Politics and Sectors Still Go Together? 178
   Mark Huberty

PART II | A (RE)NEW(ED) NEED FOR THE STATE: THE RESPONSE BY THE ALREADY WEALTHY?
   Dan Breznitz and John Zysman

8. This Time It Really Is Different: Europe, the Financial Crisis, and "Staying on Top" in the Twenty-first Century 207
   Mark Blyth

9. The Fragility of the U.S. Economy: The Financialized Corporation and the Disappearing Middle Class 232
   William Lazonick

10. Energy Systems Transformation: State Choices at the Intersection of Sustainability and Growth 277
    Mark Huberty

11. How the Nordic Nations Stay Rich: Governing Sectoral Shifts in Denmark, Finland, and Sweden 300
    Darius Ornston

12. Directionless: French Economic Policy in the Twenty-first Century 323
    Jonah D. Levy

13. Japan's Information Technology Challenge 350
    Steven K. Vogel

Conclusion: A Third Globalization, Lessons for Sustained Growth? 373
   Dan Breznitz and John Zysman

INDEX 397

Acknowledgments

Dedication by John Zysman: For my late mother who always wanted me to write books and had a deep concern with the impact of the economy on people

The authors wish to thank the Alfred P. Sloan Foundation, in particular Gail Pesyna, for financial and intellectual support; and the Berkeley Roundtable on the International Economy (BRIE), especially Kate Goldman and Constance McCarney, for research and administrative support. We would also like to thank the editors of *Governance*, Alasdair Roberts and Robert Cox, and the participants of the special issue on "governance after the crisis," in particular David Coen, who created the intellectual forum in which we could first present and develop the concept of the State in a Double Bind. Dan Breznitz would like to acknowledge that this book is partly based upon work supported by the National Science Foundation under Grant SES-0964907; and to also thank the Kauffman Foundation for its generous financial support.

Contributors

Editors

Dan Breznitz is an associate professor at the Scheller College of Business, Georgia Institute of Technology with courtesy appointments at the Sam Nunn School of International Affairs and the School of Public Policy, and a 2008 Sloan Industry Fellow. His first book, *Innovation and the State: Political Choice and Strategies for Growth in Israel, Taiwan, and Ireland*, won the 2008 Don K. Price for best book on Science and Technology; his second book (co-authored with Michael Murphree), *The Run of the Red Queen: Government, Innovation, Globalization, and Economic Growth in China* was selected as the 2012 Susan Strange Best Book in International Studies. In addition, he has published across several disciplines in social science and engineering, and served as an advisor on and initiator of innovation policies for international organizations, MNCs, and local and national governments in Latin America, the United States, Asia, and Europe. For these efforts, he was awarded the GTRC 75th Anniversary Innovation Award for Public Service, Leadership, and Policy.

John Zysman has been a member of the University of California, Berkeley faculty, teaching European politics and political economy since 1974, and is co-director of the Berkeley Roundtable on the International Economy (BRIE) since its establishment in 1982. He has written extensively on European and Japanese policy and corporate strategy; his interests include comparative politics, Western European politics, and political economy. His path-finding book, *Manufacturing Matters: The Myth of the Post-Industrial Economy*, remains an enduring driver of economic development policy and strategy for both governments and companies. Within the last two years, he has hosted international events and been a featured panelist at numerous industry and policy conferences including Green Growth Leaders, Danish Technology Institute, ETLA, Transatlantic Policy Network, Copenhagen Climate Council, and several others.

Contributing Authors

Bartholomew C. Watson is a visiting assistant professor in political science at the University of Iowa. He received his PhD from the University of California, Berkeley in 2011 for his dissertation: "Nations of Retailers: The Comparative Political Economy of Retail Trade."

Crystal Chang is an instructor of political science at the University of California, Berkeley, where she received her PhD in political science. She holds an MPIA degree in international management from the Graduate School of International Relations and Pacific Studies at the University of California, San Diego, and a BA in international relations from Stanford University.

Darius Ornston is an assistant professor in the Department of International Affairs at the University of Georgia. He is the author of *When Small States Make Big Leaps: Institutional Innovation and High-Tech Competition in Western Europe* (Cornell University Press, 2012).

Gregory W. Noble is a professor at the Institute of Social Science at the University of Tokyo. His most recent books include *Collective Action in East Asia: How Ruling Parties Shape Industrial Policy* and *The Asian Financial Crisis and the Structure of Global Finance* (co-edited with John Ravenhill).

Jonah D. Levy is an associate professor of political science, director of undergraduate affairs, and vice chair of the Charles and Louise Travers Department of Political Science at the University of California, Berkeley. His recent books include *The State after Statism* (Harvard University Press, 2006) and *Reluctant Reformers: The Left and Economic Liberalization* (forthcoming in 2014).

Jonathan Murray is executive vice president and chief technology officer of Warner Music, and was previously vice president and worldwide public sector technology officer at Microsoft.

Kenji E. Kushida is the Takahashi Research Associate in Japanese studies at the Shorenstein Asia-Pacific Research Center at Stanford University, and an affiliated researcher at the Berkeley Roundtable on the International Economy (BRIE). He received his PhD in political science at the University of California, Berkeley, and his BA and MA degrees from Stanford University in economics and East Asian studies.

Mark Blyth is a professor of international political economy in the Department of Political Science at Brown University and a faculty fellow at Brown's Watson Institute for International Studies. He received his PhD in political science from Columbia University in 1999, and taught at the Johns Hopkins University from 1997 until 2009.

Mark Huberty is a PhD candidate at the University of California, Berkeley. His research focuses on the political economy of technological and economic change, climate and energy policy, and the application of large-scale data analysis to comparative political economy. Mr. Huberty received the Fulbright-Schuman fellow in the European Union, and the United States Environmental Protection Agency's STAR fellowship. Prior to his academic work, Mr. Huberty consulted in the United States and India with the international consultancy Accenture. He has degrees in chemistry from Harvey Mudd College, and European politics and international economics from the Johns Hopkins University School of Advanced International Studies.

Michael Murphree is a research project director at the Sam Nunn School of International Affairs at the Georgia Institute of Technology. His work considers how innovation occurs in emerging economies without defined institutions, property rights, or competitive rules, and the political economy of technology standards.

Niels Christian Neilsen is a Danish business consultant with board seats on a variety of U.S. and Danish firms. He was a founding member of the Danish Technological Institute (DTI), Chairman of 2M Invest A/S from 1995 until its successful initial public offering in 2000, and was also behind the creation of the Danish government's Learning Lab. Mr. Neilsen has written extensively on knowledge, innovation, networks, international competitiveness, and the future of education.

Rafiq Dossani is a senior research scholar at Stanford University's Shorenstein Asia-Pacific Research Center (Shorenstein APARC) and erstwhile director of the Stanford Center for South Asia. Dossani's most recent book is *Knowledge Perspectives of New Product Development,* co-edited with D. Assimakopoulos and E. Carayannis, and published in 2011 by Springer. Dossani currently chairs FOCUS USA, a non-profit organization that supports emergency relief in the developing world.

Steven K. Vogel is professor of political science at the University of California, Berkeley. He specializes in the political economy of the advanced industrialized nations, especially Japan. He is the author of *Japan Remodeled: How Government and Industry Are Reforming Japanese Capitalism* (Cornell, 2006) and co-editor (with Naazneen Barma) of *The Political Economy Reader: Markets as Institutions* (Routledge, 2007). His earlier book, *Freer Markets, More Rules: Regulatory Reform in Advanced Industrial Countries* (Cornell University Press, 1996) won the 1998 Masayoshi Ohira Memorial Prize.

Stuart Feldman is vice president of engineering at Google, and a former president of ACM (Association for Computing Machinery).

William Lazonick is professor of economics and director of the UMass Center for Industrial Competitiveness (University of Massachusetts, Lowell). His book, *Sustainable Prosperity in the New Economy? Business Organization and High-Tech Employment in the United States* (Upjohn Institute, 2009) won the 2010 Schumpeter Prize.

THE THIRD GLOBALIZATION

Introduction: Facing the Double Bind
MAINTAINING A HEALTHY AND WEALTHY ECONOMY IN THE TWENTY-FIRST CENTURY

Dan Breznitz and John Zysman

SUSTAINING THE GROWTH of employment and productivity to ensure expanding real incomes of citizens is a classic policy problem and political necessity for all governments. In this era, those who command the state—those who would govern the economy—find themselves in a double bind. In psychiatry, a double bind is defined as a dilemma in communication that leads to acute distress, in which someone receives two or more conflicting messages from others to whom they attach great importance (such as a parental figure), and thus one message cancels out the other (Bateson et al. 1956). This creates a situation in which a successful response to one message results in a failed response to the other (and vice versa), so the person will answer incorrectly, regardless of his response. The double bind occurs when the person cannot confront this inherent dilemma and therefore cannot resolve it or opt out of the situation.

Such is the predicament in which policy makers find themselves today: They are called on to unleash creative capitalism and, at the same time, to intervene directly to make certain markets work optimally or to accomplish particular objectives, as in the case of climate change.

Governments have long been called on to protect society against the consequences and disruptions of the market. This is the classical Polanyi "double movement," which argues that society cannot survive under conditions of a completely free market, so "freeing" the market will always lead to a counteraction as society tries to save itself.

By contrast, the double bind that concerns us here is a dilemma in which policy makers who fully believe in market economics are called on to unleash creative capitalism by getting "out of the market" but, at the same time, are asked to forcefully intervene to "optimize" it and save it from itself. In a basic sense, this is an enduring debate. What is distinctive about the tension we now face is that appeals and requirements for purposive state action collide with the potential of the market. The imperatives and ideologies involved in this simultaneous call for often-disruptive economic growth and citizen welfare have always pulled in opposite directions. The current manifestation of this tension is what concerns us here.

The recent financial debacle, which required significant state intervention, was preceded by a long and complex evolution in the way in which firms create value and are organized. The fragmentation of production, intense global competition, and the transformation of services as a result of its intersection with information and communications technology (ICT) are all part of a story framed by the ideologies of deregulation and self-regulation. This evolution in business strategy and market competition fueled corresponding demands for market rules that would permit extensive innovation and experimentation.

A significant driver of these transformations of value creation and the reorganization of production has been the cascading waves of innovation in ICT. The process was co-evolutionary: There were a series of political and regulatory decisions that responded to and facilitated the potential of the new technologies. Thereafter, new business models and new ways of organizing innovation and production followed, which, in turn, spawned a new set of political conflicts, choices, and decisions. Those choices and decisions, in turn, influenced the subsequent development trajectory of ICT as well as other industries (Breznitz 2007a, 2007b; Zysman and Newman 2006b). The realization of all the new possibilities required new rules. The move toward market deregulation in telecommunications, for example, began with the simple effort in the United States to connect the Carterfone to the AT&T network, which led to a cascade of judicial and policy decisions, culminating in the deregulation—or, rather, re-regulation—of American telecommunications and, eventually, to a reconfiguration of telecommunications around the world (Cowhey and Aronson 2009).

The policy debates accompanying the rule changes and the shift in the logic of value creation, however, turned ideological. Those policy debates were coupled with the ascent of neoliberal thinking, which often focused on the purported need to get government out of the market and on the supposedly diminishing ability of national governments to shape their own markets and economies (Cerny 1995; Genschel 2004). The debates on "deregulation" and "globalization" had many sources, but they were consistent with the policy concerns of firms that were spreading production across diverse borders, of strong new competitors in Japan and China, and of the ICT-enabled reorganization of industry and services. Just as these rediscovered, or invented, "truths" about the role of state in the market turned into the ruling neoliberal economic paradigm, the financial crisis erupted.

For three decades, the state had been told to get out of the way to facilitate ICT-enabled innovation and adaptation and the effective deployment of these in sectors such as finance.

However, the same deregulation and self-regulation that facilitated innovation and adaptation laid the foundation for the financial crisis. The capacity to process information is one thing; the ability to process information *wisely,* however, is another matter.

The financial debacle of 2008 must be seen as the first major economic collapse of the information era. All the elements that contribute to the particular character of this bubble and crash, from the particular products to the new markets on which they are traded, are products of the information revolution. Collateralized debt obligations, the aggregation of individual securities into packages that supposedly reduced risk by reducing dependence on particular outcomes, are possible only with computers. The complex, ill-fated derivatives require complex mathematical formulas and powerful computing. The notion emerged that complex computer models with massive computing could remove the risk from the resulting financial bets and increase profits for both new and old financial organizations in the process. The integration of international markets and massive trading strategies requires communications networks to have an ever-larger capacity. The reforms arguably repaid the bets handsomely, generating massive gain for the winners and cushioning the consequences for the losers. Hidden from view in the heady days of frothy profits was the fact that this "self-regulating" market was actually a myth.

In Chapter 8, Mark Blyth argues that this time really is different: The failure to distinguish "risk" from "uncertainty" accounts for the fundamental misunderstanding of the crisis by many analysts and policy makers. As important, the crisis was the turning point in a profound transformation of the global financial system. This turning point shows up not only in the financial statistics but also in the debate over the relative power of the advanced and newly wealthy emerging economies in the control of global financial institutions such as the International Monetary Fund and the World Bank.

Unleashing the market and the force of information technology was one aspect of the dilemma. Then, as we approached the precipice of a depression after the financial crash, there suddenly were insistent demands that governments fix things and that the market rules, particularly financial market rules, be reset. Consequently, the state now finds itself in the double bind, in which it is asked simultaneously to unleash the power of market "innovation" to generate value by and to manage and maintain the market system to avoid catastrophic consequences, such as the financial crash.

For many, this was a painful rediscovery of the simple truth: All markets are built on rules that allow them to function, without rules there are no markets. The choice of rules powerfully influences not only the stability of the market, but also who benefits and who does not, or crudely, who wins and loses. Arguments about the validity and necessity of state action, which lay dormant until now, resurfaced. For some, the financial crisis was seen as an illustration of the limits or the failure of the American capitalist model, which was often equated in the popular conception with market deregulation and restrictions on state action. In Japan, the Ministry of Economy, Trade, and Industry and the Ministry of Communications pointed to a crisis in the financial markets and the commercial success of Korea as a justification for relaunching a debate on industrial policy. At the same time, reinforcing this shift in attention to the need for some state action, the debate over global warming produced a call for the state to take the lead in transforming the use of energy.

There is an emerging conundrum that policy makers must resolve as they seek the appropriate blend of policy, regulation, and government action with a combination of market operation and private initiative: how to address the gap between the issues, policies, and debates that were stressed before the meltdown of the financial markets and those that were emphasized after the meltdown.

Part I. Before the Meltdown

The dramatic recent evolution in the ways that companies create, and are politically allowed to create, value is entangled with the development of ICT. ICT is a current (and, at present, the most important) example of the rise of general-purpose technologies, whose impact is widespread across all sectors of the economy (Helpman 1998; Helpman and Trajtenberg 1998). As Levy and Murnane (2004) argue, the digital revolution requires a basic shift in education and training to capture advantage and sustain employment. The explosive growth in computing technologies—processing power, memory, storage, transmission, and sensors—was consolidated in a series of *innovation ecologies* that created new potential business strategies and production organization and opened an era of experimentation. The scale of the increase in information technology is difficult to fathom. The simplest and most suggestive measure of this scale, namely, the ability to process information, increased more than a trillion-fold in the past century. Since 1940, computing power has been increasing at roughly 50 percent a year (Nordhaus 2002). At least as important, each platform, from mainframes to minicomputers to personal computers to networks to the Internet, and now to "the cloud," necessitates radically different forms of organizations, skills, rules, and (social) roles. The ICT revolution unleashed, and in turn has been shaped by, a constant revolution in social and market organization. This constant experimentation and reshuffling and the creation of new business models generate demand for new rules and new approaches to governance. Two dramatic shifts occurred: the decomposition of production and the transformation of services enabled by ICT.

THE DECOMPOSITION OF PRODUCTION

Production is no longer organized in vertically integrated companies focused on home locations. This process of decomposition has been under way and understood for some time (Arndt and Kierzkowski 2001; Hirst and Zeitlin 1991; Sabel 2004). The ICT industry has been at the forefront of this transformation of the organization of work, while also producing the tools that facilitated the decomposition of production. As is widely discussed in the case of manufacturing, companies have broken up the components of production, from research to final assembly, and sourced them throughout the world, whether from within the firm or from outside suppliers (Sturgeon 2000, 2002). For our purposes, decomposition refers to the geographic and organizational recasting of operations that run from actual manufacturing to research and development (R&D) and strategy. It refers to *outsourcing*, purchasing goods or services outside the boundaries of the particular firm, and *offshoring*, whether by moving internal activities to another country or by buying from a supplier in another country. A detailed look at decomposition would consider component production, modules, and subsystems, their definitions and boundaries, and how the puzzle of the final product is constituted in the end. It would consider when activities are kept within the firm and when they are moved out of the firm, when they are kept at home and when they are moved "offshore." The contemporaneous geographic recasting of production tasks across borders and its recomposition in final products have come to be known as supply networks. The notion of value networks or webs of components, modules, subsystems, and service bundles, as opposed to a simple value chain, suggests the constant reorchestration and relocation of the components of value creation and, importantly, the imaginative reintegration of the constituent elements. As we discuss below, just as manufacturing has been decomposed, so ICT-enabled services have been unbundled and redistributed geographically and organizationally.

These developments were assisted, and in turned empowered, by a series of policy choices, particularly by U.S. governments, from trade policy to competition policy. In developed countries, new definitions of the rules of competition encouraged and even legally demanded modularity and compatibility between equipment and components produced by different vendors. This is as evident in the Internet browser wars still going on, as it was in the earlier deregulation of AT&T (Cowhey and Aronson 2009). In developing countries, political and industrial leaders seized the market opportunities created by the decomposition and redistribution of production to link themselves to the global economy and ensure increased economic growth (Breznitz 2007b). Indeed, as the first section of this book describes in detail, this is the core difference between the current rise of China and India, and the challenges they pose to those who are already rich, and the earlier rise of Japan and South Korea. Although the decomposition of the production of goods and services is increasingly recognized, its implications for governance are less discussed and its implications for business strategy are increasingly confusing. Although we firmly believe that fragmentation is with us to stay, it is important to note a series of recent efforts to reintegrate production and some dramatic examples of heavy capital investment to maintain position in integrated facilities.[1] The decomposition and recomposition do not mean that every major corporation now looks the same in terms of its production processes—quite the opposite. Boeing, Cisco, Samsung, Dell, and Apple have rather different production systems, but they all use global production networks extensively in the delivery of their goods and services.

This decomposition of manufacturing and services, the pervasive reorganization and experimentation, however described, has three consequences.

First, each production element (a component, a subsystem, a module, or service bundle) suddenly becomes a potential product, a point of competition with possible new competitors in interfirm and international trade (Breznitz 2007b). For some firms, regions, and countries, that might mean a loss of competitive advantage or diminished price premiums; for others, it represents an array of new opportunities: opportunities to enter new businesses or to tweak or reformulate older offerings.

Second, the resulting intense competition led to commodification, which has been driving a constant search by firms and locales for the "sweet spot" in competition (a momentarily defensible point to capture distinctive advantage and profits). Firms must have the capacity to judge which modules or components will be decisive in creating advantage, which must be developed in-house, and which can be safely sourced from outside. That judgment must include an estimation of which elements will evolve radically and determine which in-house skills are needed in order to compete. What is required are not just the critical skills needed to produce particular artifacts or subroutines or merely the ability to create a system to reintegrate the decomposed outsourced components and constituent elements, but a combination of both. Similarly, locales must develop the ability to design policy that both attracts outside firms and skills and assists existing local firms in finding the "sweet spots." The semiconductor industry is a perfect example. Firms once had to both design and fabricate their chips. At present, although some firms, such as Intel, remain integrated, most of the industry is decomposed into companies that focus on fabrication and those that focus on design. New competitive pressure appeared at all stages of production (Fuller, Akinwande, and Sodini 2003). Taiwan, as a policy initiative, created a "sweet spot" through the business organizational model of the "pure-play" foundry, that is a firm whose sole business is to fabricate for other companies the chips they designed (Breznitz 2005, 2007b; Fuller 2007; Fuller, Akinwande, and Sodini 2003). Locales must also have the judgment to invest in appropriate skills and infrastructure. More broadly, the search for the "sweet spot" can involve the reinvention of the very business. For example, although Apple's iPod is extremely well designed, it is the iTunes service that anchors its position in the market. Apple understood before others that a simple mp3 device, in this case the iPod, was the portal to a service. The iTunes model, payment for media, also addressed the problem of the violation of intellectual property rights and significant loss of revenues to media companies, that file sharing often represented. As such, Apple, which views the hardware as its main profit source, managed to secure the backing of the media companies to sell their products—songs—at one low rate to secure a winning market share for its relatively expensive hardware.

Third, if Charles Wilson, as CEO of General Motors, was ever right in proposing that "what's good for General Motors is good for America"—that the interests of giant integrated companies and their home communities are closely aligned—he would certainly find it hard to make the argument now.[2] The core location of innovation, not just employment, is at issue. Often governments invest in the stimulation of R&D projects by "their" national companies in the hope that such investment will translate into new jobs and industries created within their national borders. However, those same firms then often locate the downstream activities, where job creation and economic growth benefits are often maximized, elsewhere, in locations that offer unique advantages unrelated to novel product innovation (Breznitz 2007b; Breznitz and Zehavi 2010). To compete, places and firms must develop both competencies and assets that allow them to retain high-value-added activities and good jobs (Zysman et al. 2007). Of course, that objective means different things for firms and places—and different things for different places.

This book explores the decomposition of production through the first new challengers to the dominance of the already wealthy to emerge on the cusp of global production decomposition: China and India.

Starting with China (Chapter 1: China's Run—Economic Growth, Policy, Interdependences, and Implications for Diverse Innovation Policies in a World of Fragmented Production), Dan Breznitz and Michael Murphree present a theoretical framework for understanding the rise of China as an innovative manufacturing hub within the constraints of a global system of fragmented production and a domestic political economy striving to create a capitalist society ruled by a communist party—an environment they call *structured uncertainty*. In so doing, Breznitz and Murphree also present a detailed account of the global decomposition of production and the rise of the Chinese ICT industry.

Gregory W. Noble (Chapter 2: The Chinese Auto Industry as Challenge, Opportunity, and Partner) then presents in detail how the interaction of the Chinese political economy of structured uncertainty with global production networks led to the specific evolution of the Chinese auto industry. Noble stands our notion of control and power on its head, showing how decomposition allows "less advanced" Chinese firms to "offshore" more "technologically advanced" activities to the best firms in the West to beat the established Western auto brands at their own game.

In the last chapter on China (Chapter 3: Center-Local Politics and the Limits of China's Production Model: Why China's Innovation Challenge Is Overstated), Crystal Chang complements Noble's work by focusing on the politics behind the development of the auto sector, in particular, the central/local divide, hence, tying the auto industry case back to the argument presented by Breznitz and Murphree.

Turning to India, Rafiq Dossani takes a deeper look at the services transformation and the use of the business models enabled by this transformation, and asks whether Indian ICT has finally arrived (Chapter 6: A Decade After the Y2K Problem: Has Indian IT Emerged?) The core argument is that significant corporate organizational innovation and national policy, not low wages per se, are central to the growing success of Indian ICT.

In sum, this story of decomposition has two important lessons. First, the dominant thrust of debate in an era of decomposition and experimentation, trying to ride the successive waves of ICT technology, was about deregulation. Second, the various locations in the value chain call for different policies and approaches. A core governance choice for firms and places has been where to specialize and whether to emphasize the constituent elements or putting the whole back together again. Just as firms had multiple choices and various models of success, diverse national successes demonstrated that a variety of viable regulatory regimes and strategic growth options are possible (Breznitz 2007b; Rodrik 2007).

THE ICT-ENABLED TRANSFORMATION OF SERVICES

The application of ICT tools to services drives a second shift of critical importance: the creation of a category of ICT enabled services. Once thought to be a sinkhole of the economy (Baumol 1986), services have been transformed by ICT into a significant driver of productivity (Baumol 2007; Zysman 2006a).

What we call the services transformation is *not* about the growth in quantity or value of the activities we label "services." Rather, we refer to the transformation of service activities that resulted from the application of rule-based information technology, which alters the template on which service activities are conducted and facilitates the application of ever more powerful computing tools. The data suggest that this transformation has resulted in a surge in productivity of either newly created or recast services to generate a permanent improvement in the growth prospects of service industries (Jorgensen 2001; Triplett and Bosworth 2004). From the point of view of the state, encouraging this steady surge in productivity through the ICT enabled transformation services establishes a real need to reframe rules of markets that govern service activities.

Service activities are transformed when they are converted into formalizable, codifiable, computable, information-based processes with clearly defined rules and algorithms for their execution. Information-based goods, whether in finance or in libraries, became highly automated. The consequences are pervasive for both business processes and personal services. For example, physical goods, such as cars or refrigerators, can be integrated into service networks. Business processes, from finance and accounting to customer support and customer relations management (CRM), are altered when they can be treated as matters of information and data management. The algorithmic transformation of services permits routine and manual functions to be automated, which enables a fundamental reorganization of activities. It also permits the unbundling of the many activities and tasks that constitute a service, parallel to decomposition in manufacturing. As in production, these changes facilitate outsourcing and the easy relocation of activities.

Many changes made possible by the services transformation cut to the core of societal political-economic decisions that were settled over several decades of intense debates. Consider two examples. Some aspects of security already substitute "brain" for "brawn," transforming a service based on the presence of people into an activity monitored from a distance by some kind of machine. A similar process is at work in home-care nursing when sensors at a distance substitute in some ways for nurses and attendants on site. Decisions about how much, in what ways, and under what conditions these services are provided by people or machines are certainly not dictated by technology but, rather, are shaped by market rules and community norms and by politics broadly conceived. Thus, they are decided differently in different locales.

This is exactly the dynamic that Bartholomew C. Watson uncovers (Chapter 5: Platforms, Productivity, and Politics: Comparative Retail Services in a Digital Age). Offering a deep comparative analysis of one service sector that has been completely transformed by ICT technology—retail—Watson shows how political battles on questions such as labor, skills, and zoning influenced the development and the use of similar ICT technologies in Europe and the United States. The political battles led to the growth of equally successful, though significantly different, retail business models, all of which employ ICT to the same degree, but in very different ways, to achieve dominance in specific markets. Watson also reminds us that our current neoliberal casting of the double bind—deregulate, liberalize, or face innovative stagnation—might be factually incorrect. In retail services, the Danish, the Germans, and the French are at least as innovative and ICT-based as the Americans, but in different ways with distinct consequences for the organization of work and the distribution of gains from the innovations. The technology allowed productivity-generating innovation, but there are several paths to that outcome. Watson's message is that as long as choices matter, politics rules.

Equally important, the algorithmic services transformation changes the way in which firms compete and create value, as John Zysman, Stuart Feldman, Kenji E. Kushida, Jonathan Murray, and Niels Christian Nielsen explain in depth (Chapter 4: Services with Everything: The ICT-Enabled Digital Transformation of Services). Although it radically alters the nature, organization, and delivery of services, this transformation is not just a matter of reorganizing, automating, outsourcing, and offshoring existing service. Services become central to strategy as a response to commodified production, whether those products are manufactured goods or software. Companies such as IBM that used to embed services in their product offerings began to offer services with hardware embedded. Even in traditional industries, this transformation revolutionizes the ways in which firms think about what that they do and who they are. For example, Kone, a hundred-and-two-year-old Finnish industrial company that is one of the world's leading producers of elevators and cranes, is repositioning itself to provide "elevation services" rather than merely producing elevators and cranes.

Various firms follow different strategies. Although IBM is shedding more and more of its hardware-production legacy, Oracle, one of the quintessential software giants, bought Sun Microsystems specifically to add specialized and dedicated hardware to its service offerings.

Services have become central to value creation and critical to the effort of firms, including manufacturing companies, to escape the quagmire of being only a producer of commodities. Two important aspects services are significant in this new configuration for analytic understanding and policy debate.

First is the old notion that a defining feature of services—they are consumed as they are produced, for example, cutting hair or grass—is not appropriate to the digital age. Services are increasingly produced and stored. ICT-enabled services are delivered as part of ICT systems, and the capacity to deliver is stored in those constructed systems of information processing, storage, and distribution. Consequently, the notion of production, which has traditionally centered on manufacturing, has expanded to include the "production" of services, software, and web-based activity.

Second, capturing the value added made possible by information technology will require not just new corporate engineering and business models but also substantial social reorganization. Capturing the productivity gains made possible by the ICT tools will mean reconstituting services. This algorithmic transformation is not a mechanical or purely technological process. Services—finance, health, accounting, and media—are embedded in social rules and regulations. Therefore, national rules about services, and the politics of those rules, powerfully influence how the services transformation will unfold around the world (Zysman and Newman 2006a). This inevitably means that economic policy becomes directly enmeshed in the complex politics of social rules and regulations, institutions, status, and position. Thus, policy debates will go beyond the terms of market competition as narrowly defined. Political disputes will break out over social rules and regulations, institutions, status, and position, for example, fights about who can read X-rays, about whose private information is available to whom, and about how to distribute the gains from these new sources of productivity (Newman 2008, 2010). Consequently, in issues from privacy to financial markets, many of the old "settled" political-economic debates will be reopened (Zysman and Newman 2006b).

Three ideal types can help express the way in which ICT is influencing firms, competition, and productivity. Imagine a spectrum of services from the purely automated to the hybrid to those that are irreducibly delivered by people.

A first ideal type of services that firms offer are entirely automated, such as search services from Google, Yahoo, and Microsoft; they include data-networking services that manage communications. These activities, however, do not escape commoditization. Their providers fight against commoditization through continuous innovation in the service and its process, through intellectual property, and through network effects.

A second ideal type comprises companies that offer hybrid services. These come in various types. Some are created when products are woven into a system that is partly or entirely digitized. One example of this kind of company is OnStar and its plethora of competitors, such as Lexus Link and BMW Assist, which offer a service that includes the car and its on-board technologies (radio, video screen) in a network of ICT services for the benefit of the driver and passengers. Other hybrid services arise when personal services are digitized through the use of electronic tools (such as sensors) for monitoring, measuring, and recording information. Home health care and other medical services are rapidly becoming hybridized through the development of digital monitoring tools that can sense a patient's vital signs (heart rate, blood pressure, temperature, etc.) and alert a professional when human intervention is necessary. Other hybrid services are created when digital systems for communicating and manipulating information are deployed to let customers serve themselves when, where, and how they prefer. We see this type of hybridization, for example, in the bank-at-home systems now provided by most financial services companies, which allow customers to conduct basic transactions on their own, without the mediation of a bank employee.

The third ideal type, at the other end of the spectrum, consists of personal services, which fundamentally rely on human talent. Even at this end of the spectrum, ICT tools can make workers more productive. The work of a trial lawyer, for example, is irreducible—there is no movement afoot to develop robot attorneys that would use voice synthesis to plead cases in court. But there is no doubt that trial lawyers and their supporting teams of professionals have greatly boosted their productivity by using online databases to research legal precedents, word-processing software to write and rewrite briefs, videotape to record depositions, and so on. Yet the number of billable hours that a law partner must devote to a thorny case has not dramatically changed as a result of ICT, which is why most legal services fall into the irreducible category.

Services that have been transformed by ICT have experienced massive gains in productivity. The greatest gains come in the automated sectors, then in the hybrid sectors, and to a lesser extent in those primarily personal services that take advantage of these tools (Watson 2011).

ICT-enabled services depend on capital-intensive equipment and infrastructure that has to be built as networks and server farms. The services have to be designed, or built, as software applications. The availability of the services depends on the reliability of the ICT infrastructure, of course, but also on the capacity of the networks, in the sense that the server capacity creates redundancy and operates like inventory in manufacturing. Moreover, there is a services equivalent of the older question asked about manufacturing: Can you control what you can't produce (Cohen and Zysman 1987)? If a company or country loses the capacity to produce a product, can it compete effectively? To answer this question, we need also to know whether unbundling and outsourcing a service, or modularizing and outsourcing a manufacturing process, grants the advantages of corporate focus and arm's-length market pricing or, instead, fragments the underlying knowledge in a way that makes ongoing innovation difficult and transfers control over critical information and competencies to suppliers.

In summary, both the decomposition/recomposition of production and the ICT-enabled services transformation involved constant experimentation and reorchestration of business models and organization. To facilitate that reorchestration, firms sought regulatory flexibility.

This need for regulatory change emerging from the shifting logic of competition and value creation was transformed by the rise of a neoliberal ideology into a broad claim about the need to reduce the role of government in the economy more generally. The purported intent was to restrict the role of government in actively shaping markets and to restrict governments from direct intervention in outcomes. For example, important aspects of financial markets were said to be self-regulating, and new risk management techniques facilitated by and built with information technologies were said to diminish the need for government to ensure proper market functioning. Self-regulation by private actors in markets, we were told, not only would be sufficient to ensure the proper and appropriate functioning of the markets but also would be superior in its outcomes in terms of the efficient allocation of resources throughout the economy.

Many, we among them, believed that the debate over deregulation was badly framed. Demands for deregulation disguised arguments about how to "re-regulate" segments of the economy (Vogel 1996). It is not a matter of whether governments can act but, rather, how they do it and to whose benefit. The re-regulation of markets, which is a more accurate depiction of what occurred under the guise of deregulation, shifts the rules to influence who was advantaged and who was discomfited and who controlled and who lost control. This was clear to anyone who paid close attention, for a range of sectors from finance to media.

THE DIMINISHED STATE IN A GLOBAL WORLD

Almost as a complement to the debate about deregulation, many believed that there was an inexorable movement toward an ever more integrated "global" economy in which government influence was restricted by market forces. The argument was that market forces in a global economy limit governments so much that, beyond basic macroeconomic policy and deregulation, their policy strategies are simply rhetoric and hapless floundering (Berger and Dore 1996). The debates on "globalization" and "deregulation" had many sources, but they were consistent with the policy concerns of firms that were spreading production across diverse borders, of the strong new competitors in Japan and China, and of the ICT-facilitated globalization and reorganization of finance and telecommunications.

Interestingly, throughout this debate, the already-wealthy countries in Europe and the United States—particularly in the liberal economies of Britain and the United States—focused on the *constraints* that globalization placed on government and the costs of the decomposition of production, trying to make themselves into "competition states" and hold onto jobs (Cerny 1995, 2005; Hay 2004; Hay, Lister, and Marsh 2006; Jessop 2002; Levi-Faur 2003). Meanwhile, the emerging challengers focused on the role of the state in promoting growth and on using decomposition to engage in global production, all the while devising new models of state-led economic growth.

Part II. Enters the Great Recession: The Return of the State

Then came the financial crisis, a debacle that, it should be remembered, had its roots in the application and use of ICT tools: the use of both computing power to produce new financial products and the intimate integration of markets using data networking. These tools, the new products created, and the trades possible using ICT were facilitated by the looser regulatory regime, which supported the argument that the use of these products reduces systemic risk and allows for a more efficient allocation of resources. It is, therefore, not surprising that in the aftermath of the crisis, the debates changed focus. The emphasis is moving from arguments about limiting the state and liberating markets to arguments about what the state should do in, and to, the markets.

PRESSURES ON THE STATE

State action can come in three kinds: compensation, market rules, and purposive action.

Compensation

Compensation comprises the classic demand that the state cushion society against the dislocations created by markets, in this instance by compensating the "losers" for its outcomes. This is the archetypal Polanyi notion of the double movement, in which the market creates counter forces (Polanyi 1944). In its more sophisticated forms, such as Danish flexicurity, the question becomes how protection against social dislocation can, in fact, augment the ability of economies to adjust and adapt (Schulze-Cleven, Watson, and Zysman 2007). Darius Ornston (Chapter 11: How the Nordic Nations Stay Rich: Governing Sectoral Shifts in Denmark, Finaland, and Sweden), considers the responses of the Nordic countries to demonstrate that positive adaptation to the challenges of global markets is possible, and that social supports to cushion the adaptations can be mechanisms by which firms adjust what they produce, and how, to the emerging requirements of competition. By contrast, Jonah D. Levy (Chapter 12: Directionless: French Economic Policy in the Twenty-first Century) demonstrates that in France, unlike in Scandinavian countries, the claims for protection against the changes in value creation and competition can lead to a directionless morass, rather than competitive adjustments. France, a wealthy advanced polity, has drifted without direction or any coherent strategy as to how to stabilize its decline or how to devise new growth strategies.

Market Rules

The notion of the double bind also emphasizes the demand that the state make markets function more effectively, that is, for rules to make the market system function and remain stable. Such a demand always exists, but it was significantly sharpened in the aftermath of the financial crisis. The choice of rules powerfully influences not only the stability of the market but also who benefits and who is dislocated. The double bind is not about whether or not to have rules, but about the purposes of the rules. Indeed, the deregulation discussion obscured the fact that market rules were being recast to suit the realities of the digital era, as the extensive debates about intellectual property, online transactions, digital security, and privacy suggest (Lessig 2006; Newman 2008). These demands circle back to some basic questions about markets.

Likewise, to function, markets require rules about legitimate transactions that define the roles and responsibilities of intermediaries and traders, as several notorious cases from Enron to Madoff showed at great cost to many. The questions are endless. What is a tradable service, and who regulates the services that are "traded" across borders? Which jurisdiction decides who should be allowed to read lab and radiology tests, and who is to blame in the case of misdiagnosis? Are Indian radiologists licensed to judge the information about patients in California? What is "private information," and what constraints are there on the companies that collect that information (Lessig 2006; Newman 2008)? The implications of the answers given to these questions for American policy and development have been a motivation and focus of our work.

William Lazonick argues that the United States has failed to consider the implications of rules for the financial markets for the production side of the economy (Chapter 9: The Fragility of the U.S. Economy: The Financialized Corporation and the Disappearing Middle Class). The new rules, with their relentless focus on financial gains, specifically in stock price, and the extensive incentives that they give managers to focus on short-term fluctuations in stock price, have led to erosion in the U.S. economy's ability to invest in production capabilities. Lazonick suggests that, at the same time that ICT industries have propelled the growth of the U.S. economy, they have brought with them a new mode of business organization, the "New Economy business model" (NEBM). This model, based on the financialization of the American business, has led to a rapid increase in employment instability and inequity in the distribution of income. Furthermore, it undercut the development and maintenance of skills in the United States and therefore its prospects for long-term recovery. Can the United States, wedded to the stock market and the idea that corporations, even these whose main line of business is the production of goods and services, should be viewed solely as financial assets, overcome the growing competition and challenges that it faces with the rise of China and India? Lazonick argues that the problems are structural. Because financialization has been their main mode of operation since the 1990s, American ICT corporations have tended to demand skilled but lower-wage labor. This means that they prefer to employ younger rather than older workers and workers in developing countries rather than workers in the United States. Thus, even if U.S. corporations achieve growing profits and sales, they have already delinked themselves from the U.S. labor force. Hence, the problem is not one of jobs that are moved outside the United States but of jobs (and demand for skills) that are never created in the United States in the first place.

Purposive Action

In addition, demands arise for the state to accomplish specific objectives and purposes and to use the market to do so. Apart from the practical matter of which particular actions a government should take, the notion that purposive state action can be productive collides ideologically with demands for deregulation and "unleashing" creative capitalism. Indeed, Steven K. Vogel shows the failure of Japan on exactly this point (Chapter 13: Japan's Information Technology Challenge). More or less at the same time as the financial crash, concern over energy use and its implications for climate change, economic security, and political security came to the fore—which renewed important questions about the purposive role of state action. Mark Huberty addresses these issues (Chapter 10: Energy Systems Transformation: State Choices at the Intersection of Sustainability and Growth). The current science, technology, and innovation policy debate is over whether the state should promote a shift from a system based on high-carbon fossil fuels that is inefficient to one that is low carbon and more efficient. Regulation is an instrument of purposive action, when the regulations are used primarily to achieve particular outcomes. As Huberty illustrates, significant changes in energy systems have always been driven, facilitated, or impeded by government. In this case, the debate becomes one about the appropriate role of markets and states, what requires state action and what is best accomplished through private market actors, and how the two are interwoven (Zysman and Huberty 2010, n.d.). Influenced in part by the experience of ICT and the deregulation of AT&T in the United States, pressures accumulated to break up the energy utilities to achieve greater efficiency and competitiveness. The breakup would come about by introducing competition while separating production and distribution. The California story suggests that the particularities of the energy sector, including the need for balancing electrical loads (too much electricity produces shutdowns and too little produces brownouts), meant that the classic story of deregulated markets might not apply. Now, with the proposed transition to a lower-carbon energy system, the question is whether, for example, government should dictate the rebuilding of the electrical grid to transform it from an industrial-era grid into the smart grid of an ICT era or, as in the case of ICT, principally create rules to guide private investment and competition as a means of accomplishing particular objectives?

National energy strategies are increasingly influenced in the post-crash era by the question of whether green energy can create jobs and growth and whether some national political economies have an advantage in this transformation (Zysman and Huberty n.d.). That question itself highlights the debate between proponents of the deregulatory strategies and those advocating state action. Some might propose that the green-tech leadership come from Silicon Valley innovation, in which case the United States would "rule the green waves." However, a more state-centered successful model of energy innovation is evident. The cost of imported oil and the economic and fundamental security vulnerability that comes from importing energy led some governments to try to wean themselves off fossil fuels and imported fuels completely, with the deliberate goal of changing energy systems. The French emphasized nuclear power, radically altering the structure of their energy system, while the Danes emphasized energy efficiency and wind, dramatically changing their consumption patterns. The innovation models of the two countries differ greatly and are distinct from models emanating from Silicon Valley. Certainly, the energy stories call into question the glib conclusions that so-called liberal market economies are more effective at innovation (Taylor 2004).

A CHANGING VIEW OF THE "GLOBAL" ECONOMY

Just as the notion of a self-regulating market was dismantled after the crash, so the notion of an inevitable globalization came under pressure and began to be more widely challenged.

First, quite simply, national approaches to the crisis have differed significantly: how to restart growth, how to reregulate markets, and what the structure of the international currency system should be, in particular the proper role of the dollar. They have been different enough to prompt the question: "Has the era of financial globalization ended?" (Norris 2009). If globalization is not dead, then at least the simple version as promoted by neoliberal economists has been badly wounded by the financial market collapse.

Second, the crash revealed that the current globalization was built on fundamental imbalances. The global economy was divided between those who produced too much and those who consumed too much. In the end, all that decomposition of production, the modularization, unbundling, and redistribution of work really meant was that some countries, such as China and Germany, were doing a disproportionate part of the producing and other countries, such as the United States, were doing a disproportionate amount of consuming. The producers, moreover, were financing the consumption of the others, and in the United States, the standard of living predicated on the global consumer as the engine of growth was sustained by borrowing, ultimately from the producers. The financial extravagances built on these basic imbalances.

Significantly for the developing countries, resolving those imbalances suggests that export-led development, the one successful development formula in the past six decades, may not be sustainable. Resolving the dilemma presented by financial and consumption balances, on the one hand, and growth in the emerging market countries, on the other, will undoubtedly involve a more active role for governments in both the emerging market countries and the advanced industrial countries. In this case, as in so many others, the conversation is turning back to the role of the state in economic growth (Cohen and DeLong 2010).

Third, the notion of globalization highlights that production and economic activity are at once geographically dispersed and highly interconnected. This dispersion and interconnection, however, obscured—or diverted attention from—enduring diversity and national differences.

The first source of enduring diversity lies in the historically rooted differences in national structures and abilities. A country's historical heritage shapes and limits the array of policy choices that it might make and, hence, the lessons that it can draw from a different experience. France and the United States represent sharp contrasts: one with a highly centralized administrative and political system that provides leverage for concerted action by the central government on projects and the other with a decentralized federal system. Not surprisingly, their approaches to policy on energy and finance are sharply different. Their governance and policy appear to be on separate, distinct trajectories. As the crash underlined, the neoliberal consensus was hardly a foundation for success. The countries that opted to be more neoliberal in their economic policies were less successful and much worse off after the crisis than those with more pragmatic and eclectic policies, such as China, Brazil, and South Korea (Rodrik 2007).

The second source of diversity in policy is that, quite evidently, the problems that countries must solve. The diversity comes not from differences in the sectoral composition of an economy, but from their location in the value network. There are high-value nodes (i.e., locations) in textiles and low-value nodes in electronics. The skills and abilities required for the assembly of cars and electronics may be quite similar, and quite distinct from the skills and abilities of designing either. The result is that places now often specialize in specific phases of production and can be characterized by where they fit into the production networks as much as by the sectors of final products. Thus, rather than specializing in electronics in general, Silicon Valley clearly specializes in the conception, design, and development of fundamentally new goods and services. Various phases, if not precisely stages, in the development, design, and production of goods and services allow for particular sets of innovation and economic growth opportunities while necessitating specific sets of abilities and competencies.

As has been argued by Breznitz (2007b), specific policies lead to the development of unique abilities that guide different states to diverse growth trajectories and control over particular stages within the global production network of specific industries. By competency, we mean a specific set of skills, institutions, and resources that allow a locale to develop and retain an industry specializing in a particular stage of production (Zysman et al. 2007). For example, both Taiwan and Israel have had successful policies that allow them to excel in semiconductors working in the same markets. However, Israel focused its attention on private companies as the locus of R&D and defined R&D as the invention of novel products and technologies. Taiwan, by contrast, opted to create huge public research institutes, which specialized in transferring technology developed abroad and developing it into specific products that it then transferred and diffused to industry (Breznitz 2007b). Within two decades of following these two very different, if successful policies, Israeli companies acquired unique capacities in novel technology development, at the same time that the Israeli business environment developed a set of institutions to finance such business models and trained the labor necessary to succeed in it. Taiwanese companies perfected the business model of working as original design manufacturers for global companies and innovation and development at the level of components and already defined products.

Therefore, the question for locales is what investments to make, and how, so that firms there can develop distinct strategies for generating specific advantages.

But how should we think about the relevant domains of competencies and capacities? One method for identifying "phases" or "roles" in the value network, and the appropriate policy approaches for each role, is to consider the flow from conception of products and services to their actual production. We consider four broad "roles or phases." Those phases tend to be located in different places. Although, in reality, the exact borders between such stages and particular locales are murky, they still serve as a useful tool of analysis. Likewise, we emphasize that a country, or even a specific region, can be home to more than one of these "stages" or phases. However, the requirements for success in each are specific, and consequently the requirements can conflict (Breznitz 2007b; Sturgeon 2002, 2003).

The *novelty* stage, associated in the popular mind with innovation and Silicon Valley, is fundamentally novel product creation, often resulting in the creation of entire markets and new industries. This stage comes in several variations. One is the Silicon Valley version of the entrepreneurial company driving change. Cisco with the Internet router, Intel with the integrated circuit and the microprocessor, and Apple with the Apple 1 and the iPod may be the embodiments of this model. A different variation involves fundamental system innovation. Innovation in the system of providing electricity was often undertaken by individual entrepreneurs, such as Thomas Edison, who were able to imagine and develop the entire system. Now, such radical system shifts are more complicated. In Chapter 10, Mark Huberty argues that the energy systems must shift from high-carbon, low-efficiency energy systems to low-carbon, high-efficiency alternatives. Success requires the development, commercialization, and diffusion of many "suites" of complementary energy technologies throughout society. The innovative agent in these cases is often a government forcing significant changes. Each variation of fundamentally new product development, company-entrepreneurial and systems-driven, requires a distinct set of competencies, beginning with conception, definition, and design. There is a major difference between the ability to come up with a new product, or a new system, and the ability to define it and design it. That competency must be distinguished from production engineering. It is in this stage that the famed "communities of innovation" are the most crucial. This is the cornerstone of what makes this stage quite "sticky" to specific places (Markusen 1996).

The next stage, although not exactly in sequence, is *second-generation product and component innovations.* This stage, incorrectly seen by some as only that of "fast following" or "incremental" innovation, is often the unsung and despised hero of economic growth (Rosenberg 1983). Fascination with novelty obscures its importance. Firms working at this stage specialize in how to make existing products and technologies better, more reliable, and more appealing to wider groups of users. Accordingly, one of two modes of operation is usually followed in this stage of second-generation product and component innovations. Most evident is that, working within the confines of established products and markets, companies improve, expand, and often redefine these products. At least as important, however, is innovation in the underlying components and constituent elements of products in integrating science and technology advances. This can be innovation in screen technology or microprocessor design, the production technology for semiconductors, or car engine technology.

Before production is the stage of *design, prototype development, and production engineering*. If the ideal production and assembly firm takes fully defined product designs and makes them a reality, then the design and production engineering companies take product concepts that were only partly defined by their customers and make them into reality, using an array of production and assembly suppliers and subsuppliers. Apart from design competencies, the design and delivery (production engineering) companies also bring to the table the ability to create a working product or a system from an array of components and subsystems produced by many different, and constantly changing, companies. Any modern ICT product contains thousands of different components and subsystems. The ability to make them work together and fit them all within the ever-shrinking confines of the latest gadget gives the design and delivery companies significant competitive advantages. Taiwan is seen by many as the locale that mastered this stage of production in the ICT industry. However, looking at different industries, such as the life sciences, different countries, such as Denmark and Singapore, have become specialized locations for design, prototype development, and production engineering.

The most basic role in terms of ability and competency is *production and assembly*. At this stage, whether in services or in manufacturing, the focus of the activities is in creating a product that has been fully defined and designed elsewhere, often assembling high-value components that were manufactured or produced elsewhere. Some might view this stage as utterly commoditized, relying solely on cheap labor. However, some highly defensible strategies at this stage go beyond the use of cheap unskilled labor. For example, many view South China, particularly the Pearl River Delta region next to Hong Kong, as the optimal locale for this faceless and brandless manufacturing service and argue that this is exactly its Achilles' heel, predicting that the region will face severe economic crisis in the not too far future (Steinfeld 2004). However, the truth is that in order to truly excel in the production and assembly stage, companies must be able to produce within a few short weeks an array of extremely sophisticated products, such as tablet computers, smartphones, or ebook readers or, in the case of software, supply a working corporate-scale software system to spec. Furthermore, these companies must, at a moment's notice, be able to ramp up production to millions of units within a couple of weeks or fully abort it, incurring all the risk and the cost and still somehow staying profitable on extremely low margins. This is a feat that most, if not all, American and European companies are incapable of performing. Accordingly, South China's competitive advantage does not rely on sweatshops employing a few thousand workers in inhumane conditions but on the full mastery of flexible mass production (Breznitz and Murphree 2011).

The enduring diversity rests on the interplay of national, or regional, heritage and the requirements of place in the value network. We emphasize interplay because countries, or regions, as Breznitz has shown, find themselves fitting into those places in the value system, adopting growth strategies that call for their particular mix of abilities (Breznitz 2007b).

In sum, globalization comprises a series of national stories played out on a larger stage (Breznitz 2007b; Zysman and Borrus 1997). The financial crash highlights that this globalization has borders, and in it new emerging national players from Japan to Finland could pursue their development in larger markets (Berger 2006; Zysman 2006b; Zysman et al. 2007). National strategies for rapid growth in a variety of countries and regions, including Finland, Ireland, South Korea, France, and Japan, demonstrates that governments were outpaced by circumstances, if not simply wrong. The empirical reality has been that although the increasing complexity of global production and novel national strategies for growth took advantage of new possibilities, more traditional approaches came up against limits.

Conclusion

What, then, is a poor state to do, caught in a double bind between pressures that seem to pull in different directions? Demands for deregulation to support creative capitalism and innovation were couched in the vocabulary of neoliberalism, while demands for purposive state action recalled the necessities of fixing and directing the market. The policy problem is complicated even further because the decomposition of production and ICT-enabled transformation of services alter the political logic as well as the policy problem. Our understanding of the constituent political elements and dynamics of a political economy will need to be revisited.

Policy shifts, of course, are not intellectual debates judged by some independent authority. Policy reformulations always involve political conflict. Significant policy shifts that involve changes in the role of the state are usually accompanied by new political coalitions and, often, the emergence of new political parties, movements, and groups. In some cases, fundamental new policy directions are required, as are changes in the purposes of, and political support for, government. Indeed, in the past all major transformations of the organization and management of production have led to major upheavals in the social organization of societies and states. During the Great Depression, a sequence of policy experiments took place and an active state emerged as a result of a diverse, and often unexpected, series of political deals among labor, farmers, and business interests (Gourevitch 1986). In other cases, seemingly narrower fights, the revision of old rules, and their extension to new circumstances can cumulatively produce very significant shifts. Privacy and property rights that built up, seemingly over centuries, are subtly but significantly altered when applied to a digital world (Zysman and Newman 2006a).

A classical method in comparative political economy for explaining, or at least examining, policy change is to look at economic sectors, or segments of sectors, and the core functions within them to locate the interests of groups in society. Steel makers and cotton growers, runs the contemporary argument from Gourevitch to Rogowski, are distinct groups and often have different interests (Gourevitch 1986; Rogowski 1990). Workers as a group in the steel industry have common interests that differ from those of their managers or the company's owners. From that vantage point, the production profile of an economy, what is made and how, purportedly will provide an easy initial starting point to define lines drawn lines of political interest and conflict. We infer groupings and interests from the production profile as a useful source of propositions, and thus the production profile, the argument goes, can offer a starting point or a source for initial propositions. Of course, in reality, political groupings can never be determined from the contours of the economy. Political groupings are created through political acts.

Alexander Gerschenkron and, later, Peter Gourevitch recount how the various agricultural interests in what is now Germany were aggregated and defined by Prussian landlords (Gerschenkron 1962; Gourevitch 1986). Similarly, 100 years later, the integrated steel companies in the United States defined the political interests and policy objectives of the sector as a whole. Political actors transformed potential interests, understood from their position in the market, into political interests and policy preferences.

However, as Mark Huberty shows, the decomposition of production and the rise of services are blurring the borders between sectors (Chapter 7: The Dissolution of Sectors: Do Politics and Sectors Still Go Together?). The result is that the politicians and bureaucrats who must manage the competing pressures, establish priorities among the problems, and develop innovative solutions will find it hard to define the political terrain for policy and identify the interests of their constituencies, so interests will be continuously reconfigured. The beginnings of the changes are evident. Crucially, establishing coalitions of labor and business in the face of foreign competition, for example, in the steel or auto industries in the 1950s and 1960s, is no longer so straightforward and often impossible. Major firms are no longer automatically tied to the fate of their home country governments.[3] When production can move overseas, the interests of management and the workforce over issues such as trade policy can be divided. And while factories could be built overseas to enter new markets or benefit from lower wages to bring components and product back to the home market, workers stay home. Capital can move, but not labor.

The next step is that the modularization of manufacturing and unbundling of services sharply differentiate the interests of different sets of workers, even those with seemingly similar roles. The differentiation of interests takes place equally for firms within industries, not just workers. After the emergence of semiconductor firms such as Intel and AMD, the interests of the electronics industry fragmented. A new trade association, the Semiconductor Industry Association (SIA), emerged as the producers of semiconductors found their interests clearly different from those of the users of chips in products. As a consequence, the politics part of political economy will become ever more critical. As

Huberty discusses in Chapter 7, where does the interest of the music industry lie in terms of intellectual property rights laws and lobbying, in view of the fact that the music industry is becoming more and more a part of Apple, Google, and Microsoft's core offering?

As the production of services and goods is deconstructed, political interests are fragmented even further; they become granular. The fracturing of sectoral interests is even more fundamental. It is not just that workers and management have different interests or that workers are relatively immobile and capital is mobile. Nor is it simply that the interests of subgroups of workers or subgroups of capital have different, often contradictory interests. Rather, the modularization in production of goods, as well as the decomposition and growing tradability of service offerings with the often-abrupt relocation of jobs, makes it difficult to identify how the interests of different groups are affected by the changes of the global economy, where the boundaries around economic interests are, and what the groups are in the first place.

As the economic foundations of political groupings become less clear, the politics of creating groups and interests in the political economy becomes more critical. Political and even economic groupings must be seen more clearly for what they are: *political* constructs. As industries decompose, sectors fragment, firms outsource and offshore, and services transform, the ability to define political interests from a production map of the economy is diminished. The modularization and unbundling of activities further fragment the interests of the workforce, including management. Because the effects are diverse in their fundamental nature, the question of how political groups are constituted and reconstituted and how interests are formed, defined, and redefined becomes crucial.

As we have seen, technological advances that lead to economic changes in the ways value is being created are intertwined with political changes about how markets have been ruled. Those changes are leading to a specific set of demands on the state. At the same time, the state is increasingly asked to intervene to limit, if not outright prevent, future crises as well as to press toward defined goals, such as promoting a low-carbon energy system, a central task in addressing climate change.

Hence, after a crisis induced by both technological advances and political-economic deals to get the state "out of the way," the state finds itself asked, on the one hand, to let the markets regulate themselves and experiment in order to maximize growth and, on the other, to regulate these markets so that these same experimentations will not lead to yet another crisis. Certainly, one might argue that different problems call for different policies, and the strategies should be adapted to the problem at hand. But it is difficult to go in two seemingly opposite directions at once, and the ideological debates usually have disguised the complex policy choices. Governments will probably do what they have done in the past—that is, try to make the problem that they confront fit the solutions that they have available (Zysman 1977). They will do so because it is hard to shift the institutional constraints on choices. Similarly, most politicians will seek solutions within the theoretical frameworks with which they are most comfortable. Those frameworks not only define the problem and suggest the solutions, but also "inform" politicians and the public at large what the legitimate state actions are for each polity (Abdelal, Blyth, and Parsons 2010; Adler 1994; Blyth 2002, 2003; Breznitz 2012; Gao 1997; Hall 1989, 1993). Before the crisis, advocates of a strong role for government in the advanced industrial countries were often on the political defensive. The ideological center of gravity has undoubtedly shifted since then, yet nothing appears to have challenged neoliberal economics from its paradigmatic domination as the benchmark of policies there.

Political economy has not challenged that paradigmatic sway of the neoliberal view of globalization, regulation, and governance either. The belief that perfectly competitive markets actually exist on this earth is still a strong intellectual drug. Therefore, this financial crisis also highlights a deep crisis in political economy, showing a deep division about what states can and should do. It will be some time before it is clear whether a new ideological center of gravity has emerged or whether the substantive variety of policy, and the emergence of significant new players, will lead to any intellectual diversity. For now, comparative political economy, like the state, is in a double bind.

Acknowledgements

The authors wish to thank the Alfred P. Sloan Foundation for financial support and the Berkeley Roundtable on the International Economy (BRIE) for research and administrative support. Breznitz would like to acknowledge that this book is partly based upon work supported by the National Science Foundation under Grant SES-0964907; and to thank the Kauffman Foundation for its generous financial support.

Notes

1. Those efforts at reintegration seemed to be inspired by three things: costs, the way modularization influences the innovation process (Glimstedt, Bratt, and Karlson 2010), and some spots in the value network where more integrated operations have shown advantage.

2. Nonetheless, in a perfect example of the double bind in which states find themselves, when Detroit came calling, the Obama administration answered. It is an ironic twist of fate that the once-proud GM, whose managers truly believed that the interest of the United States are best served by advancing the interest of their company, is now part-owned by American taxpayers and desperately needs not only to succeed but to explain to itself and to the world what it means to be a U.S. conglomerate in a decomposed world.

3. Yet the fate of company and country is often more woven together than is generally acknowledged. Samsung's success is tied to Korean policy. The difficulty of Japanese firms in finding a firm global footing in the present generation of mobile telephones is rooted in national regulatory policies. Similarly, Intel's initial success was built on national policies, including, ironically given its present legal difficulties, antitrust policies that constrained AT&T and IBM. Last but not least, GM was saved by the U.S. federal government in 2009, specifically because it was deemed a local company, the American national champion of the car industry.

References

Abdelal, R., M. Blyth, and C. Parsons. (2010). *Constructing the International Economy*. Ithaca, NY: Cornell University Press.

Adler, Emanuel. (1994). "Cognitive Evolution: A Dynamic Approach for the Study of International Relations and Their Progress." In *Progress in Postwar International Relations*, edited by E. Adler and B. Crawford, 43–88. New York: Columbia University Press.

Arndt, Sven W. and Henryk Kierzkowski. (Eds.) (2001). *Fragmentation: New Production Patterns in the World Economy*. Oxford: Oxford University Press.

Baumol, William J. (1986). "Productivity growth, convergence, and welfare: What the long-run data show." *The American Economic Review* 76(5): 1072–85.

Baumol, William J. (2007). "On Mechanisms Underlying the Growing Share of Service Employment in the Industrialized Economies." In *Services and Employment: Explaining the U.S.-European Gap*, edited by M. Gregory, W. Salverda, and R. Schettkat, 63–80. Princeton, NJ: Princeton University Press.

Bateson, G., D. D. Jackson, J. Haley, and J. Weakland. (1956). "Toward a theory of schizophrenia." *Behavioral Science*, 1: 251–64.

Berger, Suzanne. (2006). *How We Compete: What Companies Around the World Are Doing to Make It in Today's Global Economy*. New York: Doubleday.

Berger, Suzanne, and Ronald Dore. (1996). *National Diversity and Global Capitalism*. Ithaca, NY: Cornell University Press.

Blyth, Mark. (2002). *Great Transformations: Economic Ideas and Institutional Change in the Twentieth Century*. Cambridge: Cambridge University Press.

Blyth, Mark. (2003). "Structures do not come with an instruction sheet: Interests, ideas and progress in political science." *Perspectives on Politics* 1: 695–703.

Breznitz, Dan. (2005). "Development, flexibility, and R&D performance in the Taiwanese IT industry—Capability creation and the effects of state-industry co-evolution." *Industrial and Corporate Change* 14: 153–87.

Breznitz, Dan. (2007a). "Industrial R&D as a national policy: Horizontal technology policies and industry-state co-evolution in the growth of the Israeli software industry." *Research Policy* 36: 1465–82.

Breznitz, Dan. (2007b). *Innovation and the State: Political Choice and Strategies for Growth in Israel, Taiwan, and Ireland*. New Haven, CT: Yale University Press.

Breznitz, Dan. (2012). "Ideas, structure, state action and economic growth: Rethinking the Irish miracle." *Review of International Political Economy* 19(1): 87–113.

Breznitz, Dan, and Michael Murphree. (2011). *Run of the Red Queen: Government, Innovation, Globalization, and Economic Growth in China*. New Haven, CT: Yale University Press.

Breznitz, D., and A. Zehavi. (2010). "The limits of capital: Transcending the public financier—Private producer split in industrial R&D." *Research Policy* 39(2): 301–12.

Cerny, P. G. (1995). "Globalization and the changing logic of collective action." *International Organization* 49: 595–625.

Cerny, P. G. (2005). "Political Globalization and the Competition State." In *The Political Economy of the Changing Global Order*, edited by R. Stubbs and G. R. D. Underhill, 376–86. Oxford: Oxford University Press.

Cohen, Stephen S., and J. Bradford DeLong. (2010). *The End of Influence: What Happens When Other Countries Have the Money*. New York: Basic Books.

Cohen, Stephen S., and John Zysman. (1987). *Manufacturing Matters: The Myth of the Post-Industrial Economy*. New York: Basic Books.

Cowhey, Peter F., and Jonathan D. Aronson. (2009). *Transforming Global Information and Communication Markets: The Political Economy of Innovation*. Cambridge, MA: MIT Press.

Fuller, Douglas B. (2007). "Globalization for nation-building: Taiwan's industrial and technology policies for the high-technology sectors." *The Journal of Interdisciplinary Economics* 18: 203–24.

Fuller, Douglas B., Akintunde Akinwande, and Charles G. Sodini. (2003). "Leading, following or cooked goose: Successes and failures in Taiwan's electronics industry." *Industry and Innovation* 10: 179–96.

Gao, Bai. (1997). *Economic Ideology and Japanese Industrial Policy: Developmentalism from 1931 to 1965*. New York: Cambridge University Press.

Genschel, Philipp. (2004). "Globalization and the welfare state: A retrospective." *Journal of European Public Policy* 11: 613–36.

Gerschenkron, Alexander. (1962). *Economic Backwardness in Historical Perspective, a Book of Essays*. Cambridge, MA: Belknap Press of Harvard University Press.

Glimstedt, Henrik, Donald Bratt, and Magnus P. Karlson. (2010). "The decision to make or buy critical technology: semiconductors at Ericsson, 1980–2010." *Industrial and Corporate Change* 19(2): 431–64.

Gourevitch, Peter. (1986). *Politics in Hard Times*. Ithaca, NY: Cornell University Press.

Hall, Peter. (1989). *The Political Power of Economic Ideas: Keynesianism Across Nations*. Princeton, NJ: Princeton University Press.

Hall, Peter. (1993). "Policy paradigms, social learning, and the state: The case of economic policymaking in Britain." *Comparative Politics* 25: 275–96.

Hay, C. (2004). "Re-Stating politics, re-politicising the state: Neo-liberalism, economic imperatives and the rise of the competition state." *The Political Quarterly* 47: 38–50.

Hay, C., M. Lister, and D. Marsh. (2006). *The State: Theories and Issues*. New York: Palgrave MacMillan.

Helpman, Elhanan. (1998). *General Purpose Technologies and Economic Growth*. Cambridge, MA: MIT Press.

Helpman, Elhanan, and Manuel Trajtenberg. (1998). "A Time to Sow and a Time to Reap: Growth Based on General Purpose Technologies." In *General Purpose Technologies and Economic Growth,* edited by Elhanan Helpman, 55-84. Cambridge, MA: MIT Press.

Hirst, Paul, and Jonathan Zeitlin. (1991). "Flexible specialization versus post-Fordism: Theory, evidence and policy implications." *Economy and Society* 20(1): 1–56.

Jessop, B. (2002). *The Future of the Capitalist State*. Cambridge: Polity Press.

Jorgensen, D.W. (2001). "Information technology and the US economy." *American Economic Review* 91: 28–32.

Lessig, Lawrence. (2006). *Code and Other Laws of Cyberspace*. New York: Basic Books.

Levy, Frank and Richard J. Murnane. (2004) *The New Division of Labor: How Computers are Creating the Next Job Market*. Princeton, NJ: Princeton University Press.

Levi-Faur, David. (2003). "New Regimes, New Capacities: The Politics of Telecomunnication Nationlization and Liberation." In *States in the Global Economy*, edited by L. Weiss, 161–78. Cambridge: Cambridge University Press.

Markusen, Ann. (1996). "Sticky places in slippery space: A typology of industrial districts." *Economic Geography* 72: 293–313.

Newman, Abraham. (2008). *Protectors of Privacy: Regulating Personal Data in the Global Economy*. Ithaca, NY: Cornell University Press.

Newman, Abraham L. (2010). "What you want depends on what you know: Firm preferences in an information age." *Comparative Political Studies* 43: 1286–1312.

Nordhaus, William D. (2002). The progress of computing. Working Paper, Version 5.2.2, Yale University Press and NBER.

Norris, Floyd. (2009). "A retreat from global banking." *New York Times*, http://www.nytimes.com/2009/07/24/business/economy/24norris.html.

Polanyi, Karl. (2001, 1944). *The Great Transformation*. Boston, MA: Beacon Press.

Rodrik, Dani. (2007). *One Economics, Many Recipes: Globalization, Institutions, and Economic Growth*. Princeton, NJ: Princeton University Press.

Rogowski, Ronald. (1990). *Commerce and Coalitions: How Trade Affects Domestic Political Alignments*. Princeton, NJ: Princeton University Press.

Rosenberg, Nathan. (1983). *Inside the Black Box: Technology and Economics*. Cambridge: Cambridge University Press.

Sabel, Charles. (2004). "Flexible Specialization and the Re-emergence of Regional Economies," In *Post-Fordism: A Reader*, edited by Ash Amin, 101–56. Malden, MA: Blackwell Publishers.

Schulze-Cleven, Tobias, Bartholomew C. Watson, and John Zysman. (2007). "How wealthy nations can stay wealthy: Innovation and adaptability in a digital era." *New Political Economy* 12: 451–75.

Steinfeld, S. Edward. (2004). "China's shallow integration: Networked production and the new challenges for late industrialization." *World Development* 32: 1971–87.

Sturgeon, Timothy J. (2000). "Turnkey Production Networks: The Organizational Delinking of Production from Innovation." In *New Product Development and Production Networks*, edited by U. Jurgens, 67–84. New York: Springer.

Sturgeon, Timothy J. (2002). "Modular production networks: A new American model of industrial organization." *Industrial and Corporate Change* 11: 451–96.

Sturgeon, Timothy J. (2003). "What really goes on in Silicon Valley? Spatial clustering and dispersal in modular production networks." *Journal of Economic Geography* 3: 199–225.

Taylor, Mark Zachary. (2004). "Empirical evidence against varieties of capitalism's theory of technological innovation." *International Organization* 58: 601–31.

Triplett, Jack E., and Barry P. Bosworth. (2004). *Productivity in the U.S. Services Sector*. Washington, D.C.: Brookings Institution Press.

Vogel, Steven K. (1996). *Freer Markets More Rules: Regulatory Reform in Advanced Industrial Countries*. Ithaca, NY: Cornell University Press.

Watson, Bartholomew. (2011). *Nations of retailers: The comparative political economy of retail trade*. Ph.D. diss., The University of California, Berkeley.

Zysman, John. (1977). *Political Strategies for Industrial Order: State, Market and Industry in France*. Berkeley: University of California Press.

Zysman, John. (2006a). "The 4th service transformation: The Algorithmic Revolution." *Communications of the ACM* 49: 48.

Zysman, John. (2006b). "Creating Value in a Digital Era: How Do Wealthy Nations Stay Wealthy?" In *How Revolutionary Was the Digital Revolution?* edited by J. Zysman and A. Newman, 23–52. Palo Alto, CA: Stanford Business Books.

Zysman, John, and Michael Borrus. (1997). "Globalization with borders: The rise of Wintelism as the future of global competition." *Industry and Innovation* 4: 141–66.

Zysman, John, and Mark Huberty. (2010). "An energy system transformation: Framing research choices for the climate challenge." *Research Policy* 39: 1027–29.

Zysman, John, and Mark Huberty. (n.d.). *From Religion to Reality: Energy Systems Transformation for Sustainable Prosperity.* Palo Alto, CA: Stanford University Press. Forthcoming.

Zysman, John, and Abraham Newman. (2006a). "Frameworks for Understanding the Political Economy of the Digital Era." In *How Revolutionary Was the Digital Revolution? National Responses, Market Transitions, and Global Technology in a Digital Era,* edited by J. Zysman and A. Newman, 3–22. Stanford, CA: Stanford Business Press.

Zysman, John, and Abraham Newman. (2006b). *How Revolutionary Was the Digital Revolution? National Responses, Market Transitions, and Global Technology.* Palo Alto, CA: Stanford University Press.

Zysman, John, Niels C. Nielsen, et al. (2007). Building on the past, imagining the future: Competency-based growth strategies in a global digital age. BRIE Working Paper Series.

PART I

The New Terms of Competition: Challenges and Challengers

Preface
Dan Breznitz and John Zysman

TWO SIGNIFICANT CHANGES occurred before the financial crisis in the way things and services are produced and sold in the global economy. The first is the fragmentation of production, which has been transforming the ways in which both states and companies interact, define themselves, and create value, jobs, and economic growth. The second is the rise of new competitors whose strategy of development is based on this new logic of competition. The chapters in this part analyze these changes from three different angles. The first angle analyzes production fragmentation, looking at both diverse industries and sectors. These chapters offer a deeper understanding of the processes of fragmentation and their impact on industries and countries in both services and manufacturing. The second angle analyzes the rapid growth of the two giants, China and India, whose development strategy has been built on the logic of globally fragmented production. The third angle analyzes the impact of fragmentation and the development of information and communications technology (ICT)-delivered services on the central unit of political, social, and economic analysis: industrial sectors.

Before we present the main lessons to be learned from these diverse stories, let us elaborate on these changes and explore the logic behind the overall inquiry of the chapters in this part. In order to understand this logic, we have to elaborate on the economic competition and, hence, the tasks faced by those who were already wealthy as they worked to remain rich until the late 1980s. If the external challenges to the already wealthy are embodied in the rise of China and India, the challenges of the 1970s to the early 1990s were embodied in the rise of Japan and South Korea. That earlier story was of a highly integrated production system developed behind market barriers with the transforming innovation of the just-in-time/lean production system for complex electromechanical products. That production innovation created advantage, first for Japanese and then for Korean producers, in an array of products and sectors. As a result of this challenge and the rapid fall from grace of American companies in sectors as diverse as consumer electronics and automobile production, a debate began in the United States over whether a firm, or country, could control or fully participate in the developments of sectors in which it could not competitively produce the goods. Many American firms had neither the understanding nor the internal capacity to innovate in production themselves. Furthermore, the American trade policy of quantitative restrictions worsened the problem faced by companies via tax and tariff policies that encouraged American firms to segment production and move parts offshore and, at the same time, encouraging foreign competitors to move from the low end of product markets to higher-value segments. Partly in response to the Japanese production advantages, partly because of available pools of low-cost labor and management, and partly because of growing technical complexity of products, American firms responded by outsourcing and offshoring production, generating a world of globally fragmented production, governed by supply networks, diffused innovation, and spatial specialization in specific production stages. In this new era, the question becomes which constituent elements of a product are so strategic and so linked to actual production that they must be kept in-house and which elements are commodities that are best to buy in an open spot market. The decomposition of production leads to the crucial question: Who controls the recombination into distinctive products and the definition of next-generation products?

It is here that a deeper understanding of the rise of China and India, and the strategic challenges and opportunities they pose to the already wealthy, is of greatest importance. Our authors offer a nuanced understanding of these dynamics. First, we look at the rapid growth of China and analyze it, giving an explanation based on an analysis of both the domestic political economy and the impacts of international (what some, wishfully, call global) political economic dynamics on its development trajectory. Here the first three chapters, by Dan Breznitz and Michael Murphree, "China's Run—Economic Growth, Policy, Interdependences, and Implications for Diverse Innovation Policies in a World of Fragmented Production," Gregory W. Noble, "The Chinese Auto Industry as Challenge, Opportunity, and Partner," and Crystal Chang, "Center-Local Politics and the Limits of China's Production Model: Why China's Innovation Challenge Is Overstated," debate among themselves to present the reader with a nuanced and coherent understanding of China's ascent as well as the dynamics of global production fragmentation. Looking at both the great protagonist of modern mass production—the car industry—and the great protagonist of global production networks—ICT hardware—the three chapters consider not only China, but also the particular challenge it poses to the already-wealthy countries.

We then move on to the other fundamental change in the global system of production: the rise of services and the role of ICT in transforming them from an economic sinkhole to the greatest source of productivity growth. We do so by both elaborating on the changes in ICT-enabled services and by offering a deep analysis of the most formidable protagonist of ICT-enabled services growth, India. In order to offer such an understanding, Zysman et al. in Chapter 4, "Services with Everything: The ICT Enabled Digital Transformation of Services," explore how with the algorithmic revolution, the ICT-enabled transformation, services shift from being a "black hole" in the economy to a driver of productivity. Baumol's dilemma—that services are an increasingly important segment of the economy but are immune to productivity increases—is resolved by Moore's law, the fact that computer processing capacity has increased a trillion-fold in the past century. ICT applied to services, which are information-rich activities, permits the fundamental reorganization of activity not only in fully automated information systems, such as Google search, or network hybrid network systems, such as iTunes or OnStar, but in fundamentally human services from medicine to restaurants and retail.

Consequently, ICT-enabled services are produced and consequently look ever more like manufacturing. Services from Facebook and Google search to OpenTable and Zagat restaurant recommendations and reservations are based on constructed capital-intensive systems in which latent capacity acts as inventory. This story of services with everything will accelerate as the next ICT innovation and ecosystem, cloud computing, becomes established. Cloud computing comprises not just being on line but, rather, a distinctive computing architecture that provides computing as an enhanced dynamic "utility" to users, large and small, while resting on scalable capital-intensive systems best provided by giants.

The capacity to adopt and adapt to these service possibilities will be critical for advanced industrial countries. There is no single solution, no single best way of implementing the possibilities of ICT in services. Bartholomew C. Watson, in Chapter 5 "Platforms, Productivity, and Politics: Comparative Retail Services in a Digital Age," considers comparative changes in retailing and shows that this key services sector has at least three quite distinct, and equally productive, solutions to implementing ICT. Crucially, political fights placed each case on a specific trajectory of ICT development and usage. Furthermore, by detailing these three different trajectories, Watson shows that, at least in part, the double-bind dilemma is a constructed one—both "restrictive" economies, such as Germany and Denmark, and "free-market experimentation" economies, such as the United States and the UK, experimented, innovated, and used new technologies to the same degree. Thus, a solution to the double bind might be thinking about the "how" of innovating and experimenting, instead of the formal "rules" on innovating and experimenting. Being an innovating and experimentation country might not necessarily mean kicking the state out of the way to ride the waves of the "free market" until a crisis hit, and only then expecting the state (and the taxpayers) to clean the mess and pay the bills.

Based on both a theoretical and empirical understanding of the ICT-enabled services transformation and the challenges it poses in the already-rich world, Rafiq Dossani offers, in Chapter 6, "A Decade After the Y2K Problem: Has Indian IT Emerged?," a comprehensive analysis of the rise of India as the first challenger to ride the new realities of ICT-enabled services in a world of fragmented production. India's presence in the global economy is affirmed by its undoubted progress in providing developed country enterprises with ICT-enabled services. It is argued that India's success is due to low costs arising from adequate supplies of software engineers and other knowledge workers, managerial skills, knowledge of English, and a first-mover advantage. Armed with these advantages, India, it is implied, can become the "China of services," with negative consequences on the size of the services sector, employment, and wages in the developed economies. Given that developed economies overwhelmingly rely on services, the negative impacts can be large indeed. As Dossani argues, many of the foregoing assumptions are true, but the implications do not necessarily follow. He first explains the industrial organization of the industry—the types of firms that constitute the Indian ICT-enabled industry, the markets they operate in, and their strategies. Second, he examines the role of the state. Armed with this knowledge, Dosanni then approaches the issue of national competitive advantage.

Last but not least, we take these insights on the changes and challenges that arose before the financial crisis and show how they transformed the political economy of the already wealthy in a way that renders old methods of analyzing them less useful. The transformations in production and the interlinking of services and products blur the borders between sectors. In the concluding chapter of this part, Mark Huberty, in Chapter 7, "The Dissolution of Sectors: Do Politics and Sectors Still Go Together?," shows us that our units of analysis, understanding of interests, and therefore the modus operandi of political-economy research has been transformed—a transformation in the empirical reality that has yet to be matched with a theoretical transformation in the way we think.

1 China's Run—Economic Growth, Policy, Interdependences, and Implications for Diverse Innovation Policies in a World of Fragmented Production
Dan Breznitz and Michael Murphree

IF THERE IS one economic growth "miracle" which is significantly transforming the global economy, and with it, some might argue, the very ability of already rich countries to stay wealthy, it is China's. The country, the most populous in the world, has enjoyed the longest period of rapid economic growth in history with over two decades of more than 10 percent annual GDP (gross domestic product) growth (NSBPRC 2001–10; OECD 2006). As it continues to grow, by 10.3 percent in 2010, even while the advanced industrialized economies of Europe and the United States suffer their worst economic crisis since World War II, understanding the specificities of China's trajectory of growth and its implication is crucial theoretically as well as practically.

We argue that China's economic growth trajectory stems from two intersecting forces: the global fragmentation of production and China's domestic environment of structured uncertainty (Breznitz and Murphree 2011). The fragmentation of production (i.e., that the production of products, components, and services now occurs in discrete stages around the world) provided the points of access for new companies in emerging locales to the global economy (Breznitz 2007). China's domestic structured uncertainty has been shaping the ways in which China's companies develop and the specific capabilities they bring to the table. We define structured uncertainty as an agreement to disagree about the goals and methods of policy or economic action, leading to intrinsic unpredictability and inherent ambiguity in implementation by political or economic actors (Breznitz and Murphree 2011).

The dynamic interactions of these two processes, fragmentation of production and structured uncertainty, has enabled Chinese companies to develop strong capabilities in incremental, process, organizational, and business innovation, all of which allow for flexibility and resilience in the face of rapidly changing market demands. Fragmentation provided an array of new points through which to access the global economy and structured uncertainty forced enterprises to develop highly flexible business models emphasizing short-term innovation, quantifiable gains, and low risk. However, the other side of this same development has been a lack of long-term R&D (research and development) projects necessary for fostering novel product/technology innovation capabilities. Nevertheless, thanks to the ever-growing fragmentation of global production and the interdependencies it creates between Chinese and Western companies, we contend that this trajectory of growth should be sustainable for at least the midterm.

Despite the strengths of China's economic and innovation system, the status quo is not that envisioned by reformers in 1978, nor is it that desired by the current political leadership. Since the beginning of opening and reform, China's central government has sought to build a novel product innovation capability and independent technology innovation base. The government continues to push myriad centrally administered and funded programs and policies designed to encourage the development of highly innovative, and independent, state-owned national champions. These include the 863 and Torch Programs, the "mega-projects" under the fifteen-year Science and Technology Plan, and the high-technology certification requirements (863 2008; Cao, Suttmeier, and Simon 2006; ChinaDevelopmentGateway 2004; ChinaTorch 2006; CTN 2008).[1]

China's innovation system excels in producing second-generation innovations by running quickly enough to remain just at the cusp of the global technology frontier while not advancing the frontier itself. We called this system the Run of the Red Queen (Breznitz and Murphree 2011). As we explored in greater detail in prior research, China exhibits a behavior not unlike the fast worldview of the anthropomorphic chess piece queen in Lewis Caroll's *Through the Looking Glass and What Alice Found There*. Just as the Queen must run fast to stay in place, China's companies follow rapidly but do not push the technological frontier. Instead, they make use of the global fragmentation of production to generate growth and jobs by utilizing innovations first proposed, evaluated, and tested elsewhere. Indeed, China's ability to follow on innovations developed elsewhere is now so fast that some Western Venture Capitalists (VC) estimate software or online applications developed in Silicon Valley are usually adopted and adapted in China within a matter of weeks (authors' interviews).

Reinterpreting Innovation and the New Logic of Globally Fragmented Production

Too often, innovation is thought of only in terms of "invention." However, it behooves us to remember that innovation encompasses the whole array of activities from invention to the supply of new or improved products and services in the market. Thus invention is only one small part of the act of innovation. Furthermore, in a world of fragmented production, it is not clear which kinds of innovation lead to the best local economic growth outcomes. Schumpeter himself argued that invention matters less than its application to create or improve products and industrial processes (Elliot 1983; Schumpeter [1934] 1961). Indeed, as Rosenberg and Birdzell noted three decades ago, scholars and policy makers keep forgetting the true heroes of innovation-based economic growth, such as incremental innovation, while attributing too much to novelty (Rosenberg 1983; Rosenberg and Birdzell Jr. 1986).

The story of globalization is in many ways the story of fragmentation of production (also known as modularization, decomposition, or unbundling). Industries and services are increasingly spatially fragmented such that activities, but not necessarily whole industries, are now geographically clustered, creating regional stage specialization (Breznitz 2007; Gereffi 1994, 1996; Sturgeon 2000, 2002, 2003; Zysman and Newman 2006).

Global fragmentation means goods and services are no longer produced or provided by integrated hierarchical companies based in national economies. Instead, many organizations separate activities into discrete modules and outsource or offshore them (Arndt and Kierzkowski 2001a, 2001b; Dossani and Kenney 2003; Gourevitch 2000; Kenney and Florida 2004; Langlois and Robertson 1992; McKendrick, Doner, and Haggard 2000; Sturgeon 2002, 2003; Zysman and Newman 2006). This global reorganization of production and services offers a new logic of value creation as well as a new set of specialization and innovative capacities; hence, we must rethink what innovation means and what the best strategies for investment might be (Breznitz 2007; Rodrik 2007; Steinfeld 2010). Two specific self-reinforcing dynamics have a significant impact on how organizations develop profitable innovation capabilities: production-stage economies of scale and scope and production-stage specialization.

"Production-stage economies of scale and scope" refers to the effect in which suppliers at each stage of a fragmented production chain pool the demand of many customers, creating economies of scope and scale that in-house divisions cannot (Breznitz 2007). For a firm operating at a given stage of production, this means that the firm can combine many customers and improve its ability to specialize around a given niche in production without having to concern itself or develop costly capabilities in other areas of the production chain. Once specialized at a given level, economies of scope and scale enable suppliers of a component or service to become more efficient and allow them to profitably operate on margins significantly lower than those acceptable to in-house manufacturing divisions. This cost advantage enables them to lower their prices while offering products of the same or higher quality, speeding the trend toward outsourcing of this stage's manufacturing or service-provision activities (Sturgeon 2000, 2002).

The most famous example for such a scale-and-scope operation in China is the mass-flexible production capacity of Foxconn's nearly 500,000-worker factory campus in the Bao'an District of Shenzhen in the Pearl River Delta, where the iPhone, iPod, iPad, and various Intel, Dell, Motorola, and Sony products are made (Dean 2007; Johnson 2011).

Foxconn is one of Taiwan's largest private companies and the largest exporter of high-tech products in China. In total, Foxconn employs one million workers across China. Foxconn's business strategy is built around the unique capabilities of the Chinese ICT (information and communications technology) hardware industry: the ability to inexpensively design, integrate, source, assemble, and ship variegated products from a common facility and still earn profits. Taiwanese ownership matters much less than the capabilities it has developed in China, such as networks of suppliers and armies of engineers skilled at design for production and improving existing products. These are not easily transferable. While American companies once had the organizational and innovational capabilities to run large-scale manufacturing operations (such as Ford's River Rouge Complex in the 1920s and 1930s), the American production system was focused on mass production and could not flexibly produce such an array of products in the same place on the same production lines. Capabilities of ultra mass-flexible production are increasingly unique to China (Breznitz and Murphree 2011).

The second dynamic is "production-stage specialization," which is the process by which companies develop superior capabilities at particular stages of the production or service network in response to decomposition (Breznitz 2007). Recent examples of this in the IT (information technology) industry are Indian IT software consultancies such as TATA, Wipro, and HCL, which are by far the most efficient IT consultancies in the world, basing their competitive position on unique capabilities and tools they developed in project management (Arora et al. 2001; Arora and Athreye 2002; Arora and Gambardella 2005; D'Costa and Sridharan 2004; Dossani and Kenney 2003, 2007, 2008). Such specialization enables companies to become better and more efficient in a narrow set of activities. It also helps them acquire specialized capabilities and knowledge that more vertically integrated firms cannot.

These capabilities, once acquired, enable firms to excel in innovation around the particular production or service stages and sets of components in which they specialize. Over time, these two related advantages, in skills and in innovation capabilities, provide these companies with even more advantages over in-house divisions in vertically integrated companies. We observe this process in high-technology areas such as power supplies but also in more traditional industries, such as bicycles, where product-chain fragmentation allowed one company, Shimano, to become the innovator and market leader in drive-train components (Galvin and Morkel 2001). This in turn means that firms and countries need different modes of innovation in order to thrive in different stages of production. Furthermore, once a country starts to develop innovation capabilities that allow it to excel in a certain stage of production, a process of self-reinforcing sequences will significantly increase the probability that its national industry will follow a particular trajectory of growth that utilizes these capabilities. This creates a situation of interdependency among firms that constitute global production networks, each set of which has unique innovational capabilities in some stages of production but not in others. Consequently, different nations can achieve rapid and sustainable growth by focusing their innovational activities on particular stages of production and thereby supplying unique outputs and services to global markets (Breznitz 2007).

Armed with this understanding of how the global economic system has changed, let us now look at how Chinese firms have evolved to take advantage of the opportunities presented by the increased global fragmentation of production.

Adaptations to Structured Uncertainty

China's entry into the world of fragmented production has not been occurring in a vacuum. Business in China developed in an environment highly imbued with structured uncertainty. Chinese firms developed specific sets of innovative capabilities which allow them to maximize their profits while minimizing the risks specific to China. These capabilities in turn shape the types of innovations Chinese enterprises can do while inhibiting others.

Structured uncertainty may be defined as an agreement to disagree about the goals and methods of policy, leading to intrinsic unpredictability and, hence, ambiguity in implementation and enforcement of economic policies and rules. Structured uncertainty cements multiplicity of action without legitimizing any specific course or form of behavior as the proper one. This ambiguity leads to some tolerance for multiple interpretations and implementations of the same policy.

For Chinese companies seeking new opportunities, at the same time that plurality of policy actions is tolerated, punishment for deemed transgressors can be severe, abrupt, and seemingly arbitrary. The limits of tolerance are undefined, adding to the ambiguity. Structured uncertainty can thus be thought of as an institutional feature that guarantees that a plurality of behaviors will be followed in any specific domain, with none of the actors knowing in advance the appropriate ways to conduct themselves. Structured uncertainty exists to a certain degree in almost all policy domains in most countries. Indeed, it is the main reason why street-level bureaucracy is so important in every society (Wilson 1968). However, it takes on a different qualitative and quantitative manifestation in the Chinese system due to the specificities of its halting but continuous transformation from a revolutionary society to a more organized, bureaucratic, and rule-bound one.[2]

Structured uncertainty has particularly pronounced effects on R&D undertakings. As succinctly argued by Kenneth Arrow, even under conditions of perfect market competition there is a tendency for private economic agents to underinvest in R&D (Arrow 1962). Structured uncertainty, through its impact on the ability to appropriate and increased uncertainty, augments R&D's inherent characteristics of indivisibility, inappropriability, and uncertainty, reducing private incentives to underwrite R&D.[3] Under structured uncertainty the great puzzle for economic theory is why some Chinese companies even perform significant R&D.[4]

Under these conditions, Chinese organizations use multiple approaches, both official and unofficial, to mitigate uncertainty. These approaches have led to the emergence of a strongly innovative organizational ecosystem, but one different from the West in its focus, and decidedly different from the one envisioned and coveted by China's central government. This innovation ecosystem fosters a wide array of innovation activities but not novel product innovation.

To ensure an incentive for productive activities, innovators must be able to appropriate returns without resorting to extralegal means. Organizations must ensure they are secure from predatory officials if they are to seek productive activities. To do so in China, organizations adopt multiple ownership forms and cultivate back-channel relationships with officialdom to ensure protection from the fickle winds of state and to guarantee their chosen market remains viable. Organizations can choose to establish themselves as wholly owned foreign enterprises, collectives, private enterprises, and state-owned ones as well as more amorphous ownership forms such as *minying* (Breznitz and Murphree 2011; Segal 2003). By redefining ownership, merging different types of ownership, and extending ownership rights to government at various levels, uncertainty regarding the behavior of officials can be partly mitigated. We can see across China's high-technology industries that this is the case: an industrial structure of mixed ownership types that offer greater assurance as to the ability to appropriate returns, but with relatively ambiguous channels of management authority by Western standards.

In terms of innovation capabilities, adapting to structured uncertainty means Chinese firms are relatively well able to avoid predations by the state but are less able to move forcefully in any area that demands commitment to high-risk activities with long time frames, exactly what is needed for novel product R&D. However, this limitation does not mean Chinese enterprises have no incentives to innovate. It is critically important to remember the flipside of structured uncertainty. If there is one agreed-upon benchmark with which to judge whether a policy or action by business is "proper," it is revenue growth and job creation. These are seen as categorical goods by both political and economic actors; hence, they are pursued over and above all else. The goal of public policy and research conducted by or within business is to maximize revenue and job creation as fast as possible while generating and sustaining the least amount of risk. It follows, therefore, that enterprises will emphasize short-time horizons and incremental activities in proven technologies and market niches.

Second, organizations in China seek means of appropriating returns in an environment that lacks fully enforced formal property rights. The strategy organizations adopt derives from the industry sector in which the organization operates as well as the resources, human and otherwise, available to it. Most frequently, Chinese enterprises release incrementally improved models of their products and services with a very short lag time between new versions. This strategy limits the value of copying by would-be competitors and ensures the company manages to keep a profitable edge. China's strengths in flexible manufacturing enable rapid turnarounds and short runs of products, thus making this a workable innovation strategy.

A second approach, exercised by large-scale enterprises with major internal resources, is to specialize in innovation of production methods or large-scale equipment design and fabrication. For these industries, the value of imitation is lower since prospective imitators would require massive capital assets of their own as well as—and more important—tacit knowledge in order to successfully pirate the organization's technology. Such high-end capital-intensive innovation strategy lends some protection copying by competitors even in the absence of property rights.

Third, the most advanced local organizations or, more commonly, branches of foreign MNCs (multinational corporations) opt to use the highest-end local human resources to conduct highly theoretical or abstract research.[5] Such primary research does not lend itself readily to imitation and requires the embedded tacit knowledge and technology transfer practices of the innovating firm in order to capitalize on any findings and deploy them in a final product.

Finally, when dealing with the financial system, firms in China adopt approaches to ensure access to capital. China's financial organizations, even those styled as venture capital, are generally highly risk averse with the partial exception of state financing. Risk aversion privileges large-scale enterprises, proven business models using already developed technologies, or foreign enterprises (authors' interviews; Breznitz and Murphree 2011; Fuller 2005, 2010; Huang and Qian 2008; Segal 2003; Tsai 2002). The relative scarcity and weaknesses of both traditional investment capital and venture capital mean that the role of government is greatly enhanced. However, the central state often opts to support only those ventures that accord with its development plans and its specific understanding of innovation. This means firms developing technologies outside the state's vision are largely excluded, but those in chosen industries can enjoy privileged access to capital. Nonetheless, the general lack of patient venture financing limits the range of R&D activities in which firms may engage, thus further encouraging their specialization in non–novel product innovation niches.

That is not to say that Chinese firms do not or cannot derive lasting advantages from their innovations. Under fragmentation of production, Chinese enterprises aggressively pursue enduring advantages *within specific phases of production.* Global production networks not only make this strategy viable but also supply China with the needed inputs in terms of novel ideas developed elsewhere, and the necessary market demand for innovations across the production cycle to make it sustainable. *For innovative Chinese organizations, specialization under the new global conditions is significant because it provides types of embedded knowledge that, similar to novel product innovations, are valuable in granting lasting competitive advantage.* Accordingly, the resulting benefits to the organization in terms of securing a competitive advantage in the marketplace are the same. Stage specialization and development of the related skills enable a firm to continue to innovate and grow at a given level without a strong need to excel in novel product innovation.

The fragmentation of production allows Chinese companies to access and succeed in the global marketplace. The story of China's rise is one of international engagement and changes in the domestic political economy to enable firms to capitalize on shifts in the world economy. It is a story of industrial co-evolution that has been going on a trajectory drastically different from the plans of the central government. To illustrate, we now look at ICT hardware production in southern China.

ICT Hardware Production—Innovation Outside State-Approved Domains

Looking at the intersection of the global fragmentation of production and the pragmatic adaptations of firms to the pressures of structured uncertainty, the Pearl River Delta's (PRD) ICT hardware industry offers a typical example of success in domains that lie outside industries slated for innovation and promotion by the central state.[6] The PRD is geographically defined as a rough triangle in central Guangdong province with vertices at Guangzhou, Hong Kong, and Macao. It includes the major industrial cities of Shenzhen and Dongguan as well as other manufacturing bases including Zhongshan and Zhuhai. Successful firms have all found means of innovating in the absence of strong IPR (intellectual property rights) protection, with undefined rules of the competitive game, and while being shut out from central state funds and bank financing.

The PRD is the production base of China's ICT hardware industry. The ICT hardware industry here emerged in tandem with major changes in the global industry. During the 1960s and 1970s, production of electronics began to fragment, with final assembly and component production increasingly occurring in Asia's emerging economies, such as Taiwan, Singapore, and Hong Kong (Hobday 1995; Scott 1987; Sturgeon and Lester 2004). By the late 1970s and early 1980s, however, even these economies faced rising land and labor costs that squeezed their profits. When the Shenzhen Special Economic Zone (SEZ), opened in 1980, Hong Kong's and other Asian entrepreneurs found a solution to their rising costs. The SEZ authorities provided subsidized land, utilities, and infrastructure to foreign investors. As a further incentive to invest, the SEZ offered a corporate income tax rate of 15 percent, half of the national tax rate (Shen et al. 2000). Investment flooded in and the economy boomed. Shenzhen's economy grew by 44 percent per year from 1980 to 1986, and 29 percent per year from 1987 to 1995 (Guo and Feng 2007). What had been a collection of fishing villages rapidly became the wealthiest Chinese city per capita, with over ten million residents, relying heavily on the ICT industry (SSB 2008). Electronics and ICT exports accounted for 76.8 percent of total exports in 2009 and 52.6 percent of industrial value added in 2010.

By the end of the 1980s, companies like ZTE and Huawei, now the two leading Chinese telecommunication equipment manufacturers, had commenced operations. The ICT industry continued to expand throughout the PRD as other cities and townships began offering similar preferential policies and incentives to the Shenzhen SEZ. However, as a first mover, the Shenzhen SEZ remained a major site for foreign and domestic investment. As the SEZ developed, manufacturing moved out from the three SEZ districts directly adjacent to the Hong Kong border and spread across the region (Walcott 2003).

The PRD has since come to dominate China's production of electronics and ICT hardware. In the process, the region—which had very limited high education and research infrastructure at the time it began to engage with the global economy—has developed a formidable innovation capability, although not one in novel product innovation. Guangdong province produces 35.6 percent of China's high-technology exports and the largest share of its electronics exports (GSB 2011). Interestingly, despite its reputation as a locale of low-value-added activities, Guangdong produces significantly more patents than Beijing and Shanghai—receiving 119,346 in 2010 versus 34,000 and 48,200 for Beijing and Shanghai, respectively (GSB 2008). Even cities such as Dongguan, which still lacks a traditional research university, produce significant numbers of design or improvement patents (DSB 2008). The PRD's success in innovation is largely the result of a tight integration of suppliers and producers. This symbiosis among firms encourages a high degree of efficiency in production and innovations to further enhance these skills. As one entrepreneur explained when discussing his reason for investing the Dongguan township of Qingxi:

> I chose Qingxi because [the ICT hardware] industry's production base is in Qingxi. The suppliers are all located here. If I had my company in Beijing, then I would have needed to ship all the parts to from here to Beijing. Since all the parts are manufactured in Qingxi, it is a great advantage for my company to be here. For example, even if, in the morning, I realize that I am missing critical parts, I just call my friends, and within a few minutes, these parts are sent and delivered to me. (Authors' interview)

Access to locally produced and inexpensive inputs alone is insufficient to foster innovation—no matter how broadly it is defined. For an enterprise to innovate, companies must have an incentive to seek productive activities. This means they must be safe from predatory officials. ICT enterprises in the PRD have secured such protection in part through seeking innocuous forms of ownership or even making the state a partial partner. In different regions of China, and particularly in different industries, bringing the state in as a partial owner and partner is more common than in the PRD. Although, as explored by Bachman, local state enterprises led the move into market-based electronic production in the 1980s and established some of the first Sino-foreign joint ventures in Guangdong, the governments of PRD cities have generally refrained from opening companies under state ownership (Bachman 2001).[7] Despite the region's reputation as a bastion of private companies, most firms explicitly refuse to describe themselves as private and prefer to claim the title minying, or "people run." "Minying," pragmatically speaking, is a largely undefined term (Segal 2003). The reticence to describe themselves as "private," even among founders who started businesses with their own funds, is due to the fact that by defining themselves as minying, they do not run the risk of falling afoul of possible regulatory changes directed at a given class of enterprises. Uncertainty over the future of property rights, combined with both the central state's disregard for pure hardware manufacturing and local authorities' particular aversion to creating state-owned enterprises (SOEs), led companies to fully embrace the ambiguous and politically neutral "minying."

Second, in order to innovate, enterprises must be able to secure returns from their investments in innovative activity (such as R&D). In the West, this is done through reliance on intellectual property rights. However, intellectual property rights in China are unevenly and somewhat arbitrarily enforced. In the PRD, ICT firms generally, although not universally, opt to innovate incrementally and rapidly but not radically as a means of ensuring a non-property rights reliant source of competitive advantage. Acknowledging local innovation patterns, regional officials take a rather broad expansive view of innovation, particularly when compared with the central government which mostly considers innovation in terms of novel product inventions:

> Here we view incremental innovation on existing platforms very much as indigenous innovation. So long as there is improvement or new features, it counts; we do not need to come up with a wholly new product to have self-innovation. (authors' interview)

Development of a tightly integrated manufacturing industry cluster in the region enables fast incremental innovation. Starting from highly codified models and overseas orders, companies begin with the simplest assembly operations and gradually increase the amount of research they perform with the *designs explicitly geared toward ensuring ease of production.* Where production is one's specialty, increasing efficiency and quality at a constant or lower cost is a powerful competitive advantage. As domestic and especially overseas clients come to trust the producer, their degree of design freedom increases, allowing the company to increase investment in R&D and to further differentiate its products from others'. Companies work with their suppliers to improve the quality of components in accordance with the needs or preferences of customers, thus bringing even more companies into a network of production-oriented innovation.

The PRD's leading ICT hardware firms have followed this development pattern since the 1980s, moving from low-profit margin assembly-based operations to technology and production innovation and (for some firms) independent brands. In industries as diverse as power supplies, mobile telephony network equipment, and assembled ICT hardware, PRD companies lead China. In power supplies, firms such as Zhicheng Champion have steadily upgraded their capabilities and moved into line-interactive and online systems at ever higher volt-ampere ratings—making them able to compete with world-leading Taiwanese firms in the global marketplace. Similarly, Huawei has moved away from its origins in maintenance and resale of foreign telecommunications equipment, to the point where it now produces late-generation mobile telecommunications equipment for markets from Asia and Africa to the European Union.

PRD firms from new national leaders such as ZTE, Tencent, or Huawei to smaller subcomponent suppliers have managed to successfully upgrade their technology such that the leading firms are now widely perceived as being as capable as any foreign competitor at producing current-generation technology while still retaining lower costs.

In interviews, many PRD SMEs (small and medium enterprises) explicitly dismissed novel product innovation as a categorical good. Entrepreneurs and officials repeatedly considered the virtues of using and producing technology appropriate for market needs, making incremental improvements, and shortening the time to market to be superior to the allure of high technology and novelty. One interviewee was particularly frank in his ambivalent view toward novel product innovation under the industrial conditions he observed in China:

> Before I started this company, I was in the Chinese Academy of Sciences. Once I moved to industry, I quickly learned that the higher the technology, the less likely [that] products would enter the market, at least in a timely fashion. There are three highs: high price, high tech, and high time consumption. These are the three highs people fear. Thirty years ago, wireless technology would be unbelievable, but now it's real. If you had tried to make it thirty years ago [in China], it would have cost a lot and failed. (authors' interview)

Incremental improvements and short time to market ensure the company's products will still be in demand and thus provide an edge over fast-approaching competitors. Indeed, the region's top ICT hardware firms—the telecommunications hardware companies Huawei and ZTE—owe their rapid rise to prominence largely by eschewing novel product development and specializing instead in the development of technologies seen as obsolete by foreign MNCs and China's national leadership. For example, ZTE grew rapidly through the production of personal quasi-mobile phone system handsets and equipment, known in China as Xiaolingtong. Although the central government tried to ban or severely restrict Xiaolingtong technology due to its lack of novelty and comparative backwardness compared with 2G and 3G mobile, market demand for inexpensive mobile telephony made it wildly popular—attaining some 91 million users by 2006. ZTE eschewed novelty and capitalized on this demand, becoming one of China's four dominant equipment providers (Lin 2003; Yuan et al. 2006).

A feature that allows the PRD's ICT SMEs to engage in continuous innovation is the gradual development of product-based industrial agglomerations around specific townships throughout the region. Many of these agglomerations take on more and more features associated with classical manufacturing-based Marshalian or North-Italian clusters (Marshall [1890] 1920; Piore and Sabel 1984). These clusters include specialized suppliers and companies that together encompass most of the stages of development and production—from R&D to final assembly—each focused on a specific variety of products.

As explained by a manager of a Guangzhou-based hardware company when asked about locational decisions:

> Why Guangzhou? Simple: the industrial chain is in Guangzhou. For example, within a radius of fifty kilometers, we can collect all of the components for the products we produce. But in the north, there is no condition like that. Does Shanghai have a complete industrial chain for electronics production? No, it does not! The entire Chinese electronics production chain is in Guangdong, Shenzhen, and especially Dongguan—not the north. (authors' interview)

This environment is highly conducive to the opening of new firms and suppliers in the PRD as both subsuppliers and market opportunities abound. Local leaders in Dongguan, for example, pride themselves on their locale's "complete" production chains as they see these as the region's source of sustained economic growth and competitive advantage:

> Why is the [ICT] industry able to operate like this? It is because the production chain is complete. Why is Qingxi able to make computer cases, LCD screens, mice, keyboards, and entire IT systems or lines? It is because Qingxi's production chain is very complete. Our full industrial chain is our greatest advantage in stimulating growth and attracting new investment. (authors' interview)

The tight, dense network of related suppliers allows individual companies to focus on a narrow set of activities in which they can excel and constantly improve. Even high-end components are typically sourced within the PRD, although software and integrated circuits frequently come from the local branch companies of foreign MNCs rather than truly local companies. Up to 90 percent of the necessary components for locally produced systems, such as uninterruptible power supplies, are sourced from other companies rather than produced in-house. That companies source so many of their components locally testifies to the degree of completeness of the local industrial chain and the extent of specialized firms' local integration.

Finally, we found the ICT SMEs in the PRD have been blocked from the formal banking and financial system. In interviews managers and owners noted this problem had only grown worse in recent years:

> Financing is a problem for the entire non-state sector. Minying enterprises cannot get loans. In the PRD, you could before, but not now. The national banks keep themselves really tight when making loans to minying enterprises. (authors' interview)

Isolated from the formal lending system, the industry has developed two separate but complementary means of securing growth and development capital: rotating financing and local state support.[8] Rotating financing are agreements among suppliers, producers, and customers to ensure smooth production, working and start-up capital, incentivize cooperation, and sanction cheating, without the need for state regulation or the need to utilize the legal system (Geertz 1962; Putnam 1993; Uzzi 1996).

An example of such an informal financing institution is intercompany credit. Under such agreements, "credit" from suppliers is used to finance expansion. A typical arrangement involves obtaining necessary components based on a commitment to pay for them once the finished products are sold. In turn, these same companies extend credit to their resellers or OEM-brand clients (original-equipment manufacturing). The system is based on unofficial promissory notes made between enterprises without formal legal contracts. Such a system is highly susceptible to cheating, but tight spatial concentration and tight networking of industry act as a deterrent. The blacklisting of suppliers and individuals who fail to repay on time involves excluding them not only from lines of credit but also from the industry as a whole. Since the necessary components for nearly any ICT hardware are all produced in Dongguan, falling from favor would result in an enterprise and individuals being forced out of business. A manager from an enterprise involved in one such financing network explained how it works:

> The whole operation is based on trust. If you cannot be trusted, you will be kicked out of the business. In ancient China, total costs were calculated once per year. So people would trade and keep track of their balance sheets. At the end of the year, each merchant would collect their credits and pay their debts. This is traditional trust. When we first set up this company, I invested my money first. Suppliers helped me, since my own capital was insufficient. They provided me with the needed capital goods and first components, assuming I would pay once I sold the final products. We didn't borrow any money from the government. In the end, it was even better than having a loan from a bank, because had I had a loan, I would have to pay interest; now I don't. The entire business is based on trust to this day. For example, if my company needs $500,000 worth of inputs, but I only have $50,000 dollars in cash, all my suppliers support me. And I support my customers too. It's a trust cycle from beginning to end. (authors' interview)

Constant and repeated interactions within the manufacturing-based ICT hardware cluster of Dongguan enable enterprises to conduct transactions based on trust. This informal financial system also extends to the creation of new enterprises. Since the start-up phase for a manufacturing facility involves a large capital investment and a time lag before any revenue is generated, such an up-front investment would be difficult to sustain without credit. In Dongguan, trust-based pooled credit among enterprises enables start-ups to commence operations and secure orders in advance by purchasing capital equipment and parts on credit with promises to repay once a revenue stream is established. However, such a system encourages investment in proven business models that are well understood by all participants in the network and involve manufacturing ventures which can secure orders in advance of, or very shortly after, commencing operations.

The second major source of capital, and one more specifically focused on improving innovative capabilities, is local and provincial government investment. As the national government and the centrally run banking system have not been involved in the development and growth of the sector, the local government can and has acted as an alternative.[9] The local state has been an important source of supplemental development capital. Realizing that the formal financial sector is largely closed to the local ICT SMEs, local governments subsidize expansion and capital-equipment upgrading through subsidies and tax rebates. The belief is that savings on capital-goods imports encourage companies to buy more advanced equipment and train the local workforce in its use, further enhancing the region's competitive advantage which relies on a highly skilled manufacturing workforce. The idea that successful innovation depends on raising the skill levels of manufacturing laborers is entrenched in local government policies. In some sectors, such as power supplies, leading companies draw a large part of their R&D financing from local-government grants. Dongguan's Municipal Science and Technology Commission annually earmarks funds for projects designed to improve the R&D capabilities and technology quality of Dongguan's SMEs. In 2008, the city established a new fund of one billion RMB (renminbi) to help SMEs and newly established enterprises (NanfangRibao 2008; Zhao 2008). These grants go directly to companies, in the amount of millions of RMB per year to each firm. Since other sources of financing are limited, the importance of local-government aid for the viability of the cluster should not be underestimated.

The ICT firms in the PRD have mostly successfully adapted to take advantage of new spaces in the global production chain. They have also effectively navigated around the constraints imposed by structured uncertainty and shown considerable resilience.

Discussion and Conclusion

Although it is clear China accomplished itself as an innovator and critical node in global production of ICT hardware, are the same forces that have enabled its emergence as an ICT powerhouse at work in other sectors?

As Chapter 7 (in this volume) demonstrates, in the case of the car industry the answer is affirmative, even with the significantly different structure of the industry. Automobile production has been a highly capital intensive industry which typically includes long production runs of single products—updated annually. Automobile production has also traditionally involved much tighter integration of companies. Even though companies increasingly source components from specialized providers such as Bosch, Denso, Johnson Controls, Lear, TRW, and Magna, different components and subsystems (such as instrument panels) often remain unique to different brands and models (Sturgeon and Florida 2004). The lack of standardization of components limits the ability of suppliers to produce for multiple brands as each part—such as a transmission—must be uniquely designed to the demands of each customer.

In Chapter 2 (in this volume), Noble presents a strong case for the emerging capabilities of Chinese automobile firms (Noble 2011). Although their export markets remain small, and the market is still dominated by foreign brands, new players such as BYD, Chery, and Geely are introducing new models, technologies, and designs and forcing other companies to adapt. As Noble explores, and we argue here, the process of China's automobile industry development has continually capitalized on the advantages afforded by China's industrial adaptations to structured uncertainty.

China is, perhaps, the first example of an outsourcing and modularized automobile industry. Rather than emphasizing the development of wholly unique cars with an integrated design and production system—as was the case with the United States, Germany, Japan, and Korea—China's new producers have been happy to use other company's parts and designs. For example, Chinese brands made use of Mitsubishi Motor's China-based factories' overcapacity for engines and bought them wholesale for use in Chinese-body cars. Chinese firms then turned to Chinese and foreign components suppliers which worked for and with the major Sino-foreign JVs (joint ventures) or foreign assemblers. The development of capable local suppliers and networks for components was particular successful in areas like Shanghai where the local state coordinated investment and development with an eye toward forming a complete local industry chain—albeit one with high degrees of foreign ownership (Segal and Thun 2001).

Noble argues that this reliance on outsourced components hurt the novel innovative capabilities of Chinese firms and prevented meaningful brand distinction. However, it enabled companies to launch large numbers of models quickly and have reliable if unremarkable quality. This rapid enlargement to scale has benefited the Chinese consumer in less expensive vehicles and the Chinese companies by enabling them to learn from the best even as they capitalize on advantages in manufacturing and a large, educated labor force.

Second, Chinese firms take advantage of knowledge in supply chain management and how to integrate fragmented production into products of acceptable quality. This includes a willingness to buy expertise off the shelf. Unlike Japanese or Korean firms, Chinese companies heavily utilize foreign design and engineering consulting firms from Italy, Germany, Britain, and Austria. This helps them rapidly generate high-quality new models without having to develop the capabilities in-house. Rather, they can concentrate on ever-improving their integration and manufacturing capabilities. These designs and technologies were bought outright as an outsourced service, thus giving the Chinese companies full rights and the ability to improve or alter them in the future, further building on incremental capabilities.

Finally, recent trends may encourage even greater successes in China's auto industry. Thun's study of the automobile industry found very different institutional arrangements shaping the development of the auto industry in different parts of China (Thun 2006). Since his research, however, there has been the emergence of private or local state-owned automobile companies which rely even more heavily on outsourcing and modularization.

Furthermore, such automobile firms' greatest advantages may come as a result of the skills in design and production of electronics and power sources—skills learned through fierce competition in the electronics and ICT industries. Firms such as BYD are leading China in the development of hybrid and particularly wholly electric vehicles by relying on existing skills in production of inexpensive but reliable batteries. The same specialization that facilitated the development of a wide array of ICT firms, each with its own component niche, is supporting development of new types of automobiles by allowing for the use of commoditized and inexpensive power sources.

As we have shown in this chapter, China should be seen as an innovative economic giant, one that has specialized in different stages of innovation, both enhancing and competing with novel product R&D innovation, the focus of policy in the United States. There is a precedent for emphasizing production and incremental improvements. Japan's most famous industries—consumer electronics and automobiles—were neither invented nor commercialized nor mass produced first in Japan. Rather, the country successfully built its industry and long-term innovative capacity from the bottom up. Japan's ability to produce novel innovations arose from the factory floor. Thus, we would not be surprised to see similar capabilities evolving in China over time. However, as the current innovation system in the product of a very specific political economic institutional environment, to attempt and force a rapid move toward novel product innovation in China would likely be highly counterproductive. It would waste resources and harm otherwise highly successful and competitive business models.

To understand whether China is a challenge to the developed West, we must understand how it operates. China's rise was enabled by the global fragmentation of production. The ability to modularize production processes continues to benefit China in a wide array of industries. China's particular political economic institutional environment shapes the innovative skills of companies in very specific and recognizable patterns. These patterns stand in contrast to the declared goals of China's central government, which has long desired for China to become a global leader in the development of new technologies and products. Chinese enterprises, through skill and necessity, have successfully adapted to this environment. They innovate by entering niches enabled by the global fragmentation of production and specializing intensively in all innovation activities apart from novel product. In the ICT industry, manufacturing skills and tightly integrated production clusters have enabled firms to develop innovative capacities for ease, speed, and cost of production and design. Thus even as costs rise, China will be able to remain competitive and profitable in many ICT niches from assembly to design and applied R&D. In the automobile industry, the mass of the Chinese market and the scale of its production capacity have, under conditions of increasing fragmentation, enabled the rise of new brands. Great competitive pressure has been exerted on foreign brands and joint ventures to increase their rate of new model design and to reduce their prices. Despite wide divergence from central plans, China's enterprises—through their successful adaptation to the limits and risks of structured uncertainty—have developed an array of innovative capabilities.

For the developed West, this poses a unique challenge. China's industries are not competing with Western ones to lead at the cusp of novel product innovation. Rather, they are competing by successfully mastering all other stages of innovation and production. In so doing, although the largest shares of profits continue to be reaped overseas, the Chinese gain greater broad-based employment and economic growth. They also gain an intimate understanding of a wide variety of technologies, exactly the sort of understanding necessary for an eventual leap into "higher" forms of innovation. Thus the China challenge is whether or not the modern economic model in the developed West which relies on specialization at only the top of the innovation pyramid is sustainable when the remainder of the pyramid, with its skills and jobs, has moved elsewhere.

Acknowledgments

The authors wish to thank the Alfred P. Sloan Foundation for financial support and the Berkeley Roundtable on the International Economy (BRIE) for research and administrative support. Breznitz would like to acknowledge that this book is partly based upon work supported by the National Science Foundation under Grant SES-0964907 and to thank the Kauffman Foundation for its generous financial support.

Notes

1. The 863 Program began in March 1986 with the purpose of facilitating development of high-technology and scientific research projects and rapidly commercializing scientific discoveries. The 1988 Torch Program explicitly called for creation of science and technology industry zones and works on improving the environment for high-technology industrial development. In 2006, China launched a fifteen-year plan for science and technology development which included investment in major centrally chosen products such as wide body aircraft and supercomputers. Since the 1980s, China's government at the central and regional level has provided an array of incentives for the development of high-technology businesses, including the provision of tax breaks and subsidies. In order to qualify, a firm must be certified as a "New and High Technology Enterprise" or its product as a "New and High Technology Product." Since 2006, the requirements for these certifications have become much more stringent in the hope of mandating firms to move into more R&D-intensive activities and investing more heavily in research and development.

2. For more on structured uncertainty, see Chapter 2 of Breznitz and Murphree (2011).

3. A prime example occurred in the telecommunications market. The Ministry of Posts and Telecommunications (MPT) took the first step toward liberalization in 1994 when it permitted China Unicom to begin competing with the incumbent—China Telecom. As a new entrant, China Unicom faced a highly uncertain environment. Unsure where the boundaries lay, it tried various experimental practices. Most notably, it developed a system known as China-China-Foreign where Unicom would form a joint venture with another Chinese firm with a foreign joint venture partner. Foreign capital could thus be funneled indirectly into China Unicom. By 1998 there were

forty-nine such collaborations completed or under negotiation when the MPT abruptly declared three of them "illegal" and the remainder "irregular" leading to their immediate termination. What had been a creative interpretation of policy, pragmatic for business development, had suddenly been deemed a bridge too far and crushed by central authorities (DeWoskin 2001; Harwit 2008; Low 2005; Wu 2009).

4. We should note, however, that today there are strong and growing constituencies in China that are seeking change. Leading Chinese companies such as ZTE, Huawei, Lenovo, and Tencent have come to understand that in order to continue to be globally successful, their interest must now lie with encouraging greater certainty in China's political economy. While we expect change, it will be a long and incremental process in which both central and local government actors as well as business interests will play a significant role.

5. The best example of this type of research strategy is exemplified by Microsoft Research Asia in Beijing. This research center is one of the most productive in the world, having an output of papers in leading computer science journals as good as or better than the world's leading universities and research centers. Such a concentration on pure science or technology (such as algorithm development) does not lend itself immediately to commercial applications and thus reduces the benefit from piracy.

6. Although the central government (seeing the success of PRD-based industries in the early 1980s) encouraged hardware production and export-oriented assembly industries in the first years of reform, this sector of the fragmented global electronics and ICT industry is increasingly disdained due to its relative low value added, reliance on high-value imported components such as proprietary processors, and use of energy and pollution. While not banned, activities in this area are increasingly discouraged and central government support—particularly financial support or promotional policies—has generally been withdrawn.

7. This is not to say that it has not happened or that the local government does not take a very active role in spurring the development of desired industries. ZTE, a telecommunications hardware manufacturer and one of the region's most successful firms, is a mostly local government-owned enterprise. Similarly, ports, transportation companies, and investment firms are also frequently enterprises owned by the local or provincial government.

8. Researchers have been increasingly noting that China's financial system privileges large and SOEs and largely neglects small and medium sized private or minying enterprises. In the 1980s and 1990s, this was attributed to lack of reform in the official banking system and the resulting lack of knowledge for how to evaluate loan applications, as well as an unspoken understanding that loan officers making loans to state enterprises, even if they went bad, would be forgiven, while bad loans to private companies would not. More recent scholarship has found that loan patterns continue to favor large and established enterprises. Even ostensibly venture capital firms do not provide early-stage investment to research-intensive enterprises. Finally, much of the national research funding goes to megaprojects, and those conducted by well-connected enterprises or institutes, leaving small companies out in the cold (authors' interviews; Breznitz and Murphree 2011; The Economist 2009; Fuller 2010; Tsai 2002).

9. This pattern held true even for early adapters which have since become national champions. Both Huawei and ZTE were largely ignored by the central state in their early formative years. Only after they had achieved success did they begin to get central government funding and loans. In their formative years, they were outside the plan (Harwit 2007).

References

863. (2008). "863 Jian Jie (Introduction to 863.)" [In Chinese.]. Retrieved March 1, 2008 (http://www.863.org.cn/863_105/863brief/index.html).

Arndt, Sven W., and Henryk Kierzkowski. (Eds.). (2001a). *Fragmentation: New Production Patterns in the World Economy.* Oxford: Oxford University Press.

Arndt, Sven W., and Henryk Kierzkowski. (2001b). "Introduction." In *Fragmentation: New Production Patterns in the World Economy*, edited by S. W. Arndt and H. Kierzkowski, 1–16. Oxford: Oxford University Press.

Arora, Ashish, V. S. Arunachalam, et al. (2001). "The Indian software services industry." *Research Policy* 30: 1267–87.

Arora, Ashish, and Suma Athreye. (2002). "The software industry and India's economic development." *Information Economics and Policy* 14(2): 253–73.

Arora, Ashish, and Alfonso Gambardella. (Eds.). (2005). *From Underdogs to Tigers: The Rise and Growth of the Software Industry in Some Emerging Economies.* New York: Oxford University Press.

Arrow, J. Kenneth. (1962). "Economic Welfare and the Allocation of Resources for Invention." In *The Rate and Direction of Inventive Activity: Economic and Social Factors*, edited by R. R. Nelson, 609–25. Princeton, NJ: Princeton University Press.

Bachman, David. (2001). "Defense industrialization in Guangdong." *The China Quarterly* 166: 273–304.

Breznitz, Dan. (2007). *Innovation and the State: Political Choice and Strategies for Growth in Israel, Taiwan, and Ireland.* New Haven, CT: Yale University Press.

Breznitz, Dan, and Michael Murphree. (2011). *Run of the Red Queen: Government, Innovation, Globalization, and Economic Growth in China.* New Haven, CT: Yale University Press.

Cao, Cong, Richard P. Suttmeier, and Denis F. Simon. (2006). "China's 15-year science and technology plan." *Physics Today* 59(12): 38–43.

ChinaDevelopmentGateway. (2004). Planning: Torch Program. Retrieved August 8, 2008 (http://en.chinagate.com.cn/english/446.htm).

"China is spending to recover." (2009). *The Economist*, June 1. Retrieved July 30, 2009 (http://www.economist.com/agenda/displaystory.cfm?story_id=13765331&fsrc=twitter).

China Tech News. (2008). "Foxconn not a high-tech enterprise under China's new standard?" Retrieved October 27, 2008 (http://www.chinatechnews.com/2008/06/18/6887-foxconn-not-a-high-tech-enterprise-under-chinas-new-standard/).

ChinaTorch. (2006). "Mission of the China Torch Program." Retrieved October 10, 2006 (http://www.chinatorch.gov.cn/eng/other/Mission.htm).

D'Costa, Anthony P., and E. Sridharan. (Eds.). (2004). *India in the Global Software Industry: Innovation, Firm Strategies and Development.* Basingtoke: Palgrave Macmillan.

Dean, Jason. (2007). "The Forbidden City of Terry Gou, the biggest exporter you never heard of." *The Wall Street Journal*, August 13.

DeWoskin, Kenneth J. (2001). "The WTO and the telecommunications sector in China." *The China Quarterly* 167: 630–54.

Dossani, Rafiq, and Martin Kenney. (2003). "'Lift and shift': Moving the back office to India." *Information Technologies and International Development* 1(2): 21–37.

Dossani, Rafiq, and Martin Kenney. (2007). "The next wave of globalization: Relocating service provision to India." *World Development* 35(5): 772–91.

Dossani, Rafiq, and Martin Kenney. (2009). "Service provision for the global economy: The evolving Indian experience." *Review of Policy Research.* 26(1–2): 77–104.

DSB. (2008). *2007 Nian Dong Guan Shi Guo Min Jing Ji He She Hui Fa Zhan Tong Ji Gong Bao* [2007 Dongguan City People's Economic and Social Development Statistics Report]. Dongguan, China: Dongguan Statistics Bureau.

Elliot, John E. (1983). "Schumpeter and the theory of capitalist economic development." *Journal of Economic Behavior & Organization* 4(4): 277–308.

Fuller, Douglas B. (2005). *"Building Ladders Out of Chains: China's Technological Upgrading in a World of Global Production."* Political Science, MIT, Cambridge, MA.

Fuller, Douglas B. (2010). "How law, politics and transnational networks affect technology entrepreneurship: Explaining divergent venture capital investing strategies in China." *Asia Pacific Journal of Management* 27: 445–59.

Galvin, P., and A. Morkel, (2001), "The effects of product modularity on industry structure: The case of the world bicycle industry." *Industry and Innovation* 8(1): 31–47.

Geertz, Clifford. (1962). "The rotating credit association: A 'middle rung' in development." *Economic Development and Social Change* 10(3): 241–63.

Gereffi, Gary. (1994). "The Organization of Buyer-Driven Global Commodity Chains: How the US Retailers Shape Overseas Production Network." In *Commodity Chains and Global Capitalism*, edited by G. Gereffi and M. Korzeniewicz, 95–122. Westport, CT: Praeger.

Gereffi, Gary (1996) "Commodity chains and regional divisions of labor in East Asia." *Journal of Asian Business* 12(1): 75–112.

Gourevitch, Peter. (2000). "Globalization of production: Insights from the hard drive disk industry." *World Development* 28(2): 301–17.

GSB. (2008). *2007 Nian Guang Dong Guo Min Jing Ji He She Hui Fa Zhan Tong Ji Gong Bao* [2007 Guangdong People's Economic and Social Development Statistics Report]. Guangzhou, China.

GSB. (2011). "2010 Nian Guang Dong Sheng Gao Xin Ji Shu Chan Pin Jin Chu Kou Qing Kuang Fen Xi [2010 Guangdong Province New and High Technology Product Import and Export Situation Analysis]." Retrieved April 15, 2011 (http://www.gdztc.gov.cn/News/2875/Info.aspx)."

Guo, Wanda, and Yueqiu Feng. (2007). *Special Economic Zones and Competitiveness: A Case Study of Shenzhen, the People's Republic of China*. Islamabad, Pakistan: Asian Development Bank.

Harwit, Eric. (2007). "Building China's telecommunications network: Industrial policy and the role of Chinese state-owned, foreign and private domestic enterprises." *The China Quarterly* 190: 311–32.

Harwit, Eric. (2008). *China's Telecommunications Revolution*. New York: Oxford University Press.

Hobday, Mike. (1995). "Innovation in East Asia: Diversity and development." *Technovation* 15(2): 55–63.

Huang, Yasheng, and Yi Qian. (2008). "Is entrepreneurship missing in Shanghai?" Paper presented at the National Bureau of Economic Research Conference on International Differences in Entrepreneurship, Savannah, GA.

Johnson, Joel. (2011). "1 million workers. 90 million iPhones. 17 suicides. Who's to blame?" [Wired]. Retrieved April 14, 2011 (http://www.wired.com/magazine/2011/02/ff_joelinchina/all/1).

Kenney, Martin, and Richard L. Florida. (2004). *Locating Global Advantage: Industry Dynamics in the International Economy*. Stanford, CA: Stanford University Press.

Langlois, Richard N., and Paul L. Robertson. (1992). "Networks and innovation in a modular system: Lessons from the microcomputer and stereo component industries." *Research Policy* 21: 297–313.

Lin, Qiang. (2003). The development of ZTE & PHS. Retrieved March 26, 2009 (http://www.phsmou.org/events/GMMaterials/ZTEIntroduction.pdf).

Low, Brian. (2005). "The evolution of China's telecommunications equipment market: A contextual, analytical framework." *Journal of Business & Industrial Marketing* 20(2): 99–108.

Marshall, Alfred. (1920). *Principles of Economics*. London: Macmillan and Co., Ltd. (Orig. pub. 1890.)

McKendrick, David, Richard F. Doner, and Stephan Haggard. (2000). *From Silicon Valley to Singapore: Location and Competitive Advantage in the Hard Disk Drive Industry*. Stanford, CA: Stanford University Press.

Nanfang Ribao. (2008). "Dong Guan 10 Yi Yuan Bang Fu Zhong Xiao Qi Ye Rong Zi Qi Ye Xu Wu Bu Liang Xin Yong Ji Lu" [Dongguan's One Billion RMB to Support SMEs—Enterprises Must Not Have an Unhealthy Credit Record]. Retrieved January 19, 2008 (http://www.gd.gov.cn/govpub/rdzt/nxcfz/knxds/200811/t20081124_73933.htm).

NSBPRC. (2001–10). *2000–2009 Nian Guo Min Jing Ji He She Hui Fa Zhan Tong Ji Gong Bao* [2000–2009 Citizens' Economic and Social Development Statistics Reports]. Beijing: National Statistics Bureau of China.

OECD. (2006). "China, Information Technologies and the Internet." In *Information Technology Outlook 2006* (Ch. 4). Paris: Organization for Economic Cooperation and Development.

Piore, Michael J., and Charles F. Sabel. (1984). *The Second Industrial Divide: Possibilities for Prosperity*. New York: Basic Books.

Putnam, D. Robert. (1993). *Making Democracy Work*. Princeton, NJ: Princeton University Press.

Rodrik, Dani. (2007). *One Economics, Many Recipes: Globalization, Institutions, and Economic Growth*. Princeton, NJ: Princeton University Press.

Rosenberg, Nathan. (1983). *Inside the Black Box: Technology and Economics*. Cambridge: University of Cambridge Press.

Rosenberg, Nathan, and L. E. Birdzell Jr. (1986). *How the West Grew Rich: The Economic Transformation of the Industrial World*. New York: Basic Books.

Schumpeter, Joseph Alois. (1961). *The Theory of Economic Development: An Inquiry into Profits, Capital, Credit, Interest, and the Business Cycle*. Cambridge, MA: Harvard University Press. (Orig. pub. 1934.)

Scott, Allen J. (1987). "The semiconductor industry in Southeast-Asia." *Regional Studies* 21(2): 143–60.

Segal, Adam. (2003). *Digital Dragon: High-Technology Enterprises in China*. Ithaca, NY: Cornell University Press.

Segal, Adam, and Eric Thun. (2001). "Thinking globally, acting locally: Local governments, industrial sectors, and development in China." *Politics & Society* 29(4): 557–88.

Shen, Jianfa, Kwan-Yiu Wong, et al. (2000). "The spatial dynamics of foreign investment in the Pearl River Delta, South China." *The Geographical Journal* 166(4): 312–22.

SSB. (2008). *Shenzhen Shi 2007 Nian Guo Min Jing Ji He She Hui Fa Zhan Tong Ji Gong Gao* [Shenzhen City 2007 People's Economic and Social Development Stastics Report]. Shenzhen Statistics Bureau: Shenzhen, China:.

Steinfeld, S. Edward. (2010). *Playing Our Game: Why China's Economic Rise Doesn't Threaten the West*. Oxford: Oxford University Press.

Sturgeon, Timothy J. (2000). "Turnkey Production Networks: The Organizational Delinking of Production from Innovation." In *New Product Development and Production Networks*, edited by U. Jurgens, 67–84. New York: Springer.

Sturgeon, Timothy J. (2002). "Modular production networks: A new American model of industrial organization." *Industrial and Corporate Change* 11(3): 451–96.

Sturgeon, Timothy J. (2003). "What really goes on in Silicon Valley? Spatial clustering and dispersal in modular production networks." *Journal of Economic Geography* 3: 199–225.

Sturgeon, Timothy J., and Richard Florida. (2004). "Globalization, Deverticalization, and Employment in the Motor Vehicle Industry." In *Locating Global Advantage: Industry Dynamics in the International Economy*, edited by M. Kenney and R. L. Florida, 52–81. Stanford, CA: Stanford University Press.

Sturgeon, Timothy J., and Richard Lester. (2004). "The New Global Supply-Base: New Challenges for Local Suppliers in East Asia." In *Global Production Networking and Technological Change in East Asia*, edited by S. Yusuf, A. Altaf and K. Nabeshima, 35–88. Oxford: Oxford University Press.

Thun, Eric. (2006). *Changing Lanes in China: Foreign Direct Investment, Local Governments, and Auto Sector Development*. Cambridge: University of Cambridge Press.

Tsai, Kellee S. (2002). *Back Alley Banking: Private Entrepreneurs in China*. Ithaca, NY: Cornell University Press.

Uzzi, Brian. (1996). "The sources and consequences of embeddedness for the economic performance of organizations: The network effect." *American Sociological Review* 61: 674–98.

Walcott, Susan. (2003). *Chinese Science and Technology Industrial Parks*. Burlington, VT: Ashgate.

Wilson, James Q. (1968). *Varieties of Police Behavior: The Management of Law and Order in Eight Communities*. Cambridge: Harvard University Press.

Wu, Irene. (2009). *From Iron Fist to Invisible Hand: the Uneven Path of Telecommunications Reform in China*. Stanford, CA: Stanford University Press.

Yuan, Yufei, Wuping Zheng, et al. (2006). "Xiaolingtong versus 3G in China: Which will be the winner?" *Telecommunications Policy* 30: 297–313.

Zhao, Dianchuan. (2008). "Dong Guan Shi Zhang Li Yu Quan: 10 Yi Yuan She Li Zhuan Xing Sheng Ji Zhuan Xiang Ji Jin" [Dongguan Mayor Li Yuquan: 1 Billion RMB establishes reform promoting specialized fund]. *Nanfang Wang* (August 18, 2008). Retrieved January 19, 2009 (http://news.southcn.com/dishi/dsrdzt/content/2008-08/18/content_4550807.htm).

Zysman, John, and Abraham Newman. (Eds.). (2006). *How Revolutionary Was the Digital Revolution? National Responses, Market Transformations, and Global Technology*. Stanford, CA: Stanford Business Books.

2 The Chinese Auto Industry as Challenge, Opportunity, and Partner
Gregory W. Noble

CHINA'S REMARKABLY RAPID and sustained economic upsurge has presented a serious challenge to firms, governments, and workers in advanced industrial countries. The Chinese government regularly protects and promotes local firms, while remaining relatively lax about environmental standards, working conditions, and infringement of intellectual property rights. From textiles to steel, foreign firms have found themselves struggling to compete with the "China price." The challenge is not limited to cheap or low-end products. China is churning out ever-increasing numbers of engineers and scientists. It has surpassed Japan as the second-largest source of academic papers, and was on track to pass Japan and the United States in 2011 in patent applications. If questions about the current quality and significance of Chinese research remain widespread, experts agree that the direction is clearly and strongly upward, especially in such crucial areas of industry as telecommunications and chemicals (Adams, King, and Ma 2009; Rovner 2010).

China's extraordinary rise is particularly visible in the automotive industry. In 2009, China shot past the United States as the world's largest automobile market, and will soon pass it in value of output as well. China's exports of automotive products ranked seventh in 2009, and grew far more rapidly in the preceding decade than those of any other significant exporter (World Trade Organization 2010: 101). Most of those exports comprise automotive parts. Exports of whole vehicles are modest and for now, at least, largely limited to developing countries. An initial flurry of reports that Chinese auto firms would export to North America proved premature, but Chinese companies are exporting cars to the peripheries of Europe, and have set up assembly operations not only in the developing world but also in Russia and the Ukraine. Almost unnoticed, China has become a major world force in trucks, buses, and diesel engines, exports of which are also rapidly increasing. Perhaps most surprising, China has gathered attention as a new force and crucial marketplace for next-generation automobiles such as hybrid and electric vehicles, not least because the Chinese government is determined to become a leader in e-vehicles (Roland Berger 2010).

China is becoming the world's leading industrial power and it will indeed challenge many firms and industries in developed countries. In some areas, such as modularization, it may also challenge existing ways of conducting business. Yet China will not present as monolithic a challenge as the Japanese did in the 1960s, or the Koreans in the 1990s and early years of the new century. Foreigners are far more deeply involved in Chinese industry via ownership and trade than they are even today in Japan and Korea. Indeed, foreign firms dominate many industries in China and have been major beneficiaries of Chinese growth. General Motors (GM), for example, already sells more vehicles in China than in the United States. To be sure, all are produced in joint ventures, and many are small and inexpensive, but over time the total profits accruing to GM and other foreign producers are likely to surpass those originating in North America, Germany, or Japan. Moreover, even as China plays an increasing role in final assembly, it increases its imports of parts and equipment, a trend that should accelerate as the Chinese currency, the *renminbi* (RMB), appreciates.

The rest of this chapter fleshes out the question of where the Chinese auto industry is a challenger, where it could be a game changer, and where it is primarily an opportunity and partner. The first section considers the degree to which China follows—and diverges from—the Japanese and Korean developmental path, emphasizing China's much earlier and greater interpenetration with global firms and markets. The second section examines China as a force for price reductions, a force that stems not just from low wages, cheap land, and subsidized inputs but from a profusion of young engineers, the selective application of dramatically cheaper Chinese machinery, and a level of domestic competition far exceeding that found in Japan or Korea. The third section looks at the extensive use of modularization and outsourcing in China, especially the shifting reliance on European and domestic design and engineering houses. The final section explores China's alternative energy vehicle strategy and closely examines three Chinese companies developing next-generation vehicles. China relies heavily on foreign sources of technology at the same time that it is pouring resources into hybrid and electric cars and the batteries to power them.

China as a Variant on the Japanese and Korean Developmental Path

China's progression recalls that of Japan and Korea, two other east Asian countries that grew into major auto exporters on the basis of skilled and disciplined low-wage labor, inexpensive but productive engineers, and extensive government protection and promotion. Prospects for the Chinese auto industry also draw a great deal of skepticism, however. Chinese vehicles are still prone to defects, indifferently designed, and lacking in brand power. The quality of management in Chinese companies remains suspect, labor costs are rising, and sooner or later the Chinese government will have to allow the RMB to appreciate.

China echoes many aspects of the targeted industrial policy pursued by the developmental states in Japan and Korea in the post-war period (Johnson 1982). Lacking comparative advantage and facing imposing barriers to entry, the Japanese and Koreans resorted to virtually complete protection against imports of vehicles, and they strictly limited and controlled the entry of foreign capital. They gained access to foreign technology largely through licensing, the terms of which the governments strictly monitored (Mardon 1990; Mason 1992). Governments also intervened in myriad other ways, such as implementing tax policies that favored production of a narrow range of engine sizes, thus contributing to attainment of economies of scale.

This stylized account of state promotion and protection in Japan and Korea has attracted three major critiques, each of which has some validity, but none of which undermines the thrust of the argument. The first critique claims that government was generally not that closely involved in the development of the Japanese automotive industry, and to the extent it was, it failed, most notably in plans in the 1950s and again in the early 1960s to force consolidation of the industry (Henderson 1983; Trezise 1983). This claim is ill-informed and mostly incorrect. First and foremost, the Japanese government provided Toyota, Nissan, and other Japanese producers with virtually full protection against imported cars and foreign capital well into the 1980s. The second merger plan was fairly successful, and similar but less publicized efforts in parts were even more successful (Tate 1995). Government banks were significant supporters of the auto parts industry into the 1980s (Yamazaki 2003), and loans from long-term credit banks deeply influenced by government were crucial to both assemblers and suppliers (Calder 1993). To this day, technology diffusion policies help small parts makers provide larger suppliers and assemblers with inexpensive, high-quality parts (Ruigrok and Tate 1996). The Japanese government is also actively supportive of efforts to move to hybrid and electric vehicles.

Similarly in the Korean case, while Kim (1997) and especially Amsden (1989) emphasize the entrepreneurship of Hyundai, the government provided a degree of protection surpassing even that of Japan, saved Hyundai and the rest of the industry from collapse on several occasions, and in the early to mid-1980s, engineered the most thoroughgoing and successful consolidation policy in the history of the global auto industry (Noble 2010, 2011). Policy support for small suppliers, though less extensive and consistent than that in Japan, was also important in increasing quality and technological sophistication.

A second critique is that promotion of worker skills, the perfection of flexible and "lean" production techniques, and cooperative relations between assemblers and suppliers, were the keys to success in Japan, not the support of government (Koike, Hiroyuki, and Sōichi 2001; Womack, Jones, and Roos 1990). Subsequent research tends to support the contention that close relations with suppliers are a crucial and enduring element in Japanese competitive success (Fujimoto 2003), but doubts have arisen about both just how skilled Japanese labor really is and whether Japanese production is as distinctively lean and flexible as advertised (Coffey 2006; Ihara 2007; Tate 1995). As for Korea, repeated efforts to mimic the Japanese approach to labor and suppliers foundered on the authoritarian oligopoly of Korea's conglomerates (*chaebol*). Instead, the quality and speed of management—combined with still inexpensive labor and engineering costs— proved decisive (Noble 2010).

The third critique argues that even if protection and promotion were once crucial to both Japan and Korea, they have declined radically. More important, protection and promotion are increasingly ineffective in the age of liberalized trade and finance and ever more finely disarticulated global production chains. This historical critique has much to commend it. After the mid-1980s, the Japanese auto industry grew essentially independent of government support, though support for cutting-edge technology development continued. After 2000, much the same can be said for Korea. Still, if protection and promotion are mostly gone, they lasted throughout the drive of the Japanese and Korean auto industries to international triumph, and in the case of Korea, are not entirely absent, even today. Moreover, China remains at an earlier stage of development. Tariffs and other barriers to trade and investment remain significant even after WTO (World Trade Organization) entry; government intervention is still ubiquitous, and China retains capital controls and a controlled exchange rate (Noble, Ravenhill, and Doner 2005).

China shares many important similarities with Japan and Korea, but it also differs from them in crucial ways, some of which will accelerate China's ascent. The crucial difference is that China is far more complex and internationalized. China began its drive to modern industrialization saddled with a poor and isolated population and a quixotic system of socialist ownership and planning that undermined market signals, constrained competition, and, ironically, prevented attainment of economies of scale. The long negotiations and eventual terms of accession to the WTO greatly lowered tariffs and disciplined Chinese industrial policy without eliminating it. In particular, China insisted on limiting foreigners to no more than 50 percent ownership of assembly operations, and used a variety of means to pressure foreign firms to transfer technology to local partners. With WTO entry, Chinese industrial policy became far more adept at working with market forces, though the government still has a weakness for announcing specific numerical targets and attempting to impose consolidation through administrative fiat. Fortunately, efforts at consolidation have mostly failed, and the entry of new and often private firms has shaken up the industry. The government's bias against smaller and more independent firms is slowly declining, and policy has become more focused on development of independent technology, brands, and design, largely in reaction to concerns that commodification of the value chain drains all the profits away from China, and pressure from foreign firms to reduce infringement of intellectual property rights (IPRs) (Noble, Ravenhill, and Doner 2005).

China's situation also differed from the experience of Japan and Korea in several other ways. First, the progressive decomposition of global production into commodity chains or networks was far more advanced by the time of China's WTO entry. No longer can China or any other country rely on a national champion like Toyota or Hyundai to propel an entire industry. The size, weight, and complexity of automobiles have prevented decomposition of production from progressing as far as in the electronics of some other industries, but Chinese firms are simultaneously exporting low-end parts, taking advantage of modularization, and struggling to catch up in more lucrative areas such as engines and transmissions.

Second, China is rising to prominence at the same time as the shift to new power plants has gathered momentum. China is well behind leaders such as Japan technologically, and the far lower income levels make it hard to convince Chinese consumers to pay more for hybrid and electric vehicles. At the same time, China is able to build upon rapidly expanding industrial capabilities such as batteries and motors first developed in consumer electronics and industrial applications. Chinese government officials and business executives see an opportunity to leapfrog to the forefront in new technologies where Chinese firms can compete on a more even basis.

Third, China's complex structures of ownership, management, and regulation reflect both the legacy of socialism and the long, winding path away from it. Where automakers in Japan and Korea are privately held, the Chinese state remains an active shareholder in China's largest enterprises. As Breznitz and Murphree (2011) emphasize, stiff opposition by some party leaders forced Deng Xiaoping and his allies to introduce, in many cases ratify, economic reforms gradually, starting far from the capital. The diverse structure of the Chinese auto industry and the mind-boggling number of auto assemblers reflects both the socialist legacy and the piecemeal and locally specific character of reform (Thun 2006).

China's first Five Year Plan led to the creation First Auto Works (FAW), a massive complex of state-owned factories built with Russian assistance in the northeastern city of Changchun. At first, FAW was largely dedicated to producing medium-sized trucks. The decentralization of the Great Leap Forward encouraged Shanghai, Nanjing and other cities to establish local auto and truck producers, notably the forerunner of Shanghai Auto Industrial Corporation (SAIC). In the mid-1960s, the Sino-Soviet split spurred the creation of another major truck maker, Second Auto Works, later dubbed Dongfeng, in the hills behind Wuhan city, far from Russia.

When the Chinese companies proved unable to meet the sudden outburst of demand for taxis and other cars that accompanied "reform and opening" in the early 1980s, the leadership authorized the creation of joint ventures with foreign automakers. The first ventures, Beijing Jeep and Guangzhou Peugeot, proved disappointing. After years of patient effort to improve quality and upgrade suppliers, Shanghai VW succeeded in creating a competent local vehicle with high levels of local content. Budgetary pressures spurred the military to open a number of auto factories, the largest of which was Chang'an Auto in Chongqing city.

In 1997, in return for promises to introduce new vehicles in a huge plant and transfer considerable technology, GM won the right create a new joint venture with SAIC called Shanghai GM, which subsequently pressured Shanghai VW to lower its prices and increase the speed of new product development. Other major municipal governments were also active, as Beijing Auto formed a joint venture with Hyundai, while Guangzhou Auto created joint ventures with Toyota, Honda, and later Mitsubishi. Smaller local governments supported the creation of China Brilliance (*Huachen*) and Chery (*Qirui*), while private firms such as Zhejiang Geely, Great Wall of Baoding, and BYD in Shenzhen emerged in the late 1990s. As China's market exploded in the 1990s and 2000s, the influx of foreign companies both threatened local firms and provided them with high-quality inputs.

These diverse firms brought different strengths and limitations to the competitive landscape. Centrally owned firms such as FAW and Dongfeng, and to a lesser extent Chang'an, enjoyed scale and easy access to funding from government banks, but they also had to support huge complexes of retirees and inefficient suppliers and suffered periodic interference from the government. Joint ventures with municipally owned firms such as Shanghai VW, Shanghai GM, Beijing Hyundai, and Guangzhou Auto's Japanese joint ventures enjoyed the best balance of support and relative autonomy. Smaller public firms such as China Brilliance and Chery struggled to gain recognition and support from the central government, while private firms faced active discrimination and found it difficult to raise funds from domestic banks, though they also enjoyed the greatest degree of freedom in decision making, and grew the fastest, partly because being located in smaller, more remote areas helped lower their costs and made them better able to appeal to rapidly growing demand in smaller cities and towns. Personnel flows from the larger state firms, such as the defection of a team of Dongfeng designers to Chery, strengthened the independent firms, while the rise of the independent firms stimulated the larger firms to cut costs and speed up the rate of new product development. In this complex and rapidly moving environment, the Chinese government faces a constant tension between promoting Chinese firms and promoting China as a hub for innovative and high-tech activities by all firms, local and foreign.

In sum, while China shares many similarities with Japan and Korea, including protection and promotion policies that are still very much in place, its domestic auto industry is far more fragmented, competitive (domestically), and internationalized (see Table 2.1).

Price Pressures: Not Just Cheap Labor and Land, but Engineers and Machinery

The most obvious threat from China comes in the form of cheap labor. Direct assembly labor now accounts for a relatively modest proportion of the total cost of producing an automobile, but when the impact of inexpensive salaried workers and procurement of

TABLE 2.1

EAST ASIAN AUTO GIANTS DURING THEIR RISE TO INTERNATIONAL COMPETITIVENESS

	Japan (1960s–70s)	Korea (1970s–90s)	China (1990s–Present)
Role of the State			
Protection: imports	Virtually complete	Virtually complete	Moderate (25% tariff)
Protection: inward foreign investment	Very strong	Strong, but inconsistent	Partial: 50% limit on assembly; none on parts
Financial support	Moderate, staged (first autos, then parts)	Moderate, often indirect	Initially high, but complex, not transparent
Interference in management	Low	Sporadic	SOEs (especially central): high Private: fairly low
Support for new powertrains: hybrids, electric cars, etc.	N/A (1990s-: Early, moderate)	N/A (1990s-: Late, moderate)	Late, powerful
Market Features			
Size	Large: 3 million units, 1973; peaked at under 8 million units, 1990	Modest: peaked at 1.3 million units in 1996	Huge: 2 million units in 2000, 17 million units in 2010
Growth	Rapid	Rapid	Very rapid, sustained
Structure	Oligopoly: 3 major players (Toyota, Nissan dominant, Honda distant third)	Oligopoly: 2–3 major players (but Hyundai dominant)	Competitive, complex (state-foreign JVs; independents)
Firm-Level Features			
Wages and salaries relative to Europe, NA	Lower	Much lower	Far lower
Shop floor skills	High	Medium	Low-medium
Engineering capacity	High	Medium	Low, but rapidly improving
External Links			
Export dependence (vehicles)	High: c. 50% in 1973	High: 35–50%	Very low
Parts exports	Strong, but mostly following vehicles	Initially weak; followed vehicles	Strong, preceding vehicles

continued

TABLE 2.1
(CONTINUED)

	Japan (1960s–70s)	Korea (1970s–90s)	China (1990s–Present)
Outward investment	US, Europe, following trade conflict (1980s)	US, Europe, following trade conflict (2000s); Daewoo to developing countries, 1990s, but failed	To developing countries, 2000s. To Eastern Europe (late 2000s), preceding exports
Technology decoupling (multiple licenses; independent development)	Yes (especially Toyota)	Yes (especially Hyundai, after borrowing technology for initial Pony)	Initially, mostly no. From late 1990s, emergence of new, independent firms
Use of external design, engineering centers	Late, supplementary	One-time early (Hyundai, 1970s), then supplementary	Early, frequent, followed by growth of domestic centers and in-house capabilities

inexpensive local parts is considered, labor costs are still crucial. The global automobile industry has witnessed a clear shift from higher-wage locations such as the United States, Canada, and northern Europe to lower-cost locations, including Mexico, Brazil, Spain, the Czech Republic, Thailand, and, of course, China. In developing countries, auto work is usually relatively prestigious and high paying compared to other blue-collar manufacturing employment. Chinese assemblers require at least a high school degree, and the job attracts many workers with junior college degrees.

The labor supply in China is not only inexpensive but relatively flexible. The proportion of temporary or contract employees has increased even more in China than in Japan or Korea, and even "permanent" employees enjoy less security of tenure. Lower labor security reflects in part the harsh competitive conditions in China. The low buying power of consumers combines with the limited technological specialization and brand loyalty of Chinese auto firms to create intense price competition. The rise of independent brands based in second- or third-tier cities has exacerbated that price competition. Chinese auto companies have developed an inexpensive, flexible workforce, but at the cost of rising insecurity and discontent (Zhang 2010).

Some signs suggest that the era of cheap labor may be coming to an end. China's once-young population is rapidly aging. Younger workers are much better educated and have far higher expectations than did their predecessors even a decade ago. Factories on the southeast coast are finding it harder to attract migrant workers as economic growth and infrastructure development provide more opportunities for workers from inland regions to find employment closer to home. Partly as a response, the Chinese government in

2007 allowed a vigorous national debate that culminated in much stronger labor contract laws that assured payment of social security contributions, guaranteed equal pay for equal work, and allowed temporary employees to join labor unions. The global financial crisis of 2008–09 caused the government to move somewhat more slowly on these initiatives, but implementation on the whole has basically continued (Ho 2009; Pomfret 2009). Widespread strikes at auto parts suppliers in 2010 led to sharp wage increases and raised the prospect that Chinese manufacturing would lose international competitiveness.

Most observers doubt that the increase in labor costs will make a major dent in Chinese autos or manufacturing more generally. Wages remain far lower than in Mexico or Brazil, and much less than in Korea or Japan. Productivity growth has matched wage increases, capping unit labor costs. Automation, already increasing before the strikes, has accelerated. Manufacturers still have room to move many labor-intensive activities in-land, where wages and costs are far lower.

At least as important as the low wages of production workers is the plentiful supply and low salaries of engineers and managers. For a poor country, China has a surprisingly well-educated population. Virtually all 15–24-year-olds are literate, and an explosion of university enrollments in the 1990s and the early years of the new century allowed nearly one-quarter of all students to proceed to college or university. The government allocates a high proportion of openings at university to science and engineering departments, and China now graduates about three times more engineers every year than does the United States (National Science Board 2010; Wadhwa, Gereffi, and Ong 2007).

A similar pattern applies specifically to the auto industry. The origins of auto engineering departments at the country's two leading engineering schools, Beijing's Tsinghua University and Shanghai's Tongji University, date back to the 1930s. In 2009, Chinese universities poured out over 6,000 bachelor's degrees in automotive engineering, 1,764 master's degrees, and 175 doctorates (Zhongguo qiche jishu yanjiu zhongxin and Zhongguo qiche gongye xiehui 2010). Chinese assemblers, particularly the independent brands designing their own models, have ramped up their engineering staffs at a furious rate. Even before it bought Volvo in 2010, Geely deployed a research staff of about 3,600 (Yang 2010), while Chery and BYD each employed automotive R&D (research and development) staffs of around 5,000 (Zhongguo qiche jishu yanjiu zhongxin and Zhongguo qiche gongye xiehui 2010: 404, 425). Great Wall also boasts 5,000 engineers, with plans to increase to 10,000 by 2015 (Auto.163.com 2010). All these numbers easily surpassed the R&D workforce employed by assemblers in Brazil, another flourishing auto producer with a much longer history (Quadros and Consini 2009).

If the sheer quantity of Chinese engineers is breathtaking, many foreign observers question their quality. Chinese engineering students, they claim, may get a good background in mathematics and theory, but their practical skills, initiative, and English fluency leave a great deal to be desired, and after the top ten to fifteen schools, quality drops off drastically (Wadhwa, Gereffi, and Ong 2007). Without question, Chinese students trail far behind their Indian counterparts in English proficiency and exposure to international business practices, and for a time in the early years of the century, faculty recruitment trailed the explosion in student enrollments, leading to a temporary bulge in student-teacher ratios. But it is far from clear that Chinese students are fundamentally different from their counterparts in India or other developing countries. A wide range of foreign engineers, managers, and consultants actively working with Chinese engineers and interviewed by the author between 2006 and 2008 agreed that Chinese and Indian students were more alike than different, and what both lacked were experience and exposure to global best practice rather than basic training or intelligence. After a training period of six months to a year in England or America, they could take the initiative in projects and work effectively with foreign counterparts.

Chinese companies can also take advantage of another crucial resource that complements purely domestic capabilities: returnees and ethnic Chinese from more developed areas. Chinese students have not just matriculated at home but have surged abroad in huge numbers. In almost every major country, Chinese rank in the top three among all overseas students. In the United States, Chinese lead all foreign students (Institute of International Education 2010; National Science Board 2010). In Japan, Chinese students account for 60 percent of all foreign students. They are also the leading group in other leaders in automotive technology such as Germany, the United Kingdom, and Australia, and second in France (Federal Ministry of Research and Education 2009: 5). In recent years, China's rapid growth and the strenuous efforts of the Chinese government, universities, research institutes, and firms have succeeded in attracting numerous "sea turtles" (*haigui*), a Chinese pun for returning emigrants, to return home. For example, Zhao Fuquan received a doctorate in engineering at Japan's Hiroshima University in 1997 and worked his way up to research executive for engines and power plants at Daimler Chrysler before returning to China, where he became director of Geely's R&D institute (Wang 2010).

Ethnic Chinese from Hong Kong, Taiwan, Singapore, and other countries are also a great resource. Many of the top officials of Ford's operations in China, for example, have spent time at the company's long-established subsidiary in Taiwan, Ford Lio Ho. Linguistic facility and cultural similarity enable Taiwanese and to a lesser extent other overseas Chinese to serve as a link between China and Japan, the United States, and Europe. Returnees and ethnic Chinese have supplied workers who are familiar with global practices and have experience in devising and managing complex projects. Returnees and moonlighting Japanese contributed to Korea's rapid development as well, but in a much more modest way. Japan was, and remains, far more closed to foreign nationals.

The diversity of China's industrial structure has provided more opportunities for information, skills, and talent to diffuse in China. Returnees, for example, typically take positions at the high-paying Sino-foreign joint ventures, but after gaining further experience, they move on to private companies. The smaller firms have also been able to use foreigners and overseas Chinese in a more flexible and ad hoc fashion.

Equally as important as the relative price of labor is the price of land. Land is cheaper in China not only because per capita income remains low but because China's land ownership is still in a transition from notional socialism, giving local governments great discretion in the allocation and pricing of land. Utility rates are lower and environmental regulations less onerous, particularly at smaller factories and workshops which are far from the attention of inspectors. Many of these cost advantages, however, are transitory and already eroding. Local governments face more pressure to allocate land at market prices; utility reform is pushing up rates for water, electricity, and waste disposal; and environmental and labor conditions are visibly improving. During a tour of Beijing Hyundai's just-opened billion-dollar plant, a German auto consultant remarked that everything about the plant looked like new assembly plants in Germany and other leading industrial countries (author's site visit, Beijing, April 18, 2008).

Less recognized is the dramatic cost reductions made possible by substitution of local machinery for expensive imports. Chinese machinery can cost as little as one-tenth as imports. In 2009, China surpassed Japan and Germany as the world's largest producer of machine tools. The sophistication of Chinese machine tools has also dramatically improved. The share of machine tools guided by computer numerical control (CNC), just 8 percent in 2000, rose to 24.8 percent in 2009 (Research in China 2010), in part thanks to a wave of investment by Japanese and Taiwanese tool makers that boosted local capacities so greatly as to alarm the American government (U.S. Department of Commerce 2009).

To be sure, Chinese tools and machinery are often less sophisticated, as befits China's more labor-intensive style of production. And, in some cases, Chinese machinery is not yet up to critical applications. Most Chinese auto assemblers, for example, still rely on foreign firms such as Germany's Dürr for painting equipment. Yet for most applications, Chinese machinery is adequate and far cheaper. Chinese companies, particularly the independent brands, tend to avoid importing expensive turnkey factories, instead showing great ingenuity in mixing and matching equipment from around the world (author's interview with Zhou Jianqun, General Manager, Wanxiang, Hangzhou, February 2, 2007). China has a particularly big advantage in the production of low-cost dies, molds, and jigs, which are crucial inputs to the auto industry. The quality of molds and dies depends heavily upon machine tools, but it also depends upon the skills of their operators. Japanese firms retain a big lead in quality and speed, but their products are far more expensive. And as Japanese workers age, they are finding it difficult to compete with Korea and China, leading to a wave of bankruptcies and mergers in Japan.

Modularization and Outsourcing

The conventional wisdom holds that automobiles are a classic example of an industry in which seamless product integration is crucial to competitive success (Fujimoto 2003). This implies that outsourcing will run into clear limits and that close links between assemblers and suppliers, such as the closely knit corporate networks in the case of Japan and reliance on trusted affiliates in Korea, can be crucial to competitive success. This view has much truth to it. After all, mastery of integration is one of the main reasons Japanese firms lead the global automotive industry.

And yet, outsourcing has steadily increased, reaching around 70 percent for most auto assemblers. American, European, and even Japanese companies are steadily increasing procurement of low-end parts from China and other low-cost countries. European assemblers increasingly rely on massive first-tier suppliers to provide whole modules such as instrument panels or lights. Japanese firms have proved more reluctant to delegate so much authority, but they, too, are moving in the same direction, and analysts urge them to move more quickly.

Chinese firms have pushed even further (AllianceBernstein 2005). Younger assemblers procure the great bulk from outside firms, often from the army of foreign auto suppliers that moved into China after the late 1990s. Mitsubishi Motors provides a revealing example. Smaller than its Japanese competitors and late to the Chinese market, Mitsubishi struggled to sell vehicles in China. Stuck with overcapacity, its engine factories sold much of their output to smaller Chinese companies. Though auto firms often insist on controlling the engine, which is a crucial element of competitive strategy, Chinese companies boast of their reliable Mitsubishi engines and cut costs by procuring other, less important parts from domestic suppliers. Reliance on Mitsubishi and other outside engines increased costs and slowed progress toward the creation of independent brand identity, but it allowed Chinese firms to get under way quickly and provide a diversity of models without excessive investment.

As Chinese assemblers have gained volume and experience they have largely brought production of engines in-house. They still rely, however, on Germany's Bosch and Japan's Denso for engine controllers, and most still procure transmissions from a variety of foreign sources. Relations with suppliers are still very much arm's-length and price-based. Chinese assemblers have relied on rapid decision making and a high level of outsourcing to churn out a profusion of models. That strategy has proved successful for assemblers, though it hurts suppliers who complain of abrupt changes in orders and unrelenting pressure to cut prices. Lack of continuity makes it difficult for the two sides to establish relations of trust that would facilitate the exchange of knowledge and expertise. High levels of outsourcing, then, are not without drawbacks. Nonetheless, outsourcing is a dominant trend in the industry and Chinese firms may propel that trend even faster.

Chinese firms have applied a similar logic of outsourcing to basic design and engineering. Independent Chinese firms started out in the 1990s with little skill or experience, and unlike the Koreans or Japanese, they faced global assemblers already well entrenched on local soil. At first, the Chinese companies mainly copied or at best heavily reverse-engineered foreign models, but leading companies such as GM and Toyota began suing the independents and protesting with increasing vehemence to the Chinese government, effectively blocking exports of infringing models to the advanced countries.

In contrast to Korean firms like Hyundai that quickly weaned themselves off help from foreigners (Hyun 1999), Chinese firms continue to rely heavily on outside expertise. Improvements in telecommunications and computers eased international cooperation, while the greater openness of the Chinese market and the spread of the Internet meant that Chinese consumers were far more aware of world standards than Korean car buyers in the 1970s or 1980s. A rapid ratcheting up of regulations on emissions and fuel efficiency also virtually forced Chinese automakers to rely on external expertise. China imposed only minimal "Euro 1" regulations in 2000, but by 2010, the government applied the "Euro 4" standard, nearly catching up with Europe, which introduced "Euro 5" standards from January 2011. To design a flood of new models and constantly upgrade engines to meet ever-tougher requirements for emissions and fuel efficiency, independent Chinese firms have relied heavily on Italian design studios (e.g., Pininfarina and Italdesign) and engineering consultancies from Germany (e.g., FEV and Porsche), Austria (e.g., AVL), and Britain (e.g., Ricardo and Lotus).

By purchasing foreign technology and designs rather than copying or licensing them, the Chinese acquire full intellectual property rights, giving them freedom to modify the technology or export products containing it. Foreign consultants such as Ricardo came to accept that the Chinese assemblers are developing considerable basic capabilities, and marketed themselves as purveyors of cutting-edge technology. Ricardo opened local offices to support the ever-more important Chinese market.

As the Chinese market boomed and contracts with European design studios and engineering houses multiplied, domestic design studios also sprang up. The first and biggest domestic consultancy, TJ Innova Engineering and Technology, appeared in 1999. In just a decade, TJ Innova employed a staff of over 1,500 and claimed responsibility for developing 10 percent of all the automobiles in China, including one-third of all independent models. As it gained experience and built up a huge digital library of design components, TJ Innova offered to take over much of the design and development work of local assemblers, allowing them to focus on a narrow core competency, and to pump out new models at high speed and costs a fraction of those required by European and even Japanese automakers. The second largest design house, Beijing's IAT, is especially strong in creating concept cars for auto shows, including electric vehicles. Founded in 2002 by a "sea turtle" who had received a doctorate in Japan and worked for a number of years at Mitsubishi, IAT soon built up a staff of 700, including over 70 foreigners, mainly from Korea and Japan (IAT company website 2011).

In addition to building up internal design and engineering capacities and making extensive use of outside design and development houses, Chinese automakers are establishing overseas offices and acquiring foreign firms. Many Chinese companies established small offices in Turin, the heart of the Italian auto design industry. Others invested in engineering outposts in Germany, Britain, and Japan. When China and Taiwan signed an economic cooperation agreement in 2010, Chery announced that it would establish a research unit in Taiwan specializing in electric automobiles.

A bolder move has been investing in overseas acquisitions. SAIC led the way, acquiring a controlling share in the Korean firm Ssangyong, and then taking over the assets of Britain's MG Rover. The Ssangyong acquisition proved an expensive and humiliating failure, as conflict with Korean unions, lack of experience in overseas management, and a decline in demand for sports utility vehicles in the wake of oil price increases pushed Ssangyong into bankruptcy. Through 2010, the Rover initiative looked to be a modest success. SAIC revived the MG brand, designed new spinoffs from Rover to be sold under SAIC's own brand, Roewe, and continued to employ several hundred engineers in Britain. As noted above, when bankruptcy forced GM to divest its Saab brand, Beijing Auto acquired two platforms and associated engines for a modest price. A bolder demarche came from Geely, which acquired Volvo from Ford, thanks in part to support from central and local governments, as well as an investment of over $330 million from Goldman Sachs (Autoevolution.com 2009). Volvo was renowned for safety, but too small to compete in a world of auto giants. Managing foreign assets and foreign employees effectively, as well as transferring technology and management skill back to the domestic operations, will be major challenges for the relatively inexperienced Chinese brands, but such opportunities, if managed well, could propel these firms more quickly into global markets.

"Indigenous Innovation" and Resulting Pressures on Joint Ventures

When China opened up to the world economy in the 1980s, the Chinese government found it had little choice but to rely on joint ventures. After some struggles over the slow increase in domestic content, the deal seemed to be a success as Chinese firms improved production techniques and quality control. However, the success of joint ventures led FAW, SAIC, and other Chinese assemblers to largely abandon the development of their own brands. The emergence of new independent brands around 2000 raised questions about the reliance of the state-owned automakers on their foreign partners. If a little firm like Chery could build its own brands and models, why couldn't FAW or Dongfeng or SAIC?

These debates soon joined into larger policy struggles over the proposition that Chinese firms should engage in "autonomous" or "indigenous" innovation (*zizhu chuangxin*). Engineers and nationalists argued that China needed to end dependence on foreign technology and foreign-dominated supply chains in which Chinese firms were relegated to the lowest and least profitable segments. Some Chinese economists and incumbent firms such as FAW argued that the time for putting huge resources into R&D had not yet come, that foreign technology and foreign investment remained vital, and that China should follow comparative advantage.

In the end, the engineers and nationalists won a resounding victory, as the Party and government incorporated the language of "indigenous innovation" in official rhetoric and policy planning. The actual impact of the change, however, was less obvious, as many firms dressed up licensed or purchased technology as "independent." As is often the case in China, broad policies left plenty of room for flexible implementation, but everyone recognized the medium-to-long-term imperative to cultivate distinctive brands and redouble efforts at innovative R&D.

Independent Chinese brands have appeared in three waves. Smaller firms, such as Geely and BYD, adopted independent brands because they were unable to find foreign partners and could not convince the government to support them. These independent firms have been the most entrepreneurial, and they are the most active in exporting and making overseas investments. Chery, for example, exported about 100,000 units in 2010, largely to support 16 overseas "assembly plants" that mostly bolted together completely knocked-down kits imported from China (Chen 2010). SAIC, the most advanced of the state-owned firms, started the second wave with its overseas acquisitions and development of the "Roewe" brand. Other state-owned automakers like FAW and Dongfeng were more reluctant, but eventually they formed a third wave. They could see the commitment of the Chinese government, which hinted that it might delay or deny permits to companies that failed to establish independent brands.

Initially, foreign automakers viewed with great suspicion any attempt to weaken their brands or control over the joint operations, but as the Chinese market grew by leaps and bounds and independent Chinese firms mounted a spirited challenge in the lower-priced segments, foreigners began to see possible advantages to creating locally oriented brands. Thus, SAIC-GM-Wuling created the "Baojun" brand, Guangzhou-Honda introduced the "Linian," and Dongfeng-Nissan the "Qichen" (China Auto Web 2011; General Motors News 2011; Honda News 2010). So far, these efforts have been tentative and not terribly original, but the trend seems clear.

Underneath debates over independent brands is a long-standing tension. Foreigners fear that Chinese auto companies will learn (or steal) all of their secrets, and then, with the help of the Chinese government, use the newly acquired skill to push out their foreign partners. The Chinese side fears eternal domination by the foreign giants, which often procure parts from wholly owned subsidiaries at high prices, thus transferring the profits away from the joint venture, especially the Chinese partners. Already Chinese industry representatives have strongly rebutted the call of a leading Chinese policymaker to eliminate the 50 percent limit on foreign ownership of assembly operations (Shi 2010).

Promotion of Hybrids, Electric Cars, and Alternative Energy Sources

A crucial battlefront for innovation centers on the race to create fossil fuel alternatives. As an executive of America's Delphi observed, China not only has the largest market and the lowest costs but the most receptive customers and the biggest government subsidies for electric and hybrid vehicles (Wu 2010). The Chinese government has multiple motivations to move beyond the conventional internal combustion engine. Green cars would improve air quality in China's horribly polluted cities where environmental consciousness is rapidly growing. Global warming is also a concern, both because of foreign pressure and because China could suffer severely from the melting of the Himalayan snowpack.

China's economic development is highly energy intensive. China is now the world's biggest energy consumer, and in the next decade is likely to surpass the United States as the largest oil importer. The tremendous volatility of oil prices represents a far greater threat to China than to the advanced countries, which are more energy-efficient and dominated by services rather than manufacturing. The consumption of motor vehicles is of particular concern. The twelfth Five Year Plan anticipates annual auto output by 2015 of around 30 million units, close to twice that of the United States at its peak. The Chinese look at their history of hypergrowth and skyrocketing demand for oil, and realize that steep price increases are inevitable even under the most optimistic scenarios. Even with increased fuel efficiency, the current path of development in China is unsustainable. Of the seven strategic industries targeted by the National Development and Reform Commission in 2010, three directly involved energy (including "new energy automobiles") and three others indirectly touched on energy efficiency (Auto.sina.com 2010).

Industry and government leaders hope to make an opportunity out of a crisis. Chinese firms lag far beyond Toyota or Honda in the development of efficient internal combustion engines, but they hope to start out on more of an even basis in the development of new green technologies. A passionate advocate of such a technological leapfrogging strategy is Wan Gang, head of the Ministry of Science and Technology (MOST). After receiving a doctorate in engineering in Germany, Wan worked for a decade as a researcher on alternative energy technologies at Audi. He returned to China to promote a new plan for green car technology and take up a position at Tongji University, where he became president. Not long after that, Wan became the first non-Party member in decades to be named a minister in the Chinese cabinet.

In the face of technological uncertainty, the Chinese government is trying to keep its policy options open. For example, it is increasing emissions and fuel standards to pressure automakers to improve the efficiency of conventional engines. State-owned enterprises such as Shanghai's Baogang Steel and numerous research institutes are working on stronger, lighter-weight steels. Research on fuel cells continues. The overall thrust of Chinese policy is to favor hybrid and electric cars. But because Japanese producers such as Toyota, however, already have staked out a big lead in hybrid technology, the Chinese government would like to move fairly quickly to full electric vehicles. Electric cars emit no local pollution, and they may become a storage mechanism for the electricity grid, making it more feasible to rely more heavily on intermittent sources such as wind and solar power.

Wan Gang and the MOST support electric vehicles as a cleaner break with conventional internal combustion engines. Electric cars can build on China's formidable capacities in consumer electronics and chemicals, including a strong presence in lithium-ion batteries. China also has a crucial economic partner in Taiwan, which has an even stronger electronics industry and a similar capacity to ramp up investments quickly. Taiwan's auto market is saturated, and its firms see China as their only realistic opportunity for growth (author's interviews, Taiwan, June 2010). China faces many of the same challenges confronting other countries, particularly the limitations of electric batteries (Boston Consulting Group 2010). To penetrate mass markets, electric car producers must extend driving range, assure durability and reliability, maintain power even in cold climates, decrease recharge times, and, above all, decrease costs.

Electric vehicles, however, face special challenges in China. Low incomes make Chinese households reluctant to fork out the high up-front price of pricey hybrid cars. Toyota, for example, has found no success in selling the Prius in China. In the first three quarters of 2010, Honda sold over 475,000 gasoline-powered cars in China, but only sixty-three hybrids (Greimel 2010). Inexpensive fuel prices in China undermined incentives to seek alternatives to traditional cars, though in 2009 fuel prices began to approach international levels. Driving distances in China tend to be short, which eases the recharge problem but at the same time undermines the economic incentive to seek alternatives to gasoline-powered cars. The paucity of single-family dwellings and attached garages means that most Chinese will struggle to find a place to recharge at night. And for all the talk of leapfrogging, China is well behind the Americans in research and behind the Japanese and Koreans in mass production of electric vehicles and especially batteries and power systems.

To be sure, China also has some advantages. It produces tens of millions of electrically powered bicycles and motorcycles, which are potentially huge markets for lithium-ion batteries (Argonne National Laboratory 2009). Precisely because China is less developed, it still has room to shape the auto fleet and to plan infrastructure such as charging stations in growing urban areas. Surveys show that the Chinese populace is far more open to alternatives to gasoline-powered vehicles than car buyers in advanced countries. The Chinese are open to the idea of alternative vehicles, but they demand that electric vehicles become completely competitive in price (Dumaine 2010).

The future of alternative vehicles in China will come down to the determination and persistence of the Chinese government and whether it can sustain a transformation toward hybrid and electric vehicles. So far, the Chinese appear extremely determined, though the specifics and actual implementation can be frustratingly difficult to pin down. Minister Wan told the American journal, *Foreign Policy*, "China is committed to developing clean and electric vehicles...Batteries and clean vehicles are a national strategic priority" (LeVine 2010: 88). China's "863" program is in some ways analogous to the competitive funding process organized by the National Science Foundation in the United States, but it is often more oriented to increasing capacity for import substitution than to basic research. The program provides state support for many projects in the automobile industry (Osnos 2009). In addition, MOST's spending on "new energy vehicles" during the eleventh Five Year Plan is expected to exceed $150 million. In 2008, MOST outlined plans to promote purchase of 1,000 hybrid or electric vehicles by governments and other public agencies in ten cities. By 2010, the plan expanded to twenty cities.

In June 2010, the government announced a trial plan for five cities to provide hefty subsidies of up to RMB 60,000 ($8,900) for the purchase of an electric vehicle and up to RMB 50,000 ($7,400) for plug-in hybrids (Reuters 2010b). These subsidies, however, do not apply to conventional hybrids such as the Prius. The five designated cities were not necessarily the most polluted cities, but they were home to China's major domestic automakers: Shanghai (SAIC), Changchun (FAW), Shenzhen (BYD), Hangzhou (Geely), and Hefei (Chery). The following section looks closely the next-generation vehicle development plans of BYD, Chery, and Geely. As these case studies show, their development plans are deeply entwined with those of foreign firms.

Three Case Studies in Electric Cars: BYD, Chery, and Geely

The most aggressive and best known of the Chinese firms working on next-generation vehicles is BYD, the first automaker in the world to sell a mass-produced plug-in hybrid. BYD has made bold claims about the performance of its batteries and its intention to become the biggest energy and auto company in the world. Partly because of BYD's background in consumer electronics, it has eschewed the "modularization" approach of most other Chinese automakers and instead followed Hyundai's "Fordism light" (Noble 2010) strategy of deepening vertical integration to take advantage of low local costs and high volumes. BYD's plants rely heavily on manual assembly rather than automation, leading to doubts about the uniformity and thus quality and safety of its batteries, though the company claims that its iron phosphate–based lithium batteries are inherently safer and more robust than competing technologies. The company employs about 10,000 engineers, including 5,000 in its auto R&D center, 500 of them working exclusively on automotive batteries.

BYD's home base in Shenzhen is the center of world electronics manufacturing, and the city government is extremely supportive of BYD. City taxi fleets were the first purchasers of BYD's hybrid and electric models. The same day the central government announced its subsidy program, Shenzhen announced an additional subsidy of up to RMB 30,000 for hybrids and up to RMB 60,000 for electric vehicles (Automotive News China 2010). While BYD's long-term goal is to become the dominant producer of electric vehicles, in the short run, it has had to depend on sales of gasoline-powered cars. It achieved extraordinary growth on the back of its "F3," which looked like the Toyota Corolla but cost only half as much. In late 2008, BYD garnered extraordinary global attention when Warren Buffett's MidAmerican Energy bought 10 percent of BYD for $230 million (Gunther 2009).

Not surprisingly, skepticism of BYD soon set in. While BYD excels at low-cost production of single-cell batteries, it has not yet demonstrated mastery of battery packs and the complex electronics to control auto battery systems. Initial sales of BYD's "F3DM" hybrid were minuscule, both because refinement left something to be desired and because the car cost twice as much as the gasoline-powered version, though at about $22,000, it still costs roughly half as much as a Prius in China or a Chevrolet Volt in the United States. Following some negative press coverage, BYD announced that it would restrict consumer sales of its all-electric "e6" to a few Shenzhen taxi companies, partly because construction of the factories meant to produce it was frozen in a land planning dispute. Outsiders were unable to confirm BYD's bold claims of 300 km driving range, roughly twice that of Nissan's Leaf. Most important of all, sales of BYD's cash-cow conventional cars slumped in 2010, revealing the dangers of relying on one mass-produced model for two-thirds of sales.

Through 2009, BYD was the most profitable of any Chinese assembler, and even when sales slumped in mid-2010, the company remained in the black. The more important long-term question may be whether it can mobilize the managerial skill and financial resources to sustain the heavy investments necessary to maintain its vertical integration strategy simultaneously in batteries, mobile phones, conventional cars, and electric vehicles. Unlike Hyundai of the 1970s and 1980s, BYD does not enjoy the support of a huge conglomerate and the absolute protection by its government. The one potential bright spot is in BYD's foreign alliances, including creation of a joint venture with Germany's Daimler to conduct joint research and create a joint brand in China for hybrid and electric vehicles. BYD is to provide expertise in batteries, while Daimler will take primary responsibility for vehicle design. BYD has also signed a Memorandum of Understanding with Volkswagen.

BYD's closest rival among the independent brands is Chery. Chery began by almost completely outsourcing (and copying) both designs and engineering, though today it produces its own engines, engine management systems, and automatic transmissions. Chery just completed what it claims is the largest automotive R&D center in Asia. In November 2010, it introduced an electric vehicle, for which it claimed a range similar to that of Nissan's Leaf. Yet Chery remains reliant on outsourcing to develop hybrid and electric models. So far, all of its lithium-ion batteries come from China BAK, a major producer of batteries for consumer electronics. Like BYD, BAK uses an iron phosphate technology that is slightly less powerful but inherently safer and potentially less expensive than the cobalt and manganese formulas favored in Japan. Chery also created a joint venture with Taiwan's electronics supplier BenQ to build battery separator films, the most profitable element in electric batteries, and the one for which China has relied most heavily on imports (Tian 2011). Chery has also formed a joint venture with the noted American startup, Better Place, to build electric vehicles with replaceable electric batteries, and it has a production joint venture with Better Place's major stockholder, Israel Corporation (Reuters 2010a).

The third major independent brand, Geely, is even more reliant on international alliances. In 2009, Geely announced that it has teamed up with Taiwan's Yulon Motor to produce and sell electric cars in Taiwan. Geely will export semi-knocked-down kits of its Panda compact to Taiwan to be assembled into an electric car, which will then be sold under Yulon's Tobe brand (Jin 2009). That same year, Geely also signed an agreement to develop electric technology with the American battery supplier Johnson Controls (Reuters 2009). Finally, Geely will also rely on its recent acquisition of Volvo, as well as its partnerships with two small Danish suppliers, Lynx Motors and Danish Positive Batteries (Presswire 2011; Welch 2010).

While it is unclear whether one of these Chinese companies will produce the world's first low-cost electric car, it is increasingly evident that the extensive use of modularization and outsourcing at the intersection of the Chinese electronics and auto industries is opening up a wide range of new partnerships and exciting product possibilities.

Conclusion

In a single generation, China has made an extraordinary rise from a stifling socialist system producing a handful of atrocious vehicles for a tiny market into the world's largest producer and consumer of cars. China's auto industry is also unprecedented in its range and diversity of producers. Though that diversity contributes to many inefficiencies, it is also an underestimated source of competitive dynamism, as firms with very different resources, skills, strategies, and niches engage in a Darwinian-like struggle for survival. In the midst of this struggle, the Chinese government tries to foster domestic firms and "indigenous" Chinese capacities, as well innovative activities by foreign firms on Chinese soil.

Does China constitute a dangerous new challenge to producers in advanced countries? It is certainly not a dominant new force in the auto industry the way Toyota was in the 1980s and 1990s, or Hyundai is in the new century. Chinese firms are still far from possessing the technological and especially managerial skills deployed by Toyota and Hyundai, and they are still strongest in China and developing countries, which are less sophisticated and lucrative and will be slower to adopt next-generation vehicles.

The Chinese market is also far more open to foreign participation than were the Japanese and Korean markets a generation or two ago, or even today. Foreigners dominate both assembly and the supply chain and play a major role in important parts of the service sector, such as auto loans. The Chinese government and Chinese firms are making a major push into hybrid and electric vehicles, but virtually all of the major Chinese players have entered into cooperative agreements with foreign firms. From an American and European perspective, the Chinese firms may provide a competitive aid in the battle against the more self-reliant Korean and especially Japanese firms. Western auto companies are also partnering with Chinese automakers to penetrate other emerging markets. GM and SAIC, for example, are making inroads into India.

Even if no Chinese firm looks likely to turn into the next Hyundai, could the Chinese way of doing business, which drives down prices and accelerates transition to new technologies, pose a fundamental challenge to the status quo? Possibly. The influence of low-wage Chinese labor and inexpensive parts and machinery cannot be discounted.

Exports from China by Sino-foreign joint ventures are likely to expand, and already "the China price" has affected strategies throughout the global auto industry. Chinese firms may also accelerate the use of outsourcing for design and engineering functions and production of major modules. The Chinese government's tremendous push to promote hybrid and electric vehicles, not least through extraordinarily high subsidies, could prove crucial in making the transition to an era in which green vehicles can compete more evenly in price.

If these developments do alter the dynamics of global competition, we must put them in perspective. Even in manufacturing, automakers assemble most vehicles where they sell them, so a flood of Chinese exports or a complete move of production capabilities to China is unlikely. For the foreseeable future, Chinese firms will rely on close relations with foreign partners both in the Chinese market and abroad. Chinese auto companies are simultaneously a challenge, an opportunity, and an increasingly important group of partners.

Acknowledgments

The author wishes to thank the Alfred P. Sloan Foundation for financial support and the Berkeley Roundtable on the International Economy (BRIE) for research and administrative support.

References

Adams, Jonathan, Christopher King, and Nan Ma. (2009). Global Research Report, China: Research and Collaboration in the New Geography of Science. Leeds: Evidence Ltd. (Thomson Reuters).

AllianceBernstein. (2005). The New Industrial Revolution: De-verticalization on a Global Scale. New York: AllianceBernstein.

Amsden, Alice. (1989). Asia's Next Giant: South Korea and Late Industrialization. New York: Oxford University Press.

Argonne National Laboratory, Energy Systems Division. (2009). *Advanced Battery Technology for Electric Two-Wheelers in the People's Republic of China*. Argonne, IL: Argonne National Laboratory.

Auto.163.com. (2010). "Independent R&D investment of 5 billion to upgrade to build the Great Wall Auto Technology Center." *Auto.163.com*, October 26. Retrieved November 1, 2011 (http://auto.163.com/10/1026/12/6JU0A6LO00084JTJ.html).

Auto.sina.com. (2010). "Detailed National Development and Reform Commission blueprint for the development of new industries and taxation of financial support." *Auto.sina.com*, October 22. Retrieved November 1, 2011 (http://auto.sina.com.cn/news/2010-10-22/0853666487.shtml).

Autoevolution.com. (2009). "Goldman Sachs invests in Geely, Geely eyeballs Volvo," September 23. Retrieved November 1, 2011 (http://www.autoevolution.com/news/goldman-sachs-invest-in-geely-geely-eyeballs-volvo-11239.html).

Automotive News China. (2010). "Shenzhen offers big sales subsidy for BYD hybrids," July 13. Retrieved October 30, 2011 (http://www.autonewschina.com/en/article.asp?id=5405).

Boston Consulting Group. (2010). *Batteries for Electric Cars: Challenges, Opportunities, and the Outlook to 2020*. Boston, MA: Boston Consulting Group.

Breznitz, Dan, and Michael Murphree. (2011). *Run of the Red Queen: Government, Innovation, Globalization, and Economic Growth in China*. New Haven, CT: Yale University Press.

Calder, Kent. (1993). *Strategic Capitalism: Private Business and Public Purpose in Japanese Industrial Finance*. Princeton, NJ: Princeton University Press.

Chen, Zhijie. (2010). "Car exports from 'guerilla warfare' to 'trench warfare.'" *Nanfang Daily*, October 19. Retrieved November 1, 2011 (http://auto.sina.com.cn/news/2010-10-29/0901669354.shtml).

China Auto Web. (2011). "Dongfeng-Nissan Venucia (Qichen) concept sedan unveiled, mystery remains." *China Auto Web*, April 20. Retrieved November 1, 2011 (http://chinaautoweb.com/2011/04/dongfeng-nissan-venucia-qichen-concept-sedan-unveiled-mystery-remains-auto-shanghai-in-pictures-10/).

Coffey, Dan. (2006). *The Myth of Japanese Efficiency: The World Car Industry in a Globalizing Age*. Cheltenham, UK: Edward Elgar.

Dumaine, Brian. (2010). "China charges into electric cars." *CNN Money*, October 19. Retrieved November 1, 2011 (http://tech.fortune.cnn.com/2010/10/19/china-charges-into-electric-cars/).

Federal Ministry of Research and Education. (2009). *Internationalization of Foreign Students—Foreign Students in Germany—German Students Abroad*. Berlin, Germany: Federal Ministry of Research and Education.

Fujimoto, Takahiro. (2003). *Nōryoku Kōchiku Kyōsō: Nihon Nojjidōsha Sangyō Wa Naze Tsuyoi No Ka* [Competition on the Basis of Constructing Capabilities: Why the Japanese Auto Industry Is Strong]. Tokyo, Japan: Chuokoron-sha, Inc.

General Motors News. (2011). "Baojun 630 from SAIC-GM-Wuling begins national launch tour," August 9. Retrieved November 1, 2011 (http://media.gm.com/content/media/us/en/gm/news.detail.html/content/Pages/news/cn/en/2011/Aug/0809).

Greimel, Hans. (2010). "Japanese automakers make new push in China." *Automotive News China*, November 16. Retrieved October 30, 2011 (http://www.autonewschina.com/en/article.asp?id=6125).

Gunther, Marc. (2009). "Warren Buffett takes charge." *CNN Money*, April 13. Retrieved November 1, 2011 (http://money.cnn.com/2009/04/13/technology/gunther_electric.fortune/).

Henderson, David R. (1983). "The myth of MITI: Individual initiative, not central planning, is the main source of Japan's growth." *Fortune*, August 8: 113–16.

Ho, Virginia E. (2009). "From contracts to compliance? An early look at implementation under China's new labor legislation." *Columbia Journal of Asian Law* 23(1): 35–107.

Honda News. (2010). "Honda announces "Li Nian S1" the first model from Guangqi Honda's original brand, at the 2010 China Guangzhou International Automobile Exhibition." *Honda News*, December 20. Retrieved November 1, 2011 (http://world.honda.com/news/2010/4101220Li-Nian-S1/).

Hyun, Young-suk. (1999). "The new product development capabilities of the Korean auto industry: Hyundai Motor Company." *International Journal of Vehicle Design* 21(1): 8–20.

IAT company website. (2011). "IAT 2001 annual meeting," February 20. Retrieved November 1, 2011 (http://www.iat-auto.com/cn/news_view.asp?id=11).

Ihara, Ryoji. (2007). *Toyota's Assembly Line: A View from the Factory Floor* [Trans. H. Clarke]. Melbourne, Australia: Trans Pacific Press.

Institute of International Education. (2010). *Opendoors 2010 Fast Facts*. Washington, DC: Institute of International Education.

Jin, Vivien. (2009). "Geely teams with Taiwan's Yulon on EVs." *Edmunds Inside Line*, December 11. Retrieved October 31, 2011 (http://www.insideline.com/geely/geely-teams-with-taiwans-yulon-on-evs.html).

Johnson, Chalmers. (1982). *MITI and the Japanese Miracle: The Growth of Industrial Policy, 1925–1975*. Stanford, CA: Stanford University Press.

Kim, Linsu. (1997). *Imitation to Innovation: The Dynamics of Korea's Technological Learning*. Boston, MA: Harvard Business School Press.

Koike, Kazuo, Chūma Hiroyuki, and Ōta Sōichi. (2001). *Monozukuri No Ginō: Jidōsha Zangyō No Shokuba De*) [The Skill of Making Things: The Workplace of the Automobile Industry]. Tokyo, Japan: Toyo Keizai, Inc.

LeVine, Steve. (2010). "The great battery race." *Foreign Policy* 182: 88.

Mardon, Russell. (1990). "The state and the effective control of foreign capital: The case of South Korea." *World Politics* 43(1): 111–38.

Mason, Mark. (1992). *American Multinationals and Japan: The Political Economy of Japanese Capital Controls, 1899–1980*. Cambridge, MA: Council on East Asian Studies, Harvard University.

National Science Board. (2010). *Science and Engineering Indicators 2010*. Washington, DC: National Science Foundation.

Noble, Gregory W. (2010). Fordism light: Hyundai's challenge to coordinated capitalism. BRIE Working Paper 186, Berkeley Roundtable on the International Economy, Berkeley, CA.

Noble, Gregory W. (2011). "Industrial Policy in Key Developmental Sectors: South Korea versus Japan and Taiwan." In *The Park Chung Hee Era*, edited by Byung-Kook Kim and Ezra F. Vogel, 603–28. Cambridge, MA: Harvard University Press..

Noble, Gregory W., John Ravenhill, and Richard F. Doner. (2005). "Executioner or disciplinarian: WTO accession and the Chinese auto industry." *Business and Politics* 7(2): Article 1.

Osnos, Evan. (2009). "Green Giant: Beijing's crash program for clean energy." *The New Yorker*, December 21. Retrieved October 29, 2011 (http://www.newyorker.com/reporting/2009/12/21/091221fa_fact_osnos).

Pomfret, James. (2009). "Chinese labor laws buckle as economy darkens." *Reuters*, January 27. Retrieved November 1, 2011 (http://www.reuters.com/article/2009/01/28/us-china-workers-labourlaw-idUSTRE50R0D820090128).

Presswire. (2011). "Geely made huge impact at COP15 with electric car," December 31. Retrieved October 19, 2011 (http://www.presswire.com/releases/Geely_made_huge_impact_at_COP15_with_electric_car/450).

Quadros, Ruy, and Flávia Consini. (2009). "Innovation capabilities in the Brazilian automobile industry: A study of vehicle assemblers' technological strategies and policy recommendations." *International Journal of Technological Learning, Innovation and Development* 2(1/2): 53–75.

Research in China. (2010). "Global and China machine tool industry report, 2009–2010." Retrieved October 30, 2011 (http://www.researchinchina.com/Htmls/Report/2010/5980.html).

Reuters. (2009). "Geely signs up with Johnson Controls as parts supplier," December 16. Retrieved October 31, 2011 (http://www.reuters.com/article/2009/12/17/geely-johnsoncontrols-idUSTOE5BG03820091217).

Reuters. (2010a). "Better Place to work with Chery on electric cars," April 24. Retrieved November 1, 2011 (http://www.reuters.com/article/2010/04/24/us-betterplace-chery-idUSTRE63N1GQ20100424).

Reuters. (2010b). "China to subsidize hybrid, electric car purchases," June 1. Retrieved November 1, 2011 (http://www.reuters.com/article/2010/06/01/china-economy-cars-idUSTOE65007Z20100601).

Roland Berger. (2010). *Powertrain 2020: China's Ambition to Become Market Leader in E-Vehicles.* Munich, Germany and Shanghai, China: Roland Berger Strategy Consultants.

Rovner, Sophie L. (2010). "China ascendant." *Chemical & Engineering News* 88(2): 35–7.

Ruigrok, Winified, and John Jay Tate. (1996). "Public testing and research centres in Japan: Control and nurturing of small and medium-sized enterprises in the automobile industry." *Technology Analysis and Strategic Management* 8(4): 381–406.

Shi, Baohua. (2010). "Dongyang: Firmly opposed to open the joint venture shares than the bottom line." *Sohu.com*, November 4. Retrieved November 1, 2011 (http://auto.sohu.com/20101104/n277150319.shtml).

Tate, John Jay. (1995). *Driving Production Innovation Home: Guardian State Capitalism and the Competitiveness of the Japanese Automobile Industry.* Berkeley, CA: Berkeley Roundtable on the International Economy (BRIE).

Thun, Eric. (2006). *Changing Lanes in China: Foreign Direct Investment, Local Governments, and Auto Sector Development.* New York: Cambridge University Press.

Tian, Alfred. (2011). "Chery, BenQ to jointly mass produce batter separators." *China Automotive Review*, June 13. Retrieved November 3, 2011 (http://www.chinaautoreview.com/pub/CARArticle.aspx?ID=6103).

Trezise, Philip H. (1983). "Industrial policy is not the major reason for Japan's success." *The Brookings Review* 1(3) 13–18.

U.S. Department of Commerce. (2009). *Critical Technology Assessment: Five Axis Simultaneous Control Machine Tools.* Washington, DC: Office of Technology Evaluation, Bureau of Industry and Security.

Wadhwa, Vivek, Gary Gereffi, Ben Rissing, and Ryan Ong. (2007). "Where the engineers are." *Issues in Science and Technology* 23(3): 73–84

Wang, Xiaoling. (2010). "R&D pipeline: Geely's new engine." *Hexun.com*, February 8. Retrieved November 1, 2011 (http://news.hexun.com/2010-02-08/122642082.html).

Welch, David. (2010). "Geely buys Volvo. Believe it or not, it could work." *Bloomberg Businessweek*, March 29. Retrieved October 31, 2011 (http://www.businessweek.com/autos/autobeat/archives/2010/03/geely_buys_volvo_believe_it_or_not_it_could_work.html).

Womack, James P., Daniel T. Jones, and Daniel Roos. (1990). *The Machine That Changed the World.* New York: Rawson Associates.

World Trade Organization. (2010). "International Trade Statistics 2010."

Wu, Qiong. (2010). "The core components of domestic production in the United States will be equipped with electric cars." *Shanghai Securities News*, November 5. Retrieved November 1, 2011 (http://auto.sohu.com/20101105/n277166903.shtml).

Yamazaki, Shuji. (2003). *Sengo Nihon No Jidosha Sango Seisaku* [Postwar Japan's Automobile Industry Policy]. Tokyo, Japan: Legal Culture Publishing.

Yang, Jian. (2010). "Geely to acquire special vehicle maker and build new technology center." *Automotive News China*, March 3. Retrieved November 1, 2011 (http://www.autonewschina.com/en/article.asp?id=4448).

Zhang, Lu. (2010). "From Detroit to Shanghai? Globalization, market reform, and dynamics of labor unrest in the Chinese automobile industry." Working Paper, Research Center for Chinese Politics & Business, Indiana University, Bloomington, IN.

Zhongguo qiche jishu yanjiu zhongxin and Zhongguo qiche gongye xiehui. (Eds.). (2010). *Zhongguo qiche gongye nianjian 2010 ban* [China Automotive Industry Yearbook 2010]. Tianjin, China: China Automotive Industry Yearbook Publisher.

3   Center-Local Politics and the Limits of China's Production Model

WHY CHINA'S INNOVATION CHALLENGE IS OVERSTATED

Crystal Chang

HOW CAN GOVERNMENTS in the advanced countries generate and retain highly productive activity in the face of increasing competition from emerging economies such as China? In Chapter 1 (in this volume), Breznitz and Murphree suggest that in order to understand whether China is a challenge to the developed West, we must first understand how it operates. Their research leads off our analysis by explaining the way in which China's ICT (information and communications technology) companies developed strong competencies by adapting their business models to the global fragmentation of production and China's domestic environment of "structured uncertainty." In Chapter 2 (in this volume), Noble reinforces this narrative of globalization by showing how entrepreneurial Chinese automakers like BYD, Chery, and Geely quickly ramped up their operations on a limited budget by purchasing off-the-shelf parts and modules and outsourcing research and development (R&D) to foreign design and engineering firms. Noble suggests that this Chinese outsourced model of production could propel Chinese automakers to the forefront of next-generation automobiles.

This chapter further explores these two key themes in an attempt to more accurately characterize the nature of "China's innovation challenge." By illuminating the inherent limitations of China's outsourced production model and the often murky domestic politics that drive industrial development at the local level, this chapter concludes that the threat that China's current innovation ecosystem poses to the advanced countries may be overstated. A key aspect of Breznitz and Murphree's argument focuses on adaptations to structured uncertainty, China's ambiguous institutional environment in which there is considerable tolerance for multiple interpretations and implementations of the same policy. As the authors point out, the resultant innovation ecosystem in China is at the cusp of the technology frontier but does not advance the frontier itself. While it is true that the ability to quickly and cheaply commercialize existing technologies has been quite beneficial to China's rapid economic development, growth, and employment, in the case of the auto industry, being at the cusp has also resulted in a situation in which Chinese automakers are ever more—rather than less—reliant on foreign technology.

While structured uncertainty creates room for creative business model experimentation at the firm level, it has also had unexpected consequences for China's innovative capacity and the industrial organization of the auto sector. Specifically, adaptations to structured uncertainty by local governments have resulted in the proliferation of politically backed but inefficient automakers, which complicates the central government's call for industrial consolidation. The desire of local officials to protect and promote regional automotive champions could preclude the emergence of Chinese automakers capable of achieving the economies of scale necessary to become global players.

This chapter attempts to debunk several common misperceptions about China. The first misperception is that a Chinese industrial initiative, such as the "indigenous innovation" campaign mentioned in Chapter 2 (in this volume), will be effective as long as it has strong financial and policy support from the central government. In reality, in those policy areas where the goals of the central government are not aligned with those of local governments, the former often finds it difficult to enforce its will over the latter. The second misperception is that Chinese companies will inevitably challenge the technological leadership of established multinationals. While it is true that Chinese firms are fierce and formidable competitors in commoditized product markets (e.g., televisions and refrigerators), they are far less competitive in sophisticated product and service markets in which value is perceived as much more than cost (e.g., smart phones and financial services). The last misperception is that global competition is ultimately a zero-sum game between "us," the advanced countries, and "them," the emerging countries. On the contrary, the most competitive economies and profitable firms will be those that embrace rather than eschew cross-border transactions and partnerships. More often than not, the capabilities of Chinese enterprises are complementary to those of established multinationals.

The rest of this chapter is organized as follows. First, I explain how China's deep integration into global production networks has resulted in a production model that relies on outsourcing and perpetuates the dependence of Chinese automakers on foreign technology and expertise. Second, I describe how China's domestic environment of structured uncertainty has led to runaway economic initiatives at the local level and a domestic auto industry that is increasingly fragmented, which will delay—and possibly preclude—the emergence of Chinese automakers with innovative capabilities and scale economies that can compete with today's leading global automakers. Third, I assert that, rather than creating real competitors to the auto industries of the advanced countries, China's integration into global production networks has opened up new avenues of collaboration between Chinese and foreign firms that could lead to breakthroughs in next-generation vehicles. Technology leadership need not be a zero-sum game.

The evidence presented in this chapter comes from both secondary sources and fieldwork conducted between 2007 and 2009. During that time, I analyzed original Chinese policy documents, collected data on the Chinese auto industry, and conducted over eighty interviews in Beijing, Shanghai, Baoding, Guangzhou, and Shenzhen. The names of interviewees have been kept anonymous, except when the interviewee has explicitly agreed to be identified.

The Limits of China's Production Model

The effects of China's foreign direct investment (FDI) policy on the development of the domestic auto sector have been mixed. On the one hand, the policy has attracted billions of dollars of foreign investment, established a modern automotive supply network, ignited domestic automobile production, created hundreds of thousands of jobs, and improved mobility for millions of Chinese citizens. From an economic development perspective, then, China's FDI policy can be considered an astounding success, environmental consequences notwithstanding. In the early 1990s, China produced and consumed one million vehicles per year, less than 10 percent of which were passenger cars (China Automotive Technology and Research Center 2007). The few passenger cars that were produced were built from complete knock-down kits imported from Germany (i.e., no parts were sourced in China) and used to either transport government officials or supply state-owned taxi fleets. At that time, the automotive supply chain was nonexistent and private car ownership was not permitted. By 2010, however, China produced over 18 million vehicles, the majority of which were built with parts made in China (OICA 2010). Furthermore, over 70 percent of those vehicles are now passenger cars. China's car ownership is expected to reach 75 million by 2011 (People's Daily Online 2010). For better or for worse, the introduction of the passenger car has transformed patterns of urbanization and the very social fabric of Chinese society.

On the other hand, China's open FDI policy has ultimately failed to create technologically independent and globally competitive automakers capable of representing China in the international marketplace. How do we know the government intended for the Chinese auto industry to develop independent capabilities? Although China's call for "autonomous" or "indigenous" innovation (*zizhu chuangxin*) has received a lot of international press coverage in recent years, government officials have long been encouraging domestic firms to develop independent R&D capabilities. In its announcement of the 1994 Automotive Industry Policy, the sector's first comprehensive policy, the State Council clearly emphasized the need for Chinese automakers to "enhance product quality, the level of technology and equipment, and international competitiveness" and stated that the "country encourages and supports automotive enterprises to establish independent research and product development capabilities through the absorption of foreign technology" (State Council 1994: chap. 4 art. 14).

Through joint ventures (JVs) with foreign automakers, the government hoped that backward state-owned automakers would learn from foreign firms and build up their own product development capabilities. But to the dismay of the Chinese government, this has not happened. More than three decades after the first automotive JVs, Chinese state-owned firms are still heavily reliant on their foreign partners. China's integration into the auto industry's global production networks has resulted in an interdependent production model in which Chinese state-owned firms continue to rely on foreign partners for both key technologies and marketing expertise. And as Noble notes in the Chapter 2 (in this volume), even China's new private automakers outsource much of their design and engineering to foreign firms. What are the origins of China's outsourced production model?

At the beginning of the reform period, Chinese leaders were faced with modernizing the country's backward auto factories. In 1976, there were 1,950 factories scattered around the country ostensibly producing trucks, sedans, motorcycles, and parts based on antiquated Soviet technology (Harwit 1995: 21). After much internal deliberation about the potential merits and consequences of foreign participation in the domestic economy, Chinese officials decided to open the once highly protected auto sector to foreign investment. In an effort to appease those within the government who feared the denationalization of the domestic auto industry, a provision was added that forced foreign firms to form JVs with state-owned factories and capped their ownership to 50 percent.

Of the early JV experiments, only the partnership between Shanghai Tractor and Automobile Corporation (STAC), a local state-owned factory, and Germany's Volkswagen would prove successful. It took more than six years of negotiation before a deal was finalized in 1984, and then another ten years of hard work before the Shanghai Volkswagen (SVW) joint venture bore fruit. By the mid-1990s, SVW was responsible for establishing China's first automotive supply network and mass producing China's first passenger sedan, the Santana. The local content rate of the Santana increased from 2.7 percent in 1987 to 92.9 percent in 1997 (Thun 2006: 105). As the local content rate rose, overall costs declined while production volumes increased dramatically. For many years, the Santana was the best-selling sedan in China, largely because it was the first domestically made car available in consistent quantities. Despite—or perhaps because of—the success of the Santana, Volkswagen was reluctant to share its more sophisticated technologies with its Chinese partner. In the words of a former Shanghai official who helped negotiate the SVW deal and manage the JV, "Shanghai was frustrated because Volkswagen did not share technology or bring its Chinese partner into the product development process" (author's interview, Shanghai, March 11, 2009). This frustration eventually led Shanghai to look for another foreign partner.

In the 1990s and 2000s, nearly every major multinational automaker and component supplier rushed to form a JV in China to produce cars and parts for the domestic market.

According to government statistics, total investment commitments into the motor vehicle and related industries totaled nearly $60 billion during the 1990s alone (Gallagher 2006: 40). In 1997, General Motors (GM) committed $1.5 billion to form a joint venture with Shanghai Automotive Industry Corporation (SAIC), the successor to STAC. Not only was the Shanghai GM (SGM) deal considered the single largest foreign investment ever in China, but GM was the first foreign automaker to agree to create a joint technical center with its Chinese partner. The Shanghai government made this an explicit condition of the new JV because of what it considered Volkswagen's unwillingness to help upgrade STAC's technological capabilities. The Pan-Asia Technical Automotive Center, a separate $50 million JV with SAIC, was set up to provide engineering support to SGM and other auto companies in China.

Yet although GM followed through on its promise to exchange technology and foster Chinese managerial and professional development, SAIC has not acquired significantly enhanced technological and marketing capabilities. According to Kelly Sims Gallagher, whose research analyzes the extent of technology transfer in automotive joint ventures, "GM did not try to cultivate its Chinese partner's technological capabilities beyond what was needed to make the manufacturing operation efficient and profitable..." (Gallagher 2006: 77). A SAIC manager interviewed for this study echoes Gallagher's findings. In his words, "Chinese firms still lack real R&D capability, despite the number of engineers they claim or the amount of money they have...It will be very difficult for China to develop its own brands. The country cannot rely on JVs, it is a dead path" (author's interview, Shanghai, September 9, 2008).

Where can we see evidence of SAIC's R&D deficiencies? Even though SAIC is currently China's largest producer of passenger cars, the vast majority of the cars it manufactures are developed and sold under brands owned by Volkswagen and GM. In 2010, the market share of SAIC's own Roewe brand amounted to only 1.1 percent of passenger cars sold in China (Automotive Resources Asia 2010). Furthermore, SAIC did not design the Roewe series from initial concept but instead modified existing (and somewhat outdated) MG Rover designs it purchased from the defunct British automaker in 2004. As one American GM engineer stationed in Shanghai puts it, "Even though SAIC is big, it doesn't really seem to have the ambition to develop its own cars from beginning to end. It is in a pretty cozy position with GM and VW and making plenty of money without having to bear the brunt of the risk. Why try harder? The Chinese government might be pressing SAIC to build their own cars but SAIC might not be hungry enough" (author's interview, Shanghai, December 26, 2007). Gallagher (2006: 76) similarly notes that "SAIC has been slow to exert itself to enhance its own technological capabilities."

China's other major state-owned automakers—Dongfeng Motors, First Auto Works (FAW), and Chang'an Automobile Group—also lack the initiative to design, produce, and sell sedans under their own brands. According to market research firm, Automotive Resources Asia, Dongfeng sedans garnered less than 1 percent of the passenger car market in 2010, while FAW's Xiali subcompact series fared only slightly better at 1.1 percent.

The Xiali series is based on outdated technology licensed from Toyota. Similarly, FAW's Besturn compact car series is built with a Mazda designed engine, transmission, and chassis. In fact, the Besturn shares the same assembly line as the Mazda 6 sedan, which is produced by the JV between FAW and Mazda. Although these state-owned companies have had modest success in the development of heavy and light commercial vehicles, market segments in which the major foreign automakers are not significant players, they are hardly the technologically self-reliant automakers envisioned by past or current Chinese leaders.

In sum, after years of cooperation, Chinese state-owned automakers have not developed adequate R&D, product development, or marketing capabilities. At an industry forum in October 2011, Xu Liuping, president of state-owned Changan Automobile Group, admitted that domestic automakers are struggling with "unprecedented" challenges in technology, product quality and brand recognition (Yang 2011). State-owned firms are little motivated to pursue the development of their own brands, a strategy which is capital-intensive, risky, and unproven. This point echoes what Breznitz and Murphree argue in Chapter 1 (in this volume): Chinese firms with soft budget constraints under structured uncertainty have little incentive to move up or engage in risky activities. An ex-SVW executive from Germany puts it this way, "state-owned enterprises have some potential to build their own brands, but many obstacles stand in the way. Companies are run by government bureaucrats. They are more concerned about the profitability of their JVs, their low-risk cash cows. State-owned enterprises are too risk averse to run an entrepreneurial unit" (author's interview, Shanghai, April 13, 2009).

Commanding a total of 13.5 percent of the domestic passenger car market in 2010, the brands of China's four leading independent automakers are making greater headway compared to their state-owned counterparts. Independent automakers constitute a category of firms that are distinct from traditional state-owned automakers in terms of their management styles, corporate organization, and production model. These nascent firms were mostly formed in the 1990s and received neither support from the central government nor any foreign investment. Put simply, independent automakers were not beneficiaries of industrial policy and essentially emerged outside the central government's plan. While some independent automakers, such as Chery, are owned and managed by local governments, others, such as BYD, Geely, and Great Wall, are mostly privately held with shares listed on the Hong Kong stock exchange. In many cases, however, the underlying equity structure of the so-called private automakers is somewhat murky. The Baoding government, for example, owns about 25 percent of Great Wall (author's interview, Baoding, December 3, 2008).

These complex and creative ownership structures are evidence of what Breznitz and Murphree call adaptations to structured uncertainty, which can help to mitigate the often fickle behavior of the state. Luo (2005), Li (2009), Chin (2010), and Noble (Chapter 2, in this volume) also employ the term "independent" when referring to this group of companies. In this context, the term "independent" emphasizes the nature of their business model rather than the composition of their ownership structure. How did these little known and independent start-ups overcome the auto industry's historically high financial and technological barriers to entry without the support of the central government or foreign automakers?

Not only did these firms often receive significant support from local governments in the form of investment, government procurement contracts, cheap land leases, and tax incentives, they also benefited tremendously from the fragmentation of—and modularization within—global automotive production networks, which allowed them to outsource much of their vehicle design and component production. These firms are the antithesis of the vertically integrated automaker. Rather than rely on foreign JV partners to provide component and vehicle designs, independent automakers built a network of partnerships with a variety of foreign firms to provide design, integration, and production assistance. Outsourcing and joint development partnerships enabled these firms to create what Breznitz and Murphree (2011) call ultra mass-flexible production and to churn out new models at a rapid clip without building up expensive R&D teams internally.

However, this heavily outsourced production model, like the JV model, has significant drawbacks. First and foremost, independent automakers do not control the key value-added technologies in their vehicles. As a result, these firms continue to rely on foreign component suppliers like Germany's Bosch and Japan's Denso for electronic subsystems and engine controllers, and many still procure transmissions from foreign sources. Those firms that have transmission manufacturing capabilities purchased those designs rather than developed them on their own. A second drawback is that an overreliance on outsourcing constrains the profitability of independent automakers, which in turn limits the amount of capital available to reinvest in R&D. This is probably one of the reasons independent automakers continue to emulate popular foreign car body designs and struggle to develop more sophisticated luxury cars. Put simply, the outsourced model could end up trapping these firms in the low-end segment of the market. One critical case will be whether Geely's 2010 acquisition of Volvo will be enough to propel it up the value chain.

The lack of novel product innovation capabilities in Chinese firms is particularly pronounced in the design of next-generation vehicles. Because state-owned firms have made little progress in the development of hybrid and all-electric vehicles (EVs), the central government has opted to use political leverage to pressure foreign firms to "share" their technology with their Chinese JV partners. For example, the Chinese government has refused to let the Chevrolet Volt qualify for subsidies totaling up to $19,300 a car unless GM agrees to transfer the engineering secrets for one of the Volt's three main technologies to a JV in China (Bradsher 2011). Without these subsidies, the Volt would be out of the reach of most Chinese consumers. In order to appease the Chinese government, GM reportedly agreed to co-develop an EV architecture with its partner, SAIC. The majority of Japanese and European automakers are holding back on making similar deals to sell their new hybrids and EVs in China for fear of losing trade secrets if they are forced to share their newest technologies with Chinese companies. That the Chinese government feels compelled to apply political pressure on foreign firms to share their EV technology implies that the capabilities of Chinese firms continue to lag behind foreign firms.

Because they cannot rely on the government to do their bidding, independent automakers are proactively forging new partnerships with foreign firms to penetrate the domestic EV market. Like state-owned firms, independent automakers are not equipped to develop EVs without the help of foreign partners. Though highly publicized, BYD's EV models have not reached mass production. Almost an admission of its own weaknesses, BYD formed a $90 million JV with Germany's Daimler to co-design and produce an EV for sale in 2012. Meanwhile, Geely has partnered with two Danish companies to develop an electric version of its Panda small car. The electric motor system for the electric Panda is supplied by a Danish EV company, Lynx Cars, while the lithium polymer battery pack is supplied by Lynx Car's sister company, Positive Batteries. Similarly, Chery has partnered with California-based technology firm, Better Place, to jointly develop switchable battery EV prototypes for the Chinese market.

Like the ICT companies Breznitz and Murphree write about in Chapter 1 (in this volume), China's independent automakers depend on cost control, incremental improvements, and time to market to ensure that their products will be in demand. This strategy requires continually adapting not only to new openings in the global production chain to capture value but also to the domestic environment of structured uncertainty to protect against the fickle nature of central government policies. However, as the following section will show, operating in an environment of structured uncertainty also has had significant consequences for the industrial structure of the Chinese auto sector.

Structured Uncertainty and the Problem of Runaway Local Economic Initiatives

In their conceptualization of structured uncertainty, Breznitz and Murphree (2011) describe it as an implicit agreement to disagree about the goals and methods of policy or economic action. Structured uncertainty cements multiplicity of action without legitimizing any specific course or form of behavior as the proper one, which results in some tolerance for multiple interpretations and implementations of the same policy. This is true for both political and economic actors. As in the ICT sector, Chinese firms in the auto sector adapt to structured uncertainty by adopting a variety of ownership forms and back-channel relationships with government officials. From the perspective of local governments, the environment of structured uncertainty gives them leeway to adapt national policy directives to meet local conditions. What are the origins of structured uncertainty?

As part of its reform strategy in the late 1970s, the Chinese central government expanded both the decision-making authority of local governments and their ability to retain the majority of the revenue generated within their jurisdictions. Many scholars have carefully studied the incentive structure that resulted from decentralization and encouraged local officials to pursue and promote local development (Blecher 1991; Breznitz and Murphree 2011; Duckett 1998; Lieberthal and Oksenberg 1998; Oi 1992, 1995; Shirk 1993; Thun 2006). Given different resource endowments and varying levels of development, it is not surprising that local government participation in the economy has taken different forms.

Marc Blecher (1991) and Jane Duckett (1998) have argued that "state entrepreneurialism," the direct participation of the state in business activities, has been an effective way in which local governments throughout China have adapted to market reforms. In what she calls local state corporatism, Jean Oi (1992) asserts that local officials can often be much more than entrepreneurs. They are often the primary coordinators of all economic and social activity within their jurisdiction. The "corporate good" in these cases is defined more broadly than economic interests and profits and includes social interests such as employment. As these and other scholars have noted, the adaptability of the local state in China runs contrary to assumptions about state resistance to market reform found in the neoclassical economics literature, especially the modern public choice literature, which emphasize the state's bureaucratic inflexibility and preferences for established working practices and rent-seeking behavior (Bauer 1971; Collander 1984; Lal 1983).

The development of the Chinese auto industry reflects the wide range of economic initiatives taken by local officials. In those regions with an established state-owned automaker, such as Shanghai, Changchun, Wuhan, and Chongqing, local governments worked closely with the central government to find suitable JV partners. In those regions without an established state-owned automaker, local officials searched for creative ways to build up a local auto industry beneath the radar of the central government which sought to restrict market entry. More entrepreneurial officials started their own regional automakers (e.g., Chery), while other officials opted to take a minority interest in semiprivate automakers (e.g., Great Wall). Some regional governments preferred a more hands-off approach by supporting private automakers through government procurement contracts, tax incentives, and privileged access to government-controlled land (e.g., Geely and BYD). Local governments were eager to support locally based firms because a thriving regional auto manufacturing hub could generate jobs and tax revenue, not to mention create spillover opportunities in upstream and downstream industries.

Yet unchecked economic ambition at the local level presents a quandary for the central government. While Chinese leaders realize that excessive centralization stifles local initiative, as was the case under the central plan, excessive decentralization can produce chaos and detract from the pursuit of national development objectives. The relationship between the central government and regional governments is the subject of continual debate and reform, as Chinese leaders seek an appropriate blend of national uniformity and provincial autonomy (Lieberthal and Oksenberg 1998: 139). Though Beijing has periodically attempted fiscal recentralization in the 1980s and early 1990s, local governments retain considerable control over economic decision making within their respective jurisdictions.

The development of the Chinese auto industry thus far indicates that the central government has yet to find the optimal balance between uniformity and autonomy. Although local support of independent automakers has generated competitive pressure on the JVs and helped to bring down car prices for the average consumer, local ambitions have also led to what many experts inside and outside China view as excessive industrial fragmentation. As Phil Murtaugh, the former president of SGM notes, "the central government passes a lot of regulations that the provinces simply choose to ignore. For example, although the government has been promoting consolidation since the early 1990s, the local governments have not heeded. There were 120 some automakers in the early 1990s and there are about the same number now" (author's interview, Shanghai, February 27, 2009). Expressing a similar sentiment, a representative of the European Automobile Manufacturers Association's Beijing office notes, "there are too many of them [Chinese automakers], many of which are locally protected" (author interview March 2009).

The extraordinary surge in Chinese auto production and pent-up demand from China's bourgeoning middle class have together masked the problems inherent in China's fragmented industry. Fears of production overcapacity did not materialize when demand grew at a rapid clip, but such concerns are beginning to resurface. In September 2010, Chen Bin, a top official at China's National Development and Reform Commission, warned that "serious overcapacity will lead to negative market competitiveness, a loss in enterprise efficiency, factory stoppages, and other problems" (Waldmeir 2010). During that news conference, Chen predicted that production capacity could reach 31 million vehicles per year by 2025, twice the size of the current domestic market. Chen's primary concern is that the domestic market will not be able to absorb that many vehicles; those outside China are worried that excess product will be dumped cheaply on world markets. As consumption growth begins to slow, as it has in 2011, there will be mounting pressure for smaller and less efficient automakers to shut down or merge with larger firms. The question is whether officials who support local automakers will be willing to let them go into bankruptcy or be merged with bigger companies, or whether they will instead decide to keep unprofitable firms afloat through funds from local state-controlled financial institutions such as investment arms and banks.

Efforts by the central government to encourage consolidation into the largest and most established state-owned firms have not been effective. Previous policy slogans have included "Big Three, Small Three" in 1988, "Grasping the large, Letting go of the small" in the early 1990s, and "Big Four, Small Four" in 2009, to name a few. Though the details vary, the main thrust of each campaign is always the same. In addition to the largest state-owned firms, the government identifies three to four smaller state-owned firms to receive policy support. Not one of these campaigns has included a privately held Chinese automaker, even though BYD sold more Chinese-branded cars in 2009 than any of the "Small Four." To this day, there are over 100 Chinese enterprises spread out around the country that claim to be engaged in auto assembly. With a few exceptions, the central government's calls for consolidation have fallen on deaf ears, a sign of the resistance Beijing faces in the periphery.

The center-local tension can also be seen in the promotion of EVs in China. Increased auto and oil consumption is forcing a reconsideration of how energy is governed. In the twelfth Five Year Plan, the Chinese government designated "new energy vehicles" as one of China's seven "strategic emerging industries." To encourage the development and deployment of new energy vehicles, the government has pledged more than RMB 100 billion ($15 billion) in state funding (World Bank and PRTM Management Consultants 2011). But the promise of funding alone will not be sufficient to fuel China's leadership in next-generation vehicles. Why?

For one, the widespread adoption of EVs will require a number of common national standards. Key standards include the plug interface between the EV and the charging station, vehicle charging methods (alternating current vs. direct current), charging network communications and billing protocols, and the range of acceptable temperatures for charging, to name a few. Some in the industry are also calling for a standard size and interface for EV battery packs, which would enable an EV owner to swap out a battery pack at a designated EV service station rather than take the time to fully charge his or her EV battery. Without such standards, it will be difficult for the central government and EV manufacturers to build a national interoperable charging infrastructure that can convince potential consumers that EVs will not be limited by battery range. As Yasuaki Hashimoto, the president of Nissan (China) Investment Company, has said, "It's inevitably important to have these standards, otherwise we cannot start the mass market" (Reuters 2010).

Unfortunately, the lack of national standards has not stopped local governments and their partners from investing in local EV charging stations based on local preferences. In cooperation with China Southern Grid Power Grid, one of China's two main utility companies, the Shenzhen government put into service China's first EV charging stations in 2009 (Popper 2010a). In August 2010, the Beijing municipal government announced its own list of standards for EV charging stations to be built in four districts within the city's jurisdiction—Hangtianqiao, Majialou, Xiaoying, and Sihui (Luo 2010). Meanwhile, the city of Hefei announced its own EV charging standards in November 2010 (Popper 2010b). At the end of 2010, seventy-six charging stations based on differing specifications had been built in forty-one cities across China. In a sense, pioneering the adoption of EVs is an extension of the race between locales to become the country's premier auto manufacturing hub. Rather than having one central Detroit-like hub, China has multiple—as many as eight to ten—regional manufacturing hubs spread out across the country, from the coast to inland cities.

To complicate matters further, agencies within the central government are competing to take control of standard setting. In November 2010, the Ministry of Industry and Information Technology (MIIT) released a document outlining steps toward a unified charging station standard (ifeng.com 2010). Instead of outlining a set of standards, the MIIT document calls for the formation of a committee composed of representatives from industry, the China Electric Vehicle Research Center, the China Association of Electricity Producers, and the China Scientific Electrical Appliance Research Institution to create a bill proposing common standards. When, or if, this MIIT-led effort will produce a unified charging station standard is unclear.

At the same time, the influential Ministry of Science and Technology (MOST) has separately announced that it is working with both the General Administration of Quality Supervision Inspection and Quarantine and the Standards Administration of China "to set up a [e-car] standardization system in accordance with the characteristics of domestically innovated products and technology" (Lan 2010). The national standard-setting process is a classic example of what Lieberthal and Oksenberg (1998: 22) refer to as China's "fragmentation of authority," which leads to a "policy process that is protracted, disjointed and incremental." The lack of a Chinese energy superministry with full and undisputed authority to set EV standards perpetuates the ambiguous environment of structured uncertainty.

To be sure, China is not alone in the fight over EV standards. In the United States, the J1772 charging plug designed by the Society of Automotive Engineers is the leading standard for 120V and 240V charging, and it is compatible with the leading alternative energy vehicles available today. In Europe, a group of manufacturers led by Daimler have chosen a different plug that is often referred to as the Mennekes plug, which can support 240V and 360V charging, though some French and Italian automakers object to the German specifications (EurActiv.com 2011). In Japan, Tokyo Electric Power Company has developed a specification solely for high-voltage fast charging in conjunction with Mitsubishi, Nissan, and Subaru, which can support fast charging up to 500V. These three plugs have different numbers of connectors and vary in size.

The fact that nearly all of the world's leading automakers have JVs and influential political partners in China could further complicate the Chinese government's efforts to settle on a common set of national EV standards. And given China's history of ambivalence in standard setting, the auto industry could end up with multiple EV charging standards. This is what happened in the telecommunications industry. China not only adopted the Global System for Mobile Communications (GSM) standard from Europe and the Code Division Multiple Access (CDMA) standard from the United States, it also developed and deployed its own standard called Time Division Synchronous Code Division Multiple Access (TD-SCDMA) (Yu and Tan 2005).

Yet even if China is unlikely to lead the world in the adoption of EVs, it is becoming a hub for EV development and technological collaboration between Chinese and foreign firms. The following section examines new forms of Sino-foreign collaboration that have the potential to produce the world's first low-cost, mass-produced EV.

New Forms of Sino-Foreign Collaboration

In Chapter 2 (in this volume), Noble asks where the Chinese auto industry is a challenger, where it could be a game changer, and where it is primarily an opportunity and partner. Noble and I both find that rather than posing a real threat to the auto industries of the advanced countries, the Chinese auto industry presents ample opportunity for Sino-foreign collaboration. The most innovative and competitive next-generation vehicles are likely to be products that combine sophisticated technology and engineering from the advanced countries and ultra-flexible and low-cost production in China.

For example, CODA Automotive, a privately held company headquartered in Santa Monica, California, is a start-up with ambitions to become a global leader in EVs. To keep development and production costs manageable, CODA looked to China for partners in technology development and production. Its first electric car, the CODA, is modeled on the body of a Chinese-built vehicle, the Hafei Saibao, with engineering help by Italian design firm, Pininfarina. The lithium iron phosphate battery system is co-developed and produced with a Chinese battery company, Lishen Power Battery. Though many parts, including the body and chassis, will be built in China, these parts will be assembled along with the electric motor and battery pack in the United States. In an effort to shore up its Chinese operations, CODA named long-time industry veteran, Phil Murtaugh as its CEO (chief executive officer) in early 2011. Murtaugh, former CEO and chairman of GM China, is largely credited with the success of the SGM joint venture.

Another EV start-up, Atlanta-based Wheego, is also leveraging China's automotive supply base. Wheego's first EV is a small, two-seat model called the Wheego LiFe, a play on the elemental symbols of its battery technology, lithium (li) and iron (fe). For the chassis and body of the LiFe, Wheego partnered with Shijiazhuang Shuanghuan Automobile Company. Rarely mentioned, of course, is the fact that the LiFe body is based on the body of the Shuanghuan Noble minicar, which bears an uncanny resemblance to the body of Daimler's Smart ForTwo. In any case, the ability to source the body and chassis from China should save Wheego tens of millions of R&D dollars. The first LiFe cars were delivered to U.S. customers in 2011.

The purpose of these examples is not suggest that one of these firms will lead the global EV revolution but, rather, to point out the range of new Sino-foreign business arrangements and product development models that are emerging from the fragmentation, modularization, and intersection of global automotive and electronics production networks. As a result of collaborations between Chinese and foreign firms, we may soon find electric cars in our local dealerships that are designed and assembled in the United States, but with modules made in China.

Conclusion

Due to China's extraordinary growth over the last few decades, it has become commonplace—particularly in the media—to exaggerate the threat posed by China's so-called innovation challenge to the established multinationals of the advanced countries. Such claims tend to ignore that fact that China's rise was in large part enabled by the global fragmentation of production. During that process, the capabilities of Chinese firms developed in close conjunction with, and not independently of, the capabilities of foreign firms. Chinese manufacturers developed superior skills at particular stages of the production network, but not at every stage, especially the high value-added stages which require large investments in R&D.

With the increasing level of modularization of auto components and the ability to outsource vehicle design and engineering, China's independent automakers were able to establish low-cost and ultra-flexible product development and assembly processes. These specialized capabilities give Chinese firms a distinctive edge over more rigidly organized foreign automakers with respect to cost control and time to market. However, these firms have not developed novel product innovation capabilities. The decomposition of automotive production allowed them to "borrow" or buy technology instead of developing it on their own. The current Chinese automotive production model necessitates rather than negates the need for foreign partnerships. This Chinese model is very different from that of Japanese and Korean automakers which have preferred to work closely and almost exclusively with suppliers in their home countries.

Another distinctive feature of China's auto industry development is the role played by local governments. Although ambitious local officials should be credited with adapting national level industrial policies to local conditions and spurring local economic development, they are also largely responsible for creating a fragmented Chinese auto industry plagued by scale inefficiencies and overinvestment of scarce resources. In order for China's auto industry to mature, significant consolidation of China's more than 100 automakers will be required. However, because many of these automakers have local political support and in many cases equity ownership by local governments, mergers and acquisitions will require prickly political negotiations. This fragmented industrial structure will continue to complicate the central government's efforts to promote a few domestic automakers capable of challenging the established multinational automakers in global markets.

Nonetheless, technology leadership does not need to be a zero-sum game. As this and previous chapters have shown, there is ample room for even deeper Sino-foreign collaboration, especially in the development and manufacturing of next-generation vehicles. Bill Russo, an expert on the Chinese auto industry, recently put it this way, "While China possesses several resource and infrastructure advantages, it is clear that Chinese automotive manufacturers lack overall vehicle and drivetrain systems engineering capabilities that will be needed to achieve the necessary breakthrough to drive market acceptance of EVs. Such capabilities should be developed in partnership with multi-national players in order to accelerate the process" (Russo 2011). China's value proposition has been, and will continue to be, to assimilate technology from the best global companies with the goal of making breakthrough innovations affordable. The Chinese government and the governments of the advanced countries would best serve their respective auto industries by creating incentives that encourage and facilitate new forms of Sino-foreign collaboration.

Acknowledgments

The author wishes to thank the Alfred P. Sloan Foundation for financial support and the Berkeley Roundtable on the International Economy (BRIE) for research and administrative support.

References

Automotive Resources Asia. (2010). *China Automotive Monthly*. Shanghai, China: J.D. Power and Associates.

Bauer, P.T. (1971). *Dissent on Development: Studies and Debates in Development Economics*. London: Weidenfeld & Nicholson.

Blecher, Marc. (1991). "Developmental State, Entrepreneurial State: The Political Economy of Socialist Reform in Xinji Municipality and Guanghan County." In *The Road to Crisis: The Chinese State in the Era of Economic Reform*, edited by G. White, 265–91. London: Macmillan..

Bradsher, Keith. (2011). "Hybrid in a trade squeeze." *New York Times*, September 5. Retrieved October 19, 2011 (http://www.nytimes.com/2011/09/06/business/global/gm-aims-the-volt-at-china-but-chinese-want-its-secrets.html?pagewanted=all).

Breznitz, Dan, and Michael Murphree. (2011). *Run of the Red Queen: Government, Innovation, Globalization, and Economic Growth in China*. New Haven, CT: Yale University Press.

Chin, Gregory. (2010). *China's Automotive Modernization: The Party-State and Multinational Corporations*. New York: Palgrave MacMillan.

China Automotive Technology and Research Center. (2007). *2007 Automotive Industry of China*. [In Chinese.] Tianjin, China: China Automotive Technology and Research Center (Zhongguo Qiche Jishu Yanjiu Zhongxin).

Collander, David. (Ed.). (1984). *Neo-Classical Political Economy: An Analysis of Rent-seeking and DUP Activities*. Cambridge, MA: Ballinger.

Duckett, Jane. (1998). *The Entrepreneurial State in China*. New York: Routledge.

EurActiv.com. (2011). "Electric car makers fight over plug standard," April 7. Retrieved October 24, 2011 (http://www.euractiv.com/innovation-enterprise/electric-car-makers-fight-plug-standard-news-503854).

Gallagher, Kelly Sims. (2006). *China Shifts Gears: Automakers, Oil, Pollution, and Development.* Cambridge, MA: MIT Press.

Harwit, Eric. (1995). *China's Automobile Industry: Policies, Problems, and Prospects.* Armonk, NY: M.E. Sharpe.

ifeng.com. (2010). "Gong Xin Bu Jiu Dian Dong Che Cong Dian Jie Kou Biao Zhun Zheng Qiu Yi Jian," November 26. Retrieved October 24, 2011 (http://auto.ifeng.com/roll/20101126/475331.shtml).

Lal, Deepak. (1983). *The Poverty of Development Economics.* London: Institute of Economic Affairs.

Lan, Xinzhen. (2010). "Shifting into a new gear." *Beijing Review*, October 14. Retrieved October 24, 2011 (http://www.bjreview.com/quotes/txt/2010-10/14/content_303508.htm).

Li, Zejian. (2009). The role of international technology transfer in the Chinese automotive industry. Manufacturing Management Research Center Discussion Paper Series, M. M. R. Center, The University of Tokyo. Retrieved October 24, 2011 (http://merc.e.u-tokyo.ac.jp/mmrc/dp/pdf/MMRC269_2009.pdf).

Lieberthal, Kenneth, and Michel Oksenberg. (1998). *Policymaking in China: Leaders, Structures and Processes.* Princeton, NJ: Princeton University Press.

Luo, Jianxi. (2005). The growth of Chinese independent automotive companies. International Motor Vehicle Program (second draft for discussion), Massachusetts Institute of Technology. Retrieved October 19, 2011 (http://global-production.com/scoreboard/resources/luo_2005_independent-chinese-automotive-companies.pdf).

Luo, Linda. (2010). "Beijing issues EV charging station standards." *China Automotive Review*, September 3. Retrieved October 24, 2011 (http://www.chinaautoreview.com/pub/CARArticle.aspx?ID=4749).

Oi, Jean. (1992). "Fiscal reform and the economic foundations of local state corporatism in China." *World Politics* 45(1): 99–126.

Oi, Jean. (1995). "The role of the local state in China's transitional economy." *The China Quarterly* 144: 1132–49.

OICA. (2010). "2010 production statistics." Retrieved October 31, 2011 (http://oica.net/category/production-statistics/).

People's Daily Online. (2010). "Car ownership in China expected to overtake Japan next year." Retrieved October 31, 2011 (http://english.peopledaily.com.cn/90001/90778/90860/7006415.html).

Popper, Kevin. (2010a). "China moves towards creating unified EV charging station standards." *Electric Vehicle News China*, November 10. Retrieved October 24, 2011 (http://www.evnchina.com/2010/11/china-moves-towards-creating-unified-ev.html).

Popper, Kevin. (2010b). "Hefei announces extensive EV infrastructure plan." *Electric Vehicle News China*, November 28. Retrieved October 24, 2011 (http://www.evnchina.com/2010/11/hefei-announces-extensive-ev.html).

Reuters. (2010). "Nissan has no timetable to sell Leaf in China." November 15. Retrieved June 11, 2011 (http://www.reuters.com/article/2010/11/15/us-nissan-idUSTRE6AC0QV20101115).

Russo, Bill. (2011). "China's innovation challenge: Reinventing the automobile." *Sohu.com*, October 10. Retrieved October 29, 2011 (http://auto.sohu.com/20111010/n321685069_1.shtml).

Shirk, Susan. (1993). *The Political Logic of Economic Reform in China.* Berkeley: University of California Press.

State Council. (1994). "State Council notification of the issuance of the 'automotive industry policy.'" March 12. Retrieved October 31, 2011 (http://www.law-lib.com/law/law_view.asp?id=57739).

Thun, Eric. (2006). *Changing Lanes in China: Foreign Direct Investment, Local Governments, and Auto Sector Development*. New York: Cambridge University Press.

Waldmeir, Patti. (2010). "Glut warning for China's auto industry." *Financial Times*, September 20. Retrieved October 24, 2011. (http://www.ft.com/cms/s/0/d36fc25c-c40c-11df-b827-00144-feab49a.html#axzz1bocR9hcc).

World Bank and PRTM Management Consultants. (2011). "The China New Energy Vehicles Program: Challenges and opportunities." World Bank Transport Office. Retrieved April 24, 2011 (http://siteresources.worldbank.org/EXTNEWSCHINESE/Resources/3196537-1202098669693/EV_Report_en.pdf).

Yang, Jian. (2011). "'Chinese CEOs get a hard dose of reality.'" *Automotive News China*, October 14. Retrieved October 19, 2011 (http://www.autonewschina.com/en/article.asp?id=7692).

Yu, Jiang and Kim Hua Tan. (2005). "The evolution of China's mobile telecommunications industry: Past, present and future." *International Journal of Mobile Communications* 3(2): 114–26.

4 Services with Everything
THE ICT-ENABLED DIGITAL TRANSFORMATION OF SERVICES
John Zysman, Stuart Feldman, Kenji E. Kushida,
Jonathan Murray, and Niels Christian Nielsen

Introduction

A fundamental transformation of services is under way, driven by developments in information and communications technology (ICT) tools, the uses to which they are being put, and the networks on which they run. Services were once considered a sinkhole of the economy, immune to significant technological or organizational productivity increases.[1] Now, they are widely recognized as a source of productivity growth and dynamism in the economy that is changing the structure of employment, the division of labor, and the character of work and its location (Triplett and Bosworth 2004). Yet, the actual character of this transformation is often obscured by the increase in jobs labeled as services and by a focus on the digital technologies that, certainly, are facilitating this transformation.[2] This transformation, central to the growth of productivity and competition in the economy, poses basic policy and business choices.

The core of our story of the services transformation is not about the growth in quantity or value of the activities labeled services, the conventional emphasis of much of the writing about services. Nor is it about the revolution in digital technology. Rather, it is about how the application of rule-based information technology tools to service activities transforms the services component of the economy, altering how activities are conducted and value is created. When activities are formalized and codified, they become computable. Processes with clearly defined rules for their execution can be unbundled, recombined, and automated. The codification of service activities allows the rapid replication, analysis, reconfiguration, customization, and creation of new services. We call this the *algorithmic revolution* (Zysman 2006). Traditional business models can be made more productive; they can be extended with ICT tools; and entirely new business models can be created, offering services previously impossible at any price. The algorithmic revolution in services is profoundly changing how firms add value.

There are significant implications for how firms compete. Services are increasingly the way firms seek to avoid the ever-faster commodization of products—that is competition among similar market offerings based solely or principally on price. However, the unbundling of services activities themselves accelerates this commodification, since competitors have the same efficiency-enhancing business process and infrastructure services available to them. Firms increasingly become bundles of services purchased on markets, and at the same time some of those in-house business functions that are maintained are then offered as services. A consequence is that the distinction between products and services blurs, as manufactured products are increasingly embedded within and recast as services offerings. Clearly, traditional sectoral boundaries break down, as information and services offerings bring previously unrelated firms into direct competition.

Likewise, the consequences for business organization, production, and work are profound, just as work was transformed by the evolution of manufacturing. The automation of basic activities frees, but also requires, professionals to perform more advanced tasks. And the analytical tasks of managing information flows generated by ICT-enabled services often require a different set of skills than providing the service itself.

Capturing the possibilities from the services transformation presents new policy challenges for governments and regions. Services are deeply rooted in social rules, conventions, and regulations. Consequently, capturing the value possibilities inherently means recasting the rules, regulations, and conventions in which the services are embedded.[3]

Our argument unfolds in three parts. The first part depicts the dramatic and pervasive transformation of services. The second part introduces several analytic concepts and provides a framework for analyzing the transformation. The third part explores the policy challenges raised by the transformation and outlines several recommendations.

The Services Transformation Unfolding

The transformation of services with ICT tools is dramatic, pervasive, and far-reaching. Activities are transformed, and firms are turning to services in pursuit of value. Traditional boundaries are breaking down between products and services, manufacturing and services, and traditional industrial sectors.

THE ALGORITHMIC REVOLUTION TRANSFORMS ACTIVITIES

With the algorithmic revolution, tasks underlying services can be transformed into formalizable, codifiable, computable processes with clearly defined rules for their execution. The inexorable rise in computational power means that an ever greater range of activities are amenable to expression as computable algorithms, and a growing array of activities are reorganized and automated (Nordhaus 2002). Indeed, core activities in services—from finance through nursing—can be captured and expressed as digital information. The examples abound, and they become commonplace. Bank ATMs (automated teller machines) have automated simple bank transactions, and consumers increasingly book airline tickets and car rentals online. In major enterprises, payroll processes have been reorganized and largely automated. Few employees, if any, within major firms still know how to compute payroll checks, with their myriad deductions, overlapping tax districts, reporting restrictions, and other variables. Instead, the knowledge and process details are embedded in software, usually offered as external specialist services.

Existing activities, when converted into computable processes, often take on new purposes and create new forms of value. For example, the act of making a purchase at a supermarket or retailer has transformed from a simple monetary transaction to a data-generating activity. At the beginning of the application of ICT to retail, of course, inventories were monitored (Bar and Borrus 1985). Then, increasingly fine-grained information of not only inventories but customers began to be collected to be analyzed—to capture consumer preferences and consumption patterns, as well as manage inventories and supply chains, and sometimes, be sold to third parties. In another example, Accenture transformed its data management service into a new value-added service of data monitoring. Its initial service, offered to pharmaceutical companies, was to manage the latter's clinical trial data. Accenture then leveraged its ability to analyze this data, offering back to pharmaceutical firms a service to monitor the reactions of test subjects to drugs ("Outsourcing: External affairs" 2007).

In-house business functions become available as services for purchase. That is, firms can choose to outsource those previously internal business functions, purchasing them as services in the market. A firm may, conversely, package and sell those services to others. As the range of in-company business tasks that can be digitized and manipulated expands, activities can be *unbundled*—separated from surrounding processes and tasks— with ever-finer levels of granularity. Combined with the increasing ability of heterogeneous ICT systems to exchange information with others,[4] tasks can be moved outside companies and offered as services. Business functions ranging from accounting, computing, payroll, supply chain management, and even semiconductor manufacturing and R&D (research and development) can now be purchased on markets. More than ever before, firms are becoming an agglomeration of services offered by others, linked by ICT systems.

This *unbundling* of service activities is the counterpart to the decomposition of manufacturing, in which modularity in product design enabled manufacturing supply chains to be broken apart and spread across multiple corporate boundaries (outsourcing) and national borders (offshoring) (Baldwin and Clark 2000; Borrus, Ernst, and

Haggard 2000). In both cases—the unbundling of services and decomposition of manufacturing—it is the recomposition that is critical to sustaining market position and driving productivity. The issue is how the elements are constituted into products and services, both in constituent modules/bundles and in final offerings, requiring constant innovation.

REPOSITIONING SERVICES TO AVOID COMMODITIZATION

Intense global competition, the array of newcomers from diverse countries, and the rapid diffusion of technology mean that many products face intense price competition. That is, the products become commodities, largely interchangeable from their rivals and hence competing principally on price—even if they become more sophisticated. As firms seek to avoid ever-faster commoditization, many are repositioning the role of services in their core business models. Increasingly, firms see services as the solution to creating defensible positions in markets (see, e.g., Frei 2008; Shankar, Berry, and Dotzel 2009). They use them in a variety of ways.

Firms' hardware offerings are increasingly enhanced in value by ICT-enabled services offerings. Apple's iPod is more than an attractively designed MP3 player. Its integration with the iTunes software was critical to its commercial success, and Apple's online music store revolutionized the way music is sold.[5] Komatsu, a Japanese construction machinery firm, sells products with embedded sensors; these sensors send detailed information not only about the deterioration of parts but also about fuel usage and other information to the company's headquarters. As a result, Komatsu can notify its customers in developing countries if fuel is being siphoned, and it can even remotely halt the operation of machines if lease payments are overdue.[6] Similarly, John Deere offers agricultural equipment that embeds an array of services. Location-referenced soil samples can be collected, analyzed, and sent wirelessly to a remote database, which both helps "map" the fertilizer applied and adjusts the fertilizer mixtures in real time.

Some firms go further, *shifting their core businesses from selling products toward offering services, often delivered via ICT networks*. IBM, for example, transformed itself from a product company in which services support provided competitive advantage to a services company embodying products in its offerings.[7] Emblematic of this transformation was IBM's sale of its computer division, including the emblematic Thinkpad notebook computers, to the Chinese company Lenovo, and its acquisition of PricewaterhouseCooper's consulting arm. While still deriving significant profits from its hardware offerings, IBM's central focus has been on its service offerings, which include management consulting, running firms' ICT operations, and providing a wide range of functionality for firms with its software. Others are following suit. Hewlett-Packard (HP) purchased EDS in 2008 for almost $14 billion, announcing in 2011 that it would jettison its entire consumer computing operations—though this was later retracted. Dell acquired Perot Systems for approximately $4 billion in 2009 (Cusumano 2010: 71).

Not all firms turn to services out of strength, however. Some turn to services as their product markets collapse, a result of new services-based business models. Siebel, once a leader in enterprise customer relations management (CRM) software is a prime example. Faced with an onslaught by Salesforce.com's service and platform, Seibel's sales plummeted in the early 2000s, leading to its acquisition by Oracle in 2005 (Cusumano 2010: 87, 101).

This shift from products to services is not only in software or traditional high-tech areas. Large electronics retailers are experimenting with the idea of selling televisions and computers as a service rather than a product. In this case, for an annual fee, you get a new computer every three years. Or for a separate offering, an annual fee gives you a new television every five years or so. They are essentially transforming the "products" of personal computers (PCs) or televisions into services—computing or television viewing—with a guarantee that the products do not get terribly obsolete.

Even in the heavy industries, major blue-chip firms are repackaging their products into services (though not delivered through ICT networks, in this case). GE, rather than selling industrial refrigerators, now sells "refrigeration services." The Finnish elevator company Kone has repackaged its offerings into "solutions," embedding their products into services that follow the life cycle of the building.

Not all of this is simple rebranding. Examples can get quite interesting. For example, in the mid-2000s, an Austrian company introduced wireless fastener services, enabling the reconfiguration of such things as airline seats. The fastening devices could be controlled remotely, enabling mechanics to operate a handheld device to wirelessly unlock blocs of seats for their repositioning or replacement. The company also had security-oriented offerings, such as thick doors with no externally accessible locking mechanism; only a wireless device with the correct encrypted code could unlock the door. This particular company, Intevia, was bought out by one of its partners, TZ Limited, but the trajectory of its thinking portends the broader sea change in the transformation from products to services we currently face.

These examples reveal how the traditional distinctions between products and services, never completely discrete in the first place, are becoming ever less clear. *Products themselves can be transformed into services when delivered via ICT networks.* For example, software, which used to be a product distributed on physical media, is now increasingly repositioned as a service. Quicken, a software product if purchased on a CD in a box, becomes a service if the same software engine runs on the web, charging for access. Enterprise software for large companies increasingly takes the form of "Software-as-a-Service" (SaaS), with software delivered via the Internet and billed by usage. Even products as basic as data servers and computer processors are transformed into services delivered over ICT networks. Known collectively as "Cloud Computing," a large number of firms are offering storage and processing power, applications, and software development platforms remotely, with pay-as-you-go payment schemes (Kushida, Murray, and Zysman 2011, 2012).

The implications of software's transformation are far-reaching. Updates, for example, can be automated and continuous. It is now quite common for software to be released in "continuous Beta," which evolves incrementally and frequently. Software piracy also becomes a less serious and pervasive issue, since copying discs or a CD for stand-alone installations is far easier than counterfeiting an online authentication process. So, are Windows and Office now products or services?

The line between products and services becomes even more blurred when the software source code is never installed on the user's machine. Google Docs resides entirely in Google's data centers, requiring no user installation. Salesforce.com revolutionized the CRM software industry by hosting the software on its own servers, with users paying for the amount of access rather than for a local installation on users' machines. Upgrades can be truly continuous, with version numbers having little meaning—what's the point of knowing that you're accessing Google Docs version X.Y when there is essentially only one Google Docs offering that everybody uses, and there is no going back to older versions? Users of Facebook, for example, frequently discover major changes to the user interface and features, since the social networking company is constantly tinkering and experimenting.

Products can become portals to services, or are embedded in services. In many cases, the success of products that are tightly linked with services depends on whether the services are effective portals to the service or successful platforms for services. Of course, it is critical that the services themselves are valuable.

By portal, we mean an easy-to-use access method into the services offered. Apple products' seamless integration into iTunes Music Store is the most obvious example of an effective portal. Plug the iPod into your machine and it communicates seamlessly with the iTunes software. A simple click connects iTunes to the Music Store, providing access to search tens of thousands of songs (approximately 200,000 in 2003 when it was first introduced). A clunky interface or lack of seamless integration between product, software, and service would not have enabled the iPod to take off as it did.[8]

The Amazon Kindle e-book reader also offered an effective portal to the Amazon marketplace. When first introduced in 2008 and 2009, the Kindle surprised many by offering cellular wireless capabilities, enabling users to purchase books on the Amazon web site and have them delivered instantly and wirelessly to their Kindle device. Kindles could also access the Amazon e-book marketplace and download free samples from anywhere with a cellular signal—without requiring a separate cellular contract. Moreover, since users' credit card information resided in Amazon's web service, with each Kindle linked to an Amazon account, users could purchase e-books from their Kindle without entering credit card information each time. Free samples of the first part of each book ended with a link that allowed users to purchase the entire book with a simple click on their Kindle device. The elegance of this service integration, combined with the depth of Amazon's e-book selection, was unmatched by its competitors, the Barnes and Nobles Nook and the Sony e-Reader.

The computer peripherals world is littered with failures, such as clunky interfaces, difficult-to-use software, and problems delivering performance from web-based interfaces on the back end.

The concept of *platforms* has gained renewed attention with the advent of smartphones and the battles between iPhone and Google's Android operating system. In essence, platforms are a set of rules and interfaces that permit third-party entities to innovate and deliver services, and in doing so, third parties can enhance the value of the platform itself. Microsoft Windows is the quintessential platform, enabling third-party software developers to write software that takes advantage of its functionality, enhancing the value of the Windows platform as they do so.

Cloud Computing service providers are jockeying for a position as platform provider. For example, one of the major drivers in the success of Salesforce.com was its expansion from an online (Cloud-based) CRM service to a platform offering, Force.com. Using tools provided by Force.com, third-party application providers could write specialized or other value-added applications that Salesforce.com itself did not offer. The ecosystem of Force.com applications enhanced the value of Salesforce.com's offerings themselves.

Mobile apps for iPhone and Android have become major factors in the competition in smartphones and mobile services.[9] With the iPhone and Android apps platforms offering by far the most robust ecosystem of apps, alternative operating systems disappeared rapidly, such as Nokia's Symbian and Meego and HP's WebOS. As these firms are discovering, devices that are not part of the dominant platforms for apps are unattractive to users, regardless of the attractiveness of the operating system or devices themselves. Hardware manufacturers, especially previously successful ones such as Nokia, seem particularly challenged by this new logic of platform services-based competition.

It is also worth noting that the product cycles for smartphones can be slower than the conventional phones they replace. Mobile cellular handsets were quickly following the route of commoditization when Apple changed the game with its iPhone. Thereafter, major iPhone releases occurred basically once a year. Contrast this with the multiple lines of phones released every three to six months by manufacturers of conventional phones for much of the late 1990s and 2000s.

Conventional sectoral distinctions are collapsing into "value domains," in which the digitization of information brings previously physically distinct products and sectors into competition with one another, over less clearly defined customer bases.[10]

Without going into excessive detail, the convergence between mobile phones, personal digital assistants, music players, digital cameras, digital video cameras, and portable gaming consoles has been dramatic. Ten to twelve years ago, each was a distinct product offering, with different sets of firms competing against one another: Nokia, SonyEricsson, and Motorola for mobile phones; Palm, HP, and others for personal digital assistants; a variety of name-brand and commodity manufacturers for portable CD players and early MP3 players; Canon, Nikon, Sony, Kodak, Olympus, and Fuji Film for digital cameras; Sony, Panasonic, JVC, and other consumer electronics firms for video cameras; and Nintendo and Sony for portable gaming devices. Today, smartphones are increasingly offering capabilities that cover these all these areas, which are no longer distinct products areas but are instead a series of value domains in which firms find themselves with a new array of competitors. The collapse of traditional sectors into value domains for personal computers, laptops, netbooks, tablets, and e-book readers is unfolding as well.

Thus, competition within distinct sectors has extended into competition over "value domains." More players are involved, and there is less clarity over the boundaries of previously distinct product and user categories.

BLURRING THE BOUNDARIES BETWEEN MANUFACTURING AND SERVICES

As the market border between products and services is eroded, the analytical distinction, and therefore the policy debates, between manufacturing and services is also blurred. The distinction between products and services was never completely clear; a window washer in a GM plant was classified as a manufacturing worker if employed by GM but became a service worker if employed by a subcontractor, even if the person and the task remained unchanged (Cohen and Zysman 1987).

This distinction between manufacturing and services has long been a fundamental assumption underlying economic analyses and policy debates. As the algorithmic revolution extends the range of computable activities, and as developments in software, processing power, and ICT networks enable increasing portions of corporate activity to be outsourced, the breakdown of this distinction is accelerating.

In the current era, manufacturing itself is offered as a service, with examples ranging from Taiwanese "fabless" semiconductor manufacturing firms to a company such as Flextronics, which manufactures electronic products under contract to brand-name suppliers (original equipment manufacturing, or OEM). For national accounting purposes, to understand sources of productivity, and to analyze the nature of labor and employment for policy debates, the question is whether these OEM firms should be considered manufacturing or service firms. On the other side, firms such as Apple and Amazon design their iPhones and Kindle electronic reader devices but manufacture them on an OEM basis; does this mean they are not engaged in manufacturing?

The reality is that firms and their suppliers are often increasingly intertwined, especially at the higher ends of production. The most sophisticated toolmakers for firms such as Ford, Audi, BMW, and Boeing often colocate their activities on manufacturing shop floors. Yet, they are offering services. The question is whether to consider these third-firm employees, working on the floor of an aircraft or automobile factory, helping to design the assembly line, as manufacturing or service workers.

Finally, the myriad accounting, legal, marketing, and other service firms that take on formerly in-house tasks performed by large "manufacturing" firms blur the distinction further.

Understanding the Services Transformation

The services transformation is pervasive. Consequently we need some tools to sort through the developments. First, we distinguish the underlying services activities, placing them on a spectrum ranging from irreducible to automated. We then consider the implications for productivity gains for each type of activity and lay out the limits of the transformation—a case for the enduring role of human judgment. Then we turn to a range of transformations in the business models built on top of the services.

THE SERVICES SPECTRUM

There is a range of services activities to consider, from irreducible to hybrid to automated (see Figure 4.1).

Irreducible services rely on humans to deliver them. They are provided strictly by human beings, either because they require personal skills or attributes that only humans can offer or for simple reasons of practicality and cost. Examples include the services provided by hairdressers, judges, psychologists, and priests.

In most cases, irreducible services are created at the same time and in the same place where they are delivered and used; such services cannot truly be said to "exist" apart from their delivery by humans in a particular moment and location. Irreducible services originally constituted the full range of services available in the economy, and they still make up the majority of services sold. The constant evolution and growing power of ICT tools constantly increases the range of services that can be "transformed" into automated or hybrid services.

By contrast, ICT *automated services* rely on digital ICT to manage information and deploy it in ways that are useful and valuable to customers. The services provided by a bank ATM, an Internet travel agency, or electronic systems for collecting road and bridge tolls are familiar examples.[11]

Some automated services compete with and threaten existing manual services, or extend their reach. In one sense, eBay's online auctions compete with traditional suppliers of human-based auctions services, such as Sotheby's, Christies, and hundreds of

Irreducible Services	Hybrid Services	Automated Services
Rely on humans to deliver services, which are typically created at the same time and in the same place they are delivered.	Rely on a combination of humans and electonic tools to deliver services, using ICT and other systems to leverage or enhance human capabilities. This combination is often constituted as a system.	Rely on ICT or other technologies to deliver services that have been codified, digitized, and made available, often using electronic communication or distribution tools.

FIGURE 4.1 The Services Spectrum

local auction houses. However, their real business success rests on extending the auction model to products and communities that the model could never reach without ICT tools.

Others offer entirely new services that could not be provided manually—for example, Google's online search capability can perform functions analogous to those of a traditional human librarian or research assistant, but with a degree of speed, efficiency, accuracy, and thoroughness that no human service provider could ever hope to duplicate. On-demand delivery of video content by companies such as Netflix, allowing consumers to stream content previously only available on DVD or through illegal downloads, is another example.

Finally, *hybrid services* combine human and machine-based capabilities, either harnessing technology to improve and leverage the abilities of people or depending on human talents to augment, deliver, customize, personalize, or otherwise add value to automated services. (They are not simply services in which some of the information involved in the process or transaction is captured electronically—such as a massage therapy business using digital software to manage reservations and accounting. Rather, a central element in the creation of value is digitally processed.)

A growing fraction of the most valuable and popular services are now hybrids. For example, accountants often rely heavily on software containing significant information about tax rules, bookkeeping systems, and financial principles that is able to store, analyze, update, and manipulate large amounts of data with ease, speed, and accuracy. However, they supplement the power of the software with personal judgment that helps them provide advice and insights suited to particular situations. Similarly, travel agencies handle most transactions digitally but use human agents to handle complex cases and particularly high-value customers.

This system is highly dynamic, with particular services, service companies, and even entire industries moving, rapidly or slowly, from one position on the spectrum to another. As new technology and business systems are devised, the nature of possibilities continues to evolve. Services once practically unobtainable—access to vast stores of information now provided by a routine web search engine, for example—can now be obtained at virtually no cost in terms of time, money, or effort. The local limitations that constrain the availability of traditional human-delivered services are also reduced or eliminated by digitization.

The Services Spectrum and Potential for Productivity Gains, Transformations

Fully automated systems offer the greatest potential productivity gains. Because they rely on digital systems, the power, efficiency, and affordability of algorithmic services can be expected to improve in accordance with exponential increases in computing capabilities. As chips improve and multiply, and the networks they form become exponentially more powerful, the possibilities for fully automated digitized services expand dramatically.

It is in the hybrid sector, where human delivery is combined with automation, that the deepest economic transformations are occurring. The value of hybrid services depends on human capabilities being augmented by increasingly sophisticated ICT systems.

The Limits of the Transformation: The Need for Human Judgment

The ultimate limits of the domain of the computable have been a significant source of debate among many observers, including the authors of this chapter. One extreme view is that the domain of the computable will eventually push out human judgment altogether. The opposite view is that human knowledge will continue to dominate—that core facets of knowledge can never be reduced to algorithms. Our view is that while the domain of human activity that can be codified and automated increases, human judgment will continue to be critical.

We consider the financial debacle of 2008 to be the first major crisis of the information era.[12] Whatever its other implications, it will stand as a stark demonstration of the new logic of value creation, the transformed character of the service economy, and—paradoxically—the *heightened importance of human judgment* in a world where electronic tools for gathering, analyzing, and managing information are more ubiquitous and powerful than ever (Nielsen and Nielsen 2006).

Modern finance is possible only with the ability to analyze enormous amounts of data, to perform complicated mathematical calculations, and to act in real time. But how those possibilities are used—whether they create widespread benefits or generate disaster—depends on the judgments and talents of people.

In the case of the financial innovations of the 1990s and 2000s, disaster struck for a variety of reasons having to do with the mismanagement of financial knowledge. The possibility of complex computation often hid, and hid from the practitioners, the problems with the information they were using and the nature of risk itself.[13]

The lesson: Those who live by information also can die by it. Once again, the old information technology (IT) slogan, "Garbage in, garbage out," was validated.

Steve Lohr put it this way:

> ...the larger failure...was human—in how the risk models were applied, understood and managed. Some respected quantitative finance analysts, or quants, as financial engineers are known, had begun pointing to warning signs years ago. But while markets were booming, the incentives on Wall Street were to keep chasing profits by trading more and more sophisticated securities, piling on more debt and making larger and larger bets. (2008: B1)

We see the same message in many other industries, though delivered in less dramatic fashion.

Now that we have covered the spectrum of how services activities are transformed by the algorithmic revolution, led us turn to how they affect business models built on top of service activities.

A RANGE OF SERVICES BUSINESS MODEL TRANSFORMATIONS

The algorithmic revolution makes a range of model transformations possible. Many business models entail delivery of the services themselves. Others are extended or transformed by the underlying tools available to them. (See Figure 4.2.)

At one end, firms can use *ICT services to enhance traditional business models*, often by increasing their efficiency. For example, life insurance was among the first industries to transform its business models with the massive application of computing resources and algorithms. Wal-Mart's early and extensive use of ICT to link suppliers and distribution radically increased its operational efficiency.

Firms can also *extend traditional business models with ICT-enabled activities.* Amazon extended a catalog retailer's business model with an online storefront and user-generated reviews and ratings. A Chilean mining company provides an interesting example, in taking its traditional business of operating mining machines and shifting them to ICT-enabled remote operations; once machines are remotely operated, it can offer remote mining operations as a service worldwide.

Existing firms often progress from one step to the next; they first enhance their traditional business model to improve efficiency, then they move to extending the business model in new ways. Wal-Mart and other big box retailers' moves into online retailing are examples.

For new entrants, the ability to begin afresh with new business models that extend traditional ones offers an array of entry points. Amazon, for example, was not a traditional bookseller or retailer, starting from the ground up with an ICT-extended business model.

At the far end of the spectrum, *entirely new business models are invented.* Google is the prime example, linking advertising revenue to search. An interesting example of an entirely new business model can be found in virtual currency: users using real money to purchase virtual gifts, avatars, or other virtual goods within an online game or social networking site. Some estimates put the total spending on virtual currency at over $2 billion—only for the United States (Verna 2011). There are relatively few examples, but many hope to discover and develop the next completely new business model.

| ICT Services Enhance Efficiency of Traditional Business Models | Traditional Business Models Extended with ICT Services | Completely New Business Models through ICT |

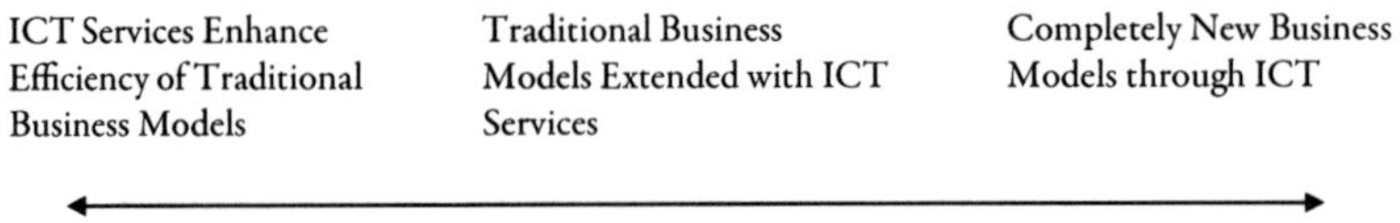

FIGURE 4.2 The Range of Business Model Transformations

THE SERVICES DILEMMA

We have seen that the ICT-enabled services transformation involves both including a services component in the business model and transforming services activities, particularly routine activities, into computable processes. This is just the beginning of the competitive story.

The services dilemma pits potential productivity gains against the threat of commoditization. If the services component of a business model or activity is primarily irreducible, it will tend to avoid commoditization resulting from other firms applying ICT tools to achieve similar results. However, it is then susceptible to Baumol's productivity trap. On the other hand, if the services component is highly codified and automated, productivity can be won, but at the cost of a continuing threat of commoditization. Thus, the need for innovation in offerings, processes, and business models continues.

DRIVERS OF THE TRANSFORMATION: WHY NOW AND WHY SO FAST?

The transformation of services has been unfolding rapidly, accelerating in the last decade or so. In order to understand why it is unfolding now, and why it is unfolding so fast, we need to look at what is driving the services transformation. The primary drivers of the services transformation are technological developments in the areas of computing, storage, software and networking, and competitive pressures in a global, digital world. The result is that production is being decomposed, manufacturing modularized, and services unbundled into their basic activities. Technology extended and intensified competition, changed how firms operated, and provided new solutions to the ever intensifying competition.

Two matters must be noted. First, the application of ICT to existing service activities, the automation of existing activities, is always the beginning of the story—a cycle. What one firm automates, another firm copies; the initial "automation" provides short-lived limited advantage. Continuous learning and innovation are therefore required. The final offerings need to be rethought, reconceived, and implemented anew.

Second, even for radical new services, such as online search or Twitter, which open entirely new domains, the competitive problem is how to maintain advantage. Google's constant introduction of new functionality and new possibilities is part of its effort to hold its users, and hence its advertising rates.

The Spiral of Ever-Increasing Commoditization and Competition: Pressure from a Global, Digital Era

There has been a spiral of intensifying competition and a resulting commodification of goods and services that is increasing competition based on price alone as more and more competitors emerge for the routine and established. That spiral is driven by a digitization of information and globalization of markets.

We know that as information is digitized, it can be stored, moved, and manipulated, allowing information-based activities to be relocated, transformed, and recombined. Information takes on new value. For example, many financial services are essentially encapsulated information, with algorithms determining patterns of trading and the composition of derivatives-based products. For digital media, such as CDs and DVDs, streamed video content, and online databases, the information itself is the product. Moreover, the digitization of information drives the breakdown of traditional sectors into value domains, as noted earlier. Firms in traditionally distinct sectors are brought into competition, adding to the pressure to find differentiated business models or defensible points in the market.

These same ICT tools facilitated the communication that encouraged an extension of competition. New competitors from countries seeking to industrialize entered the marketplace. The new competitor usually began with basic products, either borrowing technology and producing for its home markets or sending basic exports to wealthier, more advanced countries. Meanwhile, companies from the advanced countries moved production off shore. Sometimes those advanced country firms produced off shore themselves; sometimes they contracted with other firms to produce off shore for them, outsourcing abroad. As ICT tools became ever more sophisticated, producing both goods and services abroad, developing products abroad, and managing the complex operations this implied, all became easier and less expensive. The consequence, though, was straightforward. Competition for standard products—products that were in essence commodities differentiated by price or by branding—became ever more intense. The competitive pressures that have accelerated commoditization in a global, digital era are pushing firms toward seeking value in ICT-enabled services.

ICT-enabled services are one competitive response to the market and price pressures of commodization. There are two mechanisms, which we have already noted. One is that firms increasingly include a services component in their business model to avoid the consequences of the commoditization of the product itself, with Apple's iPod perhaps the most discussed example. Second, the application of ICT can transform all services. Yet, though ICT enabled, they are no panacea. That which is routine is likely to be automated. And while automating routine operations may create temporary benefits, they remain routine. And automation of the routine is easily copied. So, decisive advantage comes by sustaining the pace of automation of the routine, by innovative ways of approaching traditional activities to create new and distinct values, and by generating entirely new ICT-based products and services.

We have a particular vantage on globalization. Globalization is not simply a story of worldwide convergence—it is also a story of national innovations played out on a larger stage. In the classic view, global competition begins with falling transport and communication costs leading firms to do more and more business over distance. In this view, it becomes a flat world in which ICT tools, cross-national production networks, outsourcing, and offshoring allow corporations to reconstitute themselves as orchestrating Lego block-like nodes of activity, buying R&D from here, production capacity from there, and so forth (Friedman 2005; Berger and MIT Industrial Performance Center 2006). The decomposition of value chains with outsourced manufacturing allowed multiple points for innovation and entry by new actors. Governments are constrained in this vantage, since activities of home-grown firms can relocate anywhere, with "immobile resources" chasing "mobile assets."

However, we contend that although the global does mean a larger set of points for innovation, more competitors, and factor price convergence, it is still a story about national developments interacting on a global stage (Kushida and Zysman 2009). Lean production, developed in Japan, clearly diffused to production processes around the world. Although not all Japanese companies adopted the Toyota production innovation, lean production would not have developed were the Japanese nascent auto industry not protected from imports and direct investment while gaining access to the U.S. and global export markets. Similarly, the Finnish firm Nokia was a unique firm within Finland, but much less likely to have dominated global mobile handset markets if Nordic roaming standards had not been adopted, followed by GSM as a European standard, giving Nokia access to broader markets.[14] China's current trajectory of development was rooted in cross-national production networks and policies harnessing inflows of foreign investments. India's success as a business process outsourcing and offshoring destination was initially sparked by the combination of educational strength and telecommunications liberalization within India, the rapid buildout of transpacific fiber cable in the context of the U.S. dot-com boom, and the shortage of software engineers in the United States.[15]

The sequence of national stories produces a series of challenges in the form of new competitors and new competitive strategies for companies and countries. The result is an enduring tension between the dislocations and challenges of the global against adaptations and adjustments of particular firms and places.

In short, competition in the global, digital era is characterized by unexpected, constant disruption, both from countries and companies. Myriad new entrants in various points along value networks and production processes, combined with the increasing ability for granulized production and the purchase of business processes on markets, cause firms to experience an intensified struggle against ever-faster commoditization.

Technology Drivers: Evolving Computing Platforms, Captured by Organizations

The technology drivers of the services transformation include the exponential growth in computing power, the increasing speed of networks, the evolution of software, and the progression of computing platforms.[16] Computing platforms evolved along two dimensions—from stand-alone to networked, and from mainframe computers to PCs.[17] The result was an ever-increasing power to digitize information and then process, store, and transmit information in digital form.[18] Each techological step opened new possibilities for the application of ICT to services. The ever-increasing processing power, expanded storage, and connectivity meant a whole variety of things. All that brought greater functionality to the desktop, but it also meant small phones, increasing connectivity, and distributed sensors embedded in everything. The advent of the Internet as a platform for the delivery of services and business activities ushered in the contemporary era in the transformation of services.

An evolution to the next computing platform is currently under way. Cloud Computing, a combination of technologies and business models, will kick off another major round of innovations and new entrants. Cloud Computing, in essence, offers (1) computing resources (such as applications, services, and data) on demand via networks, which (2) can be scaled up or down rapidly according to the users' needs (providing users with the illusion of infinite scalability), and (3) are often offered as pay-as-you-go schemes, requiring no up-front commitment.[19] For users, Cloud Computing allows computing to become a "dynamic utility" (Kushida, Murray, and Zysman 2011, 2012). Firms can avoid capital expenditures of building their own data centers, instead paying for computing resources as they need. Entry barriers into computing-intensive areas are lowered, capabilities for experimentation are increased, and it becomes easier than ever for start-ups and new entrants to scale up rapidly to become major players.

The technologies, of course, do not produce their own use and do not generate their own value. The services transformation is not simply a technology story; the advantage of ICT tools is captured by organizations. The argument put forth by Stephen Cohen, Bradford DeLong, and John Zysman to understand the first phase of the ICT revolution still stands: "At each point in the past forty years the critical step in the transformation of technical potential into economic productivity has been the discovery by users of information technology of how to employ their ever-greater and ever-cheaper computing power to do the previously-impossible" (2000: 15).

Innovative lead users, in the form of large and small firms discovering new uses for information technology, were critical. Information technology was adopted to solve a particular problem, or to cut costs. Innovative users then discovered new uses. For example, Citibank took advantage of flat-rate telephony, moving its back offices not only into the area surrounding Manhattan but all the way to South Dakota. The organizational shift enabling this move—modularizing the back-office operations—facilitated moving select back-office operations much further, to places such as India. Continual organizational experimentation and innovation, adopting new technologies, and finding new business models and services possibilities will continue to drive the services transformation.

Thus, the interplay of technology, organizations, competition in a global, digital world creating pressure to escape commoditization, and the evolving computer platforms are driving the services transformation.

Capturing the Services Transformation

The question for firms and government is how to capture the value possibilities opened up by the services transformation. Before we turn to the policy and strategy issues, we need to develop the two notions that have been implicit in our discussion. First, services are a form of production ever more supported by Information and Communications Technologies. Second, precisely for that reason, ICT-enabled services are driving productivity growth.

To capture this productivity growth and the potential benefits from the services transformation, we focus on three areas: (1) connectivity—the availability of ICT tools and infrastructure, (2) people—the skills and capacities to implement technology, and (3) government—not only as a promoter and educator, but as a rule-setter and user.

We turn first to recasting the notion of services, including them as part of the conception of production.

ICT-BASED SERVICES AS PRODUCTION: RECASTING THE POLICY DEBATES

Classic conceptions of services revolved around the notion that services were market activities that did not produce or transform material goods. Consequently, they could not be stored or shipped and were consumed in the same moment and at the same place they were created. This is still mostly true for traditional services. ICT-based services differ because they often require massive (and ongoing) investments on a new industrial scale to support the future services.

With the application of ICT tools, services can be incorporated into larger systems—systems that change the level and character of investment required for delivery. Google invests massively in creating automated systems that create and deliver the actual services at a later time, anywhere. ICT-based services can often be scaled far beyond traditional services.

The development and deployment of ICT-enabled services should be considered a form of production. ICT-based services have to be built and produced, or at least the ICT systems have to be designed, developed, built, and implemented. The tools, including software, have to be "built," and the online services themselves have to be "constructed."[20] Consequently they are very much open to innovation and productivity increases. From a policy standpoint, the question is how to conceive, design, develop, and build and deploy the new system. The "good" jobs (high value-added functions) are in the innovative development and deployment of these systems. Policy makers need to employ strategies that will help communities and firms to develop the competencies required for this new form of production.

The continuing debate in political, economic, and public policy circles about the relative value of manufacturing jobs and service-sector jobs is increasingly irrelevant to policy debates in the real economy. Just as it is inaccurate to assume that manufacturing jobs are secure and well paid, it is also inaccurate to consider service jobs to be dead-end, low-wage, unskilled positions. This model ignores not only the lawyer and physician but also the computer programmer, the financial analyst, and the web designer—each a high-paid, highly skilled service worker. Rather than focusing on the increasingly irrelevant distinction between manufacturing and services, the conversation should be recast. If the word "production" includes not only traditional manufacturing but also the development of IT-based services—with the know-how, skills, and tool mastery they require—then we see that, in this broader sense, production remains of vital importance in the digital age, not just in the traditional manufacturing industries but in the services sector as well. And production workers—including not only assembly-line employees but also many kinds of knowledge workers in services industries ranging from finance, health care, and IT to education, media, and entertainment—are now more important than ever.

SERVICES DRIVING PRODUCTIVITY

Services were once seen as a sinkhole of the economy, immune to significant technological or organizationally driven productivity increases. As Baumol and Bowen (1966) put it in the 1960s, it still takes the same amount of labor to play a Beethoven quintet. "Baumol's Cost Disease," as it became known, pointed to services as a drag on aggregate economic growth as their role grew in the economy.[21] It didn't work out that way. At the same time that Baumol was writing, another article announcing Moore's law pointed the way to the explosive expansion of digital information processing (Moore 1965). That capacity, as Baumol himself notes, is transforming the services industry and the economy (Baumol 2007).

Services are now widely recognized as a source of productivity growth and dynamism in the economy. The United States experienced a rapid labor productivity surge starting in 1995. Baumol's disease was cured; new data showed that services, which we contend were transformed, drove the productivity surge. That transformation was every bit as important as investment and innovation in the manufacturing sectors (Triplett and Bosworth 2004, 2006).[22]

Services were originally a "residual" in national accounting after manufacturing and agriculture. Since "services" was a catch-all category not thought to be central to the processes of innovation and productivity, little attention was given to how to measure them or the productivity increases. And they are inherently difficult to measure in any case; measures of services price, quantity, and quality are problematic (Griliches et al. 1992). Let us consider a few instances. For major industries driving productivity growth, which include banking, insurance, securities, and real estate, among others, there is debate over what constitutes a unit of output. Measures of value added can be influenced by stock market bubbles. Investment activities that fall outside traditional business categories may not be captured—insurance firms invested in derivative hedging operations, for example. Other sectors, such as retail, have benefited from reorganization and shifting the format and product mix of retail stores, not captured by traditional performance indices. The quality of output for medical services, for example, is difficult to determined, and the output "product" of business services such as management consulting is also problematic (Triplett and Bosworth 2000). Since measures of productivity rest on output units or value added, measurement errors in the data are likely to have played a significant role in the observed slow productivity growth of services until 1995.[23] (The measures have since improved (Triplett and Bosworth 2000).)

The adoption of ICT is now clearly identified as a driver of productivity growth in services.[24] New data and improved measures available from the early 2000s revealed that ICT contributed to the surge of U.S. aggregate labor productivity since 1995. This resolved the confusion until then, that the data did not show ICT contributing significantly to productivity growth—the "productivity paradox" (Jorgenson, Ho, and Stiroh 2005, 2008). Of the aggregate labor productivity growth from ICT industries and implementation, services industries contributed a majority—80 percent, according to Triplett and Bosworth.[25]

CAPTURING THE BENEFITS OF THE TRANSFORMATION

To capture the benefits of services transformed by ICT tools, government policies surrounding ICT will play critical roles. Put simply, the key areas are connectivity, people, and government as a direct actor.

Connectivity

By connectivity, we refer broadly to the availability of ICT networks and tools. The notion of connectivity has evolved over time, causing a parallel shift in the potential role of the government in ensuring connectivity.[26]

The original notion of connectivity consisted of ensuring universal telephone access to remote geographic regions and across all income levels. With the advent of the Internet, connectivity expanded to cover Internet access, with concerns over the "digital divide" between those with and without access. More recently, connectivity was expanded to include broadband speeds, with different countries defining different throughput thresholds. The diffusion of mobile technologies further widens the notion of connectivity, as the Internet may be best accessed through mobile networks, especially in developing regions.

Although the notion of connectivity continues to evolve, it is clear that without connectivity, very little is possible in the way of taking advantage of the production and consumption of digitally transformed services.

Rapidly shifting technologies and market conditions have made the government's task in ensuring broad public connectivity both more difficult and easier. The old argument was that government should adopt policies to push for broadband for public access. Cross-subsidization schemes, the expansion of funds for increasingly broadly defined universal service, and direct subsidies to public telecommunications carriers were among the traditional policy tools. Over the past few years, the ownership of infrastructure has been evolving. The role of public telecommunications carriers is changing. Increasingly, infrastructure is privately held and operated by services firms. For example, Google has built high-speed access points around the world and invested in global fiber optic infrastructure, including transpacific and transatlantic fiber networks. As a result, data connections over the Internet jump onto Google's private network increasingly early on, especially in developing countries. Thus, in Africa, for example, connections jump onto Google's private network at a very early point, circumventing as much of public networks as possible. The rise of private networks as conduits of Internet traffic is shown clearly in recent data (Labovitz, Lekel-Johnson, et al. 2009). The emerging policy debate is over what market needs are to be provided by public and private actors.

People: Skills and Capacities

Even if technology and connectivity are available, they are useless without people capable of using and implementing them. This is clearly understood; human skills affect what can be done.

While purely routine tasks will become increasingly automated, human tasks remain. There will always be new problems to be solved, new processes to be codified, and new services to be automated through the creation of algorithms. For example, in the automation of health care, as medical knowledge is advanced, new systems need to be constructed, new monitoring and intervention patterns will be needed, and human interventions will still ultimately be necessary.

There will also remain an almost endless array of services relying on the application of both tacit knowledge and pattern recognition. Competitive companies will continue to depend on human abilities to identify and integrate sources of new knowledge and insight, to communicate this information with others through rich verbal and written interactions, to apply expert judgment based on tacit knowledge and pattern recognition, and to understand the significance of an entirely new problem and devise ways of addressing it.

A first implication is that we need a new definition of literacy at the level of basic education. Reading, writing, and arithmetic—the traditional basics of elementary schooling—are no longer enough. Instead, basic education must also focus on abstract reasoning and communication skills—the ability to identify, structure, and solve problems, both qualitative and quantitative; to access and organize information; and to communicate ideas and logical connections to others. The high school graduate (or equivalent) of tomorrow must be prepared either to help build the new technologies or to apply them in a human context—that is, either to work in services design and production or in services delivery.[27]

A second implication of the new workforce dynamic is that the balance between specific skills and general skills is shifting.

Until recently, the specific skills developed by years on a particular production line or in a particular business function (marketing, finance, design) were vitally important to organizations. Today, the value of such specific skills is rapidly eroding. With the accelerating introduction of new products and new services based on new technologies and new production methods, and with the growing use of IT-driven tools to automate processes that are purely routine, knowledge of "how things have been done" is increasingly perishable.

By contrast, such general skills as the ability to understand and cope with the unusual and the unexpected, and the ability to learn quickly in ever-shifting environments are becoming more and more critical. People who can pull together information from various expert systems and knowledge bases, crossing domains and identifying patterns and connections will create the most economic value in societies. This kind of abstract thinking—the ability to combine sensory data with an intuitive sense of what is right and wrong in terms of the meaning and quality of data—is extremely difficult to reduce to a digital algorithm, and it will probably remain so for many years to come. Therefore, this uniquely human capability needs to be emphasized and developed as much as possible in both educational systems and in knowledge-management programs at the company level.

The implications for worker training and recruitment programs have yet to be worked through. How does a country or a company maintain the capacity to sustain vital skill domains (e.g., cutting metal) when the technologies and techniques dramatically change (as when lasers replace diamond-tipped tools in metallurgy)? It is not just a matter of hiring smart, well-educated people, but about hiring people whose greatest skill is the ability to develop, absorb, and communicate ever-changing knowledge.

Government as an Actor

Governments play several roles: as major users of technology, they can shape the ICT environment; as regulators, they create the market rules that influence how the private sector deploys and uses new technologies; as promoters, they can identify distinctive opportunities.

Governments are major users of information technology. There is a running debate over the continuing importance of the government as a buyer, and whether or how it will shape industry. Government spending on IT is certainly not trivial. In 2008, for example, Gartner estimated that in worldwide IT spending, governments were the third largest spenders, behind financial services and manufacturing, a pattern projected to continue in 2009 (Gartner Newsroom 2009).[28] The U.S. government spent an estimated $80 billion a year on IT for the past few years (Thibodeau 2009), and in Europe, the UK alone planned to spend $36.8 billion in 2010 (IDC Government Insights 2010). These expenditures dwarf those of major companies, which might spend about $5 billion in a year at the high end.

Some contend that government will be a significant driver in the current round of IT investments to consolidate data centers and increase the efficiency of IT utilization.[29] In this vantage, initiatives such as the one launched in early 2010 by the U.S. government for a sweeping consolidation of the government's data centers are likely to affect the development of IT. They can accelerate the adoption of Cloud computing, which can offer increased efficiency in data center utilization, for example.[30] Others argue that the slow time scale of government spending will limit governments' effects on the development of industry.[31]

Competitive markets throughout the value chain have been central to the development and rapid diffusion of the new ICT tools. For example, when the technology giants IBM and AT&T declined to enter the nascent semiconductor industry because of direct and indirect antitrust implications, a new array of companies pushing the use of the new digital technologies emerged. Similarly, the rapid development of the Internet grew from the competition unleashed by judicial deconstruction of the monopoly phone company. Policy makers should be on guard against monopolistic or oligopolistic control of emerging technology fields and take appropriate steps to encourage the emergence of multiple companies to encourage competition and drive innovation.

An important task for policy makers in this new economic era is to find ways to promote effective capacities that enable companies and communities to maintain a competitive advantage. Here we list three:

- First, they need the capacity to *develop new technologies*—the classic research and development function that has long been emphasized (correctly) as a vital tool for innovation.
- Second, they need the capacity to *recognize and harvest new technologies* from around the world and from diverse sectors.
- Third, they need the capacity to *combine, absorb, and apply diverse innovations and sources of knowledge* into whatever production processes they are engaged in.

Conclusion

We have argued that a fundamental transformation of services is under way. It is being driven by developments in ICT tools and the uses to which they are being put. The application of rule-based information technology tools is transforming services activities, altering how activities are conducted and how value is created. Services sectors have transformed from a productivity sinkhole to a source of dynamism and productivity growth. The algorithmic revolution enables tasks underlying services to be formalized, codified, and transformed, and firms are increasingly turning to services to add value. In-house business functions are available as services, firms are ever more comprised of bundles of services purchased on markets, and manufactured products are increasingly embedded and recast as services offerings. Traditional sectoral boundaries are breaking down as information and services offerings bring previously unrelated firms into direct competition.

We have offered some analytical vantages to understand how the services transformation is unfolding. We introduced a spectrum of services activities, ranging from irreducible to hybrid to automated. While the latter offer the highest potential productivity gains, we contend that human judgment will continue to be critical. We also introduced a range of business model transformations made possible from the algorithmic revolution, ranging from enhancing the efficiency of traditional business models to extending traditional business models with ICT to creating completely new business models. We showed why the transformation is unfolding now, and so rapidly, by contextualizing it in the competitive pressures from a global, digital era and the evolution of computing technologies and platforms.

The challenge for firms and governments is in capturing the benefits of the services transformation. We call for recasting the policy debates by considering ICT-based services as "production." For firms, capturing the gains from the implementation of new technologies requires new business models, new organizational strategies, and cultivating new skills. For governments, this requires providing connectivity, an environment to foster the ability to continually learn new skills, and creating rules to facilitate experimentation and implementation. At the same time there must be attention to the classic market problems of assuring consumer rights, competition, and the like.

Services are deeply rooted in social rules, conventions, and regulations. Consequently, capturing the value possibilities in the algorithmic transformation inherently means recasting the rules, regulations, and conventions in which the services are embedded.

The present debates about intellectual property, about the rights of Google to copy the world's libraries, of media companies to shape how MP3 files are shared, are all part of that basic debate about the new rules of market for a digital services age. Writing the new rules is not a matter of just saying, we have established principles. Those established principles about, for example, property and privacy are in fact complex bargains often created and institutionalized over decades if not centuries. It is not enough to say apply those bargains in a digital age. New digital capabilities raise new issues. Who should manage the world's libraries? Or who should have the benefits from the genome of particular populations? As important, reopening the old bargains to deal with the new issues makes re-striking the bargain necessary and may change the original principles. There are implications both for the process of transformation, what it takes to accomplish the transformation, and for the kinds of services and tools that evolve.[32]

The implementation of new technologies, and the adoption of new business models and strategies, involves complex transitions. Managing these transitions means recasting rules and conventions. These transitions are not just about adopting a new technology, or about a shift from one market equilibrium to another, but rather a broader shift from one policy regime and set of market signals to alternate policy regimes and sets of market signals. Social and economic transformations always involve winners and losers, and hence are, in both a large and small sense, political. It is a tumultuous process as economic well-being and social positions are recast and reinvented.

In a small political sense there will be the struggles around and within the organization of companies, about shifts in required work skills, the relocation of work, and the displacement of workers. Again, even these smaller stories are never just technical, but, involving shifts in position and roles, they are always fraught with conflict.

In a larger political sense there will be battles about the rules of providing services, who can be providers, how quality is maintained, and who gets to use what information, as well as about how losers are compensated and potential winners supported. Those who would implement the new tools and reorganize services and service delivery must understand, almost begin with, the entrenched social character of services, of market regulation, and of labor market dynamics. That will apply to the end user, a health care company or a bank, to the ICT services company, or to the regulator.

As the political debates and battles unfold across the world, policy makers, analysts, and scholars may be tempted to see a narrower set of issues and problems with a smaller set of solutions. Our view is that only by understanding the fundamental transformation of services, which are driving the emergence of these issues and debates, can we see the disparate issues as part of a larger complex, systemic transition—a transition entailing different sets of bargains and solutions that will unfold differently across the globe.

Acknowledgments

The authors wish to thank the Alfred P. Sloan Foundation for financial support and the Berkeley Roundtable on the International Economy (BRIE) for research and administrative support.

Notes

1. William Baumol wrote in the 1960s that it still takes the same amount of labor to play a Beethoven quintet (Baumol and Bowen 1966; Baumol 1967). In the past years he has come to recognize the power of the ICT transformation of services (Baumol 2007).

2. The conventional view, summarized effectively by the National Academy of Sciences (NAS), is that growth since the mid-1990s was largely driven by the rapidly falling cost of processing power (following "Moore's law," which predicted that the number of transistors in integrated circuits—roughly, processing power—would double every two years) and heavy corporate investments into ICT (Jorgenson, Ho, and Stiroh 2005; Jorgenson and Wessner 2007).

However, remarkably, the NAS report only notes the significance of services and ICT in a couple sentences: "A structural change most associated with the New Economy today is the transformation of the Internet from a communication media to a platform for service delivery [which has] contributed to the remarkable growth of the U.S. service economy...new business models, enabled by the web...will contribute to sustaining the productivity growth of [sic] U.S. economy" (Jorgenson and Wessner 2007: 22–23). What they treat as an end point, this paper takes as the beginning.

3. For more on the first round of market and policy transformations in a digital, global, era see Zysman and Newman (2006).

4. Firms usually installed IT systems by adding new systems to existing legacy ones. By the late 1990s, most large enterprises were running several different legacy systems that were not always compatible with each other. Waves of M&A (mergers and acquisitions) activity exacerbated the situation. However, increases in the sheer number-crunching ability, combined with "glue-code"— pieces of code that bridged the heterogeneous system—increasingly enabled heterogeneous IT systems to be connected. Within companies, this increased efficiency, but more important, it facilitated the connections of IT systems across company borders, facilitating the outsourcing of an increasing array of activities.

5. Until Apple's music store became hugely popular, it was not obvious that consumers were willing to pay for music downloads. The rise of Napster, which allowed users to freely share MP3 music files of copyrighted music, was sometimes argued to have had such a pervasive cultural effect that people would be unwilling to pay for any content downloaded from online.

6. The company can also use data from the levels of usage of its machines to generate supply-demand predictions for countries or regions in which statistics about economic trends are unreliable.

7. IBM mainframes were leased to major enterprises and manned by specialists.

8. For more on the Apple iPod versus the Microsoft Zune, see Huberty, Chapter 7 (in this volume).

9. For more on the smartphone operating system battles, see Kenney and Pon (2011).

10. Many thanks to Erkki Ormala of Nokia who first made this argument at a lunch in Helsinki.

11. But not all automated services use digital ICT. For example, a self-service laundromat is an automated provider of services that typically does *not* employ ICT, except to the extent that modern washing machines use microchips to control some functions.

12. The dot-com bubble and crash of 2000 was the result of misplaced investments and optimism, but it was a classic bubble; the dot-com bubble was not about the underlying IT tools and how they were deployed and used.

13. First, loan companies and mortgage grantors took heavy advantage of the seeming clarity of credit scoring systems reduced to computerized algorithms, such as Fair-Isaac's FICO. Produced by credit bureaus, credit card companies, and specialists with access to tens of millions of loan records and the ability to analyze, these systems were found to be better predictors of repayment than the personal judgments of most loan officers. But tools like these work *only* if the factual underpinnings are correct and the models valid. Neither was the case in the subprime lending market—no-verification loans became quite common and were known among some bankers by the affectionate title of "liar's loans," while the possibility of massive foreclosure episodes was not taken into account in the scoring process.

Second, the pricing of derivatives is based on massive simulations of risk scenarios; the most complex multilevel derivatives require astonishing amounts of computing power to evaluate. These derivative products became feasible only when investment firms gained access to supercomputer-grade hardware and expert computer scientists and mathematicians. Certainly, the models were only as good as the assumptions and data underlying them; for example, most models did not take into account the nation-wide decrease in house values. As important, many of the models rest on finding fits to historical data, rather than considering how the parameters and variables evolve, which makes them inherently immune to significant innovations in business strategies and unforeseen market conditions. (For one of the most readable tales of the limited financial modeling, see Lewis 2010.)

Third, the trading of securities, options, and other derivatives is dominated by "program trading"—computers making decisions and placing bids in thousandths of a second. This increased volatility, as programs kicked in response to swings in prices and other conditions stipulated in their code.

Finally, the securitization and sale of complex instruments became a global business, pulling in capital from around the world over networks. Few actually understood, for example, the real risks in the mortgages underlying the packaged securities. Few individuals or companies had anticipated the true counter-party risks that were being undertaken. Crucially, there was a lack of transparency in the system, which hid how risk was increasingly concentrated rather than diluted. The result was global financial disruption, and, very nearly, a catastrophic depression.

14. Finland's concerted efforts toward attaining mobile prominence occurred in the context of a broader Finnish move away from supplying the Soviet Empire to become a technology-based innovator. (See Hyytienen et al. 2006.)

15. The software engineer shortage was acute, as the Y2K problem demanded a massive quantity of relatively basic mechanical coding. After the dot-com bubble burst, transpacific fiber became cheaper, and intense pressures on major firms to cut costs led to a deluge of outsourcing to India. (See Dossani and Kenney 2009; Friedman 2005.)

16. Computing power has increased exponentially, following the principle known as Moore's law. Derived from the prediction made by Gordon Moore, founder of Intel, in 1965, Moore's law states that the number of transistors that can be placed inexpensively on an integrated circuit would continue to double approximately every twelve to twenty-four months. This principle has held until now, leading to exponential rises in computing power and decreasing cost (a typical laptop today has as much computing capacity as the *world* did in 1960).

Networking has also speeded up radically. In the 1970s, the fastest links between computers were about 1.5 megabits per second; today 10 gigabits (10,000 times as fast) is typical. The transatlantic cables of the 1950s carried an equivalent bandwidth of a few megabits, while the most recent international cables have a theoretical capacity in the terabits (one million times as much). Transmission costs have fallen by comparable amounts, partly since cables' carrying capacities can be improved with new equipment at the end, without replacing the installed fibers. Thanks to the resulting proliferation of high-speed networking, computing power can be dispersed rather than having to be concentrated in or near corporate headquarters—and when knowledge is dispersed, so, to a significant extent, is power.

Software, too, has undergone a series of dramatic evolutionary steps. In the early days of computing, programs closely mimicked what people were already doing. The earliest scientific programs implemented formulas already in use, and the first payroll systems simply did elementary calculations on time cards and printed checks. With growing experience and increasing technological power, new algorithms were designed to do ever-larger numeric computations and to perform them more quickly than ever.

17. Let us go into more detail about the evolution of *computing platforms*—combinations of hardware, software, and usage patterns that fit together in a particularly useful fashion. Although the history of modern information technology involves several different platforms, it also exhibits a single major divide—that between IT systems that are fundamentally independent and systems that are highly interconnected.

The *stand-alone era* began with the platform of mainframe computers in the early post-World War II years. Database systems were first designed for mainframes, and the maintenance of such databases (along with the processing of transactions and reports) is still a dominant function of the mainframe platform. The original uses were all batch-oriented and off-line due to hardware limitations. The mainframe platform entailed centralized management, control by a highly trained priesthood of experts, and utter dependability purchased at a high price.

After a series of transitional stand-alone computers, PCs became the new paradigm from the 1980s. The so-called Wintel PC used Intel-based processors and Microsoft-based operating systems and software (with Apple's Macintosh computers and the Linux operating system providing an alternative). The key technology breakthrough was the development of the computer whose processing capability was contained on a single chip. Thanks to Moore's law, what began as a toy quickly became a powerhouse. Although the operating system and hardware change every year, significant backward compatibility was retained, and over time, the existence of this long-lasting *de facto* standard has encouraged the growth of a major ecosystem of software and hardware producers.

The low cost, simplicity, and ease of use of the PC revolutionized the role of IT in business. Individuals became direct users of information technology, no longer reliant on a priesthood of experts. They were free to create their own data, manipulate the data as they liked, load new applications, or create their own. Inside corporations, work groups equipped with PCs could operate almost independently in providing services to themselves and to others. Freelancers and small businesses could create applications and manage information as easily as large corporations. And all the while, costs were plummeting. In companies based on the mainframe model, the IT budget was typically 15 percent of revenues; in companies based on PCs, the figure was just 2 percent.

The *connected era* had roots in the 1960s or earlier, but it came of age with the advent of the World Wide Web and the Internet. Even predating the Web and the Internet, increasing standardization, openness, and bandwidth enabled IT to attain *locational independence* (the data could reside and computations could be performed anywhere), *distributed processing* (the ability to combine information and calculations without physical relocation or permission), and *federation* (the ability to combine data and processes across organizational boundaries and ownership domains).

The Internet, in its essence, is a system for easy networking, a universally accepted way of communicating among machines (whether mainframes, microcomputers, or terminals) using open protocols—that is, the way different machines are accessed is the same everywhere. These open protocols, designed for the U.S. government and supported by a volunteer standards body, together with an underlying philosophy of end-to-end communication, have led to a huge and rapid growth in networked computing by making it possible to add data sources, services, and human users quickly, easily, and cheaply.

The new communication and information formats created for the Internet had enormous impact, becoming the key standards for the 1995–2010 era. As processing and software capabilities are extended, the interactions between systems over the Internet are extended. While the Internet is basically a message-based model, with simple interactions, systems can now interact through a service model. With a service model, the basic unit is a request from one system to another for a service to be performed. A service is characterized not only by what is wanted but also by the expectations of service level (such as promptness and reliability) and by business-like attributes (such as cost and ownership of information).

There are a variety of competing protocols for services, but the underlying Internet and Web mechanisms enable interoperability while details are being agreed. Since services have defined interfaces of various sorts, it is possible to build services that use other services as components, held together by what programmers call *glue code*. The work can be done at various levels of software engineering rigor, from quickly written mash-ups (web applications that combine data from more than one source into a single integrated tool assembled on a rapid, *ad hoc* basis) to carefully built service frameworks.

18. The combination of today's computer hardware, vast interconnected networks, and enormous databases has enabled the development of entirely novel sets of algorithms that mine data and draw inferences using statistical techniques from large data sets. They have started to replicate many of the analytical tasks previously done by skilled knowledge workers; the resulting change, which is as much qualitative as quantitative, is radical.

The analytic powers thus liberated made possible such remarkable applications as the creation of useful, real-time weather forecasts, enormous improvements in the accuracy and detail of demographic projections for use by insurance companies, and the expansion of basic payroll programs into full-scale human resources systems that maintain records of employee compensation, roles, training, skills, and so on.

19. Since Cloud Computing is still new, there is still disagreement and confusion over definitions. The characteristics here are from Armbrust et al. (2009).

20. This is particularly true for Cloud Computing-based services, in which new services are often literally "constructed" by combining other Cloud services as building blocks.

21. The logic was that while the productivity of a large portion of services did not increase, wages increased, pulled up by the sectors in which productivity did grow, such as manufacturing (Baumol 1967).

22. Until the surge from 1995, observed in the early 2000s, the lack of productivity gains from ICT observable in economic data had been puzzling economists—it was referred to as the "productivity paradox."

23. It is possible that the previous slow growth of productivity in services despite heavy ICT investments was due to measurement and data problems. As Triplett and Bosworth (2004) have noted, a large proportion of ICT investment in the United States goes into the particular service industries with the most serious measurement problems, such as finance, wholesale trade, business services, communications, and medical care.

24. Until the productivity surge from 1995 became apparent in the early 2000s, economists had puzzled over a "productivity paradox"; massive ICT investments were not showing up in productivity growth data.

25. "ICT in services industries accounted for 80 percent of the total ICT contribution to U.S. labor productivity growth between 1995 and 2001" (Triplett and Bosworth 2004: 2).

26. In the evolving ICT world, other aspects of connectivity in addition to raw connectivity to the networks become important. For example, access to data, collaborative activities, and the availability of digital tools should be included. We will expand upon this point in subsequent versions of this chapter.

27. Note that this "new literacy" does *not* imply a reduction of the elementary and secondary curricula to courses in math, English grammar, and perhaps computer programming. Many subjects, including such traditional ones as history, can be used as vehicles for the teaching of analytic skills, problem solving, logic, communication, and the other talents needed by the knowledge workers of tomorrow.

28. The top ten worldwide IT spenders in 2008 according to Gartner were (in billions of dollars): (1) Financial Services 559; (2) Manufacturing 483; (3) Government 420; (4) Communications 368; (5) Services 190; (6) Retail Trade 153; (7) Utilities 128; (8) Transportation 106; (9) Healthcare 86; (10) Wholesale Trade 81.

29. The current round of IT rationalization by governments is in response to the financial crisis that has increased pressure on governments to cut IT expenditures. After the dot-com bubble burst in 2000–01, firms rationalized their IT systems in response to pressures to increase efficiency, but governments did not undertake similar measures until now.

30. The program, the "Federal Data Center Consolidation Initiative" was announced in February 2010 by the Federal Chief Information Officer's Council, a new position created by the Obama administration.

31. This is a point of contention among the authors.

32. Scholars on services innovation fail to make the comparative analysis of regions; for most authors, regions are flat and strategies are fungible across time and space. We counter that this is not true.

References

Armbrust, Michael, Armando Fox, et al. (2009). "Above the clouds: A Berkeley view of Cloud computing" [Technical Report No. UCB/EECS-2009-28]. Retrieved February 10, 2009 (www.eecs.berkeley.edu/Pubs/TechRpts/2009/EECS-2009-28.pdf).

Baldwin, Carliss Y., and Kim B. Clark. (2000). *Design Rules*. Cambridge, MA: MIT Press.

Bar, François, and Michael Borrus. (1985). Telecommunications development in comparative prospective: The new telecommunications in Europe, Japan, and the U.S. BRIE Working Paper 14, Berkeley Roundtable on the International Economy, Berkeley, CA.

Baumol, William J. (1967). "Macroeconomics of unbalanced growth: The anatomy of urban crisis." *American Economic Review* 57: 415–26.

Baumol, William J. (2007). "On Mechanisms Underlying the Growing Share of Service Employment in the Industrialized Economies." In *Services and Employment: Explaining the U.S.-European Gap*, edited by Mary Gregory, Wiemer Salverda, and Ronald Schettkat, 63–80. Princeton, NJ: Princeton University Press.

Baumol, William J., and William G. Bowen. (1966). *Performing Arts, the Economic Dilemma: a Study of Problems Common to Theater, Opera, Music, and Dance*. New York: Twentieth Century Fund.

Berger, Suzanne, and MIT Industrial Performance Center. (2006). *How We Compete: What Companies Around the World Are Doing to Make It in Today's Global Economy*. 1st ed. New York: Currency Doubleday.

Borrus, Michael, Dieter Ernst, and Stephan Haggard. (2000). *International Production Networks in Asia: Rivalry or Riches?* [Routledge Advances in Asia-Pacific Business], 11. London and New York: Routledge.

Cohen, Stephen, J. Bradford DeLong, and John Zysman. (2000). *Tools for Thought: What Is New and Important About the "E-Conomy."* Berkeley: Berkeley Roundtable on the International Economy, University of California at Berkeley.

Cohen, Stephen S., and John Zysman. (1987). *Manufacturing Matters: The Myth of the Post-Industrial Economy*. New York: Basic Books.

Cusumano, Michael A. (2010). *Staying Power: Six Enduring Principles for Managing Strategy and Innovation in an Uncertain World (Lessons from Microsoft, Apple, Intel, Google, Toyota and More)*. Oxford and New York: Oxford University Press.

Dossani, Rafiq, and Martin Kenney. (2009). "Service provision for the global economy: The evolving Indian experience." *Review of Policy Research* 26(1–2): 77–104.

Frei, Frances X. (2008). "The four things a service business must get right." *Harvard Business Review* 86(4): 70–80.

Friedman, Thomas L. (2005). *The World Is Flat: A Brief History of the Twenty-First Century*. 1st ed. New York: Farrar Straus and Giroux.

Gartner Newsroom. (2009). "Gartner says worldwide vertical market IT spending will be flat in 2009" [press release], February 23. Retrieved April 12, 2011: http://www.gartner.com/it/page.jsp?id=893512).

Gibson, Rowan. (Eds). (1998). *Rethinking the Future: Rethinking Business Principles, Competition, Control and Complexity, Leadership, Markets and the World*. London: Nicholas Brealey Publishing.

Griliches, Zvi, Ernst R. Berndt, et al. (1992). *Output Measurement in the Service Sectors*. Chicago: University of Chicago Press.

Hyytienen, Ari, Laura Paija, et al. (2006). "Finland's Emergence as a Global Information and Communications Technology Player: Lessons from the Finnish Wireless Cluster." In *How Revolutionary Was the Digital Revolution?: National Responses, Market Transitions, and Global Technology*, edited by John Zysman and Abraham Newman, 55–77. Stanford, CA: Stanford Business Books.

IDC Government Insights. (2010). "IDC government insights says government IT spending in western Europe will reach $68.6 billion by 2013" [press release], February 5. Retrieved April 12, 2011: (http://www.idc-gi.com/getdoc.jsp?containerId=prIT22198510).

Jorgenson, Dale W., Mun S. Ho, and Kevin J. Stiroh. (2005). *Productivity Volume 3: Information Technology and the American Growth Resurgence*. Cambridge, MA, and London: MIT Press.

Jorgenson, Dale W., Mun S. Ho, and Kevin J. Stiroh. (2008). "A retrospective look at the U.S. productivity growth resurgence." *Journal of Economic Perspectives* 22(1): 3–24.

Jorgenson, Dale W., and Charles W. Wessner. (Eds.). (2007). *Enhancing Productivity Growth in the Information Age*. Washington, D.C.: National Academies Press.

Kenney, Martin, and Bryan Pon. (2011). "Structuring the smartphone industry: Is the mobile Internet OS platform the key?" *Journal of Industry, Competition and Trade* 11(3): 239–61.

Kushida, Kenji E., and John Zysman. (2009). "The services transformation and network policy: The new logic of value creation." *Review of Policy Research* 26(1–2): 173–94.

Kushida, Kenji E., Jonathan Murray, and John Zysman. (2011). "Diffusing the fog: Cloud computing and public policy." *Journal of Industry, Competition and Trade* 11(3): 209–37.

Kushida, Kenji E., Jonathan Murray, and John Zysman. (2012). "The Gathering Storm: Analyzing the Cloud Computing Ecosystem and Implications for Public Policy." *Communications and Strategies* 85: 63–85.

Labovitz, C., S. Lekel-Johnson, et al. "Atlas Internet Observatory 2009 annual report." Retrieved March 15, 2010: (http://www.nanog.org/meetings/nanog47/presentations/Monday/Labovitz_ObserveReport_N47_Mon.pdf).

Lewis, Michael. (2010). *The Big Short: Inside the Doomsday Machine*. New York: W. W. Norton.

Lohr, Steve. (2008). "In modeling risk, the human factor was left out." *New York Times*, November 5: B1.

Moore, Gordon. (1965). "Cramming more components onto integrated circuits." *Electronics* 38(8): 114–17.

Nielsen, Niels Christian, and Maj Cecilie Nielsen. (2006). "Spoken-About Knowledge: Why It Takes Much More Than Knowledge Management to Manage Knowledge." In *How Revolutionary Was the Digital Revolution? National Responses, Market Transitions, and Global Technology in a Digital Era*, edited by John Zysman and Abraham Newman, 242–66. Stanford, CA: Stanford Business Press.

Nordhaus, William D. (2002). *The Progress of Computing, Version 5.2.2*. New Haven, CT: Yale University and the National Bureau of Economic Research. Retrieved (http://nordhaus.econ.yale.edu/prog_030402_all.pdf).

Omae, Ken ichi. (1999). *The Borderless World: Power and Strategy in the Interlinked Economy*. Rev. ed. New York: HarperBusiness.

"Outsourcing: External affairs." (2007). *The Economist*, July 28: 65.

Shankar, Venkatesh, Leonard L. Berry, and Thomas Dotzel. (2009). "A practical guide to combining products and services." *Harvard Business Review* 87(11): 94–99.

Strange, Susan. (1996). *The Retreat of the State: The Diffusion of Power in the World Economy*. Cambridge, UK and New York: Cambridge University Press.

Thibodeau, Patrick. (2009). "White House appoints its first federal CIO," March 5. Retrieved March 15, 2011: (http://www.cio.com/article/483180/White_House_Appoints_Its_First_Federal_CIO).

Triplett, Jack E., and Barry P. Bosworth. (2000). *Productivity in the Services Sector*. Washington, D.C.: Brookings Institution Press.

Triplett, Jack E., and Barry Bosworth. (2004). *Productivity in the U.S. Services Sector: New Sources of Economic Growth*. Washington, D.C.: Brookings Institution Press.

Triplett, Jack E., and Barry P. Bosworth. (2006). "'Baumol's Disease' Has Been Cured: It and Multifactor Productivity in US Services Industries." In *The New Economy and Beyond: Past, Present and Future*, edited by Dennis W. Jansen, 34–65. Cheltenham, UK and Northampton, MA: Edward Elgar.

Verna, Paul. (2011). "Virtual goods and currency: Real dollars add up." *eMarketer*.

Zysman, John. (2006). "The 4th service transformation: The algorithmic revolution." *Communications of the ACM* 49(7): 48.

Zysman, John, and Abraham Newman. (Eds.). (2006). *How Revolutionary Was the Digital Revolution? National Responses, Market Transitions, and Global Technology in a Digital Era*. Stanford, CA: Stanford Business Press.

5 Platforms, Productivity, and Politics
COMPARATIVE RETAIL SERVICES IN A DIGITAL AGE
Bartholomew C. Watson

Introduction

The economies of the advanced, formerly industrial democracies are undergoing a radical transformation. Similar to other economic revolutions, this metamorphosis is entangled with technology. Unlike previous industrial divides, however, this transformation is driven by services, not manufacturing (Zysman et al. 2007). Services, once a productivity quagmire, are now recognized as a source of productivity growth and an engine of the economy. These changes are altering the structure of employment, the division of labor, and the location of value in the economy (Levy and Murnane 2004; Triplett and Bosworth 2004).

One of the most radical reorganizations of services has occurred in the retail trade sector. Over the past thirty years, information technology (IT) has both transformed the sector—including its major players, its geographic location, and the character of its firms—and the basic equation of how value is captured in consumer retailing. The genesis of this transition has been the move of retailing into the category of hybrid services discussed in the introduction, where products and services are woven into digitized systems. The application of IT in retailing has sparked a wave of accelerated growth in nearly every national economy, underwritten by two common, interwoven movements: the increase in the advantages of and the presence of scale in retailing and a dramatic rise in the power of retailers through information gathering and analysis.

The radical transformation and growth in the retail sector, and other hybrid service sectors like it, offer evidence that the double bind facing states—the dilemma of balancing the need to deregulate in order to innovate with the need to protect against the catastrophic crises brought on by deregulation—may be partially false. This realization emerges from a puzzle: despite similar technology and expectations of global convergence, retailing strategies have continued to follow national trajectories. Across a variety of regulatory regimes retailers have found ways to innovate, create jobs, and successfully defend their markets with homegrown competitive advantages.

Table 5.1 demonstrates the incredible similarity in the growth of hybrid services (wholesale and retail trade, financial intermediation, and transport and storage) across three national economies (the United States, France, and Denmark) and the EU-15 from 1977 to 2007. In all three countries, labor productivity hybrid services grew at an average annualized rate of 2.7 percent. This falls between the more dynamic growth rate of automated services (such as telecommunications) and the still stagnant growth of irreducible services (social and personal services like education, health, hotels and restaurants). Importantly, hybrid services, like automated services, were a driver of

TABLE 5.1

LABOR PRODUCTIVITY GROWTH IN IRREDUCIBLE, HYBRID, AND AUTOMATED SERVICES AND THE TOTAL ECONOMY (TOTAL AND ANNUALIZED) IN THE UNITED STATES, DENMARK, FRANCE, AND THE EU-15, 1995–2007 AND 1977–2007

	Total		Annualized	
	1995–2007	1977–2007	1995–2007	1977–2007
United States				
Irreducible	3.8 (%)	0.1 (%)	0.3 (%)	0.0 (%)
Hybrid	53.4	119.8	3.6	2.7%
Automated	83.8	198.6	5.2	3.7
Total Economy	26.4	54.4	2.0	1.5
France				
Irreducible	3.9	19.9	0.3	0.6
Hybrid	26.5	119.8	2.0	2.7
Automated	158.0	674.4	8.2	7.1
Total Economy	21.4	95.0	1.6	2.3
Denmark				
Irreducible	−3.1	−5.6	−0.3	−0.2
Hybrid	34.2	119.9	2.5	2.7
Automated	103.4	362.2	6.1	5.2
Total Economy	7.7	59.7	0.6	1.6
EU-15				
Irreducible	2.5	−0.7	0.2	0.0
Hybrid	31.8	88.7	2.3	2.1
Automated	135.9	453.0	7.4	5.9
Total Economy	18.6	81.2	1.4	2.0

Source: EU KLEMS Database.

national growth and productivity over this thirty-year period, growing faster than national labor productivity growth.

National solutions to the problems of services growth run counter to the predictions in the literature in both economics and political science. In economics, an extensive convergence literature argues that technology will hasten the move toward the Fordist organizational structures seen in liberal environments. These authors argue that were it not for overburdensome labor and product market regulations, firm strategies would converge on a singular best practice largely synonymous with the American model (Delpla and Wiplosz 2007; Gordon 2004; McGuckin, Spiegelman, and Van Ark 2005; Nicoletti and Scarpetta 2003). These studies typically base their analyses on evidence from the U.S.-Europe "productivity gap" in the mid-1990s, suggesting that America leads and Europe lags in IT-using services like retail trade and finance due to labor and product market barriers that slow innovation and dampen competition (O'Mahoney and Van Ark 2003; Van Ark, Monnikhof, and Mulder 1999; Van Ark, O'Mahoney, and Timmer 2008).

A second literature, stemming from political science, contests the notion of global convergence, instead emphasizing the inherent challenges from national economic growth based on low-productivity service sectors. The basis of these arguments is William Baumol's (1967) "cost disease" theory.[1] As the share of services in national economies has grown, so has the view that advanced countries face trade-offs, most commonly between high-wage jobs and employment creation in the service sector (see Becker 1996; Organisation for Economic Co-operation and Development 1994, 1996). Iversen and Wren (1998) have made the most visible elaboration of this logic, positing that in "food and fun" services (such as retail trade) countries face a "trilemma." The notion is simple: countries must choose between three unappealing alternatives. If services cannot grow in productivity, wages must fall in these jobs (inequality), job growth must fall (unemployment), or the state must pick up the tab through public-sector job growth (lack of budgetary restraint). In all three cases, post-industrialization becomes an epithet for the troubles of the advanced economies.[2]

When broadening our time horizons, however, a puzzle emerges: neither of these theories is supported by the empirical evidence. Table 5.2 shows productivity data for various service sectors across five countries and the EU-15 from 1977 to 2007. Note that retail productivity growth exceeded national growth in four of the five country cases.[3] These are not small changes. Distribution is a large sector that captures 10–15 percent of the jobs and value in every advanced economy. It is also located between producers and consumers, making it ideal to study the conflicts between social and economic goals inherent to the service sector.

The data, therefore, show that retailing provides an excellent case to examine solutions to the double bind for two reasons. First, the pace of retailing growth has undeniably changed. Second, examining firm outcomes in retailing, it is clear that business strategies cannot be reduced to either a technodeterminist convergence story or simply a tale of

TABLE 5.2

AVERAGE ANNUAL SERVICE LABOR PRODUCTIVITY GROWTH, 1977–2007

	Denmark	Germany	UK	U.S.	France	EU-15
IT Using Service Sectors						
Retail Trade	*2.4*	*1.3*	*2.8*	*2.2*	*3.1*	*1.8*
Financial Intermediation	4.3	1.9	2.4	1.7	2.1	2.1
Average	3.3	1.6	2.6	1.9	2.6	1.9
Non-IT Using Service Sectors						
Community, Social, and Personal Services	0.4	1.1	0.3	−0.1	0.8	0.4
Hotels and Restaurants	−1.8	−0.5	0.2	0.3	−1.0	−0.5
Real Estate, Renting, and Business Services	−1.2	0.4	1.0	−0.1	0.1	−0.5
Average	−0.9	0.3	0.5	0.0	0.0	−0.2
Total Economy	1.6	2.2	2.2	1.4	2.3	2.0

Source: EU KLEMS Database.

labor markets, wages, and labor skills. The problems of markets and hierarchies in retailing are in fact being resolved by a variety of political negotiations, demonstrating once more that technical outcomes are not determined by the technology itself but by social and political rules.

The transformation from nations of shopkeepers to nations of retailers, therefore, provides both an intriguing case and a perfect comparative window into how technology transforms not only a sector, its employment, and its firms but also its political actors, political fights, and an enormous value domain in the economy.[4] Unlike manufacturing, however, where scholars of political economy could compare the efficiency of firms through the market competition of products such as cars or semiconductors, the comparative strategies of retail firms must be analyzed through a different set of arguments and evidence.

Sector-specific research in comparative context provides an essential tool for examining the services transformation. Although preferences and sectors may no longer be as tightly aligned as in the past (as seen in Huberty, Chapter 7, in this volume), sectors control for a variety of issues, highlighting where variation in political, social, and institutional variables alter market and firm outcomes. Sector cases, therefore, allow an investigation of how common technological developments are mediated and interpreted across different sets of formal institutions, political coalitions, markets, and social settings. If we accept that political and even economic groups are political constructs, studying sectors also allows insights into the correct level of analysis for studying how these groups change. The nodes of contestation evolve during any economic transformation, and level-of-governance questions are particularly important for Europe with its patchwork of political actors and regulations. Sector studies illuminate at which level the primary political action is occurring, quickly updating models of political, technological, and economic change.

This study, in addition to the empirical data presented in this chapter, is informed by approximately 100 interviews with sectoral stakeholders, including retail firms, labor unions, policy makers, business associations, and sectoral analysts, all in an attempt to unwind the political foundations of different national arrangements of the economy.

The evidence shows that the retail revolution has unfolded quite differently by country and that a variety of viable strategic growth options are possible. Faced with common economic problems, different sectoral features emerged across borders, including variations in the relationships between firms and their workers and suppliers, power relations in the economy, and tangible outcomes like wage and price levels for workers and consumers. This chapter uses the large-scale chain retailing case as a test case for the larger services transformation research agenda. The evidence shows that the importance of the services revolution goes beyond the growing contribution services to economic activity in the advanced economies. In addition, retailing underlines a broader story about how digital technology transforms service activities, reorganizes the service components of the economy, and reshuffles relationships between service firms, workers, producers, and policy makers. In doing so, it highlights the numerous challenges and conflicts that emerge in a political economy where IT-enabled services are central to employment and productivity. It also suggests areas of the economy where regulation may not place a bind on innovation and economic growth.

Importantly, the retailing revolution is both influenced by and has radical implications for politics and coalitions. How retailers organized politically to win fights with independent small-shop retailers over rules on such issues as prices, planning, opening hours, and store size locked in particular modes of interaction with suppliers and workers, prompting unique business-model configurations in the search for efficiency and competitive advantage (Watson 2011). Tracing forward, these initial political and economic plans continue to shape the business strategies and political alliances of large retailers in the current era—one where growth stems from using technology in core processes to create innovation.

Although the marriage of technology and scale has opened a variety of new business strategy opportunities for retailers, firms have implemented quite different scale processes of routinization, data analysis, and value capture. This chapter highlights three competitive strategies in modern general merchandise retailing. Each has a different primary focus for creating value and exhibits variation in how technology is used, product strategy, labor strategy, supplier-relations, and value-added strategy. In addition, we see very different levels of each across different political settings.

The argument is not that these managerial modes are the only game in town, as each may be present at different levels within a country or even a particular firm.[5] Rather, the argument is that the choices firms adopt about make, buy, or partner decisions has been strongly influenced by national political foundations.

Retailers did not adopt one or another of these strategies simply because any one was initially more economically efficient. In fact, the basic business models of retailers across the affluent economies in the 1960s and 1970s were highly similar, built on the same basic economic ideas, and even disseminated by a limited number of retail gurus, most notably Bernardo Trujillo of National Cash Register. Strategies began to diverge, however, as national political actors, institutions, and levels of power forced retailers to form coalitions with a variety of political partners (including labor, suppliers, and broad political party coalitions). How retailers managed these political choices then shifted firm economic calculations, pushing retailers toward three ideal types, each of which makes money, distributes value, and works with other economic and political actors in very different ways. Again, each strategy is not about differing levels of efficiency but different, politically conditioned trajectories of growth, competition, and value creation.

The first is the American strategy of *lean retailing*.[6] Lean retailing is a cost-squeezing strategy, best embodied by the American behemoth Walmart, but it can be equally applied to other large American retailers in mixed goods (Target), grocery (Kroger), or specific product categories (Home Depot in home improvement and Best Buy in consumer electronics).[7] Lean retailing emerged where political outcomes were based on market logic and retailers could use market advantages to dominate other partners.

Retailers in the United States typically employ a low-cost, low-service, high-turnover strategy based on squeezing costs and contested relationships with labor, suppliers, and local governments. For instance, Walmart only makes $1 by selling $35 worth of goods. Walmart has an operating profit margin of 3.5 percent in 2005, compared with a U.S. average closer to 6 percent.[8]

Retailers pass some of the cost savings on to consumers, while largely excluding workers and suppliers from the gains.[9] Looking at workers, over 66 percent of retail workers hold limited sales or service positions and a corresponding percentage (70 percent) have less than a college degree (National Retail Foundation 2010), which means that workers have limited roles in store. This is reflected in their wage levels. In 2004, for instance, Walmart made around $6,400 (profit) per employee, which works out to around $3 profit an hour/per employee over a typical year, even though the UFCW (United Food and Commercial Workers) reports that the average Walmart associate only earns $11.75 an hour.

Technology has helped retailers gain the upper hand in these relationships, as firms use technology to gather information and use the information gathered as a weapon. This is particularly true for small suppliers. Bloom and Perry (2001) find that suppliers with a small share of their respective market perform relatively more poorly when they have Walmart as a primary customer, but that suppliers with a large share of their market do better than competitors with Walmart as a primary customer. Consequently, suppliers without power suffer, as they are dominated and forced to align with the preferences of retailers. Walmart is aware of this process and tends to negotiate net prices with suppliers only after extensive analysis of their value chains (Colla and Dupuis 2002).

Relational contracting, seen in the Danish case and the German case, is a cost-sharing strategy built on a base of broad political coalitions. Firms following this model compete by creating long-term savings from cooperative political and economic relationships with workers, suppliers, and social partners.

Labor cooperation provides retailers with two categories of benefits: better, more productive workers and effective recruitment, training, and internal job ladders. Both these benefits reduce costs. Well-trained Danish workers are able to work more effectively for Danish employers and the focus on training by both workers and employers has strengthened in recent years.

Coop Denmark, the largest Danish retailer, offers in-house commercial education degrees, which are recognized throughout the Danish retail industry. Interviews highlighted how this improved training increases worker autonomy, improves productivity, decreases employee theft, reduces employee turnover and future training costs, and creates a ready supply of managers. Its main competitor, Dansk Supermarked (DSM), has a similar worldview. In addition to a training system designed to provide basic training for all employees, the DSM system focuses on building applied knowledge, with an extensive system of options for both in-house and external training for motivated individuals and managers.[10] This supports DSM's goal to have 80 percent of its managers recruited internally.

Retailers use technology as an enabler in these relationships, allowing them to up-skill workers and identify areas of collaboration with suppliers.[11] These results are supported by other, corresponding economic structures. For instance, logistics, quality control, and other activities that typically fall under the purview of retail firms in lean retailing and vertical integration countries are often an expected component of manufacturing firms in Germany and to a lesser extent Denmark (Christopherson 2007).

The final strategy is *vertical integration* seen in France and the United Kingdom.[12] It is a complementarities strategy where retailers compete by adding value through additional services, value-added products, or private label products in store. In general, vertical integration firms have developed much higher service value-added strategies in both stores and products than their lean retailing counterparts have. In a broad survey of European retailing, Müller-Lankenau, Wehmeyer, and Klien (2005–06) found that all of the French retailers surveyed (including Casino, E. Leclerc, Intermarché, Auchan, and Carrefour) had "extensive use of value-adding features" (2005–06: 97). They also note that hypermarkets, a dominant French format, tend to "offer a wide range of services and other customer-retention measures" (2005–06: 96).

Private labels are another way to capture value added. Unlike low-price generic products in the United States, French and British private labels are typically not solely focused on competing on price or forcing manufacturers to lower costs. Rather, they are a core component of the value proposition offered to customers. Taking direct control over product strategy presents vertical integrators with a unique set of opportunities and challenges. Controlling more of the value chain carries higher risks and rewards. Although vertical integrators have better quality control and can match product features with carefully targeted customer niches, they also carry promotional and design costs not borne by lean retailers.

Again, this is not to say that vertical integrators are the only retailers carrying private labels. Similarly to lean logistics, some level of private label strategy is ubiquitous among large retail firms. The level is the key; in vertical integration countries like France, private labels are a default strategy for scale retailers, occupying a much larger portion of sales.

In these countries retailers compete against suppliers but have formed more limited coalitions with political and labor partners. In fact, retailing policy in these countries has developed into an area of perpetual contestation, where retailers consistently struggle with workers and suppliers over the rules of the game. Consequently, retailers employing the vertical integration model use technology to break free of past relationships and add value to product and service offerings.

This chapter presents evidence not only that each of these strategies exists but also that each is persistent and highly competitive. Nevertheless, they should not be interpreted as the only strategy available to retailers but simply as archetypes of nation-specific tendencies. Many of the features discussed—such as the use of product data in supplier negotiations, technology to train workers, or added services and private labels—are features of leading retailers across the world. What is different, however, is the level and character of each across national borders.

The rest of this chapter traces the development of these managerial styles. The next section highlights the variety of potential opportunities opened by the marriage of digital technology and scale, elaborating the political decisions that pushed firms down different paths, and presenting evidence of each strategy and its mode of competition. The next section suggests how new technology platforms may affect each model in different ways. Finally, the conclusion outlines how these changes coupled with retail globalization shift the priorities of policy makers working on the retail sector.

From Bricks to Clicks: Stages of Retail Development

As with other IT-enabled service sectors, the evolution of the retail sector occurred in stages. Across sectors, the application of rule-based IT tools alters how service activities are conducted and how value is created. Retailing was no different. As retailers grew in size, they first used digital tools to capture information and routinize processes, such as checkout, ordering, or stocking. Next, more sophisticated demand management tools began analyzing the data streams from point-of-sale (POS) databases, opening the opportunities to reorganize shop floors, supply chains, and find complementarities (McKinsey & Company 2001).[13]

We can identify several major stages of the digital revolution in retail trade. While the precise timing of each varies cross-nationally, the first stages began in retailing during the 1970s and expanded in the 1980s while shifts in value capture began in the 1990s and continue today.

TABLE 5.3
SELECTED COUNTRY RETAIL CHARACTERISTICS

United States	
Leading Retailers	Walmart, Kroger, Target, Costco, Albertsons, Safeway
Labor Conditions	6% unionization (2009), 42% below 2/3 median wage (2003), 28% part-time (2007), $12.75 average wage (2007)
Key Policies	N/A
United Kingdom	
Leading Retailers	Tesco, J Sainsbury, WM Morrison, Kingfisher, Marks & Spencer
Labor Conditions	14% collective bargaining coverage (2006), 49% below 2/3 median wage (2003), 51% part-time (2006), $15.23 average wage (2007)
Key Policies	Spatial planning
France	
Leading Retailers	Carrefour, Casino Group, Auchan, Intermarché, E. Leclerc
Labor Conditions	3% unionization (2009), 18% below 2/3 median wage (2003), 28% part-time (2006), $16.09 average wage (2007)
Key Policies	Spatial planning, price/sales rules, high employment protection legislation
Denmark	
Leading Retailers	Dansk Supermarked, Coop Danemark
Labor Conditions	30% unionization (2010), 72% bargaining coverage (2006), 23% below 2/3 median wage (2003), 50% part-time (2006), $21.84 average wage (2007)
Key Policies	Spatial planning, high levels of labor cooperation/negotiation

Sources: Russell Sage Foundation (2008), U.S. Bureau of Labor Statistics-Current Population Survey (2010), Organisation for Economic Co-operation and Development (2010), Danmark Statistik (2010), UK Office for National Statistics (2010), Institut national de la statistique et des études économiques (2010).

The earliest stages involved the use of technology to *increase economic and informational power*. Retailers first used barcode technology, scanning system, and basic purchasing software to *codify information and routinize activities*. Next, they began using more complicated merchandise planning and demand management software to begin *organizing and analyzing* the stream of sales data that routinization produced. Along with complementary store changes (such as decreased warehouse space and increased sales floor space) these technologies allowed larger stores, larger store networks, and increased product diversity and knowledge, all while reducing nonsales inventories. Increased scale led to clashes with small shopkeepers and national politicians around store size, location, purchasing power, price rules, and antitrust and competition issues.

The marriage of technology and scale led to both *new business possibilities and contests over information use*. Once retailers had implemented basic digital technologies and built large-scale retailer networks, they sought to use both their informational and economic power to *capture new value and offer new services*. Retailing began to shift from a simple value chain to a value network, with significant opportunities to relocate, reorchestrate, or control value creation in consumer retail services.

IT together with improved data allowed increased supplier integration, network rationalization, customer niche targeting, efficient customer response (ECR) technologies, loyalty programs, reduced risks with private labels, worker upskilling, and more. Opportunities for business model extensions included offering new services in store (financial, basic medical, food services, advertising, etc.), controlling and streamlining distribution and wholesaling, or creating and branding products. Competition between retailers and with suppliers and wholesalers created political clashes around data use (privacy), supplier relations (including terms of payment), and even what services retailers could offer.

The postwar period was not the beginning of large retailers, as enormous retail firms have existed for some time. However, digital technology has changed the retail market from one where large firms were the exception to one where they are the rule. It has done so by reducing the risks associated with scale, increasing the advantages of that scale, and providing tools for scale management.

For example, in 1945, sales at Sears and Roebuck, the largest U.S. retailer for the majority of the postwar period, passed $1 billion (around 0.45 percent of U.S. GDP or $11.90 billion in 2009 equivalent dollars).[14] Sears struggled with its size. In 1946, General Wood, then president of the company, noted its problems, stating, "I have been in an unusual position to observe the problems that 'bigness' brings to a business" (Emmet and Jeuck 1950: 365). The solution was massive decentralization, breaking the firm into five almost wholly autonomous territories, and within each stores still had considerable flexibility. In 1964, a *Forbes* article described Sears as "number one in the U.S., and also number 2, 3, 4, and 5" (Katz 1987: 15). Even with its successful decentralization, Sears was the anomaly, able to succeed at its size only because it set the market, telling consumers what to buy rather than simply providing it, which helped reduce demand management risks.

Fast-forward to 2009. That year, Walmart totaled $406 billion in sales, the equivalent of 2.84 percent of U.S. GDP,[15] six other retail firms (Home Depot, CVS, Kroger, Costco, Target, and Walgreens) had revenue equivalent or larger than Sears's 1945 level of GDP, another five (Sears, Lowe's, SuperValu, Best Buy, and Safeway) had sales above $40 billion, and eleven more had revenues at or above $11.90 billion, the 2009 dollar equivalent of Sears's 1945 level.[16] In dollar equivalents, all twenty-three of these firms would have been America's largest retailer in 1945. How was this explosion of enormous retail empires possible? The answer begins with the barcode.

Digital information has fundamentally changed retail firm size by allowing retailers better information about sales, faster response times, improved communication with store networks, and reduced risk through more accurate demand management. The beginning of the scale revolution in retail trade was the digital routinization of basic activities. Prior to the full onset of the digital era, earlier technological advances, such as electronic registers, had moved the sector partially in this direction. With the implementation of barcode technology (see Nelson 1997), scanners, and the digital storage of sales and stock information, however, in-store operations and automation jumped forward. These basic digital technologies allowed the automated gathering and storage of information and provided the basis for each of the other stages described below. The fundamental feature of the digital revolution is the ability to create, store, transfer, and manipulate digital information, and barcode technology is the point at which digital information is created. Basic digital product and sales information then cascades through the rest of these stages.[17]

The ability to store information about product price and stock levels through barcodes revolutionized store operations. In addition to accelerating the movement toward self-service in retail, stores were able to reduce inventory checks (a timely and costly procedure), speed up checkout times, and generally create the types of innovations toward larger-volume formats, reaping the benefits of greater scale while keeping organizational challenges in check.[18] In addition, IT also provided a valuable tool for headquarters to effectively manage large chains of stores. IT allows a central location to communicate with stores, gather the incredible stream of information from various locations for analysis, and coordinate larger distribution networks more seamlessly. Data on electronic data interchange (EDI) systems, which are used to automatically place orders with suppliers, shows the increasing routinization of retail. Hwang and Weil (1998) find that the use of EDI by retail firms increased from 33 percent to 83 percent from 1988 to 1992 alone.

Once product information is digitized, retailers can begin analyzing sales information, allowing superior management of both inventories and price decisions. Retailing occupies a critical economic location between manufacturers and consumers. For retailers, therefore, a fundamental component of providing retail services is understanding what products consumers demand and at what price. While barcode technology allowed retailers enormous labor savings, equally large savings have accrued from the analysis of the POS data that barcodes generate. Since the mid-1990s, nearly every major global retailer has kept data on every purchase made across its store networks, often using loyalty cards to tie these purchases to particular customers.[19] The analysis of these data allows firms to better understand and manage consumer demand in a number of ways, including better matching of inventory to customer demand, even below the product level to features such as color; better understanding of the relationship between prices and sales; more efficient use of shelf space and more efficient store layout through recognition of sale complementarities; reduced inventory and fewer out-of-stock situations; and the potential to evaluate and optimize advertising, even at a personal level.

Again, this is not simply about cost cutting but also about improving sales through better store layouts, keeping goods on the shelves, and generally matching demand. Dobson, Waterson, and Chu (1998) find that in the United Kingdom, retail sales (in real terms) per outlet increased by 53 percent and per employee by 23 percent between 1980 and 1994.

Technology also allows reduced overheads and smaller stock warehouses, which can be seen in data on assets and liabilities in retail trade over time. Looking at French retailers, Dawson (2005) finds that assets and liabilities were down to 47.4 percent and 53.6 percent of sales, respectively, in 2001 as compared to 63.1 percent for assets and

59.4 percent for sales in 1984. Gaur, Fisher, and Raman (2005) support this finding from a new direction, demonstrating that greater capital intensity leads to increased inventory turnover (and lower margins). In other words, investing in IT has helped retailers to further increase turnover and lower inventories relative to sales, increasing returns on capital. As a percentage of sales, retailers can hold on to fewer goods and incur fewer liabilities as a percentage of assets. Taken together, therefore, effective demand management allows productivity gains on capital, space, and labor. The ability to keep items in stock allows storage space to be reduced or even eliminated, increasing productivity in terms of sales per square foot. Buying products from suppliers as they are needed cuts down on overstocked inventory, increasing capital productivity. Finally, retailers can now place goods in complementary locations, carrying more of what consumers want placed by other goods they buy them with, which increases sales of both products.

To recapitulate, digitally captured sales information and analysis allowed retailers to routinely achieve scale and use scale advantages to handily outcompete small independent retailers without similar capacity. The Holmes (1999) report for the Federal Reserve Bank of Minneapolis summarizes many of these findings. It models the adoption of new information technologies in the retail industry, arguing that barcodes and increased delivery offered a variety of new business strategies built around increasingly large retail networks.[20]

Increasing business opportunities have been multiplied by similar IT transformations of industries that complement retail, such as transportation. On-board computers (OBCs) and electronic tracking have increased capacity utilization and tied transportation more tightly into firm networks. This follows the expectation of Bresnahan and Greenstein (1996), who argue that productivity growth in services requires co-invention across firm networks.[21]

Once firms reached scale and had a steady information stream about what customers were buying, when they were buying, and under what store and price conditions, they faced an array of new business challenges and opportunities. How should they integrate technology into existing patterns of labor implementation—should they use information to automate or enable workers? Should they share sales data with their suppliers? How should they gather information from and connect with customers to better individualize service provision? Finally, what additional value opportunities were available? Which should be seized with partners and which should be captured alone?

The answers to these questions are neither simple nor inherent in the technological capabilities of digital tools. Looking ahead to the outcome, we find that firms have solved them in a multitude of ways. Why? The answer lies in political deals about the distribution of wealth in the economy, as political negotiations pushed firms toward nationally specific calculations about the market, firm, and relational contracting choice for firms posed by Williamson (1985).

Interestingly, many of the divergences in digital strategy appeared before digital technology was central to core retail processes (for a much longer discussion of the political competitions, their national character, and the outcomes sketched below, see Watson 2011). The majority of powerful retailers in the global economy are actually relatively new firms. Unlike many industries, essentially every major global retailer is a recent company, with few leading retailers existing in any size prior to the 1950s.[22] By the 1960s, a new class of retailers had emerged across the affluent economies. These retailers were spurred by common social and economic changes in the post-war period and process innovations including self-service, ample automobile parking, larger stores, and more product diversity. In all countries, scale retailers emerged in a similar fashion, promoting self-service and the "stack it high and sell it cheap" philosophy.

The rapid growth in scale retailers, however, soon created clashes with independent shopkeepers, long a fixture of both the economy and the ballot box. Independent shopkeepers wanted protection from what they saw as either unfair or socially disruptive aspects of scale retail development, including predatory pricing, out-of-town development, large stores, and, more generally, their sheer scale. A political conflict was brewing, and both sides began to mobilize coalitions to lobby for their preferred regulatory outcomes. How retailers built these coalitions was determined quite differently by national location, motivated by different political challenges from opposition groups of varying power and institutional resources.

Retailers are among the most connected actors in the economy, interacting with a variety of economic, political, and social groups. Politically, they must manage relationships ranging from international trade organizations and national regulators down to municipal governments. Within national economies, they connect with consumers, suppliers and producers, manufacturing firms, and wholesalers.

The development of the three national models of retail capitalism previously described is best explained by how retailers built these political partnerships. The construction of political groupings drove subsequent nation-specific business strategies and altered how retailers reorganized their networks to capture value from digital tools; building and maintaining successful coalitions not only forged economic partnerships, it also influenced ongoing regulatory strategies for national retail sectors.

Retailers facing the most fragmented and decentralized national environments (as in the United States) faced the least organized opposition and consequently needed the fewest political partners. They faced the most liberal regulatory environments and formed lean retailing business strategies built on low levels of cooperation with workers, suppliers, and governments. In the most highly consensual and corporatist countries, by contrast, powerful external and internal opposition groups led retailers to build broad political coalitions that germinated relational contracting business models. These business strategies forced retailers to integrate labor and manufacturing partners into business strategy or face political, social, and economic consequences. These coalitions agreed to higher levels of buffering regulation in return for political and economic alliances. Finally, vertical integration retailers emerged in environments with powerful but fragmented opposition groups by mobilizing weak, short-term coalitions that were

TABLE 5.4

ECR IMPLEMENTATION STRATEGY STATUS, U.S. VS. EUROPE

ECR Strategies (percent of firms responding yes)			
	U.S. (1995)	Europe (1997)	Difference
Efficient Store Assortment	55	29	26
Efficient Promotions	54	21	33
Efficient Replenishment	47	31	14

Source: Kurt Salmon Associates, as reported in Kurnia, Swatman, and Schauder (1998).

advantageous for development, such as local political partnerships, minor worker concessions, and selective cooperation with industry (for a more detailed analysis of these coalitions, see Watson 2011).

Each coalition reshaped the economic calculations of retail firms, pushing them toward different strategies of labor relations, supplier connections, product strategies, value-added services, and ultimately the digital strategies that now underpin each of these dimensions of business competition. Although it is not in the scope of this article to fully detail each model, the data in Table 5.4 provide quick evidence that they are real and sustained.

Comprehensive data on technology strategies are difficult to assess, but data in Table 5.4, from Kurt Salmon Associates on ECR, are a good proxy for the digital interactions among retailers, suppliers, and customers, and show a large difference in the lean retailing U.S. versus European firms.

A similar divergence in product strategy development has emerged, driven by the vertical integration cases. Data in Table 5.5 show not only that the vertical integration

TABLE 5.5

PRIVATE-LABEL SALES AS A PERCENT OF TOTAL SALES, FOOD RETAILING

	1995	1997	2002	2003	2005
Lean Retailing					
U.S.	8	14	16	12	14
Vertical Integration					
UK and France	23	24	30	30	32
*Relational Contracting**					
Denmark and Germany	12	11	19	18	25

* The relational contracting countries have closed the gap a bit, but it should be noted that this small convergence is driven largely by German hard discounters, whose strict low-cost private label focus is qualitatively different than the broad basket of private-label goods seen in the UK or France.

Sources: Boston Consulting Group (2003), A.C. Nielsen (2005).

countries lead in private labels as a percentage of sales but also that there has been little convergence. Sales of private labels in the UK and France were 15 percent higher than in the United States in 1995 and 18 percent higher in 2005. In addition, these numbers hide qualitative differences in how private label goods are used, primarily simply as low-cost alternatives in the United States versus high value-added products at a variety of price and quality points.[23] Note that private labels are only one dimension of the value capturing strategy of vertical integrators, which also includes additional services in-house and value-added products such as fresh prepared meals in food retailing.

From Bricks to Clicks: New Platforms, New Politics

The next technology platforms will create similar potential, perils, and politics. Accordingly, it is appropriate to examine how each of the different models of physically based retail capitalism will fare going forward, as retailers will face new pressures, including purely electronic retail services and the commodification of existing digital strategies. Digital technology also opens new opportunities, including the opportunity to offer new digital services or open new distribution streams based on new technologies.[24] What value domains might retailers tackle next based on the trajectory of both national firm tendencies and domestic political coalitions? Where are the political pressure points that will arbitrate new distributions of wealth? Once again, retailers appear to be reorganizing the provision of services based on political as much as economic foundations.

Understanding how retailers will incorporate future technology platforms is critical, because although the scope of the existing retail transformation has already been vast, there are signs that further transformations await. The changes described previously have pertained primarily to traditional brick-and-mortar stores. Although still in its infancy, experiments in and the expansion of e-commerce (Internet-based) and mobile commerce (cell phone–based) have also increased the number of retail business models. As the ways in which consumers can connect to manufacturers have increased, so too have the ways in which retailers have offered services to connect to them, from companies that offer a wide variety of products like Amazon.com to niche sites that connect consumers with hard-to-find items. With the increasing use of code, automated warehouses, and algorithms over salespeople and stockers, these forays mark the beginning of a new form of retailing that moves beyond hybrid service into full automation.

Table 5.6 shows the rise of e-commerce as a force in American retailing, with Internet retailers constituting the vast majority of the "non-store retailers" category.[25] The data show that non-store retailers were the only subsector that significantly increased market share from 1992 to 2007. In addition, this figure shows that where consumers spend across subsectors is largely static in the United States, with the exception of non-store

TABLE 5.6

AMERICAN RETAIL SUBSECTOR MARKET SHARE, 1992 AND 2007

NAICS Code	Kind of business	1992	2007	Change*
	Per capita spending, total	7,120	13,259	
	Total (excl. motor vehicle and parts dealers)	5,475	10,249	
	Percent Share			
441	Motor vehicle and parts dealers	23	23	0
442	Furniture and home furnishings stores	3	3	0
443	Electronics and appliance stores	2	3	0
444	Building mat. and garden equip. and supplies dealers	7	8	1
445	Food and beverage stores	20	14	−6
446	Health and personal care stores	5	6	1
447	Gasoline stations	9	11	2
448	Clothing and clothing access. stores	7	6	−1
451	Sporting goods, hobby, book and music stores	3	2	−1
452	General merchandise stores	14	14	1
453	Miscellaneous store retailers	3	3	0
454	Nonstore retailers	4	7	3

*Numbers may not compute due to rounding.
Source: U.S. Census Bureau, Economic Census data.

retailers and the decline in food and beverage stores.[26] Note that $7,120 in 1992 is roughly the equivalent share of GDP per capita as $13,259 in 2007 (Measuringworth.com).

Additionally, these numbers largely exclude the next rising retailing stream: mobile commerce. Although mobile commerce sales totaled only $69 billion in 2010, they are expected to explode in the next five years, and projections suggest that mobile commerce sales will total more than $600 billion by 2014 (Kenney and Pon 2011). Although still relatively small compared to the global retail market, $600 billion is 50 percent more than the total sales for Walmart in 2010 ($405 billion).

The purely digital provision of retail services via e-commerce will intensify many of the trends started by the digital revolution while opening new lines of conflict, especially in Europe where e-commerce will place increasing pressure on national regulatory differences, price levels, and product offerings. It will also open new political confrontations between physically and digitally based retailers over the rules of the game. Extending the arguments of this chapter forward, the prediction would be that these political battles—over digital signatures, privacy, consumer protections, content regulation, copyright, new distribution patterns, and taxes[27]—would follow the established patterns of policy making.[28] There are suggestions that this is the case, with American e-commerce rules being driven by market forces and market winners, French rules being hotly contested by the retailers and producers, and Danish frameworks being heavily negotiated by a variety of social partners.[29]

Similarly, e-commerce and accelerating productivity will also bring changing relationships with national governments which have slowly updated their view of retailers as simply sheltered domestic players. This suggests that once again there will be political conflicts over the distribution of wealth as retailers press to protect their formerly sheltered sector and the negotiations of the 1970s are replayed, this time with the previous victors on the defense.

Conclusion: New Dilemmas and Global Markets

For firms, digital competitors are not the only worries. Although the evolution of technology is certainly driving further reorganizations in the strategies of retailing firms, the increase in retailing regionalization and globalization has the potential to be equally transformative. Changes driven by the spread of transnational retailers both within regional free trade associations like the European Union (EU) and the North American Free Trade Agreement (NAFTA) and around the globe are forcing retailers to reexamine their competitive models. As with the transnationalization of product markets, however, retailing is experiencing a globalization with borders.

Pressure on national retailing tendencies has come from foreign as well as domestic competition. These new entrants bring with them strategies honed in very different regulatory settings. In the short term, challengers have often been ill-equipped for competition in new markets. As the growing literature on transnational retailing is increasingly finding (Coe and Wrigley 2007), entrants remain enmeshed in the national social practices of their host economy. This has typically led to difficult transitions for new entrants, highlighted by Walmart's colossal failure in entering (and early exit from) the German market in the late 1990s and early 2000s. Many of the challenges are still political. Walmart struggled to cut deals with wholesalers, producers, and workers who were used to a very different way of doing business. The technical specifications of Walmart's strategy may have worked, but the political dimension was an utter failure (Christopherson 2007).

Walmart's failure is not an isolated case. Despite considerable global growth, particularly in developing markets, Carrefour—the world's number two retailer—has also had numerous failures, including flops in Japan, Russia, Korea, and the United States. Nevertheless, the increasing number of cross-border success stories suggests that retailers are finding better ways to adapt their business models to new regulatory environments, preserving the strengths they honed at home while addressing the weaknesses of these models abroad.

Regionalization, particularly within the EU, has been one solution, as regional markets are more likely to approximate the regulatory conditions of home markets. In grocery retailing, Mesic (2009) reports that in 2004 the ten leading retailers in Europe averaged 30 percent of their sales in foreign markets, the majority of which are within Europe.

In all, the transformation of the retailing sector modifies how we should view the binds on national governments as they struggle to formulate policy in an era of digital services. Whereas in the past the service sector was a sheltered haven from competition and a bastion for job growth, today governments face the same challenge as in manufacturing, where productivity increases drive slower employment creation.

Employment patterns in retailing are clearly changing in response to digitization. The rise of digital retailers (of both physical and digital goods) coupled with the increasing replacement of workers with digital tools (such as self-checkout kiosks) has begun to change the link between economic growth and employment in the retail trade sector. Retailing growth has traditionally been highly linked with retail employment; in the past retailers that sought to increase output had few alternatives other than simply increasing hours worked. As Figure 5.1 demonstrates, showing the hours and output of the constituent retail subsectors, this relationship is weakening.

From 1987 to 1996, the line fitted to an index of hours worked to an index of output has a slope of 1.04. An extra hour worked increased output by another unit. From 1998 to 2005, the slope of this line is 2.05. In 2005, an extra hour worked increased expected output by two units. Suddenly, retailers have options other than adding labor when they seek to increase output.

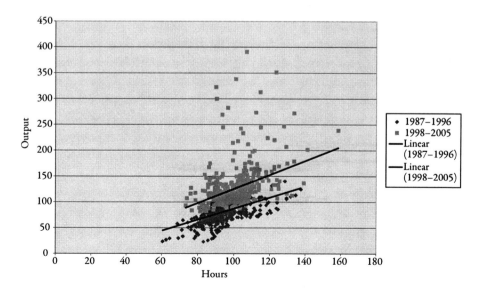

FIGURE 5.1 Output vs. Hours, U.S. Retail Trade, 1987-2005

The change in the way that retailers view employment has been starkly apparent during the current Great Recession. In the past, during downturns, retailing was often a fairly sheltered sector, where firms kept employment steady even during tough economic times. For instance in the recession of 1974–75, total nonretail private employment dropped by 2.6 million jobs (−4.2 percent of total private employment) while retailing only lost 61,000 jobs (−0.6 percent of total retail jobs). Similarly, during the 1981–82 recession, total nonretail, private employment dropped by 2.6 million jobs (−3.5 percent of total private employment) while retailing only lost 40,000 jobs (−0.4 percent of total retail jobs) (Bureau of Labor Statistics 2010).[30] In both cases, by the time that the rest of the private sector returned to its previous level of employment, the retail sector had seen around a 5 percent increase in jobs.

In contrast, from March 2008 to March 2011, retailing lost over one million jobs, representing 14.9 percent of the total private-sector job losses for the period (Bureau of Labor Statistics 2011). This percentage is roughly in line with the retail sector's percentage of jobs in the economy and shows that in this downturn retailing moved more like a productive sector of the economy than a Baumol-afflicted sheltered sector.

Together, this means job creation strategies will need to account for the growing difficulty of creating jobs in the retail sector. In his 2011 State of the Union address, President Barack Obama referred to "all the good jobs from manufacturing to retail" that have come as the result of technological innovation. Unfortunately for Obama's argument, the United States lost 4.2 million manufacturing jobs between 1997 and 2007 (EU KLEMS database). There are signs that retailing jobs may be the next to go.

Nevertheless, the final view of the retail revolution should not be a gloomy one. There are enormous opportunities from retail's transformation, from better (if perhaps fewer) jobs to new value to be captured in foreign markets. Certainly, accelerating productivity, retail internationalization, and e-commerce will all necessitate changing relationships between national governments and retailers. Those countries slow to update their view of retailers as simply sheltered domestic players will miss out while those attentive to the needs of retailers and consumers may reap considerable benefits. If there is one lesson of this work, it is that policy makers should closely evaluate their national retail market rather than assuming a one-size-fits-all policy derived from leading global firms. Changes to existing rules about labor or supplier relations, prices, and information or privacy rules may simply open the door for equally efficient foreign entrants rather than boosting the efficiency of domestic players.

How the benefits from retail growth will be distributed, therefore, remains a question that will be resolved by politics and policy makers. As for policy, the changing nature of services within political economy should force governments to rethink the relationship between governments, markets, and services growth. Charlie Wilson once famously remarked that "what was good for the country was good for General Motors and vice versa." The same could arguably be applied to Renault, Toyota, Volkswagen, or a host of other national car producers. Can this same claim be applied to Walmart, Carrefour, and Dansk Supermarked today? The answer is a qualified yes. Retailers are now among the economic actors most critical for directing and improving the national economy. Nevertheless, they are good for their countries only if they stand for the goals of policy makers and the citizens they represent.

Writing in 1955, Joseph Palamountain Jr. declared that "for the most part, however, mass distributors have not developed sufficient unrestrained power to endanger our economic, social, or political values" (262). Economic, social, or political values, however, are not simply dependent variables. The political process captures economic, social, and political values and translates them into political outcomes. As retailers' power continues to grow across national economies, it will be up to those involved in that process to ensure that political outcomes continue to reflect local, rather than global, goals.

Acknowledgments

The author wishes to thank the Alfred P. Sloan Foundation for financial support and the Berkeley Roundtable on the International Economy (BRIE) for research and administrative support. Thanks in particular go to Kenji Kushida, Derek Wong, Jonathan Murray, and Mark Huberty for help in developing the ideas about services and technology in this chapter. In addition, the editors of this volume, Dan Breznitz and John Zysman, provided ideas, support, and patience at various stages.

Notes

1. Baumol first noted the productivity growth problems of the service sector, pointing out that performing arts services were performed in much the same manner, at the same speed, and with the same quality as hundreds of years ago. The only difference was the cost. It is important to note that Baumol (2007) has since modified his position, distinguishing between "stagnant" and "progressive" (productivity-enhanced) services.

2. Similar formulations stress the same core concept: as the service sector increases as a share of economic activity, countries now face trade-offs they did not in the era of manufacturing (see Esping-Andersen 1999; Iversen 2005; Organisation for Economic Co-operation and Development 1994, 1996; Pierson 1998). Herman Schwartz may have best summed the set of fears surrounding services as recasting "the Malthusian tension between agriculture and industry as a tension between services and industry" (2001: 19).

3. The one country where it did not, Germany, can largely be explained by the strain reunification placed on innovation in the service sector.

4. Retailing services were traditionally just the final step in delivering producer products to consumers, but as we will see, the value networks controlled by retailers have rapidly expanded to cover nearly every facet of consumer goods (including branding, marketing, and even production), basic consumer services such as finance, and even technology domains such as data analysis or web hosting. It is notable that when WikiLeaks, the controversial nonprofit, came under web attack in November 2010, it initially turned to Amazon.com, an online retailer, to host its site.

5. Other studies of industrial sectors have shown extensive within-country variation in lean operations (Schroeder and Flynn 2001) and in vertical integration (Monteverde and Teece 1982).

6. The name invites parallels to lean production, with its focus on just-in-time production, lean inventories, and horizontal networks of suppliers organized around a final "assembly" firm. The parallel with lean production should not be taken too far, however, as there are numerous differences. Outside of the logistics, "lean" inventories, and just-in-time delivery, lean retailing resembles Fordism more than it does a Japanese automaker, with unskilled workers and repetitive tasks. Whereas some of the logistics features of lean production are present in all of the successful models of retailing—most notably a reduction in inventories in relation to sales and more frequent just-in-time delivery of goods, the lean retailing model best approximates the acute cost focus across the board. It is also worth noting that the term "lean production" was first applied to the automobile industry as a comparison with supermarkets (Magee 2007).

7. The term "lean retailing" has typically been used to describe a wide variety of modern retailing formats. The goal in using it here is to differentiate those models that simply have lean logistics from those where cost squeezing is the dominant logic throughout the organization.

8. The 3.5 percent operating profit margin reflects a profit of $11.2 billion on $315.7 billion in sales. Low margins for large retailers are not unique to Walmart. Walmart's largest global competitor, Carrefour, only had a margin of 1.9 percent in 2005. Note, however, that the system of "back margins" used by French retailers makes cross-national comparisons difficult.

9. Previous work has shown the welfare benefits of buyer power for consumers, although excessive buyer power may harm consumer welfare (Wang 2010).

10. In addition, DSM will pay for workers who want to take courses through HK, the Danish retailing union. In addition to internal training—they have built their own training center in Jopland—DSM offers continuing vocational training, a collaboration project cosponsored by Danish employers and Danish unions.

11. The relational contracting model is often accused of either being caused by high wages or simply being supported by high prices. Although wages are certainly higher than in the lean retailing United States, a causal arrow should not be drawn from high wages to firm strategies. For one, other nations with high wage levels (such as France) have quite different firm tendencies. In addition, wages are often well above minimum wage levels and their persistence suggests benefits to retailers, which will be elaborated later in this chapter. On costs, there is little evidence that they explain the majority of firm strategies or productivity in these countries and—as Walmart learned in Germany—they are often quite competitive with more liberal countries. If anything, high costs are the result of the same factors that drove firm strategies: broad coalitions more focused on social concerns than simply lowering consumer prices.

12. The name "vertical integration" is a bit of a misnomer, as many "vertical integration" firms are not vertically integrated (i.e., they do not physically control production of goods). What is different, however, is the level of control throughout the value chain and the constant desire to add value through complementary activities such as branding, marketing, or design.

13. McKinsey found four major areas where retail firms use IT, all of which have consequences for how information is gathered and used and corresponding organizational change. McKinsey broke their retail IT systems into central functions (store solutions, merchandise planning and management, and supply chain systems) and support IT systems.

14. According to the Consumer Price Index, using a GDP (gross domestic product) deflator method, it is equivalent to around $9.90 billion in 2009.

15. This is not to say that Walmart (or Sears) accounted for this portion of U.S. GDP (since the sale price includes far more value added than that produced by the retailer alone), simply that the dollar value of their sales was equal to this percentage.

16. And this only counts pure retail firms—the list would certainly be longer if we included sales of firms with retail as part of their portfolios. The firms are Rite Aid, Publix, Amazon.com, Staples, Macy's, TJX, J.C. Penney, Kohl's, The Gap, Toys "R" Us, and Office Depot, which neared bankruptcy in 2009, until receiving a large infusion of cash from BC Partners.

17. It is likely that the next round of base technologies, this time driven by sensor technologies like Radio Frequency Identification (RFID), may send similar upward ripples through the sector, reshaping activities just as dramatically as the barcode.

18. The benefits of digital systems are neither automatic nor universal. Jones, Kalmi, and Kauhanen's (2011) study of enterprise resource planning (ERP) implementation in a retail chain initially dropped sales and inventory turnover by 7 percent. Sales recovered, but more rapidly when workers had broad training regimes. Finally, timing matters. Those establishments that established ERP later saw inventory turnover recover faster.

19. Rules about how firms can gather and disseminate individual sales data are critical and subsequent firm strategies vary by location.

20. In a telling American-centric slip, the author of the Federal Reserve study titled the report "Barcodes lead to frequent deliveries and superstores," focusing on how increased delivery will increase store size. Arguments on size have clear limits, as the largest retail stores today need more than one truck delivery per day to keep stocked. A Walmart Supercenter can stock 200,000 unique products, and daily sales are far more than one semitruck. While it is true that small stores may not have sufficient sales to fill up a large truck's space, this argument misses the ability of dense small store networks, such as those found in Japan, with German discounters, or Danish co-ops, to make use of the potential of more frequent delivery to multiple stores.

21. Co-invention may provide an explanation for why later adoption leads to more seamless integration of new technology tools (Jones, Kalmi, and Kauhanen 2011).

22. This is particularly unusual in Europe, where only 29 percent of its 156 FT Global 500 firms were founded after 1901. Eighteen firms on the list were primarily retailers. Of these, only one was founded prior to 1901. Twelve were founded after 1946 and eleven were founded in 1957 or later. For data, see the Bruegel database of corporate birthdates (http://www.bruegel.org/8358).

23. For instance, Tesco, a British firm, has eleven private label orange juices at eight price points and eight private label yogurt brands at seven price points (Kumar and Steenkamp 2007).

24. An example of the new service opportunities can be seen in the burgeoning cloud computing business of Amazon.com. Although this strategy certainly emerged partially due to Amazon's technological expertise, its server capacity and technical infrastructure are not wholly unique in the retailing world. Other large retailers have similar opportunities, should they choose to expand their digital strategies.

25. The category also includes the forerunner of e-commerce firms, the catalog retailer.

26. This oversimplifies a bit. Even a static group may actually have a high level of internal change. For instance, even though the general merchandise stores category (North American Industry Classification System 452) shows little change, this hides the fact that within the subsector, department stores experienced declines in sales (as a percent of per capita spending) while discount and warehouse mass merchandisers experienced sharp increases in sales.

27. See Gibbs, Kraemer, and Dedrick (2003) for a somewhat dated view of which countries have passed e-commerce specific regulations in which areas.

28. Some rules will cut across the digital-physical divide and become more general societal fights. One good example is data privacy, which matters for both physical and online retailers as they gather information about their customers (and, for online retailers, their visitors). For physical stores in the United States and increasingly the UK, loyalty cards are the primary method of linking sales data to individual customers, but loyalty cards are not the only way to tie consumer information to sales data. Ito-Yokado, the firm that now owns the 7-Eleven franchise, has workers enter basic customer information (age, gender, local or visitor) into computers before ringing up purchases. The way data are gathered is certainly one of the variables most affected by regulation, notably with regard to privacy laws. Differential privacy laws mean that European companies are more likely to collect aggregate data from the cards instead of customer-specific data. In addition, it is harder for them to share the data with third parties. If they were to gather individual data, they would need a consent agreement on the front end. This also makes future mergers harder if merged companies want to use any individual data across products. See Newman (2008) for more on cross-national data-privacy regulation and a special thanks to Abe Newman for helping me think through this complicated subject.

29. In France, the political contests are often about whether to replicate/update the rules that existed in physical distribution. For instance, the 1981 Lang Law prohibited the sale of books at prices less than 5 percent below the price set by publishers. In November 2010, the French government extended the law to include e-books.

30. Historical, seasonally adjusted monthly employment data, measured from peak of employment prerecession to nadir. The term "recession" does not follow the National Bureau of Economic Research (NBER) definition but simply matches the period of employment fall below its pre-recession levels during the downturn.

References

A.C. Nielsen. (2005). "The Power of Private Label 2005." Executive News Report from A.C. Nielsen Global Service.

Baumol, William. (1967). "Macroeconomics of unbalanced growth: The anatomy of urban crisis." *American Economic Review* 57: 415–26.

Baumol, William. (2007). "On Mechanisms Underlying the Growing Share of Service Employment in the Industrialized Economies." In *Services and Employment: Explaining the US-European Gap*, edited by Mary B. Gregory, Wiemer Salverda, and Ronald Schettkat, 63–80. Princeton, NJ: Princeton University Press.

Becker, G. S. (1996). "Why Europe is drowning in joblessness." *BusinessWeek,* April 8: 22.

Bloom, Paul N., and Vanessa G. Perry. (2001). "Retailer power and supplier welfare: The case of Wal-Mart." *Journal of Retailing* 77(3): 379–417.

Boston Consulting Group. (2003). *Private Label: Threat to Manufacturers, Opportunity for Retailers.* Chicago: Boston Consulting Group.

Bresnahan, T., and S. Greenstein. (1996). "Technical progress and coinvention in computing and in the uses of computers." *Brookings Papers on Economic Activity, Microeconomics,* 1–83.

Bureau of Labor Statistics. (2010). "Table B-1. Employees on nonfarm payrolls by industry sector and selected industry detail" (www.bls.gov).

Christopherson, S. (2007). "Barriers to 'US style' lean retailing: The case of Wal-Mart's failure in Germany." *Journal of Economic Geography* 7: 451–69.

Coe, N., and N. Wrigley. (2007). "Host economy impacts of transnational retail: The research agenda." *Journal of Economic Geography* 7: 341–71

Colla, Enrico, and Marc Dupuis. (2002). "Research and managerial issues on global retail competition: Carrefour/Wal-Mart." *International Journal of Retail and Distribution Management* 30(2): 103–11.

Danmark Statistik. (2010). "Labour force" (http://www.dst.dk/en/Statistik/emner/arbejdsstyrke.aspx).

Dawson, J. (2005). "Output considerations in retail productivity." *International Review of Retail, Distribution, and Consumer Research* 15(3): 337–492.

Delpla, J., and C. Wiplosz. (2007). *La Fin des Privilèges: Payer Pour Reformer*. Paris: Haceheet Littératures.

Dobson, P., M. Waterson, and A. Chu. (1998). The welfare consequences of the exercise of buyer power. Office of Fair Trading Research Paper 16.

Emmet, B., and J. Jeuck. (1950). *Catalogues and Counters: A History of Sears, Roebuck and Company*. Chicago: University of Chicago Press.

Esping-Andersen, Gøsta. (1999). *Social Foundations of Postindustrial Economies*. Oxford: Oxford University Press.

Gaur, V., M. Fisher, and A. Raman. (2005). "An econometric analysis of inventory turnover performance in retail services." *Management Science* 51(2): 181–94.

Gibbs, J., K. Kraemer, and J. Dedrick. (2003). "Environment and policy factors shaping global e-commerce diffusion: A cross-country comparison." *The Information Society* 19(1): 5–18.

Gordon, R. (2004). Why was Europe left at the station when America's productivity locomotive departed? NBER Working Paper 10661, National Bureau of Economic Research.

Holmes, T. (1999). "Bar codes lead to frequent deliveries and superstores." Federal Reserve Bank of Minneapolis Research Department Staff Report 261.

Hwang, M., and D. Weil. (1998). The diffusion of modern manufacturing practices: Evidence from the retail-apparel sectors. Working Paper 97-11, Center for Economic Studies, Boston.

Institut national de la statistique et des études économiques. (2010). "Income-wages" (www.insee.fr).

Iversen, Torben. (2005). *Capitalism, Democracy, and Welfare*. Cambridge: Cambridge University Press.

Iversen, Torben, and Anne Wren. (1998). "Equality, employment and budgetary restraint: The trilemma of the service economy." *World Politics* 50: 507–46.

Jones, D., P. Kalmi, and A. Kauhanen. (2011). "Firm and employee effects of an enterprise information system: Micro-econometric evidence." *International Journal of Production Economics* 130(2): 159–68.

Katz, D. (1987). *The Big Store: Inside the Crisis and Revolution at Sears*. New York: Viking.

Kenney, M., and B. Pon. (2011). Smartphone industry convergence: Is the Mobile Internet OS Platform the key? Paper presented at BRIE-ETLA Collaborative Research Program Conference, January 21–22.

Kumar, N., and J. Steenkamp. (2007). *Private Label Strategy: How to Meet the Store Brand Challenge.* Cambridge, MA: Harvard Business School Publishing.

Kurnia, S., P. Swatman, and D. Schauder. (1998). Efficient consumer response: A preliminary comparison of U.S. and European experiences. Paper presented at the 11th International Conference on Electronic Commerce, Bled, Slovenia, June 8–10.

Levy, F., and R. Murnane. (2004). *The New Division of Labor.* New York: Russell Sage Foundation.

Magee, D. (2007). *How Toyota Became #1: Leadership Lessons from the World's Greatest Car Company.* New York: Portfolio.

McGuckin, R., M. Spiegelman, and B. Van Ark. (2005). "The retail revolution: Can Europe match the U.S. productivity performance?" The Conference Board, Research Report R-1358.

McKinsey & Company. (2001). "IT and productivity growth in the retail sector." McKinsey Global Institute.

Mesic, I. (2009). "Structural changes and global trends in European Union trade." *Interdisciplinary Management Research* 5: 25–32.

Monteverde, K., and D. Teece. (1982). "Supplier switching costs and vertical integration in the automobile industry." *Bell Journal of Economics* 13: 206–13.

Müller-Lankenau, Class, Kai Wehmeyer, and Stefan Klien. (2005–06). "Multi-channel strategies: Capturing and exploring diversity in the European retail grocery industry." *International Journal of Electronic Commerce* 10(2): 85–122.

Nelson, B. (1997). *Punched Cards to Bar Codes: A 200 Year Journey.* Peterborough, NH: Helmers.

Newman, A. (2008). *Protectors of Privacy: Regulating Personal Data in the Global Economy.* Ithaca, NY: Cornell University Press.

Nicoletti, G., and S. Scarpetta. (2003). Regulation, productivity, and growth: OECD evidence. World Bank Policy Research Working Paper Series, #2944.

National Retail Federation. (2010). "Retail employees by occupation, age, and education" (www.nrf.com).

O'Mahoney, M., and B. Van Ark. (Eds.). (2003). *EU Productivity and Competitiveness: An Industry Perspective: Can Europe Resume the Catching-up Process?* Luxembourg: Office for Official Publications of the European Communities.

Organisation for Economic Co-operation and Development. (1996). "Making Work Pay." In *OECD Employment Outlook,* 25–58. Paris: Organisation for Economic Co-operation and Development.

Organisation for Economic Co-operation and Development. (1994). *The OECD Jobs Study: Evidence and Explanations.* Paris: Organisation for Economic Co-operation and Development.

Organisation for Economic Co-operation and Development. (2010). "Labour force statistics" (stats.oecd.org). Paris: Organisation for Economic Co-operation and Development.

Palamountain, Joseph Cornwall Jr. (1955). *The Politics of Distribution.* Cambridge, MA: Harvard University Press.

Pierson, Paul. (1998). "Irresistible forces, immovable objects: Post-industrial welfare states confront permanent austerity." *Journal of European Public Policy* 5(4): 539–60.

Russell Sage Foundation. "Retail Jobs in Comparative Perspective." Contribution by the cross-national retail team to the Russell Sage Foundation Low-wage Work Project." September 1, 2008.

Schroeder, R., and B. Flynn. (Eds.). (2001). *High Performance Manufacturing: Global Perspectives.* New York: Wiley.

Schwartz, H. (2001). "Round up the Usual Suspects: Globalization, Domestic Politics, and Welfare State Change." In *The New Politics of the Welfare State*, edited by Paul Pierson, 17–44. New York: Oxford University Press.

Triplett, J., and B. Bosworth. (2004). *Productivity in the U.S. Services Sector.* Washington, D.C.: Brookings Institution Press.

UK Office for National Statistics. (2010). "Annual survey of hours and earnings" (UK ASHE) (http://www.ons.gov.uk/).

U.S. Bureau of Labor Statistics-Current Population Survey. (2010). "Labor force statistics" (http://www.bls.gov/cps/).

Van Ark, B., E. Monnikhof, and N. Mulder. (1999). "Productivity in services: An international comparative perspective." *Canadian Journal of Economics* 32(2): 471–99.

Van Ark, B., M. O'Mahoney, and M. Timmer. (2008). The productivity gap between Europe and the U.S.: Trends and causes." *Journal of Economic Perspectives* 22(1): 25–44.

Wang, H. (2010). "Buyer power, transport cost and welfare." *Journal of Industry, Competition and Trade* 10(1): 41–53.

Watson, Bartholomew. (2011). *Nations of retailers: The comparative political economy of retail trade.* Ph.D. diss., The University of California, Berkeley.

Williamson, O. (1985). *The Economic Institutions of Capitalism: Firms, Markets, and Relational Contracting.* New York: Free Press.

Zysman, J., N. C. Nielsen, D. Breznitz, and D. Wong. (2007). Building on the past, imagining the future: Competency based growth strategies in a global digital age. BRIE Working Paper 181, Berkeley Roundtable on the International Economy, Berkeley, CA.

6 A Decade After the Y2K Problem
HAS INDIAN IT EMERGED?
Rafiq Dossani

Introduction

India's presence in the global economy is affirmed by its undoubted progress in providing developed country enterprises with information technology–enabled services (ITES). Such services, which include Internet and software services (IT services), business processes, and research and development (R&D), are an essential component of every modern enterprise's operations.[1]

The Indian prowess in ITES is sometimes argued to parallel China's rise in manufacturing—it is argued that India's success is due to low costs arising from adequate supplies of software engineers and other knowledge workers, managerial skills, knowledge of English and a first-mover advantage (see, e.g., Athreye 2005). Armed with these advantages, India, it is implied, can become the "China of services," with negative consequences on the size of the services sector, employment, and wages in the developed economies. Given that developed economies overwhelmingly rely on services, the negative impacts can be large indeed.

As this chapter argues, many of the foregoing assumptions are true, but the implications do not necessarily follow. This chapter first explains the industrial organization of the industry—the types of firms that constitute the Indian ITES industry, the markets they operate in, and their strategies. Second, the chapter examines the role of the state. Finally, the chapter approaches the issue of national competitive advantage.

My approach compares the Indian ITES industry in 1999 with its condition a decade later, in 2009. In 1999, the so-called Y2K problem galvanized the developed world's IT industry, as it sought to debug a problem created in the 1980s by the high costs of computer disk drive memory. Indian companies played an important role in resolving the problem. Though a simple activity, debugging Y2K brought India to the forefront of the world's IT industry. The capabilities then displayed by Indian engineers and Indian IT firms were believed to assure its grand future in IT. This chapter asks the following question: A decade later, has India delivered on this promise?

The Industrial Organization of India's ITES Sector

India's ITES sector dates to 1974. The industry, consisting of over 3,000 firms, exported $59.4 billion of ITES in 2010 (NASSCOM 2011: 6). Operating margins consistently exceed 20 percent.[2]

Unlike the high-technology industry in Silicon Valley, a handful of firms drive the Indian ITES sector. The Big 6, as they are known, account for 55 percent of industry revenue (see Table 6.1). Further, these are firms that are at least two decades old; some of them, such as TCS, Tech Mahindra, and PCS were large by 1990.

The large firms' position appears to be stable: their market share increased in recent years, margins are higher, and they earn more per employee than do smaller firms.[3]

The origin of large-firm importance lies in the role of the state at the time of the origination of the industry in the early 1970s. The national government's stance toward industry was "statist, protectionist and regulatory" (Rubin 1985). State policy through the 1970s was extremely important for every single industry. The national government had declared its intention of achieving state-owned enterprises' (SOEs) control of every sector of national significance. No new industrial venture could be begun by private interests without acquiring an operating license from the national government. Such licenses were issued based on the concept of residual capacity: the state first

TABLE 6.1
THE BIG 6 OF INDIAN ITES, AS OF 2009

Name	Year of Founding	Market Share of Indian Software Exports (%)
TCS	1968	16.7
Infosys	1981	13.6
Wipro Technologies	1977	12.6
HCL	1976	6.7
Tech Mahindra	1986	3.8
Patni Computer Systems	1978	2.1
Total		55.6

Note: Software includes software services and research, development and engineering services, but excludes BPO services.

Source: Companies' annual reports, NASSCOM various years: 245.

determined what SOEs would produce. The remainder was licensed to the private sector. Production capacity per private licensee was restricted to prevent any single private firm from growing too large.

In contradiction to policy objectives, large private firms controlled private industry in consequence. This was because licensing required credible commitments of capital and expertise. The banks, which were mostly state-owned, would fund licensed projects only on similar terms. Only large firms could provide such commitments. Since licensing policy prevented them from controlling industries, they diversified instead. As a result, each industry's private sector consisted of conglomerates whose industry output was a small share of both the industry and the conglomerate's revenue.[4]

In such a restrictive environment, only a few industries were controlled by the private sector. These included industries where technology was owned by the private sector. The computer industry was one such, and it was then dominated by multinational corporations (MNCs)—IBM, ICL, and Burroughs were the main players, of which IBM was the largest (Heeks 1996: 56). Their firms' clients were mainly government departments.

The MNCs, in a strange marriage of convenience, were content with this arrangement. Neither the state nor the MNCs were interested in the growth of a flourishing domestic private computer industry and colluded to keep them out (Sharma 2009).

The state wanted, over the longer term, to bring such sectors under public control. As a first step, the government imposed a new law, the Foreign Exchange Regulation Act of 1973 (FERA-1973). Under FERA-1973, a foreign firm was allowed to operate in India only with a minority interest (foreign ownership was restricted to a maximum of 40 percent). IBM, after several rounds of negotiations with the Indian government, closed down in 1978 citing concerns about loss of intellectual property under a FERA structure. The government awarded a monopoly for the maintenance of all IBM computers in India to an SOE, the Computer Maintenance Corporation (Heeks 1996: 58).

By the mid-1970s, several MNC computer companies had accepted the FERA strictures and formed joint ventures. These included Burroughs, in a joint venture with the Tatas in 1974 (in a separate unit from TCS, which continued to do in-house work for the Tata Group), Digital, and Data General. These companies focused on domestic business, still mainly from the state sector.

Meanwhile, in 1967, a doctoral student at MIT, Lalit Kanodia, wrote a project report for the Tata Group, India's largest conglomerate, on setting up an in-house data processing unit for the group. Kanodia returned to India the next year to create and head this unit, which later would become known as Tata Consultancy Services—TCS (Sharma 2009). Kanodia was later to start Datamatics, a joint venture with Wang Computers, a well-known minicomputer MNC.

Kanodia was the first of a number of returnee engineers, armed with a U.S. technical education, who were interested in the computer business. The other founders in today's top 6 who were U.S.-trained returnee engineers were Wipro's Azim Premji (Stanford) and PCS's Narendra Patni (MIT). They initially were interested in the domestic business, but, given the draconian rules, they were unable to do anything in that sector and so turned to exports.

Exports began in 1974 with the mainframe manufacturer, Burroughs, asking its India sales agent, Tata Consultancy Services, to export programmers for installing system software for a U.S. client (S. Ramadorai, CEO of TCS, pers. comm., November 29, 2002). Burroughs was later to set up a joint venture with the Tatas for similar purposes.

By 1980, there were twenty-one software exporting firms; the firms that controlled the business were the two Tata firms. TCS and Tata-Burroughs accounted for 63 percent of industry revenue (Heeks 1996: 88).

The Tata Group stands out as being the only Indian conglomerate of significance to enter the field from the beginning. This was due to the role played by three board directors of the Tata Group at the time, Ratan Tata, F. C. Kohli, and Minoo Mody. Ratan Tata graduated in engineering from Cornell University in 1962 and turned down a job with IBM to return to India. F. C. Kohli earned his master's degree in electrical engineering from MIT in 1950. Minoo Mody, also an engineer, was instrumental in the Tata-Burrough's collaboration.[5]

These leaders, like the freshly returned engineers, saw in software exports a way to escape the state's controls, which were directed to domestic businesses.

The first initiatives by these firms were small and oriented toward manpower supply to meet the needs of foreign clients rather than software creation. Even as of 1980, the industry's revenue was just $4 million. Reputation with clients was key, given high country risk; it was this rather than production economies of scale that favored established rather than new firms. Small firms also found it difficult to raise capital due to the absence of developed private equity markets and unavailability of bank finance for services. The top eight firms accounted for 90 percent of industry revenue in 1980 (Heeks 1996: 89). Six of them were started by established business houses (though Tata was the only large conglomerate) and seven were headquartered in Mumbai.

The clients of the Indian exporters were initially large computer makers and data processing firms; this reflected the industrial structure of the client industry in developed countries in the 1970s. In developed countries at the time, the computer makers and some large data processing firms, such as General Electric, owned the computers and applications, while enterprises leased usage from such firms (Steinmuller 1996).

Technological developments in the 1980s changed the structure of the industry in the developed world. Declining computing costs due to the invention of the workstation and standardization of Unix as the programming language led to a standardized programming platform. This standardization allowed the programming function to be made independent of the other parts of creating software, such as the requirements analysis.

Due to the decline in computing costs, enterprises shifted from leasing computing power to owning it; vendors started offering applications and writing code to client requirements. Thus, the client base shifted from computer firms to enterprises, while the vendor base shifted from large computer makers to independent firms.

A consolidation among client industries, particularly financial services firms, occurred in the 1980s (Jones and Critchfield 2008). This influenced the vendors, among whom scale became important.

While these changes were afoot in the developed world, in India, the state changed stance and started encouraging private-sector software exports through reduced import duties, tax benefits, access to bank capital, and infrastructure. Combined with the above-noted technological developments overseas, this led to a change in the business model, from manpower supply to software creation in India.

This encouraged the entrance of hundreds of new firms. By 1990, the number of firms rose to 700 from 35 in 1984 (Heeks 1996: 87). This number included firms started by employees working at some of the larger firms (see Table 6.2). The new business model required large campuses where earlier none were needed. Commercial space being expensive in Mumbai and the supply of engineers being the largest in South India, firms started looking south to set up the business. In the process, Bangalore as a location for the Indian IT industry was created (Dossani 2007a).

In summary, the structure of the ITES business in India in the 1980s was defined by technological and business developments in the developed countries as well as changes in national policy at home. The outcome was a flourishing of the business with a large role for the big ITES firms. Small IT firms also flourished, catering to the needs of smaller clients. The center of the IT business started to move away from Mumbai.

TABLE 6.2
EMPLOYEES OF THE EARLY IT FIRMS WHO WENT ON TO START SUCCESSFUL IT FIRMS

	Original Employer	Founded
Ashok Soota	Wipro	Mindtree
Arjun Malhotra	HCL	Headstrong
Narayan Murthy	PCS	Infosys
Lalit Kanodia*	TCS	Datamatics
Revathi Kasturi	Tata Burroughs	Tarang Software
Sanjay Sharma	Tata Burroughs	Tata Interactive Systems
S. Gopalan	Tata Burroughs	Global Automation
B. V. R. Mohan Reddy*	ECIL	Infotech Enterprises
P. V. Kannan	TCS	24x7
Rajesh Hukku*	TCS	i-Flex
Harish Mehta*	Hinditron	Onward Software
Saurabh Srivastava*	IBM & Tata Burroughs	IIS Infotech

Note: * Indicates whether engineering training done overseas.
Source: Author's compilation.

This structure has not changed significantly since 1990. As of 2009, large firms' strategies are built around servicing large overseas clients. The large Indian firms' client profile is similar to that of large MNC service providers (with the exception of the MNCs' public-sector clients). Financial services predominate in that client profile.[6]

In consequence, the industry's structure has followed a stable pattern for the past two decades. Large firms are essentially similar firms, reliant on a few industries, particularly financial services firms, as noted. The smaller firms cater to smaller and more varied types of clients.

Just like their MNC counterparts, the Indian IT services firms are not leaders in innovation. Stable, mature processes, whether they are the creation of a software application or managing an outsourced information system, are what their clients need and what the vendors seek to deliver. For innovations, vendors rely on software product firms, such as SAP, on whose products and platforms the services are provided.

These innovative product firms are located almost entirely in the developed world. In turn, they rely on service providers to install their products and platforms for their clients. They all partner with ITES vendors for that purpose. Such partnerships are important for Indian ITES firms, just like their MNC counterparts, as a source of learning about new technologies.

The developed country MNC IT services firms can access additional sources of learning unavailable to Indian IT firms: engineers from product firms, independent professionals, and university research. Such resources are outside the ambit of the Indian IT firms, largely for locational reasons. Increasingly, however, the larger Indian IT firms are setting up developed-country campuses to tap such talent and resources.

The section "How Indian Firms Catch Up" uses a case study of a leading semiconductor design services firm to chronicle how important these last-noted factors are as sources of learning.

The Role of the State

In most countries' national systems of innovation, the role of the state is significant. States are expected to support private-sector and academic innovation through subsidies and contracts, infrastructure, localization requirements, finance for small businesses, and so on. This section considers the role of the state in India, beginning with its role in supporting the private sector.

In India, I showed that private industry did not receive state support in the beginning. On the contrary, the state was antagonistic toward the domestic private sector.

This changed, as noted previously, in the mid-1980s, and the state in India provided tax benefits, set up industrial parks, reduced import tariffs, and welcomed MNCs through new foreign direct investment (FDI) rules. While the fiscal incentives were available nationally, a key driver of a future cluster was the location of state industrial parks in large cities. This was also an important factor in MNC location.

The cities that benefited the most were in states ruled by the then-monolithic Congress party. This included Maharashtra, whose capital is Mumbai, and Karnataka, whose capital is Bangalore. The first export processing zone that housed TCS and other technology companies was established in Mumbai in 1973.[7] Bangalore's MNCs were assured bandwidth under a special program set up by the national government in 1985, an important reason for the 1986 decision by Texas Instruments and, in 1989, by HP, to locate their India operations in Bangalore.

The Indian political system is federal by design, but, until 1990, it was centralist in practice. From the 1990s, an era of coalition government began, in which national parties formed coalitions with regional parties with state-level interests (Dossani 2007b).

As regional politicians gained power, they used this coalition government to foster high-technology sectors in their states of origin. Perhaps the most impressive case is that of Andhra Pradesh, whose Chief Minister at the time, Chandrababu Naidu, leveraged his political support to the NDA (National Democratic Alliance) national government in the period 1998–2004 to obtain resources for building up the state's IT sector in the state capital, Hyderabad.

Hyderabad's case is interesting because it, Bangalore, and Chennai were the prime targets for an IT cluster when the business model shifted from manpower supply to software creation in the 1980s (see the earlier section "The Industrial Organization of India's ITES Sector"). All three cities are located in southern centers of educational excellence. Bangalore had a further advantage of being the location of a cluster of state-owned high-tech enterprises. However, politics played an important role. Between 1982 and 1989, Andhra Pradesh was ruled by the TDP, a party in opposition to the Congress. As such, the national government thwarted development in Andhra Pradesh during this period and Hyderabad, its capital, lost out. Chennai, the capital of Tamil Nadu state, also ruled by opposition parties during this period, suffered similarly.

With the advent of regionalized politics, this changed. Naidu, especially during the time that the NDA was in power in New Delhi, sought to develop Hyderabad's IT sector. His initiatives included (1) reserving 5,000 acres of land for an IT cluster; (2) convincing Microsoft, Deloitte, GE Capital, and HSBC to locate their Indian IT services and developmental headquarters in Hyderabad in return for subsidized land and fiscal incentives; and (3) investments by state departments in IT services, contracted out to local firms.[8]

Hyderabad thus rose in importance from 2000, and was, as of 2010, the fourth largest cluster after Bangalore, Mumbai, and Delhi. Chennai was fifth.

A second important effect of regionalization was on higher education. Education is a joint responsibility of the national and state governments, under the Indian Constitution. The national government is solely responsible for determining standards for teaching and research. The state governments are supposed to establish universities and colleges that meet these standards, are supposed to allow private colleges to affiliate with universities, and are responsible for the universities' funding and management.[9]

Prior to 1991, the national government took the view that all higher education should be state-provided. The failure of this policy until 1991 was met with calls by the national government for greater public investment in higher education. With regionalization, the state governments took control of higher education. A few states, notably Andhra Pradesh, Karnataka, and Tamil Nadu, decided that they would support nonprofit private providers through subsidies.

Private provision subsequently dramatically affected supply in these states. From a negligible presence up to 1990, as of 2010, private providers accounted for half of total undergraduate enrollment and over 75 percent of the number of degree-awarding institutions. In engineering studies, as of 2010, private providers accounted for 95 percent of graduates.

India, as a consequence, over the past decade, saw a large increase in the number of enrollments. As of 2011, 3.3 million students were enrolled in four-year undergraduate engineering degree programs. While the quality of the education varies, a study of colleges in the Bangalore area showed that the quality as ranked by global companies was technically adequate (Dossani and Patibandla 2010).

A related issue is whether skills other than technical skills are acquired. Indian engineering students' courses are skewed toward basic science and technical courses, which account for 88 percent of their course load; in a typical American university program, at least a third of courses are taken outside the basic sciences and technical courses. The skewed load does not necessarily mean that Indian students are more technically skilled, since hours worked, quality of teaching, and infrastructure all affect outcomes (Carnoy and Dossani 2011).

Knowledge of the English language among the technically skilled is likely high, though no formal estimates exist. However, all engineering colleges teach science and technical courses only in English.

In summary, the national government affected the ITES sector in several ways. Its decision to locate industrial parks and infrastructure in politically friendly provinces influenced the growth of Mumbai and Bangalore as centers of IT in the 1980s. In the 1990s, the provincial governments' role increased. Hyderabad's growth as an IT cluster was significantly influenced by the state's advocacy and incentives. The enormous increase in output of trained engineers was due to the shift by some provinces to support private provision.

How Indian Firms Catch Up: Case Study of Semiconductor Design

In this section, we ask how India-based IT firms address a key strategic challenge: keeping up with technological change. As noted in an earlier section, Indian firms are unable to easily access the best talent from product firms, consultants, and universities for locational reasons. This leads to new forms of learning. One such method is illustrated by a case study of the activities of a leading Indian IT firm, Wipro, in semiconductor design services over the period 2000–09.

The design services industry is about two decades old. India entered the field around 2000. The users of semiconductor design services are large and small semiconductor firms. Technological change is rapid and occurs at the level of both start-ups and large firms. We first describe the client profile as of 2009 and then consider the outsourcing industry.

ESTABLISHED FIRMS IN WESTERN COUNTRIES

For such firms, design is a part of core IP and tends to be done in-house using focused teams of sizes ranging from as few as 5 engineers to over 200 engineers (the larger teams would be found in cutting-edge projects such as GPUs), with an average of 20 engineers. Such engineers tend to be highly paid, earning average wages of $250,000. They need to be knowledgeable about the domain as well as about the electrical, analog, and digital properties of the chip.

The use of outside consultants is limited at the initial stages to a few application-specific engineers to help conceptualize the project and the chip's design (or micro-architecture).

The use of outside consultants increases for back-end work, such as converting the design into code and verification of the physical, electrical, and system properties. Outside consultants are also widely used for second-generation chip design. Such engineers tend to be cheaper and focused on the digital side.

The established firms may be categorized further by size. First, there are the large firms, which we define as those employing 1,000 engineers or more. Most of these are U.S.-headquartered. There are about twenty large firms (either pure design or IDMs) in the business, which account for two-thirds of industry revenue and employ about 250,000 engineers. Over the past decade, the large firms became regular users of outsourced design services, including offshored services. Many work through subsidiaries overseas for the purpose of accessing outsourced services.

The second type consists of medium-sized firms with average employment of 100 engineers. There are about 250 such firms, many of which are vertically specialized. These are mostly located in the United States, with some in Europe and Israel. Such firms do not usually locate globally and their outsourcing requirements are more episodic because of a limited number of products. Such firms do use outsourcers, but not as much as the large firms. Unlike start-ups (see below), they do not face severe cost pressures and often do not find it worthwhile to outsource when compared with the managerial effort needed to manage outsourcing. This is especially true for offshored outsourcing, which consumes significant management time.

ESTABLISHED FIRMS IN EAST ASIA

Japan and the rest of East Asia also have large, sophisticated semiconductor design industries. Their industries are dominated by larger firms such as Sony, Samsung, and

MediaTek. They tend to focus on consumer products, but exceptions exist, and include processor families, such as from Toshiba, and platform development, such as by Samsung. Mid-size companies have grown faster of late in East Asia than in the West.

Although these companies do outsource design services, this is limited relative to Western companies. The logic for in-house work is that the labor cost in these countries, excluding Japan, is low. Japan also does its semiconductor design work mainly in-house despite higher labor costs, largely to achieve tighter process flow. Some Japanese firms have begun outsourcing design work, including sophisticated firms such as Docomo, NEC, Renesas, and Toshiba. Their contractors are mostly in East Asia but also India.

Taiwanese design services firms control the market for outsourced design services to the rest of East Asia (but lack a significant presence outside East Asia), while Indian design services firms are insignificant in this market.

China's design industry consists of mostly small and a few mid-sized semiconductor design firms, developing chips for the local consumer appliances market. Their designs are mostly done in-house. Since chips for the consumer goods produced in China largely do not require using the latest generation of design tools, many Chinese firms get by with using freeware or pirated old-generation design tools (note that the latest-generation design tools can cost up to $4 million each)—although this is going down with time. The state tries to reduce costs for using legally acquired tools by acquiring them and making them available to smaller firms, especially within incubators, at heavily subsidized costs. China is neither a potential client country nor a significant competitor to Indian design services firms.

START-UPS

For start-ups, flexibility and speed while managing costs is a critical requirement. As of March 2009, there were about 250 such firms, mostly located in Silicon Valley. At these firms, employment ranges from twenty-five to fifty engineers. Start-ups are invariably under immense economic pressure. For such firms, semiconductor design is again a part of core IP; however, due to cost constraints, there is frequent use of consultants to assist with aspects of the design process for which expertise is not available in-house. Such outside expertise tends to vary with the start-up and can include even core IP support. For the most sophisticated start-ups, such as those typically found in Silicon Valley, back-end functions, of course, tend to be more readily outsourced.

Design Services Environment in India and Other Countries

From the foregoing, it is apparent that, until 2000, the use of outside consultants by Western independent consulting (IC) firms was mostly limited to lower-end work given to local consultants. This limited the scalability of such work in expensive-labor environments like Silicon Valley. Independent consultants were, therefore, the most common form of outside consultants. The few organized design services firms that existed were small, employing twenty engineers on average. These prospered by specializing in horizontal capabilities, both low-end and high-end, rather than in the full range of capabilities or in verticals.

As of 2000, which marked the peak of domestic outsourcing, about 15,000 people worked in the design services industry globally, of whom about 12,000 were in the United States, mostly in Silicon Valley. They represented only about 5 percent of the total semiconductor design industry workforce. They were hired at rates of about $15,000 p.m. FTE (full-time equivalent) for lower-end work in Silicon Valley, a rate that has remained unchanged until the present time.

India, by 2000, had about 1,000 design engineers in the services business, mostly organized in small firms. The work by Indian firms was mostly in quality assurance and design verification. The Indian industry grew out of a few returnees and ex-employees of multinationals. As noted previously, they mostly formed small firms, of about twenty engineers on average—thus mimicking their U.S. counterparts, though doing lower-end work.

By 2009, the U.S.-based design services industry had shrunk to less than half of its peak and employed about 6,000 engineers. While individual consultants still predominate, average firm size is larger, about 100 engineers on average, and is more vertically specialized, while focusing on relatively high-end horizontal capabilities within verticals.

Meanwhile, the Indian design services industry has seen rapid growth and employs about 7,000 engineers. This does not include personnel within multinational firms such as Intel and Texas Instrumets that are experienced in design. Including them, the Indian design sector is closer to 15,000. The Indian sector has also seen the emergence of a few large players, led by Wipro.

As a result, the low-end outsourcing work, particularly the digital work, has substantially shifted to India; as noted earlier, Silicon Valley outsourcers are mostly high-end providers, with a bimodal organizational system—mostly independent contractors, but the firms that exist are larger than before.

A larger outsourcer offers several advantages over smaller outsourcers for those client firms that are small, particularly for start-ups. The first is access to tools. Small firms are unable often to afford design tools; often, using an outsourcer is driven by this factor. Second, size enables firms to offer deep manpower benches to enable rapid up- or downscaling at low cost. Finally, size enables the creation of institutional memory for competence progression, accompanied by the potential for good documentation (often otherwise neglected in start-ups and small firms).

The large outsourcer disadvantages start-up client firms in one significant respect: stability of the labor pool. The personnel assigned to a small client rarely stay the same over successive projects largely because of the uncertainty of such projects. Over time, this adversely affects the quality of work done. This is because high-end work is best done by a more experienced designer who is already familiar with the work of a particular client.

A larger outsourcer is also more advantageous for large client firms than a smaller outsourcer, but for a different reason: the advantage is that it can offer predictable scale for doing low-end work at low costs.

Most large outsourcing firms seek large clients, even though they are less profitable per employee, to scale up both in tools and manpower. This then allows them to meet the needs of smaller clients.

While there is little sign of the emergence of a design services industry in East Asia for servicing Western firms, Europe and Israel's design services industry emerged, jointly accounting for a total employment of about 2,000 engineers as of 2009.

From the foregoing numbers, it may also be seen that global employment in design services is unchanged at about 15,000 engineers since 2000. This is despite the enormous growth in the revenue of the semiconductor industry during this time. This constancy is due to several factors, primary among them being convergence to fewer design platforms and greater automation of the design process. This happened even as the complexity of work done increased substantially due to lower bandwidth of circuitry and requirements of higher performance.

The attraction of India for design services that emerges from the foregoing discussion is similar in some ways to what drove the outsourcing of software services to India: scale, mature processes, and good documentation.

However, there are differences between software services and IC design services that affect how the work is done. The first is technical: the development of chips is via a parallelized process of design and coding, with considerable interaction between the design and coding phase. Thus, algorithmic verification feeds back to architectural coding in a different way than software. The core difference can be summarized in this way: the cost of a bug in IC design is vastly higher than that of software design and implementation. The cost increases as the project moves forward in time as well. This makes functional verification and design far more important to be tightly integrated and controlled. This results in the organization of IC architecture and RTL coding to be very different from the sequentially driven process of designing and coding computer programs in C. Specifically, these functions cannot, as of 2009, be separated in the way that they can in software. This is why outsourcing to India focused on post-RTL coding work, starting with physical verification and now largely encompassing functional verification.

The parallelized process also makes verification a critical function, accounting for about 70 percent of the FTE of labor time in chip design, compared with about 25 percent in the case of software services. Since verification is relatively low-end work, the potential for outsourcing is high, but the operational model is different from the more compartmentalized model of software development—proximity and close coordination are more important than in software development.

A nontechnical, but also a key, difference is that design outsourcing is project based rather than process based. This is a challenge that used to confront software services until the development of the Internet—note that until the mid-1990s, Indian software outsourcers focused on programming set pieces of work handed down to them by their clients' design consultants, which they completed and handed back to their clients' system integrators. Since then, software services changed from largely project work to more of process work.

The IC industry's outsourcing remains project based. The cause for this is the limited shelf lives of chips. In addition, the industry's relatively low firm survival rates due to a two- to three-year cycle make it difficult to retain clients, especially smaller clients.

Of course, problems like these create opportunities. One of the looming challenges for large outsourcing firms is to convert project to process work, through innovative thinking and proactive moves on initiating and sequencing second-generation work, for example. Without this, client stickiness will always be an issue. Most Indian outsourcers do report high rates of client churn, especially among the smaller clients.

I noted previously that India became a destination for chip design because of its reputation in software services, notwithstanding some key differences. In some other ways, India is naturally suited to the business of design services, because such work is labor intensive and requires limited infrastructure. Another factor is the relatively satisfactory quality of labor available in India. Note that chip design is an activity where experience is extremely valuable. The value of a chip designer with more experience in comparison to one who is less experienced bears a considerably higher ratio than the comparables in software services. Given that TI started designing chips in India in 1986, and that many other firms, including Intel, located sizable and sophisticated operations in India, there is a depth of VLSI talent and experience at hand. The industry's average engineer experience was three years even by 2003, growing substantially since. Further, thanks to such sizable design presence, the main tools manufacturers such as Cadence and Synopsys are present in India, even offering certification programs for their tools. Finally, India's legal environment enabled good regulation of IP.

There are challenges, as well. One is how to move up in sophistication. Indian firms succeeded in showcasing more sophisticated work and were successful at functional verification, analog and mixed-signal design, and RTL coding. However, the reluctance of large firms, on which the business largely rests, to outsource high-end work due to IP concerns means that most of the work of the Indian design services industry is focused on physical verification and back-end engineering change orders.

Skills are developing in India, though not at the pace that Silicon Valley is moving, creating challenges. For example, in video chip design, India, as of 2009, lacks capabilities right down to the power estimation stage. Some of these skills issues can be addressed through scale and pooling of knowledge workers, employing overseas consultants and training.

HOW WIPRO DESIGNS CHIPS

Wipro's semiconductor design division developed EagleWision (EW), a methodology for ensuring that the firm's designs are up-to-date, follow mature processes, are scalable, and result in the progressive building of competence within the firm. The first part of EW is that an experienced team of engineers, who might at any time be involved in implementing projects as well, works with a design team throughout the design process. They perform the role of an expert consultant on process, domain knowledge for all phases, and creating client and internal documentation. A second aspect of EW is that, through EW, all processes are standardized and documented, providing a ready resource for the design team.

The rationales for creating EW—note that it is not needed for software services or found in IC design firms—are as follows: first, to standardize the chip development process to the extent possible, so that replicability, documentation, and the creation of in-house tools becomes possible while achieving acceptable quality; and, second, to standardize the design team's technical capabilities to minimum acceptable levels.

By contrast, in software services, the costs of post-project changes are relatively low, as discussed earlier. Perhaps equally important, the Indian education system produces software engineers who are mostly at or above the minimum required quality. Such is not the case with hardware engineers (the availability of high-quality hardware engineers in developed countries explains why, in Western countries, it is not necessary to create an external consultancy team). Even the IITs' EE/EP majors mostly focus on digital design skills, not analog or mixed-signal design. Those that do teach analog and mixed-signal design, such as in IITM, use curricula that are behind what the industry requires as a stepping stone to industrial projects. Recruiters in the United States commonly complain that Indian-trained design engineers are relatively weak on process even as they are strong in conceptualizing of design. Hence, the usefulness of EW in overcoming these challenges and in helping to ensure process maturity and consistency cannot be doubted (which was acknowledged in our interviews).

EW involves substantial costs for Wipro since the costliest in-house expertise must be carved aside for the purpose of creating the expert team. It also raises moral hazard issues: does the design team perform at a level below its true capabilities because it knows that the expert team will do the "real work" during its review? Another hidden cost is that EW can perpetuate hierarchical thinking because it can create the expectation that the design team is answerable to the expert team.

To analyze this issue, we can categorize clients into the two categories presented earlier: established firms and start-ups. The former contract out both second-generation designs and the mainstreaming of cutting-edge products. The latter are at the cutting edge of technology and deal with designs that cannot be systematized (note that their competitive edge exists largely due to the newness of the process).

For the former type of client, increased standardization is a plus. Hence, for second-generation and low-end work, the focus of EW's efforts is on its second aspect: getting the chip-design process even better standardized and documented.

This includes the following considerations:

1. Setting relevant benchmarks within the time frame of chip development (rather than the longer time frame of software development), and revising them to accommodate changed circumstances.
2. Client and internal documentation needs to be standardized and written at the right level of abstraction.
3. Reviewing tools, analyzing their appropriateness to a particular project, ensuring that the most up-to-date review methods are used, and creating metrics and standard response templates.
4. Improving the review cycle at all levels, up to the microarchitecture level.

EW also seeks to build in thinking of how to convert project to process work for large client firms with a sizable second-generation pipeline. This, as noted previously, requires innovative thinking and proactive moves on *initiating* and *proposing* second-generation work.

For start-ups wanting sophisticated work done, standardization is not possible, as discussed earlier (except for low-end work). Hence, my interviews indicated that the greatest concern lay with the high incentives toward standardization motivated in part by EW. Start-ups mostly equated standardization with hierarchy; that is, they inferred that the use of standardized processes was because Wipro wanted to tightly control the process of chip design within a hierarchical framework, rather than something that helped the design process.

The last concern is an important one because of the Indian working environment which tends to be hierarchical in any case. Hierarchy can, of course, be advantageous in some circumstances. For instance, the expectations of performance are more straightforward, as is the flow of information, and it is an advantage when working with hierarchical client firms, as is the case in many large firms everywhere.

But, it is a disadvantage in the IC design services business, particularly when a key objective is to raise employees' creativity. While standardization, as noted, may help raise productivity in repeatable processes, it may reduce productivity in creative processes. Hence, one of the questions is whether EW helps institutionalize already latent hierarchy.

Start-ups' concerns with hierarchy may be summarized as follows:

1. The onus for creativity may devolve on the client, thus raising the burden on the client.
2. Rapid team changes, in order to accommodate an engineer's desire for progression up a hierarchy that is usually desired by those working in large outsourcing firms.
3. Reluctance to hire external consultants: accepting hierarchy means accepting that skills are distributed along the hierarchy and that to acquire new skills, one merely must find the right person and slot that person into the appropriate position in the hierarchy. This can significantly slow down chip development

until the vendor recruits or otherwise acquires the necessary skills in-house. In some cases, if the skills are not available in-country, they need to be obtained from overseas on a consultancy basis.
4. Reluctance to make experienced hires: India now has a cadre of experienced design engineers who represent the country's biggest competitive advantage over other developing countries. Yet many outsourcing firms report that it is difficult to hire such persons as it would disrupt the existing hierarchy.

WIPRO'S STRATEGIC CHALLENGES AND RESPONSES

Wipro responded to these concerns by creating an "engineering track." Unlike the typical Indian IT firm, where the natural hierarchical progression for an engineer is to become a specialized project manager, Wipro's engineering track allows engineers to stay as engineers, while rising up the corporate hierarchy. Following this track ties closely into our earlier observation that experience is worth much more in hardware engineering than in software engineering.

Clients also changed their operational style to spend more on coordination. My interviews indicated that the successful chip-design projects involve coordination well above that needed in the typical software project.

In fact, it is now not unexpected that a client and Wipro may agree that both sides' senior engineers travel to their counterparty's locations for a few weeks *prior* to the commencement of the project. Such face-to-face contact plays a critical role in setting expectations correctly and assessing mutual skills and complementarities. More such travel may be indicated prior to tape-out. Weekly calls at levels that may require senior management time in the client firm may also be needed.

Such interaction also becomes a source of learning, since clients are obvious sources of learning. But an overdependence on clients for learning may be disadvantageous because they are usually not diverse or numerous enough. It is also disfavored by clients who expect that they will learn from their consultant rather than conduct a purely transactional relationship.

Going beyond the client's knowledge levels can happen in two ways: a large pool of clients allows knowledge gained from each to be used for other clients. This would be a good method if the client base is sufficiently diverse—which is not usually the case. A better way is to learn from those outside the client base by tapping the largest extant knowledge base: the network of independent professionals which exists globally.

Tapping into this global (and vibrant) community of professionals requires investing in attending conferences, joining professional associations, and maintaining consultant networks. Ideally, it should be implemented along with the creation of an engineering track. Wipro's success is probably due to its willingness to invest in this network, but such a network is episodic, lacking the regular interaction that is needed to stay at the cutting edge.

Another option is for Wipro's design services group to locate a branch in Silicon Valley for undertaking sample, showcase-level designs. This strategy's disadvantage is the raising of costs, of course. But a significant payoff is access to better communities of practice in the field. Another payoff is the ability to show new and existing clients what the firm is capable of.

This will also help manage a long-term challenge to the business: the trend toward consolidation of the industry, with the likelihood of there being fewer medium-sized players. Its implications are that first, medium-sized players and start-ups are more willing to give out sophisticated, IP-sensitive work to service firms. The reduction in their market share is likely to affect this adversely. Second, the tendency to create binational firms from the beginning means that when a large firm buys a smaller rival, it is likely that the rival already is global. Consolidation requires at least a change in organizational style (e.g., the smaller firm is likely to be less horizontally divided between headquarters and branch office). If multiple locations are involved—for example, the established firm's development office might be in India, while the acquired firm's development office may be in China—it raises further challenges. Further, it is possible that one of the country locations may close down.

This implies that, for a design services firm, it is important to build a presence in clients' headquarter locations in order to showcase capabilities. This way, when consolidation occurs, the design services firm will be in a position to attract business.

India's Competitive Advantage

As a share of world trade in services, India is still a bit player. It accounted for 2.7 percent of world services exports in 2009.[10] By comparison, the United States accounted for 14.1 percent and China accounted for 3.8 percent of world services exports.

In these terms, India makes less of an impact than its emerging market rival, China. However, looking just at ITES, a different picture emerges, as Table 6.3 shows.

TABLE 6.3
INDIA'S SHARE OF OFFSHORED ITES

2010	Total ($ bn)	India ($ bn)	India (%)	China ($ bn)
IT Services	574			
Of which, offshored	57	33.5	58	1.6*
Business Processes	158			
Of which, offshored	50	14.1	28	Negligible

Source: 1. NASSCOM 2009: 7, 21, 26, 36, 37, 58, 200, 201, 202, 204. Not included in the Indian export numbers are India's R&D and product software exports for 2008 equaling $7.3 billion.

2. Retrieved December 22, 2009 (http://www.chinadaily.com.cn/china/2009-02/12/content_7467488.htm). The largest firm in China is Neusoft, with 12,000 employees in 2009, whereas each of India's top 3 firms employs over 100,000. China figures are for 2008.

3. See also http://www.businessweek.com/magazine/content/06_05/b3969412.htm, retrieved December 24, 2009, for a list of the major global outsourcers.

The two messages from Table 6.3 are, first, that India is a significant player in offshored ITES, accounting for 58 percent of IT services and 28 percent of BPO (business process outsourcing) services. That is the good news for India. It confirms our earlier discussion of the centrality of India to most ITES projects that are globally sourced. India is well ahead of any of its global peers in this respect.

The bad news is that the proportion of such services that are offshored is small—10 percent of IT services and 32 percent of BPO services; further (not shown here), the ratio remains unchanged since 2000.

This raises the questions as to why offshoring remains so small a share of ITES and, relevant for India, whether it implies a limit to the potential for offshoring.

Is there a limit to cost savings, a starting point for arguing why offshoring exists? Consider the following comparisons. As of 2011, a fresh undergraduate engineer from a top-tier Indian institution earned about $9,000 a year, including benefits, in India. In the United States, a fresh engineer's wage ranged from $42,000 to $65,000, exclusive of benefits. Neither figure is significantly different from a decade earlier. Incidentally, the comparable wage in China was $18,000.[11]

Hiring that engineer's services as part of a vendor's offerings, of course, likely costs more since the vendor may offer project management and maintenance services as well. The firm's revenue per employee is thus another way to compare cost differences. As of 2011, the revenue per employee of the Indian exporting IT sector, including R&D and product software exports as well as IT services, is $39,400 (NASSCOM 2011: 260, 263). By comparison, CSC, a large U.S.-based competitor with revenue of $16 billion in 2009, employed 91,000 persons, with revenue per employee of $176,000.[12] To get a sense of the trends, consider that the revenue per employee in India was $33,000 in 1999, while CSC's was $152,000.[13]

As these numbers indicate, the cost differences are substantial, about a 5:1 differential in labor costs and vendor costs—but, its stickiness indicates that it is an insufficient argument, or else, wage rates and revenue per employee would have converged over the past decade. On the contrary, the absolute wage differential increased.

Before we move to the reasons, we deal with a possible countervailing factor—supply of engineers. Conceivably, American labor supply may be dwindling relative to India-based supply. Despite the reality of migration and the availability of the H1-B visa, this, it may be argued, is the reason why American wages remain high: there are fewer and fewer workers in the United States.

However, this is not the case. As of May 2010, there were 3,178,030 in computer science-related occupations, including programmers, software engineers, and database and network specialists. As of May 1999, the comparable figure was 2,347,030, indicating a 35 percent increase between 1999 and 2010.[14] As of May 2010, the mean wage was $77,230, 40 percent above the mean wage in 1999, which was $54,930.

Further, all the large developed country service providers established large Indian offices. The second largest staff pool of the U.S. Big 6, as they are sometimes called, after the United States, is in India. CSC's India office, for example, employed 20,000 in 2010.[15]

Instead, it appears that Indian engineers do more of the lower-end work, evidenced by the share of Indian exports of software projects in lower-end work versus global proportions, as seen in Table 6.4. Note the continued concentration, though with some improvement, of the proportion of low-end work since 2000.

Though low value added relative to the other components, applications development and testing still require engineering skills. Most of these skills should be portable to higher-end work, such as system integration, design, and consulting. In addition, managing large development projects requires project management skills as well.

This, then, raises what we posit as the real puzzle of outsourcing ITES to India: its stability at the low end over the past decade with limited potential for change—despite possessing the skills to do so.

As the Wipro case study showed, skills—as defined by project management and technical skills—are inadequate to move up the value chain. Further, as noted earlier, the Indian firms' competitors among MNCs are not innovators. Keeping up with the latest technologies is as critical for them as it is for the Indian firms. While some strategies can be used by both types of firms—such as partnering with product firms—it is the ability to tap into professional networks that are locationally based in developed countries that appears to be a key difference.

Conclusion

This chapter studied the industrial organization of the Indian ITES sector. It showed that from its beginnings the industry was dominated by large firms. The large firms' importance grew from state policy that favored established firms for bank capital and, later, from reputation effects among foreign clients. Several technically skilled engineers returned to India from the developed world after their overseas education to play key roles in the large firms' growth.

The changes in clients' requirements due to the availability of new technologies and sectoral consolidation furthered the importance of large IT services vendors, both in the developed world and in India.

TABLE 6.4
INDIAN ITES FIRMS' SHARE OF COMPLEX WORK

2010	Design & Consulting	System Integration	Applications Development & Testing
Complexity	High	Medium	Low
Global Spending (%)	29	51	20
Indian exports (%)	4	19	77 (2000 = 88%)

Source: NASSCOM 2011: 260; NASSCOM various years: 29.

The sector as of 2011 faces an ongoing challenge of being innovative. In part, this is because innovation originates outside the services sector, even globally. It resides instead with small and large IT product firms, most of which are located in the developed world.

The large IT services firms, whether located in India or in the developed world, therefore rely on software product firms for innovation, through joint ventures. However, developed country IT services firms can and do access additional sources of learning that are largely unavailable to Indian IT services firms: engineers from product firms, independent professionals, and university researchers. The impact of lack of access could be significant: the share of low-end work done in India continues to be dominant, at 77 percent of revenue for the past decade, as a result.

Although these additional global networks of learning are still relatively inaccessible to Indian firms, learning does occur and the large Indian firms are accelerating the pace through setting up developed-country campuses. A case study in semiconductor design services illustrated how learning occurs and the importance of global networks of learning for keeping up to date.

I argued that in most countries' national systems of innovation, the role of the state is significant and that India was no different. From the mid-1980s onward, the state in India sought to help the Indian IT industry through fiscal incentives, incentives for FDI, and improved infrastructure.

Political developments were to play a significant role. Initially, the benefits were directed to locations that were politically close to the ruling party. Among these, two of the country's leading centers of educational excellence, Mumbai and Bangalore, were important beneficiaries. On the other hand, two other leading centers of educational excellence, Hyderabad and Chennai, lost out because their political leaders were in opposition to the ruling Congress party.

The regionalization of politics that occurred from 1991 helped the industry by helping to solve regional infrastructural imbalances in locations of high labor supply. Hyderabad and Chennai both emerged in the 1990s as IT clusters owing to the policies in education and infrastructure provision established by local politicians.

To the question posed in the title of this chapter—Has the Indian ITES sector emerged a decade after Y2K?—the answer is as follows: despite increasingly sophisticated skills and strategies, I found that the Indian ITES industry stabilized over the past decade at the low end of the global ITES industry, the high end being provided by developed-country firms. The promise of 1999 remains unfulfilled a decade later.

What can be done? As of 2011, this remains an open question. Perhaps a new industrial structure in India—one less controlled by large firms, for instance—might change this situation. Perhaps the educational system needs to improve. Until then, despite an environment consisting of adequate supplies of technical and managerial labor, infrastructure, and a supportive state, the impact of Indian IT on Western economies will likely continue to be limited.

Acknowledgments

The author would like to thank the Alfred P. Sloan Foundation for financial support, and the Berkeley Roundtable on the International Economy (BRIE) for research assistance.

Notes

1. The term "IT-enabled services" might not convey to the reader the range of services that are exported from India. They potentially include any service that can be delivered electronically using digital technologies. While, initially, the exports were confined to software programming and, later, call centers, since 2000, the range and depth of work have changed dramatically. The list now includes scientific R&D, financial services, market research, data-mining, and a host of other services. Largely, the services are located in the vertical-termed "professional, scientific and technical services."

2. Author's calculations for 1999–2009 of the Big 6 Indian IT companies.

3. The Big 6's market share was 36 percent in 2004; their revenue per employee was $42,873 for 2008 versus the Indian industry average of $36,000.

4. The conglomerates were not necessarily dissatisfied with this arrangement: it kept newcomers out and markets were guaranteed because output was restricted by licensing (Dossani 2007a).

5. Minoo Mody was to later lose out in a power struggle with Ratan Tata for control of the Tata Group. This was to affect the prospects of the Tata-Burroughs joint venture that he headed versus TCS. Retrieved December 21, 2009 (http://www.tata.com/media/reports/inside.aspx?artid=onWXO0FDn8M=), and author's interviews with Tata-Burroughs officials.

6. The top three firms, TCS, Infosys, and Wipro, rely on financial services for 40 percent of their revenue, as of 2010.

7. Retrieved December 27, 2009 (http://business.mapsofindia.com/epz/history.html).

8. Retrieved December 24, 2009 (http://www.expressindia.com/news/hyd-bang/fullstory.php?content_id=70540; http://www.financialexpress.com/news/mncs-flock-to-hyderabad-for-ites/68588/).The perils of such strategies must also be noted. One Hyderabad firm, Satyam Computers, which rose on the back of government patronage to become the fourth largest exporting firm, collapsed due to fraud in January 2009. The firm was subsequently sold to the Mahindra Group.

9. Note that the university in the Indian higher education system has a different meaning than in America. Indian universities are largely "affiliating" universities at the undergraduate level.

10. Retrieved September 6, 2011 (http://stat.wto.org/CountryProfile/WSDBCountryPFView.aspx?Language=E&Country=IN).

11. Retrieved September 6, 2011 (http://www.payscale.com/research/US/Job=Software_Engineer_/_Developer_/_Programmer/Salary).

12. The U.S. services industry's aggregate statistics are unavailable. However, a review of leading providers, IBM, Accenture, CSC, HP, ADP, and ACS, indicates a range of revenue per employee similar to that of CSC.

13. CSC in 1999 employed 50,000 persons and earned $7.6 billion in revenue. Retrieved September 6, 2001 (http://www.csc.com/investor_relations/ds/32578/34134-csc_annual_reports).

14. Retrieved December 25, 2009 (http://www.bls.gov/oes/2008/may/oes150000.htm), codes 15–1011/21/31/32/41/51/61/71/81, May 99; total 2,347,030, retrieved December 25, 2009, and September 6, 2011 (http://www.bls.gov/oes/1999/oes_15Co.htm).

15. Retrieved September 6, 2011 (http://en.wikipedia.org/wiki/CSC_India).

References

Athreye, S. (2005). "The Indian Software Industry." In *From Underdogs to Tigers: The Rise and Growth of the Software Industry in Brazil, China, India, Ireland and Israel*, edited by A. Arora and A. Gambardella, 7–40. Oxford: Oxford University Press.

Carnoy, M., and R. Dossani. (2011). Governance of higher education in India. Working Paper, Stanford University.

Dossani, R. (2007a). "Entrepreneurship: The True Story Behind Indian IT." In *Making IT: The Rise of Asia in High Tech*, edited by H. Rowen, M. Hancock, and W. Miller, 221–66. Stanford, CA: Stanford University Press.

Dossani, R. (2007b). *India Arriving*. New York: AMACOM Books.

Dossani, R., and M. Patibandla. (2010). "Technology and Educational Challenges in a Globalizing World—Case Study of India." In *The Handbook of Technology Management*, edited by H. Bidgoli, 845–861. Hoboken: John Wiley & Sons.

Heeks, R. (1996). *India's Software Industry*. New Delhi: Sage.

Jones, K. D., and T. Critchfield. (2008). "Consolidation in the U.S. Banking Industry." In *Handbook of Financial Intermediation and Banking*, edited by Anjan V. Thakor and W. A. Boot, 309–46. Amsterdam: Elsevier.

NASSCOM. (Various years). *The IT-BPO Sector in India: Strategic Review*. Delhi: National Association of Software and Services Companies.

Rubin, B. (1985). "Economic liberalization and the Indian state." *Third World Quarterly*, 7(4): 942–57.

Sharma, D. (2009). *The Long Revolution: The Birth and Growth of India's IT Industry*. New York: HarperCollins.

Steinmuller, W. (1996). "The U.S. Software Industry: An Analysis and Interpretive History." In *The International Computer Software Industry: A Comparative Study of Industry Evolution and Structure*, edited by D. Mowery. Oxford and New York: Oxford University Press.

7 The Dissolution of Sectors
DO POLITICS AND SECTORS STILL GO TOGETHER?
Mark Huberty

Introduction

The political economy literature has long used the concept of industrial sector as a way to aggregate business behavior, interests, and political preferences. The utility of sector as an analytic device depends on two implicit assumptions: (1) that its aggregation of firms and workers captures a fairly homogeneous set of ways in which value is derived from economic activity and (2) that the boundaries of aggregation are reasonably stable under the forces whose effects the analyst is trying to understand. Together, these assumptions allow the analyst to consider how exogenous economic or political developments affect behaviors inside sectors, and how these effects may change the way a sector understands its political interests. Implicitly, then, these assumptions suggest limits to the usefulness of sectoral analysis. In conditions where the value-creation mechanisms inside a sector, or the boundaries between sectors, are in flux, a sectoral analysis that assumes their stability will find it difficult to understand some political or economic behaviors.

I argue that many industries today are experiencing exactly this flux. The other chapters in this book discuss the political implications of increasing heterogeneity of value creation within sectors. This chapter addresses the impact of firm strategies that erode sectoral boundaries. The argument proceeds in five steps: (1) that firms are increasingly crossing sectoral boundaries to deploy integrated product-service strategies; (2) that these strategies tend to alter the value-creation mechanisms of the sectors they enter; (3) that as firms do so, they adopt political preferences consistent with these value-creation mechanisms; (4) that these preferences may not correspond to the settled preferences of the sectors they have entered; and (5) that the ensuing competition between different strategies and business models with different embedded political preferences disrupts the political bedrock on which old sectoral definitions rested, and in so doing reorders the political economy landscape. At the root of these evolving strategies is a series of general technological changes that are altering the value-creation mechanisms of long-standing industries (Zysman et al., Chapter 4, in this volume). Amidst these changes, a sectoral framework offers less purchase for understanding the resulting politics of economic value creation and competition. Sectors no longer necessarily aggregate a homogeneous set of economic actors within a set of stable boundaries. Rather, the political variable becomes the business models these strategies support. I argue that many industries today display the sectoral flux caused by this sequence of events, making sectoral analysis an imperfect tool for understanding the contemporary politics of economic and political change in the face of technological disruption.

This chapter proceeds as follows: I first describe how the model of sectoral boundaries emerges from the early writing on political economy. Case studies of Apple, Inc., Microsoft Corporation, Nokia, and Medtronic then demonstrate the limits of this model in an environment of sectoral flux. The music industry, and its late difficulties in adapting to digital content, shows sharp contrasts in the strategies pursued by Apple, Microsoft, Nokia, and the recording companies, each with different sets of political preferences even as they operate in the same sector. The entry of Medtronic, traditionally a medical devices firm, into the business of medical information collection, provides a study of a much different industry. There, Medtronic's preferences for regulation of private medical data contrast sharply with those of the other major gatherers of personal medical data—doctors, nurses, and clinical researchers.

These case studies suggest that though information technology (IT) played an important role in each of these cases, the disruption of sectoral politics is a general phenomenon, present in many different sectors throughout the economy. Thus the increased application of information and communications technology (ICT) in traditional sectors will play a disruptive role to patterns of interest formation and aggregation, translating the tension between emerging and long-standing modes of value creation into new "double-bind" dilemmas for policy makers.

Sectors in Political Economy

As an analytic tool, the sector has played an important role in the analysis of interest formation in industrial economies. Gourevitch (1987) argued that sectoral conflicts have formed the basis of economic policy making since the early industrial age. Maier (1975) has documented how the class politics of the pre-1914 industrial revolution became, through the 1920s, the sectoral politics of corporatism as the bourgeoisie struggled to contain the revolutionary tendencies of labor. He argues that the successful completion of this process of containment and institutionalization of labor-capital disputes in the various forms of corporatism, co-determination, and unionization in the postwar advanced industrial democracies brought sector politics to the fore (Maier, 1981).

These modern arguments continue an analytic tradition that dates to the establishment of political economy as a discipline. Adam Smith's notion of the division of labor implies a sectoral structure. Just as workers gain efficiencies through task specialization, so did firms gain efficiencies through specialization in production domains. The notion of sectors, if not explicitly stated, is there in Smith's pin factory: one sector for metallurgy, another for pin manufacture, another for textiles, and another for retail. As in the factory, so in the economy.

Ricardo (1996) also grounded his notion of sector on the basis of productivity. But where Smith saw only task specialization, Ricardo, writing a half-century later, also finds technology, such that advantages in trade and exchange derive from "the advantage of skill and machinery." Countries, it seems, are relatively more efficient at producing some goods than others. This "comparative advantage" creates the preconditions for trade. Comparative advantage applies to interfirm trade as well as intercountry trade. If one nation trades with another in order to reap the benefits of superior relative productivity derived from national assets in technology, geography, and knowledge, then so too would firms wish to trade on the basis of their comparative advantages.

Finally, modern analysts have debated whether this applies to services industries as well as goods. Baumol (1967) rejected the universality of the Ricardian idea of regular productivity growth through the application of machinery. Services, he argued, were usually administered by individuals with specialized knowledge, who had natural limits on the number of tasks they could perform. Swenson (1991a, 1991b) and Pontusson and Swenson (1996) have suggested several cases where the resulting differences in productivity led to sectoral politics trumping class politics, via cross-class coalitions of labor and capital in high-productivity industries opposing the preferences of lower-productivity sectors. But as the arguments in this book make clear, the development of ICT may have weakened this distinction.

The resultant narrowing of the productivity gap between sectors may provide incentives for firms to cross what formerly were seen as rigid sectoral boundaries. As firms cross these sectoral boundaries, three political possibilities emerge: they could adopt the preferences of the sector they are entering; they could bring with them the preferences of the sector from which they come; or they could adopt wholly new preferences. The standard definition of sectors—as firms that produce the same outputs and compete in the same markets—would suggest that the first would occur. If so, then blurring of sectoral boundaries within the firm will have little effect on the evolution of the political economy. If the last possibility pertains, however, the economy will see the weakening of established sectoral boundaries and their accompanying forms of contestation, replaced by new conflicts between new entrants and established players. The location and form of those conflicts will create new forms of political contestation.

The following sections explore the breakdown of sectoral boundaries and the politics that typically accompanied them. I first use the recent dynamics of the music industry to argue that integrated goods-services product strategies are blurring both the traditional sectoral separation of device makers and content makers and the politics of intellectual property protection that went with them. I then turn to a completely different industry, medical devices, to argue that these dynamics are not limited to the IT industry but in fact are present in very different sectors across the economy.

Digital Music and the Politics of Copyright Protection

THE MUSIC INDUSTRY IN AN ANALOG AGE

The music industry before the advent of digital technology provides a good example of a sectorally defined economic landscape. The modern industry consisted of two distinct but mutually dependent sectors: those that made and sold content and those that made and sold devices for playing content. The recording sector was principally concerned with identifying, developing, and promoting musical talent and distributing its output. The devices sector was principally concerned with much more technical problems: sound quality, portability, aesthetic design, and compatibility with related systems like televisions or speakers. The need for one sector's output to cooperate with the other's created the need for intersectoral standards, as with those created for long-play records or cassette tapes or compact discs. But as long as those standards were stable and uncontested, neither sector had much reason to interfere with the other. Technological developments induced changes in the structure of the content industry, through changing the costs of entry. But device manufacturers remained on the periphery of content production and distribution, and vice versa (Alexander 1994).

The political economy of the industry cleaved along these sectoral lines. Content was a product that depended on intellectual property rights for its value. The recording sector was thus a staunch protector of copyright legislation, and an aggressive prosecutor of copyright violations. In contrast, the devices sector built physical goods, whose value it protected through patent law, an entirely different intellectual property regime. The recording sector showed little concern for patent law. The devices sector limited its concern over copyright to the perpetuation of the fair use clause, codified in the 1976 Patent Act, which ensured that device makers could not be prosecuted if their customers used their devices for copyright violation.[1]

For this case, output-based sectoral distinctions make sense. Content and devices are obviously different finished products, require different skills to assemble and market, and display different factor intensities. Productivity of devices factories was subject to Ricardo's improvements in "skill and machinery." That of composers, performers, and producers fell under Baumol's purview. Likewise, sectors making content displayed different political priorities and interests than those making devices on which to play content. The requirements of production translated into different requirements of the legal and political system. Collaboration between the two took place in a contractual or standards-specification format, consistent with Coasean ideas of interfirm contracting, and by extension, sectoral boundaries. The patterns of economic behavior translated well into patterns of political behavior.

THE DIGITAL TRANSFORMATION OF FIRMS AND PRODUCT STRATEGIES

Analog music is rapidly becoming a thing of the past. Three developments in digital technology drove its disappearance. The introduction of the compact disc meant that, by the mid-1990s, most popular music was distributed in digital form.[2] Then, when personal computers for the consumer market became sophisticated enough to read from and write to CDs, it was possible to reproduce the content of master copies like commercially produced CDs rapidly and with little perceptible loss of quality. Finally, when online data transfer became commonplace, digital content that had been moved from one CD to another could now be made available online for instantaneous, costless reproduction.

This digital transformation led music device makers like Apple, Microsoft, and Nokia to enter the content markets directly. In doing so, they had to choose the business models and product strategies they would deploy. Three different versions are apparent. Apple's model derives most of its profit from the device, treating content as a necessary but perhaps not money-making service. Microsoft's initial model attempted to extract value from both devices and content services. Finally, Nokia's strategy uses content services to sell devices, as a means of differentiating their product in a crowded cellular market.

The digital transformation and the entry of new competitors with new strategies have thrown the recording industry's traditional business model into doubt. In the old music industry, the main source of value lay in the ownership of monopoly rights to music. Recording companies secured preferential access to these rights by establishing elaborate and expensive production, marketing, distribution, and sales channels. Musicians wishing to access these channels faced a choice of either signing over the rights to their musical creations to the recording companies on very generous terms or else being shut out of the most lucrative markets. In turn, the recording companies charged monopoly prices for the music they controlled, and they are alleged to have colluded to keep these prices high (Deutsch 2002).

Digital technologies meant the end of monopoly restriction on music supply. The volume of music that became available quickly eroded a profit model based on its uniqueness. That volume simultaneously generated a consumer demand for products to help store, manage, and use this new oversupply of music. The devices sector was uniquely positioned to respond to this demand, with integrated hardware-software-content suites that seamlessly managed content across multiple platforms—computers, music players, and even phones. The digital revolution, then, shifted the central point of the music market away from the copyright owners that had dominated it to the firms that could deliver means of organizing the vast quantity of content now freely (if perhaps illegally) available.

The shift in value creation has disrupted sectoral interests around intellectual property. The business models deployed by the device makers embed very different preferences for copyright protection, with potentially very different effects for the viability of a recording industry business model based on the sanctity of copyright. Even though Apple, Microsoft, and Nokia all adopted strategies as music distributors, only one of their models, which Microsoft experimented with only briefly, is fully compatible with the legacy recording industry's set of preferences. As I will show, the ensuing competition for users became a competition over preferences, even as the firms offered similar products in the same market.

This development is difficult to understand under the old model of sectoral politics. Goods firms have decided to enter services markets; they have adopted preferences different from each others' and from those of firms already present in those markets; and they have competed not just on the superficial qualities of their products but also on the political preferences embedded in those products. None of these developments would be expected under sectoral models, either those of a productivity-driven or product-driven cleavage.

Apple

Apple's music strategy derives value from devices, not from music. In 2009, Apple, Inc. earned 42 percent of its revenue from computer sales, 46 percent from sales of a music device or music-capable phone (the iPod and iPhone), and 12 percent from various music-related services including music sales through its iTunes Music Store (iTMS).[3] Responding to the digital transformation discussed above, its product strategy emphasizes the seamless integration of several different products and services. Music bought on iTMS is loaded seamlessly into the iTunes music software provided with every computer Apple sells. These computers in turn integrate seamlessly with the music libraries stored and played on the iPod music player. iPod ownership has become a point of entry for purchase of Macintosh computers and iTunes music, and vice versa.[4]

These products are not, however, modular outside the Apple suite: iTunes will not integrate with most other competing music players. Likewise, much iTMS music cannot be played on any other music software than iTunes, due to proprietary copyright protection. Thus Apple's product strategy emphasizes the integration of content and hardware across multiple proprietary platforms, a services channel for content distribution, and a proprietary system of interlinkages. Value is created not just via any one element of this system but from the system itself, with the device at its center. This is fundamentally different from the predigital behavior of the music industry, where content and devices were linked through open standards and the value model for each was distinct. It is also highly successful: Apple commands 70 percent or so of the digital music player market.

The iPod/iTunes suite came embedded with a bifurcated set of copyright preferences. On the one hand, users could load anything they wished from their own collections; on the other, music purchased through iTMS came with heavy copyright restrictions. This inconsistency reflects the origins of the iPod's success and the market power that it gave Apple to establish a new model for digital music sales. The rapid expansion of illegal music piracy gave Apple a hook into establishing an online music distribution channel—something which the recording companies had been slow to do. In effect, the debut of the iPod and its open-format design helped cement the dominance of unsecured music formats and supported the already large trade in illegally copied music. These twin developments helped create the willingness by the recording companies to try to capture some of that lost revenue via a more secure online distribution channel that Apple itself was well-positioned to create. That Apple held the power in this partnership is apparent in the technical details of the copyright protection mechanisms used by iTMS.[5]

In entering the music distribution and sales sector, then, Apple did not adopt the copyright preferences of the recording firms that traditionally dominated that sector. The iPod device has minimal copyright protection for content not obtained through iTMS. The success of the iPod, moreover, has been symbiotic with the rapid growth in music piracy, the cost of which the recording industry has estimated in the billions of dollars annually. Indeed, Apple estimates that only a tiny fraction of the capacity of the millions of iPods sold to date is taken up by legally acquired digital music (Jobs 2008). The company has done little to modify its devices to prevent their use with illegally copied content. Music sold through iTMS has stricter limits on copying and sharing, as required by the recording industry. But former Apple CEO Steve Jobs openly called these copyright protections bad for consumers, and he indicated that he would prefer to be rid of them. Finally, this open opposition to copyright protection has not prevented Apple from partnering with a recording industry heavily damaged by the piracy that the iTunes suite implicitly tolerates.

These copyright preferences are also inconsistent with the industry from which Apple originates. In its computer software and hardware business, Apple is notoriously protective of the proprietary nature of its software and hardware, to the point of refusing to license the designs to either and actively prosecuting firms that attempt to reverse-engineer core Apple products to run on non-Apple platforms. In the trifecta of possibilities for preference adoption, then, Apple neither adopted the old preferences of the sector it entered nor brought its own preferences with it. Rather, wholly new preferences accompanied a wholly new product strategy.

Thus the sectoral analysis misses some key details for a company like Apple. It has entered the music distribution and sales sector with products that compete with traditional physical means of distributing content. But it has not adopted the same preferences as other firms in that sector, or even of its partners on which it depends for content.

Classic sectoral boundaries fail to capture the dynamics of Apple's behavior in the modern music industry. Its output cannot easily be separated into content and devices. The copyright preferences embedded in that output do not correspond well with either its positions on copyright in its own sector or with those of the sector it has entered.

Microsoft

In contrast to Apple, Microsoft's initial strategy for music distribution and sales sought to make money from the music itself as well as the device. It thus tracked much closer to the preferences of the sector it was entering. In 2006, it introduced a media player (the Zune), an online content distribution channel (Zune Marketplace), and a set of software for managing content on the user's personal computer. Zune Marketplace launched with 2 million songs, from many of the same recording companies that supplied content to Apple's iTMS. The Zune product group had other features that Apple did not, including integration of Zune Marketplace with the preexisting media marketplace supporting Microsoft's successful XBox game console, the ability to share media wirelessly with other Zune users, a larger screen for viewing movies, and a music subscription alternative to per-song purchasing. Zune also took advantage of Microsoft's large installed Windows user base, which had traditionally been a source of strength for other Microsoft product lines. Early reviewers thought that this collection of advantages and additional features would make the Zune a formidable competitor to the iPod (Elgan 2006).

Unlike Apple's iPod, however, the Zune suite also embedded a set of preferences about copyright enforcement more closely resembling those of the recording industry. Zune's wireless song-sharing capability was initially launched with a "three plays or three days" limitation: users could share music with other Zune owners, but only for three days of use or three plays. That limit applied not only to content purchased through the Zune marketplace but in fact all content stored on the device. In fact, the Digital Rights Management (DRM) was built into hardware, not software, and thus treated all content as potentially suspect. Users saw this as an attempt to impose rigorous copy protection on a wide variety of content regardless of whether or not it was illegally obtained.[6]

The Zune Marketplace subscription service initially showed much closer attention to copyright concerns. Users could purchase flat-rate monthly subscriptions allowing unlimited media download. But that content remained usable as long as the user renewed his or her subscription. When the subscription lapsed, the user lost all use of the media he or she had downloaded. The reasons for such a design appear straightforward: it guaranteed an ongoing revenue stream for both Microsoft and the recording companies; it prevented consumers from using a one-month subscription to download massive amounts of material for perpetual use; and it protected the value of the recording industry's intellectual property. But users responded negatively to the idea that they would retain absolutely no rights to music they viewed as paid for, should they ever decide to end their subscription. They also thought the DRM restrictions violated what they saw as legitimate fair use rights. Thus while users liked the idea of a subscription-based option, which iTunes did not offer, this emphasis on copyright enforcement over usability appears to have diluted the attractiveness of Microsoft's offering.

Finally, Microsoft revealed that a portion of revenue from each Zune sold was forwarded to Universal Studios, whose content was sold on Zune Marketplace. This "Zune Tax" appeared to assume that the devices would be used for illegal content, and that therefore users should pay an up-front cost to the recording companies to offset their losses. This presumption of guilt appears not to have been well-received by consumers (Leeds 2006).

This internal technical orientation toward greater embedded copy protection appeared to correspond with its public positions. While he was still involved in day-to-day operations, William H. Gates III made no public statement on par with that of Steve Jobs's open letter of 2007. Gates had apparently made statements in interviews to the effect that DRM as currently structured does not work, imposes too high a cost on users, and constrains fair use. But he followed these comments with indications that he envisioned a different kind of DRM, not the end of DRM altogether.[7]

In time, however, it appears that Microsoft has converged on a position closer to that of Apple.[8] To the extent that differences remain, such as the different DRM provisions in the Apple and Microsoft operating systems, these differences reflect different technology design decisions rather than different political orientations. For instance, Windows Vista deployed elaborate DRM protections largely in order to comply with the licensing requirements for supporting high-definition DVD content, a feature that Apple does not support in OS X. Meanwhile, the copyright terms offered by Apple and Microsoft for iTMS and Zune Store sales are broadly similar. Both remain quite different from the preferences of the recording industry, in large part because of differences in the mode of value creation.

Thus Microsoft, in its initial entry to the consumer digital media market, behaved much more like the firms in the sector it was entering than Apple did. Its product-services strategy attempted to maintain the value of copyrighted material. It thus paid attention to digital rights management and assigned a higher value to protecting media against copying than to deploying a seamless goods-services market strategy. It also took steps to tie its business model to that of the recording companies, via revenue-sharing from device sales. In time, however, the positions of the two firms appear to have converged around a business model that presents serious challenges to the copyright preferences of the recording firms.

Nokia

Finally, in contrast to both Apple and Microsoft, Nokia pursued a business model that used a music distribution service to create demand for its device but did not provide a revenue source *per se*. This reflects its origins in telecommunications, where similar strategies have become commonplace. Starting in 2007, Nokia began to introduce a new music subscription service in Europe called "Comes with Music." The service had a very different business model: purchase of a Comes with Music-enabled device gave the user twelve months of unlimited music downloads from Nokia's store (Nokia 2009). Once downloaded, music can be freely transferred to digital music players or computers. Users do not lose access to downloaded music if their subscription expires. Nokia's strategy emphasizes unlimited music access, in contrast to the monopoly provision of content preferred by the recording industry.

The revenue model for Nokia and the telecommunications firms is familiar. Nokia profits from device sales; the music service makes its devices more attractive to users who might otherwise choose an iTunes-enabled iPhone or other device. The telecommunications firms profit from bandwidth sales, which increase as the demand for network-provided services like streaming music increase. Both Nokia and its telecommunications collaborators benefit from the use of services to differentiate their product from competitors.

But the unlimited-use subscription model represents a radical break with the music industry's royalty-per-song compensation model. It also breaks the differential pricing for albums versus individual songs, and differential pricing for new or popular or niche music. In this model, all music is created equal. In contrast, iTMS and the Zune Store continue to maintain differentiated pricing for new music sales based on these and other factors. The commodification of content represented by Nokia's generic subscription model, if it persists, will mark a sea change in the range of legitimate business models for music distribution, one which is much less reliant on the monopoly control of content.

It remains unclear how Nokia and the recording firms worked out compensation from device and bandwidth sales (Lindvall 2008). But clearly the intellectual property embedded in a single piece of music is, in this model, derivative of the device and the service itself, rather than of the recording-distribution framework traditionally provided by the recording companies. This represents a very different model than even the iPod or Zune: commodified content, shorn of market power, becomes a loss-leader service for the sale of hardware devices.

Nokia thus brought with it from telecommunications a model that used services as incentives to sell devices in a crowded and highly competitive market. This model is quite different from that of Apple, which invented a new business model as it created a market for digital media players; and from that of Microsoft, as it entered that market. Where Apple's business model expressed a set of political preferences distinct from both the sector it left and the sector it entered, and Microsoft's model attempted to reconcile the two, Nokia clearly tried to export the model that had proven successful in the cellular market in the past.

COMPETITION AND ITS CONSEQUENCES

The ensuing competition between Microsoft, Apple, and Nokia thus was not merely among similar product suites (devices and content services) against a backdrop of stable preferences. Rather, it was a competition of product strategies and their embedded preferences about copyright protection and copyright enforcement. Apple and Microsoft converged on a model that embedded a very favorable reading of the fair use clause for third-party content, but which took pains to lock down content sold via their own online services. Nokia, in contrast, appears to have had little regard for the ongoing differentiation of music content and instead treated it like a commodity whose presence was merely one factor in driving hardware sales and cell phone adoption. Market choices about product suite thus became choices about politics as well.

Moreover, these choices were made in a situation where all companies were in strict compliance with the law. Whatever Steve Jobs's statements on digital rights management, iTMS continues to either sell copy-protected content or, with the permission of content providers, charge a premium for DRM-free content. Microsoft maintains that its copyright protection measures have little effect on legally obtained content. Nokia's unlimited music service is not a Napster-like free-for-all. None of these companies are breaking the law. Rather, each has adopted different preferences that improvise on a set of legal and political outcomes of an earlier analog era. Up for grabs is the question of how those outcomes will be interpreted for the digital era of the future.

Attempts by the recording industry to direct this improvisation were largely unsuccessful. In 1998, 200 recording companies and devices firms launched the Secure Digital Music Initiative (SDMI) to establish a competing format to the open, unsecured MP3 format. By 2001, it was a defunct organization, and the SDMI format was nonexistent. Analyst Eric Schreier argued that the SDMI represented an attempt by the recording sector to align the interests of device makers with its own interests in rigid copyright protections. In exchange for building very secure devices, the device makers would get access to the recording sector firms' music libraries (Schreier 1999). But the market got away from the recording industry. By 2001, the success of Napster and other file-sharing services had made MP3 the *de facto* standard. Devices firms, seeing a huge market for integrated consumer electronics products, were loath to adopt a new format and configure their devices to gradually phase it in and exclude a large established base of content. Negotiations between the two sectors, which in the past had collaborated successfully on standards definition, fell apart.[9] Instead, these firms chose in favor of freedom in adopting product-service strategies, and in favor of market competition to work out the preferences landscape of the future.

The apparent victory of Apple's business model, which creates value largely through device sales and is agnostic about copyright protection, left the recording industry vulnerable. It has had no success building distribution channels on its own, and so must rely on the device makers and their integrated product strategies. Apple's integrated delivery chain has sold over 2 billion legal, copy-protected songs since its inception in 2003, generating approximately that much revenue in dollars, of which it appears the recording industry receives about 70 percent (Leeds 2005). But the industry continues to lose income from ongoing music piracy enabled in part by the work of those devices firms, losses not made up by online distribution channels. It has not attempted to restrict device capabilities, possibly for fear of alienating the devices firms that manage the only legitimate digital distribution channels.[10] Thus, despite its slipping hold on the most lucrative part of the music business, the recording industry has decided to fight copyright protection only at the consumer level,[11] not at the device level, a fight it appears to be losing.[12] The industry's discomfort with its position may explain why it felt it had to sign on to a distribution channel like Nokia's, despite the commodification of intellectual property that it implies.

Of course, the market's reception of different devices may have little to do with consumers' perception of the differences in copyright protection between Apple, Microsoft, and Nokia. Quality of services, quality of industrial design, usability, and myriad other factors no doubt influenced consumers' choice for the iPod over the Zune. But this is a separate issue from the main argument about the decomposition of sectoral preferences. If firms were competing on these factors alone, with devices that embedded identical copyright protection preferences, then the sectoral boundaries would be clearer. But this is clearly not what has occurred. Microsoft's initial attempts to balance copyright and openness looked very different from Apple's. Apple's copyright agnosticism horrifies the recording industry. Nokia's subscription model is in some ways *more* subversive than Apple's, treating as it does music as a bulk commodity. All three are competing in the market, and the consequences of that competition will determine not only market share but also the politics of copyright in the future. That market outcomes are shaped by factors besides copyright protection does not change the dynamics of shifting preferences, improvisation, and market competition over political outcomes.

Thus, in entering the music distribution sector, Apple, Microsoft, and Nokia all adopted product-service suites. But each represented different preferences on intellectual property and copyright law that were distinct from each other and from the sector they were entering. Apple sought value through its device by making it open to content regardless of copyright; Microsoft initially attempted to balance openness and copyright protection; and Nokia has adopted a business model that turns copyright on its head. Common products offered in common markets—heretofore called a sector—did not imply common political preferences. As business models shifted the location of value creation away from copyrighted content and toward the seamless integration of content and devices, these firms adopted political preferences consistent with the business model, not the economic sector. Technological change drove business model changes that fragmented traditional sectors. In this context, the sector as a unit of analysis breaks down.

Beyond IT: Medical Devices and the Politics of Privacy

The case of the music industry suggests three things: (1) that major firms are adopting integrated goods-services product strategies to pursue new markets; (2) that such strategies aren't merely one-off curiosities but in fact are central to establishing and maintaining market position; and (3) that these strategies may require the adoption of political preferences inconsistent with a sectoral model of political cleavages. Nevertheless, it could be argued that the IT industry bears little resemblance to the rest of the economy. Its products are knowledge-rich, enjoy declining cost curves, can often be moved almost costlessly across large distances, and employ a common set of generic technological innovations (silicon chips, display screens, radio-frequency transmitters) to deliver a vast set of products.[13] Many industries don't enjoy these features. If these features are the determining factor for delivery of integrated product strategies, then the blurring of sectoral lines may be unique to those industries proximate to IT.

I argue that the blurring of sectoral distinctions is in fact a more general phenomenon. To demonstrate this point, the following subsection outlines the case of a medical devices company, Medtronic. Medical devices are very different from consumer software: they are physical goods which result from complex engineering; they often require labor-intensive final assembly; they face significant regulatory and compliance costs in major markets like the United States and Europe due to rigorous clinical testing and approval processes; they do not have zero-marginal-cost mass production; and, as devices, face expensive and location-contingent installation costs, as with the surgical implantation of pacemakers. Despite these differences, device makers like Medtronic have begun to adopt integrated product-service strategies. With these strategies have come new political preferences that don't correspond well with those of the sectors they have entered.

MEDTRONIC AND REMOTE DELIVERY OF MEDICAL SERVICES

Medtronic has long been a major player in the medical devices field. It presently markets many different varieties of pacemakers, blood sugar monitoring devices, ophthalmic surgery implements, remotely controlled surgery robots, and neurostimulators. These devices have traditionally put Medtronic squarely in the goods-production sector of the medical devices delivery process. It designed, manufactured, and distributed devices, but the final installation of devices in patients and the monitoring of those patients was controlled by the medical profession. The responsibility for gathering data necessary for doctors and nurses to detect, diagnose, and treat the various ailments for which the devices were designed—for instance, heart arrhythmia—was collected by the medical personnel themselves. Medtronic's responsibility for the device was limited to its mechanical functioning.

These distinctions fit well with the older sectoral divisions between goods and services. High-value manufacturing, amenable to mass production methods, occupied the attentions of one set of firms, Medtronic among them. Low-productivity services such as surgery or nursing care were taken care of by a different set of firms. Cooperation between the two sectors was, of course, necessary, both for the devices firms to receive feedback on their products and for the doctors and nurses to correctly install and administer them. But little crossover business existed between the two sectors.

In 2001, Medtronic launched the first version of a service known as Carelink.[14] It consisted of two parts: medical devices that, in addition to performing their primary function, could store and transmit data about the health of the patient they were implanted in or used by, and a service that aggregated that data and made it available remotely to that patient's doctors and nurses. It was a move to an integrated product strategy: the device data was inaccessible without Carelink, and Carelink was useless unless patients were using Medtronic devices. As with Apple's introduction of a platform that integrated content acquisition, storage, and use, Carelink was compatible with a diverse set of medical devices, and was in some cases retroactively compatible with earlier versions of Medtronic devices already in use. As a product, Carelink operated with one major goal in mind: to allow the regular remote monitoring of many patients by a few doctors, at costs much smaller than those of frequent office visits; and to thereby improve patient health via faster and more accurate diagnoses of adverse health events for patients suffering from chronic health problems like heart failure or diabetes. The ongoing provision of the data-gathering and distribution service constituted a new revenue stream for Medtronic.

As with Apple and iTunes, Carelink marked Medtronic's move into a different sector. Now it overlapped with the traditional medical information-gathering role of the medical profession. What doctors and nurses traditionally had read off of charts and monitors in a hospital, Medtronic could now read remotely via wire leads and telecommunications. A sectoral model might suggest that political interests would track with these similar economic processes. But in fact that is not the case.

One issue in particular stands out. Carelink made Medtronic the middleman in the handling of vast amounts of patient medical information, just as such information was coming under heavy regulation to protect patient privacy. At Carelink's 2001 launch, the U.S. Department of Health and Human Services was in the final stages of issuing the medical privacy regulations mandated by the 1996 Health Insurance Portability and Accountability Act (HIPAA). Compliance with other aspects of HIPAA had generated substantial compliance costs for health insurers, health care providers, and clinical researchers, mostly around major changes needed in patient identification and data protection. Compliance with the privacy regulations was expected to generate similar costs. All three groups, while agreeing in concept to the idea that patient privacy should be protected, objected to what they viewed as excessive compliance costs.[15]

Medtronic, in contrast, appears to have little objection to the HIPAA privacy regulations that govern the use of the data it collects via Carelink. In fact, Medtronic cites its compliance with these regulations as a selling point for its devices and services.[16] In an environment where patients have become concerned about improper or unauthorized use of personal medical information, Medtronic has adopted HIPAA compliance as proof of its reliability and trustworthiness as a data handler.

Thus, just as Apple entered the music content distribution sector but adopted political positions opposed to established players in that sector, so it appears that Medtronic has adopted positions at odds with other groups that collect, analyze, and use health data. That said, there may be many reasons for Medtronic's deviation from its competitors, which have little to do with sectoral decomposition. First, Carelink was not launched until 2001, five years after the authorizing HIPAA legislation passed. Medtronic thus may have faced a settled regulatory landscape that it had little chance of changing. Second, Medtronic was building Carelink as a new service and thus could build in HIPAA compliance from the foundations up; its counterparts faced the onerous task of retrofitting existing systems and business processes. Thus Medtronic's compliance costs may have been far lower. Finally, Medtronic's exposure to patient health data is limited: it collects data, processes them, and transmits them. The number of human beings interacting with the data along the way is limited. Thus, very few unique business processes or systems interfaces had to be built. It was instead a problem of bulk data privacy protection. Most of the compliance issues for the Carelink system remained with the health care providers who interacted with individual patient files.

Evidence from the development of Carelink suggests that these competing possibilities cannot explain Medtronic's decision to adopt different attitudes toward health privacy legislation. While Carelink was launched in 2001, the final HIPAA privacy regulations were not issued until 2003, leaving Medtronic ample time to object to anything in the rule-making process. Furthermore, Medtronic would have had Carelink in development for several years prior to 2001, which would have made it sensitive to the cost and uncertainty of a large new rule-making process. Finally, though Medtronic's exposure to the details of patient data was limited compared to that of a doctor or nurse, that exposure was much broader. Carelink currently processes data for at least 225,000 patients, far more than any doctor would see in a year. Mishandling patient data could expose Medtronic to large class action lawsuits, as has occurred with other cases of loss or inadvertent release of confidential information.

With these caveats, however, the value-creation paradigm, invoked to explain the conflicting preferences of Apple and the rest of the music industry, fits the politics of medical devices as well. For medical professionals, patient data have no intrinsic value of their own. Doctors aren't paid to collect data. Rather, the medical profession creates value by using its specialized knowledge to turn data into diagnoses and treatments. Regulation of that data, to the extent that it complicates or makes more expensive the process of diagnosis and treatment, runs contrary to their interests as both stewards of patient health and economic actors. In comparison, all the value of Medtronic's Carelink system is contained in the data themselves. Medtronic's supply of data is predicated on patients' confidence that the data will be handled well. Where the medical profession treats the HIPAA data privacy regulations as an interference in its value-creating process, Medtronic sees a regulatory framework that will help guarantee it a supply of valuable data. As with the music industry, an integrated product-service strategy has changed the location of value in a given business process. In doing so, it has created political interests that do not follow sectoral boundaries.

Broader Implications

I've argued that technological change has weakened the sectoral model's utility for understanding political preferences, even within long-standing sectors. Both its foundational elements are eroding: a heterogeneous set of firms now deliver goods and services in a diverse set of ways, within a constantly shifting set of boundaries. Firm competition increasingly occurs on the basis of integrated product-service strategies embedding both differences in product design and political preferences. The competition between Apple and Microsoft for market share in the digital music market is a competition not just over the merits of the iPod or the Zune but over the copyright protection preferences embedded in each. The case of Medtronic suggests that these phenomena are not limited to the IT industry alone.

Amidst such change, the concept of a sector, as a rubric for categorizing firms by firm output, no longer accurately aggregates modes of economic value creation. The boundaries of aggregation are unstable, and the aggregated firms are not homogeneous. By extension, it also no longer suffices as an analytic device to identify and aggregate coherent interest groups. Both the recording companies and the devices firms maintain music distribution and sales channels. But as I have shown, intersection of output—in this case music distribution and sales services—no longer means intersection of political interests. One group of firms remains wholly dependent on value derived from monopoly pricing of copyrighted material. The other uses the sales and distribution channel as one part of an integrated product strategy that relies in large part on openness to a large variety of content, copyrighted and otherwise. Despite common output, the first group remains dedicated to copyright protections while the second is at best ambivalent. Common output is thus no longer a sufficient classificatory variable, as it ignores where the value in that output lies. Likewise, Medtronic has deployed a goods-services strategy that attaches real value to the process of medical data collection. Regulation that protects that value is acceptable, even as it is unacceptable to the traditional data gatherers in the medical profession.

These cases are not unique. In fact, it is part of a larger transformation of political economy, what Zysman (2004) and Kushida and Zysman (2009) have called the Fourth Services Transformation. Similar arguments between content producers and content organizers over issues of reproduction and distribution can be seen in the print industry (between Google Books and the publishing industry), and in the news industry (between online news search engines and the individual publishers) (Helm 2005; New York Times Staff, 2007).

Watson (Chapter 5, in this volume) shows that this process of intrasectoral fracturing has also occurred in the very different retail sector, which he argues is now poised to undergo the *second* wave of dissolution. Thirty years ago, digitization of inventory control through the use of barcodes set in progress a first wave of disruption whereby large retailers, in different ways across countries, established durable competitive advantages over smaller competitors. Now those large retailers, having mastered the command of ICT-driven supply chains, face a new wave of threats from the incorporation of huge new information flows from e-commerce, RFID (Radio Frequency Identification) tagging, and other technologies that may threaten their own dominant position and lead to divergent preferences between giant retailers like Walmart and Amazon.

Other forms of innovation—such as the synthesis of third-world human capital development, managerial improvement, and communications technology that culminated in the outsourcing phenomenon—have done the same, by separating the production of goods (whether shoes or computer hardware) from value-added services (engineering or design or marketing), thus changing the structure of value-generating economic activity and associated interest in national economies (Kaplinsky 2004; Schulze-Cleven, Watson, and Zysman 2007).

Nevertheless, the phenomena observed in the cases explored here clearly don't appear everywhere. The American auto industry, or the global steel industry, shows few signs of the kinds of transformation overtaking the music or medical industries. What determines whether a sector is experiencing this flux? The examples here were all susceptible to the application of IT services to tasks typically performed by humans—music retail and collection of patient medical information. Digitization of these services created substantial value added for first-mover companies and became part of integrated strategies. But other industries appear less vulnerable. Steelmaking would seem mostly to still concentrate on physical goods. The auto industry has experimented with add-ons like navigation services, and cars today are more computerized than ever before, but what services have been built on these platforms appear to be largely optional rather than integrated in the fashion of the iTunes-iPod suite or Carelink.

The character of these cases suggests several possible explanations for their different susceptibility to digital services-led change. First, those industries that deal most closely with information appear most open to infiltration by digital services. The music industry had used encoded information since Thomas Edison invented the record player. Digital services required developments in technology but not in concept. Medical devices had long transmitted data to various monitors in the exam room. Lengthening the cable connecting patient to monitor was a problem of aggregation and transmission. In contrast, cars or steel beams are less obviously data devices.

Second, since digital services typically involve large amounts of protected data—copy protected music, personal medical information—the existence of a regulatory regime for that information (even one that, as in the music case, is under dispute) may provide sufficient protection for companies entering new sectors, and the consumers affected by those moves. The automobile industry may wish to record detailed information on individuals' driving patterns. It could provide a range of services to help them drive more safely, maintain their cars better, or entertain their children on road trips. But what regulatory regime could Ford or its customers refer to that would provide guidance on what either party might do with that data? Medtronic could refer to HIPAA for proof of its privacy *bona fides*; Ford has no such option. Concerns on privacy abound. Could, for instance, owners be cited or fined for neglecting their brakes? Should Ford detect when an owner needs new tires and have Goodyear contact him or her? What of actual traffic violations? Without the regime to delineate the responsibilities of both companies and consumers, companies may be reluctant to deploy services even when they could.

Finally, it may be the case that industries currently deploying integrated strategies are those that already have higher services content in their home sector. The advent of East Asian computer plants and microprocessor fabs means that Apple today is mostly an engineering and industrial design company. Much the same is true of Medtronic. Firms in which services already form a great part of the core competency—even if in service of the creation of a physical product—may find the managerial transition to supporting pure services easier than firms like Ford that still focus on physical manufacturing plants. These limits may, in time, be pushed. When this happens, the same kinds of forces presently affecting the music and medical sectors may come into play in autos or steelmaking. There's no reason to expect the effects to be any less disruptive.

To return to where this chapter started, it should by now be clear that integrated product-service strategies, often based on digital technology, are reclaiming for Ricardo what Baumol took away. Apple's iTunes retail establishment is vastly more efficient in selling inventory than is a record store. Medtronic's Carelink data service collects, aggregates, and summarizes data from thousands of patients much faster than a team of medical professionals could, and without the added costs and potential complications of hospital visits. These are real productivity gains that couple skill with machinery for the improved efficiency of services.

These productivity gains, however, have come with costs. The sectoral tensions outlined here challenge the state with intrasectoral rifts across what this book has called the double bind. Growing new industries fueled by ICT promise new forms of wealth creation. But as ICT has entered traditional service sectors like music and medicine, it also threatens to create significant losers who press the state with claims that are not compatible with many aspects of the ICT revolution. The recording industry has found that producers and composers work only so fast, even with new technology, and that protecting their wages (and, perhaps more important, the wages of the agents and producers) requires some kind of monopoly rents that digital technology has put under assault. Doctors and nurses may soon find that the introduction of services like Carelink has unpleasant effects on their own wages. If one nurse can, with the aid of Carelink, monitor the health of several times as many patients as he or she could otherwise, presumably the demand for nurses will slacken, and wages with it. Or perhaps the hospitals will simply offshore the entire operation, as they have begun to do with radiology. As Ricardo noted, "I am convinced that the substitution of machinery for human labor is often very injurious to the interest of the class of laborers" (1996: 270). Not all services appear equally subject to the productivity gains possible through the application of digital technology to services. The boundaries of the gains mark new boundaries of political contestation, even if they no longer delineate industrial sectors with unique outputs.[17]

Conclusions

We thus have a different industrial landscape before us. Technological change has enabled a wide range of companies in different sectors to deploy integrated goods-services product strategies and business models. Those strategies embed particular political preferences that are tightly linked to the firms' conceptions of how value is best created in the market. The ensuing competition between firms thus also becomes a competition between preferences. In this situation, sectors as an analytical unit may fail to give much purchase on the political economy of industrial competition and change. They represent neither a stable set of market boundaries nor aggregate firms with homogenous interests and preferences.

Finally, this process of change clearly contributes to the "double bind" facing state policy makers. Do they, on the one hand, embrace changing modes of value creation that promise entirely new sets of goods and services, and potentially new sources of employment and productivity growth? Or, in the face of a range of other threats to economic prosperity, do they act to buffer existing, successful business models from these changes? With firm preferences inside sectors fragmenting, policy makers no longer receive clear signals as to how to approach economic policy making in a diverse range of industrial domains. Thus sectoral dissolution simultaneously creates conflicting demands on policy makers and confuses the inputs they receive on how best to respond.

The decomposition of economic sectors amidst this competition between business models therefore suggests that political economy pay closer attention to the dynamics of competition between firms rather than sectors, to better understand where the new boundaries of sector and political cleavage will emerge. I have suggested in this chapter that it is possible to do so, to make reasonable predictions about how these competitive processes play out, and to see the consequences for the political and regulatory system. More work to establish how this process affects a broader set of industries will add to our understanding of where and how technological change and sectoral decomposition go together, and with what effects.

Acknowledgments

The author wishes to thank the Alfred P. Sloan Foundation for financial support and the Berkeley Roundtable on the International Economy (BRIE) for research and administrative support. Many thanks to Dan Breznitz, Kenji Kushida, Jonathan Murray, Bart Watson, John Zysman, and unnamed individuals at Microsoft Corporation for their helpful comments and insights. All errors remain my own.

Notes

1. The history of a related industry turns on this distinction. The early years of home video recording systems witnessed an important lawsuit by Universal Studios against Sony Corporation over its Betamax product. Universal alleged that since Betamax could be used to make high-quality copies of copyright-protected media, it was facilitating crime and should therefore be declared illegal. The court ruled against the motion picture industry on the grounds that illicit copying was only one of many possible uses, and that Sony was not liable for the behaviors of its customers after their purchase of its products. Since then, of course, home video rentals and sales have become a lucrative business for the motion picture industry, suggesting their initial paranoia was unjustified. For a discussion of the history of the jurisprudence of the case, see Lloyd and Mayeda (1986–87).

2. In 1990, the dollar value of shipped media was nearly equal for CDs and cassette tapes. Eight years later, the dollar value of shipped CDs was eight times that of cassettes. See *Yearend Statistics* (1999).

3. In 2007, Apple, Inc. earned 49 percent of its revenue from computer sales, 39.5 percent from sales of a music device or music-capable phone (the iPod and iPhone), and 12 percent from various music-related services including music sales through iTMS. As of 2009, these figures were 42 percent from computer sales; 46 percent from iPod/iPhone sales, and 12 percent from iTMS. See Apple, Inc. (2007, 2008, 2009).

4. Apple's iPod strategy has persisted to its entry into the telecommunications market. Unlike Nokia's strategy, outlined in section 3.2.3, Apple's move into the cellular phone market maintained the iPod model of music storage and sales that maintained a distinction between illegal but free "pirated" music and legal, price-discriminated sales through iTMS. In contrast, Nokia adopted a subscription model that treated music as a commodity in all cases.

5. The specifics of the copyright provisions are not public information. However, Steve Jobs alludes to them in his open letter on music. See Jobs (2008).

6. Initial prelaunch publicity made it sound as if all songs transferred wirelessly between Zune devices would have their file contents altered to encode DRM in the song file itself. This turned out not to be true: DRM was managed by the device, not the software. Thus the song format went unmodified, but the device still treated all shared songs as valid for only three days or three plays. Microsoft later removed the "three plays" limitation. For the initial Microsoft clarification, see its public relations weblog. Retrieved July 11, 2008 (http://zuneinsider.com/archive/2006/09/19/980.aspx).

7. These comments were made in an interview with technology bloggers, for which transcripts are not available. For Gates's comments as paraphrased by one of the participants, see Arrington (2006). For corroboration of these remarks, see Rubel (2006). Gates's remarks contrast with Steve Jobs's explicit desire to eliminate copy protection from iTunes. See Jobs (2008).

8. The public press obscures this point. Background interviews in late 2009 with Microsoft suggest that they see minimal differences between the two companies' orientation to the market.

9. Anecdotal evidence indicates that tensions continued even after the launch of iTMS. Recording industry firms attempted to pressure Apple into raising prices and introducing a more complex pricing model, apparently to little effect (Leeds, 2005). This is yet another instance of the shifting locus of value creation. The recording firms' most important value stream came from music sales, hence their desire for a more profitable, differentiated pricing structure. Apple's revenue came from sales of all parts of its integrated system, hence its willingness to take lower profits on music

sales in exchange for higher profits on the system as a whole. These incompatible positions on the correct pricing model for the same distribution channel appear to have been resolved in favor of Apple, reinforcing the argument that devices firms have been empowered by digitalization.

10. It has, though, attempted to use its control over content to change the iTMS pricing structure. In 2005, news reports indicated that the recording industry wished to raise per-song prices and introduce a more complex pricing structure (Leeds 2005). They apparently made little headway, as iTMS prices for copy-protected music have remained unchanged.

11. Here, the recording industry has had substantial success convincing policy makers that the correct solution to the "double bind" dilemma between technological disruption and the protection of existing modes of value creation lies in protection. The Digital Millennium Copyright Act, and aggressive pursuit of international copyright protection treaties, put the state in the position of acting at the recording industry's behest. But that is a fight that both the state and the industry appear to have lost.

12. Some attempts to penalize device makers and, by extension, consumers, have been made. At the firm level, the "Zune Tax" discussed earlier appears to be its only success. Apple, far and away the market leader, has no similar program. Political attempts to legislate such a tax industry-wide include Canada's proposed iPod Tax, which would implement a sliding tax based on a device's storage capacity, the revenues of which would compensate artists. This tax was declared illegal by the Canadian courts in early 2008 (Schneider 2008). The Japanese had implemented a similar tax on storage media for earlier technologies like cassette tapes and DVDs but chose not to extend this to dynamic storage devices (Mehra 2008). A similar tax has been proposed by the United Kingdom's Music Business Group (2008).

13. For a discussion of what is and is not unique in information technology, see Shapiro and Varian (1999) and DeLong (1998).

14. See http://www.medtronic.com/Carelink/ for more detail from Medtronic.

15. For the concerns of the research community see, for example, Melton (1997), McCarthy et al. (1999), and O'Herrin, Fost, and Kudsk (2004). The American Hospital Association (AHA) issued a report in 2000 on the pending regulatory implementation citing compliance costs as high as $22.5 billion. The AHA president at the time noted that "this sweeping proposal goes beyond what Congress had intended and has the potential to interfere with the treatment we provide patients" (Mitchell 2000). See Tieman (2000). For post-passage disputes over the complexity and cost of regulations, see McGinley (2001). This included both the direct cost and the opportunity cost of increased barriers to collaboration between doctors or researchers, less effective or accurate insurance underwriting, and potentially higher rates of patient lawsuits over alleged violations of privacy statutes.

16. See, for instance, Medtronic Corporation News Release (2005).

17. Kushida and Zysman (2009) develop in greater detail the dimensions of political contestation resulting from the expansion of digital services, such as those discussed here.

References

Alexander, P. J. (1994). "New technology and market structure: Evidence from the music recording industry." *Journal of Cultural Economics* 18: 113–23.
Apple, Inc. (2007). *Annual Report*. Cupertino, CA: Apple, Inc.
Apple, Inc. (2008). *Annual Report/10k*. Cupertino, CA: Apple, Inc.

Apple, Inc. (2009). *Annual Report/10k*. Cupertino, CA: Apple, Inc.
Arrington, M. (2006). "Bill Gates on the future of DRM," December 14. Retrieved July 10, 2008 (http://www.techcrunch.com/2006/12/14/bill-gates-on-the-future-of-drm).
Baumol, W. J. (1967). "The economics of unbalanced growth: Anatomy of an urban crisis." *American Economic Review* 57(3): 415–26.
DeLong, J. B. (1998). "Rules, new and old, for tomorrow's economy." *Worldlink: The Magazine of the World Economic Forum*.
Deutsch, C. H. (2002). "Suit settled over pricing of music at 3 chains." *The New York Times*, October 1.
Elgan, M. (2006). "Why Zune scares Apple to the core." *Computerworld*, September 28.
Gourevitch, P. (1987). *Politics in Hard Times*. Ithaca, NY: Cornell University Press.
Helm, B. (2005). "A new page in Google's book fight." *Business Week*, June 22.
Jobs, S. (2008). "Thoughts on music."
Kaplinsky, R. (2004). "Spreading the gains from globalization." *Problems of Economic Transition* 47(2): 74–115.
Kushida, K., and J. Zysman. (2009). "The services transformation and network policy: The new logic of value creation." *Review of Policy Research* 26(1–2): 173–94.
Leeds, J. (2005). "Apple, digital music's angel, earns record industry's scorn." *The New York Times*, August 27: A1.
Leeds, J. (2006). "Microsoft strikes deal on music." *The New York Times*, November 26.
Lindvall, H. (2008). "Why Nokia's Comes With Music package comes with a price." *Guardian Music Blog*, October 16.
Lloyd, F. W., and D. M. Mayeda. (1986–87). "Copyright fair use, the first amendment, and new communications technologies: The impact of betamax." *Federal Communications Law Journal* 59: 59–101.
Maier, C. (1975). *Recasting Bourgeois Europe*. Princeton, NJ: Princeton University Press.
Maier, C. (1981). "Two postwar eras and the conditions for stability." *American Historical Review* 86(2): 327–52.
McCarthy, D. B., D. Shatin, et al. (1999). "Medical records and privacy: Empirical effects of legislation." *HSR: Health Services Research* 34(1): 417–25.
McGinley, L. (2001). "Health-care industry, consumer groups clash over medical privacy rules." *The Wall Street Journal*, February 9: B10.
Medtronic Corporation News Release. (2005). "Medtronic Carelink network reaches significant patient milestones," November 14. Retrieved July 11, 2008 (http://wwwp.medtronic.com/Newsroom/NewsReleaseDetails.do?itemId=1131743209106&lang=en_US).
Mehra, S. (2008). "The iPod tax: Why the digital copyright system of American law professors' dreams failed in Japan." *University of Colorado Law Review* 79(2): 12.
Melton, L. J. (1997). "The threat to medical records research." *New England Journal of Medicine* 337: 1466–70.
Mitchell, R. N. (2000). "Study says privacy rule costs underestimated and questions to ask your vendor about HIPAA." *ADVANCE for Health Information Executives*.
Music Business Group. (2008). "Response to UK IPO consultation on copyright exceptions." [Technical report]. London: The Music Business Group.
New York Times Staff. (2007). "News agency and Google end dispute over use of material." *The New York Times*, April 7: C2.

Nokia. (2009). "Music has changed." Retrieved February 2, 2009, Helsinki, Finland (http://www.nokia.com/NOKIA_COM_1/Press/Materials/White_Papers/pdf_files%/backgrounders_2009/Nokia_History_Music_Backgrounder.pdf).

O'Herrin, J. K., N. Fost, and K. A. Kudsk. (2004). "Health Insurance Portability and Accountability Act (HIPAA): Effect on medical record research." *Annals of Surgery* 239(6): 772–78.

Pontusson, J., and P. Swenson. (1996). "Perspective institutions: The Swedish employer offensive in comparative labor markets, production strategies, and wage bargaining." *Comparative Political Studies* 29: 233.

Ricardo, D. (1996). *Principles of Political Economy and Taxation*. London: Prometheus Press.

Rubel, S. (2006). "Our sixty minutes with Bill Gates." Retrieved July 10, 2008 (http://www.micropersuasion.com/2006/12/our_sixty_minut.html).

Schneider, J. (2008). Canadian court overturns iPod tax, an Apple victory. Bloomberg.com, January 11.

Schreier, E. (1999). The end of SDMI. *mp3.com*, October 15.

Schulze-Cleven, T., B. C. Watson, and J. Zysman. (2007). Innovation and adaptability in a digital era: How wealthy nations stay wealthy. BRIE Working Paper 177, Berkeley Roundtable on the International Economy, Berkeley, CA.

Shapiro, C., and H. Varian. (1999). *Information Rules: A Strategic Guide to the Network Economy*. Cambridge, MA: Harvard Business School Press.

Swenson, P. (1991a). "Bringing capital back in, or social democracy reconsidered: Employer power, cross-class alliances, and centralization of industrial relations in Denmark and Sweden." *World Politics* 43(4): 513–44.

Swenson, P. (1991b). "Labor and the limits of the welfare state: The politics of intraclass conflict and cross-class alliances in Sweden and West Germany." *Comparative Politics* 23(4): 379–99.

Tieman, J. (2000). "One huge HIPAA." *Modern Healthcare* 30(52): 8.

Yearend Statistics. (1999). Washington, D.C.: Recording Industry Association of America. Retrieved May 12, 2008 (http://76.74.24.142/01F751EA-7C8C-5D03-E206-D26FEB360519.pdf).

Zysman, J. (2004). Creating value in a digital era: How do wealthy nations stay wealthy? BRIE Working Paper 165, Berkeley Roundtable on the International Economy, Berkeley, CA.

PART II

A (Re)New(ed) Need for the State:
The Response by the Already Wealthy?

Preface
Dan Breznitz and John Zysman

THE FIRST PART of this book analyzes the challenges and challengers to the already wealthy that emerged as part of the long-term changes in the way things are made, to global economic governance, and the growing importance of information and communications technology (ICT)-enabled services. Thus it reflects the main tasks we had in mind when we started this project. However, things dramatically changed after the financial crisis unfolded. This part, therefore, has two aims. First, it presents the two new challenges and sources of demands for renewed state intervention: the financial crisis and the growing importance of climate change. Second, it combines the insights of both parts to look at some of the diverse responses of those who are already wealthy, from the United States to Japan, France, and the Nordic countries.

Since the outbreak, and continuous aftershocks, of the financial crisis in the past four years, a dramatic rise in the demand for direct state action to address the ills, access, and, often, plain neglect of their current economic system erupted in the advanced industrial countries. The need for the state to respond, shape markets, and take directed action, and not just allow experimentation and business innovation, became especially clear at the same time that climate change came to the fore in the new millennium. A distinctive feature of both the financial and climate crises is their systemic character.

The climate problem is, at its core, a story of the need for a fundamental shift in the energy system. This global energy crisis is not about the scarcity of resources and the "limits" to growth; rather, it is about the consequences of growth. The shift in the energy system must be from a high-carbon/low-efficiency system to a high-efficiency/low-carbon system. That problem, argues Mark Huberty, Chapter 10, "Energy Systems Transformation: State Choices at the Intersection of Sustainability and Growth," must be understood as a system change; the systemic character of energy is central to the climate problem. A true energy transformation—which is a systemic innovation—calls for much more expansive state intervention. Unless there is a fundamental systemic change, "green growth" will not prove to be the great "job accelerator" in the wealthy countries that it is hoped to be. The chapter considers what would be required for even a highly successful global energy system transformation to drive growth. Illuminating this problem permits a consideration, particularly in comparison with ICT, of how technology transformations generate growth.

The financial collapse resulted in significant part from a failed understanding of the nature of the financial system and its relation to the real economy. Mark Blyth, Chapter 8, "This Time It Really Is Different: Europe, the Financial Crisis, and 'Staying on Top' in the Twenty-first Century," argues that the inability to distinguish between two rather different things facilitated the illusion that new ICT tools could both generate value *and* protect against catastrophe. First is the inability to distinguish between systemic risk and risk for a particular financial institution. Solutions that work for a single actor, individual, or bank proved catastrophic for the system. Second, for too many financiers the fascination with computation-based financial tools hid the essential distinction between risk and fundamental uncertainty. Risk can be calculated. Every insurer supposedly has the actuarial tables to calculate the chances that we will die or suffer debilitating conditions, on the basis of which it prices our policies. Uncertainty is another matter: we cannot even imagine the outcome and, hence, have no way to start thinking about quantifying its odds.

William Lazonick, in Chapter 9, "The Fragility of the U.S. Economy: The Financialized Corporation and the Disappearing Middle Class," links the fascination with financial innovation to its particular negative impacts on the prospects of the United States to sustain growth and create good jobs for its citizens. Lazonick considers how the obsession with finance, leading to the extreme financialization of U.S. corporations, has been undermining the country's ability to respond to the challenges of decomposition and service transformation and challengers such as China and India. The chapter explores the negative consequences for job creation and skill retention and the formation of this financialization, especially in the high-tech sector, from which the new "innovations" that spur new jobs and growth are supposed to originate.

Given the depth of the challenges and the strength of the challengers depicted in the first part of this book, the shifting framework dynamics of value creation, it is striking how muted, for the most part, the responses sketched by the country analyses actually are. The editors' argument in the introduction is that new national policies or strategies for growth would have to be put in place in the advanced countries to adapt to the decomposition of production and capture the possibilities presented by the transformation of services. This calls for policy packages in domains from regulation through labor markets and education that would be suited to the new requirements. In France and Japan, postwar growth models were no longer appropriate to the new tasks of the late twentieth and early twenty-first century. As the chapters by Steven K. Vogel, Chapter 13, "Japan's Information Technology Challenge," and Jonah D. Levy, Chapter 12, "Directionless: French Economic Policy in the Twenty-first Century," respectively show, neither Japan nor France has managed to put in place the mixes of policy to facilitate corporate strategic adaptations or the political underpinnings required to allocate the costs and gains of growth—a new systemic deal. In the American case, the efforts in the financial sector to capture the possibilities of ICT and financial engineering, argues Lazonick, simply distorted the industrial underpinnings of the U.S. economy. As Darius Ornston contends, in Chapter 11, "How the Nordic Nations Stay Rich: Governing Sectoral Shifts in Denmark, Finland, and Sweden," the Nordic countries offer unique insight into how the already wealthy can successfully manage the "double bind." Each of the Nordic countries experienced acute economic shocks during the late 1980s and early 1990s. These shocks threatened traditional economic institutions, including the centralized bargaining mechanisms among industry, labor, and policy makers that defined postwar adjustment. These "neocorporatist" deals were perceived to inhibit adaptation to disruptive, economic, and technological change. However, the Nordic countries responded successfully to these challenges and found ways in which these centralized bargaining mechanisms did not inhibit adaptation but, instead, supported movement into knowledge-intensive niches in new, high-technology industries. High-technology competition has, in turn, reduced their vulnerability to economic internationalization, the fragmentation of production, the services transformation, and climate change. In adapting, Denmark, Finland, and Sweden neither defended nor dismantled traditional economic institutions but, rather, "converted" centralized bargaining to perform new functions. The question for the larger wealthy countries that consider themselves great powers is whether the Nordic experience contains useful lessons for other environments. We argue that the Nordic experience suggests that growth, equity, and fiscal sanity can successfully accommodate one another.

8 This Time It Really Is Different
EUROPE, THE FINANCIAL CRISIS, AND "STAYING ON TOP" IN THE TWENTY-FIRST CENTURY
Mark Blyth

Introduction

The editors of this book want to know whether the "already rich" countries can stay rich in a transformed and increasingly volatile global political economy. They frame this question in terms of a double bind between conflicting imperatives to, on the one hand, stand back and allow "creative capitalism" to create economic growth, even if it is disruptive, and, on the other, to intervene in markets to ensure citizens' welfare (Zysman and Breznitz, Introduction, in this volume). Disruptive economic growth for these authors refers to the twin drivers of globalization, the value-chain revolution in manufacturing, and the algorithmic revolution in services, both of which were made possible by the fifth industrial revolution of information and communications technology (ICT). The editors insightfully argue, however, that the ICT revolution impacted not just the real economy of manufacturing and services but also the financial economy, through the technological "big bang" that occurred when massive amounts of computing power were applied to the financial sector in the 1980s and 1990s. They tellingly note that the causal complexity that ICT sought to control and model in the financial sector paradoxically created the complex instruments that lie at the heart of the current financial crisis. To put it more pithily, "no ICT, no CDO/CDS, no meltdown." I agree with their diagnosis and wish to build upon it by defining two specific double binds that are at play in global finance: a "risk" double bind that applies to the future governance of private finance and an "austerity" double bind that haunts the current world of public finance.

Zysman and Breznitz define a double bind as a dilemma in which a successful response to one side of the dilemma is a failed response to the other; hence the actor "cannot confront an inherent dilemma, and therefore cannot solve it or opt out of the situation" (Introduction, in this volume). I suggest in this chapter that, when policy makers attempt to confront the dilemmas in these particular cases, their inability to successfully resolve *both* horns of the dilemma means that efforts to address the problem may in fact exacerbate the problem further.[1]

The first double bind I examine stems from the ideology of risk that governs financial markets. That is, the post-1980 highly levered and hugely profitable global financial system, and all the taxes and jobs it generates, rests upon the financial world being an environment of programmable risk that can be sliced, diced, quantified, packaged, and sold. The continuing crisis, I shall argue, strongly suggests that such a view of risk is somewhat at variance with the world we actually inhabit. Yet if governments do not replicate the rules that allow the world of risk that finance depends upon to function, then like Humpty Dumpty, finance cannot be put back together again, which is bad news for states that rely on the financial sector to pay for their welfare states and produce growth.

Our second bind is the "austerity" double bind. This double bind stems from an ideological commitment that grew up in the wake of the crisis of 2007–08 to the idea that "excessive" government spending burdens the economy by introducing unacceptable sovereign debt risk and that reducing such risk is a major part of promoting growth and preventing future crises. This ideological commitment causes governments to fixate on the reduction of spending as the *sine qua non* of recovery while ignoring the fallacy of composition at the heart of such arguments: we cannot all cut our way to growth at the same time without shrinking the economy as a whole. In this case the double bind stems from the imperative for each *individual* country to cut its own debt in order to reduce sovereign risk while avoiding an economic contraction in the aggregate, which cannot be done in a context in which *all* countries are cutting.

Taken together, I argue that these two *cognitive* double binds, for they are at base a problem of ideas, threaten the future prosperity of the "already rich" far more than we like to think because the world that they envisage is, as Keynes put it over seventy years ago, "not…the economic society [where] we actually live, with the result that its teaching is misleading and disastrous if we attempt to apply it to the facts of experience" (Keynes 1936: 3).

To make this case, I first outline how we came to think of the financial world as an environment of risk, rather than one that is inherently uncertain, by detailing the architecture of a world of risk and then make the case that we most probably do not inhabit such a world. In doing so, to be clear, I am not attacking the entire project of financial modeling. Pensions still need to be paid, investments still need to be hedged, and even basic models usually beat throwing darts at the *Financial Times*' pink pages. What I am concerned with is how the view of the financial world that a reliance on the economics of risk made possible, the intellectual substructure of post-1980s finance, made the current crisis take its very specific form.

Again, I stress, *the current crisis*: not every crisis since time immemorial. As Kindleberger once remarked, financial crises are a hardy perennial. The failure of Midwestern banks in the 1920s happened without credit default swaps and Gaussian cupolas, so blaming today's models for yesterday's crises would be absurd at best. Rather, what I am concerned with here is how our ideas about risk *at this historical juncture* actually made us fragile to risk and helped push us toward the very specific financial crisis that continues to unfold today. Understanding this is, I believe, important because the lessons learned, or not learned, from the events of 2007–11, will serve as the blueprints for tomorrow's safeguards. But if those safeguards, the new rules of the road for global finance, are designed with the same understandings of risk as before, we may well be building future failure into our designs. To put it as simply as possible, agents who repeatedly make decisions based upon calculations of probabilistic risk while living in a context of uncertainty will produce the very blowups they seek to avoid.[2]

To make this case, I stress the causal importance of our ideas about finance, insofar as our desire to see the world as governed by the architecture of risk rather than uncertainty creates these effects. That is, how we see the world of finance, both private and public, matters since our ideas and models about it are themselves the technology we use to act within it (MacKenzie 2006). I then survey how such thinking continues to dominate discussions of new regulatory frameworks, especially in Europe, despite the lessons ostensibly learned in the crisis. Finally, I discuss how the "austerity" double bind that originated in German thinking about the crisis rests upon similar notions of the world being a world of risk and how such conceptions lie at the heart of the current Eurozone crisis.

In sum, whether the European "already rich" can stay rich is contingent upon the postcrisis financial reforms of such countries not making them even more vulnerable to the next financial train wreck. Given that such crises are increasing in both frequency and magnitude (Reinhardt and Rogoff 2009), what may stop the "already rich" staying rich may be their own cupidity regarding their financial and fiscal affairs as much as transformational forces stemming from revolutions in ICT and the rise of new powers, a point I return to in the conclusion.

Worlds of Risk and Uncertainty

Let us begin by comparing two possible worlds of finance. A world of risk presumes an already constituted and "knowable" world that agents perceive directly, our understanding of which is hindered by cognitive biases and incomplete information (Abdelal, Blyth, and Parsons 2010). In such a world, if informational incompleteness could be overcome, agents could then see the world *as it really is*, our theories about the world would fully correspond to that world, and our capacity to predict the future world would be very high. This is obviously a very attractive vision to financial actors whose incomes depend upon as-yet-to-be-realized future states of the world.

Leaving naked instrumentalism by the financial sector to one side, viewing the world in this way allows the further extension that the world is computable (in a Turing sense) and thus mathematically tractable. Statistical techniques can therefore help us get closer to the world "as it really is," allowing us to make probabilistic assessments of likely outcomes based upon past data. With more data and better models we should then be more certain about our world and better able to manage the risks that it produces. This risk-based view of the world, regardless of the specifics of any single firm's models that sought to contain that risk, lay behind (almost) all financial risk management strategies prior to the crisis, whether at the level of banks or at the level of regulators.

Our second world, in contrast, is a world of uncertainty. This world is not "knowable" in the same way. An uncertain world is not (Turing) programmable, since no search algorithm can assess the probability space dynamically forward, nor is the basic problem one of informational incompleteness. Rather, the problem is informational *incomputability*, given that the system itself is constantly evolving in unpredictable ways. One might think of it as a world of constant becoming rather than being. Consequently, the assumption of ergodicity that a (normal) statistical worldview presumes becomes problematic (Kauffman 2008).

Now juxtapose these two worlds. A world of risk is a world of visible generators (you get to see the dice) where sampling past outcomes can get you close to the world "as it really is." An uncertain world, in contrast, contains invisible generators that either converge to a Gaussian (normal) distribution with extremely fat tails or do not converge at all. In a risky world where sampling the past causes convergence to the real mean and real variance, massive blowups such as 2008 should be all but impossible. As David Viniar, the chief financial officer (CFO) of Goldman Sachs, reported in 2008, his firm was being hit with events that were "twenty-five standard deviation moves, several days in a row" (Dowd et al. 2008: 1), which is as close to a statistical impossibility as one can get. In an uncertain world, however, where sampling the past does not converge to a real mean and real variance since it's a moving target, blowups should be more frequent.[3] So which of these two worlds best characterizes the world of modern finance? A quick glance at the periodicity of such blowups over the past 100 or so years strongly suggests that they are in fact the rule rather than the exception, and as such, we most likely live in a world that is more uncertain than risky (see Figure 8.1).[4]

Eyeballing the data aside, in order to answer this question we need to dissect this distinction between risk and uncertainty more precisely. Confusing risk with uncertainty, and as a consequence viewing the world as more stable than it is, creates an acute double bind when it comes to writing the new rules of the road for both global finance and fiscal governance.

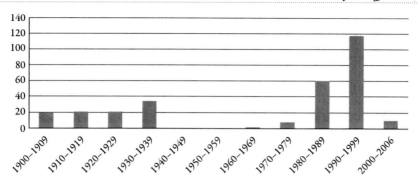

FIGURE 8.1 The Incidence of Financial Crises

The Architecture of Risk: Equilibrium Statics and Exogenous Changes

The first postulate of risk, insofar as it relates to questions of financial regulation, states that in the absence of externalities or exogenous shocks, financial markets tend to an equilibrium that is both stable and efficient. We believe this because back in the early 1980s financial theorists began to convince regulators (and economics majors who became bankers) that our understandings of aggregates, such as "financial markets," had to be grounded in credible accounts of the behavior of individuals. That is, theories of financial markets (and hence how they should be regulated) must be grounded in the appropriate microfoundations: that individuals are self-interested maximizers and that markets clear (Blyth 2003; Cassidy 2009; Eatwell 1996).

Financial theorists based this claim upon the formalization of the intuitive observation that it was highly unlikely that investors would make systematic errors in the valuation and trading of financial assets, because if they did, they would go broke. As such, errors would be random, not systematic, and agents would invest in being correct in order to stay solvent (Fox 2009). Therefore, while individual market participants may make mistakes, systematic mistakes by markets (as the sum of individually rational decisions) would be impossible. As a consequence, successful agents would share the same model of the economy such that, in the absence of large informational asymmetries, expectations about possible future states of the economy would converge, thereby promoting a stable and self-enforcing equilibrium (for a period critique of this line of thinking, see Bleaney 1985; for a post-crisis rediscovery, see Fox 2009).

Change in such a world is exogenous. Indeed, it must be so. If markets are stable in the absence of shocks and unanticipated policy interventions, and if financial assets embody the true value of their real counterparts as expressed in prices, then equilibrium becomes a rather unproblematic state. So what then would change this state of affairs? It would, by definition, have to be something exogenous, such as a supply shock, a war, or most likely, an unanticipated attempt by governments to push markets to produce specific outcomes, which would be, by definition, "off the equilibrium path" and decidedly not efficient.

Change thus assumes a discontinuous function. It should be random. It should come from outside the system itself, and like the meteor that killed the dinosaurs, appear decidedly rare and exogenous. In such a world of "efficient markets" and exogenous shocks, financial regulation either gets in the way by distorting price signals or it is irrelevant if the markets know its coming and can discount it (or can game their way around it). Either way, government intervention in markets is pointless, or toxic, or both, and "light-touch" regulation should be the only game (allowed) in town. By 2008 it was indeed the only game in town.

Invisible Generators and Complex Payoffs

The second postulate of risk, less explicitly acknowledged, and admittedly more contested, is that we can directly observe the generators of outcomes in the economic world. That is, when agents plan probabilistically from a sample of past events, they implicitly assume that they can see the generator of outcomes out there in the world: the dice are visible to all on the craps table of life, and we can all agree on the number of sides and the values on the sides, so to speak. In some cases this might be true. The U.S. Congress, for example, is directly observable and is, in principle, predictable. But as we know from the U.S. debt-ceiling debacle of August 2011, even directly observable generators with fixed rules can throw us a probabilistic curve ball from time to time.

Kick this problem up a level of aggregation and make the global economy the generator of outcomes, and agents literally can neither *see* the causal mechanisms at play nor *stand outside them*. Our impressions of them are mediated, are shared, and depend upon interpretations and imperfect data.[5] Chinese demand, for example, can be seen in increased oil imports to China, but we can also attribute many things to such a generator without it actually being true. For example, the oil price spike of 2006 being due to "Chinese demand" despite evidence to the contrary was a popular refrain until prices fell from $146 per barrel to $36 without any corresponding collapse in Chinese output. Given this opacity, sudden shifts in the output of the generators cannot be anticipated from history, not because the data is incomplete but because the generator spitting out the data, the dice in the casino of life, may throw us the occasional 113 from what we thought were two six-sided dice regardless of the systems past behavior. Now add to this the complexity of the payoffs we face when we deal with hidden generators, and the architecture of risk looks all the more uncertain.

In a risky world with visible generators, risk and reward would be calibrated. A bet of X on option Y with hedge C will produce a knowable payoff within the parameters of past data, or at least that is what we assume. But how then would we explain the collapse of one firm, say Lehman Brothers, causing the near meltdown of the global financial system? Nassim Taleb (2008) has the answer—"never cross a river that is on average four foot deep." That is, past data may tell you that the risk of an event happening is "on average" absurdly small, but somewhere in the river of data there is a fifteen-foot drop, and if you step on it you are in trouble, even if you are two feet taller than the river—on average.[6] Ignoring these factors makes our risky world much more uncertain, and much more prone to blowups, than we like to think.

Given such a view of the world, it follows that what financial actors are worried about, a quantifiable and ontologically identifiable thing called risk (credit, default, market, liquidity, etc.), should indeed be nothing more than the individual property of either an asset (some assets are more risky than others) or an individual/firm or a strategy (in a game-theoretic sense). As such, the only real policy problem becomes how to avoid moral hazard.[7] After all, if risk is individual, sliceable, and quantifiable and regulation is best left to the banks themselves since they are the ones with "skin in the game," as the regulators maintained in the run-up to the crisis, then financial governance becomes a question of *micro*-prudential regulation. Such regulations authorized banks' use of their own internal risk models and self-assigned capital adequacy requirements to ascertain how risky their world is, usually observed (after the fact) as a discoverable function of each individual bank's sum exposures.[8] This is the world we built by 2008. It was risky but stable: until it wasn't.

Risk, Uncertainty, and the Current Crisis: Evidence from 2008

Being a global financial crisis, there is no one simple way to account for it. One could begin with global imbalances and go from there to excess liquidity and then to mortgages (Schwartz 2009; Wolf 2008). One could alternatively start inside a bank and go from there to mortgages and then to global imbalances (Tett 2009). There are, to say the least, multiple points of entry. Here I juxtapose two complementary versions of the crisis: one that starts with the demand for complex instruments (micro) and one that starts with the supply of compounding bubbles (macro) (Blyth 2008). Both are, as I shall show, irreducible to notions of sliceable and knowable risk. The purpose of retelling the crisis in this particular way is to demonstrate that risk-based rules may seriously mislead us, and why this matters for the "already rich" staying rich given their current policy choices.

MICRO INSTRUMENTS

Our micro point of entry to the crisis has to start with overinvestment in real estate made possible, in part, by the transformation of relatively simply mortgage-backed securities (MBSs), a mainstay of U.S. capital markets for decades (Seabrooke 2006), into complex, tranched collateralized debt obligations (CDOs). Demand for such securities exploded during the 1990s as U.S. house prices nearly doubled between 1997 and 2008 (Economic Report of the President 2010: 40). Since a decade of rising house prices convinced the majority of investors that housing prices could only go up, such securities became thought of as safe investments, particularly by institutional investors.[9] Furthermore, because of their tranched structure (they could be split into pieces according to their estimated risk profile), they could diversify away the correlation in the underlying bond while maintaining a very strong upside. Given such features, these products became an increasingly popular way of juicing returns, and for foreigners, a nice way to recycle surplus foreign dollars as the decade wore on (Schwartz 2009).[10]

Indeed, when the security in question could be sold with an attached credit default swap (CDS), which insured the holder against the credit risk of the issuer, it made these instruments appear even safer. Credit ratings agencies were now happy to assign an AAA investment grade rating to the security if it had a CDS attached, thereby advertising the asset as being more or less risk free. This pumped demand still further, especially among institutional investors eager for AAA assets, despite the fact that such securities were, by the middle of the decade, increasingly made out of NINJA (No Income, No Job or Assets) mortgages collateralized by the eBay earnings and table-waiting tips of mortgage applicants (Goodman 2010).

Rather than hold any of this risk on their books, CDO issuers set up an originate to distribute system (contrary to what regulators believed, there was in fact very little skin in the game) where the funding and issuance of these securities was moved off-book to a special investment vehicle (SIV) "whose sole purpose was to collect the principal and interest … and pass them on to the owners of the various tranches" (Brunnermeier 2008: 4–5). These off-book issuers, most famously AIG Financial Products (an SIV), fell over themselves to issue these securities with little or no capital backstop since they were freed from the regulations that applied to their parent entities.[11] As a result, the parent entity to the SIV was heavily leveraged without it being transparent to the market or even to the parent company. Furthermore, since many of these securities were not exchange traded, especially CDSs of subprime CDOs, counterparty exposures were especially opaque.

When credit markets froze in September 2008, prices for these securities, which were by then major components of banks' portfolios, became hard to find. This constricted credit further, beginning a process of serial deleveraging where as banks' internal risk assessment models' (Value at Risk (VaR) and similar) numbers shot up, each bank sought to sell good assets to cover bad (toxic) asset losses. Unfortunately, while it is individually rational for any single bank to calculate and act upon its VaR numbers to manage risk, in an interlinked and procyclical system it is collectively disastrous for all banks to do so if there is serial correlation in the "superportfolio" of all banks, as there was with CDOs and CDS exposures (Persaud 2000). That is, if each bank holds essentially similar assets and liabilities, and they each attempt to get rid of them all at once, prices will fall through the floor; and they did just that.[12] Once this deleveraging cycle took hold it showed us that while any one bank may be diversified, the system as a whole may not be, which made the system as a whole meltdown all the faster.[13]

Note how this entire industry was predicated upon the world being an environment of calculable risk. And it was perfectly stable until it wasn't. The industry took for granted the idea that inherently low-risk (judging by limited data on historic defaults) assets (mortgages) would be made less, and not more, risky by tranching the bond pool. The industry embraced the notion that CDS was insurance, even if there was no collateral in the system, since the risks were so small as to be negligible as per the prior calculation of defaults based upon the assumption of a normal distribution of risk. This view of the world as risky made possible the belief that VaR numbers actually measured the risks faced by a bank, even when such risk cannot be reduced to a single numerical value. Finally, it made participants blind to the fact that we cannot all be liquid at once, even when we hold supposedly AAA assets. In sum, the world being modeled was, it turned out, quite different from the world that we actually inhabit.

MACRO BUBBLES

Now jump up to the macro and the same dynamic of planning for risk in an uncertain world plays out once again. In theory, market bubbles in real estate, or anything else for that matter, should be competed away by rational agents operating in efficient markets. So why are there bubbles in such a supposedly efficient system? This is the macro side of the story, which begins almost thirty years ago when the world's major financial centers deregulated their domestic credit markets and opened up their financial accounts, which gave a massive boost to global liquidity as previously isolated markets became much more interdependent (Abdelal 2006; Helleiner 1994).

This growth in global liquidity was compounded by the growth of these new financial instruments, particularly the development of derivatives. The spread of these instruments, and the leveraged positions that they allowed, pumped global liquidity all the more, and long- and short-term interest rates began to fall precipitously as a result. Beginning in 1991 the U.S. prime and Federal Funds rates (and thus global interest rates) began their long decline out of double figures to historic lows.[14] This rise in global liquidity, and the consequent "global search for yield" among investors in a low interest rate environment, persisted when the Federal Reserve under Alan Greenspan aggressively reduced interest rates following the bursting of the dot-com bubble in 1999 and again after the 9/11 attacks in 2001. As a result, bank credit skyrocketed at the same time as the privatization of former state responsibilities, especially in pensions, encouraged the growth of large nonbank institutional investors, who were all seeking "above-average" returns given the competitive nature of the new system.[15] And to stoke this fire just a little higher, Americans in particular basically gave up on saving since other countries seems only too willing to lend them back their own money (Economic Report of the President 2010; Schwartz 2009; Wolf 2008). Add all this together and the financial system as a whole had to find some way of finding "above-average" returns to stay in business: a moving average problem of planetary proportions.[16]

The problem here is one of asset classes: the limited number of categories of assets from which investors could seek such returns. There are only a few such classes around: equities (stock), cash (money market), fixed income (bonds), real estate, and commodities. If equities, bonds, and money market instruments are regarded as fungible equivalents, then global stock markets, perceived to be relatively underpriced in the early 1990s, became the first port of call to find these above-average returns. Once that particular bubble burst in 1999–2000, neither bonds nor fixed income alone would provide the above-average returns that the markets now expected. The next stop for investors was therefore the next most obvious asset class, real estate; hence the global housing boom, which began just as the tech-stock bubble deflated in the late 1990s. By 2006 this housing bubble had ran out of (good) borrowers and investors were looking for a new source of yield, with the result that the remaining class of assets, commodities, became the next bubble, with oil quadrupling in price and basic foodstuffs rising between 40 and 70 percent in a little over a year.[17] However, with the exception of oil these were comparatively tiny markets, too small to sustain such volumes of liquidity, and these bubbles burst quickly. Their collapse combined with losses in the subprime sector of the mortgage derivatives market, our micro story, to trigger the current crisis.

Note once again that these macro risks were not "calculable risks" in any meaningful sense. The rise of institutional investors all hunting yield, the ability of the United States to finance domestic consumption with foreign savings, the ability to "pump and dump" entire classes of assets on an international scale, were each conjunctural factors simply not calculable by banks or regulators. Once again, risk was in the eye of the beholder rather than in the world as a calculable property. We lived uncertainty but planned for risk, and our plans eventually came up short.[18] But what this institutionalization of an ideology of risk allowed was to make banks into their own regulators in the run-up to the crisis.[19]

Who Wrote Risk Rules for an Uncertain World?

Like the macro story previously, we begin with the move from fixed to flexible exchange rates in the late 1970s, which transferred exchange rate risk from public- to private-sector actors (Eatwell 1996). Given the deregulatory impulse of the governments of the day in the United States and the UK the private sector was encouraged to pick up this risk, and several new ones. The ICT revolution indeed played its part, as our editors suggest, with exchange automation, round-the-clock trading, and the further development of complex finance emerging as a consequence of marrying notions of calculable risk to oceans of computing power. And when the European Union made opening the capital account a prerequisite of membership in the 1990s, this deregulated risk-trading system spread itself around the world, and the risks it generated, still further (Abdelal 2006).

But what really pushed this process along was the same set of ideas noted earlier. After all, if markets found equilibrium in the absence of intervention, why intervene? If financial firms acted as rational agents who balanced risk and reward in order to maximize profit, then who better than the firms themselves to guard against risk?[20] Indeed, why not let bankers, or at least their much captured regulators, write their own rules (Tsingou 2009; Warwick Commission 2009)? It was in this context that the Basel 1 (1988) and Basel 2 (2004) capital accords were conceived, with Basel 1 establishing the principle that banks were the best judges of the risks they were running. Consequently, to make the system safe, all regulators had do was to make the individual component banks safe (and of course avoid bailouts). Basel 2 took this to a step further, effectively allowing the largest banks to become their own regulators.

The 1988 Basel banking accords (Basel 1) were designed to stop banks setting aside too little capital to cover unexpected losses (the effect of the failure of several internationally exposed banks in the 1970s and the near meltdown of the U.S. banking sector in the Latin American debt crisis of the 1980s) and to halt a regulatory "race to the bottom" by setting minimum supervisory standards as capital became more globally mobile. Basel 1 set minimum capital adequacy requirements for banks comprised of so-called tier-one (highly liquid) and tier-two capital (less liquid) that were risk weighted by category of asset. This allowed banks to set a "target standard ratio" of both tiers of capital, composed of a variety of different assets. What it also did was to put banks in the driver's seat regarding their own risk assessments, with national authorities, mainly central banks, delegated to a surveillance role (Balin 2008: 3–4).[21]

Building on Basel 1, Basel 2 (2004) took self-regulation to a whole other level. Rather than assigning crude weights to different classes of assets, banks could use published ratings by the ratings agencies (Standard and Poor's, Moody's, and Fitch) to weight their risk assessments. Furthermore, Basel 2, which was all but written by the banks themselves (Tsingou 2008, 2009), set up a system of internal risk ratings based around in-house VaR analyses where "the banks themselves, rather than the regulators, determine the assumptions of proprietary credit models" with the result that "low risk weightings translate into lower reserve requirements" (Balin 2008: 8).

In sum, Basel 2 gave a capital adequacy free lunch to banks who could build very big risk assessment departments chock-full of sophisticated computer models and risk managers. Since only the biggest banks could afford to do this, it gave them a cost-of-capital advantage over their rivals, at the same time making them ever more sensitive to shifts in their leverage ratios since their lack of capital was (in theory) made safe by their ability to price risk better than the smaller banks (Warwick Commission 2009). Basically, banks got to govern themselves, with the biggest banks being allowed to hedge their exposures the least, as long as they could model their risks, using, of course, parameters that they themselves provided. The new Basel 3 rules, which take effect beginning in 2013, require higher capital buffers in the form of 6 percent tier-one capital rather than the 4 percent required under Basel 2, but tellingly, the banks themselves still get to decide what counts as the appropriate risk weighting among their one capital asset, thereby gaming the system once again.[22]

The Price of Presumption: Risk Rules in an Uncertain World

This was the architecture within which banks structured their activities in the run-up to the crash. Markets were seen as self-equilibrating and efficient, to the point that regulatory authorities refused to even acknowledge the colossal asset bubbles forming in their economies. We were, you will recall, told that we were living in "the Great Moderation." Banks and regulators both believed that derivatives diversified risk around the system in calculable ways, and that the interaction effects of instruments were knowable *a priori* through knowledge of positions and leverage (who was holding what), while such risks could be adequately measured via VaR and similar techniques. Complications driven by hidden generators (NINJA mortgages and Chinese savings surpluses, for example) and complex payoffs (CDS insurance on Lehman almost blowing up half the U.S. financial system) were ignored as possibilities too small to worry about.

The decision by regulators not to regulate instruments and leverage directly but to rely instead on banks' own risk models to do the job highlights the importance of the belief in self-equilibration flowing from individual self-interest coupled to the belief that risk is an individual, divisible, and normally distributed property. Unfortunately, rather than equilibrium following from self-interested action, the deleveraging of 2008–11 has showed disequilibrium to be the norm as what rose together on the upside fell together on the downside with catastrophic distributional costs.

Financial crises may differ in the details; the triggering event, the asset class involved, and so on, but the disequilibrium pattern remains across cases. Some unexpected change in the system produces an initial redistribution of assets across portfolios, which alters profit opportunities. If this occurs in a period of relative stability, banks become less risk averse and expand credit in response to demand in light of these new opportunities.[23] This leads to price increases in the speculative asset class that in turn encourages more credit, thus fueling the upswing. The specific signal that "it's time to get out" will vary, but when it occurs (subprime losses, the implosion of Bear Stearns) investors all try to get out of the same assets at the same time. This drops market prices to below modeled prices, which in turn results in the liquidation of other (good) assets to cover losses in the original portfolio. The resulting cannibalization of assets is the bust that always follows the boom. This pattern has occurred at least fifty times in the history of modern capitalism (Reinhart and Rogoff 2009). It is the rule not the exception, and it shows assumptions of equilibrium and market efficiency to be deeply problematic. As such, imagining a world of risk to be the world actually inhabited and therefore acting in such a way as to "perform" that world (in a Callon/MacKenzie sense) built fragility into the world rather than making it more robust as was intended.

The causes of this crisis, whether on the micro or macro level, were neither exogenous nor normally distributed. The crisis was only a twenty-five-standard-deviation event if one thought the likelihood of such a blowup was normally distributed when it manifestly was not. The fact that so many "sophisticated participants" were blind to this possibility shows the power of financial ideas, rather than financial data and "fundamentals" to structure the financial world (Blyth 2003).[24] It was not the financial equivalent of a meteor from space. It was deeply endogenous, developing out of the interaction of complex instruments and volatile global liquidity in a wholly unpredictable manner. To take just one example, even in its tranched form a mortgage bond is a pretty innocuous instrument. Similarly, a CDS is pretty much an insurance policy with an embedded option (to generate an income stream). Both were designed to, and assumed to, reinforce one another's good sides. But place them in an environment where all the liquidity in the world dries up and the former turns into a correlation bomb while the latter turns into a naked short that lights the fuse. Such causation is emergent and inherently unpredictable (Kauffman 2008).[25] What the crisis showed us all too clearly was that while bankers and regulators may have believed that risk governed the world and that they governed risk, the crisis, a giant experiment that tested the robustness of these ideas, showed that quite different forces in fact pertained. The world may in fact be decidedly disequilibrial, fat-tailed, skewed, and endogenously unstable, inherently uncertain, and not risky.

You might think then that those designing the new rules of the financial game for a post-crisis world would try not to write essentially the same risk-based rules for an uncertain world once again. You might think this, but you would be at best half right in the world of financial governance and almost completely wrong in the world of fiscal governance. Ideas, like the institutions that they give rise to, are sticky. "Cognitive locking" into one paradigm or way of thinking often exhibits increasing returns, even in the face of empirical anomalies and disconfirming information (Blyth 2001). What we see today in Europe is a pattern where the regulators, and some of the politicians, seem to understand "what went wrong and what to do about it," in that they have authored a series of reports that acknowledged the issue detailed above (de Larosière 2009; Turner 2009; Woolley et al. 2010).

However, the adoption of the new rules recommended therein has been somewhere between partial and hamstrung. What supranational regulation that is emerging, such as Basel 3 and the new risk management committees of the European Union, is not based on what we should have, in my estimation, learned from the crisis. Regulators and politicians still view the financial world as a world of risk and seek to make it more stable through that understanding. Reforms are partial, in that these new rules will reduce the profitability of a very powerful lobby—finance—and hamstrung—in that governments' own understanding of the crisis as one of "too much debt" that now requires a period of austerity in the midst of a recession will likely make these limited reform efforts backfire. The results are the continuing cognitive double binds of risk and austerity.

The Double Bind of Rethinking Risk: European Lessons

Economic conditions in Europe in late 2011 ranged from the dire (the UK) and the desperate (Greece) to the comparatively fortunate (Germany). Nonetheless, European regulators were quick off the mark to diagnose what went wrong and what to do about it. In this regard two reports stand out, the UK's Turner Report, issued by its Financial Services Authority (FSA), and the EU's de Larosière Report, both published in 2009. What we see in both of these reports is a willingness to question the risk-based assumptions that had ruled finance to date. Strangely however, what followed this initial learning process was a set of policies and proposals that are based upon the same old regulatory architecture of risk (plus bigger airbags), a problem that the austerity double bind has only compounded.

The UK's Turner Report hit out hard at the fetish of micro-regulation and the absence of attention to the global macroeconomy of the type described above. It argues against over reliance on mathematical models, particularly VaR analysis, stating that, "short-term observation periods plus [the] assumption of normal distribution[s] can lead to [a] large underestimation of the probability of extreme loss events" (Turner 2009: 25, 47). Moreover, "systemic risk may be highest when measured risk is lowest, since low measured risk encourages behavior which creates increased systemic risks" (Turner 2009: 25, 47). Echoing the points made above, the Turner Report explicitly questions "the intellectual assumptions on which previous regulatory approaches have largely been built" (Turner 2009: 39). Building upon this critique, the Turner Report makes many sensible suggestions for reform that move beyond risk-based regulation. Unfortunately, for such policies to work, the wider institutional context in which they are embedded would have to be reformed too. That lies, sadly, in the hands of politicians who are most unlikely to do this.

For example, some of Turner's proposed reforms are uncontestable good-things, such as establishing "clearing and central counterparty systems...to cover the majority of CDS trading" and countercyclical capital charges (2009: 8). But while increasing capital adequacy ratios and establishing countercyclical capital charges are unquestioningly wise, for such rules to be effective they depend upon a prior policy of leaning against the upswing of the credit cycle. Given that there is no downside to the upside of a bubble for politicians, such a policy assumes away the very political acquiescence that it may founder upon. Similarly, if VaR and similar techniques are inherently unreliable, as Turner maintains, then supplementing them with other methods while asking the regulators to keep an eye on systemic risk, all the while using the same tools as the banks use themselves, is likely to bring about the very procyclicality via position and model homogeneity that these reforms hope to guard against.

When we move from the Turner Report to what the British government has actually implemented to date, there seems to be a shift in the recognition there that a risk-based rules framework needs to be rethought.[26] Former Labour Chancellor Alisdair Darling's one-time tax on bank bonuses and his attempt to exclude British banks from the U.S.'s new "Volcker rule" proposals were at best temporizing steps within the same framework.[27] The current Conservative government's reforms are more fundamental in some respects but more conservative in others. Their July 2010 consultative document stressed the failure of the old tripartite framework (Bank of England, Financial Services Authority,

HM Treasury) and proposed the establishment of a new systemic risk monitoring council in the Bank of England that will be equipped with the tools to monitor and deflate asset bubbles.

While this sounds promising, such policies seem to presuppose that knowledge of players' positions and leverage (a.k.a. "greater transparency") will be sufficient to alert policy makers to future crises. Yet just as the crisis showed us how CDSs and CDOs could together unexpectedly turn into correlation bombs, so knowledge of positions is insufficient to solve this problem. In an evolving system, outcomes cannot be reduced to their constituent causes. If finance is a complex adaptive system then the simple provision of "more information" alone will not reveal the risk "out there" since it's a moving target. As argued earlier, the issue is one of programmability, not transparency (Blyth 2011).

Actual British reforms brought forward in mid-2011 push back further still into a framework of risk-as-paradigm. The Report of the Independent Banking Commission (Vicker's Report 2011) advocates more competition in the retail sector and a ring fencing of retail activities such that activities in the investment banking side do not impair retail activities.[28] This is quite sensible and unobjectionable on one level, but on another it leaves risk-taking activities and, crucially, the risk assumptions of the investment banking arm, wholly unchallenged. It isolates the consumer from the casino while leaving the casino intact. Given that the crisis began in the shadow banking sector and not the regulated sector, this is a bit like locking up the bar at a temperance meeting and hoping for the best.

The EU's initial crisis report makes much the same points and then goes on to show the same limits in its policy recommendations (de Larosière 2009). While not as sophisticated as the Turner Report in its analysis, it endorses the same set of principles but then goes on to advocate strengthening of EU-level supervisory arrangements as the key to resolving the crisis. That is, to get more and better information as the policy goal, again. The main proposal to come out of the report, taking the seven current EU-level financial oversight committees and dividing them into two new mega-boards—a systemic risk board charged with macro-prudential regulation and a European System of Financial Supervisors focusing on the micro-prudential side of things—more or less recreates the UK's proposed risk-based "information plus" system on an EU-wide scale.

Why the EU is seen as the appropriate level for regulation probably says more about the need for the EU to be seen "doing something" than the need for solutions stemming from this level. Indeed, the drive to regulate finance at the EU level has historically had as much to do with the political goal of integration as it has had to do with the economic goal of getting a better financial system (Posner 2009: 185–86). As Posner reports, while the EU has "since the middle of 2008...passed (or are considering) legislation (either directives, regulations or rules) on such matters as credit rating agencies, accounting standards, insurance, clearing and settlement, bank capital requirements, alternative investment funds, packaged retail investment funds, and remuneration of directors of listed companies and employees of financial services firms" (2009: 184), when one examines these new directives, regulations and rules, the whole is much less than the sum of its parts.[29] The centerpiece of much of this activity, the European Market Infrastructure Regulation (EMIR) that seeks to standardize derivatives and centralize clearing by 2013, remains at the proposal stage three years after the crisis. Once again, its main proposals take a world of risk as the given environment and the provision of greater transparency and lower operational risk as the goals of the reforms.[30]

In sum, reform approaches and recommendations from London, Europe's financial center, to Brussels, its regulatory center, presume that more and better application of the same old rules, based upon the same old assumptions, with a few twists, will solve the problem of planning for risk in an uncertain world without really considering that these problems may be endogenous to the system itself. Despite cracks appearing in our understandings of how markets work, and therefore how they should be governed, at a European level the "already rich" have as yet to make any fundamental break with risk-based ideas and practices. As I argue next, such a stance is already biting the "already rich" in the backside far faster than they expect as the result of the risk double bind (which opens them to new sources of financial fragility) combining with an austerity double bind that compounds this error. To see how this secondary double bind arose we need to shift the focus to Germany's response to the crisis and to its very different understanding of risk to that of the British and American financial elites.

Tying the Austerity Double Bind

In contrast to the finance-dependent growth model of the UK and the United States, the export-led growth model of Germany rebounded extremely well in 2010. Yet in terms of fiscal policy, Germany was widely criticized for fretting about inflation in the middle of a deflation, effectively free-riding off its neighbors and trading partners' stimulus packages. While true, what is actually most distinctive about the German response to the crisis is how it fretted about throwing good money after bad. As Chancellor Merkel put it in late 2008, "cheap money in the U.S. was a driver of this crisis…I am deeply concerned…[with]…reinforcing this trend…[and wonder]…whether we could find ourselves back in five years facing the same crisis" (quoted in Newman 2010: 9). As Newman (2010) points out, such a policy stance speaks to the very different conception of risk that German policy makers operate with, in contradistinction to that of Anglo-American financial markets. In the Anglo-American case, risk, as we have seen, is something to be sliced, diced, quantified, and embraced. For the Germans, risk is something best avoided. Hence what emerged from Germany was a very different policy response that began to take shape in late 2008 and was pushed to the forefront with the Greek debt crisis of early 2009: a policy of fiscal austerity (a.k.a. reducing sovereign risk) as the way to control systemic risk.

By late 2011, the Eurozone was in full systemic meltdown, with Italy being in the firing line of the bond markets. Yet the basic problem with the Eurozone is not individual state budgets so much as the design of the Euro itself. As George Soros noted, "the Euro boasts a common central bank, but lacks a common treasury" (2010). This creates a problem in that when the Eurozone economy is on the upswing, the European Central Bank (ECB) mandate of "fight inflation" makes sense. However, when crisis and deflation rather than inflation is the order of the day, the ECB resembles less an effective central bank and more a currency board with an inflation target since it is constitutionally limited from active lender-of-last-resort measures.

In short, the existence of the ECB rules out either inflation or devaluation as policy responses, which leaves only internal deflation (austerity) and default (to be avoided for fear of contagion) as alternatives. Thus, when it became apparent in early 2009 that the Greeks had been less than forthcoming about the true state of their public finances, bond markets demanded a premium to hold their debt since the true risk of the asset was not reflected in its price.[31] Yields shot up, spreads against German debt widened, and CDS prices ballooned, creating both arbitrage opportunities and fear of contagion where losses in one part of the portfolio (Greece) need to be made whole by selling assets before they become distressed (Ireland, Italy), creating the very yield spikes that push these countries further into debt and create the panic that markets seek to avoid.[32]

Compounding this institutional design problem is the weakness of the underlying European banking system. Again, as Soros notes, "the continental European banking system was never properly cleansed after the crash of 2008. Bad assets have not been marked-to-market…and are instead being held to maturity" (2010: 4). Indeed we now know from BIS and other data that core banks in the Netherlands, Germany, and especially France hold as much as 20 percent of their countries' respective GDPs (gross domestic products) in impaired periphery assets, having dumped their own countries' debt for the marginal but profitable extra yield on periphery debt some ten years back when yields converged.[33] Now that the yields have shot up and prices have fallen, the "risk" has been revealed some ten years after the fact, that these banks balance sheets are seriously impaired. As such, the perceived credit risk of the European banking system, and thus of the Eurozone states themselves as their banks' backstops, has increased. This has in turn increased the costs and availability of interbank financing that only the ECB now provides, a fact more or less admitted to be the ECB's December 2011 Long Term Lending Operations (LTROs) that gave European banks a half trillion Euro for three years at effectively zero interest. Ironically then, far from reducing risk through austerity, Europe seems to be operating as a giant risk generator for the global economy, all in the name of reducing risk.

All this matters for our discussion of risk and uncertainty because seeing the European debt crisis as a problem of profligate states means that the only way to reduce the threat of contagion is to reduce government debt, which means the end of "profligate" government spending and the embrace of fiscal austerity.[34] However, and here is the double bind, while it is rational for any one state to reduce its debt, if all states do so at once, as the German-led austerity drive in Europe demands, then all we do is shrink the overall size of the economy and thus the underlying rate of growth. This is a problem because as Carlin notes, "if the nominal interest rate that the government has to pay on its debt is greater than the nominal rate of growth in the economy, the interest payments due (the numerator) will be adding to the total debt faster than growth is increasing GDP (the denominator) thereby increasing the debt ratio" (2011: 4). In other words, states collectively currently feel an imperative at the individual level to cut spending. But to achieve growth and avoid actually increasing debt ratio they must avoid shrinking the overall size of the economy, which is hard to do when both private and public sectors are deleveraging. These two imperatives cannot be reconciled. Once again, action to "do the right thing" as seen through a lens of risk produces the very outcome states are trying to avoid, and all in the name of reducing risk once again.

The European sovereign debt crisis has then added an important twist to financial reform efforts in Europe since it makes bank regulation in areas that would increase the cost of capital (adequacy ratios) or limit leverage, the main areas of reform, much less likely. After all, if one is trying to kick-start an economy by depriving it of public spending when private spending is falling and the banks are dangerously underwater, then adding "onerous" new regulations that further hamper growth when interest rates are already on the floor appears rather unlikely. In terms of actual and proposed reforms to date, what we see is a situation where the regulators "get the problem" and recommend implementing a set of rules that take the limits or risk-based finance seriously. Yet what we have ended up with is a set of reforms that are still based upon a "risk" view of the world, which is in turn compounded by a fiscal stance that allows both banks and politicians to avoid more substantive reforms. The problem in doing so is that such policies leave Europe dangerously vulnerable to a secondary banking crisis that the new risk-based rules will not obviate and that the double binds of risk and austerity will only worsen.

Conclusion: Looking Under the Lamppost for Greater Transparency

Financial crises have severe real costs. As Reinhardt and Rogoff (2009) have demonstrated, across all developed world (post-1977) financial crises (eighteen cases), asset price collapses of the order of 35 percent for housing and 55 percent for equities and unemployment increases of 9 percent above base are the norm during the bust phase of the cycle, which can be up to six years depending on the asset class. Given this, it is little surprise then that government debts surge by an average of over 80 percent as current tax receipts collapse and deficits expand as the private sector deleverages and the public sector levers up through bailouts to compensate. We have seen exactly this process in this crisis. It was a banking crisis that caused a sovereign debt crisis that was rebaptized as a profligate state crisis.

This "twin crisis" of private finance and public bailouts and their associated double binds has made the fiscal and monetary positions of many of the "already rich" countries extremely precarious. Yet despite becoming seriously impaired, the banking systems of these countries have had, by some measures, their most profitable ever year in 2010. Meanwhile, those who paid for the bailouts are being told to get ready to pay again in the form of fiscal austerity. Consequently, the impetus for fundamental financial reform fades fast as what was a problem of miscalculated risk in the financial sector is rechristened as the crisis of the profligate state.

Apart from the fiscal effects of such double binding, if we build the new rules for finance to the same specifications as before, we will likely increase the impact of the next crisis. We will do so because, tweaking the system only as far as building a risk-based world allows, we will not make the system robust enough. Given the position of "already rich" public finances for the next several years, any such crisis could signal a real disaster.

Both European and American financial systems are now too big to bail rather than too big to fail, and while banks can run 35:1 leverage rations without attracting attention, when states lever up 1:1, which we are approaching all across the OECD (Organisation for Economic Co-operation and Development) today, the costs of borrowing to safeguard against the next bust may bust the state itself. The reason we fall into this trap is that, like the proverbial drunk looking for his keys under the lamppost "because that's where the light is," our sticky acceptance of a world of risk as the world we actually live in, which leads us to a world of fiscal consolidation as the correct response, despite all the evidence to the contrary, will once again blind us to what may come next. Consider the following two examples of what might tear right through these proposed new regulatory architectures.

The first example comes from the current crisis over Greek public finances and speaks to the poverty of rule-based and informational solutions. German politicians and the neoclassical economists who advise them have one thing in common: they both think in terms of rational agents that follow rules. As such, both EMU (European Monetary Union) convergence criteria and the economic literature on rules versus discretion assume that rules are better than discretion, and that politicians should have as much of the former and as little of the latter as they can handle. The problem is of course neither German bureaucrats nor their advisors thought it at all likely that private-sector actors such as Goldman Sachs would tell politicians how to appear to abide by rules while developing the technology to break them without being caught. That type of risk can't be seen in the prior data.

The second example stems directly from this double bind of austerity and risk. Imagine you are a major European bank. A lot of your portfolio will today be concentrated in government debt, and you still have a lot of bad assets on your books such as East European mortgages. As such, you are concerned with government debt levels, and some fiscal consolidation might make you feel more secure in your bond portfolio. But what about your equity positions? Cleaning your books depends upon growth and fiscal consolidation will hurt that. As the value of your equity position drops as growth shrinks due to the fiscal consolidation you think is a good idea, growth stalls, assets fall in value, and leverage bites back once again on the downside, and the EU is quite suddenly facing a secondary banking crisis. Except this time it is from a much more exposed position since the state is just as levered up as the bank to be rescued. This time there will be no bailout since austerity politics rules that out, even if the European taxpayer could be milked one more time.

Given this, none of the architectural reforms proposed or enacted to date will make any difference whatsoever in either of these scenarios. Neither more information, nor greater transparency, nor more and better risk models run by smarter and larger risk councils, will obviate these threats. In fact, treating them as risk problems that can be modeled and anticipated while focusing on fiscal retrenchment will exacerbate the problem. After all, if austerity is a good thing, and if government debt is bad, how can more spending be good? Trapped like drunks under the risk-assessment lamppost, we open ourselves up to being caught again in a crisis of our own making.

While the editors to this book have good reason to put faith in the transformational power of technology, I try to think about how technology can often give us a false sense of security. I am therefore less confident that technology alone, as seen in these reforms, and the world that they presuppose, will be sufficient to stop the rich countries doing enough damage to themselves to severely limit their future capacity for growth.

The problem is not that it is much more difficult to write rules for an uncertain world. In many ways it is simpler. Complex systems need simple rules. Think, for example, of traffic systems. These are nonlinear complex systems. But one simple rule, we all drive on one side of the road, eliminates 90 percent of potential accidents, even in Boston. In fact, there is no shortage of simple rules that would work to stabilize an uncertain world, or at least make it more stable than the current direction of rule-making travel: countercyclical capital charges tied to growth of particular asset classes, for example, or common fee schedules and order times across exchanges to rule out regulatory arbitrage.

The problem, obviously, is that these rules would seriously curtail much of the activity on and off exchanges (think High Frequency Trading or maximizing the spread in OTC (over-the-counter) contracts with private information) that, while it has no or little social benefit, is extremely profitable. Writing the rules is not the problem: changing the incentives of the politicians and the bankers who denude and avoid them is. Those simple rules, we would be told, would curtail financial innovation and limit liquidity, as well as require a whole new funding model of politics. But we have to ask ourselves, especially on the heels of a $3 trillion blowup, if this isn't the real price that we have to pay? Maybe a precautionary principle applied to finance is the way to go in light of current events rather than more risky tweaking.

Acknowledgments

The author would like to thank the Alfred P. Sloan Foundation for financial support and the Berkeley Roundtable on the International Economy (BRIE) for research and administrative support. The author also wishes to thank Cornel Ban, Mitchell Orenstein, Danny Breznitz, and John Zysman for comments on earlier versions of this draft.

Notes

1. I do, however, wish to differentiate this argument from the so-called law of unintended consequences. First of all, there is no such law. If it was a law, then outcomes would be anticipated and thus be quite intended. Second, in its pure form, the "law of unintended consequences" is purely a rhetorical device; a perversity thesis as Hirschman (1994) had it, where reformist actions always and everywhere produce the very outcomes they are trying to avoid. What I want to stress here is that while this is not true in the general case (welfare regimes do not make most people lazy and life insurance does not cause moral hazard suicides, etc.), it is true in the particular case of global financial reform in the context of the current crisis.

2. Again, I thank an anonymous reviewer for this formulation of the problem.

3. As Taleb and Pilpel put it, in an uncertain world "before a catastrophic event [occurs]…extrapolating from past data to future behavior of such a system is *worthless*" (2004: 21).

4. Note this is frequency, not magnitude, which would require scaling with logs.

5. Indeed, our actions are part of the generating process and are therefore endogenous to that which we are trying to measure. I thank an anonymous reviewer of this chapter for this succinct formulation.

6. In more formal terms, the payoffs to strategies in systems with complex hidden generators are convex and nonlinear. This is why setting arbitrary capital buffers as reserves is at best flawed and at worse a false solution.

7. That is, if individual institutions make bad bets and go bust, bailing them out simply encourages other firms to assume that they will also be bailed out, so the optimal, and indeed only necessary policy is "no bail outs."

8. As we shall see later, this is precisely where we ended up with the Basel banking conventions as the global regulatory architecture.

9. That is, any downside is limited while the upside is unlimited (in theory).

10. The tranche structure pooled different mortgages into different risk bundles and assembled them in different risk/return combinations. It was assumed that this structure reduced correlation risk. See Tett 2009.

11. AIG Financial Products was located in London, but its regulator was the insurance regulator of Pennsylvania.

12. Add to this the problem of correlation in the supersenior (safest) tranche of CDOs (that many banks ended up keeping on-book) and what was supposed to be a diversification technique (tranching) ended up creating correlation among assets such that when one went down, they all went down, with disastrous results (Tett 2009).

13. A classic fallacy of composition where the whole does not equal the sum of the parts. As John Maynard Keynes warned us over sixty years ago, "[o]f the maxims of orthodox finance none, surely, is more anti-social than the fetish of liquidity, the doctrine that it is a positive virtue on the part of investment institutions to concentrate their resources upon the holding of 'liquid' securities. It forgets that there is no such thing as liquidity of investment for the community as a whole" (1936: 155).

14. See http://research.stlouisfed.org/fred2/series/FEDFUNDS?cid=118 and http://research.stlouisfed.org/fred2/series/CD6M?cid=121. Retrieved November 12, 2011.

15. See http://research.stlouisfed.org/fred2/series/FREQ5?cid=93 and http://research.stlouisfed.org/fred2/series/CONSUMER?cid=100 and http://research.stlouisfed.org/fred2/series/REALLN?cid=49. Retrieved November 12, 2011.

16. To see why moving average (bidding-up) creates risk problems, consider this example. If you work in finance and your bonus depends upon beating a benchmark average, and all your competitors are buying the same assets and hedges as you, then the only way to beat the average returns is to take more risk into the portfolio. But if everyone does this the total risk in the portfolio stays the same relative to the return, which makes it look like the risks being taken fall when they are in fact on the rise.

17. While real demand factors play a role here, it is not as if the population of China—the main culprit in the financial press—has quadrupled in size or doubled income in the past year and a half and then lost half that increase in the next six months.

18. To paraphrase Shakespeare, the fault Brutus, lay in the stars *and* within us.

19. I am not saying that the Basel 1 and 2 regulations caused the crisis in a linear sense. Rather, I am claiming that the move to self-regulation is emblematic of viewing the world as one of programmable risk. As such, designing risk management schemes that assumed such programmability was and still is a one-way bet if the world turns out to be a world of uncertainty.

20. Even if it turned out after the fact that very few actually had as much skin in the game as the regulatory assumed.

21. It also encouraged the securitization trend that turbo-charged mortgages since securitizing less risky loans and turning them into income streams reduced the *de jure* risk of the bank's loan book (Balin 2008: 5).

22. Retrieved November 12, 2011 (http://www.bloomberg.com/news/2011-11-09/financial-alchemy-undercuts-capital-regime-as-european-banks-redefine-risk.html).

23. "Stability produces risk and risk produces stability," as Hyman Minsky once put it.

24. Indeed, according to Reinhart and Rogoff (2009) this selfsame pattern has occurred eighteen times since 1977 with increasing frequency and severity in the developed world alone. As such, any claim to statistical normality for such events, and thus the utility of techniques that assume it to be a property of the world, falls further into question.

25. After all, there is nothing in the data that would suggest you should stress your VaR with a scenario where all the liquidity in the world dries up.

26. This suggests that the regulators knowing what to do doesn't mean that they get to do it. It is at best a necessary, but insufficient, condition of action.

27. The same can be said of the UK Treasury's October 2009 statement on liquidity standards. They were very tough, until one read that they would not be implemented until the crisis was over, by which time the government will be out of office.

28. Retrieved November 12, 2011 (http://www.ft.com/intl/cms/s/0/7321c692-dd16-11e0-b4f2-00144feabdc0.html#axzz1dWiGjFK6).

29. Take the new settlement clearing proposals. These clearly state that "the Commission evaluated the two directives in 2005 and 2006, respectively. Following extensive consultation the Commission concluded that both directives work well. . . . The Commission does therefore not propose any substantial changes but propose to amend them in limited areas in order bring them

in line with regulatory and market developments having occurred since the time of their drafting and adoption. See http://europa.eu/rapid/pressReleasesAction.do?reference=MEMO/08/267&format=HTML&aged=0&language=EN&guiLanguage=en. Retrieved November 12, 2011.

30. Retrieved November 12, 2011 (http://europa.eu/rapid/pressReleasesAction.do?reference=IP/10/1125&format=HTML&aged=0&language=EN&guiLanguage=en).

31. Retrieved August 30, 2010 (http://www.ft.com/cms/s/0/97311356-f999-11de-8085-00144feab49a.html, and http://www.bloomberg.com/news/2010-04-21/papandreou-caught-between-strikes-and-imf-as-bond-yields-surge-to-record.html).

32. Retrieved August 30, 2010 (http://www.ft.com/cms/s/0/953bfda8-117d-11df-9195-00144feab49a.html).

33. Retrieved November 12, 2011 (http://www.bis.org/publ/qtrpdf/r_qt1103.pdf). This is not to posit schizophrenic Germans who reject risk and then buy risky bonds. It is merely to point out that the people controlling the current account, the capital account, and the supervisory frameworks are all different. It's perfectly possible for prudent German savers' savings to be turned into risky sovereign debt by banks that thought they would be bailed out if they got into trouble by complacent regulators who saw no risk in current practices.

34. What this also overlooks unfortunately is that of the 39.1 percent of "extra" government debt (as a percentage of GDP) the "average" G20 country has added on to its balance sheet, only 12 percent of that debt is extra spending. Eighty-eight percent of the debt is the cost of bailing out the banks, revenue losses, and extra interest charges (IMF 2009, 2010: 14). As such, those paying for the debt are not the ones who generated it.

References

Abdelal, Rawi. (2006). *Capital Rules.* Cambridge, MA: Harvard University Press.
Abdelal, Rawi, Mark Blyth, and Craig Parsons. (Eds.). (2010). *Constructing the International Economy.* Ithaca, NY: Cornell University Press.
Balin, Bryan. (2008). "Basel 1, Basel 2 and emerging markets: A non technical analysis" (unpublished manuscript), Johns Hopkins School of Advanced International Studies, Washington, D.C.
Bleaney, Michael. (1985). *The Rise and Fall of Keynesian Macroeconomics.* London: Macmillan.
Blyth, Mark. (2001). "The transformation of the Swedish model: Economic ideas, distributional conflict and institutional change." *World Politics* 54(1): 1–26.
Blyth, Mark. (2003). "The Political Power of Financial Ideas: Transparency, Risk and Distribution in Global Finance." In *Monetary Orders*, edited by Jonathan Kirshner, 239–59. Ithaca, NY: Cornell University Press.
Blyth, Mark. (2008). "The politics of compounding bubbles: The global housing bubble in comparative perspective." *Comparative European Politics* 6(3): 387–406.
Blyth, Mark. (2011). "Beyond the Standard Model." In *Ideas and Politics in Social Science Research*, edited by Robert Cox and Daniel Beland. New York: Oxford University Press.
Blyth, Mark, and Neil Shenai. (2010). "The G20s dead ideas." *Foreign Policy,* July. Web ed.
Brunnermeier, Markus, K. (2008) "Decipering the Liquidity and Credit Crunch 2007–2008." Available at http://econ.ucdenver.edu/beckman/crisis/brunnermeier-jep.pdf

Carlin, W. (2011). "Ten questions about the Eurozone crisis and whether it can be solved" [mimeo], September 8.

Cassidy, John. (2009). *How Markets Fail: The Logic of Economic Calamities.* New York: Farrar, Strauss and Giroux.

de Larosière, Jacques. (Chair). (2009). "The high-level group on financial supervision in the EU" [Report]. Brussels, Belgium. Retrieved August 30, 2010 (http://ec.europa.eu/internal_market/finances/docs/de_larosiere_report_en.pdf).

Dowd, Kevin, et al. (2008). "How Unlucky is a Twenty-Five Sigma?" Available at http://arxiv.org/pdf/1103.5672.pdf

Eatwell, John. (1996). International financial liberalization: The impact on world development. UNDP Discussion Paper Series No. 64. New York.

Economic Report of the President. (2010). Washington, D.C.: U.S. Government Printing Office.

Fox, Justin. (2009). *The Myth of the Rational Market.* New York: Harpers.

Goodman, Peter. (2010). *Past Due: The End of Easy Money and the Renewal of the American Economy.* New York: Times Books.

Helleiner, Eric. (1994). *States and the Reemergence of Global Finance.* Ithaca, NY: Cornell University Press.

Hirschman, Albert. (1994). *The Rhetoric of Reaction: Perversity, Futility, Jeopardy.* Cambridge, MA: Harvard Belknap Press.

IMF. (2009). *Cross Country Fiscal Monitor*, November 3. Washington, D.C.: IMF

IMF. (2010). *Cross Country Fiscal Monitor*, May 10. Washington, D.C.: IMF.

Kauffman, Stuart. (2008). *Reinventing the Sacred: A New View of Science, Reason and Religion.* New York: Basic Books.

Keynes, John Maynard. (1936). *The General Theory of Employment, Interest and Money.* New York: Harcort Brace 1964/1936.

Lewis, Michael. (2010). *The Big Short: Inside the Doomsday Machine.* New York: W.W. Norton.

MacKenzie, Donald. (2006). *An Engine, Not a Camera: How Financial Models Shape Markets.* Cambridge, MA: MIT Press.

MacKenzie, Donald. (2009). "All those arrows." *London Review of Books* 31(12): 20–22.

Newman, Abraham. (2010). "Flight from risk: Unified Germany and the role of beliefs in the European response to the financial crisis." *German Politics and Society* 28(2): 156–64.

Persaud, Avinash. (2000). "Sending the herd of the cliff edge" (http://www.erisk.com/resource-center/erm/persaud.pdf).

Posner, Elliot. (2009). "Is There a European Approach to Financial Regulation Emerging from the Crisis?" In *Global Finance in Crisis: The Politics of International Regulatory Change*, edited by Eric Helleiner, Stefano Pagliari, and Hubert Zimmermann, 108–20. London: Routledge.

Reinhart, Carmen, and Kenneth Rogoff. (2008). This time is different: A panoramic view of eight centuries of financial crisis. NBER Working Paper No. 13882, Cambridge, MA.

Reinhart, Carmen, and Kenneth Rogoff. (2009). The aftermath of financial crises. NBER Working Paper 14656. Cambridge, MA.

Seabrooke, Leonard. (2006). *The Social Sources of Financial Power.* Ithaca, NY: Cornell University Press

Schwartz, Herman. (2009). *Subprime Nation.* Ithaca, NY: Cornell University Press.

Soros, George. (2010). "The crisis and the Euro." *New York Review of Books*, August 19.

Taleb, Nassim N. (2008). "The fourth quadrant: A map of the limits of statistics" (http://www.edge.org/3rd_culture/taleb08/taleb08_index.html).

Taleb, Nassim N., and Avital Pilpel. (2003). "On the Very Unfortunate Problem of the Nonobservability of the Probability Distribution." Unpublished Manuscript 2003. Available at http://www.fooledbyrandomness.com/knowledge.pdf.

Tett, Gillian. (2009). *Fool's Gold: How the Bold Dream of a Small Tribe at J.P. Morgan Was Corrupted by Wall Street Greed and Unleashed a Catastrophe.* New York: Free Press.

Tsingou, Eleni. (2008). "Transnational Private Governance and the Basel Process: Banking Regulation, Private Interests and Basel II." In *Transnational Private Governance and Its Limits* [ECPR/Routledge series], edited by Andreas Nölke and Jean-Christophe Graz, 58–68. London: Routledge.

Tsingou, Eleni. (2009). "Regulatory Reactions to the Credit Crisis: Analysing a Policy Community Under Stress." In *Global Finance in Crisis: The Politics of International Regulatory Change*, edited by Eric Helleiner, Stefano Pagliari, and Hubert Zimmermann, 21–36. London: Routledge.

Turner, Adair. (2009). *The Turner Review: A Regulatory Response to the Global Banking Crisis.* London: Financial Services Authority.

Warwick Commission on International Financial Reform. (2009). In praise of unlevel playing fields [Report by multiple authors] (http://www2.warwick.ac.uk/research/warwickcommission/financialreform/report/).

Wolf, Martin. (2008). *Fixing Global Finance.* Baltimore, MD: Johns Hopkins University Press.

Woolley, Paul, et al. (2010). *The Future of Finance and the Theory That Underpins It.* London: LSE Center for Capital Market Dysfunctionality.

9 The Fragility of the U.S. Economy
THE FINANCIALIZED CORPORATION AND THE DISAPPEARING MIDDLE CLASS
William Lazonick

Inequity and Instability in the World's Largest Economy

The United States has the world's largest economy in terms of gross domestic product. In 2010 it was the home base of 133 of the world's top 500 business corporations by revenues.[1] In 2010 the 500 largest U.S.-based corporations had $10.8 trillion in worldwide revenues, $709 billion in worldwide profits, and employed 25.1 million people in the United States and abroad.[2]

At the same time, the U.S. economy is fragile because of a failure of its leading corporations to make sufficient investments in innovation in the United States to generate the high value-added jobs for a national workforce that must compete globally on the basis of high productivity rather than low wages. The fundamental reason for this fragility, I argue, is the "financialization" of corporate resource allocation. By financialization, I mean the evaluation of the performance of a company by a financial measure, such as earnings per share (EPS), rather than by the goods and services that it produces, the customers it serves, and the people whom it employs.

The growth of the U.S. economy depends on corporate investment in innovation, defined in economic terms as higher-quality goods and services at lower-unit costs, given prevailing factor prices. Only innovation can generate the types of jobs that are sustainable in a high-wage economy as the U.S. labor force competes against qualified labor in lower wage parts of the world. Innovation is an uncertain, collective, and cumulative process. Investment in innovation is a direct investment that involves, first and foremost, a strategic confrontation with technological, market, and competitive uncertainty. Business executives who allocate resources to innovation must decide, in the face of uncertainty, what types of investments have the potential to generate higher-quality, lower-cost products. Then they must mobilize committed finance to sustain the cumulative innovation process until, through collective (or organizational) learning that transforms technologies and accesses markets, it generates the higher-quality, lower-cost products that permit financial returns (Lazonick 2010b).

The financialization of corporate resource allocation undermines investment in innovation. The high fixed-cost investments inevitably required to develop technologies and access markets reduce EPS in the short term. Hence business executives who are concerned with meeting EPS targets on a quarterly basis have incentives to avoid investments in innovation. In the process, these executives can personally benefit by exercising stock options at higher stock market prices. In the United States, the ability of a stock option holder to reap gains from exercising stock options is rarely constrained by criteria that ensure that these gains reflect the productive performance of the company for which he or she works. As we shall see, unindexed stock options enable an executive to gain from both stock market speculation and stock market manipulation. This form of compensation gives an executive an interest in touting the prospects of the company to encourage speculation in the company's stock, even in cases for which the optimistic projections are not warranted. It also gives an executive an interest in allocating resources to repurchasing his or her own company's shares with the purpose of boosting the company's stock price and hitting quarterly EPS targets. As we shall see, gains from the exercise of stock options represent the most important single component of top executive pay at major U.S. corporations, while stock repurchases have become the most important means by which corporations "create value" for shareholders, including, first and foremost, the very executives who make these corporate allocation decisions.

The ideology, prevalent since the early 1980s, that has justified the financialization of corporate resource allocation is the belief that, for the sake of superior economic performance, corporate resources should be allocated to "maximize shareholder value" (MSV). Over the ensuing decades, this ideology became firmly entrenched in the minds of corporate executives, business academics, and even government regulators. The financial crisis that resulted in the Great Recession of 2008–09 did inspire, however, one very high-profile denunciation of MSV. In an interview in *The Financial Times* in March 2009 (Guerrera 2009), Jack Welch, former CEO (chief executive officer) of General Electric, proclaimed: "On the face of it, shareholder value is the dumbest idea in the world. Shareholder value is a result, not a strategy...your main constituencies are your employees, your customers and your products" (Guerrera 2009). Perhaps in response to a look of astonishment on the face of the interviewer, Welch went on to reiterate: "It is a dumb idea. The idea that shareholder value is a strategy is insane. It is the product of your combined efforts—from the management to the employees."

Nevertheless, the fact is that, especially in the United States, this "dumb idea" rules corporate business behavior as much, if not more, after the Great Recession of 2008–09 as it did before. In this chapter, I explain why MSV is a "dumb idea" in terms of the performance of both the business corporation and the economy as a whole. Based on "agency theory," financial economists argue that among all the participants in the corporate economy, it is only shareholders who make productive contributions without a guaranteed return. Hence, as the sole risk bearers in corporate investments, the agency argument goes, shareholders are "residual claimants" to whom "free cash flow" should be distributed for the sake of the optimal allocation of the economy's resources. In contrast, "innovation theory" argues that governments and employees regularly make productive contributions to the corporate economy without a guaranteed return, and by agency theory's own logic, taxpayers and workers should also have "residual claimant status." Indeed, given that the innovation process requires "financial commitment," it is not at all clear that public shareholders, who are willing to participate in the stock market because it provides financial *liquidity*, make productive contributions to the innovation process in the first place.

Following my critique of MSV, I provide a historical summary of when, how, and why corporate resource allocation became financialized in the United States. The first transformation in corporate organization that resulted in financialization was the conglomerate movement of the 1960s in which, especially at its peak at the end of that decade, companies took on debt to acquire other companies for the sole purpose of increasing EPS, so that public investors would bid up the conglomerate's stock price. In the 1970s the collapse of the conglomerate movement provided the "junk" bonds from which Michael Milken created the high-yield bond market that would ultimately enable the hostile takeover movement of the 1980s. With the rise of a "market for corporate control," debt was used to take over companies that would then be downsized and sold off in pieces in order to make the deal pay. Meanwhile high inflation in the 1970s encouraged Wall Street to shift from helping companies raise funds for investment in long-term growth to helping stock market investors find ways to secure higher yields on corporate securities by laying hold of corporations' so-called free cash flow. Increasingly from the 1980s, the favored mode of extracting this cash flow from U.S. corporations became repurchases of the corporations' own outstanding common stock. Legitimizing these changes in financial institutions has been the ideology that superior economic performance can be achieved when companies seek to maximize shareholder value.

I then show how, driven by MSV ideology, since the early 1980s, the financialization of corporate resource allocation has contributed to the growing inequality of income, instability of employment, and disappearance of middle-class jobs in the U.S. economy. My argument is that since the beginning of the 1980s employment relations in U.S. industrial corporations have undergone three major structural changes—which I summarize as "rationalization," "marketization," and "globalization"—that have permanently eliminated middle-class jobs. From the early 1980s, rationalization, characterized by plant closings, eliminated the jobs of unionized blue-collar workers. From the early 1990s, marketization, characterized by the end of a career with one company as an employment norm, placed the job security of middle-aged and older white-collar workers in jeopardy. From the early 2000s, globalization, characterized by the offshoring of employment, left all types of members of the U.S. labor force, even those with advanced educational credentials and substantial work experience, vulnerable to displacement.

Initially, each of these structural changes in employment could be justified in terms of major changes in the industrial conditions related to technologies, markets, and competition. In the early 1980s, the plant closings that characterized rationalization were a response to the superior productive capabilities of Japanese competitors in consumer durable and related capital goods industries that employed significant numbers of unionized blue-collar workers. In the early 1990s, the erosion of the one-company-career norm among white-collar workers that characterized marketization was a response to the dramatic technological shift from proprietary technology systems to open technology systems that was integral to the microelectronics revolution. In the early 2000s, the acceleration in the offshoring of the jobs of well-educated and highly experienced members of the U.S. labor force that characterized globalization was a response to the emergence of large supplies of highly capable labor in lower-wage developing nations such as China and India.

Once U.S. corporations adopted these structural changes in employment, however, they often pursued these employment strategies purely for financial gain. Some companies closed manufacturing plants, terminated experienced (and generally more expensive) workers, and offshored production to low-wage areas of the world simply to increase profits, often at the expense of the long-term competitive capabilities of the company and without regard for the many years of service that employees had devoted to the company. Moreover, as these changes became embedded in the structure of U.S. employment, financialized business corporations failed to invest in new, higher value-added job creation on a sufficient scale to provide a foundation for equitable and stable growth in the U.S. economy.

On the contrary, with superior corporate performance defined as meeting Wall Street's expectations of steadily rising targets of quarterly EPS, companies turned to massive stock repurchases. Trillions of dollars that could have been spent on innovation and job creation in the U.S. economy over the past three decades have instead been used to buy back stock, the sole purpose of which is to manipulate the company's stock price. Legitimizing this financialized mode of corporate resource allocation has been the ideology, itself a product of the 1980s and 1990s, that a business corporation should be run to "maximize shareholder value." Through their stock-based compensation, prime beneficiaries of this focus on rising stock prices as the measure of corporate performance have been the very same corporate executives who make these financialized resource allocation decisions.

In light of my analysis of the relation between the financialization of the U.S. corporation and the disappearance of middle-class jobs, the final section of this chapter suggests ways in which the U.S. economy should be reformed to set the United States back on a path toward equitable and stable economic growth. These reforms include (1) banning of stock repurchases by established U.S. corporations so corporate financial resources that could be allocated to innovation and job creation are not wasted for the purpose of manipulating companies' stock prices; (2) indexing of employee stock options to one or more indicators of innovative performance so that executives cannot gain from speculation in and manipulation of their companies' stock prices; (3) regulation of the employment contract to ensure that employees who contribute to the innovation process share in the gains to innovation; (4) creation of work programs that make use of and enhance the capabilities of educated and experienced workers whose human capital would otherwise deteriorate through lack of other relevant employment; and (5) implementation of taxes on the gains from innovation to fund those government agencies that need to invest in the public knowledge base required for the next round of innovation. I argue that an intellectual, and political, precondition for these reforms is a rejection of the ideology that corporations should be run to maximize shareholder value. Within academia, there is a need for innovation theory to replace agency theory as an intellectual framework for understanding the achievement of superior economic performance (see Lazonick 2011b).

Shareholder Value Ideology

The ideology that, for the sake of superior economic performance, companies should "maximize shareholder value" was a product of the early 1980s (Rappaport 1981, 1983). At the same time, through agency theory, academic economists supported this ideology by propounding a shareholder-value perspective on corporate governance that is consistent with the neoclassical theory of the market economy (Fama and Jensen 1983a, 1983b). Especially in the United States, MSV remains the dominant ideology of corporate governance not only in business schools and economics departments but also in executive suites and corporate boardrooms.

For adherents of the neoclassical theory of the market economy, "market imperfections" necessitate managerial control over the allocation of resources, thus creating an "agency problem" for those "principals" who have made investments in the firm. These managers may allocate corporate resources to build their own personal empires regardless of whether the investments that they make and the people whom they employ generate sufficient profits for the firm. They may hoard surplus cash or near-liquid assets within the corporation, thus maintaining control over uninvested resources, rather than distributing these extra revenues to shareholders. Or, they may simply use their control over resource allocation to line their own pockets. According to agency theory, in the absence of corporate governance institutions that promote the maximization of shareholder value, one should expect managerial control to result in the inefficient allocation of resources.

The manifestation of a movement toward the more efficient allocation of resources, it is argued, is a higher return to shareholders. But why is it shareholders for whom value should be maximized? Why not create more value for creditors by making their financial investments more secure, or for employees by paying them higher wages and benefits, or for communities in which the corporations operate by generating more corporate tax revenues? Agency theorists argue that among all the stakeholders in the business corporation only shareholders are "residual claimants." The amount of returns that shareholders receive depends on what is left over after other stakeholders, all of whom it is argued have guaranteed contractual claims, have been paid for their productive contributions to the firm. If the firm incurs a loss, the return to shareholders is negative, and vice versa.

By this argument, shareholders are the only stakeholders who have an incentive to bear the risk of investing in productive resources that may result in superior economic performance. As residual claimants, moreover, shareholders are the only stakeholders who have an interest in monitoring managers to ensure that they allocate resources efficiently. Furthermore, by selling and buying corporate shares on the stock market, public shareholders, it is argued, are the participants in the economy who are best situated to reallocate resources to more efficient uses.

Within the shareholder-value paradigm, the stock market represents the corporate governance institution through which the agency problem can be resolved and the efficient allocation of the economy's resources can be achieved. Specifically, the stock market can function as a "market for corporate control" that enables shareholders to "disgorge"—to use Michael Jensen's evocative term—the "free cash flow." As Jensen, a leading academic proponent of maximizing shareholder value, put it in a seminal 1986 article:

> Free cash flow is cash flow in excess of that required to fund all projects that have positive net present values when discounted at the relevant cost of capital. Conflicts of interest between shareholders and managers over payout policies are especially severe when the organization generates substantial free cash flow. The problem is how to motivate managers to disgorge the cash rather than investing it at below cost or wasting it on organization inefficiencies. (1986: 323)

How can those managers who control the allocation of corporate resources be motivated, or coerced, to distribute cash to shareholders? If a company does not maximize shareholder value, shareholders can sell their shares and reallocate the proceeds to what they deem to be more efficient uses. The sale of shares depresses that company's stock price, which in turn facilitates a takeover by shareholders who can put in place managers who are willing to distribute the free cash flow to shareholders in the forms of higher dividends and/or stock repurchases. Better yet, as Jensen argued in the midst of the 1980s corporate takeover movement, let corporate raiders use the market for corporate control for debt-financed takeovers, thus enabling shareholders to transform their corporate equities into corporate bonds. Corporate managers would then be "bonded" to distribute the "free cash flow" in the form of interest rather than dividends (Jensen 1986: 324).

Additionally, as Jensen and Murphy (1990), among others, contended, the maximization of shareholder value could be achieved by giving corporate managers stock-based compensation, such as stock options, to align their own self-interests with those of shareholders. Then, even without the threat of a takeover, these managers would have a personal incentive to maximize shareholder value by investing corporate revenues only in those "projects that have positive net present values when discounted at the relevant cost of capital" and distributing the remainder of corporate revenues to shareholders in the forms of dividends and/or stock repurchases.

During the 1980s and 1990s, MSV became the dominant ideology for corporate governance in the United States. Top executives of U.S. industrial corporations became ardent advocates of this perspective; quite apart from their ideological predispositions, the reality of their stock-based compensation inured them to maximizing shareholder value (Lazonick 2010c). The long stock market boom of the 1980s and 1990s combined with the remuneration decisions of corporate boards to create this pay bonanza for corporate executives.

To some extent, the stock market boom of the 1980s and 1990s was driven by innovation, largely related to the microelectronics revolution. By the late 1990s, however, innovation had given way to speculation as a prime mover of stock prices. Then, after the collapse of the Internet bubble at the beginning of the 2000s, corporate resource allocation sought to restore stock prices through manipulation in the form of stock buybacks (Lazonick 2010c). From 2001 through 2010, 458 companies in the S&P 500 Index in January 2011 that were publicly listed in 2001 expended $2.6 trillion on stock repurchases, an average of $5.7 billion per company, while distributing a total of $1.9 trillion in cash dividends, an average of $4.2 billion per company. In 2007 alone, these companies averaged $1.211 million in repurchases and $545 million in dividends. This massive "disgorging" of the corporate cash flow manifests a decisive triumph of agency theory and its shareholder-value ideology in the determination of corporate resource allocation.

Has this financial behavior led to a more efficient allocation of resources in the economy, as the proponents of MSV claim? Elsewhere I have adduced empirical evidence at the industry and firm levels that contradicts this claim (Lazonick 2009a, 2010c). There are a number of critical flaws in agency theory's analysis of the relation between corporate governance and economic performance. These flaws have to do with (1) a failure to explain how, historically, corporations came to control the allocation of significant amounts of the economy's resources; (2) the measure of "free cash flow"; and (3) the claim that only shareholders have "residual claimant" status. These flaws stem from the fact that agency theory, like the neoclassical theory of the market economy in which it is rooted, lacks a theory of innovative enterprise (see Lazonick 2002, 2010b).

Agency theory makes an argument for taking resources out of the control of inefficient managers without explaining how, historically, corporations came to possess the vast amounts of resources over which these managers could exercise allocative control (see Lazonick 1992). From the first decades of the twentieth century, the separation of share ownership from managerial control characterized U.S. industrial corporations. This separation occurred because the growth of innovative companies demanded that control over the strategic allocation of resources to develop new technologies and access new markets be placed in the hands of salaried professionals who understood the investment requirements of the particular lines of business in which the enterprise competed. At the same time, the listing of a company on a public stock exchange enabled the original owner-entrepreneurs to sell their stock to the shareholding public. Thereby enriched, they were able to retire from their positions as top executives. The departing owner-entrepreneurs left control in the hands of senior salaried professionals, most of whom had been recruited decades earlier to help to build the enterprises. The resultant disappearance of family owners in positions of strategic control enabled the younger generation of salaried professionals to view the particular corporations that employed them as ones in which, through dedicated work effort over the course of a career, they could potentially rise to the ranks of top management.

With salaried managers exercising strategic control, innovative managerial corporations emerged as dominant in their industries during the first decades of the century. During the post-World War II decades, and especially during the 1960s conglomerate movement, however, many of these industrial corporations grew to be too big to be managed effectively. Top managers responsible for corporate resource allocation became segmented, behaviorally and cognitively, from the organizations that would have to implement these strategies. Behaviorally, they came to see themselves as occupants of the corporate throne rather than as members of the corporate organization, and they became obsessed by the size of their own remuneration. Cognitively, the expansion of the corporation into a multitude of businesses made it increasingly difficult for top management to understand the particular investment requirements of any of them (Lazonick 2004b).

In the 1970s and 1980s, moreover, many of these U.S. corporations faced intense foreign competition, especially from innovative Japanese corporations (also, it should be noted, characterized by the separation of share ownership from managerial control). An innovative response required governance institutions that would reintegrate U.S. strategic decision makers with the business organizations over which they exercised allocative control. Instead, guided by MSV ideology and rewarded with stock options, what these established corporations got were managers who had a strong personal interest in boosting their companies' stock prices, even if the stock price increase was accomplished by a redistribution of corporate revenues from labor incomes to capital incomes and even if the quest for stock price increases undermined the productive capabilities that these companies had accumulated in the past.

Agency theory also does not address how, at the time innovative investments are made, one can judge whether managers are allocating resources inefficiently. Any strategic manager who allocates resources to an innovative strategy faces technological, market, and competitive uncertainty. Technological uncertainty exists because the firm may be incapable of developing the higher-quality processes and products envisaged in its innovative investment strategy. Market uncertainty exists because, even if the firm succeeds in its development effort, future reductions in product prices and increases in factor prices may lower the returns that can be generated by the investments. Finally, even if a firm overcomes technological and market uncertainty, it still faces competitive uncertainty: the possibility that an innovative competitor will have invested in a strategy that generates an even higher-quality, lower-cost product that enables it to win market share.

One can state, as Jensen did, that the firm should only invest in "projects that have positive net present values when discounted at the relevant cost of capital." But, quite apart from the problem of defining the "relevant cost of capital," anyone who contends that, when committing resources to an innovative investment strategy, one can foresee the stream of future earnings that are required for the calculation of net present value knows nothing about the innovation process. It is far more plausible to argue that if corporate managers really sought to maximize shareholder value according to this formula, they would never contemplate investing in innovative projects with their highly uncertain returns (see Baldwin and Clark 1992; Christensen, Kaufman, and Shih 2008).

Moreover, it is simply not the case, as agency theory assumes, that all the firm's participants other than shareholders receive contractually guaranteed returns according to their productive contributions. Given its investments in productive resources, the state has residual-claimant status. Any realistic account of economic development must take into account the role of the state in (1) making infrastructural investments that, given the required levels of financial commitment and inherent uncertainty of economic outcomes, business enterprises would not have made on their own, and (2) providing business enterprises with subsidies that encourage investment in innovation. In terms of investment in new knowledge with applications to industry, the United States was the world's foremost developmental state over the course of the twentieth century (see Block 2009; Block and Keller 2011; Lazonick 2008). As one prime example, it is impossible to explain U.S. dominance in computers, microelectronics, software, and data communications without recognizing the role of government in making seminal investments that developed new knowledge and infrastructural investments that facilitated the diffusion of that knowledge (see, e.g., Abbate 2000; National Research Council 1999). As another prime example, the annual budget of the National Institutes of Health (NIH) for spending on life sciences research was about $30 billion in 2009 and 2010 and $32 billion in 2011 and 2012, about double in real terms the budget that it had in 1993 and triple that in 1985. Total NIH spending since the founding of the first national institute in 1938 through 2011 was $792 billion in 2011 dollars (Kastor 2010; Lazonick and Tulum 2011).[3]

More generally, the U.S. government has made investments to augment the productive power of the nation through federal, corporate, and university research labs that have generated new knowledge as well as through educational institutions that have developed the capabilities of the future labor force. Business enterprises have made ample use of this knowledge and capability. In effect, in funding these investments, the state (or more correctly, its body of taxpayers) has borne the risk that the nation's business enterprises would further develop and utilize these productive capabilities in ways that would ultimately redound to the benefit of the nation, *but with the return to the nation in no way contractually guaranteed.*

In addition, the U.S. government has often provided cash subsidies to business enterprises to develop new products and processes, or even to start new firms. The public has funded these subsidies through current taxes, borrowing against the future, or by making consumers pay higher product prices for current goods and services than would have otherwise prevailed (e.g., through tariff protection). Multitudes of business enterprises have benefited from subsidies without having to enter into contracts with the public bodies that have granted them to remit a guaranteed return from the productive investments that the subsidies help to finance.

Like taxpayers, workers can also find themselves in the position of having made investments without a contractually guaranteed return. The collective and cumulative innovation process demands that workers expend time and effort now for the sake of returns that, precisely because innovation is involved, can only be generated in the future. In the innovation process, large numbers of workers in the hierarchical and functional division of labor may contribute their time and effort for years on end to the development and utilization of productive resources with an expectation of future returns if and when the innovation is a commercial success. Insofar as workers involved in the innovation process make this investment of their time and effort in the innovation process without a contractually guaranteed return, they too have residual claimant status.

In an important contribution to the corporate governance debate, Margaret Blair (1995) argued that, alongside a firm's shareholders, workers should be accorded residual claimant status because they make investments in "firm-specific" human capital at one point in time with the expectation—but without a contractual guarantee—of reaping returns on those investments over the course of their careers. Moreover, insofar as their human capital is indeed firm specific, these workers are dependent on their current employer for generating returns on their investments. A lack of interfirm labor mobility means that the worker bears some of the risk of the return on the firm's productive investments and hence can be considered a residual claimant. Blair goes on to argue that if one assumes, as shareholder-value proponents do, that only shareholders bear risk and residual claimant status, there will be an underinvestment in human capital to the detriment of not only workers, but the economy as a whole.

I concur with Blair's argument that workers often have residual claimant status. From the perspective of innovation theory, however, I look at the relation between the risks that workers bear and rewards that workers may, or may not, receive differently. Quite apart from whether or not their skills are "firm specific," workers often contribute their time and effort over and above the levels required by their current level of pay to a collective and cumulative innovation process. By definition, this innovation process can only generate returns in the future, and, indeed, because the innovation process is uncertain, may not in fact generate returns. As members of the firm, therefore, workers bear the risk that the extra expenditures of time and effort will not yield the gains from innovative enterprises from which they can be rewarded. If, however, the innovation process does generate returns, workers, as risk bearers, have a claim to a share.

MSV ideology, as put forth by agency theorists, provides a flawed rationale for denying taxpayers and workers residual claimant status, and thereby excluding them from sharing in the gains of innovative enterprise. In large part the problem with agency theory is its lack of a theory of innovative enterprise that can explain the relation between the bearing of risk in and the reaping of rewards from investments in the uncertain, collective, and cumulative process that we call innovation (see Lazonick and Mazzucato 2012). Indeed, to turn agency theory on its head, on what grounds do public shareholders have residual claimant status? Put differently, what risk-bearing role do public shareholders play in the innovation process? Do they confront uncertainty by strategically allocating resources to innovative investments? No. As portfolio investors, they diversify their financial holdings across the outstanding shares of existing firms to minimize risk. They do so, moreover, with limited liability, which means that they are under no legal obligation to make further investments of "good" money to support previous investments that have gone bad. Indeed, even for these previous investments, the existence of a highly liquid stock market enables public shareholders to cut their losses instantaneously by selling their shares—what has long been called the Wall Street walk.

Without this ability to exit an investment easily, public shareholders would not be willing to hold shares in companies over the assets of which they exercise no direct allocative control. It is the liquidity of a public shareholder's portfolio investment that differentiates it from a direct investment, and indeed distinguishes the public shareholder from a private shareholder who, for lack of liquidity of his or her shares, must remain committed to his or her direct investment until it generates financial returns. The modern corporation entails a fundamental transformation in the character of private property, as Adolf Berle and Gardiner Means (1932) recognized in their landmark book, *The Modern Corporation and Private Property*. As property owners, public shareholders own tradable shares in a company that has invested in productive assets. They do not own the actual productive assets, which invariably include human assets that at any time can, in a free society, walk out of the workplace door.

Indeed, the fundamental role of the stock market in the United States has been to transform illiquid claims into liquid claims on *the basis of investments that had already been made*, and thereby separate share ownership from managerial control. Business corporations sometimes do use the stock market as a source of finance for new investments, although the cash function has been most common in periods of stock market speculation when the lure for public shareholders to allocate resources to new issues has been the prospect of quickly "flipping" their shares to make a rapid speculative return. Public shareholders want financial liquidity; investments in innovation require financial commitment. It is only by ignoring the uncertain, collective, and cumulative character of the innovation process and the role of innovation in generating the real productivity gains that bring the so-called residual into being, that agency theory can argue that superior economic performance can be achieved by maximizing the value of those actors in the corporate economy who are the ultimate outsiders to the innovation process.

Financialization of Corporate Resource Allocation

By definition, business enterprises need to avoid losses over the long term to survive. Yet investments in innovation inherently entail losses over the periods of time during which the *development and utilization* of products and processes occurs. It is only when the resultant products are sold on the market that the high fixed costs of the innovation process are transformed into low unit costs that can potentially generate financial returns (Lazonick 2010b). Investments in innovation, therefore, require committed finance, or "patient capital." In a company that has already had successful products, the foundation of committed finance is the retention of earnings out of profits. In effect, part of the gains from successful innovation of the past provides committed finance for the next round of innovation. I call this mode of corporate finance a "retain-and-reinvest" allocation regime.

In historical perspective, the U.S. industrial corporation of the immediate post-World War II decades was relatively unfinancialized. Regular distributions of dividends encouraged stable shareholding of companies listed on the New York Stock Exchange (NYSE). The corporation prudently leveraged retentions with long-term bond issues to support the growth of the organization. At established corporations, both blue-collar and white-collar workers had realistic expectations of career employment with one company. When economic downturns forced layoffs, the unemployment spells were viewed as temporary, and collective bargaining agreements often provided corporate unemployment benefits that supplemented government unemployment payments.

Stock-based compensation, which would eventually become a key source of corporate financialization, became an important component of top executive pay after the Revenue Act of 1950 allowed the gains from executive stock options to be taxed at the capital gains tax rate of 25 percent rather than at the personal income tax rate which, for income in the highest tax bracket, was over 90 percent. To gain this tax advantage, however, stock purchased by exercising an option could not be sold for at least six months from the exercise date, thus preventing an executive from benefiting from short-term increases in the company's stock price.

From the late 1950s, there was a congressional backlash against this tax privilege. The Revenue Act of 1964 required stock acquired by exercising a "qualified" stock option to be held three years from the exercise date to be eligible for capital gains tax treatment, and the Tax Reform Act of 1976 eliminated altogether this tax advantage of executive stock options (Lazonick 2010c). Graef Crystal, who would later became a leading critic of excessive executive pay (Crystal 1991), wrote that qualified stock options, "once the most popular of all executive compensation devices...have been given the last rites by Congress" (1978: 145).

Meanwhile, however, the conglomerate movement of the 1960s, which reached its peak in 1969, represented the first major movement toward the financialization of U.S. corporate resource allocation. Business schools taught that a good manager could manage anything, while many industrial organization economists argued that conglomerates enabled efficiencies in capital allocation and utilization of managerial capabilities (see Hurley 2006). Catering to a speculative stock market, however, conglomeration often became simply a method of boosting EPS of the company as a whole by using debt issues to finance the acquisition of companies with lower price/earnings (P/E) ratios. While it should have been clear to stock market investors that such short-term financial manipulation undermined the financial conditions for sustaining higher levels of EPS over the long term, stock market speculators were only interested in capitalizing on short-term changes in the market's evaluation of corporate shares.[4]

Deconglomeration of the 1970s and 1980s revealed the weakness of the conglomerate as a productive business model. Even in conglomerates in which acquisitions were not driven primarily by financial motives, strategic decision makers, isolated at the top in the conglomerate headquarters, tended to be ignorant of the types of resource allocation required for innovative enterprise in the company's many different lines of business. By the early 1970s the downgraded debt of conglomerates, "fallen angels," created the opportunity for a young bond trader, Michael Milken, at the investment banking firm of Drexel Burnham, to create a liquid market in high-yield "junk bonds." By the late 1970s, companies were issuing junk bonds directly, often to do management buyouts as the "deconglomeration" movement saw conglomerates try to divest unprofitable conglomerate divisions to become, once again, autonomous firms run by executives who understood the investment requirements of the businesses that they were managing. By the mid-1980s, Milken (who eventually went to jail for securities fraud) was using his network of financial institutions to back corporate raiders in junk-bond financed leveraged buyouts with the purpose of extracting as much money as possible from a company once it was taken over through layoffs and by breaking up the company to sell it off in pieces (Bruck 1989).

Meanwhile, in the 1970s speculative trading in corporate stocks had become much simpler and less costly through a number of transformations on U.S. securities markets. In 1971 the creation of the National Association of Security Dealers Automated Quotation (NASDAQ) System out of the fragmented over-the-counter markets dramatically increased the liquidity of the stocks of corporations that did not have the capitalization and profit record required for listing on NYSE (Ingebretsen 2002). In 1974 the passage of the Employee Retirement Income Security Act (ERISA) created the conditions for investing the vast assets of pension funds in corporate stocks on a much larger scale than previously, thus adding an immense amount of liquidity to U.S. stock markets (Carey 2010; Ghilarducci 1994). In 1975 the Securities and Exchange Commission (SEC) barred stock exchanges from charging fixed commissions on stock trading transactions, ending a practice that had prevailed on Wall Street since 1796. This change made it less costly for stock market investors to buy and sell shares to realize capital gains as an alternative to holding the shares for the sake of a stream of dividend income. Over the course of the decade, the main activity of Wall Street shifted from helping to finance the long-term investments of U.S. industrial corporations to trading in their outstanding securities (see Auletta 1986; Carrington 1987; Lowenstein 1989).

The launch of NASDAQ in 1971, with its much less stringent listing requirements than the NYSE, made it much easier for a young company with little or no profits to do an initial public offering (IPO), thus enhancing the ability of venture capitalists to use this mode of exit from their private equity investments. In the early 1970s, however, there was only a trickle of institutional money invested in venture capital, and even that flow dried up when the passage of ERISA in 1974 made corporations responsible for underfunded pensions and pension fund managers personally liable for breaches of their fiduciary duty to use the "prudent man" rule when making investments (Niland 1976). Under these circumstances, pension fund managers, who controlled the allocation of an ever-increasing share of U.S. household savings, avoided investment in venture capital funds. On July 23, 1979, however, the U.S. Department of Labor decreed that pension fund money could be invested not only in listed stocks and high-grade bonds but also in more speculative assets, including new ventures, without transgressing the prudent man rule (Ross 1979). As a result, pension fund money poured into venture capital funds.

In 1978, in response to intensive lobbying led by the American Electronics Association and the National Venture Capital Association (both of which were dominated by Silicon Valley interests), the U.S. Congress reduced the capital gains tax from as high as 49.875 percent to a maximum of 28 percent, thus reversing a thirty-six-year trend toward higher capital gains taxes (Lazonick 2009a: ch. 2; Pierson 1978). In 1981 the capital gains tax rate was further reduced to a maximum of 20 percent (Auten 1999). Venture capitalists saw lower capital gains taxes as encouraging both entrepreneurial investment in new companies and portfolio investment by individuals in the publicly traded stocks of young, potentially high-growth companies.

By the early 1980s, centered in Silicon Valley, "venture capital" had clearly emerged as an industry dedicated to the formation of new firms. Venture capital played a central role in the rise of the "New Economy business model" (NEBM). In the process the stock market became far more important to the operation of the U.S. industrial economy than had previously been the case. Elsewhere I have shown that the stock market can perform five functions in the operation of the company that can be summarized as "control," "creation," "compensation," "combination," and "cash" (see Lazonick 2009b).

Under the "Old Economy business model" (OEBM), the main function of the stock market had been to separate ownership from control; the fragmentation of share ownership of publicly listed companies left salaried managers in positions of strategic control over the allocation of corporate resources (Chandler 1977). The separation of ownership from control occurs to some extent under NEBM when companies list on the stock market. Under NEBM, however, the stock market also performs "creation," "compensation," and "combination" functions. The rise of NEBM relied on prospective stock market gains through an IPO or merger-and-acquisition (M&A) deal to induce financial capital accumulated in the Old Economy to be transferred to the New Economy in the form of venture capital that would support the creation of start-ups. Through the offer of what came to be known as "broad-based" stock option plans as an integral component of employee compensation, the rise of NEBM relied on prospective stock market gains to induce professional, technical, and administrative labor to leave secure employment at established companies for insecure employment at start-ups.[5] In addition, under NEBM it became common for companies to use their stock rather than cash as a currency to acquire other companies; the classic example is Cisco Systems which from September 1993 through July 2003 did eighty-one acquisitions for $38.1 billion, 98 percent of which was paid in stock (Lazonick 2009b).

New Economy companies tend to go public with less accumulated capital than was the case with Old Economy companies, and NASDAQ is a more speculative stock market than NYSE. As a result, the "cash" function through IPOs and secondary stock issues is relatively more important under NEBM than it was under OEBM (Lazonick 2009b; Lazonick and Tulum 2011). For the sake of financing their growth in their first decade or two of existence, New Economy companies have tended to reinvest all their earnings, paying no dividends. The innovative success of such a company has resulted in a rising stock price, which in turn strengthens the value of its stock as a compensation and combination currency.

In the 1980s and 1990s, as shown in Table 9.1, high real stock yields characterized the U.S. corporate economy. These high yields came mainly from stock price appreciation as distinct from dividend yields, which were low in the 1990s despite high dividend payout ratios.[6] With the S&P 500 Index rising almost 1,400 percent from March 1982 to August 2000, the availability of gains from exercising stock options became almost automatic. Given the extent to which the explosion in U.S. top executive pay over the past three decades has been dependent on gains from exercising stock options, there is a need to understand the drivers of the stock price increases that generate these gains.

There are three distinct forces—*innovation*, *speculation*, and *manipulation*—that may be at work in driving stock price increases. Innovation generates higher-quality, lower-cost products (given prevailing factor prices) that result in sustainable increases in EPS, which in turn tend to lift the stock price of the innovative enterprise. Speculation, often encouraged by innovation, drives the stock price higher, as investors assume either that innovation (which is inherently uncertain) will continue in the future or that there is a "greater fool" who stands ready to buy the stock at yet a higher price. Manipulation

TABLE 9.1

AVERAGE ANNUAL U.S. CORPORATE STOCK AND BOND YIELDS (%), 1960–2009

	1960–1969	1970–1979	1980–1989	1990–1999	2000–2009
Real stock yield	6.63	−1.66	11.67	15.01	−3.08
Price yield	5.80	1.35	12.91	15.54	−2.30
Dividend yield	3.19	4.08	4.32	2.47	1.79
Change in CPI	2.36	7.09	5.55	3.00	2.57
Real bond yield	2.65	1.14	5.79	4.72	3.41

Stock yields are for Standard and Poor's composite index of 500 U.S. corporate stocks. Bond yields are for Moody's AAA-rated U.S. corporate bonds.

Source: U.S. Congress (2010), Tables B-62, B-73, B-95, B-96.

occurs when those who exercise control over corporate resource allocation do so in a way that increases EPS despite the absence of innovation.

Figure 9.1 charts the roles of innovation, speculation, and manipulation as *primary* drivers of U.S. stock-price movements from the mid-1980s to the late 2000s. In the last half of the 1980s Old Economy companies that had run into trouble because of conglomeration in the United States and/or competition from the Japanese sought to manipulate stock prices through a "downsize-and-distribute" resource allocation strategy (Lazonick 2004a). The corporation sought to boost stock prices by downsizing the labor force and distributing corporate revenues to shareholders in the forms of dividends and stock repurchases. This redistribution of corporate revenues from labor incomes to capital incomes often occurred through debt-financed hostile takeovers, with post-takeover downsizing enabling the servicing and retirement of the massive debt that a company had taken on. In addition, from the mid-1980s, many Old Economy companies engaged for the first time in large-scale stock repurchases in an attempt to support their stock prices.

While Old Economy companies were manipulating stock prices in the 1980s and early 1990s, New Economy companies such as Intel, AMD, Microsoft, Oracle, Solectron, EMC, Sun Microsystems, Cisco Systems, Dell, and Qualcomm were reinvesting virtually all their incomes to finance the growth of their companies, neither paying dividends nor, once they had gone public, repurchasing stock (Lazonick 2009a: ch. 2). It was *innovation* by New Economy companies, most of them traded on NASDAQ, that culminated in the Internet revolution that provided a real foundation for the rising stock market in the 1980s and first half of the 1990s.

In the late 1990s, however, *speculation* drove the stock market as the public discovered the existence of innovative New Economy firms, and then began making bets on many dot-com start-ups that had little in the way of innovative capability. Figure 9.1 displays the extent of the speculative bubble. The rise and fall of the NASDAQ Composite Index between 1998 and 2001 make the movements of the Dow Jones Industrial Average

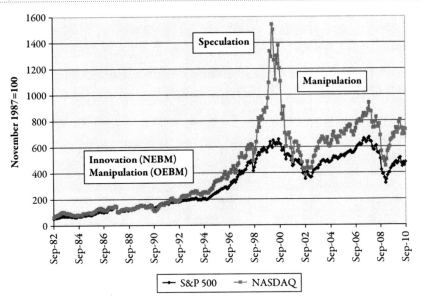

FIGURE 9.1 S&P 500 and NASDAQ Composite Indices, Sept. 1982–Sept. 2010 (monthly data, standardized for the two indices to 100 in Nov. 1987). As of September 2010 the S&P 500 Index consisted of 500 stocks, of which 406 were NYSE and 94 NASDAQ; and the NASDAQ Composite Index consisted of 2,910 stocks.
Source: Yahoo! Finance at http://finance.yahoo.com (Historical Prices, Monthly Data).

(DJIA) and the S&P 500 Index look like mere blips, even with Intel and Microsoft as the NASDAQ representatives among DJIA's thirty stocks, while larger companies listed on NASDAQ (including Intel and Microsoft) represented almost 20 percent of the S&P 500. Between March 1998 and March 2000, the NASDAQ Composite Index of over 3,000 stocks rose by 149 percent compared with 21 percent for the DJIA and 36 percent for the S&P 500 (U.S. Congress 2010, Table B-90).

Especially since 2003 stock repurchases have been the key instrument of stock market *manipulation*. A stock repurchase occurs when a company buys back its own shares. In the United States, the SEC requires stock repurchase *programs* to be approved by the company's board of directors and to be announced publicly. These programs authorize a company's top executives to do a certain amount of buybacks over a certain period of time, but with the timing and amount of actual repurchases left to the discretion of the executives. For example, on September 22, 2008, Microsoft announced that "its board of directors approved a new share repurchase program authorizing up to an additional $40 billion in share repurchases with an expiration of September 30, 2013." It was then up to the top executives of Microsoft to decide whether the company should actually do repurchases, when they should be done, and how many shares should be repurchased at any given time. Repurchases are almost always done as open-market transactions through the company's broker. Significantly, the SEC does not require the company to announce the buybacks at the time they are actually done.

Stock repurchases by large U.S. companies became an important mode of distributing cash to shareholders in the mid-1980s, and in 1997 for the first time exceeded dividends for the U.S. corporate economy as a whole (Dittmar and Dittmar 2004). With dividends, shareholders receive income by holding a company's stock, but with repurchases they receive income by selling it. That is, dividends reward stability of shareholding whereas repurchases reward volatility of shareholding. The shift from dividends to repurchases as the dominant form of distributions to shareholders reflects the corporate reorientation from investing in productive resources to trading financial securities that has been occurring in the United States over the past half century.

Among large U.S. companies, buybacks became more widespread and systemic over the course of the 1990s. In 1990–94, 373 companies in the S&P 500 Index in January 2008 that were publicly listed in 1990 expended an annual average of $25.9 billion (or $69 million per company) on repurchases, constituting 23 percent of their combined net income. In 1995–99 these same 373 companies expended an annual average of $106.3 billion (or $285 million per company) on repurchases, 44 percent of their combined net income.

Yet in the late 1990s the stage was being set for an even more massive manipulation of the market through stock repurchases, especially from 2003. Figure 9.2 shows the payout ratios and mean payout levels for 419 companies in the S&P 500 Index in January 2011 that were publicly listed from 1997 through 2010. From 1997 through 2010, these

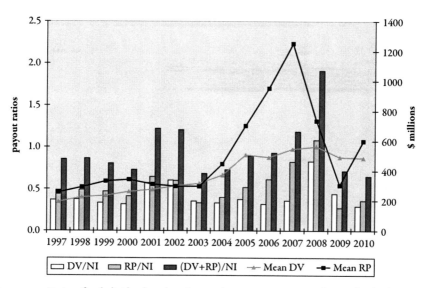

FIGURE 9.2 Ratios of cash dividends and stock repurchases to net income, and mean dividend payments and stock repurchases among S&P 500, 1997–2010. Data for 419 corporations in the S&P 500 Index in January 2011 that were publicly listed 1997–2010. Data for companies that end their fiscal years during the first six months of the calendar year are attributed to the previous year. RP, stock repurchases; DV, total dividends (common and preferred); NI, net income (after tax with inventory evaluation and capital consumption adjustments).
Sources: S&P Compustat database (North America, Fundamentals Annual, 1997–2010); company 10-K filings for missing or erroneous data from the Compustat database.

419 companies expended $2.7 trillion on stock repurchases, an average of $6.5 billion per company, and distributed a total of $2.0 trillion in cash dividends, an average of $4.8 billion per company. Stock repurchases by these 419 companies averaged $296 million in 2003, rising to $1,251 million in 2007.

Combined, the 500 companies in the S&P 500 Index in January 2008 repurchased $489 billion of their own stock in 2006, representing 62 percent of their net income, and $595 billion in 2007, representing 89 percent of their net income. Figure 9.3 shows how the escalating stock repurchases by S&P 500 companies from 2003 through 2007 helped to boost the stock market, driving the S&P 500 Index even higher in 2007 than its previous peak in 2000.

As can be seen in Figure 9.3, repurchases by S&P 500 companies declined dramatically in 2008 and 2009, as, for example (as I detail later), many banks that had been among the largest repurchasers in the previous years either went out of existence or availed themselves of a government bailout. After dropping to about $300 million per company during the financial crisis of 2008–09, repurchases doubled to around $600 million, and reached an average of $800 million per company in 2011.[7] The experience of 2003–07 suggests that, short of another financial meltdown, repurchases will continue to remain high in 2012 and beyond.

The facility with which U.S. corporations can do large-scale stock repurchases is the result of the relaxation of SEC rules against stock price manipulation. Under the Securities Exchange Act of 1934, stock repurchases can be construed as an attempt to

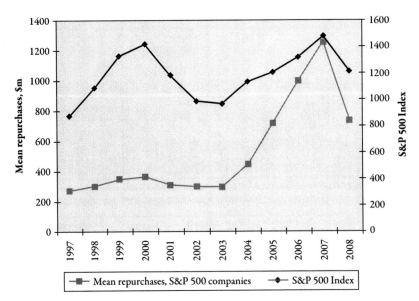

FIGURE 9.3 Stock repurchases by the S&P 500 (437 companies) and the movement of the S&P 500 Index, 1997–2008.
Sources: Standard and Poor's Compustat database (North America, Fundamentals Annual); Yahoo! Finance (http://finance.yahoo.com) (Historical Prices, Monthly Data).

manipulate a company's stock price. In 1982, however, with the promulgation of Rule 10b-18, the SEC provided companies with a "safe harbor" that manipulation charges will not be filed if each day's open-market repurchases are not greater than 25 percent of the stock's average daily trading volume over the previous four weeks and if the company refrains from doing buybacks at the beginning and end of the trading day.[8] Under these rules, during the single trading day of, for example, July 13, 2011, a leading stock repurchaser such as Exxon Mobil could have done as much as $416 million in buybacks, Bank of America $402 million, Microsoft $390 million, Intel $285 million, Cisco $269 million, GE $230 million, and IBM $220 million. And, according to the rules, buybacks of these magnitudes can be repeated day after trading day.

According to the only newspaper account of the SEC's adoption of Rule 10b-18 that I have been able to find, the *Wall Street Journal* reported that this safe harbor "made it easier for companies to buy back their shares on the open market without fear of stock-manipulation charges" (Hudson 1982). SEC Chairman John Shad was an advocate of the rule change, arguing that large-scale open market repurchases would fuel an increase in stock prices that would be beneficial to shareholders. One of the SEC commissioners, John Evans, argued that as a result of Rule 10–18b some manipulation would go unprosecuted, but then he agreed to make the SEC's vote for the rule change unanimous.

Why do corporations repurchase stock? Executives often claim that buybacks are financial investments that signal confidence in the future of the company and its stock price performance (Louis and White 2007; Vermaelen 2005: ch. 3). In fact, however, companies that do buybacks never sell the shares at higher prices to cash in on these investments. To do so would be to signal to the market that its stock price had peaked, which no CFO (chief financial officer) would want to do. It is difficult to take seriously an argument that says that top executives repurchase stock to send a signal to the stock market that their company's shares are undervalued but that these same executives will never send a signal to the market that the company's shares are overvalued by selling the company's stock.

According to the "signaling" argument, we should have seen massive sales of corporate stock in the speculative boom of the late 1990s, as was in fact the case of U.S. industrial corporations in the speculative boom of the late 1920s when corporations took advantage of the speculative stock market to pay off corporate debt or bolster their corporate treasuries (O'Sullivan 2004). Instead, in the boom of the late 1990s corporate executives as *personal investors sold their own stock* to reap speculative gains, often to the tune of tens of millions (see Gimein et al. 2002). Many of these same corporate executives as *corporate decision makers* used corporate funds to *repurchase* their companies' shares in the attempt to bolster their stock prices—to their own personal gain. Given the fact that in the United States companies are not required to announce the dates on which they actually do open-market repurchases, there is an opportunity for top executives who have this information to engage in insider trading by using this information to time option exercises and stock sales (see Fried 2000, 2001).

Indeed, as a complement to the SEC's Rule 10b-18 of 1982 which, as we have seen, effectively legalized the use of buybacks to manipulate stock prices, in 1991 the SEC made a rule change that enabled top executives to make quick gains by exercising their stock options and immediately selling their shares. Under Section 16(b) of the 1934 Securities Exchange Act, corporate directors, officers, or shareholders with more than 10 percent of the corporation's shares are prohibited from making "short-swing" profits through the purchase and the subsequent sale of corporate securities within a six-month period. As a result, top executives who exercised stock options had to hold the acquired shares for at least six months before selling them. Treating a stock option as a derivative, in May 1991 the SEC deemed that the six-month holding period required under Section 16(b) was from the grant date, not the exercise date (Rosen 1991). The new rule eliminated the risk of loss between the exercise date and the sale date and gave top executives flexibility in their timing of option exercises and immediate stock sales so that they could personally benefit from, among other things, price boosts from buybacks.

There are a number of ways in which stock options as a mode of executive compensation can be abused. A company might reprice options that are underwater by canceling an existing option and replacing it with a new option with a lower exercise price (Chance, Kumar, and Todd 2000; Ellig 2007: 434–35). As a result, an executive may be able to reap gains from stock option grants even when the company's stock price declines. In 2006 a scandal broke out over the practice of backdating stock options—that is, granting option awards today as if they were granted at an earlier date when the market price of the stock and hence the exercise price of the options were lower (Bernile and Jarrell 2009; Forelle and Bandler 2006; Lie 2005).

These abuses aside, however, the more fundamental problem with U.S.-style stock options is that they are unindexed; that is, they virtually never carry any performance criteria that would limit the gains from exercising stock options to an amount warranted by superior productive performance (Bebchuk and Fried 2004). As a result, an executive, or any other employee with stock options, can gain from a speculative stock market as distinct from an improvement in the company's productive performance.

In addition, as we have seen, executives can augment their stock option gains by allocating corporate resources to do buybacks, the sole purpose of which is to manipulate the company's stock price. Some of the stock-based compensation of U.S. executives is undoubtedly attributable to innovation, although even then there is the question of whether the amount of stock-based remuneration that executives secure is equitable relative to other contributors to the innovation process. Be that as it may, in the last half of the 1990s it was stock market speculation and in the 2000s stock market manipulation that were the main drivers of the explosion in the pay of U.S. corporate executives.

Table 9.2 shows the average compensation of the highest paid corporate executives in the United States, and the percent of that compensation derived from exercising stock options (the difference between the stock option exercise price and the market price of the stock on the exercise date) for 1992–2010. Also included in Table 9.2 are the S&P 500 Index (with over 80 percent of its component stocks being NYSE) and the NASDAQ Composite Index to illustrate the positive correlation of stock price performance with both the level of executive pay and the proportion of that pay derived from stock option exercises. The impact of NASDAQ on executive pay was especially strong in the late 1990s when speculation drove stock prices, whereas from 2003 to 2007 companies listed on NYSE as well as NASDAQ were engaged in large-scale stock repurchases that helped to push up—that is, manipulate—the S&P 500 Index.

As can be seen in Table 9.2, large proportions of these enormous incomes of top executives have come from gains from cashing in on the ample stock option awards that their boards of directors have bestowed on them. The higher the "top pay" group, the greater the average proportion of the pay of the executives in that group that was derived from gains from exercising stock options. For the top 100 group in the years 1992–2010, this proportion ranged from a low of 49 percent in 2010, when the mean pay of the group was also at its second lowest level in real terms since 1997, to a high of 87 percent in 2000, when the mean pay was at its highest level—$104.0 million in 2010 dollars. In 2000 the mean pay of the top 3,000 was, at $10.8 million in 2010 dollars, only 10 percent of the mean pay of the top 100. Nevertheless, gains from exercising stock options accounted for on average 67 percent of the pay of the executives in the top 3,000 group.

Note in Table 9.2 how the average pay of the highest paid corporate executives has risen and fallen with the fluctuations of major stock market indices. In the 1980s and 1990s, as was shown earlier in Table 9.1, high real stock yields characterized the U.S. corporate economy. These high yields came mainly from stock price appreciation as distinct from dividends yields, which were low in the 1990s despite high dividend payout ratios (see note 5). With the S&P 500 Index rising almost 1,400 percent from March 1982 to August 2000, the availability of gains from exercising stock options became almost automatic. In the 2000s, in contrast, with the stock market less speculative, the gains came primarily from manipulation, with, as we have also seen, repurchases as the instrument for boosting stock prices. Given the extent to which the explosion in U.S. top executive pay over the past three decades has been dependent on gains from exercising stock options, any policy initiatives to control executive pay must recognize the changing roles of innovation, speculation, and manipulation as drivers of the stock price increases that generate these gains. These policies should seek to reward executives, along with other corporate participants, for their contributions to innovation while eliminating the gains from speculation and manipulation.

If the stock-based character of executive pay creates a powerful incentive for top executives to allocate corporate resources to stock buybacks, the issue remains of how and to what extent stock buybacks have affected investments in innovation and job creation. In work reported elsewhere, I have examined how buybacks have adversely affected the delivery of higher-quality, lower-cost products in a range of industries from oil refining to health insurance (Lazonick 2009b, 2010c; Lazonick and Tulum 2011).

TABLE 9.2.
AVERAGE TOTAL COMPENSATION OF "NAMED" EXECUTIVES OF U.S. CORPORATIONS AND THE PROPORTION OF TOTAL COMPENSATION DERIVED FROM STOCK-OPTION GAINS FOR THE 100, 500, 1,500, AND 3,000 HIGHEST-PAID, 1992–2010, AND THE MOVEMENTS OF THE S&P 500 INDEX AND NASDAQ COMPOSITE INDEX THAT INFLUENCED THE EXTENT OF THE GAINS FROM EXERCISING STOCK OPTIONS. AVERAGE COMPENSATION (AVG $M) IN MILLIONS OF 2010 U.S. DOLLARS. AVERAGE GAINS FROM STOCK OPTION EXERCISES (AVG SO%) REPRESENT THE MEAN PERCENTAGE OF THE TOTAL COMPENSATION OF THE EXECUTIVES WITH THE "TOP" CATEGORY DERIVED FROM EXERCISING STOCK OPTIONS

	S&P 500 Index	NASDAQ Index	NASDAQ/ S&P	Top 100		Top 500		Top 1500		Top 3000	
				AVG $m	AVG SO%	AVG $m	AVG SO%	AVG $m	AVG SO%	AVG $m	AVG SO%
1992	100	100	1.00	23.1	71	9.3	59	4.7	48	2.9	42
1993	109	119	1.10	21.1	63	9.1	51	4.8	42	3.1	36
1994	111	125	1.13	18.5	57	8.1	45	4.4	35	2.9	29
1995	131	155	1.18	21.0	59	9.7	48	5.3	40	3.5	34
1996	162	195	1.20	32.4	64	13.9	54	7.2	47	4.6	41
1997	210	243	1.16	44.2	72	18.6	61	9.5	55	5.9	49
1998	261	300	1.15	76.0	66	26.7	64	12.5	58	7.5	53
1999	319	462	1.45	68.9	82	27.4	71	13.2	63	7.8	57
2000	341	614	1.80	104.0	87	40.5	80	18.7	72	10.8	67
2001	284	332	1.17	62.9	77	23.9	66	11.5	58	6.9	53

2002	237	1.06	38.1	57	17.1	49	8.8	43	5.5	38
2003	232	1.18	48.7	64	21.2	55	10.8	48	6.7	44
2004	272	1.21	55.4	75	25.0	62	12.9	55	8.1	50
2005	290	1.20	67.5	78	28.7	63	14.5	56	9.0	51
2006	316	1.47	68.9	69	29.6	59	15.4	52	9.7	47
2007	354	1.21	69.3	73	30.2	60	15.8	52	10.0	47
2008	291	1.22	47.5	58	20.7	55	10.9	45	7.0	39
2009	227	1.35	30.4	52	14.8	37	8.3	28	5.5	23
2010	271	1.43	35.9	49	18.3	40	10.4	32	6.8	28

"Named" executives are the CEO and other four highest-paid executives in a given year reported by listed companies in their annual proxy statements to shareholders.

S&P 500 Index and the NASDAQ Composite Index set to 100 in 1992 for purposes of comparison.

Total compensation (TDC1 in the Compustat database) is defined as "Total compensation for the individual year comprised of the following: Salary, Bonus, Other Annual, Total Value of Restricted Stock Granted, Net Value of Stock Options Exercised, Long-Term Incentive Payouts, and All Other Total."

Note that company proxy statements (DEF 14A SEC filings) report the compensation of the company's CEO and four other highest-paid executives. It is therefore possible that some of the highest-paid executives who should be included in each of the "top" categories are excluded. The mean compensation calculations are therefore lower bounds of actual average compensation of the highest-paid corporate executives in the United States.

Sources: Standard and Poor's Compustat database (Executive Compensation, Annual); Yahoo! Finance (http://finance.yahoo.com) (Historical Prices, Monthly Data).

Here are some examples:

- Exxon Mobil, the world's largest petroleum refiner, did $174.4 billion in buybacks during 2001–10—the most of any company—even as there is a need for large-scale investments in energy alternatives. Among the top fifty stock repurchasers in 2001–10 were two other petroleum refiners: Chevron at #21 with $25.6 billion and ConocoPhillips at #26 with $22.0 billion.
- Leading ICT (information and communications technology) companies do massive buybacks even as they shift high-tech jobs from the United States to low-wage countries and pressure the U.S. government to make larger investments in the high-tech knowledge base. In the decade 2001–10 the top repurchasers among ICT companies were Microsoft $110.0 billion (#2 among repurchasers), IBM $89.2 billion (#3), Cisco Systems $65.0 billion (#4), Hewlett-Packard $54.0 billion (#6), and Intel $48.3 billion (#11). The world's leading semiconductor company, Intel, lobbies the U.S. government to spend more on nanotechnology research (see, e.g., "U.S. could lose race ..." 2005). Yet the $48.3 billion that Intel spent on buybacks in 2001–10 was more than four times the total of $12.0 billion that, over the same period, the U.S. government allocated to the National Nanotechnology Initiative.[9]
- Pharmaceutical drug prices are at least double in the United States compared with European countries (UK Department of Health 2009: 27) The industry, including biopharmaceuticals and medical devices, benefits from U.S. federal government spending on life sciences through the NIH, the total annual budget of which averaged $31 billion in 2009 through 2012.[10] In opposing the regulation of drug prices by the U.S. Congress, the pharmaceutical companies argue that they need high prices to fund their R&D (research and development) expenditures in the United States. Yet among big pharmaceutical companies, in 1997–2010 Pfizer did repurchases equal to 64 percent of R&D expenditures, Johnson & Johnson 56 percent, and Merck 53 percent. When the substantial dividends that these companies paid are added to their repurchases, shareholder distributions exceeded R&D expenditures over this period by 32 percent at Pfizer, 17 percent at Johnson & Johnson, and 31 percent at Merck. Amgen, the largest dedicated biopharma company, repurchased stock in every year since 1992, for a total of $33.6 billion through 2010. Since 2002 the cost of Amgen's stock buybacks has surpassed the company's R&D expenditures in every year except 2004, and for the period 1992–2010 was equal to fully 100 percent of both R&D outlays and net income.
- Three of the largest corporate health insurers were among the top fifty repurchasers in the United States for the period 2001–10: UnitedHealth Group at #20 with $26.5 billion in buybacks, Wellpoint at #27 with $21.9 billion, and Aetna at #46 with $12.0 billion. As a proportion of net income over this period,

buybacks represented 88 percent for UnitedHealth Group, 101 percent for Wellpoint, and 102 percent for Aetna. When these health insurers increase their profits by raising premiums, excluding people with preexisting conditions, and capping lifetime benefits, the most likely use of those extra profits is to do more stock buybacks.
- Many of banks that were responsible for the meltdown and were bailed out under the Troubled Asset Relief Program were among the biggest stock repurchasers in the years prior to the financial crisis. They included Citigroup ($41.8 billion repurchased in 2000–07), Goldman Sachs ($30.1 billion), Wells Fargo ($23.2 billion), JP Morgan Chase ($21.2 billion), Merrill Lynch ($21.0 billion), Morgan Stanley ($19.1 billion), American Express ($17.6 billion), and US Bancorp ($12.3 billion). In the eight years before it went bankrupt in 2008, Lehman Brothers repurchased $16.8 billion, including $5.3 billion in 2006–07. Washington Mutual, which also went bankrupt in 2008, expended $13.3 billion in buybacks in 2000–07, including $6.5 billion in 2006–07. Wachovia, ranked thirty-eighth among the Fortune 500 in 2007, did $15.7 billion in buybacks in 2000–07, including $5.7 billion in 2006–07, before its fire sale to Wells Fargo at the end of 2008. Other financial institutions that did substantial repurchases in 2000–07 before running into financial distress in 2008 were AIG ($10.2 billion), Fannie Mae ($8.4 billion), Bear Stearns ($7.2 billion), and Freddie Mac ($4.7 billion). By spending money on buybacks during boom years, these financial corporations reduced their ability to withstand the crash of the derivatives market in 2008, thus exacerbating the jeopardy that they created for the economy as a whole.

U.S.-style stock options provide the top executives of U.S. business corporations, be they in manufacturing, services, or finance, with ample personal incentives to do stock buybacks even if it is at the expense of investments in innovation and job creation. The allocation of corporate resources to buybacks, moreover, is the prime way for U.S. corporations to follow the advice of Michael Jensen and agency theory more generally to "disgorge" the so-called free cash flow in order to align the interests of corporate executives with those of public shareholders for the sake of "maximizing shareholder value."

MSV ideology and its proponents among financial economists have done great damage to the performance of the U.S. economy, thus exacerbating the fragility of the U.S. economy that derives from major structural changes in the ways in which U.S. corporations employ their labor forces. Under any circumstances, an economy needs investment in innovation to generate economic growth. What renders the U.S. economy particularly fragile is that over the past three decades the financialization of the industrial corporation has gained strength, placing the repurchase of stock ahead of investment in innovation and job creation, even as major structural changes in U.S. employment have eroded the opportunities for *existing* middle-class jobs.

Disappearance of Middle-Class Jobs

During the post-World War II decades, for both blue-collar and white-collar workers, the "retain-and-reinvest" norm in Old Economy corporations was career employment with one company. When layoffs occurred, they tended to be temporary and, in unionized workplaces, on a last-hired, first-fired basis. Supported by a highly progressive income tax system, countercyclical government economic policy sought to reduce the severity of business fluctuations, while government spending, particularly on higher education, advanced technology, and physical infrastructure, complemented the employment opportunities provided by the business sector. The result was relatively equitable and stable economic growth from the late 1940s to the beginning of the 1970s (Lazonick 2009a: chs. 1, 3).

From the late 1970s, however, in industries that had been central to U.S. innovation, employment, and growth, U.S. corporations faced formidable Japanese competition. The Japanese challenge came in industries such as automobiles, consumer electronics, machine tools, steel, and microelectronics in which the United States had been a world leader. The critical source of Japan's competitive advantage over the United States was "organizational integration;" through the hierarchical integration of shop-floor workers and the functional integration of technical specialists into processes of organizational learning, the Japanese perfected the U.S. OEBM (Lazonick 1998, 2010a). Even though unionized blue-collar workers in the United States had a high degree of job security in the post-World War II decades, they had historically been excluded from the processes of organizational learning that occurred within the managerial organization. In sharp contrast, the hierarchical integration of shop-floor workers into the organizational learning processes that generated higher-quality, lower-cost products was the prime source of Japanese competitive advantage. Complementing the hierarchical integration of shop-floor workers, the collaboration of Japanese technical specialists in solving productivity problems in manufacturing encouraged the functional integration of their skills and efforts, again in contrast to the relatively high degree of functional segmentation of technical specialists in the United States.

The particular impacts of Japanese competition varied markedly across U.S. industries. Japanese competition virtually wiped out the U.S.-based consumer electronics industry. For example, in 1981 RCA was one of the leading consumer electronics companies in the world, and the forty-fourth largest U.S. industrial company by revenues with employment of 119,000. By 1986 it had been taken over by General Electric and sold off in pieces (Chandler 2001: chs. 2, 3). During the 1980s, the U.S. automobile manufacturers attempted to learn from the Japanese, but three decades later the U.S. companies were still producing lower-quality, higher-cost cars, and, not surprisingly, had lost significant market share (Platzer and Harrison 2009). In the machine tool industry, the overwhelming success of the Japanese against the major U.S. companies was followed from the 1990s by the emergence of export-oriented small- and medium-sized enterprises producing for specialized niche markets (Kalafsky and MacPherson 2002). In the steel industry, the innovative response of the United States was the emergence of independent minimills, using electric arc furnaces and scrap metal. In the 1980s, the minimills only had the technological capability to manufacture long products (e.g., bars), but, led by Nucor, the introduction of compact strip production technology from 1989 enabled the minimills to compete with integrated mills in flat products (e.g., sheets) as well (Giarratani, Gruver, and Jackson 2007).

The most perilous, but ultimately successful, U.S. response to Japanese competition was in the semiconductor industry. By the middle of the 1980s, the Japanese had used their integrated skill bases to lower defects and raise yields in the production of memory chips, forcing major U.S. semiconductor companies to retreat from this segment of the market, with Intel facing the possibility of bankruptcy in the process (Burgelman 1994; Okimoto and Nishi 1994). Led by Intel and its microprocessor for the IBM PC and its clones, U.S. companies became world leaders in chip design. Indeed, the IBM PC and its "Wintel" architecture laid the basis for the rise of NEBM, for which rationalization, marketization, and globalization of employment was in its DNA, and which by the 2000s had relegated OEBM to history (Lazonick 2009a, 2009b).

The adverse impact of Japanese competition on U.S. employment became particularly harsh in the double-dip recession of 1980–82 when large numbers of good blue-collar jobs disappeared, as it turned out permanently, from U.S. industry (Bednarzik 1983). Previously, in a more stable competitive environment, U.S. manufacturing companies would lay off workers with the least seniority in a downturn and reemploy them when economic conditions improved. Now companies were much more likely to shutter whole plants (Hamermesh 1989; Harris 1984). From 1980 to 1985 employment in the U.S. economy increased from 104.5 million to 107.2 million workers, or by 2.6 percent. But employment of operators, fabricators, and laborers fell from 20.0 million to 16.8 million, a decline of 15.9 percent (U.S. Department of Commerce 1983: 416; 1986: 386).

As Daniel Hamermesh summed it up: "Each year during the eighties, plant closings in the U.S. displaced roughly one-half million workers with three-plus years on the job" (1989: 53). Over the course of the 1980s the stock market came to react favorably to permanent downsizings of the blue-collar labor force (Abowd, Milkovich, and Hannon 1990; Palmon, Sun, and Tang 1997). While terminations could represent the initial stage of restructuring that could enhance the long-run competitiveness of a company, in what became known as the "deal decade" of the 1980s (Blair 1993), downsizing was often the result of attempts by corporate executives and corporate raiders to "maximize shareholder value" (Lazonick 2004a). As secure middle-class jobs for high school-educated blue-collar workers permanently disappeared, there was no commitment on the part of those who managed U.S. industrial corporations or the Republican administrations that ruled in the 1980s to invest in the new capabilities and opportunities required to upgrade the quality and expand the quantity of well-paid employment opportunities in the United States on a scale sufficient to reestablish conditions of prosperity for these displaced members of the U.S. labor force.

Among blue-collar workers, African Americans were extremely hard hit by the rationalization of employment in the 1980s. They were overrepresented in the Old Economy manufacturing sectors such as steel, autos, and consumer electronics that were in decline and underrepresented in the New Economy sectors related to the microelectronics revolution that were on the rise. Besides losing jobs when plants were closed, many blacks had recently moved into unionized jobs so that when some workers in an establishment were laid off, they tended to have been the last hired and hence were the first fired (see Fairlie and Kletzer 1998; Kletzer 1991; Sharpe 1993). As William Julius Wilson (1996–97) argued, the disappearance of these jobs had devastating impacts on the abilities and incentives of blacks to accumulate the education and experience required to position themselves for well-paid and stable employment opportunities.

In historical retrospect, we now know that the recoveries that followed the recessions of 1990–91, 2001, and 2007–09 were "jobless." The recovery from the recessionary conditions of 1980–82 was not "jobless" because employment opportunities created by the microelectronics boom in the first half of the 1980s offset the joblessness that remained in the traditional manufacturing sector as the U.S. economy began to grow. For example, from 1980 to 1985 employment of mathematical and computer engineers increased from 330,000 to 571,000, or by 73.0 percent, and employment of computer programmers increased from 318,000 to 534,000, or by 67.9 percent (U.S. Department of Commerce 1983: 416; 1986: 385). In the expansion of 1983–85, however, workers in traditional manufacturing industries experienced the first of four jobless recoveries of the last three decades.

As for the New Economy, the recovery from the recession of 1980–82 saw the emergence of what would become the Wintel architecture around the IBM PC (Borrus and Zysman 1997). In 1982, IBM's PC sales were $500 million and just two years later eleven times that amount, more than triple the 1984 revenues of its nearest competitor, Apple, and about equal to the revenues of IBM's top eight rivals. Subsequently, the very success of the IBM PC combined with open access to the Microsoft operating system and Intel microprocessor meant that, in the last half of the 1980s and beyond, IBM lost market share to lower-priced PC clones produced by New Economy companies such as Compaq, Gateway, and Dell (Chandler 2001: 118–19, 142–43).

As a result of the microelectronics revolution of the 1980s, these New Economy companies in the ICT industries found themselves in competition for professional, technical, and administrative labor with Old Economy ICT companies such as Hewlett-Packard, IBM, Motorola, Texas Instruments, and Xerox that offered employees the realistic prospect of a career with one company. As young firms facing a highly uncertain future, it was impossible for New Economy companies to attract labor from Old Economy companies by promises of career employment. Instead, NEBM used the inducement of employee stock options to attract and retain employees, very high proportions of whom were college educated. As the successful New Economy companies grew large, most if not all employees were partially compensated in stock options. For example, Cisco Systems had 250 employees in 1990, the year in which it did its IPO. A decade later, after it had come to dominate the Internet router market, it had over 34,000 employees, virtually all of whom received stock options (Lazonick 2009a: ch. 2).

So that stock options would perform a retention function as well as an attraction function, the practice evolved in New Economy firms of making option grants annually, with the vesting period for any annual block of option grants being 25 percent of the grants at the end of each of the first four years after the grant date. Once the options are vested, they can typically be exercised for a period of ten years from the grant date, as long as one remains with the company. Without creating the Old Economy expectation among employees of lifelong careers with the company, the perpetual pipeline of unvested options functions as a tangible retention mechanism. Indeed, for most employees, the amount of options that an individual can expect to receive is tied to his or her position in the firm's hierarchical and functional division of labor, so that the retention function of stock options is integrally related to the employee's career progress within the particular company. At the same time, under NEBM there is no expectation as there was under OEBM of a career with one company (Lazonick 2009a: chs. 2, 4).

An Old Economy company valued career employees because they had experience in the development and utilization of the company's proprietary technologies. At many of the leading companies, the corporate R&D lab was the main source of this intellectual property. Investment in new products and processes was often done on military contracts, with the adaptation of the technologies to commercial production as process technologies improved and potential unit costs declined. As Old Economy companies, taken together, passed on some of their productivity gains to their employees in the forms of higher wages, they supported the growth of mass markets on which they could attain high capacity utilization of their existing productive capabilities and for which they could develop new products.

The recession and recovery of the early 1990s witnessed the marketization of the employment relation, marking the beginning of the end of the career-with-one-company norm that characterized OEBM. The downturn of 1990–91 is known as a "white-collar recession." Although in absolute terms, blue-collar workers suffered more unemployment than white-collar workers during this recession, the extent to which professional, technical, and administrative employees were terminated was unprecedented in the post-World War II decades (Eberts and Groshen 1991; Gardner 1994). Increasingly over the course of the 1990s, including during the Internet boom in the second half of the decade, the career-long employment security that people in their 40s and 50s had come to expect under OEBM vanished as employers replaced more expensive older workers with less expensive younger workers (Lazonick 2009a: chs. 3, 7).

Given its size, reputation, and central position in the ICT industries, IBM's transformation from OEBM to NEBM in the early 1990s marked a fundamental juncture in the transition from employment security to employment insecurity in the U.S. corporate economy. Through the 1980s, IBM touted its practice of "lifelong employment" as a source of its competitive success. From 1990 to 1994 IBM cut employment from 373,816 to 219,839, reducing its labor force to only 59 percent of its year-end 1990 level. During this period, much of IBM's downsizing was accomplished by making it attractive for its employees to accept voluntary severance packages, including early retirement at age 55. In 1993 and 1994, however, after recruiting CEO Louis V. Gerstner, Jr. from RJR Nabisco to get the job done, many thousands of IBM employees were fired outright. In 1995 IBM rescinded the early-retirement offer that had helped downsize its labor force; the offer had accomplished its purpose, and in any case, IBM no longer wanted to encourage all employees to remain with the company even until the age of 55 (Lazonick 2009a: ch. 3).

Of IBM's losses of $15.9 billion in 1991–93 (including an $8.1 billion deficit in 1993, the largest annual loss in U.S. corporate history at the time), 86 percent came from workforce-related restructuring charges (including the cost of employee separations and relocations)—in effect the cost to the company of ridding itself of its once-hallowed tradition of lifelong employment. Other restructuring charges, mainly for the consolidation of manufacturing capacity and elimination of excess space—both part and parcel of the massive downsizing process—amounted to $10.6 billion over the three years. Ignoring restructuring charges, IBM recorded positive net incomes before taxes of $939 million in 1991, $2,619 million in 1992, and $148 million in 1993. Although IBM continued to downsize at a torrid pace in 1994, most of it was done outside the United States and without voluntary severance provisions. During 1994 the company booked no restructuring charges and had after-tax profits of $3,021 million. By that time, lifelong employment at IBM was a thing of the past.

In line with the IBM transition, for the period of 1992 to 1997, John Abowd et al. (2007) found a general shift in U.S. employment from older experienced workers to younger skilled workers related to the adoption of computer technologies. Using Current Population Survey data, Charles Schultze discovered that "[m]iddle-aged and older men, for whatever reason, are not staying as long with their employers as they once did" (1999: 10–11). He went on to show, moreover, that the job displacement rate for white-collar workers relative to blue-collar workers had risen substantially in the 1980s and 1990s, starting at 33 percent in 1981–82 and increasing to about 80 percent in the 1990s.

As Lori Kletzer wrote in a 1998 survey article on "job displacement":

> Job loss rates fell steadily from the 1981–83 rate, which encompassed the recession of 1981–82, through the expansion period of 1983–89. Job loss rates then rose again in 1989–91 as the economy weakened. The latest job loss figures are surprising. In the midst of a sustained (if uneven) expansion, 1993–95 job loss rates are the highest of the 14-year period: about 15 percent of U.S. workers were displaced from a job at some time during this three-year period. These high rates of job loss are consistent with public perceptions of rising job insecurity. (1998: 117)

In a more recent survey of changes in job security, Henry Farber stated that "[t]here is ample evidence that long-term employment [with one company] is on the decline in the United States" (2008: 1). Using Current Population Survey data for 1973–2006, Farber (2008: 27) showed that in the 1990s and 2000s, members of the U.S. labor force experienced shortened job tenure, with the impact being most pronounced for males. Moreover, education and experience are no longer the guarantors of employment security that they once were. Using Displaced Worker Survey data to analyze rates of job loss, Farber (2008: 35) found that those with college educations had job loss rates 22 percent lower than those with high school educations in the 1980s, but only 12 percent lower in the 2000s. He also found that workers ages 45–54 had job-loss rates 19 percent higher than workers ages 20–24 in the 1980s, whereas the job-loss rates of the older age-group were 58 percent higher than those of the younger age group in the 2000s.

In the 2000s, globalization joined rationalization and marketization as a source of structural change in the employment opportunities available to members of the U.S. labor force. In the ICT industries that were central to the growth of the U.S. economy in the 1980s and 1990s, the globalization of employment dated back to the 1960s when U.S. semiconductor manufacturers had set up assembly and testing facilities in East Asia, making use of low-paid but literate female labor (Lazonick 2009a: ch. 5). Over time, a combination of work experience at home with both multinational and indigenous companies as well as the return of nationals who had acquired graduate education and/or work experience abroad enhanced the capabilities of the Asian labor force to engage in higher value-added activities. By the beginning of the 2000s, Indians had become world leaders in the offshore provision of IT services while the Chinese had become adept in a wide range of manufacturing industries, especially in ICT. In the 2000s, the availability of a capable college-educated labor supply along with the availability of enhanced and low-cost communications networks led to a vast acceleration of offshoring by U.S. companies to China and India (Bednarzik 2005; Blinder 2007; Bronfenbrenner and Luce 2004; Hira and Hira 2008; Houseman 2009).

Offshoring depressed U.S. employment in the recession of 2001 and in the subsequent jobless recovery that stretched into 2003. Now well-educated high-tech workers found themselves vulnerable to displacement as U.S.-based companies hired workers abroad (Garner 2004; Jensen and Kletzer 2005). Given huge increases in the issuance of non-immigrant (H-1B and L-1) work visas in the United States in the late 1990s and beginning of the 2000s, there were hundreds of thousands of high-tech workers, especially Indians, who had accumulated U.S. work experience that they could now take back home. In February 2003, after more than a year of jobless recovery, *BusinessWeek* (Engardio, Bernstein, and Kripalani 2003) gained considerable attention when its cover blared the rhetorical warning: "Is Your Job Next?" The subhead read: "A new round of globalization is sending upscale jobs offshore. They include chip design, engineering, basic research—even financial analysis. Can America lose these jobs and still prosper?"

For three decades now the U.S. economy has been losing unionized blue-collar jobs. As it has turned out, Democratic administrations have been no better than Republican administrations in stanching the decline (see Uchitelle 2007: ch. 7). In 2010 the U.S.

rate of business-sector unionization was 6.9 percent, having declined steady from over 15 percent in 1983 (U.S. Department of Labor 2011). Since the early 1990s, nonunionized white-collar workers, including professional, technical, and administrative employees who are deemed to be members of "management," have found that they can no longer expect that they will have a career with one company. The shift to open-systems technologies and the globalization of high-tech jobs have rendered vulnerable the employment of well-educated and highly experienced members of the U.S. labor force.

It should be emphasized that the displacement of workers from middle-class jobs often has a productive rationale: manufacturing plants may become uncompetitive; recently educated workers may possess more relevant skills than experienced (older) workers; and the productive capabilities of workers in low-wage areas of the world may be on a par if not superior to those of workers in the United States. Nevertheless, especially once changes in the structure of employment have become widespread for productive reasons, corporations have been known to terminate employees in order to increase short-term profits for the sake of inciting speculative increases in their companies' stock prices. The tendency has then been to allocate those extra profits to stock buybacks so that manipulation as well as speculation can drive up the price of the company's stock. Legitimizing both the elimination of existing jobs and the failure to create new jobs is the ideology that companies should be run to "maximize shareholder value."

Unlike the recessions of 1980–82, 1990–91, and 2001, the Great Recession of 2008–09 was a purely financial downturn caused by speculation in and manipulation of securities markets in the financial sector of the economy. At the same time, that speculation and manipulation exploited the fragility of home ownership in an economy that since the 1980s had been eliminating middle-class jobs from the industrial sector. The jobless recovery that has followed the Great Recession has been far more prolonged than earlier ones. While Wall Street has become and remains a gambling casino, the more fundamental fragility of the U.S. economy emanates from the industrial sector. As a general rule, the executives who run the financialized U.S. industrial corporations have become focused on creating profits for the sake of higher stock prices rather than creating the high value-added jobs that are the essence of a prosperous economy.

Sustainable Prosperity in the U.S. Economy?

The objectives of government economic policy should be to support equitable and stable economic growth. Growth is equitable when those who contribute to the growth process receive a commensurate share of the gains. The equitable sharing of the gains from growth should occur at the level of the enterprise through its relations with employees, suppliers, distributors, and financiers. Tax policy should be designed to ensure that the government secures an equitable return from the business sector on government investments in physical and human infrastructure as well as subsidies that companies use to generate innovation and growth.

When certain types of participants in the economy extract much more value than they create—that is, when the distribution of income is highly inequitable—the economy becomes unstable. The relation between consumption and production is thrown out of balance. Speculative investments are encouraged. Those who extract more than they create have an interest in manipulating financial markets to increase their own gain. Government policies should be designed to reduce the possibilities for value extraction that is not warranted by value creation. Such policies would seek to preserve the incentives to innovation while reducing the possibilities for gains from speculation and manipulation.

The stock-based pay that enables corporate executives to gain from speculation and manipulation of the stock market makes the U.S. economy not only inequitable but also unstable. To reap the gains from speculation and manipulation, executives often make resource allocation decisions such as financially driven acquisitions and stock buybacks that ultimately undermine the conditions of innovative enterprise. At the same time, the U.S. economy is highly dependent on innovative enterprise not only to generate economic growth but also to create sustainable employment opportunities for the population that can, at a minimum, replace the middle-class jobs that through rationalization, marketization, and globalization the U.S. economy has lost over the past three decades. Instead, the financialization of the U.S. corporation has exacerbated the loss of jobs from these structural changes in employment.

When there is job displacement because of rationalization, marketization, and globalization, business and government must collaborate to ensure the availability of the education and training needed to reposition displaced workers to perform new productive roles in the economy. The financialized corporation tends to opt out of this collaborative effort because it operates according to an ideology that argues that it has no responsibility for the displaced workers. In doing so, the financialized corporation not only avoids a share of the cost of retraining its workers but also fails to participate in making the investments that can generate new and potentially sustainable middle-class jobs for the U.S. labor force.

Innovation and job creation require business-government collaboration (Block 2009; Block and Keller 2011; Lazonick 2008; see also Breznitz 2007). Government investment in physical infrastructures such as communication networks and transportation systems as well as human infrastructures such as higher education and research facilities provides an essential foundation for business investment, especially in high-tech fields. Government subsidies to business, often implemented through tax legislation, can serve as further inducements to business investment. As already mentioned, in the United States, government funding has been critical to the emergence and development of high-tech sectors such as computers, the Internet, and biotechnology.

But for these government investments and subsidies, the United States would not lead the world in venture capital—an industry devoted to new-firm formation and growth. Yet, in the United States, it can be argued that a disproportionate share of the returns to a successful new venture accrue to those entrepreneurs and financiers who put an innovation on the market while neglecting the contributions of other stakeholders, especially taxpayers, who made significant contributions to the innovation process (see Lazonick 2009a). In the name of "shareholder value," rewards are reaped at the expense of non-shareholding stakeholders who risked their labor and capital in the collective and cumulative innovation process.

Once a new venture has become a going concern, MSV ideology continues to hold sway. Innovation may drive stock prices for a while, and through broad-based stock options plans thousands of employees can share in the gains. But the use of stock options as a mode of compensation means that the realization of gains depends on selling, not holding, ownership stakes. Moreover, in an exploding stock market as occurred in the Internet boom of 1996–2000, the returns to option holders reflect gains from speculation much more than gains from innovation. Furthermore, even in the tight labor markets of the Internet boom, high-tech employees who could potentially reap large gains from the exercise of stock options were also vulnerable to being thrown out of work through marketization and globalization (Lazonick 2009a, 2009b).

As we have seen, in the 2000s up to the financial crisis of 2008, it was manipulation much more than innovation or speculation that drove stock prices. Through the escalation of stock buybacks from 2003 to 2007, the S&P 500 Index peaked in 2007 at a higher level than that achieved through the often wildly speculative stock valuations of 2000. In effect in the period 2003–07 major U.S. companies used escalating stock buybacks to compete with one another to boost their stock prices and manage quarterly EPS. In the Great Recession of 2008–09 stock prices tumbled as did stock buybacks. By 2010 U.S. companies were profitable again, but they both increased buybacks and still sat on huge cash reserves (in some cases augmenting these reserves by borrowing money at very low interest rates while they kept cash offshore to avoid taxation), preparing themselves, according to my prognosis, for a renewed competitive escalation of buyback activity (Jewell 2010; Krantz 2011; Lazonick 2011a). Just as the cause of the Great Recession was the financialized business corporation, so too the subsequent jobless recovery has been the result of the continued domination of MSV ideology and practice in the U.S. corporation.

In the jobless recovery that has followed the Great Recession, U.S. business corporations have been highly profitable. Indeed, even as stock buybacks escalated once again in 2011, U.S. business corporations were sitting on $1.4 billion in offshore accounts (see, e.g., Hirsch 2011), encouraged to do so by a fifty-year-old tax loophole that permits them to defer the payment of taxes on corporate profits until they repatriate them to the United States (see Lazonick 2011a). In the wake of heavy lobbying by U.S. corporations, there has been a debate going on in the U.S. Congress over whether to give corporations a substantial one-time tax reduction to encourage them to repatriate these overseas profits with a view to putting the cash to work in the sluggish economy.

That inducement was already tried under the Bush administration, and failed. As part of the American Job Creation Act of 2004, the Homeland Investment Act provided a corporate tax rate of 5.25 percent for profits repatriated in one fiscal year, with the stipulation that these profits had to be used for investments that create jobs. The Act expressly prohibited the use of these funds to pay dividends or do stock buybacks. U.S. corporations responded by repatriating $299 billion in profits in 2005, compared with an average of $62 billion in 2000–04, and a subsequent decline to $102 billion in 2006 (Dharmapala, Foley, and Forbes 2011). A study of the impacts of the tax break found that "[r]ather than being associated with increased expenditures on domestic investment or employment, repatriations were associated with significantly higher levels of payouts to shareholders, mainly taking the form of share repurchases. Estimates imply that a $1 increase in repatriations was associated with an increase in payouts to shareholders of between $0.60 and $0.92, depending on the specification" (Dharmapala, Foley, and Forbes 2011: 756). The authors suggest that companies were able to make these distributions to shareholders without violating the terms of the repatriation legislation by using the repatriated funds "to pay for investment, hiring, or R&D that was already planned, thereby releasing [domestic] cash that had previously been allocated for these purposes to be used for payouts to shareholders" (Dharmapala, Foley, and Forbes 2011: 756).

In my view, any government policy agenda that seeks to recreate the middle class in the United States needs to begin with an attack on the financialized corporation. This policy agenda then needs to engage in constructive programs in collaboration with a nonfinancialized business community to rebuild the capabilities of the U.S. labor force to engage in innovative enterprise. The policy agenda for sustainable prosperity includes five major reforms:

1. *Banning of stock repurchases by established U.S. corporations so corporate financial resources that could be allocated to innovation and job creation are not wasted for the purpose of manipulating companies' stock prices.* Once one rejects the flawed ideology that for the sake of superior economic performance, corporations should be run to maximize shareholder value, it follows that stock repurchases by established corporations serve no legitimate economic purpose. Moreover corporate executives who can think of no better way to allocate corporate resources should not be running the nation's corporations. Instead of being used to prop up stock prices, these funds can be (a) invested in innovation in areas in which the company has competence, (b) invested in new ventures and spinoffs that draw upon the knowledge and experience of corporate employees, (c) returned to employees in the form of higher wages and benefits, (d) returned to local, state, and national governments that have supported the growth of the company, and/or (e) returned to shareholders in the form of dividends, if such distributions are consistent with equitable and stable economic growth.

2. *Indexing of employee stock options to an indicator of innovative performance so that executives cannot gain from speculation in and manipulation of their companies' stock prices.* It is generally accepted, by both proponents and opponents of shareholder-value ideology, that corporate executives in the United States have developed an obsession with meeting Wall Street's expectations of quarterly EPS targets. It is also generally the case

that in their resource allocation decisions (be they the allocation of their own human capital or the resources over which they exercise control in a corporation) people will respond to financial incentives, especially when society deems those financial incentives as not only legitimate, but also consistent with the common good. Remuneration in the form of unindexed stock options that can be sold as soon as they are exercised gives the U.S. corporate executive a strong incentive to make allocative decisions that result in speculation in and manipulation of his or her company's stock price. Shareholder-value ideology legitimizes both stock buybacks and stock-based remuneration. Regulations that tie stock-based compensation to gains from innovation and exclude gains from speculation and manipulation are required to remove this perverse incentive.

3. *Regulation of the employment contract to ensure that workers who contribute to the innovation process share in the gains to innovation.* It is inherent in the innovation process that investments of productive resources, including the application of the skills and efforts of workers, are made today with the expectation of financial returns on these investments in the future. Those who contribute their labor and capital to the innovation process have a legitimate claim to an equitable share in the gains to innovation if and when they occur. Since innovation is a collective, cumulative, and uncertain process, it follows that the incentives of workers to contribute their skills and efforts to innovation depends on their expectation that these future returns will be forthcoming. At the same time, however, for these returns to be in fact equitable, they cannot be treated as an entitlement of employment. A "theory of innovative enterprise" is an essential intellectual foundation for the intelligent regulation of the employment contract so it is based on norms of distribution of the gains from innovative enterprise that are consistent with equitable and stable economic growth.

4. *Creation of work programs that make productive use of and enhance the productive capabilities of educated and experienced workers whose human capital would otherwise deteriorate through lack of other relevant employment.* Although there is little in the way of systematic evidence on the subject, there is no doubt that the combination of marketization and globalization has resulted in the displacement of large numbers of well-educated and highly experienced workers in their 40s and 50s whose accumulated human capital will obsolesce unless they are quickly reemployed in jobs that can make use of it. Such a diminution in the stock of highly qualified human capital poses a high cost to not only the individuals concerned but also society, which to some extent will have subsidized the investment in this human capital and which stands to continue to benefit from it if that investment in human capital can be put to productive use. This employment may be in the business sector or the government sector, but either way effective programs will require business-government collaboration that will maintain and enhance the capabilities of workers so that they can make productive contributions to the economy and earn decent incomes for themselves.

5. *Implementation of taxes on the gains from innovation to fund those government agencies that need to invest in the public knowledge base required for the next round of innovation.* The prevailing ideology that the free operation of markets tends to result in

superior economic performance ignores not only the role of the innovative enterprise in generating higher-quality, lower-cost products but also the role the developmental state in investing in human and physical infrastructures that support the innovation process. MSV ideology appropriates for shareholders the returns to innovation that should go to not only employees, but also the state. Notwithstanding the dominance of an ideology that says that the government should play little if any role in the allocation of productive resources, over the course of the twentieth century the U.S. government was the most formidable "developmental state" in history. In every high-tech field in which the United States has been a leader, it has been the result of a combination of resource allocation by the innovative enterprise and the developmental state (Lazonick 2011b).

It will be impossible to justify these reforms if Americans do not question the ideology that companies should be run to "maximize shareholder value." It is an ideology that results in inequity and instability and that ultimately undermines the productive foundations of economic growth. While MSV has currency throughout the world, its pervasive and unquestioned acceptance has become an almost uniquely American phenomenon. Even in the United States, it was an ideology with which the economy could do without until the 1980s—which is when the trends to permanent job displacement and income inequality set in (Lazonick and O'Sullivan 2000). The United States is engaged in global competition with highly innovative national economies in which MSV ideology does not hold sway. As long as U.S.-based corporations are permitted to be governed by this ideology, the U.S. economy will remain incapable of generating middle-class jobs on the scale that is needed to restore sustainable prosperity. Indeed, judging from the changes in not only the employment of corporate labor but also the allocation of corporate capital that has occurred in the U.S. economy over the past three decades, the persistence of this destructive ideology will mean that the achievement of equitable and stable growth in the United States will become more and more out of reach.

Acknowledgments

The author wishes to thank the Alfred P. Sloan Foundation for financial support and the Berkeley Roundtable on the International Economy (BRIE) for research and administrative support.

This chapter builds on research in William Lazonick (2009a, 2009b, 2010c). The most recent research contained in this chapter was funded by the FINNOV project through Theme 8 of the Seventh Framework Programme of the European Commission (Socio-Economic Sciences and Humanities), under the topic "The Role of Finance for Growth, Employment and Competitiveness in Europe" (SSH-2007-1.2-03) as well as by the Ford Foundation project on "Financial Institutions for Innovation and Development" and the Institute for New Economic Thinking project on "The Stock Market and Innovative Enterprise." I am grateful to Ebru Bekaslan, Yin Li, and Mustafa Erdem Sakinç for research assistance.

Notes

1. http://money.cnn.com/magazines/fortune/global500/2011/countries/US.html.
2. *Fortune*, May 23, 2011. Retrieved (http://money.cnn.com/magazines/fortune/fortune500/2011/full_list/). These numbers were all increases from 2009 when the Fortune 500 companies combined had revenues of $9.8 trillion, profits of $391 billion, and employment of 24.7 million.
3. http://www.nih.gov/about/almanac/appropriations/index.htm.
4. See the various articles on conglomeration in *St. John's Law Review*, 44, 1969–1970.
5. A stock option award gives an employee the nontransferable right to purchase a certain number of shares of the company for which he or she works at a preset "exercise" price between the date the option "vests" and the date it "expires." Typically in U.S. option grants, the exercise price is the market price of the stock at the date that the option is granted; vesting of the option occurs in 25 percent installments at each of the first four anniversaries from the grant date; and the expiration date of the option is ten years from the grant date. Unvested options usually lapse ninety days after termination of employment with the company.
6. In the 1980s, dividends paid out by U.S. corporations increased by an annual average of 10.8 percent while after-tax corporate profits increased by an annual average of 8.7 percent. In the 1990s these figures were 8.0 percent for dividends (including an absolute decline in dividends of 4.0 percent in 1999, the first decline since 1975) and 8.1 percent for profits. The dividend payout ratio—the amount of dividends as a proportion of after-tax corporate profits (with inventory evaluation and capital consumption adjustments)—was 48.9 percent in the 1980s and 55.0 percent in the 1990s compared with 39.5 percent in the 1960s and 41.6 percent in the 1970s. From 2000 to 2009 the dividend payout ratio was 61.4 percent, including a record 70.4 percent in 2007 (U.S. Congress 2010, Table B-90). The dividend payout ratio was 60.7 percent in 2010, and 59.4 percent in the first half of 2011 (http://www.census.gov/compendia/statab/2012/tables/12s0791.pdf).
7. http://www.marketwatch.com/story/sp-500-quarterly-stock-buybacks-back-to-100-billion-level-q2-2011-buybacks-up-216-from-q1-2011-2011-09-20.
8. In 2003 the SEC amended Rule 10b-18 "to simplify and update the safe harbor provisions in light of market developments since the Rule's adoption." The amendments also required that, in their 10-Q filings with the SEC, companies report the number and value of shares repurchased in the previous quarter and the average price paid per share. See http://www.sec.gov/rules/final/33-8335.htm.
9. http://nano.gov/about-nni/what/funding.
10. http://www.nih.gov/about/budget.htm.

References

Abbate, Janet. (2000). *Inventing the Internet.* Cambridge, MA: MIT Press.
Abowd, John, John Haltiwanger, et al. (2007). Technology and the demand for skill: An analysis of within and between firm differences. NBER Working Paper 13043, National Bureau of Economic Research.
Abowd, John M., George T. Milkovich, and John M. Hannon. (1990). "The effects of human resource management decisions on shareholder value." *Industrial and Labor Relations Review* 43(Special Issue): 203S–33S.

Auletta, Ken. (1986). *Greed and Glory on Wall Street: The Fall of the House of Lehman.* New York: Warner Books.

Auten, Gerald. (1999). "Capital Gains Taxation." In *The Encyclopedia of Taxation and Tax Policy*, edited by Joseph J. Cordes, Robert D. Ebel, and Jane G. Gravelle, 58–61. Washington, D.C.: Urban Institute.

Baldwin, Carliss, and Kim Clark. (1992). "Capabilities and capital investment: New perspectives on capital budgeting." *Journal of Applied Corporate Finance* 5(2): 67–87.

Bebchuk, Lucian, and Jesse Fried. (2004). *Pay Without Performance: The Unfulfilled Promise of Executive Compensation.* Cambridge, MA: Harvard University Press.

Bednarzik, Robert W. (1983). "Layoffs and permanent job losses: Workers' traits and cyclical patterns." *Monthly Labor Review* 106(9): 3–12.

Bednarzik, Robert W. (2005). "Restructuring information technology: Is offshoring a concern?" *Monthly Labor Review* 128(8): 11–21.

Berle, Adolf A., and Gardiner C. Means. (1932). *The Modern Corporation and Private Property.* New York: Macmillan.

Bernile, Gennaro, and Gregg A. Jarrell. (2009). "The impact of the options backdating scandal on shareholders." *Journal of Accounting and Economics* 47(1–2): 2–26.

Blair, Margaret. (Ed.). (1993). *The Deal Decade: What Takeovers and Leveraged Buyouts Mean for Corporate Governance.* Washington, D.C.: Brookings Institution Press.

Blair, Margaret M. (1995). *Ownership and Control: Rethinking Corporate Governance for the Twenty-first Century.* Washington, D.C.: Brookings Institution Press.

Blinder, Alan S. (2007). How many U.S. jobs may be offshorable? CEPS Working Paper No. 142, Princeton University, March.

Block, Fred. (2009). "Swimming against the current: The rise of a hidden developmental state in the United States." *Politics & Society* 36(2):169–206.

Block, Fred, and Matthew Keller. (Eds.). (2011). *State of Innovation: The U.S. Government's Role in Technology Development.* Boulder, CO: Paradigm Publishing.

Borrus, Michael, and John Zysman. (1997). Wintelism and the changing terms of global competition: Prototype of the future? BRIE Working Paper 96B, University of California, Berkeley.

Breznitz, Dan. (2007). *Innovation and the State: Political Choice and Strategies for Growth in Israel, Taiwan, and Ireland.* New Haven, CT: Yale University Press.

Bronfenbrenner, Kate, and Stephanie Luce. (2004). The changing nature of global corporate restructuring: The impact of production shifts on jobs in the US, China, and around the globe. Submitted to the U.S.-China Economic and Security Review Commission, October 14 (http://www.goiam.org/publications/pdfs/cornell_u_mass_report.pdf).

Bruck, Connie. (1989). *Predator's Ball: The Inside Story of Drexel Burnham and the Rise of the Junk Bond Raiders.* New York: Penguin Books.

Burgelman, Robert A. (1994). "Fading memories: A process theory of strategic exit in dynamic environments." *Administrative Science Quarterly* 39(1): 24–56.

Carey, Ray. (2010). "Congress designs ERISA, an economic bomb." Carey Center for Democratic Capitalism (http://www.democratic-capitalism.com/college.htm#a13).

Carrington, Tim. (1987). *The Year They Sold Wall Street.* New York: Penguin Books.

Chance, Don M., Raman Kumar, and Rebecca B. Todd. (2000). "The 'repricing' of executive stock options." *Journal of Financial Economics* 57(1): 129–54.

Chandler, Alfred D. Jr. (1977). *The Visible Hand: The Managerial Revolution in American Business.* Cambridge, MA: Harvard University Press.

Chandler, Alfred D. Jr. (2001). *Inventing the Electronic Century: The Epic Story of the Consumer Electronic and Computer Industries.* New York: Free Press.

Christensen, Clayton M., Stephen P. Kaufman, and Willy C. Shih. (2008). "Innovation killers: How financial tools destroy your capacity to do new Things." *Harvard Business Review* 86(1): 98–105.

Crystal, Graef. (1978). *Executive Compensation: Money, Motivation, and Imagination.* New York: American Management Association.

Crystal, Graef. (1991). *In Search of Excess: The Overcompensation of American Executives.* New York: W. W. Norton.

Dharmapala, Dhammika, C. Fritz Foley, and Kristin J. Forbes. (2011). "Watch what I do, not what I say: The unintended consequences of the Homeland Investment Act." *Journal of Finance* 64(3): 753–87.

Dittmar, Amy K., and Robert F. Dittmar. (2004). Stock repurchase waves: An explanation of the trends in aggregate corporate payout policy. Business School Working Paper, University of Michigan (http://webuser.bus.umich.edu/adittmar/Stock_Repurchase_Waves.pdf).

Eberts, Randall W., and Erica L. Groshen. (1991). "Is this really a 'white-collar recession'?" *Economic Commentary*, March 15 [Federal Reserve Bank of Cleveland] (http://www.clevelandfed.org/research/commentary/1991/0315.pdf).

Ellig, Bruce R. (2007). *The Complete Guide to Executive Compensation.* New York: McGraw-Hill.

Engardio, Pete, Aaron Bernstein, and Manjeet Kripalani. (2003). "The new global job shift." *BusinessWeek*, February 2 (http://www.businessweek.com/stories/2003-02-02/the-new-global-job-shift#r=lr-fs).

Fairlie, Ronald, and Lori Kletzer. (1998). "Jobs lost, jobs regained: An analysis of black/white differences in job displacement in the 1980s." *Industrial Relations* 37(4): 460–77.

Fama, Eugene F., and Michael C. Jensen. (1983a). "Agency problems and residual claims." *Journal of Law and Economics* 26(2): 327–49.

Fama, Eugene F., and Michael C. Jensen. (1983b). "Separation of ownership and control." *Journal of Law and Economics* 26(2): 301–25.

Farber, Henry. (2008). Job loss and the decline of job security in the United States. Princeton University Industrial Relations Section Working Paper No. 520, Princeton University, June 4 (http://www.irs.princeton.edu/pubs/pdfs/520revised.pdf).

Forelle, Charles, and James Bandler. (2006). "The perfect payday: Some CEOs reap millions by landing stock options when they are most valuable; Luck—or something else?" *Wall Street Journal*, March 18: A1.

Fried, Jesse M. (2000). "Insider signaling and insider trading with repurchase tender offers." *University of Chicago Law Review* 67(2): 421–77.

Fried, Jesse M. (2001). "Open market repurchases: Signaling or market opportunism?" *Theoretical Inquiries in Law* 2(2): 1–30.

Gardner, Jennifer M. (1994). "The 1990–91 recession: How bad was the labor market?" *Monthly Labor Review* 117(6): 3–11.

Garner, C. Alan. (2004). "Offshoring in the service sector: Economic impact and policy issues." *Economic Review* [Federal Reserve Bank of Kansas City, Third Quarter] 5–37.

Ghilarducci, Teresa. (1994). "US Pension investment policy and perfect capital market theory." *Challenge* 37(4): 4–10.

Giarratani, Frank, Gene Gruver, and Randall Jackson. (2007). "Clusters, agglomeration, and economic development potential: Empirical evidence based on the advent of slab casting by U.S. Steel minimills." *Economic Development Quarterly* 21(2): 148–64.

Gimein, Mark, Eric Dash, Lisa Munoz, and Jessica Sung. (2002). "You bought. They sold. All over corporate America, top execs were cashing in stock even as their companies were tanking. Who was left holding the bag? You." *Fortune* September 2 (http://money.cnn.com/magazines/fortune/fortune_archive/2002/09/02/327903/index.htm).

Guerrera, Francesco. (2009). "Welch rues short-term profit 'obsession.'" *Financial Times*, March 12 (http://www.ft.com/intl/cms/s/0/294ff1f2-0f27-11de-ba10-0000779fd2ac.html#axzz26JuHmtR6).

Hamermesh, Daniel S. (1989). "What do we know about worker displacement in the U.S.?" *Industrial Relations* 28(1): 51–59.

Harris, Candee S. (1984). "The magnitude of job loss from plant closings and the generation of replacement jobs: Some recent evidence." *Annals of the American Academy of Political and Social Science* 475: 15–27.

Hira, Ron and Anil Hira. (2008). *Outsourcing America: The True Cost of Shipping Jobs Overseas and What Can Be Done About It*. Rev. ed. New York: AMACOM.

Hirsch, Michelle. (2011). "$1.4 trillion cash stash could stole job market." *The Fiscal Times*, October 14 (http://www.thefiscaltimes.com/Articles/2011/10/14/1-Point-4-Trillion-Cash-Stash-Could-Stoke-Job-Market.aspx#page1).

Houseman, Susan M. (2009). "Measuring offshore outsourcing and offshoring: Problems for economic statistics." *Employment Research* 16(1): 1–3 (http://www.upjohninstitute.org/publications/newsletter/snh_109.pdf).

Hudson, Richard L. (1982). "SEC eases way for repurchase of firms' stock: Agency assures it won't file charges of manipulation if certain rules are met." *Wall Street Journal*, November 10: 2.

Hurley, Timothy M. (2006). "The urge to merge: Contemporary theories on the rise of conglomerate mergers in the 1960s." *Journal of Business & Technology Law* 1(1): 185–205.

Ingebretsen, Mark. (2002). *NASDAQ: A History of the Market That Changed the World*. Roseville, CA: Prima Publishing.

Jensen, J. Bradford, and Lori B. Kletzer. (2005). Tradable services: Understanding the scope and impact of services outsourcing. Working Paper 05-9. Washington, D.C.: Institute for International Economics.

Jensen, Michael C. (1986). "Agency costs of free cash flow, corporate finance, and takeovers." *American Economic Review* 76(2): 323–29.

Jensen, Michael C., and Kevin J. Murphy. (1990). "Performance pay and top management incentives." *Journal of Political Economy* 98(2): 225–64.

Jewell, Mark. (2010). "Stock buybacks increase in 3Q—Firms repurchase rather than hire." *The Commercial Appeal*, December 21 (http://commercial-appeal.vlex.com/vid/buybacks-firms-repurchase-rather-hire-233502435).

Kalafsky, Ronald V., and Alan D. MacPherson. (2002). "The competitive characteristics of the U.S. machine tool industry." *Small Business Economics* 19(4): 355–69.

Kastor, John A. (2010). *The National Institutes of Health, 1991–2008*. New York: Oxford University Press.

Kletzer, Lori G. (1991). "Job displacement, 1979–1986: How blacks fared relative to whites." *Monthly Labor Review* 114(7): 17–25.

Kletzer, Lori G. (1998). "Job displacement." *Journal of Economic Perspectives* 12(1): 115–36.

Krantz, Matt. (2011). "Companies' cash stash grows; Stock buybacks, dividends increase—but not jobs." *USA Today*, January 4: 1B.

Lazonick, William. (1992). "Controlling the market for corporate control: The historical significance of managerial capitalism." *Industrial and Corporate Change* 1(3): 445–88.

Lazonick, William. (1998). "Organizational Learning and International Competition." In *Globalization, Growth, and Governance*, edited by Jonathan Michie and John Grieve Smith, 204–38. New York: Oxford University Press.

Lazonick, William. (2002). "Innovative enterprise and historical transformation." *Enterprise & Society* 3(1): 35–54.

Lazonick, William. (2004a). "Corporate Restructuring." In *The Oxford Handbook of Work and Organization*, edited by Stephen Ackroyd, Rose Batt, Paul Thompson, and Pamela Tolbert, 577–601. Oxford: Oxford University Press.

Lazonick, William. (2004b). "The Innovative Firm." In *The Oxford Handbook of Innovation*, edited by Jan Fagerberg, David Mowery, and Richard Nelson, 29–55. Oxford: Oxford University Press.

Lazonick, William. (2008). Entrepreneurial ventures and the developmental state: Lessons from the advanced economies. World Institute of Development Economics Research Discussion Paper dp2008-01 (http://www.wider.unu.edu/publications/working-papers/discussion-papers/2008/en_GB/dp2008-01/_files/78805634425684379/default/dp2008-01.pdf).

Lazonick, William. (2009a). *Sustainable Prosperity in the New Economy? Business Organization and High-Tech Employment in the United States*. Kalamazoo, MI: Upjohn Institute for Employment Research.

Lazonick, William. (2009b). "The New Economy business model and the crisis of U.S. capitalism." *Capitalism and Society* 4(2): Article 4.

Lazonick, William. (2010a). "Innovative business models and varieties of capitalism." *Business History Review* 84(4): 675–702.

Lazonick, William. (2010b). "The Chandlerian corporation and the theory of innovative enterprise." *Industrial and Corporate Change* 19(2): 317–49.

Lazonick, William. (2010c). "The explosion of executive pay and the erosion of American prosperity." *Entreprises et Histoire* 57: 141–64.

Lazonick, William. (2011a). "The global tax dodgers: Why President Obama and Congress lack job creation plans." *New Deal 2.0*, August 18 (http://www.newdeal20.org/2011/08/18/the-global-tax-dodgers-why-president-obama-and-congress-lack-job-creation-plans-55435/).

Lazonick, William. (2011b). The innovative enterprise and the developmental state: Toward an economics of "organizational success." Paper presented at the Institute for New Economic Thinking Annual 2011 Conference, Bretton Woods, NH, April 10 (http://www.newdeal20.org/wp-content/uploads/2011/08/lazonick-innovative-enterprise-and-developmental-state-20110403.pdf).

Lazonick, William, and Mariana Mazzucato. (2012). Finance, innovation and inequality: Who takes the risks? Who gets the rewards? European Commission Finance, Innovation, and Growth (FINNOV) project working paper. In progress.

Lazonick, William, and Mary O'Sullivan. (2000). "Maximizing shareholder value: A new ideology for corporate governance." *Economy and Society* 29(1): 13–35.

Lazonick, William, and Öner Tulum. (2011). "US biopharmaceutical finance and the sustainability of the US biotech business model." *Research Policy* 40(9): 1170–87.

Lie, Erik. (2005). "On the timing of CEO stock option awards." *Management Science* 51(5): 802–12.

Louis, Henock, and Hal White. (2007). "Do managers intentionally use repurchase tender offers to signal private information? Evidence from firm financial reporting behavior." *Journal of Financial Economics* 85(1): 205–33.

Lowenstein, Louis. (1989). *What's Wrong with Wall Street?: Short-Term Gain and the Absentee Shareholder.* Boston: Addison Wesley.

Microsoft. (2008). "Microsoft announces share repurchase program and increases quarterly dividend" (http://www.microsoft.com/presspass/press/2008/sep08/09-22dividend.mspx).

National Research Council. (1999). *Funding a Revolution: Government Support for Computing Research.* Washington, D.C.: National Academies Press.

Niland, Powell. (1976). "Reforming private pension plan administration." *Business Horizons* 19(1): 25–35.

Okimoto, Daniel I., and Yoshio Nishi. (1994). "R&D Organization in Japanese and American Semiconductor Firms." In *The Japanese Firm: The Sources of Competitive Strength*, edited by Masahiko Aoki and Ronald Dore, 178–208. Oxford: Oxford University Press.

O'Sullivan, Mary. (2004). What drove the U.S. stock market in the last century? INSEAD Working Paper, Fontainebleau, France.

Palmon, Oded, Huey-Lian Sun, and Alex P. Tang. (1997). "Layoff announcements: Stock market impact and financial performance." *Financial Management* 26(3): 54–68.

Pierson, John. (1978). "Trends of higher levies on capital gains is reversed as President signs bill." *Wall Street Journal*, November 9: 14.

Platzer, Michaela D., and Glennon J. Harrison. (2009). "The U.S. auto industry: National state trends in manufacturing employment." *Congressional Record Service Report* 7–5700, August 3.

Rappaport, Alfred. (1981). "Selecting strategies that create shareholder value." *Harvard Business Review* 59(3): 139–49.

Rappaport, Alfred. (1983). "Corporate performance standards and shareholder value." *Journal of Business Strategy* 3(4): 28–38.

Rosen, Jan M. (1991). "New regulations on stock options." *New York Times*, April 27: 38.

Ross, Nancy L. (1979). "New law gives money managers breathing space." *Washington Post*, July 15: G4.

Schultze, Charles L. (1999). "Downsized & out: Job security and American workers." *Brookings Review* 17(4): 9–17.

Sharpe, Rochelle. (1993). "Losing ground: In the latest recession only blacks suffered net employment loss." *Wall Street Journal*, September 14: A1, A12–A13.

Uchitelle, Louis. (2007). *The Disposable American: Layoffs and Their Consequences.* New York: Vintage Books.

UK Department of Health. (2009). "The pharmaceutical price regulation scheme" [Tenth Report to Parliament], December.

"U.S. could lose race for nanotech leadership, SIA panel says." (2005). *Electronic News*, March 16.

U.S. Congress. (2010). *Economic Report of the President.* Washington, D.C.: U.S. Government Printing Office.

U.S. Department of Commerce, Bureau of the Census. (1983). *Statistical Abstract of the United States 1984* (104th ed.). Washington, D.C.: U.S. Government Printing Office.

U.S. Department of Commerce, Bureau of the Census. (1986). *Statistical Abstract of the United States 1987* (107th ed.). Washington, D.C.: U.S. Government Printing Office.

U.S. Department of Labor, Bureau of Labor Statistics. (2011). "Union members—2010," News Release USDL-11-0063, January 21.

Vermaelen, Theo. (2005). *Share Repurchases: Foundations and Trends in Finance.* Hanover, MA: Now Publishers.

Wilson, William Julius. (1996–97). "When work disappears." *Political Science Quarterly* 111(4): 567–95.

10 Energy Systems Transformation
STATE CHOICES AT THE INTERSECTION OF SUSTAINABILITY AND GROWTH
Mark Huberty

Introduction

The global quest for energy has entered a new phase. Where coal once replaced wood, and was in turn replaced by oil, now the industrial nations of the world seek a successor to fossil fuels of all kinds. The prospect of catastrophic global climate change has focused public attention and political interest on this search. But a desire for secure fuel sources and stable fuel supplies in a world of rapidly growing energy demand has proven an equally powerful motivator for national governments. Climate change mitigation, insulation from geopolitical instability, and long-term industrial competitiveness all point to the need for a new generation of fuel sources. The successful search for these fuels will have profound consequences for industrial competitiveness, technological innovation, and environmental sustainability.

This project puts the state, already challenged by intensified international competition and rapid technological change, in a very difficult position. Energy is the lifeblood of a modern economy. Fossil fuels remain the cheapest, most versatile way to provide it. Moving away from fossil fuels portends significant changes to how economies organize production and generate growth. The state, already troubled by the confluence of technological change and international competition, must now find a path to energy systems transformation that at the very least does not intensify these challenges.

But states have professed more ambition than just maintaining the status quo. Instead, many hope to exploit the energy challenge to improve their domestic and international economic competitiveness. Instead of only seeking some new energy source, they have sought the transformation of how their economies produce, distribute, and use energy. They hope to take advantage of the technological innovation and investment this energy systems transformation will require to drive economic growth and international competitiveness. Whether they can do so remains an open issue.

This chapter concerns itself with the comparative political economy of energy systems transformation and growth. It explores what choices states face in pursuing transformative change in their energy systems, what factors—political, economic, technological, and social—constrain those choices, and what opportunities exist for exploitation. I argue that national variation in those constraints and opportunities means that states faced with theoretically similar choices will in fact choose very different strategies. A diversity of national choices will generate new patterns of national economic competition, and in doing so affect state responses to the broader problems of technological change and international competition.

This argument has serious implications for the link between energy systems transformation and growth. As this chapter will show, there is no *a priori* reason to believe that the strategies or assumptions that underpin policy choices for energy systems transformation will translate into sustained economic growth. This does not, of course, eliminate the possibility of energy-driven growth. But it does make it incumbent upon states to articulate the link between energy and growth more clearly when making policy choices.

The chapter begins by treating energy as a systems problem. The energy system is composed of separate domains of production, distribution, and use. Each of these domains is structured by the interaction of technology, politics and regulation, and economic incentives and constraints. The particular nature of these different factors varies from country to county. As such, the degree and form with which they constrain state choices vary as well. Thus, understanding state choices requires that we begin with the system itself. Only from that basis can we infer a set of reasonable expectations about how states will respond. Moreover, this variation should inform a healthy skepticism toward universal policy solutions, notably the push for emissions pricing.

The State Between Sustainability and Growth

In the aftermath of the 2008 financial crisis, demands on the state to generate jobs and promote economic growth have intensified. In parallel, however, climate change challenges the state to gain control over the unchecked emissions of greenhouse gases. Between these two goals lies enormous tension. The emissions that cause climate change are inseparable from the fossil fuel-powered economies that create them. Economic growth, subject to no additional constraints, will necessarily drive greenhouse gas emissions higher. Yet controlling those emissions by moderating growth runs contrary to both the immediate demands on governments and the foundations of political stability in the advanced industrial economies. To resolve this particularly acute version of the "double bind," states have sought to use the technological and industrial changes required for serious emissions reduction to create new "green" foundations for growth. But this poses a dilemma of its own, between the recommendation for an arm's-length, price-based approach to emissions reduction and a call for a new green industrial policy.

Modern industrial economies have delivered enormous material prosperity to huge populations. This prosperity has had effects well beyond material well-being. The early years of industrialization were fraught with conflict over the disruptive process of economic and technological change. But this conflict ultimately gave way to political stability. From the late nineteenth century on, industrial economies generated, on balance, more than enough surplus to enrich industrial winners, compensate losers, and protect the most vulnerable in society. The institutions of a mixed economy showed, by the postwar era, that liberal polities and capitalist economies could be complements.

Unfortunately, the process of dynamic wealth creation also sowed the seeds of today's climate challenge. Rapid economic growth brought intensified use of fossil fuels and the greenhouse gas emissions they create. Even as the emissions intensity of advanced industrial economies declined, their rates of economic growth drove ongoing increases in total energy consumption. Growth overwhelmed gains in efficiency. By the late twentieth century, the potential dangers of those emissions in the medium to long term had spurred calls for action to reduce emissions and stabilize human impacts on the global climate equilibrium.

Acting on this goal has, however, proven immensely difficult. The reasons for this point to the complexity of the bind in which the state finds itself. Fossil fuels underpin modern energy systems and, by extension, the patterns of economic production that depend on them. Reducing or eliminating fossil fuel emissions without eliminating fossil fuels themselves will be very hard. Instead, progress on emissions reduction will require the large-scale replacement of fossil fuel energy sources with nonemitting sources like hydropower, nuclear energy, and renewable energy. Accommodating these changes to energy production, however, will require a range of downstream changes to the assets, markets, and regulatory frameworks that structure how energy is distributed and used. This *energy systems transformation*, which we consider in detail in the next section ("Systems and Systems Transformations"), thus poses very large-scale changes to the structure and function of industrial economies.

The scale of this transformation poses fundamental political challenges for the state. The cost and complexity alone will require significant resources for investment. But unlike earlier systems transformations, such as the adoption of coal or the shift to electrification, this transformation offers few new advantages. Indeed, today's energy systems perform admirably as energy systems—but horribly as environmental problems. Their replacements may solve the environmental problem, but they otherwise offer few immediately obvious advantages to the broader economy.

No wonder, then, that the debate over climate change policy has so far emphasized minimizing the cost of adjustment. Advocates for emissions pricing have won the theoretical argument here. Faced with the technological uncertainties surrounding how best to take emissions out of the energy system, emissions pricing promises to relieve the state of the burden of choice. Rather, it advocates pricing emissions to incentivize firms and individuals to find the most cost-effective technological, behavioral, and economic means of reducing emissions. Structured correctly, the advocates for pricing argue, economies can come close to breaking even on the cost of emissions reduction, compared with the damage of unchecked climate change.

But merely breaking even does not relieve the state of the problem of the double bind. Emissions pricing alone does nothing to assist the state in creating durable economic growth—it merely attempts to minimize the burden of transition. But without near-term growth, sustaining the level of investment and industrial change required for long-term emissions reduction will prove extremely difficult. Unlike the positive-sum game that helped stabilize the politics of industrialization, it poses a zero-sum game where a range of new innovation merely re-creates the sectors, jobs, and investment opportunities lost in the old energy economy.

A zero-sum policy game threatens both the legitimacy of the state and the durability of the climate policy regime. Sustaining emissions policy in the face of substantial opposition from both well-organized labor and industry in the energy sector and the broader economy, over a very long time frame, without economic surplus to compensate the losers, poses severe challenges to the state. And because this transformation lacks the immediate benefits that drove earlier energy systems transformations, challenges to the state represent direct challenges to the sustainability of climate policy itself.

No wonder, then, that the state has increasingly looked to how this energy systems transformation can become an opportunity for economic growth rather than simply a costly burden. To date, however, that debate has rarely looked beyond the problem of energy itself. Rather, as Huberty et al. (2011) show, most of the long-term "green growth" opportunities envisioned come primarily from two sources: export-led benefits from capturing growing overseas markets in new "green" goods like wind turbines or solar cells and increased domestic employment in the production and installation of those goods. But these sources are fundamentally limited: export competition over fixed markets risks a new zero-sum game of international trade; and domestic jobs in the renewable energy sector will replace, rather than augment, jobs lost in the coal industries.

Instead, as Zysman and Huberty (2011) have argued, escaping the double bind between sustainability on the one hand and jobs and growth on the other will require capitalizing on the transformation of the energy system to catalyze new opportunities for growth elsewhere in the economy. This puts the state back in the position of identifying how to structure the transformation in ways most likely to encourage both sustainability and growth. This process is itself fraught with risk. State action in the energy sector is no less prone to the problems of state-led industrial development than any other sector. Determining how best to navigate these risks must build on a proper understanding of the nature of the emissions problem, the challenges the problem poses, and the opportunities it might create.

Systems and Systems Transformation

The bulk of the emissions problem derives from, and is inseparable from, modern energy systems. By extension, that means that serious emissions policy will pursue the transformation, rather than modification, of today's fossil fuel-based energy systems. This is a task of immense complexity. A viable energy system for an advanced industrial economy must consistently produce energy, distribute it, and use it to power social and economic activity. These three domains—production, distribution, and use—are bound into a system by the need for technical interoperability and structural complementarity.

Interoperability is a *physical* constraint. It refers to the fundamental physical requirements that make the outputs from one domain compatible with the inputs from another. It mandates that the technologies used in any one domain fulfill the expectations for standardization and consistency of the other domains. Interoperability occurs at various levels of systems complexity. At the most basic, we observe it in standards for common electricity voltages and frequencies, or for consistent grades of gasoline that work in any appropriately designed vehicle. At greater complexity, we observe it in the requirement that electricity production constantly match consumption, in order to maintain balance in the electric grid.

The technology of the energy system does not exist in a vacuum. Rather, it is embedded in a set of political, economic, and regulatory institutions that structure and police the market for energy, and shape factors that influence energy demand. Complementarity across this set of institutions provides for the economic and market mechanisms that reinforce each domain's strengths and compensate for its weaknesses. In doing so, these institutions help ensure that the physical limits of the energy system—capacity, reliability, and scope—are not exceeded by the economy and society that depend on it. Complementarity is thus a *social* and *political* constraint, the terms of which are unique to different countries and their economic and political systems.

Thus the asset structure of energy production is tailored to a specific profile of energy demand. Energy futures and spot markets exist to ensure that the price equilibrium of energy demand reinforces the electric grid's technical need to consistently balance production and use. Regulation polices markets naturally prone to monopoly—like energy distribution—to ensure the continued smooth functioning of market-based allocation.

At equilibrium, interoperability and complementarity become self-reinforcing. Firms pursing major changes to technologies to produce, distribute, or use energy have large incentives to ensure that those changes remain compatible with the other domains. Political and economic institutions, such as public utilities or utilities regulators, exist to coordinate larger system changes to ensure that they will not create systems imbalances.

To state this more formally, an energy system requires investment in large, nontransferable assets. Having made such investments in a system that satisfies all the requirements documented previously, firms are reluctant to deviate from it for risk of suffering capital losses.[1] Therefore, all the major actors in the system, public and private, have large incentives to develop the system's abilities within its existing structure, in order to maintain technical interoperability and structural complementarity.

They do not always succeed. Recent history provides several examples of failures of both interoperability and complementarity that destabilized the equilibrium of the energy system. Energy market deregulation in California in the late 1990s decoupled the economics of retail and wholesale electricity markets. In a market of heavily constrained supply, this interfered with the ability of the market to correctly ration energy supplies. Electricity retailers were forced to buy at high wholesale prices and sell at low retail prices. The resulting imbalances led to both overconsumption and blackouts and financial insolvency for the retailers. It also forced the state to step in, at extraordinary expense, to try to maintain both market and supply equilibrium (Sweeney 2002). In this case, the failure to create complementary economic and regulatory institutions drove physical imbalances that led to systems failure, causing significant economic losses.

The New York blackout of 2003 provides an example of the failure of interoperability. There, a single high-voltage transmission line for the northeastern power grid failed, at a time of high demand due to a summer heat wave. As it failed, the load it normally carried failed over to other lines, which immediately overloaded and failed (U.S.-Canada Power System Outage Task Force 2004). The cascading failure disrupted power to most of the northeastern United States and eastern Canada. Restoration of power after these imbalances were corrected took twenty-four to thirty-six hours (New York Independent System Operator 2003). Millions of retail, commercial, industrial, and public-sector customers were left without power.

Thus the production, distribution, and use of energy constitute a system in two senses. Technically, they demand interoperability via standards and consistency across all three domains. Structurally, these domains must be complemented by economic, regulatory, and political actions that provide for the market and nonmarket measures that reinforce the need to balance the system and compensate for its weak points. Both economics and politics provide large incentives to develop a system along a trajectory that reinforces these qualities.

SYSTEMS TRANSFORMATION

Energy systems are extraordinarily sensitive to imbalances stemming from failures in either technical interoperability or structural complementarity. This sensitivity provides powerful economic and noneconomic incentives toward inertia. Major technological or structural changes to one domain of the system can force changes in all the other domains, leading to complex and expensive coordination problems. Likewise, when introducing new innovation, individual actors have strong incentives to ensure that they comply with the existing system. If they do, their products will enjoy immediate markets; if not, they face significant barriers to the use of their noncompliant products in the existing system. These incentives push energy systems toward path dependency, both politically and technically.[2]

Overcoming this path dependency requires that the energy system shift out of its existing trajectory of development, so that the incentives facing public- and private-sector actors now align with changing the system rather than maintaining the status quo. Such a transformation may require parallel changes to energy production, distribution, and use, involving both technological innovation and regulatory and market reform. However the transformation occurs, it must result in a system capable of maintaining the technical interoperability and structural complementarity that keeps the system stable as the source of energy for a modern economy.

Given this context, states face special challenges when pursuing energy systems transformation. The motivations for these changes—whether emissions reduction, energy security, or energy efficiency—do not matter. In any of these cases, major changes to how the system produces, distributes, or uses energy have the potential to disrupt the equilibrium of the system. The potential economic and social costs of such disruptions are large constraints on state choices. They also create significant incentives for private-sector actors to resist such changes unless the potential benefits are very large.

Despite these constraints, we can identify three different possibilities for energy systems transformation that all states face:

1. Replacement of existing energy sources with other sources that are equally interoperable with the rest of the energy system. Nuclear energy is the only major emissions-free option here.
2. Moderation of energy demand through changes to the structural aspects—economic, regulatory, or social—that shape energy consumption
3. Pursuit of technological transformation to production, distribution, and use of energy, with the appropriate changes to the structural context in which those technologies are deployed.

Each of these solutions poses unique challenges to the state. Presently, option 1 is only available through the widespread deployment of nuclear energy. Option 2 requires that social and economic actors accept and respond to enforced social change. Option 3, the most ambitious, exposes actors to significant technological risk and relies on the ability of the system as whole to accomplish big changes in a quasi-coordinated fashion.

Unsurprisingly, to the extent that these choices have been taken already, their success correlates closely with the capacity of the state to overcome these challenges. Three examples demonstrate this point. Option 1, the pursuit of nuclear power, was tried by many nations in the aftermath of the energy crises of the 1970s. Both the United States and France pursued nuclear energy as an alternative to imported oil. But while France succeeded, and today gets over 70 percent of its electricity from nuclear power, the United States failed.

The difference is attributed to the famously autonomous French state, compared with the porous and veto-prone American political system (for a complete discussion of the French case, see Chick 2007). Public concern about the safety of nuclear energy led to widespread opposition in many Western nations. The French state was able to ignore to a large extent public concerns, and embarked on an intensive program of nuclear power plant construction. In contrast, plant construction in the United States quickly became tangled in a web of local, state, and federal lawsuits and permitting processes. Furthermore, while the French bureaucracy maintained a commitment to nuclear power even after energy prices declined in the 1980s, American regulators and firms quickly lost interest. The French were able to maintain long-term investments in energy infrastructure due in part to bureaucratic priorities. As a result of these differences in political structure, the French have built successive generations of nuclear power plants. French firms have also become leading exporters of cutting-edge nuclear reactor technology. In contrast, no permits for new nuclear plants were issued in the United States between 1980 and 2007.[3]

Option 2, the pursuit of energy efficiency through social and economic restructuring, has had great success in the Scandinavian countries and some American cities, like Portland, Oregon.[4] But two political factors have made this much easier. First, in both cases, the project began relatively early on. Portland's decision to constrain suburban sprawl and build mass transit began in the late 1970s, well before the city enjoyed several economic booms and population growth. Scandinavian cities, like many in Europe, are dense for historic reasons. Embarking on a similar program in cities with large suburban legacies would be much harder. Second, in both cases the populations proved receptive to the regulatory framework required to push energy efficiency through building codes, land use regulations, and energy pricing.

Finally, option 3, the pursuit of substantial technological change across many different domains, challenges the state to find the means of coordinating technological, regulatory, and economic change across many different domains. As with option 1, much of this will depend on the preexisting capacities of the state. But it will also depend on the state's ability to develop and deploy technological innovation. As the work of Nelson (1993) and Lundvall (1992) demonstrated, this varies widely in the industrial economies. Thus a decision to pursue technological change *does not* imply technological determinacy. National choices in this regard will still generate substantial national diversity, owing to the capacities of the state.

Thus the viability of each of the macroscopic options for energy systems transformation depends, to a large extent, on the specific political capacities of the state.

State Goals: Energy Systems Transformation and Economic Growth

Most advanced industrial states have chosen option 3, technological innovation, as the primary route toward energy systems transformation. With the exception of France, none of the major industrial economies have pursued nuclear energy to a large degree, in no small part because of public opposition.[5] Energy efficiency, while it can contribute to the moderation of the rate of growth in demand, has shown little ability to reduce it in absolute terms. Thus although nearly all major industrial economies have become more efficient in using energy since the 1970s, energy appetites have continued to grow in absolute terms.[6] That leaves large-scale technological innovation as the remaining option.

As noted in the introduction, most countries that have taken this route have explicitly called for it to drive economic growth as well.[7] In doing so, they have implied that the technological innovation and investment required to achieve energy systems transformation are compatible with, and encouraging of, economic growth.

This section examines the goals and requirements of both energy systems transformation and economic growth. It argues that there is no *a priori* reason to believe that a successful energy systems transformation will lead to sustainable economic growth or international competitiveness. The challenges posed by new international competition remain, even if the industries they threaten are "greener" than they were in the past. It is thus incumbent on states pursuing both to examine and articulate these connections.

GOALS FOR SYSTEMS TRANSFORMATION

In pursuing a technology-driven energy systems transformation, nearly all states have adopted the same substantive goal: a new energy system that supports a modern industrial economy; requires minimal changes to patterns of economic production, prosperity, or social life; but which delivers major reductions in carbon emissions, energy imports, or both.

Let us take each of these, in reverse order. Major reductions in both emissions and energy imports imply a much larger dependence on renewable energy sources. This means, principally, solar and wind energy.[8] Biofuels, and coal energy coupled to emissions capture technology, may also play a significant role but remain largely unproven at present.

Wind and solar energy have a much different production profile than fossil fuel electricity. Unlike fossil fuels, which deliver highly reliable, very steady power, wind and solar are intermittent. The intensity of solar radiation or wind currents does not correlate with patterns of energy demand in any reliable fashion. At times, they may generate more electricity than is required. At other times, when the wind is slack or on cloudy days, they may deliver insufficient power to meet demand. Thus on their own, they have limited ability to provide constant power to the economy, or to keep demand and supply in balance.[9]

To compensate, additional technological changes are required for energy distribution and use. At present, this usually means back-up generation using gas turbines. In the future, it will probably require some form of "smart grid," coupled to energy storage, and systems that allow energy consumers to respond more quickly to changes in supply.[10] This would make for a much different system than we have today. Currently, supply is matched to demand almost entirely by manipulating energy production, turning different kinds of plants on or off as demand fluctuates over time. With these technologies, it's hoped that the system can maintain balance by manipulating demand, replenishing and discharging storage, and modulating noncritical demand.

All these technological changes imply equally substantial changes to regulation and market structure. They also imply massive public investment in infrastructure like the power grid, or public intervention in utilities markets to provide for that investment. They further demand significant coordination across many different economic sectors—from power plants to appliance manufacturers—to provide for technical interoperability. But no matter how countries choose to pursue these changes, the goal remains the same: at the end of the transformation, the structure of energy production and distribution should not make much difference to the ability of the energy system to support modern industrial society.

That means that successfully navigating all these technological, economic, and regulatory challenges will result in *no functional difference* to end users. The wind- or solar-generated electrons coming out of the plug will look almost identical to their coal- or oil-generated predecessors. There are good political and economic reasons for doing this. Politically, anything else might require a radical rethinking of the economic and social arrangements that underpin economic activity in the industrialized economies.[11] Economically, those changes might require even more radical changes to patterns of economic value creation and capital investment. Moreover, this approach is fully consistent with the general pattern of path dependency in social and political life that challenges policy initiatives in other areas of the economy.

Those more significant changes would compound a problem that already plagues energy systems transformation. Any of the goals of an energy systems transformation—emissions reduction, security of supply, or reduced dependence on imports—generate diffuse benefits. Those benefits might be cleaner air, reduced costs from global warming, lower energy price volatility, or an improved balance of payments. But these benefits are largely intangible, and they come through cost avoidance. Unlike earlier energy systems transformations, they do not deliver immediate, tangible benefits to citizens. In the meantime, they impose significant, acute adjustment costs, such as the forced obsolescence of coal-fired power plants, or the loss, through eminent domain, of land needed for a new distribution system.

Thus politically, energy systems transformation through technological innovation is optimum. It promises an energy system that requires few major social or economic changes and uses relatively uncontroversial energy sources. It cannot avoid the imposition of adjustment costs. But many of its sponsors have argued that it can offset those costs not just through avoiding other costs but also through generating jobs and economic growth. We now turn to whether that assumption is warranted.

GOALS FOR GROWTH

A technology-driven energy systems transformation will require large-scale investments in research and development (R&D), capital-intensive production and distribution infrastructure, and end-user devices ranging from automobiles to light bulbs. States facing intense international economic competition have sought to use this investment to generate durable comparative advantage and economic growth.[12] They hope that the innovation required to deploy a new energy system will build domestic firms capable of competing in international markets and offering skilled, high-paying jobs to workers. Common examples of firms in this vein include the Danish wind energy giant Vestas, the Siemens solar power division, start-up firms like SunPower or FirstSolar, and large established multisector firms like General Electric.

Whether this will occur depends on whether these investments and innovations satisfy the preconditions for economic growth. Those preconditions exist in two categories. Either the innovation and investment must create a wholly new economic sector, whose expansion generates investment and jobs, or it must replace an older sector in such a way as to fundamentally transform the possibilities for economic value creation throughout the economy.

Earlier energy systems transformations drove growth through both pathways. Consider the adoption of coal energy. It displaced wood as the primary energy source. It created a rapidly expanding coal mining industry. But it also provided fundamentally different opportunities to smelt iron and steel or generate steam power. Those spillover benefits made coal into a general-purpose technology and became the industrial revolution (Flinn 1984). Likewise, electrification initially displaced gaslight. But it also created an entirely new industry to generate and distribute electricity, and entirely new possibilities for factory organization and productivity, communications, and household devices (Hughes 1983; Perez 1983).

We can also draw analogies between energy systems and other networked technologies. The Internet, for instance, created both a new information and communications technology (ICT) sector to deliver devices and connectivity and an entirely new set of possibilities in other sectors as diverse as retail, entertainment, supply chain organization, and globalized service provision. It drove growth not only through the expansion of the ICT sector itself but also through changes to productivity and investment throughout the entire economy.

These earlier systems transformations generated growth because they created much more economic activity than was lost in the sectors that they displaced. Of course, coal mining displaced woodcutting, and electric lights displaced the gasworks, and e-mail displaced the telephone or postal service. But in every case, growth occurred because the new technology made possible a vast new set of possibilities for economic value creation, and for productivity improvements in existing forms of economic activity.

This had, of course, vast political ramifications. Tolerance for Schumpeterian "creative destruction" emerged in part because of the rising standards of living it generated. Where one lagged too far behind the other, social unrest quickly followed. The Luddite movement in Britain in the early nineteenth century is one such example. True to Ricardo's belief that "the introduction of machinery is often quite injurious to the laborer," wage gains lagged industrialization until the mid-nineteenth century.[13] As Maier (1981) has argued, the subsequent stabilization of the link between technological change, growth, and wages helped stabilize postwar European democracy.

POTENTIAL FLAWS IN THE GROWTH-ENERGY NEXUS

This articulation of the goals and preconditions of energy systems transformation and growth leaves us with a contradiction. A wildly successful energy systems transformation aims to produce an energy system that, as far as its ability to support modern industrial production is concerned, looks little different from the one it replaces. The goal minimizes the political and economic complexity of the energy systems transformation. But even so, it remains no simple technological feat.

Growth, in contrast, requires more than just substitution. The substantive outputs that a new energy system would produce would look identical to that of the old. Cars powered by such a system would, if successful, permit the same freedom of movement and personal autonomy that gasoline-powered cars do today. Thus it is unclear whether the technological innovation required to pull off energy systems transformation would generate the kinds of spillover benefits that coal, electrification, or Internet-based communications did in the past. All the investment to deploy a new energy system may constitute only substitution of jobs and investment in one sector for those in another.[14]

Furthermore, as noted previously, most of the economic value of transformation is tied up in avoidance of either direct economic costs or externalities. Unlike policies that deliver tangible positive benefits, cost avoidance has limited abilities to generate strong interest groups devoted to protecting policies against the losers they create. That the avoided costs in this case are very diffuse only compounds the problem.

Depending on the time frame under consideration, these fundamental differences between growth and energy systems transformation pose major challenges to the use of energy systems transformation to drive growth. In the short term, the need to build out substantial infrastructure will create jobs. It is unclear whether, once that initial period is over, growth will persist. If energy demand with today's technology grows at some constant rate k that is driven entirely by the growth rate of the larger economy, then there is little reason to believe that the growth of the energy economy would exceed that once the initial substitution had occurred.[15] At that point, identifiable benefits will become entirely about cost avoidance—either from imbalance of payments, energy supply volatility, or damage from unmitigated global warming. This may create serious difficulties for energy systems transformation as well as economic growth. Though cost avoidance should count as a real benefit, in practice it is rarely done. Political science has long recognized that voters tend to blame politicians for failures, credit them for visible successes, and rarely acknowledge actions that just maintained equilibrium.[16] Policy that attempts major changes that impose acute costs while delivering diffuse (albeit very real, and potentially very large) benefits, faces significant political resistance. The fraught debate over action on climate change, which at root is a debate over energy, clearly illustrates these dynamics at work. Even if it succeeds at the legislative stage, its ongoing survival, and thus its credibility as a political reality, will remain in doubt.[17]

Implications for the Political Economy of Energy Systems Transformation

Thus energy systems transformation will pose special challenges for state policy and economic growth. As the previous sections have argued, energy systems transformation imposes adjustment costs in pursuit of an energy system that will, if successful, behave about like today's. Benefits generated by that transformation will consist largely of cost avoidance—real benefits, to be sure, but diffuse and less visible than the costs.[18] And, as the prior section argued, attempts to link energy systems transformation to economic growth have not clearly articulated why we should expect substitution of one energy system for another to lead to spillover growth in the rest of the economy, in the way that earlier systemic technological change did. None of this is to suggest that energy systems transformation is an illegitimate goal: the benefits are real. But it does reveal the political constraints that states face in pursuing energy policy. As such, the choice of policy options is much more complicated.

This section reviews both the logic and the political economy of those policy options. Given the arguments to this point, it suggests that the dominant policy conversation around emissions pricing is misguided. For both technical and political reasons, emissions pricing will probably fall short in providing for the innovation and investment required for energy systems transformation. Instead, a broader policy portfolio stands the best chance of achieving a politically sustainable energy systems transformation. It also holds the best promise for finding some connection to economic growth. But it does not absolve the state from solving the more fundamental problems of growth created by intensified international competition or disruptive technological change.

POLICY OPTIONS FOR SYSTEMS TRANSFORMATION

Across the advanced industrialized countries, the debate over energy and climate policy has identified three major policy instruments at the hands of states embarking on energy systems transformation: they may penalize the use of the old energy system through emissions taxes or caps; they may support the deployment of a new system through research, development, and deployment of new technology; and they may mandate or incentivize changes through regulatory reforms. Each has flaws that make it insufficient as a single policy. More important, none provides universal solutions to the different national energy systems. Finally, none, on its own, necessarily drives growth.

Emissions pricing has received the most attention.[19] It forms the core of European climate and energy policy, and it was the centerpiece of the Kerry-Lieberman and Waxman-Markey climate change policy bills that stalled in the U.S. Congress. The logic of emissions pricing for energy systems transformation is simple: impose penalties for consumption of fuels in the present system, thus generating incentives to switch to fuels that would not incur those penalties. If the technologies do not exist to do so immediately, firms would invest in R&D to bring new goods to market to satisfy the demand created by emissions taxes. Because the policy would be a generic tax, governments would not have to engage in the messy business of choosing which technologies received subsidies; rather, the market would find the most efficient means to minimize the taxation burden.[20]

Three problems challenge the effectiveness of emissions pricing. First, the evidence on consumer responsiveness to energy prices is mixed. As both Popp (2010) and Enkvist, Nauclér, and Rosander (2007) discuss, we already know of many relatively low-cost energy-saving devices with almost immediate returns to investment, like more efficient light bulbs or better home insulation. But consumers seem slow to respond to such incentives even when the costs and benefits are clear and the technologies immediately available. Corporations are no better. For instance, despite years of incurring large energy bills as one of the biggest retailers in the world, Walmart didn't embark on a significant push for energy efficiency until its CEO (chief executive officer) chose to prioritize it (Gunther 2006). Incomplete information and structural incentives often interfere with market promotion of energy efficiency even when they promise immediate cost savings. Carbon pricing presents the same challenge.

Second, it is not clear whether prices will drive innovation across the entire system. The major success case for the use of emissions pricing to date has been acid rain reduction. There, the U.S. Environmental Protection Agency (EPA) attached a price to sulfur dioxide emissions. Subsequent research has shown that the program achieved faster reductions in emissions, at much lower cost, than program sponsors had initially estimated (EPA 2005). But as Hanemann (2009) has noted, the conditions that obtained for acid rain look nothing like those of energy systems transformation. Then, the technologies were well-known, their costs clearly understood, and the number of affected parties relatively low. Now, the technologies are yet to be invented, the costs are not well-known, and the effects will span the entire economy. In such circumstances, technological uncertainty may mean that firms reduce their tax burden mostly through reducing or moving production.

Finally, and of more relevance to the political economy discussion, the influence of prices on innovation depends on their credibility. Because R&D takes many years, firms will invest in innovation based on the price they can expect to apply when they bring the goods to market. Because that price is entirely a function of the state's ability to make long-term credible policy commitments, the expected price is some credibility-weighted function of the statutory price. There is plenty of evidence from fiscal policy, welfare policy, and tax policy to suggest that states' institutional abilities to sustain long-term fiscal commitments are variable at best and weak to nonexistent at worst. This is particularly true in the world's per-capita major emitter, the United States. This reality makes any price a much weaker signal than it would otherwise be, and it undermines the ability of emissions pricing to drive technological innovation and adoption. Credibility will clearly vary across political systems, but that variability informs against the reliance on emissions pricing as the central driver of energy systems transformation.[21]

In lieu of, or in addition to, emissions pricing, regulatory incentives have proven to be effective tools for expanding the use of renewable energy in many different energy systems. Two stand out. The German government implemented a feed-in tariff for solar energy in 1990 and expanded it to include other non-fossil fuel sources in 2000. The tariff required energy utilities to buy wind, solar, and other renewable forms of electricity at higher rates, reflective of the higher costs of those sources. In the ensuing twenty years, German solar capacity has grown at greater than 50 percent per annum, compounded (BSW-Solar 2009; Jacobsson and Lauber 2006). In Denmark, similar rates of growth for wind energy followed the adoption of a green certificates program that mandated purchases of renewable energy.

The success of both programs, however, has run into long-run problems as the share of renewable energy has risen. In Denmark, high shares of intermittent wind energy have been possible only through dependence on gas-fired back-up power and Norwegian hydroelectric power. Other infrastructure investments in the energy distribution system, to make it less sensitive to imbalances caused by wind power fluctuations, did not automatically follow with the expansion of wind energy production. The same has been true in Germany, which has only recently embarked on large-scale trials of intelligent power systems through the *e-Energie* programs. These problems are of course surmountable, but their existence informs against reliance only on regulatory reforms in the energy investment markets.

Finally, the need for new technological innovation to both create energy alternatives and drive down their cost has encouraged states to pursue energy systems transformation through financial support of research, development, and deployment. This has led to a debate over which of several models for R&D sponsorship best fits the energy challenge: big-push efforts like the Manhattan Project or Apollo missions; very diffuse programs like the National Science Foundation or the National Institutes of Health; some mixture of the two, analogous to how the U.S. national laboratories or the Max Planck Institutes operate; or some other model entirely.[22]

As Zysman and Huberty (2010) have noted, none of these options for sponsoring technological innovation will succeed on its own. The energy system is too diverse, and covers too many sectors, for one technology policy model alone to work. Instead, the choice of policy approaches must complement the technical and economic characteristics of the energy system domain being targeted. Thus nuclear fusion or carbon sequestration—capital-intensive, high-risk programs with narrow targets—may merit the kind of intensive, price-insensitive investment used in the Apollo missions. But major energy efficiency gains in buildings, appliances, and automobiles will require some combination of diverse innovation in many technical domains, coupled to some mechanism to unify those innovations into actual products, and those products into viable systems of production, distribution, and use.

Whatever the choice of policies to support technology R&D, consistency and reliability of funding remain key. As the American Energy Innovation Council (2010) has pointed out, and as Figure 10.1 shows, U.S. commitments to energy research have been both volatile in the short term and penurious in the long term. Researchers who built out substantial laboratories in the late 1970s and early 1980s, when high oil prices drove the last wave of interest in alternative energies, soon found themselves without predictable funds to continue. That kind of volatility undermines long-term research planning.

Policy Implications for Energy and Growth

Viable long-term policy for energy systems transformation will therefore require some kind of policy portfolio. Energy prices will play a role, but for both political and technical reasons may not dominate. Regulatory intervention and state support for research and

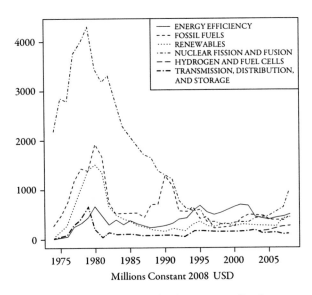

FIGURE 10.1 Patterns of American research and development spending by energy technology category, 1974–2008.
Source: Energy Information Agency (2008).

development of new technologies will be crucial. No matter the portfolio, however, the promise of carbon pricing—a single policy model suitable to all market economies—will go unsatisfied. Variation in national political economies and energy systems means that no single policy model will work best for all countries. The characteristics of national economies and energy systems will constrain the choices that states have available when looking to make long-term credible commitments to energy systems changes.

This set of economic and political developments should have significant domestic and international implications for comparative political economy. At the international level, different national policy approaches will affect the dynamics of competition in capital-intensive, high-technology industries. To the extent that expertise in specific industrial sectors can bring comparative advantage, green energy will be no different at the microlevel. Hence Denmark already benefits significantly from its early investment in wind energy, deriving billions of Euros and thousands of jobs from the wind sector. This advantage draws on Denmark's already substantial expertise in high-precision engineering and machining. But nothing specific to green energy suggests that this advantage is any more durable than in other sectors that have suffered from intense competition from developing economies. The issues that challenge the ability of the advanced industrial economies to maintain prosperity and competitiveness remain the same: skill formation and retraining, innovation, labor policy, and other factors remain problematic regardless of whether the jobs or technologies they emphasize are "brown" or "green."

Domestically, national variation in political structure and state capacity will affect the pace and structure of energy systems transformation in different countries. This outcome is already plainly visible in the very different contributions made by renewable energy to the advanced industrial countries. On the one hand, this may portend a sustainable pattern of trade in energy technology. On the assumption that all national solutions will use the same mix of technologies, but with different degrees of emphasis, then patterns of national competitive advantage will vary, potentially creating the basis of new trade patterns. However, in common technologies—such as "intelligent" grid infrastructure—early adopters may find durable competitive advantage derived from early exposure to the learning effects of large-scale systems integration. Late-movers in those technologies may find their ability to catch up on massive infrastructure technology limited.

Finally, the highly competitive developing economies pose a real threat to the advanced industrial world. Unlike the advanced countries, their energy infrastructures are often suboptimal compared with their development goals. Thus they confront no paradox of growth and energy systems transformation like that discussed in the section "Potential Flaws in the Growth-Energy Nexus." Instead, for them, a modern energy grid does offer vast new possibilities to the entire economy, just as it did to a coal-fired England during the first industrial revolution, or an electrified United States in the second. As such, they will face fewer problems of credible commitment to long-term changes in their energy infrastructure, because the tangible benefits to investment vastly outweigh the costs.

Conclusions

Regardless of the motivation, a renewable energy systems transformation will occur over the next century. This poses two substantial challenges to the state. Accomplishing transformation will require a diverse set of policy approaches tailored to the demands of markets in energy production, distribution, and use. As we have argued, these domains have very different technological and economic properties that inform against one-size-fits-all policy choices. Economically and politically, states face real difficulty in translating energy systems transformation into economic growth and political sustainability. Despite the rhetoric on "green jobs," it remains unclear how energy systems transformation will translate into growth in the broader economy. At a time when states are once again pressed to generate durable economic growth as a precursor to social and political stability, this reality poses real challenges to both the state and the viability of long-term emissions policy. If a low-emissions energy systems transformation will not translate into broader economic opportunity, then it will require policy choices that impose fewer direct costs on the economy, or are less sensitive over the short term to interests affected by those costs. Those consequences stand in contrast to the enthusiasm for carbon pricing, which makes costs obvious and acute, and which can be easily reversed. How best to structure alternatives tailored to the domestic political economy of energy systems transformation remains a question that states must answer for themselves.

Acknowledgments

The author wishes to thank the Alfred P. Sloan Foundation for financial support and the Berkeley Roundtable on the International Economy (BRIE) for research and administrative support.

Thanks also to Danny Breznitz, Stu Feldman, Michael Hanemann, Martin Kenney, Paul Pierson, Alison Post, John Zysman, and participants at the May 2010 "Sea of Change in Information Technology" conference at the University of California, Berkeley. All errors remain my own.

Notes

1. Troesken (1996) argues that the risks created by nontransferable investment were among the most significant motivators for private-sector acceptance of public utility regulation. The fear of asset appropriation by local governments gave utilities the incentive to seek regulation granting them regulated monopoly status. Absent that regulation, they risked abuse by local governments seeking to exploit their economic vulnerability for short-term political gain.

2. This kind of behavior has been identified in other networked markets. See Katz and Shapiro (1985, 1986, 1994) on network economies in telecommunications. For the political incentives that this kind of behavior creates, see Pierson (2000). He concludes that even highly contested and

controversial political decisions become harder to unseat over time, as even those who opposed the initial decision invest in compliance and thus face large sunk costs.

3. See Table 9.1 in Energy Information Agency (2008) for a history of American nuclear energy permitting.

4. See Sarzynski, Brown, and Southworth (2008) for data on U.S. urban carbon footprints. The data require a caveat that many of the best performers have favorable geographic and climatic conditions that reduce their aggregate energy demand.

5. Indeed, Germany, which had a significant amount of nuclear generating capacity, has decided to retire all of its nuclear plants even as it pursues aggressive emissions reductions. That decision, taken under the earlier SPD/*Grünen* coalition, has not been challenged under either of Angela Merkel's two governments.

6. In the G7, energy intensity per unit GDP (gross domestic product) declined 19.7 percent between 1991 and 2007. Despite this gain, energy use per capita grew 4 percent on average, and total energy consumption 14 percent. Total energy consumption declined only in Germany and the United Kingdom, 1 percent and 0.65 percent, respectively. But German success in particular came at a price: the dismantling of the East German industrial base after reunification, and the widespread East German unemployment that followed. This is, obviously, not a viable or reproducible strategy. For information on global energy consumption, see "Total Primary Energy Consumption" and its variants, in Energy Information Administration (2009), updated regularly (http://www.eia.doe.gov/emeu/international/contents.html).

7. In the United States, both the President and the Congress have adopted the language of "green jobs" associated with energy policy. The American Reinvestment and Recovery Act of 2009, designed to provide demand stimulus after the 2008 financial crisis and recession, provided billions of dollars in energy research and infrastructure investment. President Obama's transition plan clearly envisioned this as part of a broader economic growth strategy involving plug-in hybrid electric vehicles, infrastructure investment, and expansion of renewable energy. (See http://change.gov/agenda/energy_and_environment_agenda/). In Europe, the European Commission consistently articulates EU energy strategy in terms of both emissions reduction and economic competitiveness. It clearly identifies energy efficiency and renewable energy as opportunities to "create jobs, promoting innovation and the knowledge-based economic in the EU" (European Commission 2007: 4).

8. A universe of other potential solutions exists, including tidal, geothermal, and hydroelectric power. Of these, only the last is proven at scale. The utility of each of these is, moreover, even more highly geographically constrained than solar or wind.

9. In fact, the stability of the grid is threatened by relatively small amounts of intermittent energy generation capacity. The Integration of Variable Generation Task Force (2009) estimates the threshold level at about 20–25 percent of total generation capacity. The Nord Pool integrated Scandinavian energy market experienced more frequent grid destabilization because of Denmark's high proportion of wind energy. In response, it recently introduced a -200 €/MWh penalty tariff for wind farms that do not turn off their turbines at times of overproduction. See Nord Pool Spot (2009).

10. As of this writing, the term "smart grid" is overused and underdefined. For the purposes of this chapter, we treat it as a power grid capable of using information about the real-time status of microlevel sources of demand, supply, and storage nodes on the energy grid to achieve systems balance through changes in all three. The details of how that would occur we leave to the engineers.

11. This concern isn't limited to the advanced industrialized countries. It has also influenced developing countries' resistance to comprehensive international action on climate change. Recognizing the close relationship between energy and economic growth, China and India have little interest in tying their hands just as their own development has taken off. Barring significant economic compensation from the industrialized world, there is no sign of this changing.

12. In doing so, they have resurrected a debate from the early 1980s about the benefits of taxing externalities. The "double dividend" debate suggested that states could achieve both environmental benefits and economic benefits by reducing taxes on labor and capital and increasing them on gasoline—by taxing "bads" like pollution instead of "goods" like employment or investment. As Hoerner and Bosquet (2001), Koskela, Sinn, and Schob (2001), and Manresa and Sancho (2005) have noted, the evidence for such a "double dividend" is decidedly mixed.

13. See Robert Allen's wage series for confirmation. The cyclical fluctuation in wages did not turn into long-term growth until the mid-1800s (Allen 2001).

14. The developing countries are a very important exception. There, the energy system *is* a wholly new sector that creates new possibilities for economic production. This difference presents a major threat to the use of green energy as a growth sector in the advanced economies, as it lacks the scale and pace of expansion available in the developing countries.

15. It could, of course, grow faster if it managed to capture comparative advantages in the global economy. But because the new energy economy would be largely dependent on technological innovation rather than resource endowments, that comparative advantage might be fleeting. In any event, attaining that advantage has nothing to do with "green" energy and everything to do with the normal determinants of comparative advantage—skill formation, finance, trade policy, and other standard tools of economic development. To the extent that states already suffer loss of comparative advantage from failures in these areas, "green" energy offers no panacea for growth.

16. Witness the debate over the various economic stimulus packages deployed to counter the 2008 financial crisis. Most official estimates suggest that those actions staved off a second Great Depression. But with unemployment still hitting 10 percent or higher in many major industrialized countries, the argument that "it could have been worse" came as cold comfort.

17. As Patashnik (2003) has noted, policies that fail to generate their own interest groups to oppose those who suffer adjustment costs usually fail even if they make it through the legislative process successfully.

18. This is consistent with most estimates of the cost of action on climate change. Various estimates suggest that significant emissions reductions could be attained at a very reasonable price compared to the potential damage of unmitigated global warming. See, for instance, Stern (2006). But most estimates suggest that GDP will nevertheless be lower even with these benefits taken into account. That the counterfactual is valid does not mean that voters will perceive it as such.

19. In theory, emissions pricing and cap-and-trade schemes are economically equivalent. One uses price to constrain quantity; the other uses quantity constraints to impose prices. Politically, of course, taxes are received very differently from other kinds of policy instruments. Weitzman (1974, 2009) has noted that this equivalence may not hold. Here, I refer to both under the blanket of emissions pricing for convenience' sake.

20. Of course, in practice, the tax is never actually generic. The various American bills all contained large loopholes for certain industries, as well as the automobile transport and air transport sectors. The European Union emissions trading scheme does not cover automobiles and does not presently cover air travel.

21. Helm, Hepburn, and Mash (2003, 2004) formalize this argument and provide potential institutional solutions modeled on British monetary policy. But they conclude that such solutions are highly unlikely, because they would involve substantial loss of policy autonomy on the part of Parliament. The same arguments apply, albeit to a greater degree, to the U.S. political system.

22. For a full discussion of these options, see Hargadon (2010), Zysman and Huberty (2010), Mowrey, Nelson, and Martin (2010a, 2010b), and Perrow (2010).

References

Allen, R. (2001). "The great divergence in European wages and prices from the Middle Ages to the First World War." *Explorations in Economic History* 38(4): 411–47.

American Energy Innovation Council. (2010). *A Business Plan for America's Energy Future*. Washington, D.C.: The American Energy Innovation Council.

BSW-Solar. (2009). *Statistische Zahlen der Deutschen Solarstrombranche (Photovoltaik)*. Berlin: Faktenblatt, Bundesverband Solarwirtschaft e.V.

Chick, M. (2007). *Electricity and Energy Policy in Britain, France and the United States Since 1945*. Cheltenham, UK: Edward Elgar.

Energy Information Administration. (2009). *Annual Energy Outlook 2009* [Technical report DOE/EIA-0383(2009)]. Washington, D.C.: U.S. Department of Energy.

Energy Information Agency. (2008). *Annual Energy Review 2008*. Washington, D.C.: U.S. Department of Energy.

Enkvist, P., T. Nauclér, and J. Rosander. (2007). "A cost curve for greenhouse gas reduction." *McKinsey Quarterly* 1: 34–45.

Environmental Protection Agency. (2005). Acid Rain Program 2004 Progress Report: 10 Years of Achievement [Technical report]. Washington, D.C.: U.S. Environmental Protection Agency.

European Commission. (2007). *An Energy Policy For Europe. Communication to the European Parliament and European Council SEC(2007) 12*. Brussels, Belgium: Commission of the European Communities.

Flinn, M. (1984). *The History of the British Coal Industry*. Oxford: Clarendon Press.

Gunther, M. (2006). "The green machine." *Fortune Magazine*, July 31.

Hanemann, W. M. (2009). "The role of emission trading in domestic climate policy." *The Energy Journal* 30(2): 73–108.

Hargadon, A. (2010). "Technology policy and global warming: Why new innovation models are needed." *Research Policy* 39(8): 1024–26.

Helm, D., C. Hepburn, and R. Mash. (2003). "Credible carbon policy." *Oxford Review of Economic Policy* 19(3): 438–50.

Helm, D., C. Hepburn, and R. Mash. (2004). Time-inconsistent environmental policy and optimal delegation. Discussion Paper 175, Oxford University Department of Economics.

Hoerner, J., and B. Bosquet. (2001). *Environmental Tax Reform: The European Experience*. Washington, D.C.: Center for a Sustainable Economy.

Huberty, M., H. Gao, J. Mandell, and J. Zysman. (2011). Shaping the green growth economy: A review of the public debate and the prospects for green growth. Mandag Morgen and the Berkeley Roundtable on the International Economy, and Copenhagen, Denmark, and Berkeley, California.

Hughes, T. (1983). *Networks of Power: Electrification in Western Society, 1880–1930*. Baltimore, MD: Johns Hopkins University Press.

Integration of Variable Generation Task Force. (2009). *Accommodating High Levels of Variable Generation* [Technical report]. Princeton, NJ: North American Electric Reliability Corporation.

Jacobsson, S., and V. Lauber. (2006). "The politics and policy of energy system transformation—Explaining the German diffusion of renewable energy technology." *Energy Policy* 34(3): 256–76.

Katz, M., and C. Shapiro. (1985). "Network externalities, competition, and compatibility." *The American Economic Review*, 75(3): 424–40.

Katz, M., and C. Shapiro. (1986). "Technology adoption in the presence of network externalities." *The Journal of Political Economy* 94(4): 822–41.

Katz, M. L., and C. Shapiro. (1994). "Systems competition and network effects." *The Journal of Economic Perspectives* 8(2): 93–115.

Koskela, E., H. Sinn, and R. Schob. (2001). "Green tax reform and competitiveness." *German Economic Review* 2(1): 19–30.

Lundvall, B. (1992). *National Systems of Innovation*. London: Pinter.

Maier, C. (1981). "Two postwar eras and the conditions for stability." *The American Historical Review* 86(2): 327–52.

Manresa, A., and F. Sancho. (2005). "Implementing a double dividend: Recycling ecotaxes towards lower labour taxes." *Energy Policy* 33(12): 1577–85.

Mowrey, D., R. Nelson, and B. Martin. (2010a). "Technology policy and global warming: Why new policy models are needed (or why putting new wine in old bottles won't work)." *Research Policy* 39(8): 1011–23.

Mowrey, D., R. Nelson, and B. Martin. (2010b). "A response to our commentators." *Research Policy* 39(8): 1032–33.

Nelson, R. (1993). *National Innovation Systems: A Comparative Analysis*. New York: Oxford University Press.

New York Independent System Operator. (2003). *Interim Report on the August 14, 2003 Blackout* [Technical Report]. Albany, NY: New York Independent System Operator.

Nord Pool Spot. (2009). Nord Pool Spot implements negative price floor in elspot from October 2009 [Online] (http://www.nordpoolspot.com/Message-center-container/Exchange-list/Exchange-information/No162009-Nord-Pool-Spot-implements-negative-price-floor-in-Elspot-from-October-2009-/).

Patashnik, E. (2003). "After the public interest prevails: The political sustainability of policy reform." *Governance* 16(2): 203–34.

Perez, C. (1983). "Structural change and the assimilation of new technologies in the economic and social system." *Futures* 15(5): 357–75.

Perrow, C. (2010). "Comment on Nelson, Mowrey, and Martin." *Research Policy* 39(8): 1030–31.

Pierson, P. (2000). "Increasing returns, path dependence, and the study of politics." *The American Political Science Review* 94(2): 251–67.

Popp, D. (2010). Innovation and climate policy. NBER Working Papers Series, National Bureau of Economic Research, Cambridge, MA.

Sarzynski, A., M. A. Brown, and F. Southworth. (2008). *Shrinking the Carbon Footprint of Metropolitan America*. Washington, D.C.: Brookings Institution Press.

Stern, N. (Ed.). (2006). *Stern Review on the Economics of Climate Change*. London: HM Treasury.

Sweeney, J. (2002). *The California Electricity Crisis*. Stanford, CA: Hoover Institution Press.

Troesken, W. (1996). *Why Regulate Utilities?: The New Institutional Economics and the Chicago Gas Industry, 1849–1924*. Ann Arbor: University of Michigan Press.

U.S.-Canada Power System Outage Task Force. (2004). *Final Report on the August 14th, 2003 Blackout in the United States and Canada: Causes and Recommendations*. Washington, D.C.: National Energy Regulatory Committee.

Weitzman, M. (1974). "Prices vs. quantities." *The Review of Economic Studies* 41(4): 477–91.

Weitzman, M. (2009). "On modeling and interpreting the economics of catastrophic climate change." *The Review of Economics and Statistics* 91(1): 1–19.

Zysman, J., and M. Huberty. (2010). "An energy system transformation: Framing research choices for the climate challenge." *Research Policy* 39(8): 1027–29.

Zysman, J., and M. Huberty. (2011). From Religion to Reality: Energy Systems Transformation for Sustainable Prosperity. Copenhagen: Mandag Morgen.

11 How the Nordic Nations Stay Rich
GOVERNING SECTORAL SHIFTS IN DENMARK, FINLAND, AND SWEDEN

Darius Ornston

Introduction

This chapter explores how wealthy countries navigate the tension between promoting capitalism and regulating it by analyzing developments in Denmark, Finland, and Sweden. These three Nordic states offer unique insight into this double bind for three reasons. First, these small, open economies are uniquely exposed to challenges such as economic internationalization, the decomposition of production and the services transformation. Each country experienced acute economic shocks during the late 1980s and early 1990s (Fellman 2008; M. J. Iversen and Andersen 2008; Sjögren 2008).[1] Second, these shocks threatened traditional solutions to the double bind, including the centralized bargains among industry, labor, and policy makers that defined postwar adjustment (T. Iversen 1996; T. Iversen and Wren 1998; Pontusson and Swenson 1996). These "neocorporatist" deals were widely perceived to inhibit adaptation to disruptive economic and technological changes (Henrekson, Jonung, and Stymne 1996; Miller 1991; Tainio, Pohjola, and Lilja 1997). Third, the Nordic countries responded successfully to these challenges. Centralized bargaining did not inhibit adaptation, but instead supported movement into new, knowledge-intensive activities and industries (Castells and Himanen 2002; Glimstedt and Zander 2003; Kristensen 2006). As a result, these economies have proven surprisingly resilient to the challenges outlined in this volume (Gylfason et al. 2010).

In adapting, Denmark, Finland, and Sweden neither defended nor dismantled traditional economic institutions but instead converted institutionalized cooperation among organized economic actors to perform new functions. In contrast to other continental European economies, adaptation did not reflect a "competitive" pact to reduce wage and nonwage costs (Rhodes 1998). Nordic Europe instead relied on "creative" corporatist bargaining, adapting cooperation to invest in new supply-side resources such as risk capital, human capital, and research. These inputs created more space for new, entrepreneurial actors that had struggled under traditional, neocorporatist bargaining and, in so doing, facilitated rapid movement into new activities and industries (Ornston n.d.-b).

This chapter documents and explains this distinctive adjustment strategy in four steps. The section "Nordic Europe as a Critical Case in Comparative Political Economy" underscores Nordic Europe's significance as a critical case, both in terms of its vulnerability to disruptive political and economic challenges and its relative success in adapting to these challenges. The section "Explaining Sectoral Shifts: Challenges and Choices" characterizes the choices that policy makers faced during the 1980s and 1990s, including traditional corporatism, neoliberal reform, competitive corporatism, and creative corporatism. The section "Explaining National Choices: Crisis and Cooperation" explains why Denmark, Finland, and Sweden pursued creative corporatism, focusing on the interaction between crisis and cooperation. Stated most concisely, mutual vulnerability encouraged stakeholders to adapt neocorporatist institutions, while inherited patterns of cooperation enabled them to invest in sensitive inputs. The final section, "Political Constraints and Contemporary Challenges," concludes by describing the challenges that confront Nordic Europe and advanced industrialized economies more generally. Analysis is informed by 241 interviews conducted with politicians, industrialists and labor representatives in Denmark, Finland, and Sweden between 2003 and 2006.

Nordic Europe as a Critical Case in Comparative Political Economy

The Nordic countries represent an ideal point of departure for studying how disruptive economic challenges such as economic internationalization, the decomposition of production, and the services transformation impact the political economy of rich countries in general, and European countries in particular. Like their continental counterparts, these Nordic countries relied heavily on institutionalized bargaining among organized actors such as banking blocs, industrial associations, trade unions, and state agencies to manage the tension between economic change and social stability. Indeed, these Nordic countries relied even more heavily on "neocorporatist" bargaining than did their continental peers. For example, Finnish and Swedish firms were among the most reliant on long-term, bank-based finance, Danish and Swedish labor market bargaining was highly centralized, and all three countries possessed large public sectors (Fellman 2008; M. J. Iversen and Andersen 2008; Sjögren 2008).

These neocorporatist arrangements resolved the double bind in two ways. Most obviously, they tackled the challenge of embedding markets by insulating vulnerable employees, employers, and industries from disruptive economic shocks (Katzenstein 1984; Polanyi 1944). For example, employment protections and generous unemployment benefits maintained social peace by shielding workers from economic downturns (Scharpf 1984). "Universal" banks performed an analogous function, furnishing large, long-term loans in exchange for institutionalized influence over their clients (Zysman 1983). Finally, policy makers used countercyclical fiscal policies, subsidized loans, investment grants, competitive devaluations, and even nationalization to restore competitiveness in troubled sectors (Katzenstein 1984).

These deals unleashed economic growth by encouraging actors to undertake and upgrade specialized investments in capital equipment, skills, and knowledge. For example, patient capital, employment protections, and generous social benefits encouraged workers to invest in firm- or industry-specific skills (Streeck 1992). Long-term loans enabled firms to invest in progressively more modern and large-scale capital equipment (Albert 1993). Finally, industrial policies upgraded entire sectors at the national level (Katzenstein 1984). Such strategies were most effective in stable, low- or medium-technology industries. Universal banks were more willing to extend large, long-term loans to firms operating in mature industries with predictable technological trajectories, such as forestry (Lilja, Rasenan, and Tainio 1992). After committing significant capital, banks worked to protect and upgrade those investments. In doing so, however, they effectively delayed the redistribution of resources to growth-oriented firms, emerging occupations, and new industries (Henrekson and Jakobsson 2003). Neocorporatist economies were, and still are, perceived to struggle with radical technological and economic change (Casper 2007; Hollingsworth 2000; Katzenstein 1984).

Historically, Denmark, Finland, and Sweden exemplified this pattern of incremental adjustment, relying on integrated manufacturing activities in stable, often resource-extracting low- and medium-technology niches throughout the postwar period. In Finland, pulp, paper, and related forest activities accounted for over half of the country's exports into the 1970s (Lilja, Rasenan, and Tainio 1992: 139). The Swedish economy was more diversified, but mainly by virtue of its dependence on mining and metal-based industries, such as transportation equipment (Porter 1990: 332–33). Even Denmark, with its comparatively modest manufacturing sector, was engaged in an array of low- and medium-technology manufacturing activities, such as food processing and agricultural equipment (Edquist and Lundvall 1993: 276). These activities supported steady economic growth and full employment during the early postwar period but left these Nordic states uniquely vulnerable to disruptive new challenges.

These challenges started as early as the 1970s as low-cost Asian producers entered traditional manufacturing industries and rising oil costs punished energy-intensive manufacturing industries such as shipbuilding and papermaking. As John Zysman and Dan Breznitz (Introduction, in this volume) relate, new information and communication technologies accelerated the decomposition of production by making it easier to codify production and offshore manufacturing activity. By the 1990s, Nordic producers were transferring pulp and paper production from Finland to Uruguay and redirecting food processing activities from Denmark to Poland.[2] The loss of traditional manufacturing jobs created two problems. Economically, growth was now predicated on the ability to identify new activities, occupations, and industries, often in less clearly defined and more narrowly differentiated service activities (Zysman and Breznitz, Introduction, in this volume). Politically, movement into these activities threatened to undermine highly centralized, standardized, and solidaristic ties that underpinned postwar neocorporatism (Pontusson and Swenson 1996).

The Nordic countries initially responded to new competitive challenges by expanding public-sector employment or, in the case of Finland, barter trade with the Soviet Union (Fellman 2008; Henrekson, Jonung, and Stymne 1996; Pedersen 1996). Traditional neocorporatist strategies, however, only made things worse. Public-sector expansion delayed restructuring and generated large fiscal and current account deficits. By the early 1990s, each country faced unsustainable deficits, double-digit unemployment, and declining economic growth (Henrekson, Jonung, and Stymne 1996; Kalela et al. 2001; Schwartz 1994).[3] Such solutions might have worked in a slower, gentler postwar environment, but they appeared woefully inadequate for tackling disruptive new challenges. By the mid-1990s, the Nordic region looked like a cautionary tale, foreshadowing a decade of stagnant output and elevated unemployment on the European continent.

These three Nordic states, however, offered very different lessons by the end of the decade. Finland and Sweden enjoyed Western European-leading growth rates during the second half of the 1990s, and Danish unemployment fell steadily into the 2000s. Solid economic growth, declining unemployment, and balanced budgets propelled all three nations to the top in international benchmarking exercises. Finland ranked first in a series of surveys of economic competitiveness, with Denmark and Sweden not far behind (IMD 2007; World Economic Forum 2007). Indeed, the Nordic region was soon perceived as a "model" for struggling continental European economies by virtue of its ability to combine macroeconomic stability, social protection, and low unemployment (Andersen et al. 2007).

Nordic Europe's solid economic performance and enviable macroeconomic position reflects significant restructuring over the course of the last two decades. Traditional, low- and medium-technology industries have moved from traditional, integrated manufacturing activities into knowledge-intensive services such as research and marketing. The Finnish crane and elevator manufacturer KONE, for example, has redefined itself as an "elevation services" provider, coordinating activities at docks and related facilities (see Zysman and Breznitz, Introduction, in this volume). Similar developments can be found in other countries. Employment in the Danish textile industry actually increased despite high-profile factory closures during the 1990s. The industry's resilience is based in large measure on its ability to redefine itself from a producer of high-quality textiles into a leader in fashion and design.[4]

Even more intriguingly, Nordic Europe has entered fundamentally new, high-technology industries ranging from biotechnology to software and telecommunications equipment (Ornston n.d.-b). The share of high-technology manufactured exports, value added, and employment increased dramatically over the course of the decade, outstripping traditional high-technology leaders such as Britain and the United States. For example, the share of high-technology manufactured exports increased by 56 percent in Denmark, 80 percent in Sweden, and a remarkable 310 percent in Finland between 1990 and 2000 (OECD 2011).

Rapid movement into new, high-technology industries, however, generated new challenges. The information technology (IT) bubble attracted a host of new competitors, most notably from emerging economies such as India and China (Dossani, Chapter 6, in this volume; Breznitz and Murphree, Chapter 1, in this volume). Interestingly, however, employment in Northern Denmark's "mobile valley" remained roughly constant over the course of the 2000s, even as domestic firms flirted with bankruptcy and multinational corporations offshored manufacturing operations (Stoerring and Dalum 2007: 135). Similar developments prevail in Finland and Sweden, as large firms such as Nokia shifted their focus from manufacturing to software. While the share of high-technology manufactured exports in Finland and Sweden shrank dramatically after 2001, software exports have increased dramatically. Among wealthy, Western European states, only Ireland is more specialized in software exports (Rönkkö, Peltonen, and Pärnänen 2011: 15).[5]

As a result, Denmark, Finland, and Sweden have retained leadership in a range of dynamic, high-technology industries, even as the share of high-technology manufactured exports continues to plummet. For example, Sweden, Finland, and Denmark ranked first, second, and fourth in the EU-27 in the share of employment in high-technology industries in 2008 (Eurostat 2011). High-technology competition is in turn based in large measure on knowledge generation rather than cost competition. Finland and Sweden, for example, ranked first and second within the European Union in both per-capita high-technology patent applications to the European Patent Office and the ratio of high-technology patent applications to all patent applications (Eurostat 2011).

Nordic Europe's position in knowledge-intensive niches within high-technology industries has offered some protection from the current financial crisis, particularly relative to other wealthy economies described in this volume (Levy, Chapter 12, in this volume; Vogel, Chapter 13, in this volume; Blyth, Chapter 8, in this volume). In contrast to the United States, growth after the dot-com crash was based on activities such as research and design rather than nontradable services such as residential construction (Ornston 2012). While economic output was projected to fall from 4.5 percent in Denmark to 6.9 percent in Finland in 2009 (Eurostat 2011), this reflected their "virtuous" reliance on exports, rather than their exposure to "vices" such as financial debt and leverage (Elanger 2010). Indeed, the Nordic countries are better positioned to weather the current financial crisis than many of their European peers. In contrast to other wealthy states (Blyth,

Chapter 8, in this volume), government debt as a share of GDP (gross domestic product) remains below 40 percent in all three countries (Eurostat 2011) and Nordic European excellence in export-oriented industries represents a sustainable source of growth as the global economy recovers.

These Nordic states thus occupy a distinctive and enviable position within Europe. Yet the precise process by which these three states navigated these challenges is less clear. While some scholars emphasize institutionalized cooperation among industry, labor, and state representatives (Campbell and Hall 2009; Castells and Himanen 2002), these processes appeared to inhibit successful adaptation two decades ago. Other scholars emphasize liberalization or market-oriented reform (Andersen et al. 2007; Glimstedt and Zander 2003). Cooperation, however, is more pronounced than ever in some domains. Why are these neocorporatist economies enjoying such success? This chapter takes a first cut at the question by returning to the challenges of the 1980s and surveying the options that these economies confronted at the time.

Explaining Sectoral Shifts: Challenges and Choices

Nordic policy makers faced four choices entering the 1980s. First, policy makers could resist market forces, protecting existing industries and activities. A decision to do so was a decision to defend the traditional neocorporatist arrangements described above. Alternatively, policy makers could turn to the market, eliminating traditional neocorporatist deals and relying on decentralized competition among individual market actors. This shift would represent convergence on a liberal or Anglo-American economic model. Third, policy makers could convert neocorporatist institutions to reduce wages, government expenditure, taxation, and related costs. This strategy is most closely associated with "competitive" corporatism (Rhodes 1998). In fact, Nordic policy makers resolved the double bind in a fourth and novel way, creatively adapting neocorporatist networks to promote investment in new, supply-side resources such as risk capital, human capital and research (Ornston n.d.-b). This section reviews each strategy in turn.

CHOICE ONE: TRADITIONAL CORPORATISM

The first option was to resist economic pressures by relying on traditional, neocorporatist institutions. As noted earlier, universal banks could do this unilaterally, extending long-term loans to ailing firms and investing in progressively more modern capital equipment. Policy makers could support this process by subsidizing troubled banks, extending investment and employment grants, or even nationalizing bankrupt firms. Finally, and perhaps most significantly, policy makers, banks, and firms could compensate vulnerable workers, through a combination of labor market regulation, employment protection, or public-sector expansion.

These traditional corporatist strategies remain relevant in a number of European countries such as Austria, Germany, and Norway. Universal banks, for example, played an influential role in Austrian and German political economy throughout the 1990s (Hyytinen et al. 2003: 398). The European Union imposed limits on Austrian and German state aid, but employment protections remain relatively stringent in both countries (OECD 2004: 117). Finally, policy makers relied on early retirement, disability pensions, and other passive labor market strategies to insulate vulnerable workers from economic shocks (Kristensen 2011b: 32; Sherwood 2006: 3). To the extent these countries invested in human capital, training focused on core workers in established enterprises (Culpepper 2007: 625; Kristensen 2011a: 238).

The Nordic countries employed similar conservative corporatist measures in their initial response to economic shocks. Swedish public-sector outlays increased dramatically from 45 percent of GDP in 1971 to 66 percent of GDP by 1983 (Henrekson, Jonung, and Stymne 1996: 269). Denmark also relied on public-sector employment to hire works, and generous unemployment benefits to compensate the unemployed (Pedersen 1996: 566). Yet such efforts were short-lived. Financial crises bankrupted traditional financial blocs in the early 1990s, transforming the Finnish and Swedish financial systems into some of the most liberal, shareholder-friendly markets in the world (Hyytinen and Pajarinen 2003: 23). Policy makers simultaneously abandoned traditional industrial policies, reduced grant aid, and privatized state-owned enterprises (Morris 2005: 92; Ylä-Anttila and Palmberg 2005: 5–6). Finally, countries dismantled core labor market institutions, reducing unemployment benefits, restricting eligibility, and decentralizing collective wage bargaining (Cox 1998: 310; Pontusson and Swenson 1996: 231; Saari 2001: 195).

CHOICE TWO: NEOLIBERAL REFORM

The most obvious alternative to defending traditional, neocorporatist institutions was to dismantle them. Policy makers, in other words, could promote greater market competition. In financial markets, policy makers could increase protection for minority shareholders, encouraging the formation of decentralized equity markets populated by individual investors. In industrial policy, policy makers could reduce grant aid, privatize state-owned enterprises, break up monopolies, and prosecute collusion in order to increase competition among private-sector actors. In labor markets, policy makers and firms could attempt to minimize trade union influence, decentralize collective wage bargaining, eliminate restrictions on hiring, and reduce social benefits. This "neoliberal" approach to political economy gained momentum during the 1980s, as policy makers grappled with the apparent failure of traditional, neocorporatist strategies (Blyth 2002; Hall 1993).

In doing so, these Nordic countries would more closely approximate liberal market economies such as Australia, Britain, New Zealand, or the United States. Indeed, Australia, Britain, New Zealand, and, to a lesser extent, the United States made the greatest strides in this direction, deregulating financial markets, retrenching the state, liberalizing labor markets, and weakening trade unions (King and Wood 1999; Schwartz 1994). This represented a second and potentially attractive response to the new economic challenges of the 1970s and the pointed failure of traditional neocorporatist institutions during the 1980s.

Some scholars suggest that the Nordic region has witnessed a similar shift "from cartels to competition" (Steinbock 1998). Such trends are most pronounced in capital markets, where the crisis of the early 1990s literally bankrupted traditional financial intermediaries (Hyytinen and Pajarinen 2003: 23). Yet other actors, from state agencies to industrial associations and trade unions, remain influential in Nordic political economy. By some measures, institutionalized bargaining has actually increased. Finnish policy makers constructed a peak-level tripartite council to govern science and technology policy during the 1980s (Castells and Himanen 2002: 37); Denmark relied on a similar commission to restructure social policies during the 1990s (Morris 2005: 256–57); and Swedish policy makers have engaged jointly managed pension funds in early stage risk capital markets (Andersson and Napier 2005: 59). While Nordic responses are clearly inconsistent with traditional corporatism, they do not reflect liberal convergence either.

CHOICE THREE: COMPETITIVE CORPORATISM

Some scholars argue that countries can resolve the tension between corporatist continuity and liberal convergence by converting neocorporatist institutions to perform new functions. The literature on "competitive" corporatism argues that the cozy bargains that protected vulnerable firms and workers can be converted to impose painful austerity measures (Rhodes 1998). For example, policy makers can strike deals with trade unions, and employers, to restrain wage costs (Hancké and Rhodes 2005; Perez 2000) and restructure social benefits (Baccaro 2002). Tripartite pacts can also reduce nonwage costs in other areas, retrenching state expenditure and reducing corporate and personal income taxes (Hardiman 2002). This market-oriented strategy closely resembles liberalization, but it differs in that it is negotiated and implemented by societal actors, with different distributional consequences.

Many countries engaged in "competitive" corporatist strategies over the course of the 1990s, emulating the Netherlands's highly successful, tripartite program of macroeconomic stabilization and cost containment in 1983 (Visser and Hemerijck 1997). Ireland struck an identical deal in 1987, relying on a combination of wage restraint, fiscal retrenchment, and tax concessions to lure foreign direct investment (Hardiman 2002). By the mid-1990s, countries from Greece to Portugal were concluding similar social pacts. These deals sought to restrain private- and public-sector costs, as European monetary unification prevented competitive currency devaluations, restricted government spending, and pressured labor costs (Pochet and Fajertag 1997).

Denmark, Finland, and Sweden also used neocorporatist bargaining to reduce wage and nonwage costs. Finland, for example, relied on the most centralized and encompassing collective bargaining round in the country's history to contain wage growth (European Commission 1999: 33) and cut government spending (Saari 2001: 194). Yet this "competitive" picture is incomplete. Finnish trade unions agreed to restrain wages with the expectation that the resulting profits would be allocated to research and development (R&D).[6] Danish stakeholders were even more explicit in linking wage restraint to training in collective bargaining rounds (EIRO 2004). The Swedish wage earner funds were liquidated, not to reduce corporate or personal income taxation but rather to finance new research foundations and venture capital funds (Andersson and Napier 2005). In other words, neocorporatist institutions were adapted, but institutional innovation was not confined to cost-competitive and market-oriented reform.

CHOICE FOUR: CREATIVE CORPORATISM

Recent scholarship suggests that the Nordic countries adapted neocorporatist institutions in a distinctive way, embracing "creative" corporatism (Ornston n.d.-b). Creative corporatism can be defined as institutionalized cooperation to invest in new, supply-side resources, explicitly targeted at new enterprises, industries, and activities. Investments target the creation of new actors, activities, or even industries. In financial markets, countries have replaced relational ties between large banks and established firms with collaboration in risk capital markets. In labor markets, stakeholders have eliminated traditional employment and social protections but expanded cooperation in continuing education. In industrial policy, policy makers have reduced vertical employment and investment grants but engaged industry associations and firms in R&D.

This process of creative corporatist bargaining most closely characterizes Nordic responses to the economic crises of the 1980s and 1990s. Content varied, but each country adapted neocorporatism to identify and invest in new, supply-side resources. In Sweden, cooperation shifted from ailing universal banks and their increasingly fragmented industrial families to new actors such as pension funds (Andersson and Napier 2005: 59). In Denmark, policy makers reduced social insurance benefits and eligibility but relied on peak-level bargaining and local industry–labor cooperation to expand training (Morris 2005: 256–57). Finally, Finland eliminated traditional industrial policies from credit rationing to the state-owned enterprises but introduced a new, tripartite architecture to mobilize public- and private-sector support for R&D (Ylä-Anttila and Palmberg 2005: 7).

Neocorporatist cooperation in each of these domains encouraged investment in new supply-side resources. Table 11.1 provides evidence of this, using OECD (Organisation for Economic Co-operation and Development) data from the beginning of the financial

TABLE 11.1

INVESTMENT IN RISK CAPITAL, SKILL FORMATION, AND RESEARCH[a]

Country	Venture Capital Investment/GDP, 2008	Expenditure on Active Labor Market Policies/GDP, 2008	Research and Development Expenditure/GDP, 2008
Austria	0.04	0.67	2.68
Germany	0.05	0.80	2.64
Norway	0.13	0.42[b]	1.62
Finland	0.23	0.82	3.73
Denmark	0.30	1.34	2.72
Sweden	0.21	0.97	3.75
Netherlands	0.15	1.06	1.75
Britain	0.21	0.27	1.77
Ireland	0.15	0.72	1.43

Source: [a] Figures from OECD (http://stats.oecd.org).
[b] Norwegian active labor market expenditure does not include public employment services and administrative costs, which ranged from a low of 0.14 in Ireland to a high of 0.34 in the Netherlands.

crisis. It reveals that Denmark, Finland, and Sweden have each assumed a leading position in venture capital, human capital, and research relative to their European peers. Nordic achievements in this space are particularly impressive because they are so new. In contrast to traditional leaders such as Germany, Finland was among the least research-intensive countries in the OECD during the early 1980s, investing less than 1.2 percent of GDP in R&D (OECD 2011). Similar developments prevailed in venture capital and labor markets, as early postwar Sweden was dominated by conservative, universal banks (Sjögren 2008: 51) and Denmark relied heavily on passive labor market policies such as unemployment insurance and early retirement (Björkland 2000: 148).

As described elsewhere (Ornston n.d.-b), these new inputs had radically different implications for economic adjustment. Swedish software start-ups, which struggled to secure financing in earlier decades, could rely on robust early-stage risk capital markets (Glimstedt and Zander 2003: 143). In Denmark, the University of Aalborg and related technology programs mobilized skilled labor and knowledge around local radio producers, enabling them to shift from maritime radio to mobile communications (Stoerring and Dalum 2007: 133). Finally, Finnish investments in R&D enabled firms such as Nokia to experiment in risky, but ultimately lucrative new technologies, such as the digital GSM mobile communications standard (Ali-Yrkkö and Hermans 2002: 10). Denmark, Finland, and Sweden's ability to assume and maintain leadership in a broad range of high-technology activities has thus placed them in an enviable position relative to their European peers. To what extent does this approach represent a model for other countries? The following section addresses this question by explaining why these countries embraced creative corporatism.

Explaining National Choices: Crisis and Cooperation

Stated most concisely, creative corporatism was shaped by the interaction between crisis and cooperation. Neocorporatist adaptation was predicated on a crisis that threatened policy makers, trade unions, and firms. Countries that did not experience a crisis, or in which some actors were more vulnerable than others, lacked the ability or incentive to adapt neocorporatist institutions. In several historically neocorporatist countries, social actors such as trade unions could block reform. In several liberal countries, politically insulated policy makers could unilaterally dismantle neocorporatist institutions. Neocorporatist adaptation occurred when policy makers and societal actors were equally vulnerable. In countries with a weak tradition of cooperation, negotiations were more likely to privilege wage restraint and fiscal retrenchment. In countries with a strong tradition of cooperation, policy makers could get firms to share the sensitive information and scarce resources necessary to invest in new, supply-side resources. Table 11.2 summarizes the argument and, by extension, the structure of this section.

TABLE 11.2
EXPLAINING CHOICE IN CONTEMPORARY POLITICAL ECONOMY

	Uneven vulnerability	Mutual vulnerability
Strong tradition of cooperation	Traditional Corporatism	Creative Corporatism
Weak tradition of cooperation	Neoliberal Reform	Competitive Corporatism

TRADITIONAL CORPORATISM: COOPERATION AND UNEVEN VULNERABILITY

Neocorporatist adaptation was precipitated by economic crisis. Countries such as Austria and Norway, which enjoyed stable growth and low unemployment throughout the 1980s and 1990s, had little reason to reform traditional neocorporatist institutions. The former country successfully upgraded medium-technology industries from automotive components to machine tools, benefiting from expanding demand within Eastern Central Europe (Rehn 1996: 161). The latter benefited from the even more fortuitous discovery of offshore oil and gas resources in 1970 and the sector's subsequent expansion during the 1980s and 1990s (Thue 2008: 459–61). While policy makers gradually dismantled *dirigiste* instruments over the course of the 1980s (Rehn 1996: 155; Thue 2008: 461), they faced little pressure to restructure traditional social protections such as unemployment benefits, disability insurance, or early retirement (Kristensen 2011b: 33; Sherwood 2006: 3). For example, whereas the number of public employees decreased in Sweden between 1980 and 1998, in Norway it increased by 50 percent (Thue 2008: 461).

Denmark, Finland, and Sweden, by contrast, each faced acute economic crises between the early 1980s and the early 1990s. Unemployment approached 10 percent in Denmark (1993) and Sweden (1997), and a staggering 17 percent in Finland (1994).[7] Meanwhile, economic output stagnated in Denmark and declined by as much as 14 percent in Finland during the early 1990s. Partly as a result of these developments, Danish-, Finnish-, and Swedish-sector public debt as a share of GDP exceeded comparable Western European economies such as Britain, France, and Germany (Eurostat 2011). What was most distinctive about these crises, however, was the threat they posed to traditional stakeholders, most notably trade unions. Newly elected center-right governments in Denmark, Finland, and Sweden could credibly threaten trade union resources by de-indexing collective wage bargaining, cutting unemployment insurance benefits, or severing the link between social insurance and trade union membership.[8] Nor was industry immune from these developments, as the universal bank that underwrote neocorporatist arrangements collapsed. Furthermore, it did so as firms struggled to identify new export markets and more competitive products (Amin and Thomas 1996: 266; Fellman 2008: 193).

Trade union and industry vulnerability thus distinguishes Denmark, Finland, and Sweden from other, conservative corporatist countries facing deteriorating economic performance. Germany, for example, also suffered from stagnant growth and mounting unemployment during the 1990s. Policy makers, however, were limited in their capacity to threaten social actors by federal institutional structures and constitutional restrictions (Hemerijck and Vail 2006: 59). The universal banks and large firms that underpinned neocorporatist bargaining were also less interested in institutional reform, because they did not suffer the same catastrophic losses in financial assets and market share as their Nordic counterparts (Manow and Seils 2000). Institutional reform, to the extent that it occurred, transpired at the margins through the incremental dualization of the German economy into more and less neocorporatist spheres (Crouch 2005; Palier and Thelen 2010).

NEOLIBERAL CONVERGENCE: LIMITED VULNERABILITY AND WEAK COOPERATION

Limited vulnerability manifested itself differently in liberal economies such as Australia, Britain, New Zealand, and, to a lesser extent, the United States. In these countries, societal actors were more vulnerable. Industry and labor organizations were weak and decentralized and did not enjoy institutionalized influence in policy-making and production. Policy makers, by contrast, were insulated by a relatively strong and centralized state and a single party majority (Hassel 2007: 112). As a result, policy makers could respond to disruptive economic challenges by unilaterally implementing the market-oriented reforms that were in vogue during the 1980s and 1990s.

Unilateral liberalization, however, was not a viable option in Nordic Europe. Nordic policy makers were as vulnerable as the societal actors they threatened. In contrast to Britain, no political party enjoyed a clear majority and liberal politicians governed in coalition with other parties. In Denmark and Finland, liberals launched ambitious industrial policies to satisfy conservative coalition partners.[9] The Swedish center-right government was equally constrained, relying on Social Democratic support to pass economic legislation during the economic crisis.[10] Meanwhile, liberal experiments provoked fierce societal resistance. Center-right governments abandoned their most aggressive labor market reforms following a general strike in Denmark and lost power altogether after trade unions threatened to launch a similar strike in Finland.[11] In other words, Nordic governments were influential enough to threaten societal actors, but unable to implement market-oriented reform unilaterally.

COMPETITIVE CORPORATISM: MUTUAL VULNERABILITY AND WEAK COOPERATION

Mutual vulnerability generated new and innovative responses to disruptive economic challenges. Policy makers engaged societal actors to diffuse the political costs associated with adjustment. Trade unions and industry associations, meanwhile, welcomed the opportunity to influence the content of those policy reforms, particularly given the uncertain but plausible threat of unilateral reform (Baccaro and Lim 2007). In countries with a weak or conflicted tradition of neocorporatist governance, negotiated solutions resulted in competitive corporatism (Rhodes 1998). Greece, Ireland, Italy, Portugal, and Spain, each with a weak and conflicted tradition of neocorporatist coordination during the 1970s, struck social pacts to limit government expenditure and wage growth (Natali and Pochet 2009; Pochet and Fajertag 1997).

The Netherlands, the first and defining example of competitive corporatism, fits this pattern. While often treated as a paradigmatic case of consensus-based governance (Lijphart 1968), cooperation among policy makers, trade unions, and industry associations declined precipitously during the early postwar period and had deteriorated into a low-trust "stalemate" by the 1970s (Verspagen 2008: 321). When Dutch policy makers resurrected neocorporatist bargaining in 1982, they did so in an effort to facilitate wage restraint (Visser and Hemerijck 1997: 26–28). Neocorporatist bargaining, to the extent that it addressed social policy, emphasized fiscal retrenchment, often through the introduction of market-oriented social benefit reforms (Hemerijck 2003: 54–60). Countries such as Ireland, differed only in the degree to which they linked wage restraint and fiscal retrenchment to aggressive reductions in personal and corporate income taxation (Hardiman 2002: 19–20).

Fiscal retrenchment, wage restraint, and market-oriented reform were particularly attractive for countries with a weak tradition of cooperation, because they did not require trade unions or firms to share sensitive information about their capital requirements, skill profiles, and technological portfolios. Furthermore, while these bargains had distributive consequences, they did not require societal actors, firms in particular, to commit scarce resources. Competitive corporatist strategies were thus easier to sell to firms with a limited tradition of private-public or industry-labor cooperation. Indeed, efforts to replicate Nordic-style investments in training and research largely failed in this environment. In the Netherlands, public expenditure on education as a share of GDP has been virtually flat since the mid-1980s and spending on research actually declined (Verspagen 2008: 328–29). Similar developments prevail in Ireland, where efforts to promote training, research, and risk capital achieved modest results (Ornston 2012).

CREATIVE CORPORATISM: MUTUAL VULNERABILITY
AND STRONG COOPERATION

While Danish, Finnish, and Swedish policy makers, trade unions, and firms were just as vulnerable as their Dutch, Irish, or Italian peers, they operated in a very different institutional environment. More specifically, policy makers could exploit a rich tradition of peak-, industry-, and firm-level cooperation to identify and invest in new resources. As a result, policy makers could use neocorporatist institutions to gather information about industry preferences and mobilize private sector resources. In Finland, firms had a long tradition of collaborating within sector-based price-fixing cartels and cross-sectoral financial blocs (Fellman 2008: 177–80). Policy makers used existing networks to publicize and implement new technologies policies. For example, state agencies such as the Finnish Funding Agency for Technology and Innovation relied on inter-firm networks to pool resources, monitor inputs, and diffuse findings from new technology programs.[12] Corporate technology officers confirm that peer monitoring made it easier for firms to share information and curbed opportunistic behavior.[13]

Similar dynamics prevailed in Denmark, where policy makers not only struck a peak-level deal to increase investment in training (Morris 2005: 256–7), but also could delegate implementation to regional industry and labor councils (Björkland 2000: 168). Here, policy makers could draw on a well-established tradition of labor market cooperation. Corporate representatives routinely highlighted harmonious workplace relations and worker skills as a source of competitive advantage.[14] Swedish industrial relations were more antagonistic and creative corporatism was less pronounced (Vartiainen 1998). Even here, however, policy makers could convert jointly managed pension and wage earner funds, initially established to moderate wage demands and curb capitalist excesses, into venture capital vehicles, with little opposition from either industry or labor (Andersson and Napier 2005).

The Nordic turn to creative corporatism was thus shaped by the interaction between crisis and cooperation. Each country suffered sharply deteriorating economic performance beginning in the 1970s. These pressures were transmitted to societal actors as firms struggled to identify new markets, banking blocs flirted with insolvency, and center-right government threatened trade unions. After more radical liberal experiments faltered in the face of industry and trade union resistance, policy makers experimented with negotiated reform. Policy makers' ability to engage societal actors, and industry representatives in particular, within an existing, neocorporatist framework enabled them to pursue more ambitious, creative corporatist reforms. Indeed, creative corporatist bargaining was most successful where actors had cooperated in the past. Denmark, with its long tradition of industry-labor cooperation, invested heavily in education and training, while Finland, with its history of private-public cooperation, converted publicly sponsored, price-fixing cartels into research consortia (Ornston n.d.-a).

Conclusion: Political Constraints and Contemporary Challenges

What lessons do the Nordic countries hold for other advanced, industrialized economies? The Danish, Finnish, and Swedish experiences suggest that it is possible to reconcile the competing demand to unleash the forces of capitalism and shield the population from its most destructive effects (Andersen et al. 2007; Kristensen 2011b). In contrast to other accounts, the preceding analysis suggests that there is nothing intrinsically Nordic about this response. Norway has used its oil wealth to defend traditional neocorporatist policies (Thue 2008: 461), while there is nothing to prevent other countries from investing in new, supply-side resources. These supply-side strategies, however, are unlikely to succeed in countries with a weak or conflicted tradition of cooperation. As described earlier, competitive corporatist economies such as the Netherlands and Ireland have struggled to boost public or private expenditure in research, risk capital, and human capital, and large economies such as France (Levy, Chapter 12, in this volume) and the United States (Blyth, chapter 8, in this volume) face similar challenges. The countries that are best positioned to invest in new, supply-side resources may be the countries that have done the most to defend traditional, neocorporatist institutions. Indeed, continental European economies such as Austria, Germany, and even Norway have demonstrated increasing interest in risk capital, human capital, and research (Adelberger 1999; Culpepper 2007; Gergils 2006). These "stagnant" welfare states (Kitschelt and Streeck 2004) may prove surprisingly dynamic when subjected to disruptive economic shocks.

At the same time, continental policy makers may want to think twice before copying their more "successful" Nordic counterparts. After all, even Denmark, Finland, and Sweden face formidable economic and political challenges. Economically, there are diminishing returns to new, supply-side investments. For example, investments in human capital, risk capital, and research have not always generated comparable gains in economic output or employment (Edquist and McKelvey 1998; Ornston and Rehn 2006). This supply-side strategy is a necessary but insufficient response to heightened economic competition, particularly as emerging economies upgrade their investments in this area (Breznitz and Murphree, Chapter 1, in this volume; Dossani, Chapter 6, in this volume). This is most visible in Finland, where Nokia's market-leading R&D budget failed to insulate it from emerging rivals such as Samsung and LG (Boutin 2010).

Nokia's recent troubles illuminate more fundamental challenges. Denmark, Finland, and Sweden insulated themselves from labor cost and tax-based competition by moving into new, knowledge-intensive activities. In doing so, however, these countries simultaneously increased their vulnerability to disruptive technological innovations. For example, Apple's iPhone redefined the market for smartphones and, in so doing, undermined Nokia's dominance in mobile communications within two years. A single product thus precipitated what policy makers have labeled "the greatest structural upheaval that Finland has ever seen in the new technology sector" (Helsingin Sanomat 2011). While Finland is unusual in its reliance on a single firm (Nikulainen and Pajarinen 2010), the Swedish software industry and the Danish telecommunications equipment cluster have witnessed even greater turnover over the last two decades (Augustsson 2005; Stoerring and Dalum 2007).

Heightened technological competition generates political as well as economic challenges, as workers face difficult career transitions or unemployment. While the Nordic countries have creatively and successfully adapted risk-sharing institutions (Kristensen and Lilja 2011), coverage is arguably less comprehensive than in previous decades. After all, not all workers are equally well positioned to enter new knowledge-intensive industries. Swedish policy makers, for example, readily acknowledge the challenges associated with retraining in a progressively more complicated and flexible economic environment.[15] Meanwhile, the shift to an equity-based financial system and new forms of stock-based worker compensation threaten to amplify these divisions, contributing to rising income inequality in Finland during the 1990s (Pelkonen 2008). Together with the shift toward more differentiated and individualized services, these trends threaten to erode the consensus that underpins creative corporatism.

Indeed, Nordic policy makers continue to wrestle with the double bind, as recent developments simultaneously challenge their commitment to market competition and social protection. The populist right-wing Sweden Democrats achieved a significant breakthrough in a 2010 election (Castle 2010), and the True Finns secured an even more remarkable electoral victory, becoming the second-largest party in Finland in 2011 (Daley and Kanter 2011). Increasing nationalist sentiment not only threatens to undermine the sense of solidarity that underpinned neocorporatist bargaining in earlier decades (Schwartz 2010) but also reverses the region's historical commitment to open markets. Finland has attracted the most publicity by threatening to obstruct a coordinated response to the Eurozone crisis (Daley and Kanter 2011), but the Danish government has taken a potentially even more significant step in challenging European integration by reintroducing border controls (Dempsey 2011). Even the Nordic countries, despite a successful track record of institutional innovation, continue to struggle with their conflicting commitments to market competition and social protection.

Acknowledgments

The author wishes to thank the Alfred P. Sloan Foundation, the American Scandinavian Foundation, and the German Marshall Fund of the United States for financial support, the Berkeley Roundtable on the International Economy (BRIE) for research and administrative assistance, and Dan Breznitz and John Zysman for encouraging and insightful feedback.

Notes

1. Norway, with its abundant oil and gas resources, has proven less vulnerable to these shocks. As described later, stakeholders used these resources to defend traditional, neocorporatist institutions.

2. Author interviews with chief technology officer, Finnish forestry firm (November 2, 2005, Finland), and director, Agricultural Council (February 22, 2006, Denmark).

3. This crisis occurred earlier in Denmark, during the mid-1980s. Policy makers nonetheless continued to grapple with sluggish growth and high unemployment during the early 1990s.

4. Author interview with former director, Danish Employer's Confederation (March 14, 2006, Denmark).

5. Furthermore, Irish software exports are heavily influenced by transfer pricing (O'Hearn 1998).

6. Author interview with economist, Labor Institute for Economic Research (August 22, 2003, Finland).

7. By contrast, unemployment never exceeded 7 percent in either Austria or Norway (Eurostat 2011).

8. Author interviews with director, Central Organization of Finnish Trade Unions (October 21, 2005, Finland), former official, Ministry of Finance (November 21, 2005, Denmark), and former director, Ministry of Industry (October 4, 2006, Sweden).

9. Author interviews with a former member of Parliament (October 6, 2005, Finland) and director, Ministry of Science, Technology and Innovation (March 14, 2006, Denmark).

10. Author interview with former director, Ministry of Industry (October 4, 2006, Sweden).

11. Author interviews with director, Central Organization of Finnish Trade Unions (October 21, 2005, Finland), and former official, Ministry of Finance (November 21, 2005, Denmark).

12. Author interview with former director, Finnish Funding Agency for Technology and Innovation (November 1, 2005, Finland).

13. Author interview with research director, engineering firm (November 4, 2005, Finland).

14. Author interviews with former CEO, electronics firm (February 16, 2006, Denmark), and executive officer, electronics firm (March 24, 2006, Denmark).

15. Author interview, former economist, Ministry of Labor (October 4, 2006, Sweden).

References

Adelberger, Karen E. (1999). A developmental German state? Explaining growth in German biotechnology and venture capital. Berkeley Roundtable on the International Economy Working Paper #134, Berkeley, CA.

Albert, Michel. (1993). *Capitalism vs. Capitalism*. New York: Four Walls Eight Windows.

Ali-Yrkkö, Jyrki, and Raine Hermans. (2002). *Nokia in the Finnish Innovation System*. Helsinki: Taloustieto Oy.

Amin, Ash, and Damian Thomas. (1996). "The negotiated economy: State and civic institutions in Denmark." *Economy and Society* 25(2): 255–81.

Andersen, Torben M., Bengt Holmström, et al. (2007). *The Nordic Model: Embracing Globalization and Sharing Risks*. Helsinki, Finland: Taloustieto Oy.

Andersson, Thomas, and Glenda Napier. (2005). *The Venture Capital Market: Global Trends and Issues for Nordic Countries*. Malmo, Sweden: The International Organization for Knowledge Economy Development.

Augustsson, Fredrik. (2005). *They Did IT: The Formation and Organisation of Interactive Media Production in Sweden*. Stockholm: National Institute for Working Life.

Baccaro, Lucio. (2002). "Negotiating the Italian pension reform with the unions: Lessons for corporatist theory." *Industrial and Labor Relations Review* 55(3): 413–31.

Baccaro, Lucio, and Sang-Hoon Lim. (2007). "Social pacts as coalitions of the weak and moderate: Ireland, Italy and South Korea in comparative perspective." *European Journal of Industrial Relations* 13(1): 27–46.

Björkland, Anders. (2000). "Going Different Ways: Labour Market Policy in Denmark and Sweden." In *Why Deregulate Labour Markets?*, edited by Gøsta Esping-Andersen and Marino Regini, 148–80. Oxford: Oxford University Press..

Blyth, Mark. (2002). *Great Transformations: Economic Ideas and Institutional Change in the Twentieth Century*. Cambridge: Cambridge University Press.

Boutin, Paul. (2010). "Analysts: How Nokia lost the USA." *VentureBeat*, February 16 (http://venturebeat.com/2010/02/16/nokia-us-cmda/).

Campbell, John L., and John A. Hall. (2009). "National identity and the political economy of small states." *Review of International Political Economy* 16(4): 547–72.

Casper, Steven. (2007). *Creating Silicon Valley in Europe: Public Policy Towards New Technology Industries*. Oxford: Oxford University Press.

Castells, Manuel, and Pekka Himanen. (2002). *The Information Society and the Welfare State: The Finnish Model*. Oxford: Oxford University Press.

Castle, Stephen. (2010). "Swedish anti-immigration party claims seats." *New York Times*, September 19.

Cox, Robert Henry. (1998). "The consequences of welfare retrenchment in Denmark." *Politics and Society* 25(3): 303–26.

Crouch, Colin. (2005). *Capitalist Diversity and Change: Recombinant Governance and Institutional Pioneers*. Oxford: Oxford University Press.

Culpepper, Pepper. (2007). "Small states and skill specificity: Austria, Switzerland and interemployer cleavages in coordinated capitalism." *Comparative Political Studies* 40(6): 611–37.

Daley, Suzanne, and James Kanter. (2011). "Finland's turn to right sends shivers through Euro Zone." *New York Times*, April 21 (http://www.nytimes.com/2011/04/22/world/europe/22finland.html).

Dempsey, Judy. (2011). "Denmark reintroduces border controls." *New York Times*, May 12 (http://www.nytimes.com/2011/05/13/world/europe/13iht-border13.html).

Edquist, Charles, and Bengt-Ake, Lundvall. (1993). "Comparing the Danish and Swedish Systems of Innovation." In *National Innovation Systems: A Comparative Analysis*, edited by Richard R. Nelson, 265–98. New York: Oxford University Press.

Edquist, Charles, and Maureen McKelvey. (1998). "High R&D Intensity Without High Tech Products: A Swedish Paradox?" In *Institutions and Economic Change: New Perspectives on Markets, Firms and Technology*, edited by Klaus Nielsen and Björn Johnson, 131–49. Cheltenham, UK: Edward Elgar.

EIRO. (2004). "2003 Annual review for Denmark." *European Industrial Relations Observatory Online* (https://eurofound.europa.eu/eiro/2004/01/feature/dk0401102f.htm).

Elanger, Steven. (2010). "Absorbing the blows that buffet Europe." *New York Times*, March 8 (http://www.nytimes.com/2010/03/08/world/europe/08france.html?scp=1&sq=France%20Germany%20virtuous&st=cse).

European Commission. (1999). *The Economic and Financial Situation in Finland*. Luxembourg: The Office for Official Publications of the European Union.

Eurostat. (2011). "Data explorer." Retrieved February 15, 2011 (http://epp.eurostat.cec.eu.int/).

Fellman, Susanna. (2008). "Growth and Investment: Finnish Capitalism, 1850s-2005." In *Creating Nordic Capitalism: The Business History of a Competitive Periphery*, edited by Susanna Fellman, Martin Jes Iversen, et al., 139–217. New York: Palgrave Macmillan.

Gergils, Hakan. (2006). *Dynamic Innovation Systems in the Nordic Countries* (Vol. 2). Stockholm, Sweden: SNS Förlag.

Glimstedt, Henrik, and Udo Zander. (2003). "Sweden's Wireless Wonders: The Diverse Roots and Selective Adaptations of the Swedish Internet Economy." In *The Global Internet Economy*, edited by Bruce Kogut, 109–51. Cambridge, MA: MIT Press.

Gylfason, Thorvaldur, Bengt Holmström, et al. (2010). *Nordics in Global Crisis: Vulnerability and Resilience*. Helsinki: Taloustieto Oy.

Hall, Peter A. (1993). "Policy paradigms, social learning and the state: The case of economic policymaking in Britain." *Comparative Politics* 25(3): 275–96.

Hancké, Bob, and Martin Rhodes. (2005). "EMU and labor market institutions in Europe." *Work and Occupations* 32(2): 196–228.

Hardiman, Niamh. (2002). "From conflict to coordination: Economic governance and political innovation in Ireland." *West European Politics* 25(4): 1–24.

Hassel, Anke. (2007). *Wage Setting, Social Pacts and the Euro: A New Role for the State*. Amsterdam: Amsterdam University Press.

Helsingin Sanomat. (2011). "More than 1,000 Nokia employees walk out in Tampere in protest at Symbian phase out." *Helsingin Sanomat*, February 11 (http://www.hs.fi/english/article/More+than+1000+Nokia+employees+walk+out+in+Tampere+in+protest+at+Symbian+phase-out/1135263743059).

Hemerijck, Anton C. (2003). "The Resurgence of Dutch Corporatist Policy Coordination in an Age of Globalization." In *Renegotiating the Welfare State: Flexible Adjustment Through Corporatist Concertation*, edited by Frans van Waarden and Gerhard Lehmbruch, 33–69. London: Routledge.

Hemerijck, Anton C., and Mark I. Vail. (2006). "The Forgotten Center: State Activism and Corporatist Adjustment in Holland and Germany." In *The State After Statism: New State Activities in the Age of Liberalization*, edited by Jonah D. Levy, 57–92. Cambridge, MA: Harvard University Press.

Henrekson, Magnus, and Ulf Jakobsson. (2003). "The transformation of ownership policy and structure in Sweden: Convergence towards the Anglo-Saxon model?" *New Political Economy* 8(1): 73–102.

Henrekson, Magnus, Lars Jonung, and Joakim Stymne. (1996). "Economic Growth and the Swedish Model." In *Economic Growth in Europe Since 1945*, edited by Nicholas Crafts and Gianni Toniolo, 240–89. Cambridge: Cambridge University Press.

Hollingsworth, J. Rogers. (2000). "Doing institutional analysis: Implications for the study of innovations." *Review of International Political Economy* 7(4): 595–644.

Hyytinen, Ari, and Mika Pajarinen. (2003). "Financial Systems and Venture Capital in the Nordic Countries: A Comparative Study." In *Financial Systems and Firm Performance: Theoretical and Empirical Perspectives*, edited by Ari Hyytinen and Mika Pajarinen, 19–63. Helsinki: Taloustieto Ltd.

Hyytinen, Ari, Petri Rouvinen, et al. (2003). "Does Financial Development Matter for Innovation and Economic Growth? Implications for Public Policy." In *Financial Systems and Firm Performance: Theoretical and Empirical Perspectives*, edited by Ari Hyytinen and Mika Pajarinen, 379–456. Helsinki: Taloustieto Ltd.

IMD. (2007). *World Competitiveness Yearbook 2007*. Lausanne, Switzerland: IMD.

Iversen, Martin Jes, and Steen Andersen. (2008). "Cooperative Liberalism: Denmark from 1857 to 2007." In *Creating Nordic Capitalism: The Business History of a Competitive Periphery*, edited by Susanna Fellman, Martin Jes Iversen, et al., 265–91. New York: Palgrave Macmillan.

Iversen, Torben. (1996). "Power, flexibility and the breakdown of centralized wage bargaining: Denmark and Sweden in comparative perspective." *Comparative Politics* 28(4): 399–436.

Iversen, Torben, and Anne Wren. (1998). "Equality, employment and budgetary restraint: The trilemma of the service economy." *World Politics* 50(4): 507–46.

Kalela, Jorma, Jaakko Kiander, et al. (2001). "Introduction." In *Down from the Heavens, Up from the Ashes: The Finnish Economic Crisis of the 1990s in Light of Economic and Social Research*, edited by Jorma Kalela, Jaakko Kiander, et al., 3–21. Helsinki: Government Institute for Economic Research.

Katzenstein, Peter J. (1984). *Corporatism and Change: Austria, Switzerland and the Politics of Industry*. Ithaca, NY: Cornell University Press.

King, Desmond, and Stewart Wood. (1999). "The Political Economy of Neoliberalism: Britain and the United States in the 1980s." In *Continuity and Change in Contemporary Capitalism*, edited by Herbert Kitschelt, Peter Lange, et al., 371–97. Cambridge: Cambridge University Press.

Kitschelt, Herbert, and Wolfgang Streeck. (2004). "From Stability to Stagnation: Germany at the Beginning of the Twenty-First Century." In *Germany: Beyond the Stable State*, edited by Herbert Kitschelt and Wolfgang Streeck, 1–34. London: Frank Cass.

Kristensen, Peer Hull. (2006). "The Danish Business System: Transforming Toward the New Economy." In *National Identity and the Varieties of Capitalism: The Danish Experience Montreal McGill University Press*, edited by John L. Campbell, John A. Hall, and Ove K. Pedersen, 295–30. Montreal: McGill University Press.

Kristensen, Peer Hull. (2011a). "Developing Comprehensive, Enabling Welfare States for Offensive Experimentalist Business Practices." In *Nordic Capitalisms and Globalization: New Forms of Economic Organization and Welfare Institutions*, edited by Peer Hull Kristensen and Kari Lilja, 220–58. Oxford: Oxford University Press.

Kristensen, Peer Hull. (2011b). "Changing Nordic Welfare and Business Systems." In *Nordic Capitalisms and Globalization: New Forms of Economic Organization and Welfare Institutions*, edited by Peer Hull Kristensen and Kari Lilja, 1–46. Oxford: Oxford University Press.

Kristensen, Peer Hull, and Kari Lilja. (Eds.). (2011). *Nordic Capitalisms and Globalization: New Forms of Economic Organization and Welfare Institutions.* Oxford: Oxford University Press.

Lijphart, Arend. (1968). *The Politics of Accommodation: Pluralism and Democracy in the Netherlands.* Berkeley: University of California Press.

Lilja, Kari, Keijo Rasanen, and Risto Tainio. (1992). "A Dominant Business Recipe: The Forest Sector in Finland." In *European Business Systems: Firms and Markets in Their National Contexts,* edited by Richard Whitley, 137–54. London: Sage Publications.

Manow, Philip, and Eric Seils. (2000). "Adjusting Badly: The German Welfare State, Structural Change and the Open Economy." In *Welfare and Work in the Open Economy: Diverse Responses to Common Challenges,* edited by Fritz Scharpf and Vivien Schmidt, 264–307. Oxford: Oxford University Press.

Miller, Kenneth A. (1991). *Denmark: A Troubled Welfare State.* Boulder, CO: Westview.

Morris, Damon C. (2005). *State power and institutional challenges to coordinating industrial adjustment: Industrial and labor market politics in Denmark in the 1990s.* Ph.D. diss., City University of New York.

Natali, David, and Philippe Pochet. (2009). "The evolution of social pacts in the EMU era." *European Journal of Industrial Relations* 15(1): 147–66.

Nikulainen, Tuomo, and Mika Pajarinen. (2010). "Is the Innovative Dominance of Nokia in Finland Unique in International Comparison?" In *Nokia and Finland in a Sea of Change,* edited by Jyrki Ali-Yrkkö, 69–90. Helsinki: Taloustieto Oy.

OECD. (2004). *Employment Outlook.* Paris: OECD.

OECD. (2011). "OECD.Stat." Retrieved September 18, 2011 (http://stats.oecd.org/).

O'Hearn, Denis. (1998). *Inside the Celtic Tiger: The Irish Economy and the Asian Model.* London: Pluto Press.

Ornston, Darius. (2012). *When Small States Make Big Leaps: Institutional Innovation and High Tech Competition in Western Europe.* Ithaca, NY: Cornell University Press.

Ornston, Darius. (n.d.-a). "How old ideas shape new investments: Divergent pathways to a knowledge economy in Denmark and Finland." *Governance.* Forthcoming.

Ornston, Darius. (n.d.-b). "Creative corporatism: Explaining high-technology competition in Nordic Europe." *Comparative Political Studies.* Forthcoming.

Ornston, Darius, and Olli Rehn. (2006). "An Old Consensus in the "New" Economy? Institutional Adaptation, Technological Innovation and Economic Restructuring in Finland." In *How Revolutionary Was the Revolution? National Responses, Market Transitions and Global Technology,* edited by John Zysman and Abraham Newman, 78–100. Stanford, CA: Stanford Business Books.

Palier, Bruno, and Kathleen Thelen. (2010). "Institutionalizing dualism: Complementarities and change in France and Germany." *Politics and Society* 38(1): 119–48.

Pedersen, Peder J. (1996). "Postwar Growth of the Danish Economy." In *Economic Growth in Europe Since 1945,* edited by Nicholas Crafts and Gianni Toniolo, 541–75. Cambridge: Cambridge University Press.

Pelkonen, Antti. (2008). "Reconsidering the Finnish model: Information society policy and modes of governance." *TRAMES* 12(4): 400–20.

Perez, Sofia. (2000). "From decentralization to reorganization: Explaining the return to national bargaining in Italy and Spain." *Comparative Politics* 32(4): 437–58.

Pochet, Philippe, and Giuseppe Fajertag. (1997). *Social Pacts in Europe*. Brussels: European Trade Union Institute.

Polanyi, Karl. (1944). *The Great Transformation*. Boston: Beacon Press.

Pontusson, Jonas, and Peter Swenson. (1996). "Labor markets, production strategies and wage bargaining institutions: The Swedish employer offensive in comparative perspective." *Comparative Political Studies* 29(2): 223–50.

Porter, Michael E. (1990). *The Competitive Advantage of Nations*. New York: Free Press.

Rehn, Olli. (1996). *Corporatism and industrial competitiveness in small European States: Austria, Finland and Sweden, 1945–1995*. Ph.D. diss., Oxford University.

Rhodes, Martin. (1998). "Globalization, Labour Markets and Welfare States: A Future of Competitive Corporatism?" In *The Future of European Welfare: A New Social Contract?*, edited by Martin Rhodes and Yves Mény, 178–203. London: Macmillan.

Rönkkö, Mikko, Juhana Peltonen, and Dani Pärnänen. (2011). *Software Industry Survey 2011*. Helsinki: Aalto University School of Science.

Saari, Juho. (2001). "Bridging the Gap: Financing Social Policy in Finland, 1990–1998." In *Down from the Heavens, Up from the Ashes: The Finnish Economic Crisis of the1990s in Light of Economic and Social Research*, edited by Jorma Kalela, Jaakko Kiander, et al., 189–214. Helsinki: Government Institute for Economic Research.

Scharpf, Fritz (1984). "Economic and Institutional Constraints of Full-Employment Strategies: Sweden, Austria and West Germany, 1973–1982." In *Order and Conflict in Contemporary Capitalism*, edited by John H. Goldthorpe, 143–78. Oxford: Clarendon Press.

Schwartz, Herman. (1994). "Small states in big trouble: The politics of state reorganization in Australia, Denmark, New Zealand and Sweden in the 1980s." *World Politics* 46(4): 527–55.

Schwartz, Herman. (2010). "Small states in the rear-view mirror: Legitimacy in the management of economy and society." *European Political Science* 9(3): 365–74.

Sherwood, Monika. (2006). "Unemployment in Austria: Low but…" *ECFIN Country Focus* 3(3): 1–6.

Sjögren, Hans. (2008). "Welfare Capitalism: The Swedish Economy, 1850–2005." In *Creating Nordic Capitalism: The Business History of a Competitive Periphery*, edited by Susanna Fellman, Martin Jes Iversen, et al., 22–74. London: Palgrave MacMillan.

Steinbock, Dan. (1998). *The Competitive Advantage of Finland: From Cartels to Competition*. Helsinki: Taloustieto Ltd.

Stoerring, Dagmara, and Bent Dalum. (2007). "Cluster Emergence: A Comparative Study of Two Cases in North Jutland, Denmark." In *Creative Regions: Technology, Culture and Knowledge Entrepreneurship*, edited by Philip Cooke and Dafna Schwartz, 127–47. London: Routledge.

Streeck, Wolfgang. (1992). "Productive Constraints: On the Institutional Preconditions of Diversified Quality Production." In *Social Institutions and Economic Performance*, edited by Wolfgang Streeck, 1–40. London: Sage.

Tainio, Risto, Matti Pohjola, and Kari Lilja. (1997). "Economic Performance of Finland After the Second World War: From Success to Failure." In *National Capitalisms, Global Competition and Economic Performance*, edited by Sigrid Quack, Glenn Morgan, and Richard Whitley, 277–90. Amsterdam: John Benjamins.

Thue, Lars. (2008). "Norway: A Resource-Based and Democratic Capitalism." In *Creating Nordic Capitalism: The Business History of a Competitive Periphery*, edited by Susanna Fellman, Martin Jes Iversen, et al., 394–493. London: Palgrave MacMillan.

Vartiainen, Juhana. (1998). "Understanding Swedish social democracy: Victims of success?" *Oxford Review of Economic Policy* 14(1): 19–39.

Verspagen, Bart. (2008). "Challenged Leadership or Renewed Vitality? the Netherlands." In *Small Country Innovation Systems: Globalization, Change and Policy in Asia and Europe*, edited by Charles Edquist and Leif Hommen, 319–54. Cheltenham, UK: Edward Elgar.

Visser, Jelle, and Anton Hemerijck. (1997). *A Dutch Miracle: Job Growth, Welfare Reform and Corporatism in the Netherlands*. Amsterdam: Amsterdam University Press.

World Economic Forum. (2007). *Global Competitiveness Report: 2006–2007*. New York: Oxford University Press.

Ylä-Anttila, Pekka, and Christopher Palmberg. (2005). The specificities of Finnish industrial policy: Challenges and initiatives at the turn of the century. Discussion Paper 973, The Research Institute of the Finnish Economy, Helsinki.

Zysman, John. (1983). *Governments, Markets, and Growth: Financial Systems and the Politics of Industrial Change*. Ithaca, NY: Cornell University Press.

12 Directionless

FRENCH ECONOMIC POLICY IN THE TWENTY-FIRST CENTURY

Jonah D. Levy

FRANCE HAS LONG been paired with Japan as the archetypal *dirigiste* or state-led political economy (Cohen 1977; Hall 1986; Shonfield 1965; Zysman 1978, 1983). For decades following World War II, French planners aggressively manipulated an array of policy instruments—from trade protection, to subsidies, to cheap credit, to exemption from price controls—in an effort to accelerate the pace of economic modernization. State guidance operated through a series of five-year plans initially, then through ambitious sectoral plans and high-technology projects known as *grands projets* (Cohen 1992; Cohen and Bauer 1985). Through these initiatives, French authorities channeled resources to privileged groups, favoring investment over consumption, industry over agriculture, and big business over small. They also "picked winners," both specific sectors, such as coal and steel in the immediate postwar era and nuclear power and telecommunications in the 1970s, and specific firms, the so-called national champions, multinational corporations anointed as France's standard-bearers in the battle for global economic leadership.

The present context would seem to be ripe for a new round of voluntarist French initiatives. As the editors describe in the introduction to this volume, changes in digital technology and energy use provide tremendous economic opportunities for the countries and companies that are first to market. Seizing these opportunities, developing the markets of the future, is critically dependent on state support.

The current context provides not only an economic opportunity for state leadership but also, in the wake of the 2008 financial meltdown, an ideological space. The spectacular crash of the neoliberal model has eroded faith in unregulated markets. With the economy in crisis, governments everywhere, including in the neoliberal heartland of the

United States and the UK, have been intervening in all manner of ways. Bailouts, mammoth budget deficits, and calls for new kinds of regulation have become common. In this context, France's traditional *dirigiste* approach no longer seems so out of place.

Rather than a return to *dirigisme*, however, French economic policy can best be described as directionless. It is directionless in a triple sense, starting with the literal. The French verb *diriger* means "to direct," yet state authorities are not directing the economy in the manner of the postwar *dirigiste* model. Recent governments have lacked a coherent industrial policy vision, have been reluctant to tell companies what to do, and have deployed limited resources at best on behalf of industrial projects. A second way in which French policy is directionless concerns the coherence of public intervention. French authorities have not hewed to a consistent course of reform. Instead, they have moved in contradictory directions, with the same governments launching neo-*dirigiste* initiatives accompanied by vigorous denunciations of the free market and neoliberal initiatives accompanied by equally vigorous denunciations of the bloated, bureaucratic state. The third way in which French policy is directionless relates to prioritization. Successive governments have been unwilling or unable to commit to a particular policy direction. Authorities have often advocated lofty economic and social objectives simultaneously, even though they clearly lack the fiscal resources for such an agenda. French leadership has also been reluctant to choose between radical reform and the preservation of the status quo, alternating promises of dramatic change or "rupture" with reassurances that traditional commitments and social solidarity will be preserved.

The most common explanation of France's directionless policy is the governing style of the president from 2007 to 2012, Nicolas Sarkozy. Sarkozy was constantly announcing new reforms, a strategy that one leading scholar of French economic policy describes as "carpet-bombing" (Cohen 2008), but many of these initiatives were either largely symbolic or never fully implemented. Critics charge that Sarkozy's reforms were long on spin and short on substance (Cahuc and Zylberberg 2009; Szarka 2009). French economic policy was directionless, then, because the French president was directionless.

There is certainly ample evidence to support the claim that Sarkozy's economic policy was directionless. Sarkozy came to office promising a "rupture" or radical break with past French policy, which he blamed for the country's slow growth and high unemployment. Although Sarkozy avoided the "L word" (liberalism), his signature initiative, his first piece of legislation as president, was a massive tax cut, the Law for Labor, Employment, and Purchasing Power (*Loi pour le Travail, l'Emploi, et le Pouvoir d'Achat*, or TEPA). TEPA introduced deductibility for home mortgage interest, exempted overtime hours from income and payroll taxes, and enshrined a so-called fiscal shield limiting the maximum direct tax liability of any individual to 50 percent of income (Greciano 2008; Monnier 2009). Sarkozy also moved to cut government spending, which he promised to reduce by 1 percent of GDP (gross domestic product) per year. Key measures included the nonreplacement of one out of two retiring civil servants and the scaling back of the so-called special pension regimes (*régimes spéciaux*) that had enabled certain categories of public employees (mainly transportation and energy workers) to retire as early as age 50 (Howell 2008).

In response to the 2008 crisis, however, Sarkozy tacked in a neo-*dirigiste* direction. Declaring that "*Laissez-faire* is over. The market that is always right is over," Sarkozy called for a "refounding of capitalism" with "a new balance between the State and the market" (Sarkozy 2008). Toward this end, he launched a series of industrial policy initiatives that harkened back to the *dirigiste* era. One initiative was a French variant of a sovereign wealth fund, designed to support promising French firms and to protect "companies that may become the prey of [foreign] predators." Another initiative was an ambitious plan to boost French industry, complete with a series of specific targets: increasing industrial production by 25 percent in five years; boosting France's share of European industry by 2 percent by 2015; sustaining employment in industry at current levels; returning to a trade surplus in manufactured goods (excluding energy) by 2015 (French Presidency 2010).

In early 2010, Sarkozy shifted again, this time asserting that free-spending France had been living beyond its means and announcing a series of austerity measures. These measures were long on spending cuts and short on tax increases. Sarkozy announced that his top priority was pension reform, and his government produced a reform that unions charged extracted 85 percent of the savings from employees, most notably by raising the retirement age by two years (Peillon 2010). Moreover, despite accusations of favoring the rich, including from within his own political camp, Sarkozy doggedly defended his fiscal shield, which he viewed as *the* defining reform of his administration and a symbol of his commitment to reining in French taxation. Indeed, Sarkozy drew a line in the sand, declaring that he would not abandon the fiscal shield under any circumstances.

One year later, Sarkozy changed his strategy yet again. Unable to reduce France's budget deficit sufficiently by spending cuts alone and facing charges of unfairness, Sarkozy reversed course on tax increases. In short order, virtually all the TEPA tax cuts, including the fiscal shield, were sacrificed. Other taxes were raised as well. Successive plans in August and November 2011 were the polar opposite of earlier plans, with between two-thirds and three-quarters of the deficit reduction coming from tax hikes ("C'était Sarkozy: Histoire d'une ambition" 2012: 137). Thus, in five years as president, Sarkozy advanced four different economic agendas: (1) a liberalizing agenda of spending and tax cuts; (2) a revival of neo-*dirigiste* industrial policy in response to the 2008 crisis; (3) a neoliberal austerity program to reduce deficits by spending cuts alone; and (4) a tax-centered austerity program, combining significant tax increases with limited spending cuts. Rather than neoliberal or neostatist, Sarkozy's economic policy appears contradictory and directionless. The 2008 financial meltdown and ongoing sovereign debt crisis aggravated the directionless character of Sarkozy's economy policy, with each challenge pulling the French government in a new direction.

Without denying the significance of President Sarkozy's governing style or the current economic crisis, this chapter argues that the roots of France's directionless policy run deeper. Indeed, many of the same criticisms could be leveled against Sarkozy's predecessor as president, Jacques Chirac, who governed prior to the crisis and whose policies also seemed to lack any kind of ideological or strategic anchor. Moreover, although it is too early to pronounce definitive judgment, the initial economic policies of Sarkozy's successor as president in May 2012, the Socialist, François Hollande, appear equally directionless. To understand the dilemmas and dysfunctions of contemporary French economic policy, then, we must look beyond present presidential personalities.

This chapter contends that the directionless character of French economic policy today has been profoundly shaped by the decisions of French authorities long ago, notably the decisions surrounding France's break with the *dirigiste* model in the early 1980s. Three features of this break have contributed to the directionless character of contemporary French policy. First, the break with *dirigisme* was far-reaching. French authorities did not simply tinker or adapt *dirigiste* policies and institutions. Rather, they dismantled these policies and institutions altogether. Second, despite the far-reaching nature of economic reform, the government did not explain, let alone champion, its actions. Instead, the government and its successors either downplayed the movement away from *dirigisme*, engaging in what Philip Gordon and Sophie Meunier term "liberalization by stealth" (Gordon and Meunier 2001), or blamed this movement on the pressures of the European Union. Third, the break with *dirigisme* was socially compensated. In a "social anesthesia" strategy (Levy 2005a, 2005b, 2008; Levy, Miura, and Park 2006), expensive welfare and labor market programs were launched in order to soften the blow of market-led reform and to undercut potential opposition.

The fact that the break with *dirigisme* in the 1980s was institutionally far-reaching, politically masked, and socially compensated has created a series of policy dilemmas for French authorities more than a quarter-century later. Specifically, French governments confront powerful demands for both prongs of the double bind described by the editors of this volume, for both neostatist and neoliberal reforms, yet possess limited capacity to pursue either agenda. The dramatic expansion of social and labor market spending has created pressure for fiscal retrenchment, for pruning and reforming social programs. Yet the disinclination to defend neoliberal reform on its own terms and a certain degree of what might be termed "reform fatigue" following the liberalizing reforms of the 1980s have made it extremely difficult politically to enact these kinds of cuts. Liberalizing reform is, at once, economically necessary and politically elusive. In a similar vein, the enduring attachment to statist ideology and discourse has fueled calls for neo-*dirigiste* intervention to relaunch French growth and investment. However, the dismantling of the *dirigiste* apparatus and the dramatic expansion of costly social programs have deprived state authorities of the vision, policy instruments, and fiscal resources necessary to carry out ambitious neo-*dirigiste* initiatives. Neo-*dirigiste* reform is thus both politically attractive and institutionally and fiscally unavailable. The combination of multiple economic agendas and limited state capacities—an inability to move to either a neoliberal or neostatist strategy—has lent a confused, contradictory, directionless character to contemporary French economic policy.

This chapter is organized into four sections. The first section describes France's turn away from the *dirigiste* economic model and accompanying expansion of social protection. The second section points to the limits and growing dysfunctions of this social anesthesia strategy. The third and fourth sections examine the contemporary period, in which economic policy appears anemic and directionless, with state authorities unable to pursue a coherent neoliberal or neostatist approach. The third section focuses on the efforts of France's president from 1995 to 2007, Jacques Chirac, to pursue liberalizing reform, while the fourth section focuses on President Sarkozy's attempts to revive statist industrial policy. The fourth section finishes with a brief discussion of the initial policies of France's new president, François Hollande. The conclusion offers observations about the implications of the French case for the double bind.

From the *Dirigiste* State to the Social Anesthesia State

In the postwar period, France adopted a statist economic development model (Cohen 1977; Hall 1986; Shonfield 1965; Zysman 1978, 1983). State authorities did not hesitate to "pick winners," favoring business over labor and, within business, large corporations over small firms. They squeezed resources from labor through a combination of low wages, frequent devaluations, and a limited welfare state (Levy 2000). They deployed a variety of tools to steer the strategies of business from planning to selective protectionism to control over prices to access to cheap credit. And they conducted a series of voluntarist *grands projets* that catapulted France to positions of global leadership in such industries as high-speed trains, nuclear power, and digital telecommunications switches. Of course, *dirigiste* initiatives were not always successful: the Concorde supersonic airplane was a costly white elephant, while the *plan calcul* to develop a French computer industry went nowhere (Cohen and Bauer 1985; Zysman 1977, 1978). Still, within a generation, under state guidance, France was transformed from a sleepy, backward, peasant economy to one of the world's most affluent and advanced industrial powers.

In the 1970s, the performance of France's *dirigiste* model began to erode (Berger 1981; Cohen 1989; Levy 1999). An increasingly competitive, internationalized, and fast-changing environment made it difficult for planners to identify the most promising sectors and promote appropriate business strategies. Moreover, political pressures led governments to use industrial policy less and less for economic development and more and more as a way of preserving employment by propping up declining heavy industries. By the early 1980s, France was experiencing stagnant investment, rising unemployment, double-digit inflation, and large trade and budget deficits.

The erosion of the *dirigiste* state culminated in 1983, when a currency crisis threatened to push the French franc below the minimum exchange rate allowed by the European Monetary System (EMS) (Hall 1990). Under pressure from international financial markets and with growing skepticism about the effectiveness of *dirigiste* industrial policy,

Socialist President, François Mitterrand opted to abandon the government's voluntarist tack. A leftist administration that had been elected just two years earlier on a campaign to intensify *dirigisme* began instead to dismantle *dirigisme*.

The 1983 U-turn touched off a series of reforms that struck at the heart of the *dirigiste* model (Cohen 1989; Hall 1990; Levy 1999, 2000; Schmidt 1996). This shift was inaugurated cautiously by the left from 1983 to 1986, then amplified when the right returned to power from 1986 to 1988, and confirmed and completed by subsequent governments on both sides of the political spectrum. Within a decade, French authorities wound down industrial policy, privatized the vast majority of public enterprises, liberalized the financial system, lifted capital controls, reduced inflation and budget deficits to German levels, and eased restrictions on layoffs, part-time employment, and temporary employment. Looking across the wealthy democracies, one would be hard-pressed to find any country that shifted so far away from its postwar economic strategy as the France of François Mitterrand and Jacques Chirac. Certainly, compared to other statist political economies, such as Japan and Korea, France moved earlier and more aggressively against its postwar policy model (Levy, Miura, and Park 2006).

The far-reaching break with the postwar *dirigiste* industrial policy model was not accompanied by a comparable shift in political discourse. On the contrary, the Mitterrand government sought to downplay the changes that it was introducing. Officials spoke of a "pause" in reform, rather than a reversal of course; they used the phrase "rigor," as opposed to austerity. Instead of making the economic and social case for breaking with the *dirigiste* model, the left engaged in what Philip Gordon and Sophie Meunier describe as "liberalization by stealth" (Gordon and Meunier 2001), maintaining a voluntarist discourse, while conducting liberalizing reforms quietly, under the radar. Moreover, to the extent that the government admitted that it was engaging in economic liberalization, left leaders presented these reforms as having been imposed by the European Community, rather than chosen. In point of fact, the reforms in France went well beyond anything necessary for remaining in the EMS, but it was more politically expedient to say that Europe was forcing the French to reform than to take responsibility and argue that the reforms were necessary and good for France. This combination of denial and blaming of Brussels may have originated with the left, but it would become a bipartisan strategy, as conservative governments likewise sought to avoid blame for unpopular liberalizing reforms.

The rollback of the *dirigiste* model was not the only shift in French policy touched off by the 1983 U-turn. A second shift, more social in orientation, accompanied and enabled the first shift. State authorities dramatically expanded social and labor market programs, to cushion the blow to industrial workers and other groups made vulnerable by movement away from *dirigisme*. These initiatives were motivated by more than social concerns. They also reflected a social anesthesia logic; that is, they sought to permit French firms to reorganize on a more market-rational basis by pacifying and demobilizing the potential victims and opponents of economic liberalization (Levy 2005a, 2005b, 2008; Levy, Miura, and Park 2006). In a logic first articulated by Karl Polanyi, the extension of market forces was softened, made politically acceptable through the expansion of social protections for those most affected by liberalization (Polanyi 1944). Social anesthesia did not come cheaply, however. As Figure 12.1 reveals, French state spending and taxation have increased in the post-*dirigiste* period, despite the winding down of expensive industrial policy programs.

France's social anesthesia strategy centered initially on early retirement. State programs permitted workers in troubled industries like coal and shipbuilding to retire on full pension as early as age 50 (as opposed to age 55 or 60 under normal conditions). The expansion of early retirement to accommodate and humanize restructuring began under the center-right presidency of Giscard d'Estaing in the 1970s. Between 1974 and 1980, the number of early retirees more than tripled from 59,000 to 190,400 (DARES 1996: 100). The left tripled the figure again to over 700,000 workers in 1984. Beyond salving the left's guilty conscience, the widespread recourse to early retirement served a more strategic purpose—demobilizing France's working class and undercutting trade union capacity to mount resistance to industrial restructuring. The vast majority of French workers were more than willing to quit smelly, physically taxing, alienating jobs, to receive 90 percent of their previous wages without having to report to work. In such a context, France's already anemic trade unions were completely incapable of mobilizing their members to fight industrial restructuring. The effects of early retirement on the French labor market cannot be overestimated. Today, fewer than one worker in three is still employed at age 60, and France's labor force participation rate for those ages 55 to 64 is under 40 percent, among the lowest figures in Western Europe (DARES 2011b).

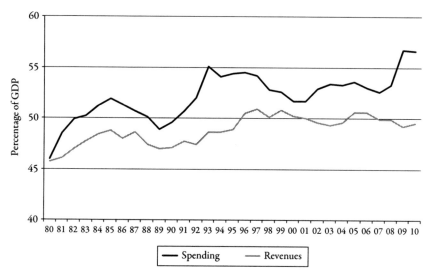

FIGURE 12.1 French Public Spending and Taxation as Percentage of GDP, 1980–2010
Source: Eurostat (2011a, 2011b).

Although social anesthesia measures were conceived of as a temporary accompaniment to industrial restructuring, they persisted and multiplied. Social anesthesia policies were deployed not only to facilitate the movement away from *dirigisme* but also to palliate the perceived limits or failings of economic liberalization, in particular, the persistence of mass unemployment. In 1988, the Socialist government of Michel Rocard established a national guaranteed income, the *revenu minimum d'insertion* (RMI). The RMI provides a monthly allowance, ranging from €445 for a single individual to €926 for a family of four (plus €176 for each additional child), on a means-tested basis to citizens and long-term residents over the age of 25. It often functions as a basic income support for adults who have exhausted or failed to qualify for unemployment insurance.

Governments of left and right alike have also multiplied labor market policies to limit the suffering of those who are unable to secure stable employment. The right has tended to focus on subsidies and tax breaks for private employers who agree to hire hard-to-place employees (youths, the unskilled, older workers) at the bottom of the wage spectrum. Such programs cost €17 billion in 2005. The left has favored training programs as well as public internships. The center-left government of Lionel Jospin, which was in power from 1997 to 2002, established the *Programme Emplois Jeunes* (PEJ), providing five-year positions in the public and non-profit sectors to some 350,000 young people at a cost of €5.3 billion. The Jospin government also presented its thirty-five-hour workweek reform as a way of creating (or sharing) jobs, although this analysis was hotly contested by economists, employers, and the parties of the right.

Looking at labor market policy globally, Figure 12.2 reveals that the number of French workers enrolled in some kind of public labor market program expanded two-and-one-half-fold during the fifteen years following the Socialists' U-turn—rising from slightly under 1.2 million in 1984, at the height of industrial restructuring, to nearly 3 million

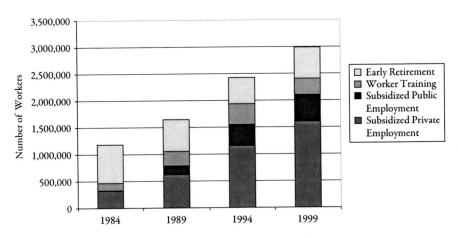

FIGURE 12.2 Number of French Workers in Public Labor Market Programs

in 1999 (DARES 1996, 2000). This total is in addition to the 2 to 3 million French workers who were formally unemployed during this time. Aggregate spending on labor market policy showed a similar increase, expanding from slightly over 2 percent of GDP in the mid 1980s to 4.66 percent of GDP in 2003 (DARES 2010b). Today, France spends as much on labor market intervention as Sweden, the Mecca of active labor market policy.

The growth of the welfare state has been equally dramatic. Social spending in France rose from 20.8 percent of GDP in 1980 to 29.0 percent in 2005 (OECD 2011). The increase in social spending has occurred steadily and has continued well beyond the period of industrial restructuring in the 1980s. Indeed, Figure 12.3 indicates that the French welfare state has become the most expensive in the OECD.

France's break with *dirigisme* in the 1980s provided a dual impetus to the social anesthesia state. The *promise* of liberalization induced authorities to commit vast resources to the transition process, to the alleviation of social pain and political resistance, in the expectation that a more flexible labor market would quickly generate enough jobs to make such costly transitional measures unnecessary (or, at least, much less necessary). The *disappointments* of liberalization and the continuing high levels of unemployment not only made it difficult to wind down supposedly transitional early retirement measures but also drove new spending in the form of employment promotion and social assistance programs. In short, "de-*dirigisation*" and the expansion of the social anesthesia state were two sides of the same (very expensive) coin.

From Solution to Problem—The Limits of the Social Anesthesia State

The social anesthesia strategy brought real benefits to the French economy. Whereas the *dirigiste* state sought to steer the market, the social anesthesia state underwrote

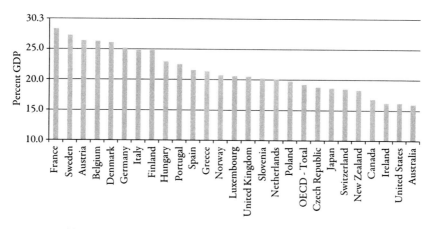

FIGURE 12.3 Public Social Expenditures as Percentage of GDP, 2007
Source: OECD (2011).

market-led, privately determined adjustment strategies. By protecting French workers from the worst effects of job loss, the state allowed employers to reorganize their companies, closing unprofitable factories and downsizing plants as necessary. In the 1980s, French industry rationalized, returned to profitability, and drew down its heavy debt. France's balance of trade shifted into surplus, as French firms met European and global competition with great success.

The social anesthesia strategy, as the label suggests, offered social as well as economic benefits. French companies were able to reorganize, much like their American or British counterparts, but worker living standards were protected. In other words, the costs of industrial adjustment were socialized to the collectivity, rather than concentrated on those who lost their jobs. The reorganization of the steel industry, described by Anthony Daley as "job loss without unemployment," exemplifies the social anesthesia state in action: employment in steel dropped from 155,700 in 1974 to 62,900 in 1987, yet thanks primarily to early retirement measures, virtually no layoffs occurred (Daley 1996: 155). French authorities have also been attentive to new social needs, establishing programs like the RMI to strengthen the safety net and address emerging gaps in the social insurance system. In short, the social anesthesia state moved France toward the market, while offering relatively humane treatment to the victims of industrial restructuring and economic liberalization.

If the social anesthesia strategy has facilitated de-*dirigisation* and industrial restructuring, it has also generated problems of its own. For starters, the social anesthesia state is very expensive. From a fiscal standpoint, the multiplication of social anesthesia measures has more than offset the savings from de-*dirigisation*. Despite the winding down of expensive industrial policy measures, state spending has increased since the early 1980s, exceeding 55 percent of GDP in 2010 (Eurostat 2011a). While one can certainly sympathize with the effort to protect the poor and vulnerable, the cost of these programs has pushed the French state to the limits of its taxing capacity.

The high cost of the social anesthesia state has also compromised public investment, a historic strength of the *dirigiste* model. In the past, French authorities invested heavily in public infrastructure and supported industrial development through lucrative government contracts. The result was an impressive array of programs and facilities—highways, high-speed trains, nuclear energy, urban transportation, advanced telecommunication, public research and development (R&D)—that enhanced the business climate. More recently, this public investment vocation has been largely crowded out by social anesthesia spending. Government spending on R&D declined from 1.26 percent of GDP in 1992 to 1.03 percent in 2002, at a time when the United States, Scandinavia, China, and India were intensifying their investments in the knowledge economy (Ministry of Industry 2004). In 2001, the government set a very high price (initially, almost €5 billion) for third-generation mobile telephone licenses (UMTS), slowing the rollout of a critical new technology in order to raise revenues to improve the country's fiscal position and offset future pension obligations (Cohen and Mougeot 2001). In 2006, having just created a special fund to reinvest the proceeds from toll roads into future highway development, the Chirac government opted to privatize the toll roads to generate funds to reduce the budget deficit. Most recently, the Chirac and Sarkozy governments seized or eliminated critical revenue sources for French local governments, which are responsible for significant investments in roads, schools, and businesses, then reneged on promises to compensate local authorities for these losses, forcing local authorities to scale back planned investments. In all these instances, social anesthesia has trumped public investment.

A second problem of the social anesthesia state concerns the labor market. The social anesthesia state is largely passive; it pays people not to work. If this represents an improvement over bailing out uncompetitive companies in order to prevent layoffs, one can imagine better uses for the money. Social democratic regimes like that of Sweden spend as much or even more than France on social programs, but the social democratic approach is centered around the so-called work line, the notion that every adult should be employed (Esping-Andersen 1990; Huber and Stephens 2001). As a result, passive measures tend to be limited, with much of the spending concentrated on "activating" policies that facilitate employment, such as education and training, relocation assistance, and low-cost public child care. Under the "active" or "social investment" model, there is an economic payoff beyond simply keeping displaced workers from protesting and blocking layoffs (Pontusson 2010). France's social anesthesia strategy offers few such benefits, few if any gains in human capital and employment.

Whatever the virtues of the social anesthesia state in facilitating the movement away from *dirigisme* in the 1980s, it has not provided a long-term solution to France's economic troubles. On the contrary, the social anesthesia state has become a problem in its own right, crowding out resources for industrial promotion and hindering employment creation. French authorities have been trying to move beyond the social anesthesia state since the mid-1990s, but as described below, their efforts have largely been checked by the legacies of the 1983 U-turn.

The Limits of Liberalism—The Presidency of Jacques Chirac

By the mid-1990s, there was widespread dissatisfaction with both prongs of French economic policy, with both market-led economic promotion and the social anesthesia state. Market-led adjustment did not seem to be reviving French growth and investment, leading to calls for renewed state direction. At the same time, the social anesthesia state seemed to be weighing on public finances and job creation, leading to calls for a curtailing of state spending and regulation.

Despite the widely expressed desire to break with France's underperforming economic model, successive governments have found it exceedingly difficult to pursue any kind of coherent economic strategy, whether inspired by neoliberal or neostatist principles. The striking feature of French economic policy in the current period is the lack of a comprehensive or even coherent approach to the double bind. French policy appears unfocused and contradictory. This is true of both neoliberal and neostatist initiatives. There have been halting efforts to move in new directions, but these attempts have generally not gone far and been contradicted by other government initiatives.

Many blame France's mercuric president from 2007 to 2012, Nicolas Sarkozy, for the directionless character of French economic policy. However, this problem predated Sarkozy. Under Sarkozy's Gaullist predecessor, Jacques Chirac, who served as president from 1995 to 2007, French policy likewise appeared anemic, contradictory, and directionless. The problem also seems to post-date Sarkozy, with the initial policies of Sarkozy's Socialist successor, François Hollande, displaying many of the same chracteristics. The reason is that French economic policy has been shaped profoundly by the legacies of the 1983 U-turn, not just presidential personalities.

This section and the next analyze some of the key initiatives of Presidents Chirac and Sarkozy. The goal is not to provide a comprehensive history of the economic policies of these two presidents but, rather, to illustrate the extent to which current government initiatives are constrained by the legacies of the 1983 U-turn. For purposes of clarity, this section focuses on Chirac's efforts to reform the social anesthesia state, and the next section focuses on Sarkozy's attempts to revive voluntarist industrial policy. The two presidents did not hew to a single economic course, however. As described briefly at the end of the next section, Chirac sought to revive industrial policy like Sarkozy, while Sarkozy strived to curb the social anesthesia state like Chirac. Moreover, a quick review of the initial policies of the Hollande presidency suggests that the forces that produced directionless economic policy continue to operate today, despite the replacement of a president of the right with a president of the left.

Chirac's tenure as president was bracketed by two failed attempts at economic liberalization: the Juppé Plan to overhaul the social security system in 1995, and the 2006 first employment contract (*contrat première embauche*, CPE), designed to increase youth hiring. These failures were due partly to poor political management and high-handed government behavior, but they stem above all else from the legacies of the 1983 U-turn.

The Juppé Plan announced in October 1995 by Chirac's prime minister, Alain Juppé, sought to curtail France's sky-high levels of social spending through a series of far-reaching reforms. These reforms included an annual parliamentary vote to set the social security budget; controls on hospitals and physicians; an increase in the retirement age and decrease in pension benefits of civil servants; and painful tax hikes, most notably in the value-added tax from 18.6 percent to 20.6 percent. Although praised initially by policy experts as a courageous response to France's Social Security deficits, the Juppé Plan was received much less favorably by the French public. Government tactics were partially to blame. The government had done little to cultivate support for the Juppé Plan. The plan had been prepared in complete secrecy, and the prime minister openly bragged that not ten people had seen his plan prior to its presentation to parliament. As a result, few actors felt any need to support a plan in which they had had no say.

Beyond tactical missteps, the Juppé Plan was undermined by two critical legacies of the 1983 U-turn. The first was the unusual trajectory of liberal reform in France. Other European countries have certainly engaged in the kinds of liberalizing reforms proposed by the Juppé Plan. They have reformed their welfare states to get spending and taxation down to manageable levels. They have also overhauled their labor markets, making them more flexible and improving the returns from employment relative to social benefits. Before launching these kinds of reforms, however, France's leaders were required to do something else first, to dismantle a dysfunctional *dirigiste* industrial policy system. They achieved this objective by expanding social protection for those who lost their jobs in the process, but this social anesthesia strategy then created additional difficulties. Thus, the French reform trajectory has entailed two rounds of liberalizing reforms—a first set of reforms to get rid of dysfunctional *dirigisme* and a second set of reforms to address some of the problems stemming from the first set of reforms, from social anesthesia measures. That is a lot of liberalizing reforms to expect from any country, particularly one not known for its love of the market.

Because of the long trajectory of post-*dirigiste* reform, the Juppé Plan ran into what might be called "reform fatigue" or "liberalization fatigue." The experience of de-*dirigisation* had led many in France to feel that they had *already* been subjected to retrenchment—and had little to show for it. Since 1983, French citizens had reluctantly accepted a series of painful liberalizing measures. Each time, they were told that the reforms in question would relaunch growth and bring down unemployment: if French inflation were held below that of Germany or Italy, then French workers would get the jobs that were going to German and Italian workers; if the state spent less on uncompetitive firms, then fast-growing start-ups would arise to take their place; if wages gave way to profits, then investment and jobs would follow; if French employers were given the right to fire, then they would be more inclined to hire. The reforms were implemented one after the other, yet economic growth remained anemic, and mass unemployment persisted. Given these disappointments, the idea embodied by the Juppé Plan that what was needed was another turn of the neoliberal screw, welfare retrenchment on top of *dirigiste* retrenchment, did not elicit great popular enthusiasm.

The second legacy of the 1983 U-turn that impeded the Juppé Plan was the unwillingness of French leaders to be honest about the government's liberalizing actions. The 1983 U-turn had been presented by the left as a slight "pause" or adjustment, rather than a radical break, and painful liberalizing measures had been blamed on Europe, rather than defended on their own terms. Although initiated by a government of the right, the Juppé Plan replicated this combination of "liberalization by stealth" and scapegoating of the EU (Gordon and Meunier 2001).

Less than six months before the Juppé Plan was announced, Jacques Chirac had secured election as president on an ambitious social agenda. Denouncing the supposed subservience of his main conservative rival to la *pensée unique*—roughly translated as "hegemonic neoliberal thought" or "Washington consensus"—Chirac pledged to increase state intervention to renew the "Republican pact" and "heal the social fracture." Yet instead of increasing social spending, Chirac and Juppé proposed to implement an austerity package.

Chirac evoked European constraints to justify the abandonment of his campaign promises; France needed to reduce its budget deficit in order to for European Monetary Union (EMU). As in 1983, a neoliberal turn was blamed on Europe, rather than defended as good for the French economy in its own right. That argument did not go over well with the French public, however. Chirac was seen as cynically casting aside his campaign promise of increased state support. He had no mandate for a liberalizing agenda; on the contrary, by embracing such an agenda so shortly after his election as president, Chirac was widely regarded as violating his mandate.

The response to the Juppé Plan was a six-week strike by civil servants and public-sector workers that paralyzed the country. What is more, French public opinion ran resolutely in favor of the strikers and against the government. In order to end the strike, Juppé was forced to abandon his public-sector pension reform. Although he maintained a tougher line toward the physicians, ultimately, this part of the reform also unraveled, leaving only the unpopular tax hikes intact.

If the Juppé Plan ruined the beginning of Chirac's tenure as president, the attempt to establish the "first employment contract" (CPE) in 2006 ruined the end. The CPE sought to address the problem of very high rates of unemployment among young people in France—on the order of double the national average (DARES 2010a). The premise behind the CPE is that restrictions on layoffs discourage employers from hiring unskilled and inexperienced workers, for fear of being unable to shed these workers should they fail to pan out. The CPE proposed to introduce a two-year probationary period for workers under the age of 26, during which time employers would be free to dismiss these employees without providing justification or compensation. The government reasoned that by making it easier to fire young people, the CPE would also make it more attractive to hire young people.

Ironically, young people, the supposed beneficiaries of the CPE, spearheaded the opposition to the reform. Once again, the government had misread public sentiment. French youths saw the CPE as relegating them to substandard employment contracts. Rather than creating jobs, the CPE would simply replace stable, secure jobs with revolving-door, two-year youth hires. Moreover, students in universities and technical institutes felt that the CPE was denying the value of their education because it lumped them in the same employment category as unskilled youths. Not coincidentally, these students formed the core of protestors against the CPE.

Like the Juppé Plan, the CPE was poorly managed politically. Chirac's prime minister, Dominique de Villepin, refused to acknowledge the students' concerns or to even meet with the protestors. Once again, though, the root problems can be traced back to the way that France broke with the *dirigiste* model in the 1980s. The expansion of the social anesthesia state increasingly deprived French authorities of the fiscal resources for negotiating deals. Whereas in the 1980s and early 1990s, governments were often trading one benefit for another—plant closings in return for early retirement, fewer industrial policy subsidies in return for greater managerial autonomy—by the late 1990s, cash-strapped governments had little to offer in the way of side-payments. Yet zero-sum reforms, when claimants are asked to give up benefits with only the vague promise of a healthier economy or public finances in return, are the most politically difficult to undertake. In the case of the CPE, French youths were offered nothing more than the hope that reducing their job security would lead to increased hiring.

Another legacy of the 1983 U-turn that worked against the CPE reform was the government's unwillingness to advocate neoliberal reform on its own terms. The CPE was framed as a social initiative, a way of addressing the suffering of French youths, rather than a neoliberal initiative. Yet the core change was to reduce the job protections of young people. If the Juppé Plan was a case of scapegoating Europe, the CPE represented "liberalization by stealth" (Gordon and Meunier 2001). Further reinforcing this stealthy image, the CPE reform was announced during school holidays in the hope of making it difficult to mobilize student opposition and was rammed through parliament, using a highly constraining confidence vote procedure (Article 49.3), to avoid prolonged debate.

Despite Prime Minister de Villepin's efforts to present French youths with a *fait accompli*, students mobilized massively against the CPE. When the unions threatened to enter the fray in support of the students, the government was forced to retreat. The abandonment of the CPE sounded the death knell of the Chirac administration's reformist efforts as well as any talk of a presidential run by Prime Minister de Villepin.

The Limits of Statism—The Sarkozy Presidency

Chirac's successor as president, Nicolas Sarkozy, issued from the same Gaullist party but positioned himself as a critic and alternative to Chirac. In contrast to the somnolence of the Chirac years, Sarkozy would be a bold reformer, a man of action (Levy, Cole, and Le Galès 2008; Sarkozy 2007). Sarkozy pledged to rehabilitate "political will," to demonstrate that political leadership could reverse economic decline and build a better France. The watchword for Sarkozy's presidential campaign was "rupture," meaning a radical break with the French past, including the actions and governing style of the Chirac administration. Initially, Sarkozy's "rupture" took the form of efforts to chip away at the social anesthesia state—to reduce government spending and taxation, while enhancing labor market flexibility. In response to the 2008 crisis, however, Sarkozy very quickly shifted to an alternative form of "rupture." France would break with neoliberal dogma and tack sharply in a neo-*dirigiste* direction.

The centerpiece of Sarkozy's response to the 2008 crisis was a revival of voluntarist industrial policy. Not all industrial policy initiatives were unique to France, of course. Like the United States and other European governments, French authorities rescued individual banks (Dexia, Caisse d'Epargne, and Banque Populaire) and put together a massive rescue package for the banking industry as a whole (OECD 2009). The €360 billion package included €40 billion in fresh capital to bolster the solvency of France's leading banks and €320 billion in loan guarantees to improve liquidity and lending. Also like other governments, the Sarkozy administration intervened to help the French auto industry (Greciano 2010). In early 2009, Sarkozy provided €7.8 billion in subsidized loans to the main domestic manufacturers (Renault, Peugeot, Citroën, Renault Trucks) along with their subcontractors and provided further support to the industry through a French version of "cash for clunkers" programs seen in the United States and Germany.

Where Sarkozy's industrial policy appeared more distinctive was in going beyond the rescue of those too big to fail. Sarkozy launched several initiatives that evoked a traditional French *dirigiste* approach not seen since the early 1980s. In November 2008, he announced the creation of the Strategic Investment Fund (*Fonds Stratégique d'Investissment*, or FSI), modeled on the sovereign wealth funds of several foreign countries (Greciano 2010). The FSI was given €20 billion in capital to invest in companies that are critical to the competitiveness of the French economy based on their potential for growth, technological mastery, savoir-faire, export potential, or brand value. In a neo-mercantilist tilt, Sarkozy also entrusted the FSI with protecting "companies that may become the prey of [foreign] predators."

The FSI was supplemented by the "grand national loan" (*grand emprunt national*) one year later. Sarkozy commissioned a study by two former prime ministers, one on the right (Alain Juppé) and one on the left (Michel Rocard), to identify priority measures for promoting French industry (Greciano 2010). Based on Juppé and Rocard's recommendations, Sarkozy launched a state loan campaign in November 2009 to raise €35 billion. Of that €35 billion, €11 billion was intended to help five to ten institutions of higher education reach world-class level, €8 billion to promote technology transfer from research to industry, €6.5 billion to support industrial small- and medium-sized enterprises (SMEs), €5 billion to fund sustainable development initiatives, and €4.5 billion to encourage France's transition to a digital economy ("Avec le grand emprunt" 2009: 2).

In November 2009, the government convened a series of meetings, the Estates General of Industry (*Etats généraux de l'industrie*), to analyze the problems of French industry. At the conclusion of the Estates General in March 2010, Sarkozy announced an aid package and spelled out a series of specific targets in the purest 1970s industrial policy style. These targets included increasing industrial production by 25 percent in five years; boosting France's share of European industry by 2 percent by 2015; sustaining employment in industry at current levels; and returning to a trade surplus in manufactured goods (excluding energy) by 2015 (French Presidency 2010).

Along with ambitious industrial policy initiatives like the Strategic Investment Fund, Grand National Loan, and Estates General of Industry, Sarkozy periodically responded to pleas and protests with pledges to save individual factories on the verge of closing (Mittal steel, Caterpillar tractors, etc.). Sarkozy also impinged on managerial decision making in ways that harken back to an earlier era. For example, in return for low-interest state loans, French auto manufacturers were required to pledge not to make any layoffs for one year and to close no plants in France for the duration of the loans. This concession did not stop Sarkozy from voicing outrage that French automakers purchase only one-third of their components from French suppliers and vowing to eventually boost the figure to two-thirds. Another source of outrage was the return of unseemly bonuses at French financial institutions in early 2009. Sarkozy responded by threatening to cancel a forthcoming €10.5 billion tranche of aid if executives did not renounce their bonuses. He established the principle that bonuses would not be allowed in companies receiving state support and imposed a one-time 50 percent tax on bonuses above €27,500 paid by banks in 2009, an initiative that was coordinated with the British government.

Sarkozy's shift in response to the 2008 financial crisis has fueled the impression that France has returned to its old *dirigiste* ways (Aghion and Cage 2010; "Leviathan Inc." 2010; "Picking winners, saving losers" 2010). Certainly, Sarkozy moved far from his initial liberalizing orientation as president. Indeed, Luc Ferry, a French philosopher and former minister of education, claims that the 2008 financial meltdown engendered an economic policy U-turn much like that of the Mitterrand administration in 1983, albeit in reverse:

> The crisis has come along and invalidated all the themes of the 2007 [presidential] campaign, the first campaign of an unabashed right finally at ease with its values. The campaign was liberal, deregulatory, and pro-American. We were going to sweep away the old world, finish with the long, Chiraquian slumber and the "French social model"! And then the crisis came. Like the left in 1983, the right makes a 180-degree turn. President Sarkozy takes on the mantle of protector, regulator, almost anti-capitalist... (Askolovitch 2010)

While appealing in its simplicity and symmetry, the argument that economic circumstances have driven a revival of *dirigiste* policy making or even a 1983 in reverse cannot stand up to close scrutiny. The claim of a new U-turn rests on a grossly exaggerated view of the changes that have occurred in French policy since 2008. More fundamentally, it ignores the powerful constraints stemming from the break with *dirigisme* in 1983.

The first constraint is intellectual or conceptual. The Sarkozy administration lacked a coherent vision or plan for French industry. It had no real strategy for the companies that it was helping. The bank bailouts initially came with no strings attached other than an obligation to increase lending in 2009, which the banks promptly ignored. It was only in the wake of the bonus scandals that the government began intervening more closely in the banks' affairs, and here, the motivation was social (to curb abusive bonus practices) rather than economic.

Much the same can be said of the aid to the automobile industry. The government did not pursue any kind of economic vision. It did not seek to accelerate the pace of investment or development of new car models. It did not condition aid on the introduction of greener hybrid or electric cars. Instead, as with the banks, the government's concerns were social—to prevent factory closings and layoffs. Far from a voluntarist industrial policy, the rescue of the bank and auto industries seems reminiscent of the worst failings of the tail-end of the *dirigiste* era, when the promotion of innovation and the industries of the future gave way to bailouts of lame ducks for the sake of putting out social brushfires and preserving jobs (Berger 1981; Cohen 1989; Levy 1999).

A second limitation on the return to state activism was fiscal. The burden of the social anesthesia state meant that the government lacked the financial resources to pursue an ambitious economic agenda. Even before the recession, France's budget deficit exceeded EMU Stability Pact rules (3.4 percent of GDP in 2008, as opposed to a legal ceiling of 3.0 percent of GDP and a Eurozone average of 1.5 percent of GDP). So, too, did government debt, which now exceeds 90 percent of GDP, some 30 percent of GDP above the level authorized by the Stability Pact (National Institute of Statistics and Economic Studies 2012). Consequently, the Sarkozy administration was extremely reluctant to establish new spending commitments.

Many of Sarkozy's signature industrial policy initiatives were constructed with an eye to limiting the government's financial obligations. The first €10.5 billion capital infusion for French banks came not from the state but rather from the state's allied financial institution, the *Caisse des Dépôts et Consignations* (CDC). The CDC receives cheap capital primarily in the form of tax-exempt funds collected by savings banks and the post office. In return, it performs various public missions, most notably funding the construction of social housing and acting as a long-term investor in many of France's most prominent companies (including about one-half of the CAC 40, or the forty leading enterprises listed on the Paris bourse). The government tapped the CDC not only for the first round of bank recapitalizations but also for one-half the costs of the Strategic Investment Fund (FSI). Moreover, just €3 billion of the government's €10 billion share represented fresh spending; the other €7 billion came from the state's transfer of its minority shareholdings in a number of privatized companies (including Air France and Renault).

The €35 billion "grand national loan" has also involved a limited financial commitment by the government. For starters, as the name indicates, the program relied on long-term borrowing, rather than direct outlays. Indeed, to avoid drawing attention to that fact, the program was renamed "investments in the future" in 2010. Moreover, €13 billion of the €35 billion came from the repayment of loans by French banks rather than new borrowing. On the spending side, €19 billion of the €35 billion was committed to higher education at a time when the Sarkozy government was cutting educational spending and employment from year to year. Thus, to some extent, the "investments in the future" wound up replacing funding cuts in the government's regular budgets. Sarkozy's plan to revive French manufacturing was even more tight-fisted. Despite the ambitious objectives (increasing industrial production by 25 percent in five years, etc.), the administration committed barely €1 billion to the enterprise.

Although this section and the last have analyzed the liberalizing initiatives of President Chirac and the statist initiatives of President Sarkozy, respectively, it is important to note that both presidents engaged in both kinds of policies. During his second term in office, from 2002 to 2007, Chirac launched several voluntarist initiatives, which confronted many of the same constraints as Sarkozy's industrial policy (Clift 2008; Cohen 2007). An "Agency of Industrial Innovation" (AII) was established to encourage French multinationals to launch high-tech projects in such areas as energy, multimedia networks, and nanotechnologies. The AII fell victim to the funding squeeze caused by the social anesthesia state, receiving less than €1 billion, and its aid to industry had to be approved by the European Commission, creating long delays. The organization was eliminated after barely two years in existence.

Another industrial policy initiative of the Chirac administration was the creation of a series of territorially based "competitiveness poles," with the idea of fostering collaboration and synergies among local companies, research centers, and universities. Like the AII, the competitiveness poles received limited funding: dozens of competitiveness poles were recognized in 2005, but the global budget was set at only €750 million. The same could be said of a new bank, Oséo, which was created to meet the needs of SMEs, especially in high tech. Oséo received little in the way of fresh money. It was essentially a repackaging of preexisting programs in support of start-ups and SMEs: the National Agency for the Commercialization of Research (ANVAR), the Bank of SMEs (BDPME), and the French Guarantee Company (SOFARIS).

Finally, in the name of "economic patriotism," the Chirac administration enacted laws to protect strategic French sectors against hostile takeovers by predatory foreign multinationals. Lacking any kind of institutionalized thinking capacity about industrial policy, however, this initiative was not accompanied by any kind of coherent definition of what made an industry "strategic." The official list of "strategic sectors" included casinos among other industries! In another sign of improvisation, the government rushed to the defense of a French food conglomerate, Danone, which was rumored to be a takeover target of the American company, Pepsi, suggesting that yogurt, too had become a strategic sector.

If the Chirac administration dabbled in industrial policy, Sarkozy gave considerable attention to economic liberalization. In contrast to Chirac, Sarkozy was relatively candid about his commitment to reducing and restructuring the social anesthesia state during his campaign for president. Initially, he enacted tax cuts and pledged to shrink state spending by 1 percent of GDP per year. The signature reform was a so-called fiscal shield, limiting the total direct tax liability of any individual to 50 percent of earnings. Even at this point, Sarkozy was more effective at cutting taxes than cutting spending, drawing warnings from the European Commission about excessive budget deficits.

When the financial crisis hit in 2008, Sarkozy expanded spending and the deficit as part of his commitment to a voluntarist response to the crisis. The move was not appreciated by Sarkozy's conservative electorate, and following the right's worst showing in the history of the Fifth Republic in local elections in early 2010, Sarkozy tacked away from Keynesian demand stimulus, announcing that deficit reduction was now his top priority. For about a year, Sarkozy attempted to eliminate France's deficit solely through spending cuts, but when the sovereign debt crisis raised the specter of a downgrading of France's rating and potential difficulty borrowing, Sarkozy shifted ground again, agreeing to make tax increases part of the deficit reduction package. In the end, he even abandoned his cherished "fiscal shield."

Thus, Sarkozy's economic policy was directionless, not only in swinging wildly between neo-*dirigisme* and economic liberalism but also in pursuing three variants of liberalism that sometimes contradicted one another: tax and spending cuts at the beginning of the administration, in 2007–08; then spending cuts without tax increases in 2010; finally, in 2011–12, both spending cuts and tax increases, including the repeal of virtually all of the administration's own tax cuts from the initial 2007–08 period. Overall, Sarkozy's fiscal policy can scarcely be described as neoliberal: from 2007 to 2010, revenues declined slightly, from 49.9 percent to 49.5 percent of GDP (Eurostat 2011b), while public expenditures surged from 52.6 percent to 56.6 percent of GDP (Eurostat 2011a). Nor did Sarkozy's actions impress the bond rating agencies. In January 2012, Standard & Poor's downgraded France's rating from AAA to AA+ ("C'était Sarkozy: Histoire d'une ambition" 2012: 140).

French economic policy was directionless under both Chirac and Sarkozy. Both leaders experimented with neo-*dirigiste* industrial policy, but they lacked the intellectual, institutional, and fiscal capacities to make a significant impact. Both presidents also dabbled with liberalizing reform. Although some changes were made, many of the most important initiatives, such as the Juppé Plan and CPE, were checked by the resistance of a population that is tired and skeptical of the virtues of neoliberal reform. In the end, the modest liberal reforms that were introduced did not suffice to stop the upward trajectory of public spending and unemployment (DARES 2011a; Eurostat 2011a).

Although it is tempting to blame Presidents Chirac and Sarkozy, the anemic and directionless character of French economic policy is the product primarily of the legacies of the 1983 U-turn, as opposed to personalities. On the one hand, the agenda of economic liberalization is highly contested due to a political discourse that has long denied the extent of liberalization taking place or blamed liberalization on the EU and to the sentiment of much of the French public that liberalization has already been tried and did not work. On the other hand, the agenda of voluntarist industrial policy has been hamstrung by limited state capacities resulting from the dismantling of many *dirigiste* institutions and policy instruments in the 1980s and 1990s and the crowding out of public finances by the social anesthesia state. Chirac and Sarkozy certainly varied greatly in their leadership styles, but they operated under the same constraints, and the directionless character of their respective economic policies attests to the salience of these constraints.

The initial policies of François Hollande, who was elected as president in May 2012, display a similar directionless character. Hollande's presidential campaign offered a synthesis of neostatist and neoliberal objectives (Hollande 2012). Hollande contended that by reversing the tax breaks conceded to affluent individuals and corporations by governments of the right over the preceeding ten years, it would be possible to both boost public investment and industrial policy, a neostatist agenda, and meet France's obligations to the European Commission to reduce its budget deficit from 4.5 percent of GDP in 2012, to 3.0 percent in 2013 and zero in 2017, a neoliberal agenda. Once in office, however, Hollande has fallen short on both counts.

On the neostatist front, Hollande called for a revival of industrial policy and created a new "Ministry of Productive Recovery" to spearhead this initiative. Like his predecessors, though, Hollande had no particular vision for how to achieve productive recovery. For the most part, the ministry's work has consisted of responding to company announcements of plant closings and mass layoffs by trying to find new investors or, at a minimum, improve the compensation package of employees who lose their jobs. The government has been willing to put small amounts of money into rescue packages, but these sums have generally been too modest to lure outside investors. In any case, the kind of work being performed by the Ministry of Productive Recovery has centered squarely on the social mission of preserving the industrial jobs of the past, as opposed to the economic mission of creating the high-tech or service jobs of the future.

Along with the commitment to productive recovery, Hollande promised a revival of public investment. Specifically, he promised to establish 150,000 subsidized jobs, mostly in the public sector, for at-risk youths, to make 60,000 new hires in education, and to construct 150,000 social housing units annually (Hollande 2012). These objectives are exceedingly modest. The last government of the left, the Jospin government created 350,000 public and non-profit jobs between 1997 and 2002, and these jobs ran for five years, rather than the one to three years in the case of Hollande's program. The 60,000 new hires in education will not suffice to replace the staffing reductions under the Sarkozy government. Moreover, Hollande has announced that total public sector employment will remain stable, meaning that most other ministries will be required to reduce staffing to offset the hires in education (Ministry of the Economy and Finance and Delegated Ministry for the Budget 2012).

As modest as the government's public investment objectives may have been, Hollande has already scaled back some of these goals. The government lacks the means to fund the construction of 150,000 social housing units annually. The mechanism that Hollande proposed was to immediately double the maximum amount of money that French citizens could place in tax-exempt savings accounts, with the proceeds then used to finance social housing and aid to small business (Hollande 2012). The problem is that boosting savings in tax-exempt savings accounts would divert savings away from private banks. Given the parlous condition of French banks as a result of the financial crisis and exposure to debt in Southern Europe, the banks were able to convince the government to water down its proposal. Instead of doubling the maximum allowable placement in tax-exempt accounts immediately, as promised, Hollande has announced that the government will raise the ceiling gradually, over the course of his five-year mandate. Of course, the growth of spending on public housing and aide to small business will be slowed accordingly.

Like his effort to renew industrial policy and public investment, Hollande's efforts to rein in France's deficits have fallen well short of expectations. The €29 billion to be raised from taxes on the affluent and corporations are insufficient to meet the government's deficit targets. Already in July 2012, the combination of slower-than-expected economic growth and increased spending by the Sarkozy goverment toward the end of a tight electoral campaign forced Hollande's administration to introduce an €8.7 billion austerity package just to meet the 2012 deficit target of 4.5 percent of GDP. In order to hit the 3.0 percent target for 2013, the government reneged on its promise that significant spending cuts would be unnecessary. The 2013 budget projects €10 billion in spending cuts along with €20 billion in tax hikes (Ministry of the Economy and Finance and Delegated Ministry for the Budget 2012). Moreover, outside analysts anticipate that further austerity measures will be necessary, most likely including increases in sales and earnings taxes that hit low-income and middle-class citizens, as economic growth continues to fall short of forecasts. Even under its own relatively optimistic growth projections, the 2013 budget concedes that France will be unable to honor its commitment to the European Commission to balance its budget by 2017 (Ministry of the Economy and Finance and Delegated Ministry for the Budget 2012).

François Hollande's election was seen by many as signaling the end of the EU's emphasis on austerity as the solution to the sovereign debt crisis. Hollande himself stated that he would not ratify the European Treaty on Stability, Coordination, and Governance (TSCG), which establishes tough new rules and punishments to ensure fiscal discipline, unless pro-growth measures were added. Yet the TSCG was not amended, and only very limited pro-growth measures have been agreed-upon at the EU level, most notably some €120 billion in new infrastructure spending, most of it coming from unspent moneys lying around various EU programs. Still, Hollande agreed to ratify the TSCG, even as France appears likely to fall under the punitive provisions for excessive deficits.

François Hollande has nearly five years left as president. Obviously, it would be premature to pass definitive judgment on his record. That said, a change of political leadership does not appear to have altered the directionless, contradictory character of French economic policy. Hollande has tacked back and forth between neostatist and neoliberal objectives, achieving little sucess in either undertaking. His disapproval rating has already surpassed 50 percent in a series of polls. Of course, the president has made mistakes, and electoral debts have had to be paid, but like Chirac and Sarkozy before him, Hollande appears to be fundamentally constrained by the fiscal, institutional, and political legacies of France's break with *dirigisme* a quarter-century ago. The government lacks the ideas, institutions, and resources for a neostatist strategy, while Hollande's campaign promise of a painless return to fiscal balance has made it difficult for him to ask for sacrifices, especially on behalf of the timeworn and increasingly contested objective of advancing European integration.

Conclusion: The Double Shift and the Double Bind

In the introduction to this volume, the authors portray states as trapped between pressures pulling in opposite directions—toward neoliberalism, on the one hand, and toward state promotion of industrial development and adjustment, on the other hand. Although this "double bind" is present in all countries, the dilemma seems especially acute in France.

Contemporary French leaders like Jacques Chirac and Nicolas Sarkozy have found it extremely difficult to pursue either prong of the double bind. Their initiatives, whether of neoliberal or neo-*dirigiste* inspiration, have consistently run up against the legacies of the 1983 U-turn: a liberalizing movement that has been disguised, rather than legitimated; a stripped-down industrial policy state, lacking the vision and tools for voluntarist action; and a set of passive social policies, paying people not to work and swallowing fiscal resources that are desperately needed for other purposes. The legacies of the 1983 U-turn have imposed powerful constraints on French leaders a quarter-century later, imbuing their economic policy with a halting, anemic, and directionless character.

The French case points to the significance of the interconnections between social concerns and the double bind. The biggest obstacle to the double bind in France today is the Polanyian double shift undertaken almost three decades ago—the social anesthesia state that accompanied and enabled the break with the *dirigiste* model. The dramatic growth of social- and labor-market spending has deprived would-be reformers of the fiscal resources to pursue either state economic promotion or neoliberal tax cutting. In other words, the social anesthesia state has crowded out both prongs of the double bind, both neoliberalism and state promotion.

Pushing the argument further, it would appear that resolving the social question is central to resolving the double bind. Whatever the virtues of neoliberalism and state promotion, respectively, France is unlikely to be able to commit significant resources to either project until the social anesthesia state has been curtailed dramatically. Because of the double shift in the 1980s, French reformers today find themselves confronting not just a double bind but arguably a triple bind or triad. To the double-bind tension between neoliberalism and state promotion has been added a Polanyian tension between neoliberal and statist economic development strategies, on the one hand, and social protection, on the other hand.

France has had a long and tortured relationship with the triple bind. The postwar *dirigiste* growth strategy privileged state guidance at the expense of the market, but also of subordinate groups, which were marginalized and neglected. That exclusionary approach was shattered by the near revolution of May 1968 and subsequent mobilization of the working class. In the 1970s and early 1980s, the pursuit of economic modernization was increasingly subordinated to social protection, and the *dirigiste* model entered into crisis. The shift from the *dirigiste* state to the social anesthesia state beginning in 1983 represented an effort to synthesize social protection and economic development—this time, centered on market promotion, as opposed to state guidance. Once again, though, the synthesis of economic promotion and social protection has proven elusive, as the social anesthesia state has impeded French economic performance and job creation. Thus, across the twists and turns of postwar policy making, French authorities have never been able to truly resolve the social question. Until they do, we can expect them to remain equally unable to resolve the double bind.

Acknowledgments

The author wishes to thank Dan Breznitz and John Zysman for their comments and suggestions on earlier drafts of this chapter along with the Alfred P. Sloan Foundation for financial support and the Berkeley Roundtable on the International Economy (BRIE) for research and administrative support.

References

Aghion, Philippe, and Julia Cage. (2010). "Repenser le role de l'Etat dans la croissance: Perspectives d'après-crise." *Regards sur l'actualité—Crise: le retour de l'Etat?* (362): 48–59.
Askolovitch, Claude. (2010). "Luc Ferry: 'Sarkozy doit revendiquer le gaullisme.'" *Journal de Dimanche*, March 26.
"Avec le grand emprunt, Nicolas Sarkozy veut r é ussir l'apr è s-crise." *Les Echos*. 20473: 2. December 15, 2009. Accessed October 4, 2012, available http://archives.lesechos.fr/archives/2009/LesEchos/20573-9-ECH.htm.
Berger, Suzanne. (1981). "Lame Ducks and National Champions: Industrial Policy in the Fifth Republic." In *The Fifth Republic at Twenty*, edited by William Andrews and Stanley Hoffmann, 160–78. Albany, NY: SUNY Press.
Cahuc, Pierre, and André Zylberberg. (2009). *Les réformes ratées du Président Sarkozy*. Paris: Flammarion.
"C'était Sarkozy: Histoire d'une ambition" [*Libération* hors série]. *Libération*, March 2012.
Clift, Ben. (2008). "Economic Policy." In *Developments in French Politics 4*, edited by Alistair Cole, Patrick Le Galès, and Jonah Levy, 191–208. Houndmills, UK: Palgrave Macmillan.
Cohen, Elie. (1989). *L'etat brancardier: Politiques du déclin industriel (1974–1984)*. Paris: Calmann-Lévy.
Cohen, Elie. (1992). *Le Colbertisme "high tech": Economie des telecom et du grand projet*. Paris: Hachette.
Cohen, Elie. (2007). "Industrial policies in France: The old and the new." *Journal of Industry Competition and Trade* 7(3): 213–27.
Cohen, Elie. (2008). "Les trois erreurs de Nicolas Sarkozy." *Telos*. (http://www.telos-eu.com/fr/article/sarkozy_le_reformateur).
Cohen, Elie, and Michel Bauer. (1985). *Les grandes manoeuvres industrielles*. Paris: Belfond.

Cohen, Elie, and Michel Mougeot. (2001). Enchères et gestion publique. CAE Report #3, La Documentation Française, Paris.
Cohen, Stephen. (1977). *Modern Capitalist Planning: The French Model*. Berkeley: University of California Press.
Daley, Anthony. (1996). *Steel, State, and Labor: Mobilization and Adjustment in France*. Pittsburgh, PA: University of Pittsburgh Press.
DARES. (1996). *40 ans de politique de l'emploi*. Paris: Direction de l'Animation de la Recherche, des Etudes et des Statistiques.
DARES. (2000). *La politique de l'emploi en 1999*. Paris: Direction de l'Animation de la Recherche, des Etudes et des Statistiques.
DARES. (2010a). "Emploi et chômage des 15–29 ans en 2009." *DARES Analyses* October (072): 1–12.
DARES. (2010b). La dépense pour l'emploi et les allègements généraux. *La dépense pour l'emploi*, French Ministry of Labor, Employment, and Health. March 25, 2010 (http://www.travail-emploi-sante.gouv.fr/etudes-recherche-statistiques-de,76/statistiques,78/politique-de-l-emploi-et-formation,84/donnees-transversales,252/la-depense-pour-l-emploi,2087.html).
DARES. (2011a). "Emploi, chômage, population active: Bilan de l'année 2010." *DARES Analyses* August (65): 1–24.
DARES. (2011b). *Tableau de bord trimestriel: Activité des seniors et politiques d'emploi*. Paris: French Ministry of Labor, Employment, and Health.
Esping-Andersen, Gøsta. (1990). *The Three Worlds of Welfare Capitalism*. Princeton, NJ: Princeton University Press.
Eurostat. (2011a). *Total General Government Expenditure % GDP* (http://epp.eurostat.ec.europa.eu/tgm/table.do?tab=table&init=1&language=en&pcode=tec00023&plugin=1).
Eurostat. (2011b). *Total General Government Revenue % of GDP* (http://epp.eurostat.ec.europa.eu/tgm/table.do?tab=table&init=1&language=en&pcode=tec00021&plugin=1).
French Presidency. (2010). *Conclusion des etats généraux de l'industrie*. Marignane, France: Dossier de Presse.
Gordon, Philip, and Sophie Meunier. (2001). *The French Challenge: Adapting to Globalization*. Washington, D.C.: Brookings Institution Press.
Greciano, Pierre-Alain. (2008). Economie: Une année mitigée. In *La France en 2007: Chronique politique, économique, et sociale*, 67–88. Paris: La Documentation Française.
Greciano, Pierre-Alain. (2010). Economie: Vers l'éclaircie? In *La France en 2009: Chronique politique, économique, et sociale*, 67–92. Paris: La Documentation Française.
Hall, Peter. (1986). *Governing the Economy: The Politics of State Intervention in Britain and France*. New York: Oxford University Press.
Hall, Peter. (1990). The State and the Market. In *Developments in French Politics 2*, edited by Peter Hall, Jack Hayward, and Howard Machin, 172–88. London: Macmillan.
Howell, Chris. (2008). Between State and Market: Crisis and Transformation in French Industrial Relations. In *Developments in French Politics 4*, edited by Alistair Cole, Patrick Le Galès, and Jonah Levy, 209–26. London: Palgrave.
Hollande, François. (2012). *Le changement, c'est maintenant: Mes 60 engagements pour la France* [Change is Now: My Sixty Promises for France], October 4 (http://www.parti-socialiste.fr/articles/les-60-engagements-pour-la-france-le-projet-de-francois-hollande).
Huber, Evelyne, and John Stephens. (2001). *Development and Crisis of the Welfare State: Parties and Policies in Global Markets*. Chicago: University of Chicago Press.

"Leviathan Inc." (2010). *The Economist*, August 7–13: 9–10.
Levy, Jonah. (1999). *Tocqueville's Revenge: State, Society, and Economy in Contemporary France*. Cambridge, MA: Harvard University Press.
Levy, Jonah (2000). France: Directing Adjustment? In *Welfare and Work in the Open Economy: Vol. II. Diverse Responses to Common Challenges*, edited by Fritz Scharpf and Vivien Schmidt, 308–50. Oxford: Oxford University Press.
Levy, Jonah. (2005a). Economic Policy. In *Developments in French Politics 3*, edited by Alistair Cole, Patrick Le Galès, and Jonah Levy, 170–94. London: Palgrave.
Levy, Jonah. (2005b). Redeploying the French State: Liberalization and Social Policy in France. In *Beyond Continuity: Explorations in the Dynamics of Advanced Political Economies*, edited by Kathleen Thelen and Wolfgang Streeck, 103–26. Oxford: Oxford University Press.
Levy, Jonah. (2008). "From the dirigiste state to the social anesthesia state: French economic policy in the longue durée." *Modern and Contemporary France* 16(4): 417–35.
Levy, Jonah, Alistair Cole, and Patrick Le Galès. (2008). From Chirac to Sarkozy: A New France? In *Developments in French Politics 4*, edited by Alistair Cole, Patrick Le Galès, and Jonah Levy, 1–21. London: Palgrave-Macmillan.
Levy, Jonah, Mari Miura, and Gene Park. (2006). Exiting *Etatisme*? New Directions in State Policy in France and Japan. In *The State after Statism: New State Activities in the Age of Globalization and Liberalization*, edited by Jonah Levy, 92–146. Cambridge, MA: Harvard University Press.
Ministry of the Economy and Finance and Delegated Ministry for the Budget. (2012). *Projet de Loi de Finances 2013: Les chiffres clés [2013 Finance Bill: Key Figures]* (Bill #235, released September 28, 2012, Paris, National Assembly), October 4 (http://www.assemblee-nationale.fr/14/projets/pl0235.asp).
Ministry of Industry. (2004). *L'effort français de recherche et développement (R&D)* (http://www.industrie.gouv.fr/observat/bilans/bord/cpci2004/cpci2004_f21b.pdf).
Monnier, Jean-Marie. (2009). Politique fiscale: Une mise en perspective. In *L'Etat de la France, Edition 2009–2010*, edited by Elisabeth Lau, 182–92. Paris: La Découverte.
National Institute of Statistics and Economic Studies. (2012). "The public debt reached 1832.6 billion Euros." In *The General Government Debt According to the Maastricht Definition—Second Quarter of 2012* (released September 28, 2012). Paris: INSEE (http://www.insee.fr/en/themes/info-rapide.asp?id=40).
OECD. (2009). *Economic Surveys: France, 2009*. Paris: OECD.
OECD. (2011). Social Expenditure—Aggregated Data. In *OECD.StatExtracts* (http://stats.oecd.org/Index.aspx?datasetcode=SOCX_AGG).
Peillon, Luc. (2010). "Retraites: 'La mobilisation devra être exceptionnelle pour entraîner le retrait' de la réforme." *Libération*, September 2, 2010 (http://www.liberation.fr/politiques/1201333-retraites-quelles-marges-de-man-uvre).
"Picking winners, saving losers." (2010). *The Economist*, August 7–13: 68–70.
Polanyi, Karl. (1944). *The Great Transformation*. Boston: Beacon.
Pontusson, Jonas. (2010). Once Again a Model: Nordic Social Democracy in a Globalized World. In *What's Left of the Left? Democrats and Social Democrats in Challenging Times*, edited by James Cronin, George Ross, and James Shoch, 89–115. Durham, NC: Duke University Press.
Sarkozy, Nicolas. (2007). *Ensemble, tout devient possible* (http://www.politiquessociales.net/IMG/pdf/monprojet_1_.pdf).

Sarkozy, Nicolas. (2008). "Le texte intégral du discours de Nicolas Sarkozy à Toulon" (speech delivered September 25, 2008 in Toulon, France). *Le Nouvel Observateur*, December 2, 2011 (http://tempsreel.nouvelobs.com/sources-brutes/20111202.OBS5859/le-texte-integral-du-discours-de-nicolas-sarkozy-a-toulon.html).

Schmidt, Vivien. (1996). *From State to Market? The Transformation of French Business and Government*. New York: Cambridge University Press.

Shonfield, Andrew. (1965). *Modern Capitalism: The Changing Balance of Public and Private Power*. Oxford: Oxford University Press.

Szarka, Joseph. (2009). "Nicolas Sarkozy as political strategist: Rupture tranquille or policy continuity?" *Modern and Contemporary France* 17(4): 407–22.

Zysman, John. (1977). *Political Strategies for Industrial Order: State, Market, and Industry in France*. Berkeley: University of California Press.

Zysman, John. (1978). The French State in the International Economy. In *Between Power and Plenty: Foreign Economic Policies in Advanced Industrial States*, edited by Peter Katzenstein, 255–93. Madison: University of Wisconsin Press.

Zysman, John. (1983). *Governments, Markets, and Growth: Financial Systems and the Politics of Industrial Change*. Ithaca, NY: Cornell University Press.

13 Japan's Information Technology Challenge
Steven K. Vogel

JAPAN HAS NOT only suffered from dismal macroeconomic performance over the past two decades but has lost its edge in areas of its greatest competitive strength, such as electronics, including information and communications technology (ICT) hardware. Meanwhile, it has failed to challenge the global leaders in areas of weakness, such as software and services, including ICT services. Japanese firms lag their competitors by many standard measures of industrial performance, such as growth, profits, and productivity. Japanese corporations continue to move manufacturing and other core functions abroad, while foreign companies are not attracted to Japan as a location for production.

So, what went wrong? In short, recent developments in the global economy—including the decomposition of production and the services transformation described in the introduction to this volume—have severely undermined Japan's institutional strengths and exacerbated its weaknesses. Yet that answer only begs another question: Why have the Japanese government and corporations failed to adapt better to these challenges? In this chapter, I argue that they have favored incremental reforms designed to reinforce valued institutions rather than to generate new sources of competitive strength. Specifically, Japanese firms have preferred strategies to preserve long-term relationships with workers, banks, suppliers, and other business partners, and to leverage the benefits of these relationships when possible. And these firms have lobbied the government to enact incremental reforms to facilitate corporate restructuring without undermining the traditional basis of their competitive advantage. Japan's IT (information technology) challenge also reflects more fundamental long-term problems: an erosion in the confidence and capacity of the government bureaucracy, a relative decline in education and training standards, and a lag in international engagement. The March 2011 earthquake, tsunami, and nuclear crisis have only exacerbated Japan's competitive challenge in the short term, straining government finances, disrupting supply chains, and constraining the power supply. In the longer term, however, the disaster could galvanize the government and industry to embrace more radical reforms.

Moreover, I postulate that the Japanese government has produced the wrong mix of industrial promotion and market liberalization in its ICT strategy. That is, the government's primary error was not in failing to emulate the American model of tough antitrust policy and aggressive procompetitive regulatory reform, or in failing to preserve its own state-led industrial policy model. The government was right to pursue a strategy that combined state support with liberalization—but it produced the wrong mix. It failed to deliver strong state support where it was most needed and procompetitive policies where they were most appropriate. In contrast, the South Korean and Nordic country governments devised more effective combinations of government policies for ICT sectors.

This chapter cannot prove or disprove these propositions, but it can achieve several more modest objectives. It will outline Japan's competitive performance, and survey government and corporate responses to recent developments. It will review the evidence for the foregoing propositions, deploying comparisons across time periods, nations, sectors, and companies to gain analytical leverage. Let us turn first to a quick survey of the facts of Japan's competitive decline, and then review the elements of the argument in turn.

Japan's Decline: The Facts

Japan's postwar economic miracle did not quietly fizzle out but, rather, exploded in grandiose fashion. In a period of market euphoria in the late 1980s—now referred to simply as "the Bubble"—investors poured money into the real estate and stock markets. When the Bank of Japan finally raised interest rates, the economy plunged into a prolonged slump from which it has never fully recovered. Japan's share of the global economy fell from 14.3 percent in 1990 to 8.9 percent in 2008, and Japan dropped from third place in per-capita gross domestic product (GDP) in 2000 to twenty-third in 2008 (METI 2010b: 5).

Japan's descent from industrial dominance arrived later, evolved more slowly, and varied considerably by sector—and yet the turn of fortunes was equally stunning. Japanese manufacturers' global market share dropped from 76 percent to 3 percent from 1987 to 2004 in DRAM chips; from 95 percent to 20 percent from 1997 to 2006 in DVD players; from 100 percent to 5 percent from 1995 to 2005 in liquid crystal display (LCD) panels; from 100 percent to 20 percent from 2003 to 2007 in car navigation systems; from 45 percent to 21 percent from 2004 to 2007 in solar energy panels; and from 90 percent to 48 percent from 2000 to 2008 in lithium ion batteries (see Figure 13.1) (METI 2010a: 3; METI 2010b: 22). One government report estimates that Japanese electronics companies produced 70 percent of an iPod in 2005 but only 20 percent of an iPad in 2010 (METI 2010a: 4). Japan's share of OECD (Organisation of Economic Co-operation and

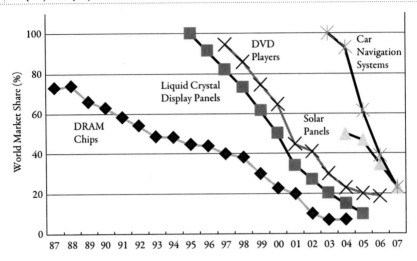

FIGURE 13.1 World Market Share, 1987–2007
Source: Ogawa (2008).

Development) ICT goods exports dropped from 20.6 percent in 1996 to 12.1 percent in 2008 (see Table 13.1).

Meanwhile, Japanese firms are losing market share in areas of weakness (less than 5 percent global market share) as well as areas of strength (greater than 25 percent of global market share).[1] Japan's share of OECD ICT services exports plummeted from 8.0 percent in 1996 to 0.8 percent in 2008 (Table 13.2). Japanese firms still have only 0.9 percent of the global market in applications software and 2.3 percent in system software. U.S. firms continue to dominate critical market segments, including operating systems (98 percent), search engines (96 percent), and database management software (85 percent) (METI 2010a: 5).

Japan also lags by some standard measures of business performance. Japanese corporate profits are considerably lower than foreign firms' in key sectors: 58 percent of foreign firm returns in IT and 36 percent in semiconductors.[2] Japanese IT firms had operating profits from 1 percent (Sanyo, NEC, Toshiba) to 8 percent (NTT Data), while their international competitors posted rates from 8 percent (Hewlett Packard) to 36 percent

TABLE 13.1
SHARE OF OECD ICT GOODS EXPORTS (PERCENTAGE)

	1996	2002	2008
Japan	20.6	15.1	12.1
United States	24.7	21.3	18.4
Germany	8.5	10.2	11.7
Korea	6.1	8.7	12.2

Source: Adapted from OECD Information Technology Outlook (2010).

TABLE 13.2

SHARE OF OECD ICT SERVICES EXPORTS (PERCENTAGE)

	1996	2002	2008
Japan	8.0	2.7	0.8
United States	19.6	13.8	11.5
Germany	11.2	11.0	10.7
Korea	2.0	0.6	0.5

Source: Adapted from *OECD Information Technology Outlook* (2010).

(Microsoft).[3] Ministry of Economy, Trade, and Industry (METI) officials note with some alarm that Samsung's profits have surpassed those of Japan's top six electronics companies combined.[4] Japan ranks twentieth among thirty OECD countries in labor productivity.[5] And Japan's rate of corporate start-ups now lags behind corporate failures, meaning that the total number of firms is declining (METI 2010b: 19).

Japanese manufacturers continue to shift operations abroad. One METI survey finds that 90 of 170 companies responding were considering moving some or all of their manufacturing operations abroad; and some were even contemplating a shift of development functions (thirty companies), research functions (eight companies), or headquarters functions (four companies) (METI 2010b: 10). Meanwhile, foreign companies are not attracted to Japan as a business location. In a survey of foreign companies selecting a location for Asian operations, Japan ceded first choice for overall operations and for R&D (research and development) headquarters to China (METI 2010b: 29).

Japan's Challenges

Japan's weak macroeconomic performance contributed to declining industrial competitiveness because it left the government and the private sector with diminished resources to invest toward future productivity gains.[6] Economic stagnation pushed government officials to stress macroeconomic recovery over long-term growth, and corporate executives to favor cost cutting over strategic investments. By the 2000s, the government's budget deficit presented a major constraint on increases in government spending for IT infrastructure and R&D. The long-term appreciation of the yen undermined Japan's export competitiveness and pushed manufacturers to move production abroad. Japan has suffered even more acute exchange-rate pressure since 2010 when the yen appreciated to the range of 80 yen to a dollar.

Furthermore, the changes in the global economy highlighted in this volume have posed particularly severe challenges for Japan. Specifically, the decomposition of production has undermined the competitive advantage of Japanese business models that rely on integral production plus long-term relationships with suppliers, banks, and workers to foster incremental advances in production processes. Japanese manufacturers have maintained a stronger competitive position in products characterized by integral production (automobiles, digital cameras) than in those with more modular production (personal computers, cellular telephones) (METI 2010b: 24). And the services transformation has tested Japanese manufacturers because it relies on capabilities in areas of their weakness—such as services, software, entertainment, and system integration—or on ties with firms that possess those capabilities.

The recent evolution of international competition in ICT sectors is not one discrete change but rather a cluster of developments, and these developments have affected different industrial sectors and different firms in Japan in distinct ways. So let us unpack the distinct challenges further before evaluating how Japanese firms and the government have responded. For example, the decomposition of production has hit Japan's integrated electronics manufacturers particularly hard. In the United States, the disintegration of the production chain drove the transformation of the electronics and information industries. U.S. antitrust policies broke up the supply chain, and regulatory reforms in finance and telecommunications fueled user-driven innovation. This heralded the "Wintelist" era (named for Microsoft Windows plus Intel), in which integrated electronics firms such as AT&T or IBM no longer controlled technological standards but shared control with downstream suppliers, including software companies and semiconductor specialists (Borrus and Zysman 1997; Newman and Zysman 2006). In the earlier period, Japan's integrated electronics producers were seen to have an advantage over American merchant semiconductor manufacturers because their computer divisions could subsidize their semiconductor operations (Borrus 1988). In the Internet age, however, this integration became a liability as Japanese electronics firms were slow to capture either the cost benefits of modular production or the innovative potential of independent software and components firms (Cole and Whittaker 2006). Some Japanese electronics companies have sold facilities to manufacturing service companies, but they have done so more as a means of cutting costs than as a strategic reorganization of the production process.

Japanese companies have not simply been slow to react to the new competitive environment: they have been reluctant to undermine the institutional foundations of their competitive advantage. For example, these companies have benefited from collaborative relationships with their suppliers in which the suppliers have customized components or software for them, have met specific standards for delivery or service, and have collaborated on product or process innovation. So they have been wary of moving toward more arm's-length relationships with suppliers or of standardizing technical interfaces.

The decomposition of production has fueled the shift toward more open architecture (Borrus and Zysman 1997). Japan's integrated electronic companies have favored proprietary technology, and they had considerable success with this model in Japan's high-growth years. Yet the information economy operates on a different logic, with more open interfaces and user-driven innovation. Japanese electronics producers have been slow to embrace this transformation. They are wary of sharing technology for fear that this will help their competitors. A METI report on industrial competitiveness stresses that those firms that have been most successful, such as Cisco and Intel, have combined an open interface with a black box of proprietary technology, and the report recommends that Japanese firms adopt this approach (METI 2010a: 8).

The services transformation discussed in this volume refers not simply to the growth of services relative to manufacturing but also to the integration of service functions into manufacturing. This also works to Japan's disadvantage because it means that its weakness in services undermines its manufacturing sector as well. Observers have characterized Japan as having a "dual economy," comprised of an internationally competitive sector focused in manufacturing and a domestic protected sector centered in services. And this dual economy has been characterized by a particularly wide gap in productivity between the two sectors (Katz 1998). Hence a shift in the locus of growth in the global economy from manufacturing to services and toward greater integration of manufacturing and services implies a shift away from Japan's comparative advantage.

The services transformation also involves the use of advanced software embedded in manufacturing, and yet Japan lags in many areas of software development (Cole 2006a; Cole and Fushimi 2011). Arora, Branstetter, and Drev (2010) contend that this shift is the single most important factor in Japan's competitive decline in the IT sector relative to the United States. They find that U.S. firms improved their relative performance over the course of the 1990s but advanced most dramatically in those areas where software competence was most critical. Moreover, IT patents granted by the U.S. government—including hardware patents—increasingly cite software technology, yet Japanese firms were less likely to cite software than their competitors, suggesting that their innovations were less reliant on advances in software.

Japan is also not well situated to take advantage of the productivity gains of the services transformation because Japanese firms are unlikely to be either competitive providers or leading users of outsourced services. Most Japanese firms cannot take advantage of high-skilled outsourcing firms that operate in English, and cannot provide outsourcing in English. Meanwhile, the Japanese government has not substantially improved the climate for high-skilled immigrants such as software engineers. Furthermore, Japanese firms lag their U.S. counterparts in sophisticated IT systems and the integration of manufacturing and services that is at the heart of the services revolution.

Japanese firms' strong orientation toward the domestic market rather than the global marketplace has hindered their ability to take advantage of both the decomposition of production and the services transformation. Commentators now commonly refer to this as the "Galapagos" phenomenon. That is, Japanese manufacturers develop high-quality products that are only suited for the Japanese market (Kushida 2011). In a classic example, Japanese electronics companies produce some of the most sophisticated cellular telephones in the world, and yet they have not succeeded in world markets because the handsets are not suited to global technical standards, their features are tailored to Japanese tastes, and their prices are too high.

Japanese firms have a strong record of innovation, but they have a greater capacity for incremental improvements in production processes than in breakthrough discoveries.[7] This balance of strength and weaknesses reflects Japan's comparative institutional advantages.[8] In some sectors, however, breakthrough innovations have become more important in recent years while production improvements are less so. In the semiconductor industry, for example, U.S. makers have had the edge in innovation and Japanese producers have excelled in production—but the production advantage was more decisive in the lean production era while the innovation advantage is more critical today. In the 1970s and 1980s, U.S. firms could not keep up with Japanese rivals that emulated their technology and achieved better quality, higher volume, and lower costs in production. Now U.S. companies prevail because the innovation cycle has accelerated and designs have become more complex (Vogel and Zysman 2002). Japanese firms continue to perform reasonably well in terms of patents overall, but they lag considerably in the fastest-growing sectors, such as software and information technology (Japan Patent Office 2010).

Japan also has a disadvantage in breakthrough innovation because it has relatively little new entry into the market. This means that Japanese firms have adjusted to new developments via incremental reform by existing companies, rather than radical innovation by new companies. In the United States, some incumbent firms have struggled to adapt to the new environment, just like their Japanese counterparts. Meanwhile, firms with radically new business models, such as Cisco, Google, and Apple, have emerged as market leaders.

We should not be too surprised that the information revolution has not played to Japanese strength. Japanese institutions fostered the lean production revolution, and Japanese companies led the shift to that paradigm and profited from it. Likewise, U.S. institutions nurtured the Internet revolution, and U.S. companies have played the leading role.

While recent developments have challenged the Japanese model, not all of Japan's institutional strengths are obsolete. Japan could still leverage its capable bureaucracy, strong government-industry ties, and close collaboration among firms, suppliers, banks, and workers as sources of competitive advantage. In fact, Japan has underemployed its advantages and allowed some to atrophy. In many areas, Japanese institutions offer both strengths and vulnerabilities. For example, Japanese firms have effective mechanisms for coordinating technical standards between government and industry and among industry players, but the Japanese government and industry have not been particularly effective in discerning when they should promote an industry technological standard, when they should adapt to an international or global standard, and when they should eschew coordination altogether.

Corporate Strategies

Japanese corporations have leveraged the government's incremental reforms since the 1990s to reduce costs and to enhance flexibility, but they have not fundamentally shifted from a strategy of quality manufacturing to one of modular production, rapid innovation, or open architecture.[9] They have sought to preserve the valued institutions at the heart of the Japanese model, such as cooperative long-term relationships with workers, banks, and other firms. Yet they have been forced to make compromises in the process: downgrading if not abandoning the "lifetime" employment system, reducing levels of corporate cross-shareholding, and sometimes even compromising quality standards to cut costs.

We can analyze Japanese corporate strategies since 1990 by deploying Albert Hirschman's (1970) concepts of "exit" (withdrawal) and "voice" (negotiation). The postwar Japanese economic model was characterized by government industrial policy, government-industry coordination, and long-term collaborative relationships between corporations and their workers, banks, and business partners. Corporations were constrained from "exit" from these relationships so they cultivated channels for "voice." This then produced a distinctive pattern of corporate restructuring. When faced with an economic downturn, Japanese companies would favor voice over exit with their partners. In concrete terms, this meant that Japanese companies would negotiate wage restraint but not lay off workers; they would press their main banks for better terms but not abandon them; and they would squeeze primary suppliers but not cut them off.

Within these general patterns, however, corporate strategies varied considerably. Based on a statistical analysis of 2,632 companies in the period 1990–2002, I found that companies in the service sector were bolder in restructuring labor relations than those in manufacturing, and that firms with high levels of foreign ownership were more aggressive in restructuring. A structured comparison among ten case study companies in the period 1990–2005 confirmed these patterns with a broader range of measures of restructuring. In addition, the cases showed that companies with foreign management, as opposed to portfolio investment, were the most aggressive. Electronics companies restructured more than automobile companies: they shifted further toward modular production, for example, by spinning off units to specialized contract manufacturers (Vogel 2006: 157–204).

As a result, Japanese firms have suffered some erosion of the traditional sources of their competitive advantage, including the stable employment system, the main bank system, and corporate groups. Employers have preserved the stable employment system for regular workers by reducing the share of regular workers in the workforce. They have also downgraded long-term employment by shifting from a guarantee of employment at the home company to a guarantee of employment within a broader corporate group. And they have restrained wages and benefits to reduce costs and have resorted to early retirement programs to accelerate attrition. Large corporations have moved away from reliance on a main bank, and corporations and their banks have reduced cross-shareholding ties. Manufacturers have loosened ties to some of their parts suppliers. They have become more selective in subcontracting relationships: strengthening partnerships that are critical to competitive advantage but procuring more standard items on a more purely cost basis.

Japan's ICT hardware sector has been dominated by NTT "family" firms such as NEC and Fujitsu that worked closely with NTT, the dominant telecommunications service provider, in building up Japan's communications infrastructure and developing high-quality equipment. These firms focused first and foremost on serving NTT and the large domestic market, and this impeded them from adjusting rapidly to the discontinuous technology of the Internet. NTT was strongly committed to asynchronous transfer mode (ATM) network technology, so it was very late in adopting TCP/IP (Transmission Control Protocol/Internet Protocol). Likewise, NTT cultivated a closed digital standard for cellular phones, the personal digital cellular standard. Japanese cellular telephone makers gave priority to developing phones for NTT DoCoMo's standards, undermining their ability to compete in the global market (Cole 2006b).

Japan's ICT manufacturers may have been more aggressive than the auto companies in restructuring, but they have still essentially adhered to the incremental pattern described previously. NEC, for example, engaged in a series of restructuring plans, beginning with modest cost-cutting plans and moving on to successive reorganization schemes including selling some production facilities to contract manufacturing companies. It merged its memory chip (DRAM) business with Hitachi in 1999, forming Elpida Memory, Inc., to share costs and invest in new technology. It experimented with a surprisingly ruthless personnel system for white-collar workers in 2002, in which managers would be asked to identify the bottom 10 percent of workers for possible demotion and a "rechallenge" program. In practice, however, it was never able to implement the program because managers designated less than 1 percent of their workers for the program. NEC also reassessed its relations with suppliers, reducing the overall number of suppliers, instituting a more systematic evaluation system for routine parts, but also reinforcing ties with core suppliers of critical technology.

Softbank, in contrast, brazenly diverged from standard Japanese business practices and aggressively challenged government policies, and it has remade Japan's IT sector in the process. Softbank was founded in 1981 as a software distribution company. It made key investments in U.S. start-ups in the Internet field, most notably Yahoo, with spectacular results. It embraced labor turnover and rapid reorganization, aggressively pursued mergers and acquisitions, and ruthlessly restructured. It took advantage of the government's telecommunications reform and relentlessly expanded its market share in broadband service to challenge NTT and to raise demand for its other Internet-related businesses. Softbank almost single-handedly drove down Japan's broadband rates and dramatically increased usage. Softbank entered the cellular telephone service business in 2005, with the same aggressive market-expansion strategy. Softbank has encountered some notable setbacks as well as successes with its maverick business style, and relatively few other Japanese companies have successfully challenged the incumbents with novel business models.

If Japanese corporations have not revamped their strategies sufficiently to adapt to the information age, then why hasn't the government been able to do more to transform the institutional context and to promote private-sector reform? In the past, the government played the leading role in reshaping Japan's market structure. So why not now?

For one thing, the core manufacturers, such as NEC and Fujitsu, have lobbied for policies that would reinforce their existing competitive strengths rather than shift the terms of competition. "We want the government to implement policies that help us with our strategy," explains Fujitsu's Tetsuro Uruno. "We want to increase the size of the market, so the government could support this by promoting the 'smart [digitally enabled] community,' for example. And we want to upgrade our products and services, so the government might invest in R&D for basic technology, information security, or information technology for the agriculture or health sectors."[10] Softbank, meanwhile, has pressed the government to build up the IT infrastructure and to break NTT's incumbent advantage in the telecommunications market. "We do not need the government to boost exports of IT products," declares Ted Matsumoto, senior executive vice president. "But it should promote the best possible IT environment, with the cheapest and the best IT services. That is the real meaning of international competitiveness."[11] To understand the Japanese government's IT strategy, however, we must not only identify industry policy preferences but also examine how these preferences are mediated in the political arena.

Government Strategies

Since 1991, the Japanese government has formulated its policies for industrial renewal and IT in the context of macroeconomic weakness. Government officials focused initially more on short-term measures to support economic recovery and resolve the banking crisis than on long-term policies to upgrade technology, enhance productivity, or promote technology. Despite popular images of paralysis, however, government officials did not fail to act. They enacted a wide range of reforms, from corporate law to labor policy and financial regulation, designed to strengthen the legal infrastructure supporting markets and to facilitate corporate restructuring. They shifted away from government promotion and protection of industry and adopted selective procompetitive regulatory reforms. They found themselves caught between two paradigms: unable to preserve the postwar model of government leadership and close collaboration among businesses and yet unable to shift decisively toward a liberal market model. To understand this pattern of reform and its pathologies, we must examine the political factors shaping the specific substance of those policies.

The government's macroeconomic policy errors contributed to the economic crisis that began in 1991 and exacerbated it afterward. Specifically, the government failed to tighten fiscal and monetary policy in the late 1980s, fueling the asset bubble and making the ensuing crash much worse. It was then slow to ease monetary policy and to expand fiscal policy after the crash. And when it did deploy fiscal stimulus, it did so in a particularly ineffective stop-and-go pattern, with spending concentrated on public works projects that did not contribute to long-term economic growth. In addition, Ministry of Finance (MOF) officials initially responded to the financial crisis with their standard repertory of measures.

They downplayed the crisis for fear that public disclosure could lead to panic; they worked closely with the distressed banks, offering regulatory breaks as necessary; and they asked stronger banks to support their weaker affiliates. They were slow to recognize that these tools would not work because the scale of the crisis was so huge, and they only turned to a more aggressive approach after the financial crisis deepened in 1997.

By the 1990s, Japanese government officials had already begun to move away from a state-led industrial strategy. They started to liberalize deposit interest rates in 1985, and they eased the regulatory barriers between commercial banks and stock brokerages in 1992. They privatized the telecommunications carrier, NTT, and introduced competition in the sector in 1985 (Vogel 1996). They then enacted a series of reforms to strengthen the legal infrastructure underpinning markets and to give corporations greater ability to reduce costs and to increase returns. The government's distinctive approach to market reforms reflected the preferences of Japanese industry. Japanese corporations sought to reduce costs while preserving their long-term collaborative relationships with workers, financial institutions, and other corporations, and the government sought to deliver reforms that would facilitate that.

The government gave employers more flexibility by allowing dispatch workers (agency temps), thus permitting a new tier of temporary workers who could be hired and dismissed at will. And it enhanced the institutional infrastructure for labor mobility by allowing private employment agencies. At the same time, however, it reinforced the long-term employment system for regular workers by codifying rules restricting layoffs. Meanwhile, the government enacted a daunting array of revisions to corporate law to give companies more options for restructuring. It permitted companies to buy back their own shares and to issue stock options; it reformed procedures to facilitate corporate spinoffs and mergers and acquisitions; and it permitted companies to adopt a U.S.-style committee board system while not requiring them to do so. The Ministry of International Trade and Industry (MITI, which became METI in 2000) also sought to promote corporate restructuring more directly, combining tax relief, regulatory breaks, subsidies, and low-interest loans to support companies to reduce capacity or invest in growth areas. It also tried to promote start-ups by eliminating capital requirements for incorporation.

The government moved most decisively in finance with the "Big Bang" reforms of 1996. It opened foreign exchange markets; deregulated brokerage commissions; liberalized mutual fund, pension, and trust markets; loosened restrictions on new financial instruments; lifted the ban on holding companies; allowed banks, securities houses, and insurance companies to enter one another's lines of business through holding companies; and shifted the MOF's supervisory duties to a new Financial Supervision Agency. The government also enacted substantial accounting reforms, including mark-to-market accounting for financial instruments and consolidated reporting for subsidiaries above a certain threshold of ownership.

In the realm of information technology, the Ministry of Posts and Telecommunications (which merged into a new ministry in 2000, now called the Ministry of Internal Affairs and Communications) had advocated competition in telecommunications since the 1980s because ministry officials had more of a rivalry than a collusive relationship with NTT, and they recognized that they could augment their own power and status by allowing competition. The ministry lost some of its procompetitive fervor after 1997, however, when it forged a delicate political compromise that broke up NTT into one long-distance carrier and two regional carriers under a holding company structure. The government's IT Strategy Council unveiled an ambitious reform program in 2000, combining procompetitive regulation, investment in infrastructure, improvements in the legal apparatus supporting electronic commerce, and measures to support electronic government. The ministry subsequently pressed NTT to lower interconnection charges and to lease unused lines, fueling a remarkable price war in digital subscriber lines (Kushida 2006). Japan's broadband service rates dropped to the lowest in the world by 2002 (MIC 2010c: 20).[12] Internet penetration surged from 21.4 percent in 1999 to 57.8 percent in 2002 and 78.0 percent in 2009 (MIC 2011: 186).

By the early 2000s, the economy finally entered a stable recovery. Prime Minister Junichiro Koizumi (2001–06) heralded a program of "structural reform," including the privatization of the postal system and the reform of special public corporations, aimed more at transforming politics than liberalizing the economy. He sought to save the ruling Liberal Democratic Party (LDP) by dismantling the public works machine, thereby attracting voters disenchanted with the old LDP politics. Koizumi was given credit for liberalizing the Japanese economy, but for the most part, market reforms during his term followed the incremental pattern of his predecessors.

Koizumi's political strategy worked brilliantly in the 2005 Lower House elections, but his successors—Shinzo Abe (2006–07), Yasuo Fukuda (2007–08), and Taro Aso (2008–09)—could not emulate his success. They lacked his personal charisma; they undercut some of his political reforms; and they struggled to guide the party. Abe declared that he would shift greater attention to promoting innovation, since productivity increases would have to drive economic growth as Japan's population was no longer rising. Yet Abe did not stay in office long enough to make meaningful progress in this area.

When the global financial crisis hit in 2008, Japan briefly appeared insulated because the financial sector had just completed a round of restructuring and it had not invested heavily in hedge funds or the U.S. housing market. But the crisis eventually struck Japan hard through a different route, as a sharp drop in global demand devastated exporters. The Japanese government responded with a relatively modest fiscal stimulus, as officials were concerned with the country's enormous fiscal deficit.

The DPJ Era

In August 2009, the LDP, which had dominated Japanese politics for more than fifty years, fell from power in a stunning loss to the Democratic Party of Japan (DPJ).

The DPJ had appealed to voters looking for a change by pledging to alter the basic logic of Japanese politics. The DPJ vowed that politicians would finally assert their proper authority over bureaucrats, and the government would scrutinize government spending and reduce wasteful public works spending. The DPJ represented a wide spectrum of views on both domestic and foreign policy issues, although it was slightly less nationalistic and more favorable toward welfare spending than the LDP. It had closer ties to labor unions and looser ties with business interests. The DPJ manifesto was remarkably short on specific policy proposals, especially given that Japan was mired in a severe economic crisis.

The DPJ administration disbanded the Council on Economic and Fiscal Policy (CEFP), which had coordinated economic policy under Koizumi. In its place, it created a National Strategy Headquarters that was supposed to integrate overall economic and foreign policy planning. The administration was hampered from the start by a dual power structure in which Prime Minister Yukio Hatoyama led the government and Secretary General Ichiro Ozawa ran the party. Both Hatoyama and Ozawa had advocated a stronger cabinet closer to the British "Westminster" system, in which the cabinet would exercise authority over the bureaucracy and the party. But this vision could not be realized since the party's strongest leader, Ozawa, found himself outside the government due to a political finance scandal. Moreover, the new National Strategy Headquarters could not take the lead on economic reform because its nominal leader, Yoshito Sengoku, did not have Ozawa's support. In any case, the administration gave top priority to its goal of reshaping politics and the policy process, moving slowly and awkwardly on policy issues. The government only unveiled its new growth strategy in December 2009, with further details in June 2010, pledging to cut corporate tax cuts, boost disposable income, promote exports, and increase IT investment.

The growth strategy's schemes for industrial and IT policy incorporated proposals that had emerged from the ministries. By 2010, METI and MIC officials were remarkably candid in their assessment of Japan's declining competitiveness, and they were proposing some creative policy responses. Yet in the DPJ era, the strained ties between political leaders and the bureaucrats would make it particularly difficult to implement these plans.

METI reports on industrial competitiveness proposed that the government should resurrect elements of an industrial policy: increasing financial support for research, actively coordinating Japanese companies, and aggressively marketing Japanese products abroad. Akira Kawamoto, Deputy Director-General, Economic and Industrial Policy Bureau, explains the ministry's turn in thinking:

> Up until the financial crisis, we had been saying that we should leave things to the private sector. But then we asked ourselves: Is that enough? The results had not been good. So we concluded that the private sector alone was a weak driver of growth. The government would have to take a more proactive role—although it would certainly not be wise or practical to go back to Japan's traditional industrial policy.[13]

The reports argued that Japan would have to shift from a reliance on manufacturing, particularly in automobiles, to growth sectors: infrastructure (railways, electric power, water), the environment and energy, culture industries (fashion, entertainment), health care, and high technology (robots, aerospace). They stressed that the government would have to actively support Japanese infrastructure exports to emerging markets and developing countries via government aid and lending. They recognized the global trends highlighted in this volume: the integration of manufacturing and services and the modularization of production. And they asserted that the government must reestablish strategic collaboration among politicians, bureaucrats, and industry and foster government-industry-academic ties to promote research and development in order to compete in this new environment (METI 2010b).

Both METI and MIC reports advocated a dramatic increase in investment in IT. Koichi Akaishi, senior director of METI's Information Policy Division, declares:

> We propose a radical change in thinking. We should no longer think of investment in IT as a cost. We should think of it as costless—since costs decrease so quickly—and develop business strategies based on that presumption.[14]

One METI report offers three explanations for Japan's weakness in IT: insufficient investment, a flawed strategy on standards, and too much focus on the domestic market (METI 2010a).

The DPJ government's first Minister of Internal Affairs and Communications, Kazuhiro Haraguchi, departed from standard practice by announcing his own personal "vision" for Japan's IT revival. Haraguchi had been strongly influenced by Masayoshi Son, the president of Softbank, who advocates 100 percent national penetration for fiber-optic broadband, electronic books for public schools, and aggressive regulation and even further breaking up NTT to promote competition. "We have a more liberal approach to telecommunications policy than the United States," Haraguchi insists, "we want to enhance competition."[15] When Prime Minister Naoto Kan reshuffled his cabinet in September 2010, however, Haraguchi found himself out of a cabinet spot and unable to press forward this vision.

Japan's Governance Problem

The Japanese government has responded to declining industrial competitiveness with incremental adjustments, not bold reform. In some sense, the government's caution is warranted. The government has sought to give corporations more flexibility to restructure while preserving the strengths of the Japanese model, including stable employment relations and coordination among firms. Moreover, the government's approach has reflected the preferences of the Japanese people, who have been wary of reforms that would deliver higher financial returns at the expense of greater risks. Thus the government's reluctance to deliver bold liberal market reforms reflects the normal functioning of the political system and not its failure (Vogel 2006: 44–45, 51–61).

Nonetheless, the Japanese government's policy record reveals some troubling weaknesses, particularly when it comes to the IT sector. By abandoning its own state-led model and yet not adopting a liberal market model either, the government risked undermining Japan's comparative institutional advantages without cultivating a viable alternative.

It is tempting to blame Japan's incoherent economic strategy on the pervasive political instability since the LDP first lost power in 1993. The unwieldy coalition that replaced the LDP lasted less than a year, giving way to a series of LDP-led coalition governments, frequent realignment among the opposition parties, and a long series of forgettable prime ministers. Koizumi was the notable exception during this period, yet even he did not substantially alter the trajectory of economic reform beyond postal privatization and the banking clean-up. Some of the signature Koizumi structural reforms, such as the reform of the special public corporations, were well under way before Koizumi took office. And on many other issues, such as labor policy or corporate governance reform, the bureaucracy simply continued on a path of incremental adjustments.

Yet Japan's postwar political system has rarely been characterized by strong political leadership on economic policy issues. Thus I would contend that Japan's lack of a coherent economic strategy since 1990 reflects a decline in bureaucratic leadership more than political volatility. The core economic ministries, particularly METI and MOF, have experienced a profound loss of prestige, confidence, and power. The government officials themselves have lost faith in the government's ability to enhance Japan's competitiveness. Meanwhile, politicians have made bureaucrat bashing a major theme in their political strategies. This shifts the blame for economic problems from politicians to bureaucrats, it appeals to popular disillusionment with the bureaucracy, and it gives divided political parties an issue to unite them.

When the DPJ took power, its attempt to uproot bureaucratic power and to overhaul the policy process rendered Japan's economic policy apparatus even less effective. The ministries were gridlocked for several months at least, as the ministers (who are politicians) tried to get up to speed on the policy issues, and the civil servants were stymied from moving forward in the absence of clear directions from their political leaders. This gradually evolved into greater tension in the case of some ministries, notably the Ministry of Health, Labor and Welfare and the Ministry of Land, Infrastructure and Transport, and to fragile cooperation in others, such as METI and the Ministry of Foreign Affairs ("Minshutou seiji-shudou no detarame" 2010).

On March 11, 2011, Japan was hit by a 9.0 earthquake centered offshore the Tohoku (northeastern) region prefectures of Fukushima, Miyagi, and Iwate. The ensuing tsunami rose more than fifty feet in some areas, killing more than 20,000 people, and wiping out many coastal communities. The earthquake and tsunami also struck the Fukushima Daiichi nuclear power plant, leading to explosions, meltdowns, and the worst nuclear disaster since Chernobyl. In the short term, the earthquake exacerbated the country's fiscal crisis and delayed progress on economic reforms. The government passed supplementary spending bills for recovery and reconstruction in May, July, and November, and it announced that it would review its economic growth strategy in light of the disaster. The disaster also disrupted supply chains in automobiles, electronics, and other key manufacturing sectors. Some Japanese firms were forced to rely more heavily on non-Japanese suppliers to maintain production. Meanwhile, DPJ and LDP politicians engaged in petty political gamesmanship despite the gravity of the situation. The LDP and even some members of the ruling party pressed Prime Minister Naoto Kan to resign, and he ultimately relented in late August.

In the longer term, however, the earthquake could push Japanese leaders to consider bolder reforms. The disaster certainly brought some of Japan's key challenges to the surface: the fiscal deficit, anemic growth, technology, energy, and the environment. Before the earthquake, the government's long-term energy plan had aimed at increasing Japan's reliance on nuclear energy from about 30 percent of electricity generation to 50 percent by 2030, adding fourteen new nuclear reactors. After the quake, the government allowed the nuclear reactors to gradually go offline for scheduled maintenance, but did not restart them due to strong local opposition. The last of Japan's fifty-three reactors went out of service in May 2012, and only two had been restarted as of September. The government's Reconstruction Design Council issued its first report in June 2011, advocating special economic zones in the Tohoku region, with fewer regulations and tax breaks to stimulate investment, plus support for the development of renewable energies.

The Wrong Policy Mix?

Recent developments in the global economy have undermined the strengths of the Japanese business model and exacerbated its weaknesses, yet does that mean that the model is obsolete? In conclusion, let us review three alternative interpretations of Japan's competitive decline, all of which capture elements of Japan's dilemma.

PROPOSITION I

Japan has failed to shift toward a new business model better suited for the information age. The global economy has moved in a direction where Japanese institutional advantages are less salient and U.S. advantages are paramount. It is no accident, of course, that U.S. companies have fared well in the information age, since the U.S. government, companies, and institutions drove the shift to the new paradigm. This paradigm rewards those features characteristic of the U.S. model: low barriers to entry, fluid labor markets, open technical standards, modular production integrated into global supply chains, and robust competition in product markets, telecommunications, and financial services. Japanese government and industry have publicly called for a shift toward a liberal market model for two decades, yet their reforms have been incremental and many have been designed to reinforce existing institutional strengths rather than to generate new ones.

Japan may not have converted to the U.S. model, yet other countries—notably the Nordic countries and South Korea—have not done so either and yet have been highly successful in key ICT sectors. Moreover, Japan's traditional strengths are not irrelevant in the information age. A competent bureaucracy, dense government-industry networks, strong bank-industry ties, good labor-management relations, and tight coordination between manufacturers and their core suppliers remain potential sources of competitive advantage today, just as they were in the past.

PROPOSITION 2

Japan has failed to preserve its own institutional strengths. The Japanese government has diminished administrative capacity as the central ministries have lost authority and loosened ties with industry. Japan has experienced a slow erosion of the core features of its distinctive model, including long-term cooperative relationships among firms, workers, banks, and suppliers.

Japan has indeed reformed its model, but for the most part the government and industry have favored tactical adjustments designed to give firms the flexibility they need to compete in hard times. On balance, this has made Japanese firms more competitive, not less. The government and industry retain the institutions of coordination, such as industry associations, but both government and industry are much less confident in deploying these capabilities.

There is some evidence, however, that Japan is losing ground at a more fundamental level. Japan shows troubling signs of decline in social performance, including education, an area of remarkable success in the postwar era. In international tests for middle-school students, Japan dropped from first place to fifth in math and from first to third in science from 1981 to 2007 (MIC 2010c: 33). In 2009, the World Economic Forum ranked Japan thirty-first in the world in the quality of the education system, thirty-third in the quality of math and science education, and twenty-fifth in Internet connectivity in the schools (MIC 2010c: 18). Japan has 7,700 doctorates in science and engineering compared to 28,000 for the United States and 14,900 for China, 12,200 for Germany, and 9,400 for the United Kingdom (METI 2010b: 33). Japan has also lost some of its social solidarity as economic inequality has risen, with a Gini coefficient increasing from 23.9 in 1993 to 37.9 in 2008.[16]

Meanwhile, Japanese are becoming less engaged internationally. This does not bode well for Japan's ability to remedy some of its key weaknesses in the information age, such as its lack of software programmers. Japan is sending fewer students abroad, although more foreign students are coming to Japan.[17] Even so, only 0.7 percent of Japan's higher education graduates come from abroad, compared to 29 percent for Australia, 26 percent for Canada, 16 percent for the United Kingdom, and 13 percent for the United States.

Among current higher education students, only 3.5 percent come from abroad, compared to 29 percent for Australia, 26 percent for the United Kingdom, and 6 percent for the United States.[18] Japan remains behind in English-language education, whereas China, South Korea, and other East Asian countries have made considerable improvements in recent years.[19]

PROPOSITION 3

The Japanese government has produced the wrong mix of policies to adapt the Japanese model to new circumstances. In this view, Japan was right to combine market liberalization with selective efforts at state-led industrial policy and government-industry coordination, but it delivered the wrong mix. It proceeded too slowly with procompetitive reform where it was most needed, and too tentatively with state support where it was most appropriate. After all, those countries that have been most successful in key ICT sectors—the Nordic countries and South Korea, in particular—have also deployed more successful mixed strategies.

To sort out the characteristics of a right mix from a wrong mix of policies, one would have to confront the daunting task of specifying the relationships between government policies, institutional capabilities, and market success in the information age. I attempt to unpack these relationships here as a first step toward considering how better to analyze them.

We cannot make useful generalizations about the linkage between national institutions and industrial performance at the aggregate level. We can begin by suggesting that Japan's distinctive set of institutions gave it a comparative institutional advantage in some sectors, such as automobiles or electronics, but a disadvantage in others, such as services, software, biotechnology, or aerospace. But these broad sectoral advantages were really embedded in more specific functional advantages. That is, Japan was better able to forge labor-management cooperation, train engineers, provide stable finance via the banking system, foster coordination across industry, and achieve incremental improvements in production. Meanwhile, the United States was better able to foster labor mobility, finance new ventures via equity markets, breed entrepreneurs, promote competition, support basic research, and generate breakthrough innovation (Vogel and Zysman 2002: 240–42).

So to apply our understanding of these functional advantages to the ICT sector, we would have to disaggregate the analysis by both type of policy and industrial subsector. For example, we might suggest that a strong central government with a well-trained bureaucracy and close ties between industry and finance would be better able to increase overall investment in the sector and to build up the ICT infrastructure. Likewise, tight government-industry and industry-industry networks could facilitate the coordination of technical standards or training programs. At the same time, however, a government with close ties between the regulator and the incumbent telecommunications carrier, or a government in which industrial promotion and regulation are fused in the same ministry, would be less well positioned to promote effective competition. So a "smart" state in the information age would have to know how best to capitalize on its capabilities for guiding investment and for mobilizing sectoral networks while recognizing when it should promote competition or to ease restrictions on international trade and investment.

With respect to subsectors, the capacity to guide investment would be most critical in areas where competition requires massive investments, such as memory chips, solar panels, and auto batteries. The South Korean government and industry have been particularly effective in challenging the Japanese leaders in precisely these areas. One METI report notes that South Korea has fewer firms in key sectors, so these firms have a larger domestic market in absolute terms even though the South Korean economy is considerably smaller than the Japanese economy. The report credits the South Korean government with orchestrating industrial consolidation under the "big deal" after the Asian financial crisis, and it suggests that this has helped South Korean firms to outspend their Japanese rivals in sectors where the scale of investment is critical (METI 2010b: 17–18). In contrast, the promotion of effective competition is more essential in telecommunications services to lower prices and thus promote usage and innovation. To its credit, the Japanese government made substantial progress in this area in the early 2000s, but by that time the United States and South Korea were well ahead (Kushida 2006).

In this light, the Nordic states and South Korea have outperformed Japan with a better mix of policies in recent years. As Darius Ornston argues (Chapter 11, in this volume), Denmark, Sweden, and Finland did not dismantle corporatist institutions but rather redeployed them to support growth in high-technology sectors. In contrast to Japan, these countries have experienced an improvement in macroeconomic performance since the mid-1990s and an improving competitive position in the ICT sector. They have neither relied on traditional corporatist coordination nor embraced rapid market liberalization. Instead, they have redesigned collaboration among government, industry, and labor to increase investment in human resources, foster risk capital, and boost R&D in high technology sectors.

South Korea provides an even closer comparative fit for the Japanese case. South Korea and Japan began in similar positions in 1990s, albeit with Japan holding a clear technological lead in most high-technology sectors. South Korea and Japan had both succeeded in the postwar era with a state-led growth strategy combined with strong government-industry ties and a highly organized private sector. And yet in recent years South Korea has been gaining market share in IT products while Japan has been losing share, and South Korea has outstripped Japan in the development of IT services and the expansion of IT usage. The South Korean government has been more aggressive than the Japanese government with market reforms since the Asian crisis of 1997. It moved sooner than Japan to promote competition in telecommunications and support IT diffusion.[20] It aggressively pursued bilateral free trade and investment packages. It encouraged Korean industry to adjust to international technical standards. Meanwhile, the Korean government has provided stronger support for IT infrastructure investment and for IT-related

R&D, and it has pressed more aggressively for coordination and consolidation in key sectors.[21] Japanese officials are acutely aware that Japanese industry has lost ground to South Korea. METI's Kawamoto summarizes his own position rather succinctly: "While we were talking about leaving things to the private sector," he laments, "South Korea passed right by us with a state-led model."[22] Overall both the Japanese and South Korean governments have opted for a mixed strategy: neither fully adhering to the old state-led model nor dramatically switching to a neoliberal one. Yet the South Korean government and corporations have crafted a more effective combination.

Acknowledgments

The author would like to thank Robert Cole, Kenji Kushida, and John Zysman for insightful comments; Ayako Hirata, Trevor Incerti, Kumiko Isono, Kazu Kanairo, and Hiroki Taniguchi for research assistance; and the Center for Japanese Studies and the Committee on Research at the University of California, Berkeley for research funding. The author also wishes to thank the Alfred P. Sloan Foundation for financial support and the Berkeley Roundtable on the International Economy (BRIE) for research and administrative support.

Notes

1. 2010 data from MIC (2010a: 2–3).
2. 2007 data from METI (2010b: 17).
3. Average operating profits for 2005–08 from METI (2010a: 6). This report notes that Japanese electronics firms achieved better results in 2009, but that cuts in research and development spending account for a substantial share of the increase in profits (METI 2010a: 10).
4. Interviews, Tokyo, May–June 2010.
5. 2008 data from METI (2010a: 15).
6. The Japanese government and the private sector have maintained relatively stable rates of R&D spending since 1990 as a share of GDP, but slow growth has naturally constrained total R&D spending. According to OECD Science, Technology and R&D Statistics, during the 1990–2009 period government-financed R&D spending has ranged from 0.52 percent (in 1997) to 0.66 percent of GDP (in 1995), and industry-financed R&D spending has ranged from 1.90 percent (in 1994) to 2.69 percent of GDP (in 2008).
7. Robert E. Cole and Tsuyoshi Matsumiya (2007) argue that Japanese high-technology firms' fixation on quality has actually undermined their capacity for innovation.
8. Herbert Kitschelt (1991) argues that Japan excels in sectors characterized by medium to long production runs and amenable to incremental production improvements, such as office machines, appliances, consumer electronics, and electronic components. Japan lags in sectors that require huge public investments in basic research and breakthrough innovation such as aerospace, biotechnology, and software. Likewise, Peter Hall and David Soskice (2001) contend that liberal market economies like the United States excel in radical innovation that is critical in dynamic technology sectors

such as biotechnology, semiconductors, and software. Radical innovation is also important for system-based products, such as telecommunications or defense systems, and for service sectors, such as advertising, corporate finance, or entertainment. Coordinated market economies like Japan and Germany excel in incremental innovation that is more critical for capital goods manufacturing, such as machine tools, consumer durables, engines, and specialized transport equipment.

9. This section and the next build on Vogel (2006).

10. Interview with Tetsuro Uruno, general manager, Government Relations Division, Fujitsu, Ltd., Tokyo, June 2, 2010.

11. Interview with Ted Matsumoto, senior executive vice president, Softbank Mobile Corp., Tokyo, June 3, 2010.

12. According to the World Economic Forum, Japan's ranking for ICT rose from twentieth in 2003 to eighth in 2005, only to slide back to twenty-first by 2010 (MIC 2010b: 4). The MIC's own index ranked Japan first among twenty-four countries in ICT base in 2009 (MIC 2010c: 19).

13. Interview, Tokyo, May 31, 2010.

14. Interview, Tokyo, May 31, 2010.

15. Interview, Tokyo, June 3, 2010.

16. The U.S. Gini coefficient has risen from 40.8 in 1997 to 45.0 in 2007, while the figure has fallen from 35.8 in 2000 to 31.4 in 2009 in South Korea, and from 30 in 1994 to 27 in 2006 in Germany (Central Intelligence Agency 2010).

17. Japanese students studying abroad declined from 60,424 in 2004 to 44,768 in 2009, while the numbers increased over the same period for students from South Korea (96,885 to 125,165), China (343,126 to 510,314), the United States (41,181 to 53,251), and Germany (56,410 to 91,928) (United Nations Educational, Scientific and Cultural Organization 2006–11). Meanwhile, foreign students studying in Japan rose from about 40,000 in 1990 to 60,000 in 2000 to more than 120,000 in 2008 (Cabinet Office 2010).

18. 2009 data from METI (2010b: 33).

19. Average TOEFL examination scores for 2011 were 69 for Japan, 77 for Taiwan, 77 for China, and 82 for South Korea (Educational Testing Service 2012).

20. South Korea leads the world with over 90 percent of households having broadband access, compared to 60–70 percent for the United States and Germany and less than 60 percent for Japan: 2009 data from *OECD Information Technology Outlook* (2010: 179).

21. South Korean government and industry R&D spending as a share of GDP has been roughly comparable to that of Japan, but South Korea leads all OECD countries by a large margin in government funding of business R&D (direct and indirect) plus tax incentives for R&D at 0.34 percent of GDP (compared to 0.23 for the United States and 0.15 for Japan) (*OECD Science, Technology and Industry Outlook* 2010: 5).

22. Interview, May 31, 2010.

References

Arora, Ashish, Lee G. Branstetter, and Matej Drev. (2010). Going soft: How the rise of software-based innovation led to the decline of Japan's IT industry and the resurgence of Silicon Valley. NBER Working Paper 16156, National Bureau of Economic Research Cambridge, MA.

Borrus, Michael G. (1988). *Competing for Control: America's Stake in Microelectronics.* Cambridge, MA: Ballinger.

Borrus, Michael, and John Zysman. (1997). "Globalization with borders: The rise of Wintelism as the future of global competition." *Industry and Innovation* 4(2): 141–66.

Cabinet Office. (2010). "Kyouiku no guroubaru senryaku" [A Global Strategy for Education].

Central Intelligence Agency. (2010). *The World Factbook 2010.* Washington, D.C.: CIA.

Cole, Robert E. (2006a). "Software's Hidden Challenges." In *Recovering from Success: Innovation and Technology Management in Japan,* edited by D. Hugh Whittaker and Robert E. Cole, 105–26. Oxford: Oxford University Press.

Cole, Robert E. (2006b). "Telecommunications Competition in World Markets: Understanding Japan's Decline." In *How Revolutionary Was the Digital Revolution? National Responses, Market Transitions, and Global Technology,* edited by John Zysman and Abraham Newman, 101–24. Stanford, CA: Stanford Business Books.

Cole. Robert E., and Shinya Fushimi. (2011). "The Japanese Enterprise Software Industry: An Evolutionary and Comparative Perspective." In *Have Japanese Firms Changed? The Lost Decade,* edited by Hiroaki Miyoshi and Yoshifumi Nakata, 41–6. Houndmills, Basingstoke, Hampshire, UK: Palgrave MacMillan.

Cole, Robert E., and Tsuyoshi Matsumiya. (2007). "Too much of a good thing? Quality as an impediment to innovation." *California Management Review* 50(1): 77–93.

Cole, Robert E., and D. Hugh Whittaker. (2006). "Introduction." In *Recovering from Success: Innovation and Technology Management in Japan,* edited by D. Hugh Whittaker and Robert E. Cole, 8–14. Oxford: Oxford University Press.

Educational Testing Service. (2012). *Test and Score Data Summary for TOEFL Internet-Based and Paper-Based Test.* Princeton, NJ: ETS.

Hall, Peter, and David Soskice. (2001). "An Introduction to the Varieties of Capitalism." In *Varieties of Capitalism: The Institutional Foundations of Comparative Advantage,* edited by Peter Hall and David Soskice, 36–44. Oxford: Oxford University Press.

Hirschman, Albert. (1970). *Exit, Voice, and Loyalty: Responses to Decline in Firms, Organizations, and States.* Cambridge, MA: Harvard University Press.

Japan Patent Office, Statistics Division. (2010). "Jouhou tsuushin kanren" [Information Technology].

Katz, Richard. (1998). *Japan the System That Soured: The Rise and Fall of the Japanese Economic Miracle.* Armonk, NY: M.E. Sharpe.

Kitschelt, Herbert. (1991). "Industrial governance structures, innovation strategies, and the case of Japan: Sectoral or cross-national comparative analysis?" *International Organization* 45: 453–93.

Kushida, Kenji E. (2006). "Japan's Telecommunications Regime Shift: Understanding Japan's Potential Resurgence." In *How Revolutionary Was the Digital Revolution? National Responses, Market Transitions, and Global Technology,* edited by John Zysman and Abraham Newman, 134–41. Stanford, CA: Stanford Business Books.

Kushida, Kenji E. (2011). "Leading without followers: How politics and market dynamics trapped innovations in Japan's domestic 'Galapagos' telecommunications sector." *Journal of Industry, Competition, and Trade* 11: 279–307.

METI. (2010a). "Jouhou keizai kakushin senryaku (gaiyou)" [Information Economy Renovation Strategy (Summary)], May.

METI. (2010b). "Sangyou kouzou bijon gaiyou" [Industrial Structure Vision Outline], June.

MIC. (2010a). "Heisei 22-nenban ICT kokusai kyousouryoku shihyou" [2010 ICT International Competitiveness Indicators], July.

MIC. (2010b). "ICT seisaku no saishin doukou" [The Latest Developments in ICT Policy], May.

MIC. (2010c). "Wagakuni no ICT kokusai kyousouryoku no genjoutou ni suite" [Japan's International Competitiveness in ICT].

MIC. (2011). "Jouhou tsuushin hakusho" [Information and Communications in Japan], Tokyo.

"Minshutou seiji-shudou no detarame" [The Democratic Party of Japan's Politician-Led Nonsense]. (2010). *Sentaku*, May 4: 6–7.

Newman, Abraham, and John Zysman. (2006). "Transforming Politics in the Digital Era." In *How Revolutionary Was the Digital Revolution? National Responses, Market Transitions, and Global Technology*, edited by John Zysman and Abraham Newman, 391–410. Stanford, CA: Stanford Business Books.

OECD Science, Technology and Industry Outlook. (2010).

Ogawa, Kouichi. (2008). From product innovation to business model innovation. IAM Discussion Paper Series #001, University of Tokyo.

United Nations Educational, Scientific and Cultural Organization. (2006–11). *Global Education Digest: Comparing Education Statistics Across the World.* Montreal: UNESCO Institute for Statistics.

Vogel, Steven K. (1996). *Freer Markets, More Rules: Regulatory Reform in Advanced Industrial Countries.* Ithaca, NY: Cornell University Press.

Vogel, Steven K. (2006). *Japan Remodeled: How Government and Industry Are Reforming Japanese Capitalism.* Ithaca, NY: Cornell University Press.

Vogel, Steven K., and John Zysman. (2002). "Technology." In *U.S.-Japan Relations in a Changing World*, edited by Steven K. Vogel, 239–61. Washington, D.C.: Brookings Institution Press.

Conclusion

A THIRD GLOBALIZATION, LESSONS FOR SUSTAINED GROWTH?

Dan Breznitz and John Zysman

THE COUNTRIES THAT are now rich can remain productive, wealthy, and healthy as the "third globalization" unfolds. Indeed, the very fact that they are facing an acute double bind might allow experimentation and force the politics of policy making to step outside the current ideological traps.

As we observed in the introduction, policy makers now find themselves in a double bind. One edge, or imperative, of the double bind in the years before the meltdown was the demand for re-regulation and deregulation of the market to permit corporate experimentation. The way firms create value and organize themselves has undergone a long and complex evolution. That evolution has been significantly shaped by at least three developments. First, the rapid advancement of information and communications technology (ICT), the main general-purpose technology of the day, changed our lives and altered the ways markets work and firms compete. Second, the decomposition of production and the rise of economic regions devoted to particular phases of production in specific industries pose long-term challenges to the preeminence of the advanced countries. Third, but not least, the development of ICT and the fragmentation of production have together led to the algorithmic transformation of services: the ability to reproduce them and supply them repeatedly without spatial limitations. In sum, the requirements for growth have changed, consequently creating a new "growth model," by changing the requirements of competition and productivity.

By a new "growth model," we mean changes in what it takes for firms to compete in markets, create value, and generate jobs. Accordingly, a "growth model" also refers to the needed evolution in the roles governments must play in sparking, sustaining, and supporting development. All these developments are part of a story framed by the ideologies of deregulation and self-regulation. This co-evolution fueled corresponding demands for market rules that would permit extensive innovation and experimentation. The demands were based on, or, rather, justified by, the neoliberal belief that "less" regulated markets can achieve sustained growth, which will then "naturally" enhance societies without the need for public intervention.

Currently, the second edge, the second imperative, of the double bind—the demands for the state to forcefully intervene in order to optimize growth—has taken equal place in policy debates or even moved to the forefront. The second edge, the second imperative of the double bind, is the painful rediscovery, which came with the recent financial debacle, of simple truths: all markets are built on rules that allow them to function, but the choice of rules powerfully influences not only the stability of the market, but also who benefits and who is dislocated. Many objectives are best addressed by direct government action. The continuing manifestations of the financial crisis that call for state action—for example, the Euro crisis and debates over austerity—have become the main drivers of policy. Arguments over the validity and necessity for state action in support of markets and capitalism, sublimated earlier, resurfaced.

The double bind expresses and extends an ongoing conflict over the character of capitalism. In a recent book, Anatole Kaletsky notes that, from the mid-eighteenth century to the early part of the twentieth century, markets and politics were seen as entirely separate domains (Kaletsky 2010). Only after the social democratic welfare state came about as a reaction to the disruption of the Great Depression did government policy change and states start to manage business cycles and compensate for the social dislocations of the market. This was followed, since the 1970s, with the "Thatcher-Reagan monetarist counterrevolution that culminated in the Bush-Greenspan market fundamentalism," the notion that markets should discipline political leaders.

It is unlikely that the Humpty Dumpty of modern capitalism will be put back together again in the same old way. The twin imperatives that define the double bind intertwine in practice even as they collide in theory and ideology. The resolution of the double bind will of necessity involve a new balance between market and state: recognition of both the limits of state action and the fallibilities of markets.

What kind of resolution is possible? How will the requirements for flexible markets facilitating experimentation be reconciled with the need for rules for a stable system? Can the conflicting ideological claims be reconciled, or will the ideological conflict prevent a practical solution? How will the political necessities of social justice, required for democratic capitalism, be achieved in an era of fiscal austerity? Can the continued efforts of the wealthy countries to sustain the growth of employment and productivity, ensuring expanding real incomes of their citizens, accommodate the needs and demands of the large emerging economies? The resolutions of these questions will define the character of the age in which we will live.

Conclusion 375

A new era, which we label the "third globalization," will emerge from the multiple national resolutions of the double bind. This is an era, we repeat, in which governments are pressed simultaneously to support the industrial and regulatory reorganization, to develop and support the required new competition and growth models, and to take direct action to address immediate pressing problems all at once. Unfortunately for the countries that are already wealthy, it is evident that these stresses have stretched their capacities to the limit. Neither the United States nor the European Union nor Japan seems capable of safely navigating the current crises, let alone planning ahead. The growing fiscal pressures on governments, moreover, are entangled with pressures on the welfare state, the set of policies that for three-quarters of a century have cushioned society against the fluctuations of capitalist markets.

In this conclusion, we *first* consider the character of this "third globalization." *Second*, we contend that the distinct challenges and problems of the "third globalization," and possible national responses, are best understood by considering how "growth models" have changed. The notion of a "growth model" focuses attention on the growth *tasks* and possibilities for firms and places at a particular moment in the international or global economy, on the one hand, and the institutional and political *capacities* required to address the problems, on the other. *Finally* we consider some policy implications.

Part I. A Third Globalization?

As this book concludes, we are stepping into the era of the "third globalization." The first globalization, in the nineteenth century, was defined by expanding trade, goods produced in one country and shipped to another, and portfolio foreign investment, investments in projects abroad without direct operational control. The financial world was "managed" by England—that is, by the then-private Bank of England. The British Empire spanned the globe, and European rivalries defined global conflicts. It was the emergence of the United States that extended the central international story beyond Europe. America was a newcomer and challenger; American grain exports in the late nineteenth century redefined European politics. That first globalization collapsed with war and depression. Out of that collapse the United States emerged as the hegemon of the Western world, and the Soviet Union arose to control the Eastern bloc—their conflict shaped the cold war era.

The second globalization, which developed in the second half of the twentieth century, has been defined, schematically, by direct foreign investment, the growth and spread of multinational corporations (MNCs) setting up operations around the world, a system of global finance facilitated by expanding electronic communications and complex financial instruments, and a continuing policy effort aimed at market opening and deregulation. The United States stood at the center of this system with the leading MNCs, a supposedly "model" financial system, and policies of deregulation creating pressures for change in Japan and Europe. Global trade and financial rules were, many would say, shaped by American preferences, and, certainly, when the United States acted in tandem with European countries, their joint preferences were largely imposed on the global system (Steinberg 2006). The ultimate negotiating tools were "access" to markets and finance on the one hand and military and security support on the other. American industrial preeminence, dating from the first part of the century, and its financial preeminence at the end of World War II provided the pillars of its global position. Its system of production, known as Fordism, gave a name to an entire epoch of industrial development.

Certainly, there were challenges over the fifty or sixty years this system held in place, but the core system remained in place. Japan in the 1970s, with its lean production system and innovation in consumer electronics, followed in the late 1980s by South Korea, were the new industrial challengers, extending the global story beyond Europe and the United States to include the emergence, or re-emergence, of Asia. In a sense, Asia was a factory aimed principally at satisfying final demand in American and European markets. The complex division of labor was expressed in the notion of cross-national production networks. Indeed, the term "globalization" began to substitute for the narrower term "internationalization" with the entry of Japan as a major player in now "global" markets and the emergence of the Asian factory.

The third globalization, the twenty-first-century globalization, was clearly announced when the European leaders asked China to help bankroll the European financial stability fund. At the moment of the Euro crisis, the Asian titan was called to the rescue of the Western banks and governments. It was quite a reversal from the stories of the 1997 Asian financial crisis only a decade earlier, when it seemed that the Washington Consensus had triumphed over the developmental state. Let us consider the features of this new twenty-first-century globalization, which sharply differentiate it from the earlier era of the second globalization.

1. *Economic governance*: The financial market crash of 2008 marks a change in global economic governance. The Western domination of the trade and finance system has eroded. It is not simply that the "Anglo-Saxon" financial system has lost its claim as the single and best model, but that the composition of the power base is shifting. Europe and the United States, in particular, will be forced to share governance with newcomers. China, now moved to a position of influence, not only publicly requested to help balance Europe financially but explicitly noted that political favors will be expected in reciprocation. This is a subtle, but important, change from the less public and less explicit American borrowing from China that allowed the Bush administration to fund the second Iraq war without taxes, and permitted American families to maintain increasing living standards without increased wages. In this new world order, American and European ability to set the global rules will be constrained, even if no alternate power is yet able to step up to dominate the discussions (Steinberg 2006).

2. *Sources of final demand*: With the rapid expansion of the Brazilian, Russian, Indian, and Chinese domestic markets, the sources of final demand to sustain global growth may soon come as much from outside Europe and North America as from within them. As a result, the Western threat to restrain market access will have less power as a negotiating tool. At the same time, concerns over climate change give power to the weaker; the threat to pollute by the weak is as crucial as the threat by the powerful to limit access to their markets.

3. *Transformation of production*: The decomposition of production in both goods and services and the full force of the revolution in information technology has changed the terms of market competition, as Mark Huberty argues in Chapter 7 ("The Dissolution of Sectors: Do Politics and Sectors Still Go Together?," in this volume), and with it the underpinning of political interests. A variety of consequences point to a new economic era. The story of the independent Chinese automakers told in their chapters by Gregory W. Noble (Chapter 2, "The Chinese Auto Industry as Challenge, Opportunity, and Partner," in this volume) and Crystal Chang (Chapter 3, "Center-Local Politics and the Limits of China's Production Model: Why China's Innovation Challenge Is Overstated," in this volume) highlights the way that supply networks making widely available components and tools permit rapid new entry into previously concentrated industries. Similarly, the emergence of the Indian software industry, depicted by Rafiq Dossani in Chapter 6 ("A Decade After the Y2K Problem: Has Indian IT Emerged?," in this volume), is an example of the deployment of globally available tools to create advantage in sectors previously dominated by the West. The infusion of service components and ICT-based functionality into an array of products, "services with everything," blurs the boundaries of industries. Canon cameras confronted competition from Nokia handsets, and Nokia handsets were ultimately trumped by smartphones with diverse functionality.

4. *Employment and inequality*: Importantly, in the advanced countries, especially in the United States, the recovery so far has been substantially jobless. Furthermore, economic inequality has risen sharply across the European Union and the United States. The debate is whether the underpinnings of the jobless recovery, lie in (a) the increasing ICT-based automation in both manufacturing and in services; (b) the expansion of production from the new titans; (c) policy that has, particularly in the United States, tilted the gains from growth toward a tiny fragment of society—really the upper .1 percent or .01 percent—and more generally failed domestic policy to support expansion and education (Hacker and Pierson 2010). The answer is the combination, the interplay of these elements. The emphasis one places, the element that one defends, of course, has consequences for policy choices and thus for political stability, future job creation, and the prospects of economic growth.

IS ANYONE ADAPTING TO THE THIRD GLOBALIZATION?

Four years have passed since the financial debacle began, but the aftershocks continue. The political struggles are more than just a debate about the "right" mix of tax and spending policies. They are part of a search for a new balance between markets and states and new conceptions of the role and organization of government in the economy. For the most part, the major Western powers have focused on recovering from the financial crisis and, perhaps, debating the character of the welfare system in the twenty-first century. Certainly, they have focused less, if at all, on how they will adapt to the competitive realities of the third globalization; until now, there has been little, if anything, to suggest that those that are already wealthy are ready to think about policies appropriate to the new requirements of growth and competition. The advanced countries seem firmly trapped by the double bind. They have not defined strategies aimed at truly addressing the transformational challenges outlined in the first section of this book.

Let us consider the general issues first. The financial meltdown of 2008 had its technical roots. It was, as we argued in the introduction, the first great financial crisis of the information age. Both the products, such as collateralized debt obligations (CDOs), and the high-speed markets for trading them would have been impossible without the computing and communication power of the information tools. Without these developments, a few small banks in Iceland could not have made bets that sank a country. It was not the tools themselves but how they were used that proved so destructive. Mark Blyth points out in Chapter 8 ("This Time It Really Is Different: Europe, the Financial Crisis, and "Staying on Top" in the Twenty-first Century," in this volume) that the inability to distinguish between systemic risk and risk for a particular financial institution helped generate the illusion that new IT (information technology) tools could not only generate value but protect against catastrophe. Solutions that work for a single actor, whether an individual or a bank, may in fact be catastrophic for the system. The classic run-on-the-bank example is that if one person discovers a bank is in difficulty, then a rational decision for that individual is to pull money out. However, if everyone tries to pull out their money at the same time, then the bank reserves are drained, and it collapses, whether or not the bank was in difficulty in the first place. This inherent fragility of the banking system, which cannot be "self-solved," lies in the need for government to publicly commit to act as lender of last resort—hoping that, in so doing, public promises would be enough to prevent the frequent financial crises and bank runs, which otherwise would be triggered by rational agents acting at the first whiff of a rumor of trouble.

Equally, the fascination with computation-based financial tools and models hid, for too many financiers, the essential distinction between risk and fundamental uncertainty. Risk can be calculated: We can calculate the odds of drawing an ace of spades from a fully shuffled deck of fifty-two cards. Uncertainty is another matter. Together, these beliefs created serious problems. The widespread belief that risk was calculable and could be managed by individual financial actors in their own self-interest led to a regime of self-regulation coupled with extraordinarily high levels of financial leverage. New ICT-facilitated financial products, new ICT-enabled financial tools, and new financial markets resting on ICT infrastructure all allowed an array of financial intermediaries to make enormous, often little understood, bets. The greater leverage made the individual banks vulnerable to smaller market movements. Moreover, this deregulated system with the technical tools that allowed lenders to offload risk onto willing asset buyers created enormous moral hazards. As a result, the quality of the assets underlying financial instruments was too often ignored. Furthermore, the protection of hedges and derivatives intended to manage individual bank risks assumed that the financial market counterparties would always be there and would always be able to make good on their deals. After the market began to tank, the high leverage and the interconnection of bets provided no protection and no immediate market floor.

Fundamentally, the financial problems were political, not just technical. The dollar's status as a global reserve currency facilitated immense borrowing for consumption by the U.S. government and private agents, instead of investment in productive capacity. In Europe, the creation of the euro, in a similar but more limited way, ultimately facilitated an increase in public and private borrowing. Constraints on public-sector borrowing eroded when France and Germany violated the very limits they intended to impose on others. Interest rates overall in the Eurozone remained low, and somehow lending to and in Greece and Spain in euros was thought to be less risky than lending in drachmas or pesos. As a result, cheap money was available, and, not surprisingly, it led various bubbles to grow in different countries, from the real estate bubble in Ireland and Spain to a public financing bubble in Greece (Lewis 2010, 2011). Therefore, the political question in the Eurozone was how to use the additional and less expensive credit permitted by the euro, at least for a moment. In only a few cases were the funds invested in ways that would finance growth and productivity, instead increasing consumption.

The financial crisis diverted energy and attention in policy making from the longer-term challenges and transformation. However, the fascination with finance itself, not just the current crisis, has had serious consequences. In the United States, as William Lazonick argues in Chapter 9 ("The Fragility of the U.S. Economy: The Financialized Corporation and the Disappearing Middle Class," in this volume), the concern with narrow stock market measures of shareholder value diverted corporate attention and resources from the more basic problem of how to compete effectively, how to innovate, and how to sustain success in the market.

How, though, have the individual countries responded to the particular challenges sketched previously? Let us reflect in turn on the troubled adaptations of Japan, France, Germany, and the United States. The Japanese financial bubble and collapse had principally domestic sources, but it left Japan vulnerable to the 2008 crisis. Japan stumbled in the transition from the state-manipulated credit-based financial market that helped, from the 1950s to the 1970s, to sustain rapid expansion over three decades to a more capital market-based system of allocating credit. In the postwar era of capital shortage, state institutions helped ensure that rapidly growing sectors would have access to capital while cushioning the segments of society and economy that were being dislocated. High savings rates that fed domestic investment supported rapid growth and generated an era of trade surpluses, but eventually there were no mechanisms to allocate effectively the savings to productive uses at home or abroad. Perhaps a trillion dollars in bad loans, often stolen assets, and overpriced assets created bubbles and crashed the financial system. Since then, Japan has found it difficult to break loose from the resulting dismal performance, which has continued for two decades. The paralysis has caused it to lose its edge in many arenas of its greatest industrial strength and to be unable to develop an advantage in crucial new areas of software and services.

Steven K. Vogel, in Chapter 13 ("Japan's Information Technology Challenge," in this volume), states that policy favored "incremental reforms designed to reinforce valued institutions rather than to generate new sources of competitive strength." Japanese firms have preferred strategies to preserve long-term relationships with workers, banks, suppliers, and other business partners, and to leverage the benefits of these relationships when possible. And these firms have lobbied the government to enact incremental reforms to facilitate corporate restructuring without undermining the prior basis of their comparative advantage.

Or consider France. France, Jonah D. Levy contends in Chapter 12 ("Directionless: French Economic Policy in the Twenty-first Century," in this volume), is directionless. The French president called for liberal reforms to free the French economy for growth at the same time that he condemned morally empty capitalism for calling for state actions to contain runaway markets.

The current American double bind, as we have emphasized, begins with a long process of deregulation in many sectors of the economy, from the telecommunication sector, with the breakup of AT&T, to transport and finance. We should be clear: not all the deregulation was destructive. The antitrust-driven breakup of AT&T and the corresponding constraints forcing IBM to unbundle software from hardware undoubtedly facilitated the diffusion of semiconductor technology, the emergence of software as an independent industry, and the advent of the Internet as the basis of digital communications. Despite later problems that derived from the extensive deregulation, there were often positive gains from increased competition in air travel and trucking, to name two examples.

However, enamored with the success of these policy innovations, American policy makers, at the urgings of American companies, then began to press these core deregulations in finance and communications on the rest of the world. Of course, the deregulatory impulse did not emanate solely from the United States. It was powerfully expressed in Britain under Margaret Thatcher. Nonetheless, the United States, the ideological and policy leader of the second globalization, was the principal champion of these deregulatory policies.

In the post-crash period, as we enter the third globalization, the United States has been constrained by ideological and partisan divides as well as financial constraints. Despite the crisis, the notion persists in many policy circles that bank self-regulation is sufficient to safeguard stability and does not create systemic risk. The financial market reforms and re-regulations are disputed and certainly are not seen as a model for the rest of the advanced world, let alone the emerging market countries and new giants.

Moreover, the United States has failed to become an international leader in the debates over climate change and energy. The Obama administration subordinated climate and energy policy to debates over health care and finance, and investments in alternative energy or energy system transformation have been entangled in partisan debates or limited by reduced funding. Most disturbing has been the emergence of a movement that denies outright the science of climate change. At the same time, many fossil fuel-based American energy companies, such as Chevron, are now asserting that affordability should be the single focus and foundation of American energy policy.[1] Finally, although American policy helped drive the information age and globalization, there has not been a real policy debate over how to maintain a strong American competitive position. Concerns over American competitiveness have often focused principally and narrowly on intellectual property issues, laments over outsourced jobs being linked to limited efforts to make manufacturing "smart," demands for a better business environment, and limited extensions of prior trade initiatives.[2]

Among large countries, Germany might seem to be the exception, the outlier that resolved the double bind. The financier of the Eurozone, it has remained a competitive exporter with continued growth. There are twists to the story that we need to analyze, however, before we declare Germany a clear example of successful adaptation (Eurostat 2011). After the trauma and financial strains at the end of the twentieth century involved in integrating the East and West German economies, reunified Germany has asserted industrial and financial primacy in Europe. Arguably, the macro-events swirling around Germany have reinforced its existing structure rather than facilitating longer-term development. Moreover, despite German financial rectitude domestically, its financial institutions remain critically vulnerable to the broader European financial chaos. The irony, of course, is that for Germany, the weaker Eurozone partners have, since the creation of the euro, helped hold down the value of the common currency, making German exports more competitive. Now the euro crisis directly lowers the euro exchange rate, providing Germany, yet again, with an exchange rate far below that which it would have had with its own currency, with the added benefit that its European competitors cannot devalue against the euro as they so often did against the mark in the postwar years. To its advantage, the German export portfolio is concentrated in capital goods that are inputs to production with the consequence that the expansion of manufacturing in China, for example, generates markets for Germany even as China floods Western markets with final products (Eurostat 2011). German manufacturers, moreover, benefited from the East European "near abroad" in its successful attempts to reorganize production, by enabling those countries to threaten labor with job relocation, threats that muted wage increases and demands. Perhaps the continued competitive success of traditional German manufacturers has limited the German interest in pursuing policies to support the ICT-enabled transformation of services. Services in Germany continue to be seen in their classic form, as an economic dead end, rather than as an ICT-enabled productivity driver. The emphasis is on the growth of services as the result of deindustrialization rather than as a capital-intensive basis of a new economic era. In a sense, Germany has sidestepped the double bind, rather than resolving it (Hassel and Williamson 2004).

The large countries reviewed here, then, seem locked into their past, ideologically and organizationally, with neither the vision nor the capacity to make the fundamental adaptations needed here. By contrast, the small Nordic advanced countries have made a serious effort to adapt and adjust. As Darius Ornston notes in Chapter 11 ("How the Nordic Nations Stay Rich: Governing Sectoral Shifts in Denmark, Finland, and Sweden," in this volume), on small country adaptations, traditional solutions, in particular the centralized bargains among industry, labor, and policy makers that defined postwar adjustment "neocorporatist" deals, were widely perceived as inhibiting adaptation to disruptive economic and technological changes. But the reality is that these once conservative institutions' and arrangements' services were repurposed to form the basis of a competitive and adaptive corporatism. Accordingly, Ornston argues, the Nordic countries turned centralized bargaining institutions to new purposes and, instead of inhibiting adaptation, they supported movement into new, knowledge-intensive activities and industries, transforming into "creative corporatism." Institutionalized cooperation among organized economics actors was converted to perform new functions. The countries invested in new supply-side resources such as risk capital, human capital, and research. These inputs created more space for new, entrepreneurial actors that had struggled under traditional, neocorporatist bargaining and, in so doing, facilitated rapid movement into new activities and industries.

Moreover, while one must be skeptical of financial market reports, and the recent European bank stress tests have widely debated flaws, the Nordic banks—Denmark, Finland, Norway, Sweden—are reported to be quite healthy and comparatively strong with very little "exposure" to the southern European debt. Interestingly, it is reported that the Nordic banks pass the stress tests even with a "uniform haircut of 50% on all sovereign PIIGS [Portugal, Ireland, Italy, Greece, Spain] holdings." Nordic banks, reportedly, learned lessons from the crisis of the 1990s.[3] As a result, these economies have proven surprisingly resilient in the face of the challenges outlined in this volume.

Part II. Models of Growth: Understanding Who Adapts to the Third Globalization

How, then, do we understand who adapts and who does not? How do we account for the national variation in adaptation to the third globalization? Is it simply the classic argument that small countries are forced by intense pressures to adapt? Are the politics in the larger countries entrenched or fragmented in ways that prevent a clear statement of objectives or a clear political deal to move forward? What features of a domestic political economy shape the ability to respond to significant changes in the economic environment?

We use the simple concept of a "growth model" to sort through these questions. The notion of a "growth model" defines what it takes for firms to compete in markets, create value, and generate jobs. It clarifies the roles that governments need to play in sparking, sustaining, and supporting development. Let us develop the notion of a "growth model" beginning with the simple and classic logic of Alexander Gerschenkron (1962). The industrialization in Britain at the beginning of the industrial revolution was a story of small-scale textile development. Later, in the second half of the nineteenth century, Germany developed around capital-intensive steel and chemicals. As Gerschenkron taught us, it is critical to understand that what was necessary in order to succeed in heavy industry was very different from the conditions for success in small-scale textiles (Gerschenkron 1962). In simple terms, your family and friends could lend you enough money to start a small textile business, but to start heavy-industry production facilities you need the sort of massive capital infusion that only a bank or a government can amass. Similarly, the textile industry requires simple mechanical skills, while the chemical industry was the first modern science-based industry and thus was deeply entwined with the rise of the new German university-industry model that underpinned the chemical industry (Arora, Landau, and Rosenberg 1998). Evidently, the *tasks* for governments and firms are different in each era; the *capacities* required to address those tasks are different, so the political problem of growth evolves. Each opportunity in the market, in the global political economy, involves particular tasks and capacities. The different ways in which states approach them define the different trajectories of growth various countries have pursued in the same period.

Considering recent decades, Breznitz analyzed the rapid innovation–based growth of Israel, Taiwan, and Ireland, three states that were poor, peripheral, and technologically backward in 1960 (Breznitz 2007). Breznitz shows that at the end of the 1960s, state-led initiatives to develop indigenous high-tech industries were launched in all three societies. At that point, all three were similar along most of the important economic dimensions, including size and population. All three had low skill intensity in their labor force (defined as the number and percentage of scientists and engineers in the population), a relatively low percentage of high school graduates, poor communication and physical infrastructures, and a high dependence upon agriculture.

All three states followed similar infrastructure policies. Despite similarities between their macrolevel and infrastructure policies, however, their micro-, that is, industry- and firm-level, policies were different. Since the late 1960s, Ireland has focused mainly on industrial development funded by foreign direct investment (FDI). Israel has focused on funding industrial R&D (research and development) activities through government grants, with project ideas originating solely from private industry. In Taiwan, the ruling party, the Kuomintang, mistrusted big private industry and feared the rise of competing powers. Hence, it prevented the creation of overarching conglomerates, controlled the inflows and outflows of investment, and relied on public research agencies such as Industrial Technology Research Institute (ITRI) and The Institute for Information Industry (III) to lead R&D efforts and diffuse the results throughout private industry.

Today, the IT industries of all three countries are undoubtedly successful. Yet the three IT industries are markedly different in the way they work, the business models they use, and the way they relate to the global IT production network. Israeli firms have succeeded in both software and hardware. The industry's role in the global IT production networks is as a supplier of high-end new technologies (or of new products based on new technologies). Thus, Israel's success is based almost solely on intensive R&D. In Taiwan, the development of its software industry has stagnated, and the IT hardware industry is embedded within the global IT production network in a very different way from that of Israel. Taiwan's industry bases its success on innovation in product design and manufacturing and focuses on second-generation innovation R&D. In Ireland, even after more than forty years of industrial policies that brought MNCs to open manufacturing facilities in the country, indigenous IT hardware growth has not been significant, and it is the local software industry that rose to prominence.

For many years in all three countries, the private market did not possess the necessary skills and capability to successfully create and manage R&D-based IT companies. Private actors, in particular, investors, shied away from even attempting to do so. Moreover, even after more than a few successes, such as the spin-off of United Microelectronics Corporation (UMC) from ITRI in Taiwan, or the several initial public offerings (IPOs) of Israeli firms on the New York stock exchanges by 1989, private financial institutions were unwilling to invest in the IT industry. Thus, the state was the only actor willing and able to start developing skills and capabilities in an attempt to spur growth of the industry.

In turn, the different ways in which Israel, Taiwan, and Ireland then addressed the common specific task of developing ICT industry after 1960 influenced the specific capacities their firms and citizens developed, the creation of specialized service industries, and the very different relationship each industry has with the global markets for goods, skills, and, most important, capital (Breznitz 2007). These, in turn, led each national industry down a different path for growth. Thus, their varying patterns of industrial evolution led each of the three states to face a different crisis when they confronted the global financial meltdown in 2008.

We emphasize that the notion of a "growth model" that we propose focuses our attention on the growth *tasks* and possibilities for firms and places at a particular moment in the international or global economy, on the one hand, and the *capacities* required to deal with the problems, on the other. The simple notion is that as the tasks change, the capacities required to address them will have to evolve as well. The *tasks* are defined by what is required to take advantage of the possibilities. A significant advantage of this approach is that it considers at its core the institutions and political arrangements that create the ability to address tasks.

Every era has universal developments that affect all economies, though there are, we have seen, a variety of possibilities and opportunities in a given historical period, particularly this one. Nonetheless, the cookbook and the possible ingredients for success evolve over time. In this volume, we emphasize the emergence of ICT-enabled services, the decomposition of production of both services and manufacturing, the continued competitive pressure of the largest emerging economies, and the problems of energy and climate. The *particular tasks* vary by country, depending on its existing production structure, institutional arrangements, and political choices. The *specific capacities* available to governments to respond likewise depend on their existing political, institutional, and market arrangements. In that respect, countries follow historically rooted trajectories, and their particular characteristics influence how they experience universal problems and how they respond. The important thing is the match, or mismatch, between "tasks" and "capacities." (Zysman 1994). If there is a match, then a country might not need to make significant adjustments in its internal arrangements. If there is a mismatch, adaptation might require a political fight to develop new capacities.

This approach stresses the specific tasks presented by a particular "growth model" and the particular capacities and tools that can be called on to develop solutions to those tasks. We have argued elsewhere how political solutions at particular moments generate trajectories of growth and technology development (Breznitz 2007; Zysman 1994). The question, as growth models change tasks, is whether a country is constrained, bound, or trapped by its previous choices about how to organize markets and governments. Certainly, initial responses to new problems are framed by existing institutions, ideological framework, and power balances. Nonetheless, national systems do evolve. The French financial system was reshaped after World War II to serve development purposes and morphed again in the 1980s with a top-down liberalization led unexpectedly by a Socialist minister of Finance. Our past is not our destiny but part of the resources with which we address the future—a discussion that remains for another work. We distinguish this "growth model" approach from a *resource* approach, the Stolper-Samuelson logic, which focuses on the way that shifting access to resources—labor, finance, or goods in a global market—influences the *interests and preferences* of groups in the domestic economy. The resource notion emphasizes that, as the global economy changes, as the opportunities and challenges evolve, groups in the domestic economy will be affected in different ways. The resulting needs of the groups will translate into political demands, and the resulting policy output will reflect the political resources of these groups. These two approaches—growth models that emphasize tasks and capacities and resource approaches that emphasized interests and political assets—are, complementary, not competing.

Let us play out the logic of the "growth model" approach. After World War II, the rapidly growing countries—France, Germany, and Japan—were rebuilding, shifting resources, people, and capital from agriculture to industry, and reorganizing both. In France, on farms, it often meant substituting tractors for animals while, in factories, it meant establishing a form of Fordist mass production. Resources had to be channeled to firms and farms that were more productive and expanded productivity, while those displaced had to be coddled or politically pinioned. The credit-based financial system in France and Japan facilitated a conservative modernization: an economic modernization dominated by existing elites.

In Japan, the particular pattern of controlled competition that characterized its conservative modernization generated the lean production model of high-volume manufacturing. The French policy focus, industrial base, and strategic position were different and generated a different pattern of industrial growth based on capital-intensive technology, such as aircraft, trains, and luxury goods (Zysman 1983).

By contrast, the countries with slower growth—the United States and Britain—had to reorganize existing industries. That meant that the productivity gains would often result from a sequence of marginal changes in existing industries, rather than significant gains from shifting resources from labor-intensive agriculture to capital-intensive manufacturing. Perhaps more important, the reorganizations required confrontation between groups, such as labor and management, that had entrenched policy and political positions in advanced economies. For the rapidly growing countries, conservative modernization strategies finessed the rural and small-town communities, often sidestepped, and sometimes politically marginalized them. Market gains, productivity growth, from the shift out of agriculture proved sufficient to provide incentives for both industry and compensation for affected communities. Whereas the Japanese, for example, expanded their automobile production system and, in the process, generated the innovative "just-in-time" production system, the British had to retool and reorganize theirs. A strategic reorientation by the firms, a restructuring of manufacturing practices embedded in existing labor relations, and a reformulation of auto sector regulation were all required, aside from the need to modernize the auto fleets. The British-owned volume automobile producers never managed the shift, and they ended up either in the hands of foreign producers or closing down. Similarly, American automakers for years failed to recognize the fundamental Japanese production innovations and tried in various ways to make marginal changes when radical reform was called for.

To be sustained, the "growth model" of each era must resolve a simple and evident simultaneous equation: *first*, either resources must be made more productive, or more resources must be accumulated; *second*, the question of allocation of the gains from growth must be settled, because otherwise the struggles over who wins and who loses will interfere with the working of the markets. The various political economy solutions to these two equations in one era are often not appropriate to the next. Firms, or places, then adapt and adjust or face relative decline.

Transitions from one growth era to another are difficult. It means moving from one "growth model" of tasks and required capacities to the next, with a different set of tasks required for productivity gains to be realized and capacities to address those tasks. These shifts, of course, are not intellectual debates, with the best policies determined by an independent judge or authority. The transition of economic governance from one era's "growth model" to another in the next often means new institutions, new relationships between governments and markets, new approaches to regulation, and new theories of the economy and politics. Policy reformulations always involve political conflict, and a shift in the framework of political economy all the more so. Consequently, policy shifts that involve changes in the role of the state are often accompanied by new political coalitions and, often, the emergence of new political parties, movements, and groups. In some cases, fundamental new policy directions are required, as are changes in the purposes of, and political support for, government. In the past, all major transformation of the organization and management of production have led to major upheavals in social organization.

After their high-growth phase, both France and Japan faced severe difficulties in adapting from their heavily subsidized financing through administrated price credit-based financial systems to the new era that required the restructuring of the financial system and the creation of a more capital market-based system. The French managed the shift with limited damage to their banks and financial system, while for the Japanese, the transition—arguably still incomplete—paralyzed the financial system with, by some estimates, a trillion dollars in bad debts. In the first phase, both managed a conservative-led industrial modernization, in which the Japanese path produced the powerful innovation of lean production. In the transition, the Japanese stumbled, unable to break from the past. Similar tasks and similar institutional structures, but different capacities and different elite politics, characterized the French and Japanese cases. Similar institutional arrangements implied similar capacities for action, but the specific ways in which conservative politics were organized in each differentiated the two countries.

Critically, when the tasks required to sustain growth and productivity shift as the growth model evolves, then the solutions of one era may not be appropriate to the problems of the next. The adaptation can be difficult, as the new tasks or solutions to those problems are not evident. Identifying and understanding the problems are difficult. New problems are likely to be addressed first using existing tools and perceived through old lenses. Long evolutions might be accompanied by real disruption as the politics of new institutions emerge.

In this sense, crises are no different. Old solutions based on existing capacities are employed to address new problems. Initially, there is not enough time to create new ones. In this current crisis, the United States, France, and Japan used old approaches that simply disguised the new problems, and so far new solutions and strategies have not emerged.

With that in mind, we argue that the market transformation underlying the new growth models emerging from the third globalization makes analyzing political economy problems more difficult. Some of the analytic tools disintegrate in our hands, because, indeed, the interests and interest groupings cannot be simply inferred from market position. More than ever, the interests and interest groupings are political creations. For example, a classical method in comparative political economy is to examine economic sectors, or segments of economic sectors, and to infer their needs and interests. Wheat growers and steel makers, runs the argument from Gourevitch to Rogowski, are distinct groups and often have different interests (Gourevitch 1986; Rogowski 1990). This approach infers groupings and interests from the production profile as a useful source of propositions. Thus the production profile, the argument goes, provides a useful starting point for initial propositions about issues and conflicts in the political economy. Although it has always been difficult to identify political interests from economic positions, we contend that it is an even greater problem now. As some of the chapters in our book have shown, interests can no longer be easily determined from the production profile of the existing economy or even the production profile of an imagined economy. The decomposition of production, including the modularization of manufacturing and unbundling of services, also decomposes political interests. In the post-World War II golden age, labor and capital often found common ground, allowing the creation of coalitions of labor and management in the face of foreign competition. When production moved overseas, the interests of management and the workforce over issues such as trade policy often diverged. The story of the fragmentation of interests continues. The present step is the modularization of manufacturing and unbundling of services. For firms, interests are defined by where they sit in the production networks and by the strategies they adopt to pursue the "sweet spots" of value added. Consequently, interests within sectors are fragmented. Now the interests of different sets of workers, even workers with seemingly similar roles, become sharply differentiated by the possibility that a firm will outsource beyond its corporate boundaries and its national home base. As a consequence, the politics of political economy will become ever more central. As interests diverge and fragment, economic interest formation cannot simply be derived from the production profile or resource pattern of an economy. Rather, interests themselves and the boundaries of sectors are political outcomes.

As the economic foundations of political groupings become more unclear, the politics of creating groups and interests in the political economy becomes more central. The question of how political groups are constituted and reconstituted, how interests are formed, defined, and redefined, becomes ever more crucial. Political and even economic groupings must be seen more clearly for what they are: *political* constructs. The politics of political economy become more central. The politics of governance become core.

III. Something Old, Something New, Something Borrowed: Can the Double Bind Be Reconciled?

We started this book with a sense of optimism about the future of the already wealthy. It might puzzle the reader, at this stage, after having read repeated accounts of drifting and directionless policies in most rich societies other than the Nordics (and perhaps Germany), that we remain optimistic. However, the real question that this volume raises is whether the conflicting demands of the double bind can be reconciled, whether demands for state action to make markets and the market system function more effectively can fit with demands for market experimentation. As we detail next, this is not going to be easy, but the fact that this task is now on the agenda, because the failure of the one-size-fit-all neoliberal solution is on full display, offers a unique period of policy experimentation and innovation. Let us consider some policy issues that emerged from the chapters in this volume.

FINANCE

The core of the financial story, as considered here, has been that policy lost sight of the central relationship between the financial system and the "real economy": the manufacture and distribution of goods and services. The policy presumption leading up to the financial crisis was that lightly regulated, or self-regulated, financial markets were the best mechanism for channeling savings to the most productive uses. As the economies of the advanced industrialized countries were "financialized," to use William Lazonick's term, and policy left finance to fend for itself, the financial system became an end in itself (Chapter 9, "The Fragility of the U.S. Economy: The Financialized Corporation and the Disappearing Middle Class," in this volume). This is a policy concern over and above the questions raised here about the danger of confusing risk and uncertainty and of managing an uncertain marketplace with conceptions of risk; of the confusion between the stability of individual banks and the system as a whole linked by common assets that dissolve in a crisis; and of the indifference to the real value of assets in an originate-and-diffuse model of CDOs. The conversation must return to the question of how the financial system can support the continued growth and development of the entire economy. Sadly, at this stage these conversations have yet to begin in any of the already wealthy countries.

CLIMATE AND ENERGY

Two core notions emerge from the discussions of climate change and energy. First, the climate problem is fundamentally a matter of shifting from a high-carbon, low-efficiency energy system to a low-carbon, high-efficiency system. The problem is that this shift cannot be achieved piecemeal; it is a transformation in which the system needs to be levered from one balance point to another. The coordination requires government action. Not all the science is yet available, and not all the incentives for the transition are in place. In addition, governments will not be able to make the endless array of technical choices and foresee which technological approaches will be most effective. Consequently, the energy system transformation will require a rethinking of the relationship between markets and governments, where government action is appropriate, where private strategies will be more effective. Ideological combat will not serve us well in this transition. Second, where successful transition has been taking place, there has always been a political deal between a segment of industry interested in profit, a segment of the government interested in solving issues of energy security, and, usually, green interest groups. Without such political deals, coordination and the creation of markets have proved elusive.

ICT-ENABLED SERVICES

ICT-enabled services are, and will remain, a central component of productivity. These services, from Google through the array of products and tools in the new financial market place to iTunes by Apple, all look more and more like manufacturing. These services are capital intensive with latent inventory in the network of servers. Accordingly, policy must address the productivity possibilities of ICT-enabled services. More generally, services are increasingly introduced into products as a means of differentiating them and of avoiding competition from low-cost global producers. Many of those services are enabled by IT, but the process is more general. This process requires a workforce with analytic judgment and problem-solving skills. The transformation of the service sector is just beginning. It will be accelerated by the development of "cloud computing," which will make computing-intensive activities available to small and medium-size companies and individuals. It will also allow rapid experimentation with and prototyping of both goods and services. As a result, policies to ensure the existence of the capacities to use these new possibilities effectively will be essential.

AN ERA OF DIFFUSED PHASES OF PRODUCTION

In this new competitive environment, locations—whether countries, regions, or cities—must focus on the core competencies underpinning diverse activities, firms, and sectors that are central to the competitive advantage of companies and consequently of locales (Zysman, Nielsen, and Breznitz 2007). In a world of commodities, the challenge is to find the "sweet spot" in the value network. There is no single path to competitive success, so regions are not necessarily rivals. Although a company must find its defensible place in a dispersed value network, the "sweet spot" of value creation, its success depends on all the other nodes and elements of that value network. Similarly, a "location" must find its defensible node, and that node depends on its relationship with other regions. The question for locations is what investments to make, and how, so that firms there can develop distinct strategies for generating specific advantages. The core task is to consider what a location is competent to do and how to deepen those competencies, expand the list, and ensure the local capacity for combining competencies into productive activity.

A critical issue in policy formulation for success in the era of the third globalization is whether the development of one set of capacities required for one role in the value network and a specific strategy with regard to energy and ICT-enabled services interferes with or supports the development of capacities for a different role. Can two different sets of competencies coexist in a particular location? Or, will they interfere with each other?

Rephrased, the proposition is that each set of competencies and capacities requires a distinct set of institutional foundations, so the question becomes whether those institutions can coexist in the same place and within the same sets of national rules. We have repeatedly stressed that there is always a need to have certain competencies from other phases and domains in order to excel in innovating in a specific one. Therefore, locations not only can, but must, maintain competencies from several phases and technological domains in order to fully master one.[4] A sensible long-term strategy for any region is to specialize, while keeping diverse competencies, allowing coordination and collaboration with other locations, and, when needed, transforming its core activities as the markets, industries, and technologies in which it specializes change over time.

Countries are not necessarily rivals. In fact, successes in one country can open opportunities in others. The Western companies' supply networks have created entry points for development in emerging countries. So the questions pose themselves: Can supply networks be ladders to development? Is the international economy, at least in some ways, a bit like training for a charity race in which all win? This image is certainly close to the classical economist's image of gains from trade. Or are countries bitter rivals in a zero-sum game that is closer to boxing, in which you win only if you knock your opponent senseless, a more mercantilist world view?

Can the diversity of experience provide lessons that one country can learn from another, as states respond to the several current crises? What clues to effective policy emerge from the diverse evolutions of national policies? Can the apparent successes of one country work in another? Can the strategies that work for one country be transported to another?

Drawing usable lessons from national cases will be difficult. One difficulty is that with the overlapping swirls of crises, the question becomes which policies are relevant to which outcomes, let alone in which specific context. In the United States, for example, the fundamental shift in the logic of value and the distribution of production, commoditization, modularization, and the services transformation produced concerns, and policies, focused on the offshoring of production. The financial meltdown, by contrast, leads to a focus on government capacities to restart the economy and the need for financial market re-regulation to avoid a rerun. Meanwhile, the climate debate and the need to enable energy transformation call for active state strategies for innovation and domestic production of new generations of energy technology.

More important, any particular national government tends to use similar approaches, to deploy its existing array of policy tools to address different problems. And even if the tools are not exactly the same, the policy processes in a particular country tend to follow similar paths setting constraints on the range of solutions. (Berger and Dore 1996; Crouch 2005; Hall and Soskice 2001; Shonfield 1965). There is a striking regularity in policy within countries across domains. Policy strategies and particular policies are embedded in specific institutional and policy contexts. Even when objectives are similar, different countries have to pursue those objectives in starkly distinct ways. Countries facing similar crises often resolve them, for the most part, in different ways.

The underlying questions of policy maker and academic, in this case, converge. Policy makers seeking innovative solutions must ask, of course, which policies worked abroad. But what worked abroad might not work at home; the institutional and policy environment might not "accept" policy strategies devised in a distinctly different institutional environment. The policy maker asking which lessons can be borrowed from abroad must evaluate whether policy made abroad can be transposed from one policy setting to another. A country's historical heritage shapes and limits the available array of policy choices and hence the methods that it can implement from a different experience. France and the United States represent sharp contrasts: one with a highly centralized administrative and political system that provides leverage for concerted action by the central government on projects and the other with a dramatically decentralized federal system. Not surprisingly, their approaches to energy and finance are sharply different. They appear to be on separate, distinct trajectories of governance and policy. It is evident that policies formulated in one environment and one set of institutions are not automatically transferable to another.

Nonetheless, thinking about growth models might allow us to go beyond this apparent dead-end. By thinking about tasks and capacities, we can look at the principles behind the ways that different states solved the same general problems. This allows us to think about whether, and how, a solution specifically developed in one political-economic environment offers lessons for creating solutions in a different environment. As a conclusion, let us focus on an example from an area both authors view as critical for sustained production innovation in the already-wealthy countries.

As Breznitz and Cowhey have recently argued (Breznitz and Cowhey 2012), there is a low level of innovation in American production small and medium-size enterprises (SMEs). Anchor American production firms (such as automakers) do not continuously invest in infusing the supply base with innovation, and many SMEs have limited capability and resources to engage in innovation. Moreover, the innovation that does take place is usually diffused slowly in this environment.

These facts have led many pundits to suggest that the United States would do well to look at how other countries have called on various public research institutes to solve those issues. The examples are many, from the Korean research institutions to the currently idolized German Fraunhofer institutes network and the Taiwanese ITRI. Using our growth model's analytical framework, we can quickly see what purposes are served by these institutes and what capacities they develop within the local environment. Indeed, these public research institutes have a similar design: Their specialized departments (or subinstitutes) focus on particular industrial niches and sets of technologies, develop long-term relationships with industry, and establish a division of labor, in which private resources are pooled and coupled with infusions of public funding, allowing the institute to concentrate on core and continuous production R&D and spread the results widely to industry, which in turn focuses mostly on final development and implementation of these technologies.[5]

Armed with this knowledge, we can start thinking about how to develop institutions and policies suitable to the American political economy, an environment in which for many years various public research institutions played a role without ever reaching the same degree of success as in South Korea, Germany, and Taiwan. Nonetheless, as suggested by Breznitz and Cowhey (2012), the United States has already developed a set of institutions to solve exactly such issues in another sector of the economy: agricultural research, which is widely credited with solving much of the world's hunger problem. Hence, a program for production innovation built around the principles exemplified by the Fraunhofer institutions can be built in the United States, but for it to work it might need to be developed following the organizational logic of agricultural research, which is based on regional specialization, and sponsored at both the state and federal levels instead of by once-centralized institutions.[6]

In short, while the third globalization necessitates that the already-wealthy develop new models of growth in order to stay rich, employing the growth model's analytical framework presented here should provide policy makers in the rich countries with the ability to learn from, and improve on, one another's experiences in a more nuanced fashion.

Acknowledgments

The authors thank the Alfred P. Sloan Foundation for financial support and the Berkeley Roundtable on the International Economy (BRIE) for research and administrative support. Breznitz acknowledges that this book is based in part on work supported by the National Science Foundation under grant SES- 0964907, and he thanks the Kauffman Foundation for its generous financial support.

Notes

1. Testimony of John S. Watson, Chairman and Chief Executive Officer of Chevron, for the Hearing on "Oil and Gas Tax Incentives and Rising Energy Prices," U.S. Senate Committee on Finance, May 12, 2011.

2. For more, see U.S. Patent and Trademark Office, "Leahy-Smith America Invents Act Implementation" (http://www.uspto.gov/aia_implementation/index.jsp 2005); Council on Competitiveness: 2005 Innovate America: National Innovation Initiative Summit and Report; Policy Brief #184, "The Comprehensive Patent Reform of 2011: Navigating the Leahy-Smith America Invents Act." The Brookings Institution (http://www.brookings.edu/papers/2011/09_patents_villasenor.aspx).

3. For more, see http://news.efinancialcareers-norway.com/newsandviews_item/newsItem Id-35563.

4. The competencies principally required for a particular role, say product design, do not entirely stand alone. They require at least access to complementary capacities—and access

to those complementary capacities demands at least adequate local resources to absorb knowledge and coordinate with others. Hence, if Israel now appears to be an embodiment of novel-product-creation focus, a deeper analysis reveals that Israel also excels in many of the activities suited to second-generation and component innovations.

5. On the German model, see http://www.eib.org/attachments/efs/eibpapers/eibpapers_ 2003_v08_no2/eibpapers_2003_v08_no2_a03_En.pdf. On ITRI, see Breznitz (2005, 2007).

6. For ideas along similar lines, see Duderstadt (2009); Duderstadt, Muro, and Rahman (2010).

References

Arora, Ashish, Ralph Landau, and Nathan Rosenberg. (1998). *Chemicals and Long-Term Economic Growth: Insights from the Chemical Industry*. New York: Wiley-Interscience.

Berger, Suzanne, and Ronald Dore. (1996). *National Diversity and Global Capitalism*. Ithaca, NY: Cornell University Press.

Breznitz, Dan. (2005). "Development, flexibility, and R&D performance in the Taiwanese IT industry—Capability creation and the effects of state-industry co-evolution." *Industrial and Corporate Change* 14(1): 153–87.

Breznitz, Dan. (2007). *Innovation and the State: Political Choice and Strategies for Growth in Israel, Taiwan, and Ireland*. New Haven, CT: Yale University Press.

Breznitz, Dan, and Peter F. Cowhey. (2012). America's two systems of innovation: Recommendations for Policy changes to support innovation, production and job creation. Connect Innovation Institute White Paper, San Diego.

Crouch, C. (2005). *Capitalist Diversity and Change: Recombinant Governance and Institutional Entrepreneurs*. Oxford: Oxford University Press.

Duderstadt, James J. (Chair). (2009). *Energy Discovery Innovation Institutes: A Step Toward America's Energy Sustainability, Blueprint for American Prosperity*. Washington, D.C.: Brookings Institution Press.

Duderstadt, James J., Mark Muro, and Sarah Rahman. (2010). *Hubs of Transformation: Leveraging the Great Lakes Research Complex for Energy Innovation*. Washington, D.C.: Brookings Institution Press.

"Europe turns to Asia for help with bailout." *Wall Street Journal: Asia Business*, October 28.

Eurostat. (2011). *External and Inta-EU trade: A Statistical Yearbook Data 1958–2010*. Eurostat: European Commission.

Gerschenkron, Alexander. (1962). *Economic Backwardness in Historical Perspective, a Book of Essays*. Cambridge, MA: Belknap Press of Harvard University Press.

Gourevitch, Peter. (1986). *Politics in Hard Times*. Ithaca, NY: Cornell University Press.

Hacker, Jacob S., and Paul Pierson. (2010). *Winner Take All Politics*. New York: Simon & Schuster.

Hall, Peter, and David Soskice. (2001). *Varieties of Capitalism: The Institutional Foundations of Comparative Advantage*. Oxford: Oxford University Press.

Hassel, Anke, and Hugh Williamson. (2004). The evolution of the German model: How to judge reforms in Europe's largest economy. Working Paper, Anglo-German Foundation for the Study of Industrial Society, January.

Kaletsky, Anatole. (2010). *Capitalism 4.0: The Birth of a New Economy in the Aftermath of Crisis.* New York: Public Affairs.

Lewis, Michael. (2010). *The Big Short: Inside the Doomsday Machine.* New York: W.W. Norton.

Lewis, Michael. (2011). *Boomerang: Travels in the New Third World.* New York: W.W. Norton.

Rogowski, Ronald. (1990). *Commerce and Coalitions: How Trade Affects Domestic Political Alignments.* Princeton, NJ: Princeton University Press.

Shonfield, Andrew. (1965). *Modern Capitalism.* Oxford: Oxford University Press.

Steinberg, Richard. (2006). "The Transformation of European Trading States." In *The State After Statism: New State Activities in the Age of Liberalization,* edited by Jonah D. Levy, 340–60. Cambridge, MA: Harvard University Press.

Zysman, John. (1983). *Governments, Markets, and Growth: Financial Systems and the Politics of Industrial Change.* Ithaca, NY: Cornell University Press.

Zysman, John. (1994). "How institutions create historically rooted trajectories of growth." *Industrial and Corporate Change* 3(1): 243–83.

Zysman, John, Niels C. Nielsen, and Dan Breznitz. (2007). Building on the past, imagining the future: Competency based growth strategies in a global digital age. BRIE Working Paper Series, Berkeley Roundtable on the International Economy, University of California, Berkeley.

Index

A

Abe, Shinzo, 361
Abowd, John, 262
Accenture, 101
African Americans, and disappearance of middle class jobs in U.S., 260
Agency theory, maximize shareholder value (MSV) ideology, 234, 238–40, 242
Agricultural interests, Germany, 21
AIG Financial Products, 214
Akaishi, Koichi, 363
Algorithmic revolution, 32, 100–102
Alternative energy sources, China, 71–74
Amazon.com, 144, 151n24
    Kindle, 104
American Electronics Association, 245
American Energy Innovation Council, 292
American Job Creation Act of 2004, 266–67
American Reinvestment and Recovery Act of 2009, 295n7
American support for energy research and development, *292*
Analog age, 181–82
Apple, Inc.
    Apple 1, 18

copyright protection, digital music, 182–85, 188–89
iPod, 6, 102
iPod strategy, 197n4
iTunes Music Store (iTMS), 183–84, 188
    revenue, 197n3
Asia, low-cost producers, 302–3
Aso, Taro, 361
Assembly, role of, 19
AT&T
    deregulation of, 5, 15, 380
    semiconductor industry, 120
Austerity double bind, 208, 222–24
Auto industry
    China, 7, 49, 57–81, 58–62
        age of workers, 64
        alternative energy sources, 71–74
        Automotive Industry Policy, 84–85
        "Baojun" brand, 71
        "Big Four, Small Four," 92
        case studies, 74–76
        and central government, 91–92
        domestic passenger car market, 87–88
        East Asian auto giants, *63–64*
        electric vehicles (EVs), 71–74, 89, 92–94, 96

397

398 | Index

Auto industry (*Cont.*)
    electric vehicles (EVs), case studies, 74–76
    engineers, 65–66
    First Auto Works (FAW), 61, 70, 86–87
    Five Year Plans, 61, 72, 74
    foreign direct investment (FDI) policy, 84–85
    foreign technology, purchase of, 69
    hybrids, promotion of, 71–74
    indigenous innovation, 70–71
    intellectual property rights (IPRs), 60
    and Japanese and Korean developmental path, 58–62
    joint ventures, 70–71, 85–86, 88
    labor, cheap, 62, 64–75
    land, 66–67
    machinery, 62–67
    modularization, 67–70
    national standards, lack of, 92–93
    outsourcing, 67–70, 88
    ownership management structure, 61
    politics and development of auto sector, 7, 82–93
    price pressures, 62–67
    production model, limits of, 84–89
    reform period, 85, 90
    renminbi (RMB), 58, 74
    Sino-foreign collaboration, 94–95
    structured uncertainty, 89–94
    Taiwan, economic cooperation agreement with, 69
    World Trade Organization (WTO), 60, 61
    France, 340
Automated services, 107–8
Auto sector, politics and development of in China, 7, 49, 82–98

B

Bank of England, 221, 375
Banks, bailouts, 257, 339
"Baojun" brand, 71
Barcode technology, 138
Basel 1, 217, 228n30
Basel 2, 217, 228n30
Baumol, William J., 122n1, 149n1, 181
    "Baumol's Cost Disease," 116, 132
Beijing auto, 62
Berle, Adolf, 242
Betamax, 197n1

"Big Four, Small Four," 92
Blair, Margaret, 241
Blue collar jobs, "disappearance of" in U.S., 263–64
Britain, industrialization, 383
Bush administration, 266
Business model transformations, services, 110, *110*
BusinessWeek, 263
BYD, 71, 74–76

C

California
    energy market deregulation, 282
    financial crisis of 2008, state actions, 15
Capacity, transformation of services, 118–19
Career employees, "disappearance" of middle class jobs in U.S., 261
Carelink, 191–92, 195
"Carpet-bombing," 324
Cash dividends, ratios of, *249*
Cash subsidies, provision of to business enterprises, 241
CDOs. *See* Collateralized debt obligations (CDOs)
CDS. *See* Credit default swap (CDS)
Chery, 69, 71, 74–76
China
    auto industry, 7, 49, 57–81, 377
    age of workers, 64
    alternative energy sources, 71–74
    Automotive Industry Policy, 84–85
    "Baojun" brand, 71
    "Big Four, Small Four," 92
    case studies, 74–76
    and central government, 91–92
    domestic passenger car market, 87–88
    East Asian auto giants, *63–64*
    electric vehicles (EVs), 71–74, 89, 92–94, 96
    electric vehicles (EVs), case studies, 74–76
    engineers, 65–66
    First Auto Works (FAW), 61, 70, 86–87
    Five Year Plans, 61, 72, 74
    foreign direct investment (FDI) policy, 84–85
    foreign technology, purchase of, 69
    hybrids, promotion of, 71–74
    indigenous innovation, 70–71
    intellectual property rights (IPRs), 60

and Japanese and Korean developmental
   path, 58–62
joint ventures, 70–71, 85–86, 88
labor, cheap, 62, 64–75
land, 66–67
machinery, 62–67
modularization, 67–70
national standards, lack of, 92–93
outsourcing, 67–70, 88
ownership management structure, 61
politics and development of auto sector, 7,
   82–93
price pressures, 62–67
production model, limits of, 84–89
reform period, 85, 90
renminbi (RMB), 58, 74
Sino-foreign collaboration, 94–95
structured uncertainty, 89–94
Taiwan, economic cooperation agreement
   with, 69
World Trade Organization (WTO), 60, 61
auto sector, politics and development of, 7,
   49, 82–98
development strategy, 31–32
economic growth, 35–56
863, 36, 51n1, 73
and European financial stability fund, 376
foreign direct investment (FDI) policy, 84–85
Foxconn, 37–38
General Administration of Quality
   Supervision Inspection and Quarantine,
   93
information and communications technology
   (ICT), hardware production, 42–48
innovation
   hardware production, ICT, 42–48
   structured uncertainty, 40–41, 83
market rules, 204
Ministry of Industry and Information
   Technology (MITT), 93
Ministry of Posts and Telecommunications
   (MFT), 51–52n3
Ministry of Science and Technology
   (MOST), 72, 73, 93
"Minying," 43
OEM-brand clients, 47
Pearl River Delta, 37, 42, 52n6
production, decomposition of
   auto industry, 7, 49

auto sector, politics and development of, 7,
   49, 82–98
production, fragmentation of
   generally, 7, 35–36
   logic of, 36–39
   production-stage economies of scale and
      scope, 37–38
Qingxi, 43, 46
research and development (R&D), 43–44, 50
rise of, 5
risk, 212
Run of the Red Queen, 36
Science and Technology Plan, 36
semiconductor design, 165
Shenzhen Special Economic Zone (SEZ), 42
small and medium size enterprises (SMEs),
   45–46
Standards Administration, 93
structured uncertainty, 35–36
   adaptation to, 39–42
   auto industry, 89–94
   foreign multinational corporations
      (MNCs) and, 41
   innovation and, 40–41, 83
   research and development (R&D), 39, 41
students, 65–66
Torch Programs, 36
unskilled labor, use of, 19
Xiaolingtong, 45
China Unicom, 51–52n3
Chirac, Jacques, 326–28, 333–37, 341
Cisco Systems, 18, 260–61
Climate and energy, double bind, 389–90
Cloud Computing, 105, 114, 120, 126nn19 and 20
CODA Automotive, 94
Cognitive double binds, 208
Co-invention, retail, 151n21
Collateralized debt obligations (CDOs), 213, 378
"Comes with Music" (Europe), 187
Commoditization, transformation of services,
   111–13
Compensation
   financial crisis of 2008, 13
   France, 13
Competition
   copyright protection, digital music, 187–89
   from Japanese corporations, 239
   production, decomposition of, 6
   services, transformation of, 111–13

400 Index

Competitive corporatism
  Denmark, Finland, and Sweden as wealthy nations, 307–8, 312–13
Complex instruments, securitization and sale of, 124n13
Computer industry, France, 327
Computing platforms, 105, 113–14, 125n17
  connected era, 125n17
  stand-alone era, 125n17
Concorde, 327
Conglomerate movement of 1960s, 244
Connected era, computing, 125n17
Connectivity, transformation of services, 117–18
Content, copyright protection, 181–82
Coop Denmark, 137
Cooperation
  Denmark, Finland, and Sweden as wealthy nations, 310–11
    strong cooperation, 313–14
    weak cooperation, 311–12
Copyright protection, digital music, 181–89
  and analog age, 181–82
  Apple, 182–85, 188–89
  "Comes with Music" (Europe), 187
  competition, 187–89
  content, 181–82
  devices, 181–82
  Digital Rights Management (DRM), 185–86, 188, 197n6
  firms, digital transformation of, 181–87
  Microsoft, 182–83, 185–86, 189
  Nokia, 182–83, 186–87, 189
  product strategies, 181–87
  Secure Digital Music Initiative (SDMI), 188
Corporate resource allocation, financialization of. *See* Financialization of corporate resource allocation
Corporatism, conserving
  Denmark, Finland, and Sweden as wealthy nations, 305–6, 310–11
Creative corporatism
  Denmark, Finland, and Sweden as wealthy nations, 308–9, 313–14
Credit default swap (CDS), 214–15, 219
CRM. *See* Customer relations management (CRM)
Crystal, Graef, 244
Current Population Survey, 262–63
Customer relations management (CRM), 103

D

Daley, Anthony, 332
Danish, Germans, and French retailing
  and politics, 146, 152n29
  and technology, 9
    private labels, 135–36
    relational contracting, 135–36, 150n11
Darling, Alisdair, 220
Data privacy, retail, 152n28
d'Estaing, Giscard, 329
"Deal decade" of 1980s, 259
Decomposition of production. *See* Production, decomposition of
Deconglomeration of 1970s and 1980s, 244
Democratic Party of Japan (DPJ), 361–64
Denmark
  energy systems, 293, 295n9
  retailing. *See* Danish, Germans, and French retailing
  as wealthy nation. *See* Denmark, Finland, and Sweden as wealthy nations
Denmark, Finland, and Sweden as wealthy nations, 300–22, 382
  challenges, 314–15
  choices of policy makers (1980s), 305–9
    competitive corporatism, 307–8, 312–13
    contemporary political economy, explaining choice in, *310*
    cooperation, 310–14
    corporatism, conserving, 305–6, 310–11
    creative corporatism, 308–9, 313–14
    explaining choices, 310–14
    neocorporatist cooperation, 308–9
    reforms, neoliberal, 306–7
    risk capital, investment in, *309*
    vulnerability, 310–12
  comparative political economy, 301–5
    double bind, 301–2
    information technology (IT) bubble, 304
    Soviet Union, barter trade with, 303
    "universal" banks, 302
  competitive corporatism, 307–8, 312–13
  cooperation, 310–11
    strong cooperation, 313–14
    weak cooperation, 311–12
  corporatism, conserving, 305–6, 310–11
  creative corporatism, 308–9, 313–14
  double bind, 301–2
  industry vulnerability, 311

Index 401

information technology (IT) bubble, 304
neocorporatist cooperation, 308–9
political constraints, 314–15
reforms, neoliberal, 306–7
risk capital, investment in, *309*
sectoral shifts, explaining, 305–9
Soviet Union, barter trade with, 303
trade union vulnerability, 311
unilateral liberalization, 311–12
"universal" banks, 302
vulnerability, 311
  limited, 311–12
Deregulation
  AT&T, 5, 15, 380
  California, energy market, 282
  debates on, 2
Derivatives, pricing of, 124n13
Design, prototype development, and production engineering stage, 19
Developing countries, financial crisis of 2008, 16
Development and utilization of products, 243
Devices, copyright protection, 181–82
Digital music, copyright protection and, 181–89
  and analog age, 181–82
  Apple, 182–85, 188–89
  "Comes with Music" (Europe), 187
  competition, 187–89
  content, 181–82
  devices, 181–82
  Digital Rights Management (DRM), 185–86, 188, 197n6
  firms, digital transformation of, 181–87
  Microsoft, 182–83, 185–86, 189
  Nokia, 182–83, 186–87, 189
  product strategies, 181–87
  Secure Digital Music Initiative (SDMI), 188
Digital Rights Management (DRM), 185–86, 188, 197n6
Dirigiste approach, France, 324–26, 333, 345–46
Displaced Worker Survey, 263
Diversity and global economy, 17
Dividends, ratios of cash dividends, *249*
Division of labor, 180
Double bind, 1–27
  austerity double bind, 208, 222–24
  climate and energy, 389–90
  cognitive double binds, 208
  current, 380
  defined, 1

Denmark, Finland, and Sweden as wealthy nations, 301–2
"double movement," 1
energy systems transformations, state choices, 180–81
finance, 389
financial crisis of 2008, 1–2, 13–20, 208
  compensation, 13
  double bind, 219–22
  global economy, changing view of, 16–20
  market rules, 13–14
France, 345–46
Germany, 381–82
ICT-enabled services, 390
information and communications technology (ICT), 2, 4
meltdown, before, 4–12
  consumption of services as they are produced, 10
  diminished state and, 12
  production, decomposition of, 4–8
  regulatory change, need for, 12
  retail, technology and, 9, 130–55
  security, 8–9
  services, ICT-enabled transformation of, 8–12
  value, creation of, 9–10
policy skills and, 20–21
production, diffused phases of, 390–92
reconciliation of, 388–93
  climate and energy, 389–90
  finance, 389
  ICT-enabled services, 390
  production, diffused phases of, 390–92
sectors, dissolution of, 198n13
sustained growth, 373–74
"Double dividend" debate, energy systems, 296n12
"Double movement," 1, 13
Double shift, France, 345–46
Dow Jones Industrial Average, 247–48
DPJ. *See* Democratic Party of Japan (DPJ)
Drexel Burnham, 244
DRM. *See* Digital Rights Management (DRM)

E

EagleWision (EW), 169–70
Earnings per share (EPS), U.S. economy, 232–33
Earthquake of 2011 (Japan), 364–65

East Asia
  auto giants, *63–64*
  semiconductor design, 164–65
ECB. *See* European Central Bank (ECB)
E-commerce, rise of, 144–45
  sub-sector market share, *145*
Economic growth
  energy systems transformations, state choices, 285–89
    "creative destruction," 288
    flaws in growth-energy nexus, 288–89
    goals for, 285–88
    networked technologies, analogies between energy systems and, 287–88
    technological changes, 286
ECR. *See* Efficient customer response (ECR)
Education level, transformation of services, 118–19
Efficient customer response (ECR), 139, 143
863, China, 36, 51n1, 73
Electric vehicles (EVs)
  China, auto industry, 71–74, 89, 92–94, 96
  case studies, 74–76
Elpida Memory, Inc., 358
EMIR. *See* European Market Infrastructure Regulation (EMIR)
Emissions
  pricing, 290
  reductions in, 285
Employee stock options, indexing of (suggested reform), 236, 267–68
Employment
  globalization, effect on jobs, 234–35
  "green jobs," 294, 295n7
  job creation, 235, 265
Employment contract, regulation of (suggested reform), 236, 268
Employment patterns, retail, 147–48
Employment Retirement Income Security Act (ERISA), 244–45
EMS. *See* European Monetary System (EMS)
EMU. *See* European Monetary Union (EMU)
Energy
  double bind, 389–90
  strategies, 15–16. *See also* Energy systems
Energy systems
  networked technologies, analogies between energy systems and, 287–88
  transformations, state choices, 18, 277–99
    American support for energy research and development, *292*
    California, energy market deregulation, 282
    "creative destruction," 288
    double bind, 180–81
    "double dividend" debate, 296n12
    and economic growth, 285–89
    economic growth, goals for, 287–88
    emissions pricing, 290
    emissions, reductions in, 285
    financial crisis of 2008, aftermath of, 278–79
    flaws in growth-energy nexus, 288–89
    fossil fuels, 277
    France, 284
    German government, 291, 295nn5–6
    goals for, 285–88
    "green growth" opportunities, 180
    "green jobs," 294, 295n7
    Integration of Variable Generation Task Force, 295n9
    networked technologies, analogies between energy systems and, 287–88
    New York blackout of 2003, 282
    policy implications, 292–93
    policy options, 289–92
    political economy, implications for, 289–92
    Portland, Oregon, 284
    possibilities for, 283
    reductions in emissions, goals for, 285
    research and development (R&D), 290–92, *292*
    scale of transformation, 279
    "smart grid," 286, 295n10
    sustainability and growth, between, 278–81
    systems transformation, 281–84
    technological changes, 286
    wind and solar energy, 285
    zero-sum policy game, 180
Environmental Protection Agency (EPA), 290
EPA. *See* Environmental Protection Agency (EPA)
Equilibrium statics, risk, 211–12
ERISA. *See* Employment Retirement Income Security Act (ERISA)
EU. *See* European Union (EU)
Euro, creation of, 379

Europe
    "Comes with Music," 187
    energy systems, 295n7
    financial crisis of 2008, wealthy persons, 209
    Nordic nations, wealth of. *See* Denmark, Finland, and Sweden as wealthy nations
    retail, technology and, 9
European Central Bank (ECB), 223
European financial stability fund, 376
European Market Infrastructure Regulation (EMIR), 222
European Monetary System (EMS), 328
European Monetary Union (EMU), 225, 336, 340
European Treaty on Stability, Coordination, and Governance (TSCG), 344
European Union (EU), 146
    energy systems, 296n20
    risk, 216, 219–22
Eurozone, 381
EVs. *See* Electric vehicles (EVs)
Executives, highest paid, 252–53, *254–55*
"Exit," concept of, 357
Exogenous changes, 211–12
Exxon Mobil, 251, 256

F
Fannie Mae, 257
Farber, Henry, 262–63
FAW. *See* First Auto Works (FAW)
FDI. *See* Foreign direct investment (FDI)
Federal Data Center Consolidation Initiative, 127n30
FERA. *See* Foreign Exchange Regulation Act (FERA) of 1973
Ferry, Luc, 339
Finance, double bind, 389
Financial crisis of 2008
    compensation, 13
    developing countries, 16
    double bind, 13–20, 208
        risk, 219–22
    and double bind, 1–2
    energy strategies, 15–16. *See also* Energy systems transformations
    energy systems transformations, state choices
        aftermath of crisis, 278–79
        generally, 233
    global economy, changing view of, 16–20
    housing boom, 216
    and manipulation, 266
    market rules, 13–14
    purposive action, demand for, 15
    risk
        austerity double bind, 208, 222–24
        double bind, 219–22
        macro bubble, 215–16
        micro investments, 213–15
        and preemption, 218–19
    state actions, 15
        California, 15
        Japan, 15
    state, pressures on
        compensation, 13
        market rules, 13–14
        purposive action, demand for, 15
    uncertainty
        macro bubble, 215–16
        microinvestments, 213–15
Financialization of corporate resource allocation, 243–57
    banks, bailouts, 257
    cash dividends, ratios of, *249*
    conglomerate movement of 1960s, 244
    deconglomeration of 1970s and 1980s, 244
    development and utilization of products, 243
    executives, highest paid, 252–53, *254–55*
    generally, 232–33
    health insurers, 256–57
    information and communications technology (ICT), 256
    innovation as force, 246–47, 265–66
    manipulation as force, 246–48
    New Economy business model (NEBM), 245–47, 260–61
    Old Economy business model (OEBM), 245–47, 258, 261
    pharmaceutical drug prices, 256
    post-World War II, 243
    qualified stock options, 244
    ratios of stock repurchases, *249*
    and signaling, 251
    speculation as force, 246–48
    speculative trading on corporate stock, 244
    stock and bond yields, average annual, *247*
    stock-based compensation, 243
    stock options, 257
    stock repurchases, 248–51, *250*
    venture capital, 245

Index

Financial services Authority (FSA), 220
Financial Times, 233
Finland as wealthy nation. *See* Denmark, Finland, and Sweden as wealthy nations
Firms, digital transformation of, 181–87
First Auto Works (FAW), 61, 70, 86–87
Fordism, 376, 386
Foreign competition, maximize shareholder value (MSV) ideology, 239
Foreign direct investment (FDI)
    China, 84–85
    India, 161
    Ireland, 383–84
Foreign Exchange Regulation Act (FERA) of 1973, 158
Foreign technology, purchase of, 69
Fossil fuels, 277
Fourth Services Transformation, 193
Foxconn, 37–38
France
    Agency of Industrial Innovation (AH), 341
    automobile industry, 340
    bank bailouts, 339
    Bank of SMEs (BDPME), 341
    borrowing, 379
    Caisse des Dépôts et Consignations (CDC), 340
    compensation, 13
    computer industry, 327
    currency crisis, 327–28
    double bind, 345–46
    double shift, 345–46
    "economic patriotism," 341
    economic policy, 323–49, 380
        Agency of Industrial Innovation (AH), 341
        automobile industry, 340
        bank bailouts, 339
        Bank of SMEs (BDPME), 341
        Caisse des Dépôts et Consignations (CDC), 340
        "carpet-bombing," 324
        currency crisis, 327–28
        dirigiste approach, 324–26, 333, 345–46
        double bind, 345–46
        double shift, 345–46
        "economic patriotism," 341
        Estates General of Industry, 338
        "first employment contract" (CPE), 336–37
        French Guarantee Company (SOFARIS), 341
        Grand National Loan, 338
        gross domestic product, 324, 340
        industrial policy, 343
        Juppé Plan, 334–37
        labor market, *330*, 330–31
        Law for Labor, Employment, and Purchasing Power, 324, 325
        liberalism, limits of, 333–37
        limits of statism, 337–45
        National Agency for the Commercialization of Research (ANVAR), 341
        Programme Emplois Jeunes (PEJ), 330
        public social expenditures, *331*
        public spending, *329*
        social anesthesia state, 327–33, 340
        social spending, 331, 333
        Stability Pace, 340
        steel industry, 332
        Strategic Investment fund, 338
        taxation, *329*
        U-turns, 328, 334, 337, 339, 345
        zero-sum reforms, 337
    energy systems transformations, state choices, 284
    Estates General of Industry, 338
    financing, 387
    "first employment contract" (CPE), 336–37
    French Guarantee Company (SOFARIS), 341
    Grand National Loan, 338
    gross domestic product, 324, 340
    industrial policy, 343
    Juppé Plan, 334–37
    labor market, *330*, 330–31
    Law for Labor, Employment, and Purchasing Power, 324, 325
    liberalism, limits of, 333–37
    mobile telephone licenses, 332
    National Agency for the Commercialization of Research (ANVAR), 341
    nuclear power, 16
    post-war growth models, 204–5
    Programme Emplois Jeunes (PEJ), 330
    public social expenditures, *331*
    public spending, *329*
    research and development (R&D), 332
    retailing. *See* Danish, Germans, and French retailing
    social anesthesia state, 327–31, 340
        limits of, 331–33

social spending, 331, 333
  public social expenditures, *331*
Stability Pace, 340
steel industry, 332
Strategic Investment fund, 338
taxation, *329*
zero-sum reforms, 337
"Free cash flow," maximize shareholder value (MSV) ideology, 237–38
Fujitsu, 359
Fukuda, Yasuo, 361

G

"Galapagos" phenomenon, 355
Gallagher, Kelly Sims, 86
Gates, William H. III, 186, 197n7
GDP. *See* Gross domestic product (GDP)
Geely, 71, 74–76
General Electric, 233, 258
General Motors (GM), 148
  China, 58, 62
    limits of production model, 86
    outsourcing, 68
    production, decomposition of, 6–7
    SAIC-GM-Wuling, 71, 86
    Shanghai GM (SGM), 86, 91
Germany
  agricultural interests, 21
  borrowing, 379
  double bind, 381–82
  government, energy systems transformations, 291, 295nn5–6
  retailing. *See* Danish, Germans, and French retailing
Gerschenkron, Alexander, 383
Gerstner, Louis V., Jr., 262
GM. *See* General Motors (GM)
Goldman Sachs, 210
Gordon, Philip, 326, 328
Great Depression, 20
Greece, real estate bubble, 379
"Green growth" opportunities, 180
"Green jobs," 294, 295n7
Greenspan, Alan, 215
Gross domestic product (GDP)
  and energy systems, 295n6
  Japan, 351
  U.S. economy, fragility of, 232
Growth, sustained. *See* Sustained growth

H

Hamermesh, Daniel, 259
Haraguchi, Kazuhiro, 363
Hardware
  Japan, 358
  services, transformation of, 102
Haroyama, Yukio, 362
Health Insurance Portability and Accountability Act (HIPAA), 191–92, 194–95
Health insurers, financialization of corporate resource allocation, 256–57
Hewlett-Packard, 102
HIPAA. *See* Health Insurance Portability and Accountability Act (HIPAA)
Hirschman, Albert, 357
Hollande, François, 326, 334, 343–45
Home health care, 11
Homeland Investment Act, 266–67
Honda, 72
Hong Kong, information and communications technology (ICT), 42
Housing boom, financial crisis of 2008, 216
Huawei, 42, 45, 52nn4 and 9
Human talent, personal services relying on, 11
Hybrid autos, China, 71–74
Hybrid services, 108
  growth of in retail, 131
    labor productivity growth, *131*
  information and communications technology (ICT), 10–11
Hyundai, 69

I

IBM, 102, 261–62
  India, 158
  PCs, 260
  semiconductor industry, 120
  value, creation of, 9
ICT. *See* Information and communications technology (ICT)
India
  Constitution, 162
  development strategy, 31–32
  Foreign Exchange Regulation Act (FERA) of 1973, 158
  information technology-enabled services (ITES), 156–77
    Big 6, 157, *157*, 173
    competitive advantage, 172–74

India (*Cont.*)
    design services environment, 165–72
    early IT firms, employees of, *160*
    foreign direct investment (FDI), 161
    industrial organization of sector, 157–61
    multinational corporations (MNCs), 158, 161
    offshore ITES, *172*, 173
    outsourcing, 166–67
    and political developments, 175
    private provision, 163
    semiconductor design (case study), 163–65
    share of complex work, *174*
    state-owned enterprises (SOEs), 157–58
    state, role of, 161–63
    technological developments, 1980s, 159, *160*
  market rules, 14, 204
  National Democratic Alliance (NDA), 162
  and political developments, 175
  production, decomposition of
    services transformation, business models and, 7, 33–34
  rise of, 5
  share of complex work, *174*
  state-owned enterprises (SOEs), 157–58
  state, role of, 161–63
  Tata Consultancy Services, 159
  technological developments, 1980s, 159, *160*
Indigenous innovation, China's auto industry, 70–71
Industry vulnerability
  Denmark, Finland, and Sweden as wealthy nations, 311
Inequity, U.S. economy, 232–36
Information and communications technology (ICT)
  algorithmic revolution, 32, 100–102
  China. *See* China
  development of, 31
  and double bind, 2, 4, 390
  financialization of corporate resource allocation, 256
  human talent, personal services relying on, 11
  hybrid services, 10–11
  ideal types of services, 10–11
  production, decomposition of, 4–5
  retail. *See* Retail, technology and service services, 10
  services, transformation of, 99–129
    algorithmic revolution, 32, 100–102
    automated services, 107–8
    benefits of transformation, 117–20
    business model transformations, 110, *110*
    capacity, 118–19
    capturing services transformation, 115–17
    Cloud Computing, 105, 114, 120, 126nn19 and 20
    commoditization, 111–13
    competition, 111–13
    computing platforms, 105, 113–14, 125n17
    connectivity, 117–18
    customer relations management (CRM), 103
    drivers of transformation, 111
    education level, 118–19
    government spending, 119–20
    and hardware offerings, 102
    hybrid services, 108
    in-house business functions, 101
    innovative lead users, 114
    intellectual property rights (IPRs), 121
    manufacturing and services, blurring boundaries between, 106–7
    portals to service, products as, 104–5
    production, ICT-based services as, 115–16
    productivity gains, potential for, 108–9
    productivity, services driving, 116–17
    products, shifts from, 102–3
    repositioning services, 102–6
    services dilemma, 111
    services spectrum, *107*, 107–8
    skills, 118–19
    social rules, services and, 121
    software, 103–4
    Software-as-a-Service (SaaS), 104
    unbundling of services, 21–22, 101–2
    unfolding of, 100–106
    "value domains," 105–6
  service transformation and, 33–34
  South Korea, 367–69
  sustained growth, 373
Information technology-enabled services (ITES), India, 156–77
  Big 6, 157, *157*, 173
  competitive advantage, 172–74
  design services environment, 165–72
  early IT firms, employees of, *160*
  foreign direct investment (FDI), 161
  industrial organization of sector, 157–61
  multinational corporations (MNCs), 158, 161

offshore ITES, *172*, 173
outsourcing, 166–67
and political developments, 175
private provision, 163
semiconductor design (case study), 163–65
share of complex work, *174*
state-owned enterprises (SOEs), 157–58
state, role of, 161–63
technological developments, 1980s, 159, *160*
Information technology (IT). *See also* Information technology-enabled services (ITES)
    Denmark, Finland, and Sweden as wealthy nations, 304
    Japan. *See* Japan
In-house business functions, transformation of services, 101
Initial public offering (IPO), 245–46
Innovations
    China. *See* China
    financialization of corporate resource allocation, 246–47, 265–66
    Israel, 383–84
    Japan. *See* Japan
    taxes on (suggested reform), 236, 268–69
Innovative lead users, transformation of services, 114
Instability, U.S. economy, 232–36
Integration of Variable Generation Task Force, 295n9
Intel, 124n16
Intellectual property rights (IPRs)
    China, 60
    services, transformation of, 121
International Monetary Fund, 3
Internet, 125–26n17
    boom, 266
IPO. *See* Initial public offering (IPO)
IPRs. *See* Intellectual property rights (IPRs)
Ireland
    expenditures, 314
    foreign direct investment (FDI), 383–84
Israel
    innovation-based growth, 383–84
    research and development (R&D), 17, 384
ITES. *See* Information technology-enabled services (ITES)
Ito-Yokado, 152n28

J
Japan
    auto industry, 58–62
    "Big Bang" reforms, 360
    competition from, 258–59
    controlled competition, 386
    corporate strategies, information technology (IT), 356–59
    Council on Economic and Fiscal Policy (CEFP), 362
    Democratic Party of Japan (DPJ), 361–64
    earthquake of 2011, 364–65
    Economic and Industrial Policy Bureau, 362–63
    "exit," concept of, 357
    financial bubble, 379–80
    financial crisis of 2008
        capitalism, 15
        state actions, productivity of, 15
    financing, 387
    governance problem, 363–65
    gross domestic product, 351
    information technology (IT), 15, 350–72, 380
        "Big Bang" reforms, 360
        challenges for Japan, 353–56
        corporate strategies, 356–59
        decline, Japan's, 351–53
        Democratic Party of Japan (DPJ) era, 361–64
        "exit," concept of, 357
        "Galpagos" phenomenon, 355
        and governance problem, 363–65
        government strategies, 359–61
        hardware, 358
        innovations, 356
        NTT "family" firms, 358–61
        Organisation for Economic Co-operation and Development (OECD), 351–52, *352–53*
        policy mix, 365–69
        production, decomposition of, 354–55
        Proposition 1, 365–66
        Proposition 2, 366–67
        Proposition 3, 367–69
        research and development (R&D), 369n6, 370n21
        services transformation, 355
        software, 355

408 Index

Japan (*Cont.*)
    "voice," concept of, 357
    "Wintelist" era, 354
    World Market Share, 352
  innovations, information technology (IT), 356
  lean production, 376
  Liberal Democratic Party, 361, 364
  MIC, 361–63
  Ministry of Communications, 3
  Ministry of Economy, Trade, and Industry, 3
  Ministry of Finance (MOF), 359, 364
  Ministry of Health, Labor and Welfare, 364
  Ministry of Internal Affairs, 360–61
  Ministry of International Trade and Industry (METI), 360, 362–64, 369
  Ministry of Land, Infrastructure and Transportation, 364
  Ministry of Posts and Telecommunications, 360–61
  NTT "family" firms, 358–61
  post-war growth models, 204–5
  production, decomposition of, 354–55
  Proposition 1, 365–66
  Proposition 2, 366–67
  Proposition 3, 367–69
  Reconstruction design Council, 365
  research and development (R&D), 369n6, 370n21
  rise of, 31–32
  services transformation, information technology (IT), 355
  students sent abroad, 366–67, 370n17
  "voice," concept of, 357
  World Economic Forum, 366, 370n12
  World Market Share, 352
Japanese corporations, competition from, 239
Jensen, Michael, 237–38, 240
Job creation, 235
  retail, 148
Job displacement
  globalization, due to, 265
  marketization, due to, 265
  and sustainable prosperity, 265
Jobs, Steve, 184, 186, 188
Joint ventures, China's auto industry, 70–71, 85–86, 88
Junk bonds, 234
Juppé Plan, 334–37

K

Kaletsky, Anatole, 374
Kan, Naoto, 365
Kanodia, Lalit, 158–59
Kawamoto, Akira, 362–63, 369
Kerry-Lieberman climate, 290
Keynes, John Maynard, 227–28n14, 342
Kletzer, Lori, 262
Kohli, F. C., 159
Koizumi, Junichiro, 361, 364
Kone, 103, 303
  value, creation of, 9
Korea, auto industry, 58–62
Kuomintang, 384
Kurt Salmon Associates, 143

L

Labor market, France, 330, 330–31
Law of unintended consequences, 227n1
Lean production, Japan, 376
Lean retailing, 135, 150nn6 and 7
Lenovo, 52n4
"Liberalization by stealth," 326, 328
Loan companies, 123n13

M

Macro bubble, 215–16
Manipulation, financialization of corporate resource allocation, 246–48
Manufacturing and services, blurring boundaries between, 106–7
Market imperfections, maximize shareholder value (MSV) ideology, 236
Marketization, 234–35, 263
  job displacement due to, 265
M&As. *See* Mergers and acquisitions (M&As)
Maximize shareholder value (MSV) ideology, 236–43
  agency theory, 234, 238–40, 242
  cash subsidies, provision of to business enterprises, 241
  damage done by, 257
  dominance of ideology, 238
  and foreign competition, 239
  "free cash flow," 237–38
  generally, 233
  Japanese corporations, competition from, 239
  market imperfections, 236
  questioning of, 269

residual claimants, 237
and stock market boom of 1980s and 1990s, 238
Means, Gardiner, 242
Medical devices, privacy and, 189–92
  Carelink, 191–92, 195
  Medtronic, 179, 190–92
  remote delivery of medical services, 190–92
Medtronic, 179, 190–92
  Carelink, 191–92, 195
  good-services strategy, 193
  and HIPAA, 194–95
Mergers and acquisitions (M&As), 123n4
Merkel, Chancellor, 222
METT report, 355
Meunier, Sophie, 326, 328
Microinvestments, 213–15
Microsoft, 182–83, 185–86, 189, 251
  Zune Marketplace, 185, 187, 197n6, 198n12
Microsoft Research Asia, 52n5
Microsoft Windows, 105
Middle class jobs, "disappearance of" in U.S., 258–64
  African Americans, 260
  blue collar jobs, 263–64
  career employees, 261
  Current Population survey, 262–63
  Displaced Worker Survey, 263
  globalization, effect of, 234–35
  and Japanese competition, 258–59
  offshoring, 263
Milken, Michael, 244
"Minying," 43
Mitsubishi, 68
Mitterande, François, 328, 339
MNCs. *See* Multinational corporations (MNCs)
Mobile telephone licenses, France, 332
The Modern Corporation and Private Property (Berle and Means), 242
Modularization, China's auto industry, 67–70
Modularization of manufacturing, 21–22
Mody, Minoo, 159
Moore, Gordon, 124n16
Moore's law, 124n16
Mortgage-backed securities (MSBs), 213
Mortgage grantors, 123n13
MSBs. *See* Mortgage-backed securities (MSBs)
MSV. *See* Maximize shareholder value (MSV) ideology
Multinational corporations (MNCs)
  China, structured uncertainty, 40
  India, 158, 161
  spread of, 375–76
Murtaugh, Phil, 91

N

NAFTA. *See* North American Free Trade Agreement (NAFTA)
Naidu, Chandrababu, 163
Napster, 188
NASDAQ. *See* National Association of Security Dealers Automated Quotation (NASDAQ)
National Academy of Sciences, 122–23n2
National Association of Security Dealers Automated Quotation (NASDAQ), 244–46
  executive pay, impact on, 253
  NASDAQ Composite Indices, 247, *248*
National Bureau of Economic Research (NBER), 152n30
National Cash Register, 135
National Institutes of Health (NIH), 240
National Nanotechnology Initiative, 256
National Science Foundation, 73
NBER. *See* National Bureau of Economic Research (NBER)
NEBM. *See* New Economy Business Model (NEBM); New Economy business model (NEBM)
NEC, 358–59
Neocorporatist cooperation, 308–9
Netherlands
  competitive corporatism, 312–13
  expenditures, 314
Networked technologies, analogies between energy systems and, 287–88
Networking, 124n16
New Economy Business Model (NEBM), 14
New Economy business model (NEBM), 245–47, 260–61
New York blackout of 2003, 282
New York Stock Exchange (NYSE), 243, 245
NIH. *See* National Institutes of Health (NIH)
NINJA (No Income, No Job or Assets), 214
Nokia, 182–83, 186–87, 189, 315
Nordic nations, wealth of. *See* Denmark, Finland, and Sweden as wealthy nations

North American Free Trade Agreement (NAFTA), 146
Norway, oil wealth, 314
Novelty state, 18
NTT, 358–61
Nuclear power, France, 16
NYSE. *See* New York Stock Exchange (NYSE)

O

Obama administration, 381
OEBM. *See* Old Economy business model (OEBM)
OECD. *See* Organisation for Economic Co-operation and Development (OECD)
Offshore ITES, India, *172*, 173
Offshoring, "disappearance" of middle class jobs and, 263
Old Economy business model (OEBM), 245–47, 258, 261
On-board computers (OBCs), 141
OnStat, 10
Organisation for Economic Co-operation and Development (OECD), 225, 351–52, *352–53*
Outsourcing
 auto industry, China, 67–70, 88
 design services environment, 166–67
 India, 166–67
Ozawa, Ichiro, 362

P

Palamountain, Joseph Jr., 149
PCs, evolution of, 125n17
Pearl River Delta. *See* China
PEJ. *See Programme Emplois Jeunes* (PEJ)
Pharmaceutical drug prices, financialization of corporate resource allocation, 256
Phases, identification of, 18
Platforms, technology, 144–46
Point-of-sale (POS) databases, 137
Polanyi, Karl
 "double movement," 1, 13
 on market forces, 328–29
Political economy, sectors in, 179–81
Portals to service, products as, 104–5
Portland, Oregon
 energy systems transformations, state choices, 284

Post-World War II
 financialization of corporate resource allocation, 243
 sustained growth, 385–88
Pradesh, Andhara, 162
Privacy, medical devices, 189–92
 Carelink, 191–92, 195
 Medtronic, 179, 190–92
 remote delivery of medical services, 190–92
Private labels, retailing, 136, *143*
Private provision, India, 163
Production, decomposition of, 21, 34, 48. *See also* China; India; Japan
 China, 7
  auto industry, 7, 49
  auto sector, politics and development of, 7, 49, 82–98
  competition, 6
  consequences of, 5–7
  and giant companies, 6–7
  offshore, movements to, 5
  potential products, 6
  semiconductor industry, 6
  structured uncertainty, 7
Production, fragmentation of
 China. *See* China
Production, ICT-based services as, 115–16
Production, role of, 19
Productivity gains, potential for in transformation of services
 services, transformation of, 108–9
Productivity gap, 180
Productivity, services driving, 116–17
Products, shifts from and transformation of services, 102–3
Programme Emplois Jeunes (PEJ), 330

Q

Qualified stock options, financialization of corporate resource allocation, 244

R

Radio Frequency Identification, 151n17, 194
Rationalization, 234–35, 263
 job displacement due to, 265
Ratios of stock repurchases, *249*
R&D. *See* Research and development (R&D)
Real estate bubble, 379

Reforms. *See specific topic*
Regionalization, retailing, 147
Relational contracting, retailing, 135–36, 150n11
Remote delivery of medical services, 190–92
Renminbi (RMB), 58, 74
Report of the Independent Banking Commission, 221
Repositioning services, 102–6
Research and development (R&D)
    China, 43–44, 50
        structured uncertainty, 39, 41
    energy systems transformations, state choices, 290–92
    France, 332
    Israel, 17, 384
    Japan, 369n6, 370n21
Residual claimants, maximize shareholder value (MSV) ideology, 237
Retail, technology and, 9, 130–55
    barcode technology, 138
    "Baumol's Cost Disease," 132
    business opportunities, increase of, 141
    co-invention, 151n21
    data privacy, 152n28
    decentralized national environments, 142–43
    and digital revolution, 137–44
    dilemmas, global markets and, 146–49
    e-commerce, rise of, 144–45
        sub-sector market share, *145*
    efficient customer response (ECR), 139, 143
    employment patterns, 147–48
    growth in services, 132
    hybrid services, growth of, 131
        labor productivity growth, *131*
    implementation strategy status, *143*
    job creation strategies, 148
    lean retailing, 135, 150nn6 and 7
    national models of retail capitalism, 142
    on-board computers (OBCs), 141
    output vs. hours, *147*
    platforms, technology, 144–46
    point-of-sale (POS) databases, 137
    post WWII period, 139
    private labels, 136
    private-label sales, *143*
    productivity across five countries, 132–33, *133*
    reduced overheads, 140–41
    regionalization, 147
    relational contracting, 135–36, 150n11
    retailing revolution, 134
    scale retailers, growth in, 142
    sector-specific research, 133
    selected country characteristics, *138*
    stages of retail development, 137–44
    vertical integration, 136, 150n12
    warehouses, size of, 140–41
Revenue Act of 1964, 243
Ricardo, D., 180, 181
Risk
    architecture of, 211–12
    complete payoffs, 212–13
    equilibrium statics, 211–12
    European Union (EU), 216, 219–22
    exogenous changes, 211–12
    financial crisis of 2008
        double bind, 219–22
        macro bubble, 215–16
        micro investments, 213–15
        and preemption, 218–19
    invisible generators, 212–13
    payoffs, 212–13
    uncertainty, failure to distinguish from, 3, 209–12
Risk capital, investment in, *309*
RMB. *See* Renminbi (RMB)
Roles, identification of, 18
Run of the Red Queen, China, 36

S

SaaS. *See* Software-as-a-Service (SaaS)
SAIC, 70
SAIC-GM-Wuling, 71, 86
Santana, 85
Sarkozy, Nicolas, 324–27, 333–34, 337–45
Schultze, Charles, 262
SDMI. *See* Secure Digital Music Initiative (SDMI)
Sears and Roebuck, 139
SEC. *See* Securities and Exchange Commission (SEC)
Second generation product and component innovations phase, 18–19
Sectors, dissolution of, 21, 34, 178–200
    digital music, copyright protection and, 181–89
    and analog age, 181–82
    Apple, 182–85, 188–89
    "Comes with Music" (Europe), 187

Sectors, dissolution of (*Cont.*)
  competition, 187–89
  content, 181–82
  devices, 181–82
  Digital Rights Management (DRM), 185–86, 188, 197n6
  firms, digital transformation of, 181–87
  Microsoft, 182–83, 185–86, 189
  Nokia, 182–83, 186–87, 189
  product strategies, 181–87
  Secure Digital Music Initiative (SDMI), 188
 double bind, 198n13
 Fourth Services Transformation, 193
 implications, 193–96
 and information technology (IT), 179
 medical devices, privacy and, 189–92
  Carelink, 191–92, 195
  Medtronic, 179, 190–92
  remote delivery of medical services, 190–92
 political economy, sectors in, 179–81
 and productivity gap, 180
 Radio Frequency Identification (RFID), 194
Secure Digital Music Initiative (SDMI), 188
Securities and Exchange Commission (SEC), 245, 248, 250
  Rule 10b-18, 251
Securities Exchange Act of 1934
  Section 16(b), 252
Security, before meltdown, 8–9
Semiconductor design, 163–65
  China, 165
  East Asia, 164–65
  India, case study, 163–65
  Silicon Valley, 165
  start-ups, 165
  Western Europe, 164
Semiconductor Industry Association (SIA), 21–22
Semiconductor industry, decomposition of production, 6
Services dilemma, 111
Services spectrum, *107*, 107–8
  services, transformation of, *107*
Services, transformation of, 99–129
  algorithmic revolution, 32, 100–102
  automated services, 107–8
  benefits of transformation, 117–20
  business model transformations, 110, *110*
  capacity, 118–19
  capturing services transformation, 115–17
  Cloud Computing, 105, 114, 120, 126nn19 and 20
  commoditization, 111–13
  competition, 111–13
  computing platforms, 105, 113–14, 125n17
  connectivity, 117–18
  customer relations management (CRM), 103
  drivers of transformation, 111
  education level, 118–19
  government spending, 119–20
  and hardware offerings, 102
  hybrid services, 108
  ICT-enabled transformation of, 8–12
  in-house business functions, 101
  innovative lead users, 114
  intellectual property rights (IPRs), 121
  manufacturing and services, blurring boundaries between, 106–7
  portals to service, products as, 104–5
  production, ICT-based services as, 115–16
  productivity gains, potential for, 108–9
  productivity, services driving, 116–17
  products, shifts from, 102–3
  repositioning services, 102–6
  services dilemma, 111
  services spectrum, *107*, 107–8
    productivity gains, potential for, 108–9
  skills, 118–19
  social rules, services and, 121
  software, 103–4
  Software-as-a-Service (SaaS), 104
  unbundling of services, 21–22, 101–2
  unfolding of, 100–106
  "value domains," 105–6
SEZ. *See* Shenzhen Special Economic Zone (SEZ)
Shad, John, 251
Shanghai Tractor and Automobile Corporation (STAC), 85
Shanghai Volkswagen (SVW), 85
Shareholders, MSV. *See* Maximize shareholder value (MSV) ideology
Shenzhen Special Economic Zone (SEZ), 42
SIA. *See* Semiconductor Industry Association (SIA)
Signaling, financialization of corporate resource allocation, 251
Silicon Valley
  design services environment, 166
  semiconductor design, 165
  venture capital, 245

Sino-foreign collaboration, 94–95
SIV. *See* Special investment vehicle (SIV)
Skills, transformation of services, 118–19
Small and medium size enterprises (SMEs), 392
   China, 45–46
"Smart grid," 286, 295n10
SMEs. *See* Small and medium size enterprises (SMEs)
Smith, Adam, 180
Social rules, services and, 121
Social spending, France, 331
   public social expenditures, *331*
Softbank, 358
Software
   engineer shortages, 124n15
   evolutionary steps, 124–25n16
   Japan, 355
   services, transformation of, 103–4
Software-as-a-Service (SaaS), 104
Sony Corporation, 197n1
Soros, George, 223
South Korea
   information and communications technology (ICT), 367–69
   rise of, 31–32
Soviet Union, barter trade with, 303
S&P 500 Index, 246, *248,* 249–50, *250*
   and executive pay, 253
Special investment vehicle (SIV), 214
Speculation
   financialization of corporate resource allocation, 246–48
      speculative trading on corporate stock, 244
STAC. *See* Shanghai Tractor and Automobile Corporation (STAC)
Stand-alone era, computing, 125n17
Start-ups, semiconductor design, 165
Steel industry, France, 332
Stock and bond yields, average annual, *247*
Stock-based compensation
   financialization of corporate resource allocation, 243
   and sustainable prosperity, 265
Stock market boom of 1980s and 1990s
   maximize shareholder value (MSV) ideology, 238
Stock options, financialization of corporate resource allocation, 257

Stock repurchases
   banning of, proposed reforms, 236, 267
   financialization of corporate resource allocation, 248–51, *250*
   ratios of, *249*
Structured uncertainty, China. *See* China
Sustainable prosperity, 264–69
   job displacement, 265
   policy agenda for, 267–69
   stock-based pay, 265
   and tax policy, 264
Sustained growth, 373–96
   China auto industry, 377
   double bind, 373–74
      reconciliation of, 388–93
   economic governance, 376
   employment, inequality and, 377
   Fordism, 376, 386
   "growth model," 373–74, 382–88
   information and communications technology (ICT), 373
   multinational corporations (multinational corporations (MNCs)), spread of, 375–76
   post–World War II, 385–88
   sources of final demand, 377
   "third globalization," generally, 375–82
      adaptation to, 378–82
      China auto industry, 377
      economic governance, 376
      employment, inequality and, 377
      Fordism, 376, 386
      multinational corporations (multinational corporations (MNCs)), spread of, 375–76
      sources of final demand, 377
      transformation of production, 377
   transformation of production, 377
Sweden as wealthy nation. *See* Denmark, Finland, and Sweden as wealthy nations
SWV. *See* Shanghai Volkswagen (SVW)

T

Taiwan
   auto industry, 72–73
   business model, 17–18
   China, economic cooperation agreement with, 69
   "fabless" semiconductor manufacturing firms, 106
   Foxconn, 37–38

414   Index

Taiwan (*Cont.*)
  Industrial Technology Research Institute (ITRI), 384, 392
  Institute for Information Industry (III), 384
  Kuomintang, 384
Tata Consultancy Services, 159
Tata, Ratan, 159
Taxation
  France, *329*
  on innovations, implementation of (suggested reform), 236, 268–69
  tax policy and sustainable prosperity, 264
Tax Reform Act of 1976, 243–44
Tencent, 52n4
Thatcher, Margaret, 380
Tokyo Electric Power Company, 93
Tongji University, 65
Top-down liberalization, 385
Torch Programs, China, 36
Toyota, 72
  outsourcing, 68
Trade union vulnerability
  Denmark, Finland, and Sweden as wealthy nations, 311
transparency, 224–26
Troubled Asset Relief Program, 257
Trujillo, Bernardo, 135
TSCG. *See* European Treaty on Stability, Coordination, and Governance (TSCG)
Tsinghua University, 65
Turner Report (UK), 220

U

Unbundling of services, 21–22, 101–2
Uncertainty, 3, 204, *211*, 378
  financial crisis of 2008
    macro bubble, 215–16
    microinvestments, 213–15
  risk, failure to distinguish from, 3, 209–12
  structured uncertainty, China. *See* China
Unilateral liberalization
  Denmark, Finland, and Sweden as wealthy nations, 311–12
United Kingdom, Turner report, 220
"Universal" banks
  Denmark, Finland, and Sweden as wealthy nations, 302
Universal Studios, 197n1

Uruno, Tetsuro, 359
U.S. Department of Labor, 245
U.S. economy, fragility of, 232–76, 381
  "deal decade" of 1980s, 259
  earnings per share (EPS), 232–33
  employee stock options, indexing of (suggested reform), 236, 267–68
  employment
    globalization, effect on jobs, 234–35
    job creation, 235, 265
  employment contract, regulation of (suggested reform), 236, 268
  financial crisis of 2008, 233
  financialization of corporate resource allocation, 243–57
    banks, bailouts, 257
    cash dividends, ratios of, *249*
    conglomerate movement of 1960s, 244
    deconglomeration of 1970s and 1980s, 244
    development and utilization of products, 243
    executives, highest paid, 252–53, *254–55*
    generally, 232–33
    health insurers, 256–57
    information and communications technology (ICT), 256
    innovation as force, 246–47, 265–66
    manipulation as force, 246–48
    New Economy business model (NEBM), 245–47, 260–61
    Old Economy business model (OEBM), 245–47, 258, 261
    pharmaceutical drug prices, 256
    post-World War II, 243
    qualified stock options, 244
    ratios of stock repurchases, *249*
    and signaling, 251
    speculation as force, 246–48
    speculative trading on corporate stock, 244
    stock and bond yields, average annual, *247*
    stock-based compensation, 243
    stock options, 257
    stock repurchases, 248–51, *250*
    venture capital, 245
  globalization, 234–35
    job displacement due to, 265

Index 415

gross domestic product, 232
growth of, factors for, 232–33
inequity, 232–36
instability, 232–36
and junk bonds, 234
marketization, 234–35, 263
    job displacement due to, 265
maximize shareholder value (MSV) ideology, 236–43
    agency theory, 234, 238–40, 242
    cash subsidies, provision of to business enterprises, 241
    damage done by, 257
    dominance of ideology, 238
    and foreign competition, 239
    "free cash flow," 237–38
    generally, 233
    Japanese corporations, competition from, 239
    market imperfections, 236
    questioning of, 269
    residual claimants, 237
    and stock market boom of 1980s and 1990s, 238
middle class jobs, "disappearance of," 258–64
    African Americans, 260
    blue collar jobs, 263–64
    career employees, 261
    Current Population survey, 262–63
    Displaced Worker Survey, 263
    globalization, effect of, 234–35
    and Japanese competition, 258–59
    offshoring, 263
1980s, ideology, 233, 235
policy agenda for, 267–69
rationalization, 234–35, 263
    job displacement due to, 265
reforms, suggested, 236
    employee stock options, indexing of, 236, 267–68
    employment contract, regulation of, 236, 268
    stock repurchases, banning of, 236, 267
    taxes on innovations, implementation of, 236, 268–69
    work programs, creation of, 236, 268
stock repurchases, banning of (proposed reform), 236, 267

sustainable prosperity, 264–69
    job displacement, 265
    policy agenda for, 267–69
    stock-based pay, 265
    and tax policy, 264
taxes on innovations, implementation of (suggested reform), 236, 268–69
work programs, creation of (suggested reform), 236, 268
U.S. Environmental Protection Agency. See Environmental Protection Agency (EPA)

V

Value at Risk (VaR), 214, 218
Value creation, 2, 9–10, 204
"Value domains," transformation of services, 105–6
VaR. See Value at Risk (VaR)
Venture capital, financialization of corporate resource allocation, 245
Vertical integration, retailing, 136, 150n12
Vicker's Report, 221
Villepin, Dominique de, 336–37
Viniar, David, 210
"Voice," concept of, 357
Volcker Rule, 220
Vulnerability
    Denmark, Finland, and Sweden as wealthy nations, 311
    limited vulnerability, 311–12

W

Wall Street Journal, 251
Walmart, 139, 145, 146, 151n15
Wan Gang, 72
Washington Consensus, 376
Waxman-Markey climate, 290
Wealthy nations. See Denmark, Finland, and Sweden as wealthy nations
Welch, Jack, 233
Wheego, 94
Wilson, Charles, 6–7, 148
Wilson, William Julius, 260
Wind and solar energy, 285
Wintel PC, 125n17
Wipro, 169–72, 174
Work programs, creation of (suggested reform), 236, 268

World Bank, 3
World Economic Forum, 366, 370n12
World Trade Organization (WTO), 60, 61
WTO. *See* World Trade Organization (WTO)

X
Xiaolingtong, 45

Z
Zero-sum policy game, energy systems transformations, 180
Zero-sum reforms, France, 337
Zhicheng Champion, 44
ZTE, 42, 45, 52nn4 and 9
Zune Marketplace, 185, 187, 197n6, 198n12

CPSIA information can be obtained at www.ICGtesting.com
Printed in the USA
BVOW031646070713

325244BV00001B/1/P

9 780199 917846